THE ESSENTIAL GUIDE TO DEVELOPMENT STUDIES

In recent years, much mainstream development discourse has sought to co-opt and neutralize key concepts relating to empowerment, participation, gender, sustainability and inclusivity in order to serve a market-driven, neoliberal agenda. Critical development studies now play a crucial role in combatting this by analyzing the systemic changes needed to transform the current world to one where economic and social justice and environmental integrity prevail.

The Essential Guide to Critical Development Studies takes as its starting point the multiple crises – economic, political, social and environmental – of the dominant current global capitalist system. The chapters collectively document and analyze these crises and the need to find alternatives to the system(s) that generate them. To do so, analyses of class, gender and empire are placed at the centre of discussion, in contrast to markets, liberalization and convergence, which characterize mainstream development discourse. Each contributor supplements their overview with a guide to the critical development studies literature on the topic, thereby providing scholars and students not only with a précis of the key issues, but also a signpost to further readings.

This is an important resource for academics, researchers, policymakers and professionals in the areas of development studies, political science, sociology, economics, gender studies, history, anthropology, agrarian studies, international relations and international political economy.

Henry Veltmeyer is Senior Research Professor of Development Studies at Universidad Autónoma de Zacatacas, Mexico, and Professor Emeritus in International Development Studies at Saint Mary's University, Canada.

Paul Bowles is Professor of Economics and International Studies at the University of Northern British Columbia, Canada.

"This book invaluably fills a vacuum in the literature. Across its nearly forty chapters, it provides the highest level of scholarship and knowledge around the history, content and scope of critical development studies, covering both material and intellectual developments in a reader-friendly fashion for researchers, students and policymakers alike." – *Ben Fine, Professor of Economics at the School of Oriental and African Studies, University of London, UK.*

"We have not reached the end of history but the story of Progress, its errors and criticisms is the most important one in social science. Here 37 experts have both charted and navigated an extensive archipelago of ideas to produce this guidebook. Not only will teachers and students find it indispensable but so also will everyone currently critical of means to the ends of the world's Sustainable Development Goals." – *Barbara Harriss-White, Emeritus Professor of Development Studies, Oxford University and Visiting Professor, Jawaharlal Nehru University, India.*

"The *Essential Guide* presents clear, historically contextualised genealogies of major trends in development theory, and problematises them with critical alternatives. Feminist theory, counter narratives such as buen vivir ('living well') and discursive analyses of Development help to show the limitations of mainstream development theory and neoliberal approaches." – *Andrea Nightingale, Chair of Rural Development in the Global South, Swedish University for Agricultural Sciences, Sweden.*

"The *Essential Guide to Critical Development Studies*, edited by Henry Veltmeyer and Paul Bowles, is the comprehensive product and theoretical culmination of some six decades of critical research on development and underdevelopment, from Paul Baran's *The Political Economy of Growth* (1957) to the present. Bringing together the analyses of many of the world's leading analysts in this area, it explains how successive waves of liberal and neoliberal developmentalism have largely failed to address the complex problems of the global South and the persistent realities of imperialism and unequal exchange. In the twenty-first century these issues have proven more important than ever, making this volume an invaluable contribution to the understanding of the epochal crises and global transformations taking place in our time." – *John Bellamy Foster, editor,* Monthly Review, *USA.*

Routledge Critical Development Studies
Series Editors

Henry Veltmeyer is co-chair of the Critical Development Studies (CDS) network, Research Professor at Universidad Autónoma de Zacatecas, Mexico, and Professor Emeritus at Saint Mary's University, Canada

Paul Bowles is Professor of Economics and International Studies at UNBC, Canada

Elisa van Wayenberge is Lecturer in Economics at SOAS University of London, UK

The global crisis, coming at the end of three decades of uneven capitalist development and neoliberal globalization that have devastated the economies and societies of people across the world, especially in the developing societies of the global south, cries out for a more critical, proactive approach to the study of international development. The challenge of creating and disseminating such an approach, to provide the study of international development with a critical edge, is the project of a global network of activist development scholars concerned and engaged in using their research and writings to help effect transformative social change that might lead to a better world.

This series will provide a forum and outlet for the publication of books in the broad interdisciplinary field of critical development studies—to generate new knowledge that can be used to promote transformative change and alternative development.

The editors of the series welcome the submission of original manuscripts that focus on issues of concern to the growing worldwide community of activist scholars in this field.

To submit proposals, please contact the Development Studies Editor, Helena Hurd (Helena.Hurd@tandf.co.uk).

1. **Moving Beyond Capitalism**
   Edited by Cliff Du Rand

2. **The Class Struggle in Latin America**
   Making History Today
   James Petras and Henry Veltmeyer

3. **The Essential Guide to Critical Development Studies**
   Edited by Henry Veltmeyer and Paul Bowles

https://www.routledge.com/Routledge-Critical-Development-Studies/book-series/RCDS

THE ESSENTIAL GUIDE TO CRITICAL DEVELOPMENT STUDIES

Edited by Henry Veltmeyer and Paul Bowles

Routledge
Taylor & Francis Group

LONDON AND NEW YORK

KH

First published 2018
by Routledge
2 Park Square, Milton Park, Abingdon, Oxon OX14 4RN

and by Routledge
711 Third Avenue, New York, NY 10017

Routledge is an imprint of the Taylor & Francis Group, an informa business

British Library Cataloguing-in-Publication Data
A catalogue record for this book is available from the British Library

Library of Congress Cataloging-in-Publication Data
Names: Veltmeyer, Henry, editor. | Bowles, Paul, editor.
Title: The essential guide to critical development studies / edited
    by Henry Veltmeyer and Paul Bowles.
Description: Abingdon, Oxon ; New York, NY : Routledge, 2017.
Identifiers: LCCN 2017004491 | ISBN 9781472483485 (hb) |
    ISBN 9781138049970 (pb) | ISBN 9781315612867 (ebk)
Subjects: LCSH: Economic development. | Development
    economics. | Social change—Economic aspects.
Classification: LCC HD82 .E757 2017 | DDC 338.9—dc23
LC record available at https://lccn.loc.gov/2017004491

ISBN: 978-1-4724-8348-5 (hbk)
ISBN: 978-1-138-04997-0 (pbk)
ISBN: 978-1-315-61286-7 (ebk)

Typeset in Bembo Std
by Swales & Willis Ltd, Exeter, Devon, UK

1/10/18

CONTENTS

PART V
Policy configurations for development: international, national and local 203

PART VI
Class and development 249

PART VII
Agrarian change and spatial reconfigurations 289

ABOUT THE AUTHORS

A. Haroon Akram-Lodhi teaches agrarian political economy. He is Professor of Economics and International Development Studies at Trent University in Peterborough, Canada; a Fellow of Food First, the Institute for Food and Development Policy; and has adjunct appointments in Canadian, American and Mexican universities. He is also the Editor-in-Chief of the *Canadian Journal of Development Studies* and an Associate Editor of *Feminist Economics*. He does extensive advisory work for UN Women and the United Nations Development Programme. Email: haroonakramlodhi@trentu.ca.

Salvatore Babones is Associate Professor of Sociology at the University of Sydney. He is the author or editor of 10 books and more than two dozen academic research articles. His research covers the macro-level structure of the global economy, with a particular focus on China. His latest book, *American Tianxia: Chinese Money, American Power, and the End of History*, will be published by Policy Press in 2017.

David Barkin is Distinguished Professor at the Universidad Autónoma Metropolitana (UAM), Xochimilco Campus, Mexico City, and was a founding member of the Ecodevelopment Centre, created by the Mexican Science and Technology Council as an independent research organization. He was a recipient of the National Prize in Political Economy in 1979 for his analysis of inflation in Mexico. He was elected to the Mexican Academy of Sciences in 1992 and is an Emeritus Researcher at the National Research Council. He collaborates with groups of communities in many parts of Mexico in their efforts to consolidate post-capitalist societies. He is visiting at Humboldt University as a Georg Forster Fellow during the 2015–2017 period.

Milford Bateman is a freelance consultant on local economic development policy, Visiting Professor of Economics at Juraj Dobrila University of Pula, Croatia, and Adjunct Professor of International Development Studies at St Mary's University in Halifax, Canada. His research and consulting interests are in local economic development and local financial systems, with particular reference to the developmental role of the local state. He is the author of *Why Doesn't Microfinance Work? The Destructive Rise of Local Neoliberalism*, published by Zed Books in 2010, and, most recently, is co-editor with Kate Maclean of a multidisciplinary study entitled *Seduced and Betrayed: Exposing the Contemporary Microfinance Phenomenon*, published by the University of New Mexico Press in 2017. Email: milfordbateman@ yahoo.com.

Walden Bello is currently Professor of Sociology at the State University of New York at Binghamton and Senior Research Fellow at the Center for Southeast Asian Studies at Kyoto University. He served in the House of Representatives of the Philippines from 2009 to 2015. He is the author of 20 books, including *Capitalism's Last Stand?* (Zed Books, 2013) and *Food Wars* (Verso, 2009). He received the Right Livelihood Award (aka Alternative Nobel Prize) in 2003 for his work on corporate-driven globalization and was named Outstanding Public Scholar by the International Studies Association in 2008.

Berch Berberoglu is Professor of Sociology and Director of the Graduate Program in Sociology at the University of Nevada, Reno. He is series editor for Routledge on 'Globalization, Crises, and Change', for Palgrave Macmillan on 'Social Movements and Transformation' and for Emerald on 'Class and Inequality', as well as 'Politics, State, and Society'. His areas of interest include globalization, political economy of development, class analysis and social movements. He has published 32 books and many articles. His most recent books include: *Beyond the Global Capitalist Crisis: The World Economy in Transition* (Routledge, 2012); *Political Sociology in a Global Era* (Paradigm, 2013); *The Global Capitalist Crisis and Its Aftermath: The Causes and Consequences of the Great Recession of 2008–09* (Routledge, 2014); and *Social Theory: Classical and Contemporary – A Critical Perspective* (Routledge, 2017).

Miguel Borba de Sá teaches Latin American Development Studies at the Pontifical Catholic University of Rio de Janeiro (PUC-Rio), where he is also a PhD candidate within its International Relations Institute. He has formerly lectured International Relations Theory at Candido Mendes University and International Political Economy at the Defence and International Strategic Management undergraduate programme of the Federal University of Rio de Janeiro (UFRJ). He is the co-author of *Bolivia: passos das revoluções* and several articles on Latin American social struggles and intellectual traditions. Since 2010, he has been a member of the Institute for Alternative Policies for the Southern Cone (Instituto PACS), where he works as a researcher and activist. He is affiliated to the Socialism and Freedom

Party (PSOL) in Brazil, where he presents seminars on political theory and Latin American progressive politics at the party's cadre formation programmes.

Paul Bowles is Professor of Economics and International Studies at the University of Northern British Columbia. He has published on China's political economy, globalization, development and the international monetary system. His work on these topics has appeared in *Review of International Political Economy*, *Development and Change*, *Journal of Development Studies*, *New Political Economy*, *Cambridge Journal of Economics* and *New Left Review*. He has also recently added an interest in extractivism and is co-editor of *Resource Communities in a Globalizing Region: Development, Agency and Contestation in Northern British Columbia* (UBC Press, 2015). Email: paul.bowles@unbc.ca.

Yin-Wah Chu is Associate Professor of Sociology at the Hong Kong Baptist University. Her research interests focus on the political economy of development, as well as social and political movements in China, South Korea and Taiwan. Her research papers have been published in *Economy and Society*, *International Journal of Urban and Rural Research* and *Urban Studies*, among others. She is editor of *Chinese Capitalisms* (Palgrave Macmillan, 2010); *The Asian Developmental State* (Palgrave Macmillan, 2016); co-editor of *East Asia's New Democracies* (Routledge, 2010); and co-author of *The Global Rise of China* (Polity, 2016). Email: ywchu@hkbu.edu.hk.

Raúl Delgado Wise is Director and Research Professor of Development Studies at the Universidad Autónoma de Zacatecas, Mexico. He is also holder of the UNESCO Chair of Migration and Development, President of the Migration and Development network, Director of the journal *Migración y Desarrollo*, and Co-Chair of the Critical Development Studies network. His most recent publications include *Espejismos del Río de Oro: Dialéctica de la Migración y el Desarrollo en México* (Miguel Ángel Porrúa, 2016); *Mexico's Economic Dilemma: The Failure of Neoliberal Restructuring*, co-authored with James Cypher (Rowman & Littlefield, 2010); and *Agrarian Change, Migration and Development*, coauthored with Henry Veltmeyer (Fernwood/Practical Action, 2016).

Ana Garcia teaches International Relations at the Federal Rural University of Rio de Janeiro, where she also coordinates the Interdisciplinary Laboratory of International Relations Studies (LIERI). She collaborates with the Institute for Alternatives in the Southern Cone (PACS) as an activist and researcher. She holds a PhD in International Relations from PUC-Rio and a degree in Political Science from the Free University of Berlin, Germany. She was a visiting researcher at York University, Toronto, Canada. She works within the field of international political economy, mainly with critical theory, multinational corporations and South–South relations. She recently co-edited *BRICS: An Anti-Capitalist Critique* (with Patrick Bond).

Barry K. Gills is Professor of Development Studies at the University of Helsinki, Department of Political and Economic Studies, and formerly Professor of Global Politics at Newcastle University, UK. He is the founding editor of the journal *Globalizations* and the book series 'Rethinking Globalizations' and a Fellow of the World Academy of Art and Science. He has written widely on world-systems history, globalization, the political economy of development, global crisis, democracy, the politics of resistance and most recently on the BRICS and South–South cooperation, and transversal cosmopolitanism.

Eduardo Gudynas is Senior Researcher at the Social Ecology Latin American Centre (CLAES), Associate Researcher with the Department of Anthropology at the University of California, Berkeley, and Arne Naess Chair on the Environment and Global Justice 2016 at the University of Oslo. His research interests include alternatives to development, and the environment and social movements. His most recent publications include a textbook on the theory of extractivism (with editions in Bolivia and Peru), and a book on nature's rights and biocentrism in Latin America (with different editions in Argentina, Colombia, Ecuador, Bolivia and Peru).

John Harriss is Professor and sometime Director of the School for International Studies at Simon Fraser University. Trained originally in social anthropology, he has worked for most of his academic life in contexts of cross-disciplinary development studies, at Cambridge University, the University of East Anglia, the London School of Economics, the National University of Singapore and now at SFU. He has lived and researched in India, and elsewhere in South and Southeast Asia, for long periods, and particularly in Tamil Nadu – where he has studied many different aspects of economy, politics and society. Outside the academy, he worked for some time as the Head of the Regional Office for South and Central Asia of the Save the Children Fund (UK).

S.A. Hamed Hosseini, PhD in Sociology and Global Studies from the Australian National University (2006), is Senior Lecturer in Sociology and Anthropology at the University of Newcastle, NSW, Australia. He is the author of *Conscientious Sociology* (H&S Media, 2013) and *Alternative Globalizations* (Routledge, 2009/2011). The latter establishes a new theoretical approach to studying the ideological elements of global justice movements. He has conducted research and published articles on 'Critical open-mindedness' (2017); 'Towards transversal cosmopolitanism' (co-authored, 2016); 'Theorizing alternatives to capital' (co-authored, 2016); 'Transversality in diversity' (2015); 'Transversalist justice' (2015); 'Transversal cosmopolitanism in Occupy movements' (2013); 'Theorizing social ideations' (2012); and 'Sociology of dissident knowledge' (2010).

Naila Kabeer is joint Professor of Gender and International Development at the Gender Institute and the Department for International Development at the

London School of Economics and Political Science. Her main areas of research include gender, poverty, labour markets and livelihoods, and social protection. She sits on the Editorial Committee of *Feminist Economics*, Advisory Editor of *Development and Change* and the Editorial Boards of *Gender and Development* and *Third World Quarterly*. Her recent books include *Gender and Social Protection in the Informal Economy* (Routledge, 2010) and *Organizing Women Workers in the Informal Economy: Beyond the Weapons of the Weak* (Zed Books, 2013).

Claudio Katz is Professor at the University of Buenos Aires and researcher at the National Council of Science and Technology. He received honourable mentions of the Liberator Award for Critical Thinking for his books *Under the Empire of Capital* (2011), *The Dilemmas of the Left in Latin America* (2008) and *The Future of Socialism* (2004). There are also several editions of his essay 'El redesign of Latin America. ALCA, MERCOSUR and ALBA' (2006), as well as 'Marxist economics, today: six theoretical debates' (2010). His most recently published book is *Neoliberalism, Neodevelopmentism, Socialism* (2015). His web page is http://katz.lahaine.org. Here can be found his contributions to the debate on social and political developments in Argentina's current conjuncture among member of a Latin America-wide network of leftist economists.

Cristóbal Kay is Emeritus Professor at the International Institute of Social Studies (ISS), Erasmus University Rotterdam (EUR); Professorial Research Associate, Department of Development Studies at SOAS, University of London; and Emeritus Professor, FLACSO, Quito, Ecuador. His research interests are in the fields of rural development and development studies, with particular reference to Latin America. He has been the editor of the *European Journal of Development Research* (EJDR) and a co-editor of the *European Review of Latin and Caribbean Studies* (ERLACS). He is currently an editor of the *Journal of Agrarian Change* (JAC). Email: Kay@iss.nl.

Peter Kragelund is Associate Professor and Head of the Department of Social Sciences and Business, Roskilde University. His main interests include changes in the global economy and how these changes affect developing countries. In particular, his research has examined how the tectonic shift brought about by 'emerging' economic actors' renewed interest in Africa has affected the political economy of the host countries. His work has been published, inter alia, in *Cambridge Review of International Affairs, Cornell International Law Review, Development and Change, Development Policy Review, European Journal of Development Research, Journal of Modern African Studies, Review of African Political Economy* and *Third World Quarterly*. Email: jpk@ruc.dk.

Kari Polanyi Levitt is Emerita Professor at McGill University, specializing in Political Economy and Economics of Development. She holds an honorary doctorate from the University of the West Indies, as well as being honorary president of the Karl Polanyi Institute of Political Economy at Concordia University and a recipient of the J.K. Galbraith Prize from the Progressive Economics Forum of

Canada and a recipient of the Order of Canada. Among her publications are *Life and Work of Karl Polanyi*, co-edited with McRobbie; *Karl Polanyi in Vienna*; *Reclaiming Development: Independent Thought and Caribbean Community*; *Essays on the Theory of Plantation Economy: A Historical and Institutional Approach to Caribbean Economic Development*, co-authored with Lloyd Best; and *From the Great Transformation to the Great Financialization: On Karl Polanyi and Other Essays*.

Charmain Levy is Professor at the University of Outaouais since 2005, teaching International Development, and a specialist in Latin America, particularly Brazil, social movements, religion and development, and urban and development studies. She is director of the Groupe de Recherche sur les Espaces Publics et Innovations Politiques; member of the Reseau Québecois d'Études Féministes; former president of the Canadian Association of Studies in International Development; and editorial director of the Development and Globalization Collection at the University of Ottawa Presses.

Fiona MacPhail is Professor of Economics at the University of Northern British Columbia. Her research programme centres on gender, work, and public policy in Canada and Asia, with particular attention to migration, and different types of paid and unpaid work. She has published in journals such as the *Cambridge Journal of Economics*, *World Development* and *Feminist Economics* and has completed consultant reports for several international development agencies. She is the book review editor for *Feminist Economics* and a member of the international advisory board for the *Canadian Journal of Development Studies*.

Ronaldo Munck is Head of Civic Engagement at Dublin City University and a visiting professor of sociology at the University of Buenos Aires, Liverpool University and St. Mary's University, Halifax. He is a labour and development specialist, having authored books such as *Labour and Globalisation: The New Great Transformation* (2002) and *Critical Development Theory: Towards a New Paradigm* (1999). Professor Munck has most recently published *Rethinking Latin America: Development, Hegemony and Social Transformation* (2013), which has established a new framework for considering the past and future of Latin America from a broadly Gramscian perspective. He is a lead author and Ireland coordinator for the International Panel on Social Progress, chaired by Amartya Sen, which aggregates social science research to explore innovative solutions to the global challenges of the 21st century.

Pun Ngai is Professor in Department of Sociology, University of Hong Kong. She is the author of *Made in China: Women Factory Workers in a Global Workplace* (2005), which received the C.W. Mills Award and was translated into French, German, Italian, Polish and Chinese. Her articles have appeared in *Modern China*; *China Journal*; *China Quarterly*; *Global Labour Journal*; *Work, Employment and Society*; *Cultural Anthropology*; *Feminist Economics*; *Current Sociology*; and *Third World Quarterly*. Her most current book is *Migrant Labor in China: Post-Socialist Transformations* (Polity Press, 2016).

Alf Gunvald Nilsen is Associate Professor in the Department of Global Development Studies and Planning at the University of Agder. His research focuses on social movements in the global South, with a particular concentration on India. He is the author of *Dispossession and Resistance in India: The River and the Rage* (Routledge, 2010) and co-author of *We Make Our Own History: Marxism and Social Movements in the Twilight of Neoliberalism* (Pluto, 2014). He has also co-edited several volumes, most recently *New Subaltern Politics: Reconceptualizing Hegemony and Resistance in Contemporary India* (Oxford University Press, 2015) and *Social Movements and the State in India: Deepening Democracy?* (Palgrave, 2016).

James Petras is Professor Emeritus in Sociology at Binghamton University in New York and Adjunct Professor in International Development Studies at Saint Mary's University, Canada. He is the author of over 60 books and numerous other writings on the dynamics of world and Latin American developments, including *Unmasking Globalization* (2001); *Social Movements in Latin America: Neoliberalism and Popular Resistance* (2011); *Imperialism and Capitalism in the 21st Century* (2013); and *Extractivist Imperialism in the Americas* (2014). His most recent book, *The Class Struggle in Latin America*, co-authored with Henry Veltmeyer and several collaborators, will be published by Routledge in 2017. A list and an actual file of his periodical writings and journal articles are maintained and can be accessed at Rebelión.com.

Sergio Rodríguez Lascano is a director of and columnist with the Zapatista journal *Rebeldía*. His most widely read essays for *Rebeldía* include 'La izquierda: entre las cenizas y el fuego' (The Left: between the ashes and the fire). The video '20 años de zapatismo' (20 years of Zapatismo), prepared for the grassroots organization La Coordinadora del valle de Chalco Libre, is available on YouTube (www.youtube.com/watch?v=pvByL1C8zSk). His writings on Zapatismo and the dynamics of social change and political developments are also published in journals such as *Herramienta: Debate y Crítica Marxista*, published in Buenos Aires by a broad network of activist scholars concerned with an analysis of capitalist development in Latin America in the current conjuncture.

Alvin Y. So is Chair Professor in the Division of Social Science at the Hong Kong University of Science and Technology. His research interests include development, class conflict and East Asia. His recent publications include *The Global Rise of China* (co-authored with Yin-Wah Chu, Polity Press, 2016) and *Class and Class Conflict in Post-Socialist China* (World Scientific, 2013).

Susan Spronk is Associate Professor in the School of International Development and Global Studies at the University of Ottawa. Her research focuses on the experience of development in Latin America, more specifically the impact of neoliberalism in the Andean region with a focus on the water sector and social policy. She coordinates the journal *Studies in Political Economy*. She is also a research associate with the Municipal Services Project, an international research project that focuses on alternatives to privatization in municipal service delivery in Africa, Asia and Latin America. Her most recent book is *Crisis and Contradiction: Marxist Perspectives on Latin America in the Global Political Economy* (Haymarket Press, 2015), co-edited with Jeffery R. Webber.

Marcus Taylor is Associate Professor in the Department of Global Development Studies at Queen's University, Canada. He has worked on various topics in the political economy and political ecology of development, including climate change adaptation, labour and livelihoods, agrarian change, microcredit and anti-poverty policies. His most recent books include *The Political Ecology of Climate Change Adaptation* (Routledge, 2015) and *Global Labour Studies* (with Sébastien Rioux, Polity, 2017).

Darcy Tetreault is Professor Researcher at the Autonomous University of Zacatecas, Mexico, in the Department of Development Studies, and an adjunct professor at St. Mary's University, Halifax, Canada. His doctoral thesis on environmental degradation and poverty in rural Mexico was awarded the national-level (Mexico) Arturo Warman Prize in 2008. His research interests include social environmental conflicts, peasant and indigenous movements, agrarian transformation, poverty and social policy, with a focus on Mexico and the Latin American context.

Joseph Tharamangalam is Professor Emeritus of Sociology and Anthropology at Mount Saint Vincent University and Adjunct Professor of International Development Studies at Saint Mary's University, both in Halifax, Canada. His earlier work focused on social movements, agrarian change and the Kerala model of development. His recent research has focused on human development, democracy and public action with particular reference to India and Cuba. His research papers have appeared in journals such as *Critical Asian Studies* and the *Canadian Journal of Development Studies*.

Henry Veltmeyer is Research Professor of Development Studies at the Universidad Autónoma de Zacatecas, Mexico, and Professor Emeritus of International Development Studies at Saint Mary's University, Canada. He is co-founder and current Chair of the Critical Development Studies network, and co-editor of the Routledge series of books on Critical Development Studies. He has authored, co-authored and edited over 40 books on Latin America and the political economy of development, including *Poverty and Development in Latin America: Public Policies and Development Pathways New Extractivism in Latin America*; *Human Development: Lessons from the Cuban Revolution*; and *The Politics of Agrarian Reform in Brazil: The Landless Rural Workers Movement*. His most recent publications include *Agrarian Change, Migration and Development*, co-authored with Raúl Delgado Wise.

Leandro Vergara-Camus is Senior Lecturer in Development Studies at the SOAS, University of London. Prior to that, he taught international political economy and development in the University of Groningen, the Netherlands and several Canadian universities. He specializes on Latin America, the Left, globalization of agriculture, alternatives to neoliberalism, social movements and the state, as well as the political economy of renewable energy. His current research is on agrofuels, nature and the global energy transition. His work has been published in the *Journal of Peasant Studies*; *Journal of Agrarian Change*; *Latin American Perspectives*, *Revista Mexicana de Sociology*; and *Capitalism, Nature, Socialism*. His latest book is *Land and Freedom: The MST, the Zapatistas and Peasant Alternatives to Neoliberalism* (Zed Books).

Elisa Van Waeyenberge is a lecturer in the Economics Department of SOAS University of London. Her research interests include the international financial institutions, changing development paradigms, alternative macroeconomic policies, infrastructure financing and more recently housing provision. Her writings have appeared in various journals and edited book collections that include *The Political Economy of Development: The World Bank, Neoliberalism and Development Research* (Pluto, 2011), jointly edited with Kate Bayliss and Ben Fine.

Fernanda Wanderley holds a doctorate in sociology from Columbia University and is the Director of the Institute for social and economic research at the Catholic University (IISEC-UCB), La Paz, Bolivia, and formerly Professor at the University of San Andres (CIDES-UMSA), Center for Development Studies and visiting professor at Gothenburg University and Padua University. She has written widely on Bolivian and Latin American development and public policy, care work, labour market, feminist economy, social and solidarity economy, and women's and children's rights. She has written many books and articles on these subjects. Her recent publications include *Theoretical and Political Challenges of Social and Solidarity Economy: Readings from Latin America* (Plural Editors, 2015) and 'The continuous negotiation of the authority of oil and gas dependent states: the case of Bolivia' in *Contested Powers* (Zed Books, 2015). Email: fernandawanderley38@gmail.com. Blog: www.fernandawanderley.blogspot.com.

Raúl Zibechi is Professor in critical pedagogy, journalist and adviser with several urban social movements in Latin America. He has published 15 books, three of them have been translated into English. His most recently published books are *Decolonizing Critical Thinking* (2014) and *The Limits of Progressivism* (2016). The weekly articles can be found in *La Jornada* (México), *Gara* (Spain) and *Rebelión*.

CRITICAL DEVELOPMENT STUDIES

An introduction

Henry Veltmeyer and Paul Bowles

It has been argued that the idea of 'development' in the post-1945 era was invented as a geopolitical project to rescue countries recently liberated from the yoke of colonial rule away from the lure of communism, and to steer them along a capitalist path (Sachs, 1992). It was in this context that Tucker (1999) could write of 'development' as a form of imperialism, the imposition of an idea advanced in the interests of imperial rule.

This notion of 'development' – the provision of overseas financial and technical assistance to the 'economically backward' countries of what would later be described as 'the Third World' – as the product of an East/West ideological conflict and a process of decolonization, is debatable. For one thing, the idea of 'development' has been traced as far back as the 'idea of progress' formulated by the *philosophes* and historians of the 18th-century Scottish and French Enlightenments, and to the associated projects to create a 'better, more just and modern society' via processes of industrialization and democratization based on the ideas of progress, equality and freedom, and associated ideologies (Cowen and Shenton, 1995).

Nevertheless, there were certain specificities of the post-1945 period that justify the notion of a post-war launch of development. In any case, it is possible to identify six 'development decades' from around 1948, when President Truman launched his Point-4 Program of International Cooperation, to the 2008 'global financial crisis' that marked the beginnings of a new post-neoliberal – and possibly post-development – era. Over the course of these six decades of developmentalism, three under the aegis of the development state and three under the aegis of the Washington Consensus regarding the virtues of free-market capitalism, both the theory and practice of 'development' evolved in a series of paradigmatic shifts both in the mainstream of development thinking and in several alternative sidestreams. The history of what we have termed 'critical development studies' – diverse ideas of alternative development and alternatives to development – can be traced out over the course or curse of these six decades.

From an idealist perspective, history can be viewed as the outcome of a struggle between conflicting and competing ideas – the 'dialectic of the idea', in Hegel's formulation. Karl Marx, however, stood Hegel's dialectic on its head, viewing it as no more than a reflection and an idealist inversion of the way history unfolded in the real world. In either case, it is possible to trace out this history at two levels – in the real world, as a process of (capitalist) development of the forces of production and the corresponding changes in the social relations of production, and at the level of development theory, which can be seen as either the driving force of this development process or as a series of efforts at social scientific explanation.

In this introduction to *The Essential Guide to Critical Development Studies*, we take the latter view. In what follows, we reconstruct the geneology and contours of the development idea in terms of its evolution in the mainstream of development thinking and a series of critical counterpoints. We then provide an introduction and overview of the book in the form of 37 analytical probes into the broad field of critical development studies.

The geneology of critical thinking in development

The evolution of the development idea can be traced out, and reconstructed, virtually decade by decade, as a series of strategic responses to changing conditions – either in an effort to advance the development project (bring about a desired set of improvements in the lives and social condition of a defined or targeted population) or to reflect on the development implications and outcomes of these changing conditions and strategic actions taken in the direction of development, however defined or understood.

Launching the development project: developmentalism in the 1950s and 1960s

As an idea, a field of study, and as a geopolitical project taken up by governments and international organizations in the 'North', 'development' can be traced back to the late 1940s, with particular reference to the pioneering ideas of development economists in the 'structuralist' rather than the 'liberal' tradition (Meier and Seers, 1984; Rostow, 1960). This tradition had two strands. Those scholars seeking economic development within the capitalist system, such as Walter Rostow (1960) and W. Arthur Lewis (1963), dominated development thinking and practice at the time. However, the writings of political economists such as Paul Baran (1957), while less influential in development circles, laid the groundwork for critiques that would emerge in the 1970s (see Kay, 1989).

In addition to the anti-colonial movements and associated nationalisms, and the emergence of an East–West ideological struggle and cold war, the basic context for this evolution in development theory was provided by a secular path of unprecedented rapid economic growth within the institutional framework of the 'world economic order' set up at Bretton Woods. French historians in this context wrote of 'the thirty glorious years' while others more generally have done so in terms of 'the golden age of capitalism' (Marglin and Schor, 1990).

Within this geopolitical context and institutional framework, 'development' was conceived in conditional terms as relative *progress* in per capita incomes and in structural terms as *industrialization* and *modernization*. So conceived, 'development' was defined primarily in economic terms and seen to entail: (i) an increase in the rate of savings and investment – the accumulation of physical and financial capital; (ii) investment of this capital in industry (each unit of capital invested in industry, in theory generating up to five times the rate of return on investment in agriculture, with strong multiplier effects on both incomes and employment); (iii) in the absence or weakness of an endogenous capitalist class, the state assumes the basic 'functions of capital' – investment, entrepreneurship and management; (iv) the nationalization of economic enterprises in strategic industries and sectors; (v) an inward orientation of production, which, together with a secular increase in wages and salaries, would expand the domestic market; (vi) regulation of this and other markets and the protection (and subsidized support) of the firms that produce for the market, insulating them from the competitive pressures of the world economy; and (vii) modernization of the production apparatus, the state and social institutions, reorienting them towards values and norms that are functional for economic growth.

This approach assumed that economic growth would be accompanied by the adoption of Western cultural and institutional practices (i.e. Western modernity) and would be led by states and their functionaries in both the South and North. Some political economists at the time, oriented towards an alternative socialist system, argued for centrally planned political and economic structures and questioned the benefits of capitalism, but, like exponents of the more orthodox approach, accepted the key role of the state in economic development and the equation between economic growth and industrial/technological progress or modernization (Hirschman, 1958).

Together, these ideas constituted a theoretical model that was used to inform analysis and government policy for at least the first two development decades (the 1950s and 1960s). In the 1970s, orthodox structural economics came under attack from a number of directions. It is in this period that a number of different approaches to development began to take shape. We now turn to their emergence, interaction and debates – a process that has dominated development debates and practice(s) from the 1970s to the present.

A decade of liberal reform: the 1970s

In the 1970s, under the conditions of a worldwide economic production crisis, the development project came under serious question, challenged from both the Left with proposals of revolutionary change, and the Right by proposals to halt and reverse the gains made by workers and smallholding producers at the expense of capital and the propertied class. The mainstream of development thinking was dominated by proponents of social reform who conceived of development in social rather than economic terms – as a state of deprivation or poverty, the inability to meet one's basic human needs, that would be remedied with a development policy and a programme of state-led social reforms (Adelman, 1986). At the same time, some of these scholars in the tradition of social liberalism began to call for a more participatory, people-centred approach to development problems in the Third World (Hollnsteiner, 1977; Rahman, 1984). Thus, by the end of the decade, the three schools of thought (economic modernization, social reformism and social liberalism) that defined and dominated the mainstream of development thinking and practice had taken form.

On the left of the political spectrum, a sidestream of development thought, oriented towards a belief in the need for radical or systemic change, emerged. Those who subscribed to this belief turned towards both Marxism and Latin American 'structuralism' to construct what came to be known as 'dependency theory' (Kay, 1989; Palma, 1978). Within the framework of the centre-periphery model constructed by the theorists of Latin American structuralism, 'dependency theorists', such as Fernando Cardoso, Theotonio Dos Santos and André Gunder Frank, argued that development and underdevelopment were two sides of the same coin, and that socioeconomic conditions were inextricably linked to the position a country happened to occupy in the 'world capitalist system'. Strictly speaking, 'dependency' constituted a school of thought among like-minded scholars rather than a 'theory'. It included Gunder Frank's (1967) proposition that development in the metropole (the industrialized countries) was predicated on the 'underdevelopment' of countries on the periphery – the 'development of underdevelopment' in Frank's controversial but popular formulation. Others argued that 'dependency' was more a 'situation' than a 'structural condition', a proposition encapsulated in the notion of a situation of 'dependent associated capitalist development' (Cardoso, 1972; Cardoso and Faletto, 1979). According to this 'reformist' notion – reformist because of its political and strategic implications – relations of dependency are neither inherently exploitative nor block the possibility of peripheral capitalist development; it just creates a situation that favours a dependent or distorted pattern of capitalist development.

In the 1970s, dependency theory in its neo-Marxist form (see the discussion in Chapter 4 by Kay in this volume) was widely circulated in academic, if not policymaking, circles. It achieved such a resonance in academe that Immanuel Wallerstein, addressing a large scholarly meeting in 1975, could declare without a murmur of dissent that its main rival – modernization theory – was 'dead'. Yet, in policymaking circles, no such consensus existed. Far from it. Voices of dissent from the political right questioned state-centred solutions to developmental problems and began to argue for global free trade as the engine of economic growth (Bauer, 1982; Lal, 1983).

Pressure to consider the problems of the poor from a people-centred perspective intensified as well. A growing number of scholars and activists, particularly in the South, argued that development would only address the problems of the poor when it involved the poor themselves, particularly local community organizations. Proponents of participatory action research (PAR) called for more grounded, localized approaches to developmental problems, ones that would actively involve the poor rather than offering prescriptions from above (Cohen and Uphoff, 1977; Rahman, 1984).

In the face of these conflicting pressures, the mainstream development project was reconstructed in the direction of liberal reform – to stave off pressures for more radical change or social revolution, as well as calls to abandon the field. The essential features of this reform were an enhanced role for the state (the government, that is) in terms of: (i) programmes that would establish the social conditions of development (education, health, social welfare); (ii) a poverty-oriented strategy designed to meet the basic needs of the poor; (iii) reforms designed to improve access to society's productive resources (land reform, etc.); (iv) redistributive 'growth with equity' policies via taxation, etc. designed to redistribute more equitably market-generated incomes; and (v) an integrated programme of rural development that corrected for the urban bias of government policies, as well as the neglect of agriculture.

In the 1970s, this model ('growth with equity', or the basic human needs approach) was advanced in the context of an extensive, at times heated, and still ongoing debate on the role of inequality in the growth and development process, and the relevant policy option priorities and trade-offs – 'growth with efficiency', 'equity' or 'growth with equity'. Simon Kuznets (1953), a pioneer of the theory of economic growth, maintained that inequalities in poor countries would inevitably widen with economic growth before levelling out. Another pioneer, the Caribbean economist W. Arthur Lewis (1963), advanced a similar argument that widening inequality was an unavoidable price poor countries would have to pay for the economic development and prosperity that would eventually ensue.

The conservative counter-revolution and the neoliberal world order: the 1980s

By 1980, the liberal reformers that had dominated the field of development practice in the 1970s had succumbed to the blows levelled against them from both the Left and the Right, leaving behind a theoretical space soon occupied by proponents of free-market capitalism[1] who saw the state (i.e. the government) as the problem rather than as an agency of development. Until the 1980s, members of this neoliberal thought collective were lonely voices in the universe of structuralist thinking, but under conditions of a conservative counter-revolution (Toye, 1987). This 'counter-revolution' in development thought and practice swept away the ideas associated with the developmentalist state and brought to the fore the idea of a 'new world order'. And it brought into play a 'new economic model' geared to a programme of 'structural reforms' in macroeconomic policy. However, it did not eliminate competing approaches to development. Indeed, development theory and practice in the 1980s is best understood as a diverse world of competing ideas and practices, characterized by three main approaches and associated models: (i) a neoliberal model based on a belief in the efficacy of a market (and other 'forces of economic freedom) liberated from the regulative restrictions of the welfare-developmental state; (ii) a wide-ranging search for an alternative form of development that is human in scale and form, people-centred and participatory, inclusive in terms of gender and the poor, and sustainable at the level of both the environment and livelihoods; and (iii) the appearance of a post-development mode of thinking based on a critique and the rejection of both liberal and structural lines of development thought and the strategies and practices based on them (Burkey, 1993; Chambers, 1987; Goulet, 1989; Korten and Klauss, 1984; Rahnema and Bawtree, 1997).

The post-Washington Consensus re-inclusive development: the 1990s and the 2000s

In the context of what David Harvey (2003) has described as the 'neoliberal era', new development issues for study emerged at the level of both academe and development practice. Hitherto, the key issue had been the respective role and the relative weight that should be assigned to the market and the state. The neoliberal doctrine of free-market capitalism tilted the balance towards the market, but by the end of the 1980s it was evident that a policy of free-market capitalism was unsustainable and that the state had to be brought back into the development process. But in the 1990s, the academic debate reached beyond this issue, turning to a concern for other issues such as the sustainability of development policies vis-à-vis the environment and rural livelihoods (Redclift, 1987; UNDP, 1997). Other issues included a concern for equity and equality as regards the distribution of wealth and income, as well as the increased participation of women in the development process (Parpart *et al.*, 2000, 2002) – as well as other 'hitherto excluded' groups such as the rural and urban poor and the indigenous communities on the margins of the capitalist system (Stiefel and Wolfe, 1994). At the academic level, frameworks for the integration of women into the development process were formulated, while at the level of policy it would become a matter of principle and priority (Moser, 1993; World Bank, 1979; see also Chapter 13 by Kabeer and Chapter 14 by MacPhail in this volume). Other concepts such as 'civil society', 'empowerment' and 'globalization' also entered the development lexicon, as did notions of 'human', 'sustainable' and 'inclusive' development. These notions were the key building blocks of diverse attempts to construct a model of development within the institutional and policy framework of a new post-Washington Consensus regarding the need for a more inclusive and sustainable form of development.

In the context of this post-Washington Consensus, the theorists and architects of the development idea in the mainstream of development thought constructed several alternative models for the redesign of development policy and practice.

In addition to the Social Capital Initiative of the World Bank (Dutra, n.d.), which was used to inform diverse models of community-based local development, the three most consequential models in regard to development policy were constructed by economists associated with the United Nations Development Programme (UNDP), the Economic Commission for Latin America and the Caribbean (ECLAC) and the United Nations Conference on Trade and Development (UNCTAD).

ECLAC was the institutional source of a model that was widely used in the 1990s and the new millennium by governments in Latin America in the elaboration of development policy in the direction of 'inclusive development' – the 'new developmentalism' (Bresser-Pereira, 2006, 2007, 2009). On this model, see our discussion below regarding Critical Counterpoint #2. As for UNCTAD, its model of 'Structural Transformation for Inclusive and Sustained Growth' (UNCTAD, 2016) was constructed with reference to the proposal advanced in a series of studies over the past two decades by economists at ECLAC as to the need for a 'new industrial policy' in the context of the latest phase in the evolution of the world capitalist system and the associated advances in the process of globalization (on this, see the various chapters in Section III in this volume). As for the UNDP, the model constructed for the purpose of promoting and bringing about a more 'human' form of (capitalist) development was inspired and based on ideas advanced by Amartya Sen (1989, 1999). As Amartya Sen saw it, (human) development was a matter of ensuring the opportunity, freedom and the capacity of each individual to realize their full human potential. On this concept of human development and the UNDP model associated with it, see Veltmeyer and Rushton (2013).

In the whirlwind of the search for alternative forms and models of development, it was also possible to discern a pronounced trend towards interdisciplinarity at the level of development studies. This trend involved the institution of academic programmes in international development studies (IDS), particularly in the UK but also in other European countries such as Finland, the Netherlands and Spain, as well as Canada.[2] See, for example, CASID's White Paper on the state of international development studies in Canada commissioned by the IDRC (CASID, 2003).

Critical counterpoints in international development studies and an agenda for the 21st century

The history of development can be reconstructed in terms of different forms of analysis and schools of thought found in the mainstream of development theory, together with a series of critical counterpoints to this body of ideas. Both the mainstream stream of development thought and these critical counterpoints need to be contextualized in terms of changing conditions in the real world.

The first critical counterpoint to mainstream approaches to development studies (such as the modernization theory of economic growth) can be found in the late 1960s in the form of Marxist-oriented dependency theory. It took the form of a neo-Marxist dependency theory constructed within the framework of an alternative political economy paradigm based on the premise that capitalism was unable to provide the necessary conditions for development understood as emancipation from structures of economic exploitation and oppression (see Chapters 4 and 23 by Kay and Chapters 2 and 34 by Munck in this volume). However, the success in the late 1970s and the 1980s of several tiers of Newly Industrializing Countries in East Asia (see Chapter 17 by Bowles in this volume) led to involution of dependency theory in the form of world-systems theory and its near-death, although it was revived, reformulated and debated two decades later in the Latin American context (Dos Santos, 1998; Hernández López, 2005; Katz, 2016; Martins, 2011; Osorio, 2009; Sotelo, 2000, 2005, 2009). The evolution and contribution of world-systems theory as a framework for analysis and research is reviewed in several chapters in this volume, but see in particular Chapter 3 by Nilsen, Chapter 7 by Babones and Chapter 9 by Hosseini and Gills. The BRICS, a source of change in the world system, are analysed in Section IX.

Dependency theory has been revived in recent years in response to conditions formed of a new relation of dependency associated with the latest advance in the process of capitalist development in the form of extractivism and globalization (Borón, 2008; Osorio, 2009; Martins, 2011; Sotelo, 2000, 2005). The renewed dependency of governments and economies in the South on both the export of the social product in primary commodity form[3] and large-scale foreign direct investment has generated a vibrant and heated debate.

The new form taken by dependency theory in Latin America today is described by Borón (2008) and Katz (2016) in the following terms. In the 21st century, under conditions of a major reconfiguration of economic power in the global economy and the advance of capitalism at the dusk of the neoliberal era, there emerged a new current of post-dependency thought that postulated the emergence in Latin America of another industrialization process based on a new industrial policy designed to take advantage of the opportunities provided by the region's integration into the global economy (Dos Santos, 2011; Guillen, 2007; Moreno-Brid, 2013). But some scholars (e.g. Sunkel, 2001) are not at all sanguine, indeed pessimistic, about the opportunities for national development provided by the global economy and Latin America's integration into it on the basis of the rules governing the current world order.[4] Others, oriented towards neo-Marxist dependency theory, reformulated by some in the form of world-systems theory and by others (e.g. Delgado Wise and Martin, 2015) along the lines of a reconstructed Marxist theory of monopoly capitalism, rejected this postulate by reference to a neocolonial system of global production in which countries on the (Latin American) periphery are forced into a new dependency on the export of primary commodities and the influx of 'resource-seeking' capital (Osorio, 2009; Sotelo, 2009).[5]

A second critical counterpoint to mainstream development thought was constructed within the developmentalist project. By 1989, just six years into the structural adjustment programme based on the new economic model of neoliberal globalization, it was evident – even to the guardians of the new world order – that free-market capitalism was economically dysfunctional (rather than activating the capital accumulation and economic growth process, the 1980s was 'lost to development' – no growth over the course of the decade – resulting in increased poverty and a deepening of social inequalities), and politically destabilizing (generating protests and powerful forces of resistance). Thus, the theoreticians and architects of developmentalism came to a new consensus as to the need to establish a better balance between the market and the state and bring about a more inclusive form of development by means of a new social policy targeting extreme poverty (Craig and Porter, 2006).

Several economists at ECLAC led the push to modify the developmentalist project – basically to save capitalism from itself (Sunkel, 1993). But several UN agencies (UNICEF, for example) also got into the act with the promotion of 'structural adjustment with a human face' (Jolly et al., 1987), and the World Bank took the lead in constructing a development strategy based on the new post-Washington Consensus (World Bank, 2007; see also Chapter 15 by Van Waeyenberge in this volume). Towards the end of the 1990s, the World Bank established a 'comprehensive framework' for the delivery of development assistance, and also a new conditionality in the form of Poverty Reduction Strategy Papers (PRSPs) that would both replace the ill-fated one-size-fits-all Structural Adjustment Program and allow developing countries to 'take ownership of their own development'.

The new consensus was solidified and put into practice in the form of what one of its leading architects, the ECLAC-affiliated Brazilian economist Bresser-Pereira (2006, 2007, 2009), described as the 'new developmentalism'. This neostructuralist approach towards national development was translated into policy by the new 'progressive' (centre-left) regimes formed in the first decade of the new millennium in conditions of widespread disenchantment and rejection of the neoliberal model (Veltmeyer and Petras, 2014: Chapter 1).[6]

A third critical counterpoint to orthodox development theory comes from the analysis of the non-economic factors in development. From the perspective of orthodox development theory, development in its diverse dimensions is predicated on economic growth (i.e. the expansion of the forces of economic production), which creates the necessary conditions for both social and economic development. The driving force of economic growth in this conception is the accumulation of capital in the form of money or finance (financial capital), infrastructure, technology and machinery (physical capital), natural resources (natural capital), and knowledge and skills or social technology (human capital). In the 1990s, however, the failure of this approach to capture the causes of growth led to revisions within the mainstream by including what came to be known as 'social capital', with reference to 'a set of norms, institutions and organizations that promote trust and cooperation among persons in communities and in the wider society' (Durston, 1999: 104). This concept can be found in the World Bank's Social Capital Initiative and was elaborated by various sociologists associated with ECLAC (Atria et al., 2004; Durston, 1999). The theory was that social capital, so understood as norms of reciprocity and social exchange based on relations of social solidarity, was a productive resource accessible to the poor, empowering them to act for themselves in a process of community-based local development (De la Rocha, 1994; Harriss and de Renzio, 1997; Solow, 2000). As noted above (but see Delgado Wise and Veltmeyer, 2016, for further discussion), with the understanding that the labour and migration pathway out of rural poverty had reached its limits, and that the incessant flow of rural migrants to the cities and urban centres were placing excessive pressures on both governments and the private sector, the World Bank shifted towards a strategy of so-called empowering the poor in a process of community-based local development. The concept of social capital was a critical factor in this approach and the theory behind it (on this, see Fukuyama, 2004; Knack, 1999; Solow, 2000; Woolcock and Narayan, 2000). The introduction of social capital into development thinking opened up the space for the consideration of the non-economic determinants of development, and as such can be seen as important in bringing back in politics and social structures, but the way in which this was done by many, including the World Bank, failed to take this approach through to its logical conclusion. For a critique of this social capital approach to development, see, inter alia, Fine (2001), Harriss (2001) and Veltmeyer (2011). From the perspective of these critics, the concept of social capital was formulated and advanced for the purpose not of poverty reduction, the stated goal of the World Bank's Social Capital Initiative, but political demobilization – to turn the rural poor away from the confrontational politics of the social movements. In contrast, many of the chapters in this volume point to the importance of political mobilization, of social movements, and of class and gender relations to an understanding of how an alternative development can be possible.

A fourth critical counterpoint to mainstream development thinking and practice took the form of several Marxist theories of uneven capitalist development and imperialism. These theories are constructed within the framework of historical materialism, a set of fundamental principles established by Marx for scientific analysis – what in the subsequent Marxist tradition we might label 'Marxist political economy'. The first principle of this materialist conception of political economy is that in the process of production, people enter into relations that are independent of their will (i.e. objective in their effects), and the structure of these relations correspond to changes and diverse phases in the development of the forces of production.

Diverse variations on and contributions to this body of Marxist theory have been constructed over the course of the six developmental decades. From this critical perspective, the development project of international cooperation was little more than a form of imperialism – the velvet glove within which was hidden the iron fist of armed force, viz. the deployment of the repressive apparatus of the state against the forces of popular resistance confronting the incessant and seemingly irresistible advance of capitalism (Petras and Veltmeyer, 2001; Veltmeyer, 2005).

Marxist critical thinking about development – about development viewed as a process (the development of the forces of development and corresponding changes in the social relations of production) – has taken two other forms. One is in the form of a metatheory of long-term, large-scale capitalist development focused on the transformation of an agrarian society based on pre-capitalist relations of production (a peasant economy of independent producers and small-landholding farmers) and a traditional communalist culture into a capitalist system based on the extension of the capital–labour relation into all areas of production. The ideas associated with this metatheory regarding the fundamental dynamics of capitalist development are brought into focus and briefly discussed by Raúl Delgado Wise in Chapter 25. As he reconstructs the theory (see Delgado Wise and Veltmeyer, 2016, for a more extended exposition of the theory), the capitalist development process hinges on the exploitation of the 'unlimited supply of surplus agricultural labour' associated with the transition towards capitalism.

Another contribution by Marxist social science to international development studies relates to the theory of imperialism as a bearer of capitalism, an agency of capitalist development. James Petras and Henry Veltmeyer, in Chapter 9, critically review the various debates that surrounded this development question (imperialism as the bearer of capitalism and an agency of development). However, what they do not discuss here is the body of theory and the debates that surround the dynamics of resistance to imperialism, which raises a political rather than development question, namely, what is the connection between the politics of anti-imperialism and the resistance to the expansion and advance of capital in the current context of a transition towards what is evidently a new form of capitalism and a new phase of capitalist development? Petras and Veltmeyer do in fact address this question in another study of the political dynamics of social change in the neoliberal era (Petras and Veltmeyer, 2001). Here, they advance the theory that development as a project of international cooperation – at least in the Latin American context – is part of a strategy designed to turn the rural poor away from the peasant and indigenous movements mounted against the neoliberal policy agenda of many governments in the region. The unstated but evident goal of the strategy was to divide the social movement and provide the rural poor a less confrontational alternative path towards social change.

A fifth critical counterpoint to orthodox development thought and practice takes a more radical form than the thinking associated with critical development theory (see Chapter 2). Whereas this school of thought was – and is – concerned with the search for an alternative form of development ('another development'), the theorists and advocates of post-development argue that the entire development project and associated enterprise is misbegotten, basically a way of colonizing the minds of people in so-called developing or poor societies as a mechanism of control, another form of neocolonial subjugation (Escobar, 1997; Sachs, 1992).

Eduardo Gudynas, in Chapter 5, deconstructs the theoretical discourse associated with this school of thought (for a more critical exposition of post-developmentalism, see Veltmeyer, 2002). As Gudynas reconstructs it, post-development is based on a post-structuralist form of discourse analysis, which is to say, on the presumption that social science does not have a privileged access to the 'truth' (a means of grasping and being able to explain what is happening in the real world of development); as Nietzsche has been quoted to argue: 'there are no facts; only interpretations' – different ways of seeing, different interpretations, different worlds – all from the perspective of the beholder or the subject of a particular action, and all with equal validity (see the discussion on this point in Veltmeyer, 2001).

A sixth critical counterpoint of critical thinking in the study of international development can be found in the ideas associated with diverse experiments in efforts constructing a social and solidarity economy (see Chapter 30). The notion of a social and solidarity economy (SSE) emerged in the early 1980s as a form of alternative development, an economic model for combatting poverty and inequality, and as a vision of social transformation (Razeto, 1993). In the 1990s, however, it turned into a 'new development paradigm' designed to expand a third sector of the economy based on social capital and a culture of social solidarity, and supported by a decentralized form of governance and a new social policy oriented towards poverty reduction and empowerment of the poor (Narayan, 2002; Rao, 2002).

Other researchers, however, conceptualized the social and solidarity economy from a local development angle and the perspective of grassroots community-based social organizations as a form of 'inclusive and sustainable development' (Vieta, 2014). Here, reference is made to a concept advanced by Peter Utting at UNRISD and a reader edited by a team brought together by the Social and Solidarity Economy Academy at Campinas, Brazil, and published by the International Training Centre of the ILO. Both publications, focused on exploring the conditions for scaling up the social and solidarity economy, point to spaces and strategies for capacity-building, institutional innovation and social change strategies for capacity-building, institutional innovation and social change in the context of existing internal constraints or oppositional forces.

David Barkin, in Chapter 30, reviews several practical experiences with this model – social, solidarity and ecological economies (SSEE), in his formulation. Barkin argues that emerging across Latin America among peasants and indigenous groups that are organized collectively in rural areas are important attempts to construct a theoretical model and forge a social and solidarity economy, which – according to Gudynas (see Chapter 5 in this volume) – takes a post-development form. The paradigmatic case of this model is the social and solidarity economy under construction on the margins of the capitalist system and beyond the reach of the Mexican state in Chiapas (EZLN, Sexta Comisión, 2015).[7]

This counterpoint of critical thinking is also associated with the indigenous Quechua concept of *Sumak Kawsay*,[8] translated in Spanish as '*buen vivir*' (Ecuador) or '*vivir bien*' (Bolivia). This concept is notoriously difficult to render into English (see Solón, 2014), but it is taken by Eduardo Gudynas (see Chapter 5) to describe a condition of living in social solidarity and in harmony with nature (see also Acosta, 2012; Dávalos, 2008). As Gudynas sees it, *vivir bien* or *buen vivir* is a form of post-development thought constructed within a 'non-capitalist paradigm' (see also Albó, 2011; Farah and Vasopollos, 2011; Medina, 2011). He formulates this idea as follows: 'postdevelopment as critique, *vivir bien* as alternative' (Gudynas, 2014). And Gudynas is not alone in this understanding (see Acosta, 2010, for example). His interpretation of *buen vivir* as the practical application of post-development, an alternative to development (i.e. as an anti-capitalist post-development approach to social change), coincides with the understanding held by Alberto Costa, an Ecuadorian leftist economist who once was very close to the government in its efforts to institutionalize the concept, but who is now one of President Correa's major and loudest critics.

Themes and issues

The first part of this introduction traced the genealogy of critical development studies from its origins in the post-1945 period to contemporary debates that include the questioning of the 'idea of development' itself. This review has demonstrated that while critical development studies can be readily defined by what it is not – the mainstream approach that views development as a primarily technocratic exercise in effective programme design and implementation – it is less easily reduced to a few sentences on what it is. As the discussion above showed, critical development studies, or CDS, is a broad field of enquiry, often interdisciplinary in approach and pluralist in scope. It tackles the big questions, does not shy away from controversy, and challenges conventional ideas and practices. It is not surprising, therefore, to find that it is also a field within which there are lively debates. Part of the *raison d'être* for critical development studies is to force us to confront how best to analyse the unequal and diverse world in which we live and to challenge us to imagine better alternatives. The authors in the volume have all risen admirably to these challenges, and the second part of this introductory chapter provides a guide to the themes of the book.

This volume opens with a chapter by Kari Polanyi-Levitt, who draws upon her experience and involvement in the development debates of the past half-century and more to survey how development theory has changed over time and makes the important links between global political, military and economic trends and events, on the one hand, and development theory, on the other. She reminds us of the brutality of the 'post-war' world, of continued colonialism, not least in the ways in which developing countries served as the laboratories for testing the policies of the international financial institutions and American universities. Her chapter also reminds us of the centrality of the US to the global economic system, a point made clear by the global financial crisis, and a theme developed in other chapters. But her chapter ends on an optimistic note, suggesting that there is no better time for students to engage with critical development studies and to take advantage of the space that has been created for understanding multiple perspectives.

Thinking critically about development is the theme for the next section. Given the influence of Marxism in the field of critical development studies, several authors take as their task the job of analysing the ways in which Marxism and its variants may be useful in understanding the contemporary dynamics of development and the ways in which it needs to be extended. Ronaldo Munck provides an examination of the work of Marx himself, setting out his main ideas about capitalist development but also pointing to contradictions within his work, as well as unanswered questions. The latter were taken up subsequently by Lenin, where the question of the peasantry and of imperialism were addressed, enduring issues that are also taken up in other chapters of this volume. Lenin, of course, was also an architect of the first example of '20th-century socialism', and Munck's chapter assesses this and other examples; attempts at constructing '21st-century socialism' in Latin America are discussed in a later chapter by Claudio Katz. Munck also shows how, as part of the modernist paradigm, Marxism has been challenged by the post-development critique, a critique that strikes at the foundations of what is meant by 'development'.

This is also the subject of Alf Gunvald Nilsen's chapter. Nilsen argues that it is essential that critical development studies continue to explicitly name and interrogate capitalism as the dominant system in need of analysis. The question, he asks, is how best to do this. Is it through the continued relevance of the work of Marx or should we look to postcolonial critiques? He argues for the former, but also for the need for a 'Marxist approach to a non-Eurocentric conception of capitalist development' that includes a rediscovery and reintegration of the concept and theory of 'uneven development' that allows nonlinearity a central theoretical place. Whether any form of 'Western theory' can be rescued is questioned further by Eduardo Gudynas. He distinguishes between two types of 'post-development': the first as critique of Western-derived, universal metanarratives; the second as the search for alternative forms of development based upon different principles often drawing on indigenous knowledge and world views captured by the term *'buen vivir'/'vivir bien'*, or living well, which offers the prospect of a post-capitalist and post-socialist form of development that respects nature. But constructing such an alternative is an enormous task requiring three levels of analysis and a large toolbox.

That 'post-development' theory should find resonance in Latin America is just the latest contribution from critical development thinkers from a region that, integrated into global empires for over 500 years, has been fertile ground for the examination of the dynamics of capitalist development and the inequalities that it has generated. Following Levitt, Cristobal Kay provides an analysis of the structuralist and dependency approaches that held sway in much of the developing world, as well as in academe, in the 1960s and 1970s. While the historical review is instructive in terms of our understanding of the origins and forms of critical development studies, it is also relevant as the basis for the neostructuralism that Kay argues is still central to the critical development studies agenda and influential in policymaking today. The arguments for neostructuralism, for greater state intervention and market guidance for example, also connect with the East Asian developmental state model analysed by Paul Bowles in Chapter 17.

The final chapter of Section II in this volume again highlights the critical development studies approach of questioning and interrogating the application of mainstream models to development issues. Francesca Wanderley does this with respect to gender issues and shows how the application of 'new home economics' models impoverishes policy discussion and fails to account for the continued and pervasive oppression of women globally. She argues that a starting point for analysis must be the recognition and inclusion of the centrality of care provision in our understating of how an economy operates. This has been a central argument advanced by feminists, and Wanderley goes on to argue for the promotion of care as a social right, an idea seemingly simple to express, but which would have profound implications for how societies organize themselves by opening up the possibility of challenging the patriarchal order and democratizing family and community. This gender perspective is also developed in subsequent chapters by Naila Kabeer and Fiona MacPhail.

Some of the major themes highlighted in this section – capitalism, imperialism and globalization – are the focus of Section III in this volume. These terms are central to critical development studies approaches but are not without their challenges and contestation. Salvatore Babones introduces the world-systems approach and argues that the structure of the world economy, and the incorporation of countries into core, semi-peripheral and peripheral zones, has been relatively stable for the past five centuries. But it is not static. In particular, Babones analyses how the rise of global cities and the organization of production into global value chains have changed the state-focused nature of the world system and how anti-systemic movements might offer (some) hope for global democracy. Berch Berberoglu's chapter provides a different account of the origins of modern capitalism more firmly rooted in the 18th-century Western European experience and the emergence of the central contradiction between capital and labour. This contradiction, and the crises that spring from it, operate just as much in the advanced capitalist countries as they do in the so-called developing world, and Berberoglu's analysis of the current crisis demonstrates how workers in all countries have been the victims of capitalism's unequalizing processes (see also the brief discussion of this towards the end of Polanyi Levitt's opening chapter).

The relative importance of states and corporations has been a subject of much debate generally. It has been prominent in different analyses of the relationship between imperialism and capitalism, for example. James Petras and Henry Veltmeyer provide an overview of the literature and argue that class and the class analysis of state power must be central to the analysis of imperialism. They further argue that the relationship between imperialism and capitalism changes over time, a point they illustrate with an analysis of the recent turn to 'extractive imperialism'.

The next two chapters tackle another contested term: 'globalization'. Hamed Hosseini and Barry Gills analyse the diverse conceptions of what they view as 'globalizations', while Walden Bello advances a 'deglobalization' perspective. Hosseini and Gills provide an overview of the origins and evolution of the concept of 'globalization', showing how it variously subsumes, runs parallel with, and interacts with the concept of 'development'. A dense and rich account, it helps make sense of a vast literature and points to areas where critical globalization and critical development studies can fruitfully engage.

Bello's deglobalization perspective, which has been closely associated with the Bangkok-based progressive think tank *Focus on the Global South*, aims at enhancing ecological equilibrium, democracy and equality while promoting the principle of subsidiarity or locating the locus of production and decision-making at the lowest level where it can be done with minimal economic cost.

The aim of the deglobalization paradigm is to move beyond the economics of narrow efficiency, in which the key criterion is the reduction of unit cost, never mind the social and ecological destabilization this process brings about. Rather, it promotes an 'effective economics', which strengthens social solidarity by subordinating the operations of the market to the values of equity, justice and community by enlarging the sphere of democratic decision-making. To use the language of the great Hungarian thinker Karl Polanyi in his book *The Great Transformation*, deglobalization is about 're-embedding' the economy in society, instead of having society driven by the economy (Polanyi, 1957: 68–76).

Moving on from these conceptual issues and the ways of thinking about the dynamics of contemporary capitalism, Section IV in this volume addresses what have come to be seen by many as the major concerns of critical development studies, namely, poverty and both social and international inequalities. While poverty became central to mainstream development studies as part of the 'saving capitalism from itself' rationale discussed above, both poverty and the multiple dimensions of inequality hold places of equal importance in critical development studies. Joseph Tharamangalam analyses the persistence of chronic poverty in the midst of plenty. He reviews the data on various poverty indices and examines why the World Bank's policy prescriptions to reduce or, better still, eradicate poverty have fallen short because the root of the World Bank's approach is to attempt to depoliticize what is inescapably a political question: How will society organize the distribution of its resources?

Poverty and inequalities are not random in whom they affect. Class dynamics are central to the understanding but so are gender dynamics, as it is women who make up the bulk of the world's poor and who are disproportionately found at the bottom of steep ladders of social inequality. The chapters by Naila Kabeer and Fiona MacPhail help us to understand why. Kabeer shows how feminist scholarship has demonstrated that women are systematically disadvantaged not only in terms of income (and the resulting poverty associated with it), but also in terms of time poverty, how gender asymmetries mean that women typically have less control over their own labour than men, and are more vulnerable to natural and policy-induced shocks. Kabeer also examines the interrelationships between class and patriarchy in determining poverty outcomes. MacPhail analyses 'work', both paid and unpaid, expanding upon some the issues raised in Wanderley's chapter. MacPhail shows that despite well-intentioned development goals, women remain subject to pervasive and, in many cases, increasing inequalities in paid work outcomes and unpaid work burdens. Using three countries – Cambodia, China and the Philippines – as examples, she shows how policy objectives fail to translate into gender equality. MacPhail's chapter also highlights the particular forms of inequality faced by women workers who migrate both intra- and internationally, a theme also considered in subsequent chapters by Pun Ngai and Delgado Wise. Inequalities arising from climate change, including their gendered impacts, are examined in Marcus Taylor's chapter.

Section V in this volume contains four chapters that analyse the policy roles of actors at the international, national and local scales and assesses their development potentialities. Elisa Van Waeyenberge provides an analysis of the post-Washington Consensus (PWC). Whereas the failed Washington Consensus was premised on counterposing the state *versus* the market as agencies for development, the PWC posited that it was the state *and* the market, working in partnership, that paved the way for development. Van Waeyenberge shows how this became operationalized as public–private partnerships where the 'private' included firms, NGOs, families and citizens. She concludes that the PWC represents a particular form of neoliberalism and is, in some important ways, still a regression from the pre-Washington Consensus.

The theme of partnerships is also evident in Peter Kragelund's chapter on international cooperation. He argues that the world of aid donors has undergone a 'tectonic shift' as a result of the emergence of new state donors (especially the BRICS, whose internal dynamics are considered in Section IX in this volume) and private aid donors, and as a result of the fall in the significance of aid flows compared to other financial flows such as trade, foreign direct investment and remittances. He then traces how this new reality has changed the bargaining position of recipient countries and asks whether it has fundamentally changed the basis of, and prospects for, development through international forms of cooperation. The new emphasis on public–private partnerships and 'win–win' outcomes provide the basis for scepticism.

Paul Bowles looks at the national level and considers the 'developmental state model', the only path to have historically led to successful late industrialization (in terms of raising average GDP per capita to advanced country levels). He outlines the elements of the model as they were found in the East Asian Newly Industrializing Countries before examining whether the model is still possible given changes in international policy space and the organization of global production (as also discussed by Babones) and whether it is desirable given the authoritarianism that accompanied its implementation. Milford Bateman analyses local economic development focusing on the claims made on behalf of microcredit, a policy tool that has become one of the most popular development tools associated with the PWC, often framed in terms of reaching the poorest, especially women, and leading to empowerment. Bateman provides a thorough analysis that demolishes these claims and suggests that other forms of local development must be sought, a task that is taken up by some of the chapters in Sections VIII and X in this volume.

One of the central concepts used by critical development scholars, and evident in many of the chapters to this point, is that of class. However, this concept is not without its ambiguities, and Section VI in this volume provides a thorough investigation both theoretically and in practice of this central concept. Henry Veltmeyer's chapter provides a useful overview of the ways in which class has been defined, measured and used by different schools of thought and disciplines. He argues that the Marxist formulation of class is the most coherent and insightful, and allows exploration of class as a structural phenomenon as well as a political one (i.e. as class struggle).

These issues are taken up in Section III. Berch Berbegoglu's chapter, following on from his previous one, pays particular attention to class formation and class struggle at the global scale in the contemporary phase of capitalist development. Pun Ngai presents an analysis of class formation in China, in particular the formation of a new migrant working class, fashioned in the context of China's emergence as the factory of the world. She argues that it is a class in the sense that migrant workers have developed a class consciousness, are aware of their subjugated position in the global capitalist system and are increasingly ardent in defending their interests.

The role of class struggle in Latin America is analysed by Susan Spronk. She argues that trade unions must be reintegrated into development studies as actors in the development process and argues that we should not exaggerate the differences between 'old' trade unionism and 'new' social movements, but rather link both to the rhythm of capitalist accumulation. Spronk's chapter also discusses women and trade unions, thereby extending the gender analysis provided by Wanderley, Kabeer and MacPhail.

One of the classes identified by Veltmeyer in his chapter is 'the peasantry'. An examination of this class is taken up in Section VIII by Kay and Akram-Lodhi. Kay's chapter considers three interlinked issues: land grabbing; the crisis of the peasant economy, the emergence of a rural precariat and the feminization of rural labour; and the financialization of agriculture. All three issues show how capitalist dynamics are affecting the peasantry and impoverishing the lives of those who work on the land in the face of the power of global capital. The processes analysed by Kay are in important ways the result of the current global food regime analysed by Akram-Lodhi. He describes that regime as a 'corporate food regime' dominated by agrofood transnational corporations, driven by world market prices and a relentless drive for commodification. He outlines the basis of this system in colonialist and capitalist practices, examines the consequences in terms of poverty and inequalities, and proposes that an alternative be constructed using the concept of 'agrarian citizenship', a concept that involves not only equitable relations between people, but also harmony between humans and nature, thereby linking with other chapters (Gudynas and Barkin, for example).

The crisis in the countryside is a main contributing factor to the flows of labour out of rural areas. Pun Ngai's chapter focused on this with respect to China, and in this section Raúl Delgado Wise provides a more general examination of migration, a spatial reconfiguration of the global labour-force. After a discussion of different approaches to agricultural transformation, Delgado Wise then focuses on one proposed pathway out of rural poverty, namely, international migration. He shows how migration has been and continues to be part of capitalist dynamics, and argues that migration has intensified during the neoliberal period, bringing precarious and exploitative working conditions for many migrants, as well as serious 'brain drain' losses to developing countries. Migration is also contributing to another spatial reconfiguration, namely, urbanization.

Urban development in the Global South is analysed by Charmain Levy. She analyses the consequences of neoliberalism on the declining capacity of the state to provide for the material needs of city dwellers, rising informality of work and rising urban poverty; one-third of the population in the Global South in 2012 lived in slums. The restriction of public services, such as water, to fee-paying customers and provided by public–private partnerships has transformed urban governance but has also spurred resistance from urban social movements at both local and international levels, offering hope for some change of direction.

In Section VIII, the book shifts towards another crisis, the environmental crisis. Darcy Tetreault asks the question of whether sustainable capitalism is possible. He provides an insightful overview of why many have answered in the negative. Tetreault continues by providing an analysis of recent trends in global capitalist development that have a high impact on the environment, such as land and water grabs (discussed by Kay and Akram-Lodhi), neo-extractivism and GHG emissions, before considering alternatives that seek to steer an ecologically sustainable course. Each of these issues is taken up in the remaining chapters of the section. Marcus Taylor discusses climate change and development. He outlines how 'climate justice' is concerned with two central questions, namely, how should the burden of reducing global emissions be shared between countries and, second, what can and should be done to address the fact that the impacts of climate change are falling disproportionately on the populations of the Global South. Taylor surveys the issues of mitigation, green development, adaptation and resilience before leaving us with the key question of whether 'degrowth' is required to save the planet.

Raúl Zibechi analyses the complex dynamics of extractive capitalism, which he sees as the latest phase in the evolution of capitalism with forms of resistance that reflect the changes in the social relations of production and particular forms of struggle that correspond to this particular phase of capitalist development. In his review of these dynamics, he identifies a number of new and emerging forms of resistance and class struggle. While the political landscape throughout the 20th century was dominated by the land struggle and the labour movement, the new frontier of extractive capital in South America has seen the formation of diverse resistances ranging from socioenvironmental movements of those affected by the destructive operations of extractive capital to organized resistance against actions and policies that restrict the access of indigenous and peasant communities to the global commons of land, water and the land-based resources used for subsistence.

Organized resistance is one response made by the dispossessed and semiproletarianized rural landless workers and peasant farmers to the forces of social change and capitalist development. Migration in the search for an alternative livelihood based on labour is another (see Chapter 25 by Delgado Wise). David Barkin, on the other hand, in Chapter 30, reconstructs an entirely different response to the expansion of capital, one that has been pioneered by the Zapatistas in Chiapas. It is to disconnect from the capitalist system and construct a social economy on the foundation of a culture of social solidarity, cooperativism and workers' self-management. Barkin reviews and reconstructs the 'social and solidarity economies' that have sprung up on the margins of the capitalist system and within spaces that have been opened up within the system through the cooperative efforts of grassroots organizations. These social and solidarity economies have sprung up in rural and/or indigenous communities across Latin America, and are highlighted as a particular critical counterpoint in the first part of this introduction. Based on a quite different understanding of the purpose of an economic system to capitalism's premise of profit-seeking, Barkin provides examples from avocados to water of communities organizing themselves in ways that provide for a quality of life that includes material goods, social relationships, equality and ecological sustainability.

The final two sections of the book present analysis of national and subnational development projects that have been initiated in the Global South, and which have gained global attention. Section VIII focuses on the 'rise of the BRICS', a turn-of-the-century phenomenon popularized by Goldman Sachs, and which has set the scene for a burgeoning industry analysing linear trends that show how a few mega emerging economies will soon dominate the world economy and replace the old North–South divide. Of course, there is some evidence for this, but before taking the leap of faith that this will lead to 'convergence' being the key trend of the 21st century, a critical development studies scrutiny is warranted. The activities of the BRICS on the international stage has already been seen in discussion of new aid donors (Kragelund) and land grabbing (Kay). The chapters in Section IX in this volume examine Brazil, India, and China further. Some of the discussion is about whether these BRICS will indeed challenge the 'old order' or whether the countries under consideration are better described as 'head servants' or 'sub-imperialists', but the main focus of these chapters is on the internal development dynamics of each of the countries, and in each case the reality between the growth numbers (or ex-growth numbers in the case of Brazil) presents a much more complex picture than popular accounts provide.

The chapter by Garcia and de Sá documents the changes to Brazil's development strategy over time and its attempts to escape from colonial and neocolonial trade patterns (i.e. the primary export model). They show how the implementation of policies consistent with the ECLAC industrialization path, then neoliberalism, and most recently the 'neodevelopmentalism' of the Lula regime, has left Brazil at something of a crossroads with a 'fragmentation and multiplicity of analyses' now competing in the search for a way forward. John Harriss, in his chapter on India, shows that since independence, successive governments have prioritized economic growth and failed to address redistribution. The need to address redistribution remains as real as ever, as economic growth has left many of the poor, especially those in the rural economy, behind. For all the hype behind India's high economic growth and the promise of 'inclusive growth', Harriss argues that 'excluded labour' is a more apt description. Part of the current Indian Prime Minister Modi's development plan is to follow the lead of China in becoming a manufacturing centre. However, So and Chu present a different account of Chinese 'success' than that which is often provided, even when it comes to considering only economic factors. They argue, in ways reminiscent of the Latin American dependency debate of the 1970s, that contemporary China is technologically dependent and heavily reliant on the US market and on multinational capital. To its external dependence must be added high levels of internal income inequality and an environmental catastrophe in the making; the 'China model' is exposed.

Those looking for alternatives might look elsewhere, and the final section of the volume considers the paths that have been adopted in Latin America over the past decade in the so-called 'red/pink tide', to see what lessons can be learned from its successes and failures. To understand what the Latin American experience can tell us, we start with a theoretical chapter by Ronaldo Munck, which asks us first to come to terms with what Latin America is: A part of the Global South? A European outpost? He argues for the concept of 'hybridity' and shows how the 'post-development' movements of the 21st century embrace parts of this. In a wide-ranging exposition, Munck shows how Latin America presents 'a rich laboratory for the study of a wide range of counter-movements', including indigenous ones. Leandro Vergara-Camus focuses on one such counter-movement, that of peasant alternatives to neoliberalism. Building on the chapters by Veltmeyer, Kay and Akram-Lodhi, Vergara-Camus analyses what constitutes 'the peasantry', an analysis necessary to understand how peasants and peasant households respond, both separately and collectively, to the forces that they confront. He discusses these responses, paying particular attention to that followed by *La Vía Campesina*.

A different peasant alternative, that of confronting capitalism and neoliberalism from outside of the state, is provided by the Zapatista movement, and the final chapter of this collection is an exposition of Zapatista thought given by Sergio Rodríguez Lascano, a columnist with the Zapatista journal *Rebeldía*. Here, we learn first-hand from one of the most important social movements in the continent, a piece with which we choose to conclude the volume, leaving the reader with the words of one of the groups and a grassroots organization actively engaged with 'development' from a critical perspective, an engagement that the preceding chapters largely analyse at an arm's-length vantage point. One idea implicit in this Zapatista discourse on confronting the 'capitalist hydra' is that any interaction with the capitalist system tends to strengthen it. For example, the development project of poverty reduction serves – even if not designed to the purpose – as a means of sustaining the system, giving it energy (capitalism can be reformed to make it more humane). Given that capitalism is like a hydra with many heads, there is no point in attacking any one of these heads (the World Bank's anti-poverty programme, for example) because it will simply grow another. The only way of confronting capitalism is not to feed or nourish 'the beast' – but to disconnect from it.

Sandwiched in between Vergara-Camus's piece on the peasant pathway to alternative development and the Zapatista's more radical post-development position is the chapter by Claudio Katz on socialism in Latin America. Drawing especially on the cases of Bolivia and Venezuela, Katz argues for the centrality of the state as the institution necessary to promote an alternative socialist form of development. This emphasis is consistent with some of the other chapters in this volume, but contrasts with others that stress the global and/or local levels as the primary sites in the struggle for a development that serves the interests of humanity and of the planet. It shows that while critical development studies may not have all of the answers, it does provide a guide to the important questions to ask.

Notes

1 These proponents of free-market capitalism constituted a neoliberal thought collective associated with the Mont Pelerin Society founded by Von Hayek and like-minded economists (see Mirowski and Plehwe, 2009).
2 The first academic programme in international development studies was established in The Hague in the Netherlands in the form of the ISS, but similar interdisciplinary development studies programmes were instituted in the UK and elsewhere. In Canada, the first such programme was established in 1985 as a consortium between Saint Mary's University and Dalhousie University in Halifax. In 1989, Saint Mary's University established a graduate programme leading to the MA in IDS, but by 2004 similar programmes were established at over 20 universities across the country. In the same year, an interdisciplinary programme of international development studies was established in Zacatecas, Mexico, as well as in La Paz, Bolivia, and several other Latin American countries.
3 On the evolution in Latin America of an extractive form of capitalism under conditions of a primary commodities boom on the world market, see Veltmeyer (2013) and Veltmeyer and Petras (2014).
4 On this 'new dependency' see, inter alia, Sunkel (2001), who argued in a recent interview that '[t]he international context is not . . . favourable. The world economy is not growing as it used to grow in the past. We have . . . in some cases become more dependent in the last 20 years on raw material exports, on exports based on natural resources. And it has now become a policy in developed countries to try to reduce the natural resource content of the goods that are being produced there as part of the new efforts of sustainable development'. Sunkel add that '[t]his is a big menace for foreign markets of our products. Social conditions have worsened. The state has fewer resources to support the poor. A lot of these natural resources being exploited now are beginning to be threatened by overexploitation. So the outlook for Latin America under these kinds of policies is pretty dim. I believe personally that we need some very substantial changes in the present policies'.
5 Although not theorized in terms of the dynamics of the new world capitalist system, this notion of a new dependency formed under conditions of a primary commodity boom and a consequent (re)primarization of exports from the region has been widely disseminated by a number of heterodox and structuralist economists (Cypher, 2010; Sunkel, 2001).
6 Behind and the fundamental cause of the demise of neoliberalism was the activism of the indigenous and peasant movements in the 1990s (Petras and Veltmeyer, 2009, 2013).
7 The Zapatistas are not alone in this conception, nor are they isolated from a broad Latin America-wide network dedicated to the promulgation of a social and solidarity economy (Coraggio, 2011; Jubeto *et al.*, 2014; Pérez de Mendiguren *et al.*, 2009; REASRed de Redes de Economía Alternativa y Solidaria, n.d.).
8 In Bolivia, the concept of 'vivir bien' is associated with the indigenous term *Suma qamaña* (Artaraz and Calestani, 2014).

References

Acosta, A. (2010). 'El Buen Vivir en el camino del post-desarrollo: Una lectura desde la Constitución de Montecristi'. Policy Paper 9. Friedrich Ebert Stiftung.

Acosta, A. (2012). *Buen Vivir. Sumak kawsay. Una oportunidad para imaginar otros mundos.* Quito: Abya Yala.

Adelman, I. (1986). 'A poverty focused approach to development policy'. In C.K. Wilber (ed.), *The Political Economy of Underdevelopment*, 4th edition. New York: Random House, pp. 493–507.

Albó, X. (2011). 'Suma qamaña = convivir bien. ¿Cómo medirlo?' In *Vivir Bien: ¿paradigma no-capitalista?* La Paz: CIDESUMSA.

Artaraz, K. and Calestani, M. (2014). 'Suma qamaña in Bolivia: indigenous understandings of well-being and their contribution to a post-neoliberal paradigm'. *Latin American Perspectives*, 20 August. Available at: http://lap.sagepub.com/content/early/2014/08/20/0094582X14547501/.

Atria, R., Siles, M., Arriagada, M., Robison, L. and Whiteford, S. (eds) (2004). *Social Capital and Poverty Reduction in Latin America and the Caribbean: Towards a New Paradigm*. Santiago: ECLAC.

Baran, P. (1957). *The Political Economy of Growth*. New York: Monthly Review Press.

Bauer, P.T. (1982). *Equality, the Third World and Economic Delusion*. Cambridge, MA: Harvard University Press.

Borón, A. (2008). 'Teorías de la dependencia'. *Realidad Económica*, 238, August–September: 20–43.

Bresser-Pereira, L.C. (2006). 'El nuevo desarrollismo y la ortodoxia convencional'. *Economía UNAM*, 4(10): 7–29.

Bresser-Pereira, L.C. (2007). 'Estado y mercado en el nuevo desarrollismo'. *Nueva Sociedad*, 210, July–August: 110–25.

Bresser-Pereira, L.C. (2009). *Developing Brazil: Overcoming the Failure of the Washington Consensus*. Boulder, CO: Lynne Rienner.

Burkey, S. (1993). *People First: A Guide to Self-Reliant, Participatory Rural Development*. London: Zed Books.

Cardoso, F.H. (1972). 'Dependency and development in Latin America'. *New Left Review*, 74: 83–95.

Cardoso, F.H. and Faletto, E. (1979 [1971]). *Dependency and Development in Latin America*. Berkeley, CA: University of California Press.

CASID (2003). *White Paper on International Development Studies in Canada*. Ottawa: CASID.

Chambers, R. (1987). *Sustainable Rural Livelihoods: A Strategy for People, Environment and Development*. Brighton: IDS, University of Sussex.

Cohen, J.M. and Uphoff, N. (1977). *Rural Development Participation: Concepts and Measure for Project Design, Implementation and Evaluation*. Center for International Studies, Rural Development Committee, Monograph no. 2. Ithaca, NY: Cornell University Press.

Coraggio, J.L. (2011). *Economía Social y Solidaria. El trabajo antes que el capital*. Quito: Ediciones AbyaYala. Available at: www.coraggioeconomia.org/jlc/archivos%20para%20descargar/economiasocial.pdf.

Cowen, M. and Shenton, R. (1995). *Doctrines of Development*. London: Routledge.

Craig, D. and Porter, D. (2006). *Development Beyond Neoliberalism? Governance, Poverty Reduction and Political Economy*. London: Routledge.

Cypher, J. (2010). 'South America's commodities boom: developmental opportunity or path-dependent reversion?' *Canadian Journal of Development Studies*, 30(3–4): 565–638.

Dávalos, P. (2008). 'Reflexiones sobre el sumak kawsay (el buen vivir) y las teorías del desarrollo'. *Eutsi – Pagina de izquierda Antiautoritaria*. Ecuador.

Delgado Wise, R. and Martin, D. (2015). 'The political economy of global labour arbitrage'. In K. Van der Pijl (ed.), *Handbook of the International Political Economy of Production*. Cheltenham, UK: Edward Elgar, pp. 59–75.

Delgado Wise, R. and Veltmeyer, H. (2016). *Agrarian Change, Migration and Development*. Halifax: Fernwood.

Dos Santos, T. (1998). *La teoría de la dependencia un balance histórico y teórico, Los retos de la globalización*. Caracas: UNESCO.

Dos Santos, T. (2011). 'Globalization, emerging powers, and the future of capitalism'. *Latin American Perspectives*, 38 (March): 45–57.

Durston, J. (1999). 'Building community social capital'. *Cepal Review*, 69: 103–18.

Dutra, S.T. (n.d). *Capital social y desarrollo: Análisis crítico de la literatura producida por la Iniciativa sobre Capital Social del Banco Mundial (1996–2001)*. Bilbao: Universidad del pais Vasco (Euskal Herriko Unibertsitatea).

Escobar, A. (1997). 'Unmasking development'. In M. Rahnema and V. Bawtree (eds), *The Post-Development Reader*. London: Zed Books, pp. 191–203.

Farah, I. and Vasapollo, L. (eds) (2011). *Vivir bien: ¿Paradigma no capitalista?* La Paz: CIDES-UMSA.

Fine, B. (2001). 'It ain't social and it ain't capital'. In G. Morrow (ed.), *An Appropriate Capitalisation? Questioning Social Capital*. Research in Progress series, Issue 1, October (special issue). London School of Economics, The Gender Institute, pp. 11–15.

Frank, A.G. (1967). *Capitalism and Underdevelopment in Latin America*. New York: Monthly Review Press.

Fukuyama, F. (2004). 'Social capital and development: the coming agenda'. In R. Atria et al. (eds), *Social Capital and Poverty Reduction in Latin America and the Caribbean: Towards a New Paradigm*. Santiago: ECLAC, pp. 33–47.

Goulet, D. (1989). 'Participation in development: new avenues'. *World Development*, 17(2): 165–78.

Gudynas, E. (2014). 'El postdesarrollo como crítica y el Buen Vivir como alternativa'. In C. Delgado Ramos (ed.), *Buena Vida, Buen Vivir: imaginarios alternativos para el bien común de la humanidad*. México: CEIICH – UNAM, pp. 61–95.

Guillen, A. (2007). *La teoría latinoamericana del desarrollo. Repensar la teoría del desarrollo en un contexto de globalización*. Buenos Aires: CLACSO.

Harriss, J. (2001). *Depoliticising Development: The World Bank and Social Capital*. New Delhi: Left Word Books.

Harriss, J. and de Renzio, P. (1997). '"Missing link" or analytically missing? The concept of social capital: an introductory bibliographic essay'. *Journal of International Development*, 9(7): 919–37.

Harvey, D. (2003). *The New Imperialism*. Oxford: Oxford University Press.

Hernández López, R. (2005). 'La dependencia debate'. *Latinoamérica*, 40, January: 11–54.

Hirschman, A.O. (1958). *The Strategy of Economic Development*. New Haven, CT: Yale University Press.

Hollnsteiner, M.R. (1977). 'People power: community participation in the planning of human settlements'. *Assignment Children*, 40, October–December: 11–47.

Jolly, R., Cornea, A. and Stewart, F. (1987). *Adjustment with a Human Face Protects Vulnerable Growth*. Oxford: Oxford University Press.

Jubeto, Y., Guridi, L. and Fernández Villa, M. (eds) (2014). *Diálogos sobre Economía Social y Solidaria en Ecuador: Encuentros y desencuentros con las propuestas para otra economía*. Bilbao: Instituto Hegoa, Universidad del País Vasco (Euskal Herriko Unibertsitate). Available at: http://publicaciones.hegoa.ehu.es/assets/pdfs/318/Dialogos_sobre_ESS_en_Ecuador. pdf?14029%2008778.

Katz, C. (2016). *El surgimiento de las teorías de la dependencia*. ALAI-America latina en movimiento, 29 July. Available at: www.alainet.org/es/articulo/179142.

Kay, C. (1989). *Latin American Theories of Development and Underdevelopment*. London: Routledge.

Knack, S. (1999). 'Social capital, growth and poverty: a survey of cross-country evidence'. *Social Capital Initiative Working Paper 7*, Washington, DC: World Bank, Social Development Department.

Korten, D. and Klauss, R. (eds) (1984). *People-Centred Development: Contributions Toward Theory and Planning Frameworks*. West Hartford, CT: Kumarian Press.

Kuznets, S. (1953). 'Economic growth and income inequality'. *The American Economic Review*, March: 1–28.

Lal, D. (1983). *The Poverty of Development Economics*. London: Institute of Economic Affairs.

Lewis, W.A. (1963 [1954]). 'Economic development with unlimited supplies of labour'. In A.N. Agarwala and S.P. Singh (eds), *Economics of Underdevelopment*. New York: Oxford University Press, pp. 131–91.

Marglin, S. and Schor, J. (1990). *The Golden Age of Capitalism: Reinterpreting the Post-War Experience*. Oxford: Clarendon Press.

Martins, C.E. (2011). *Globalizacao, Dependencia e Neoliberalismo na América Latina*. Sao Paulo: Boitempo.

Medina, J. (2011). 'Acerca del Suma Qamaña'. In *Vivir Bien: ¿paradigma no-capitalista?* La Paz: CIDES-UMSA, pp. 39–64.

Meier, G. and Seers, D. (eds) (1984). *Pioneers in Development*. New York: Oxford University Press.

Mirowski, P. and Plehwe, D. (2009). *The Road from Mont Pelerin: The Making of the Neoliberal Thought Collective*. Cambridge: Cambridge University Press.

Moreno-Brid, J.C. (2013). 'Industrial policy: a missing link in Mexico's quest for export-led growth'. *Policy Studies*, 4(2): 216–37.

Moser, C. (1993). *Gender Planning and Development: Theory, Practice and Training*. London and New York: Routledge.

Narayan, D. (2002). *Empowerment and Poverty Reduction: A Sourcebook*. Washington, DC: World Bank.

Osorio, J. (2009). *Dependencia e superexplotacao. A América Latina e os desafios da globalizacao*. Rio de Janeiro: Boitempo.

Palma, J. (1978). 'Dependency theory and its implications for contemporary development strategy'. *World Development*, 6: 881–924.

Parpart, J., Connelly, P. and Eudine Barriteau, V. (eds) (2000). *Theoretical Perpectives on Gender and Development*. Ottawa: IDRC.

Parpart, J., Rai, S. and Staudt, K. (eds) (2002). *Rethinking Empowerment: Gender and Development in a Global/Local World*. London: Routledge.

Pérez de Mendiguren, J.C., Etxezarreta, E. and Guridi, L. (2009). 'Economía Social, Empresa Social y Economía Solidaria: diferentes conceptos para un mismo debate'. *Papeles de Economía Solidaria*, 1. Available at: www.economiasolidaria.org/files/papeles_ES_1_ReasEuskadi.pdf.

Petras, J. and Veltmeyer, H. (2001). *Globalization Unmasked: Imperialism in the 21st Century*. London/Halifax: Zed Press/Fernwood.

Petras, J. and Veltmeyer, H. (2009). *What's Left in Latin America?* Farnham: Ashgate.

Petras, J. and Veltmeyer, H. (2013). *Social Movements in Latin America: Neoliberalism and Popular Resistance*. Basingstoke: Palgrave Macmillan.

Polanyi, K. (1957). *The Great Transformation*. Boston, MA: Beacon.

Rahman, A. (ed.) (1984). *Grassroots Participation and Self-Reliance*. Delhi: Oxford University Press.

Rahnema, M. and Bawtree, V. (eds) (1997). *The Post-Development Reader*. London: Zed Books.

Rao, V. (2002). *Community Driven Development: A Brief Review of the Research*. Washington, DC: World Bank.

Razeto, L. (1993). *De la economia popular a la economia de solidaridad en un proyecto de desarrollo alternative*. Santiago: Programa de Economía del Trabajo (PET).

REASRed de Redes de Economía Alternativa y Solidaria (n.d.). *Portal de Economía Solidaria*. Available at: www.economiasolidaria.org/.

Redclift, M.R. (1987). *Sustainable Development: Exploring the Contradictions*. London: Methuen.

Rostow, W.W. (1960). *The Stages of Economic Growth: A Non-Communist Manifesto*. Cambridge: Cambridge University Press.

Sachs, W. (ed.) (1992). *The Development Dictionary: A Guide to Knowledge and Power*. London: Zed Books.

Sen, A. (1989). 'Development as capability expansion'. *Journal of Development Expansion*, 19: 41–58.

Sen, A. (1999). *Development as Freedom*. New York: Alfred & Knopf.

Solón, P. (2014). *Systemic Alternatives: Vivir Bien. Notes for the Debate*. Coordinated by ATTAC France, Focus on the Global South and Fundación Solón.

Solow, R. (2000). 'Notes on social capital and economic performance'. In P. Dasgupta and I. Serageldin (eds), *Social Capital: A Multi-Faceted Perspective*. Washington, DC: World Bank, pp. 6–10.

Sotelo, A. (2000). '¿Globalización: estancamiento o crisis en América Latina?' *Problemas de Desarrollo*, 120, January–March: 31–53.

Sotelo, A. (2005). 'Dependencia y sistema mundial: ¿convergencia o divergencia?' *Rebelión*. Available at: www.rebelion.org/noticia.php?id=19642 (4-9-2005).

Sotelo, A. (2009). 'Neo-imperialismo, dependencia e novas periferias'. *A América Latina e os desafíos da globalizaca*. Rio de Janeiro: Boitempo.

Stiefel, M. and Wolfe, M. (1994). *A Voice for the Excluded: Popular Participation in Development – Utopia or Necessity?* London: Zed Books.

Sunkel, O. (1993). *Development from Within: Toward a Neo-Structuralist Approach for Latin America*. Boulder, CO: Lynne Rienner.

Sunkel, O. (2001). 'Up for debate: dependencia and protectionism in hindsight'. Interview conducted for PBS, *Commanding Heights*. Available at: www.tc.pbs.org/wgbh/commanding heights/shared/pdf/int_osvaldosunkel.pdf.

Toye, J. (1987). *Dilemmas of Development: Reflections on the Counter-Revolution in Development Theory and Policy*. Oxford: Basil Blackwell.

Tucker, V. (1999). 'The myth of development: a critique of Eurocentric discourse'. In R. Munck and D. O'Hearn (eds), *Critical Development Theory*. London: Zed Books, pp. 44–62.

UNCTAD (2016). *Trade and Development Report: Structural Transformation for Inclusive and Sustained Growth*. New York/Geneva: UNCTAD.

UNDP (1997). *Governance for Sustainable Human Development: A UNDP Policy Document*. New York: UNDP.

Veltmeyer, H. (2001). 'The politics of language: deconstructing the discourse of postdevelopment'. *Canadian Journal of Development Studies*, 22(3): 597–620.

Veltmeyer, H. (2002). 'The politics of language: deconstructing post-development discourse'. *Canadian Journal of Development Studies*, 22(3): 597–624.

Veltmeyer, H. (2005). 'Development and globalization as imperialism'. *Canadian Journal of Development Studies*, 26(1): 89–106.

Veltmeyer, H. (2011). 'Social capital and local development'. In *The Critical Development Studies Handbook: Tools for Change*. London/Halifax: Pluto/Fernwood, pp. 225–31.

Veltmeyer, H. (2013). 'The political economy of natural resource extraction: a new model or extractive imperialism?' *Canadian Journal of Development Studies*, 34(1), March: 79–95.

Veltmeyer, H. and Petras, J. (2014). *Neoextractivism: A New Model or the Imperialism of the 21st Century?* London: Zed Books.

Veltmeyer, H. and Rushton, M. (2013). *The Cuban Revolution as Socialist Human Development.* Chicago, IL: Haymarket Books.

Vieta, M. (ed.) (2014). *Social and Solidarity Economy: Towards Inclusive and Sustainable Development.* Geneva: ITC-ILO.

Woolcock, M. and Narayan, D. (2000). 'Social capital: implications for development theory, research and policy'. *The World Bank Research Observer*, 15(2), August: 225–49.

World Bank (1979). *Recognizing the 'Invisible' Women in Development: The World Bank's Experience.* Washington, DC: World Bank.

World Bank (2007). *Meeting the Challenges of Global Development.* Washington, DC: World Bank.

PART I
Reflections on history

1

HISTORY FROM A CRITICAL DEVELOPMENT PERSPECTIVE

Kari Polanyi Levitt

Neither foreign assistance nor projects at the grassroots can substitute for a national developmental state acting in the public interest of the majority population. Only an effective national government can assure the framework for the provision of the basic amenities of modern life to its citizens, including a supply of potable water to every household, a comprehensive system of public transportation, free primary and secondary education, and universal access to health services.

Liberal policies of economic globalization were and are aimed at creating a 'borderless world' for capital – but not for labour. Global capital has no address, no country and no social responsibility. By contrast, people live in societies with specific geographic, historical and cultural characteristics and support systems that enable them to survive adversity and exercise collective solidarities to improve their lives. There is no such thing as global society. 'Think globally, act locally' is the motto of development and environmentalist activists, but the problem with this approach is that at the global level, power lies with capital. At the community level, social movements cannot secure their objectives without a government able to defend society against the destructive capacities of the global market to invade, reorganize and exploit human and natural resources. Where countries are too small, this calls for regional cooperation.

Origins of the development agenda

Development came on the agenda before the end of World War II in anticipation of the decolonization of Asia and Africa. Leaders of struggles to free the colonial world from imperialist control and refugee economists from continental Europe gathered in London, Cambridge and Oxford. The early literature on development economics was produced by independent-minded scholars. A remarkable number originated from Scandinavia (Frisch, Myrdal, Nurkse), Western Europe

(Hirschman, Mandelbaum, Perroux, Singer, Tinbergen) and Central and Eastern Europe (Bauer, Georgescu-Roegen, Kaldor, Kalecki, Rosenstein-Roden, Streeten, Schumacher). Others came from Britain (D. Seers), Russia (Gerschenkron, Kuznets, Leontieff), India (V.K.R.V. Rao, Chakravarty, Mahalanobis), Burma (Myint), Argentina (Prebisch), Egypt (S. Amin), Brazil (Furtado), the West Indies (W.A. Lewis) and the US (Chenery, Rostow). The early UN provided a supportive environment, and important conferences were held in New Delhi, Rio de Janeiro and Cairo.

In 1945, the US and the Soviet Union emerged as the two most important world powers. Both enjoyed respect and influence in Europe and Asia, but neither was initially concerned with the development of underdeveloped regions. The primary concern of the US in the early post-war years was the threat of communism in Europe and Asia. A secondary objective was the dissolution of British and also French preferential economic spheres of influence and currency blocs. The Marshall Plan, a large volume of unconditional economic assistance, was successful in limiting Soviet influence to the satellite states of Eastern Europe, where communist governments were installed in 1948 after a brief period of democratic multiparty regimes. In Asia, following the defeat of Japan in 1945, US hegemony was challenged by the victory of Mao's communist revolution in 1949. The remnants of Chiang Kai-Shek's forces retreated to Taiwan. For the next 30 years, the US recognized the Nationalists in Taiwan as the legitimate government of China with a veto in the Security Council in the UN. A major war in Korea pitted a US-led UN force against China, resulting in the division of the country between North and South, with 30,000 troops on the border to this day. The US Seventh Fleet is permanently deployed in the waters of Japan, Korea and Taiwan.

A rising tide of anti-imperialist forces in Southeast Asia were engaged in struggles to free the region from Japanese occupation and attain political independence from British, French and Dutch colonialism. British India gained independence in 1947, tragically by the division of the subcontinent into India and Pakistan. India established friendly relations with the Soviet Union while Pakistan drifted into the US sphere of influence. In 1956, Egyptian President Nasser nationalized the Suez Canal, and the US refused to support British and French intervention.

In 1955, President Sukarno of Indonesia, joined by Nehru of India, Nasser of Egypt and Nkrumah of Ghana, convened a conference of Asian and African non-aligned states in Bandung. China's premier and foreign minister Zhou Enlai headed the Chinese delegation. By this time, China's relations with Russia had chilled, and Tito's role in the Non-Aligned Movement, formalized in Belgrade in 1961, was evidence that the Bandung initiative sought independence from Moscow as well as Washington.

The US used every means at its disposal in efforts to replace secular national left-wing governments, including assistance to religious fundamentalist extremists, as in Afghanistan in the 1980s. From the overthrow of Mossadegh and the installation of the Shah in Iran, to the massacre of a million supporters of the Sukarno regime in Indonesia by General Suharto in 1965, to the war in Vietnam from 1965 to

1975, and massive support for the Marcos regime in the Philippines, which hosted a principal US military base, Asia was the prize, and official development assistance was directed towards securing the gains.

Recommended reading: Polanyi Levitt (2013).

The development project takes shape

In the course of the 1950s, development studies was institutionalized, and the US State Department engaged the services of leading US universities to fashion programmes of economic development. India was assigned to Harvard, and Indonesia to MIT, and the University of Chicago played the leading role in Latin American studies. MIT professor W.W. Rostow's *Stages of Economic Growth*, subtitled *A Non-Communist Manifesto*, suggested that any country could engage in an aeronautical assent from 'takeoff' to self-sustaining growth and mass consumption, provided cultural and historical obstacles to modern business practice were overcome. The model was appealing, and the modernization approach dominated development studies in political science and sociology.

In the 1950s, Latin American states were firmly locked into friendly relationships with the US, which could at all times count on their votes in the UN. It is important to note, however, that the US did not pressure these governments to comply with free trade treaties. Brazil was particularly successful in implementing policies of industrialization. The US responded to the Cuban Revolution of 1959 by launching the Alliance for Progress. The US also imposed a trade embargo and made a number of unsuccessful attempts at regime change on the island. In 1962, Cuba was suspended from the Organization of American States (OAS); only Mexico and Canada maintained diplomatic relations. With the end of easy import substitution, political tensions mounted. In 1964, a military government took control of Brazil and exiled thousands of intellectuals and other opponents of the regime. In 1973, the democratically elected government of Allende in Chile was overthrown by a US-supported military coup. Murderous military dictatorships were also established in Argentina and Uruguay in 1976. Strong economic growth in the 1970s was driven by favourable markets for primary products, and Latin America attracted large inflows of capital from US commercial banks seeking returns higher than could be obtained domestically. The foundations of the debt crisis of the 1980s were laid.

As an increasing number of African and Caribbean countries acceded to political independence, the UN established the Conference on Trade and Development (UNCTAD) in 1964 under the direction of Raúl Prebisch to address the problems of export-dependent peripheries. But it was the Organization of Petroleum Exporting Countries (OPEC) in the Middle East with the participation of Venezuela that was effective in exercising commodity power.

In the 1970s, the General Assembly of the UN adopted the Action Plan for a New International Economic Order. Many international conferences were held, but no meaningful concessions were made by the North. It marked the end of an era in which the UN could effectively give voice to the aspirations of the developing world. In his Nobel Prize lecture of 1979, renowned development economist W. Arthur Lewis noted that there will be no new international economic order until the nations of the Global South develop their own resources, individually and collectively, to increase food production and employ their populations in productive industries and services. He noted that the 'engines of growth' of industrialized countries were slowing down, and that continued dependence on exports to these countries would ensure that they remain poor. A more equitable international economic order would have to await the rising power of the Global South. With the accession of Prime Minister Thatcher (in 1979) and President Reagan (in 1980), an economic regime change was instituted in Britain and the US. The objective was to restore the discipline of capital over labour in the industrialized world and reduce the powers of government in the developing world. A doctrinal coup at the World Bank dismissed liberal-minded economists, including Streeten and Ul Haq, who had introduced a basic needs approach to development, and installed a team of hard-nosed neoliberals, including several trade economists. Policies of domestic industrialization, which had achieved growth rates in the South equalling those of the industrialized countries from 1950 to 1980, were now deemed to be inefficient and contrary to principles of comparative advantage in international trade. Export-oriented development became the new panacea. The early pioneers of development economics were demonized as 'structuralist,' a heresy bordering on socialism.

Recommended reading: Parpart and Veltmeyer (2004).

The right to development

There was no longer a need for development economics because in the new order the laws of economics had universal validity without regard for structural or historical difference. Two prominent pioneers of development economics, Albert Hirschman and Dudley Seers, wrote eulogies with titles such as *The Rise and Decline of Development Economics* and *The Birth, Life and Death of Development Economics.*

The declaration of the right to development by the UN in 1986 was a defensive action intended to confirm the right of developing countries to engage in national strategies of social and economic transformation. However, under the influence of the rising tide of neoliberalism, the UN Universal Declaration of Human Rights of 1948, which included social and economic rights, was reinterpreted as a doctrine of individual human rights, which effectively excluded the collective right to development. Twenty-five years of structural adjustment policies imposed on African and Latin American debtor countries has systematically limited the exercise of sovereign states to achieve the goals of human development for their citizens. Development was replaced by macroeconomic and structural adjustment to demands of private and official creditors. The Washington Consensus of deregulation, liberalization and privatization became the universal prescription. The authors of the *UN Contribution to Development Thinking and Practice,* the official history of the UN, acknowledged that in the 1980s, the intellectual and policy initiative regarding development passed to the IMF and the World Bank. The UN found itself 'unable to come forward with a new agenda that offered the prospect of coping with the new problems while preserving the social and human development goals it had been advocating' (Jolly *et al.*, 2004: 150). The UN became increasingly impotent.

An extreme rise in interest rates at the opening of the 1980s plunged Latin American countries into a decade-long debt crisis. Overexposed commercial banks were rescued by the IMF and the US Treasury. Private debt was socialized and added to public debt. The blame for the debt crisis and the entire cost of adjustment was placed on the debtor countries and borne by their populations.

Africa became a gigantic laboratory for experiments in economic liberalization, as scores of countries came under the tutelage of the IMF and the World Bank. Subsidies to farmers were eliminated, and domestic food production declined as scarce resources, including water, were reserved for the production of exotic products, such as strawberries and flowers, for European markets. Where tropical agricultural commodities competed with US products, as in the case of cotton, African exports were effectively embargoed. Few economists in Africa believed in these policies, but desperation elicited compliance.

By contrast, in the 1970s and 1980s, Korea had embarked on industrial policies that combined import substitution with export promotion guided by large and effective planning agencies with the full support and direct participation of political authorities. The corporatist business organization of Korea was modelled on Japan, with close association between large productive enterprise and domestic development banks. Foreign direct investment was restricted. In Taiwan, medium-sized enterprises were favoured. The success of the so-called tiger economies owed nothing to the World Bank or the IMF, but benefited from the geopolitical interests of the US, which permitted them to engage in active industrial policies that violated neoliberal doctrine. With variations, such as the encouragement of FDI, policies combining domestic industrialization with export of manufactures were followed by Malaysia, Thailand, Indonesia and later also Vietnam. In all these cases, nationally owned enterprises were critical to successful economic development. In the late 1970s, China launched a programme of economic reform combining private with state enterprise in a unique model of a socialist market economy. This yielded unprecedented high rates of growth, based on very high rates of domestic and foreign investment, the latter principally from overseas Chinese capital from North and Southeast Asia. External markets for manufactured exports in North America and Europe were complemented by a dense network of China-centred regional trade relations. In the early 1990s, China, and to a lesser degree India, emerged as new growth poles of the world economy.

Recommended reading: Jolly *et al.* (2004).

The nation state, capitalism and development

As in the earlier case of the late industrializers of the 19th century – Germany, the US, Russia and others – no country has ever achieved economic development without the construction of an effective modern nation state, and no country has established a viable industrial base without protecting its industries from the unrestricted import of goods and capital. In all cases of late industrialization, economic development was a political project requiring a state with authority and legitimacy to negotiate conflicting interests of classes and regions.

Following the victory of the West in the Cold War and the implosion of the Soviet Union, social democratic governments in Europe embraced Anglo-American doctrines and policies of privatization. Socialism was in ideological retreat, and the social welfare state on the defensive. In Russia, a new oligarchy of former Soviet officials acquired state assets at firesale prices. Huge fortunes were made in this chaotic condition of wild capitalism, while millions descended into poverty and average life expectancy plummeted. Similar policies transformed the countries of East Europe from Soviet satellites to economic and political clients of the Western powers. NATO military installations were shifted from West to East Europe, and control over the Balkans was secured by dismantling the former Yugoslavia. In 1991, the US launched the first Gulf War against Iraq, which it had previously supported in its war with Iran.

In the rest of the world, the projection of Western economic power was aimed at securing access to markets and natural resources and, most importantly, protection of foreign investments from regulation and control by host national governments. The first attempt at a treaty designed to privilege investor rights over the sovereign rights of national governments was the Multilateral Agreement on Investment (MAI) drafted by the Organisation for Economic Co-operation and Development (OECD). This was blocked by a campaign of international NGOs. The arrangements governing mutually negotiated trade agreements under the GATT (General Agreement on Tariffs and Trade) was converted to the WTO, with binding rules and mechanisms of enforcement of all member countries, now extended to include services, intellectual property and so-called trade-related investment measures (TRIMs). Although disadvantaged in negotiations, developing countries were able to use their votes to block agreement on further extensions to include investment, government procurement and competition aimed at entrenching the privileges of the transnational corporations and proposals granting foreign investors extended rights under enhanced free trade agreements (FTAs) such as the North American Free Trade Agreement (NAFTA). Signed in 1994, NAFTA served as a template for the proposed Free Trade Agreement of the Americas (FTAA) and all subsequent FTAs. Commitments made by countries signing FTAs with the US or Economic Partnership Agreements (EPAs) with the European Community go far beyond what is required of member countries of the WTO. In the early 1990s, a word was lifted from the literature of communications and presented as describing an irreversible historical trend towards a borderless global economy: 'globalization'. For developing countries, there appeared to be no alternative to deeper integration into circuits of trade and capital flows. As Latin America emerged from the debt crisis of the 1980s, governments advised by US-trained economists and installed in central banks and ministries of finance instituted neoliberal reforms – most radically in Argentina. In Africa, debt relief failed to reverse the excess of the outflow of debt service over the inflow of official development assistance. This so-called TINA (There Is No Alternative) effect was accompanied by extravagant claims for the beneficial results of 'globalization'.

The World Development Report of 1995, entitled *Workers in an Integrating World*, suggested that globalization promised a return to the 'golden age' of 1870–1914, which could bring untold prosperity to developing countries provided they opened their economies to unrestricted imports and capital flows. The title of the report suggests that workers could be the principal beneficiaries of globalization. The authors of this flagship publication of the World Bank seem to have forgotten the fact that 1870–1914 was the Age of Empire, when European imperialist expansion engulfed all of Africa and most of Asia. Throughout this period, colonial labour exploited in the mines and plantations of Africa and Asia contributed to the accumulation of capital in the industrialized countries, impoverishing many in these areas and countries, and a deterioration in their terms of trade. Colonial possessions became captive markets for British and other European textiles, and their traditional agricultural economies were transformed to supply cotton, rubber, palm oil, jute, indigo and other agricultural and mineral commodities to the metropoles.

When Adam Smith published *The Wealth of Nations* in 1776, the living standard of an Indian peasant was no lower than that of an English agricultural labourer, and China was regarded as a model of a prosperous and stable civilization. From the Conquest of Bengal by the East India Company and throughout the 19th and early 20th centuries, British India regressed from a viable agricultural economy to an impoverished underdeveloped country. In the late 1870s, and again in the late 1890s, the failure of monsoon rains produced the greatest famines in recorded history in India and also in Northern China. British authorities failed to provide famine relief and continued to ship large quantities of grains to London on railways, the costs of which were charged to the colonial government of India. Because colonial authorities neglected to maintain traditional management of water resources of canals, wells and storage tanks to provide for drought, many millions perished unnecessarily from hunger and disease. In China, social disintegration due to the introduction of opium by the British East India Company earlier in the 19th century had weakened the capacity of the government to come to the aid of the victims of the famine in Northern China, which claimed between 8 and 20 million lives. Both in India and in China, the forced opening of the country to 'world markets' by British imperial policies turned devastating droughts into human disasters (Davis, 2002).

It is difficult to understand how an agency mandated to serve 'development' could have advocated a return to the globalization of the 19th century as a prescription for development for the 21st century. Moreover, the World Development Report of 1995, a veritable capitalist manifesto, cannot be dismissed as a lapse of memory, because the World Bank continues to urge countries to increase exports, encourage imports to compete with domestic firms to improve efficiency, open up to unrestricted flows of capital and generally to deepen integration into the world economy.

Recommended reading: Bello (2009), Bienefeld (2013), Veltmeyer (2005, 2013), World Bank (1995).

The financialization of development and the global crisis

The most serious crisis since the Great Depression has most heavily affected precisely those countries that are most deeply integrated into the financial networks of capitalism. The epicentre of the crisis is in the US, and the countries most vulnerable include the UK, Australia, Switzerland, the Eurozone, Eastern Europe and the OECD country of South Korea. Among the least vulnerable are the large developing countries, including China, Indonesia and Nigeria. For the first time since the 1970s, the IMF has extended rescue packages to European countries, including Iceland ($12 billion), Hungary ($20 billion), Latvia and other Baltic countries indebted to Western banks. By contrast, in the developing world, only Pakistan and Turkey requested IMF assistance.

The 1990s witnessed more frequent and more severe financial crises than those of the 1930s, not yet in the heartlands of capitalism, but in Mexico, Turkey, Brazil, Argentina, Russia and, most importantly, in East Asia. In some of these crises, incomes plunged not by 2 or 5 per cent, but by 20 or even 30 per cent at a time. The IMF intervened to save major international banks from losses in East Asia in 1997–1998 and facilitated the transfer of ownership of industrial enterprises from domestic to foreign capital. Following the rescue by the US Federal Reserve of a very large New York hedge fund, which threatened to bring down the world financial system, there was talk of the need for a new architecture to oversee and control global financial markets. The panic soon passed, and in 1999 legislation enacted during the Great Depression, which had prohibited deposit-taking commercial banks from engaging in the sale of stocks, bonds and insurance and issue of mortgages, was repealed by the Clinton administration at the urging of Wall Street. The firewall separating commercial from investment banks was thereby removed. For the next 10 years, an inverted pyramid of financial assets and claims was constructed on the base of the savings of millions of people in pension funds, mutual funds, insurance premiums, equities and investment in real estate, whose value appeared to be forever rising. During the Bush administration, all remaining restrictions on financial transactions were removed.

Since the mid-1980s, the returns on portfolio investments and the opportunities for capital gains have exceeded profits from investment in non-financial enterprise. Corporations moved assets from production to distribution and finance. They engaged in downsizing, subcontracting and outsourcing to cheaper labour locations to boost shareholder value and compete on stock markets with financial service industries. Some 40 per cent of total corporate profit accrued to financial enterprise. The contribution of finance, insurance and real estate now amounts to 20 per cent of GDP in the US and Britain, whereas manufacturing has declined to levels of 13 and 11 per cent, respectively. There has been no increase in median wage and salary earnings in the past 25 years.

Millions of people were employed in the unproductive activity of transferring ownership of paper claims. Billions of dollars were made by promoters, traders and insiders of this virtual casino of exotic financial products that transfer resources from producers and taxpayers to owners of legal claims to a portion of the output of the real economy. Both at the domestic and international levels, it has been an engine of inequality and instability.

Ten years after the Asian crisis, the inevitable crash finally hit the heartlands of this predatory Anglo-American variety of capitalism. The epicentre was the US and Britain, but the damage extended to Europe and to financial institutions in many other countries. The permissive condition of the extraordinary accumulation of public and private debt was the inflow of capital from the rest of the world to cover a 6 per cent external current account deficit in the US. Since 1971, when the US abandoned gold convertibility, the US dollar has served as the principal reserve currency of the world, and banks have been able to create dollar liabilities unconstrained by official reserve ratios.

Keynes's greatest fear was that finance would destroy capitalism. By this, he surely meant that the unrestricted power of financial capital could corrupt the capitalism that organized the production of useful goods and services and applied technology to improve living standards of the people. Western governments are pouring billions into the bottomless coffers of banks to save a rapacious form of capitalism that has demonstrably failed to deliver on its promises. The ideologues and institutions that preach their doctrines of 'reform', designed and serving to subordinate societies and nations to the global republic of capital, have lost all legitimacy. Henceforth, the crisis must present an opportunity to regain political and economic control of governments by the majority population in the developing world.

Globalization, it has often been said, provides challenges and opportunities, winners and losers. But history has surprises. The advocates of globalization did not imagine that the principal beneficiary of the liberalization of trade would be communist China. Nor did they anticipate that the failures of liberalization policies in Latin America would result in the election of a new generation of left-leaning political leaders. They certainly did not expect that the deregulation of powerful financial institutions would unleash the most serious financial and economic crisis since the Great Depression.

In contrast to declining output in the 'advanced capitalist countries' and also in the 'emerging market economies' of Russia and East Europe, the developing world showed reduced but significant growth. In all regions of the developing world, reduced export earnings and cancellation of investment projects substantially reduced growth rates from levels attained in 2007, but the engines of growth have not shut down. Post-global financial crisis growth is now sustained primarily by the developing world.

For 100 years or more, growth in the commodity supplying peripheries was dependent on growth in the major industrial centres. This relationship of dependence is undergoing a significant change as countries and regions of the developing world are generating a measure of self-sustaining growth. The divergent growth rates since 2009 reveal the lesser vulnerability of the Global South to the unfolding economic crisis, although this point is arguable. As noted earlier, the most vulnerable economies are those that are most closely integrated into metropolitan circuits of international commerce and finance. Export-dependent countries with diversified external (and regional) markets, such as the ASEAN countries, are less vulnerable than the countries of Latin America. Developing Asia, which accounts for roughly one-third of world output, is currently the growth point of the world economy.

What is interesting here is why Latin America, which in 1950 had GDP per capita levels approximating those of Southern Europe, accounted for half the trade of the developing world and averaged 6.1 per cent growth from 1960 to 1980, lost a decade of growth in the 1980s and failed to recover a growth momentum in the 1990s. The most striking difference between East Asia and Latin America is the extreme inequality of land ownership and of income in the latter. In Japan, South Korea and Taiwan, America instituted a thoroughgoing land reform after the end of World War II. In China, the communist revolution dispossessed landowners and reorganized agriculture, while maintaining state ownership of land. It is important to note that it is not only in China and former colonies of Japan that rural producers have been able to share in the economic growth of the country, but equality of assets and income is also far higher in Indonesia, Malaysia and Thailand than in Latin America. Only in the Philippines has the legacy of Spanish and US colonialism resulted in inequalities of land ownership approximating those of Latin America.

The deep cleavages of class and ethnicity in Latin America have their origin in the conquest and dispossession of aboriginal peoples 500 years ago and the legacy of the slave trade, which brought African labour to work the plantations of Brazil and the Caribbean, and the subsequent settlement of European populations on stolen lands. Since the beginning of the 19th century, landed oligarchies controlled and profited from the export of primary commodities, more recently accompanied by industrialization by import substitution for a domestic market that was restricted to the middle and upper levels of a highly skewed distribution of income. With the exception of Brazil, Latin American business classes did not develop manufacturing industries capable of competing in international markets; they preferred to place their savings in overseas financial institutions in Miami, New York or Toronto. There is an absence of national cohesion. Elites effectively do not pay taxes, nor can they be collected from the large informal economy in which the majority of the population is engaged. The state is in perpetual fiscal shortfall. Governments, which have largely been controlled by business interests, have welcomed transnational corporations and have been quick to sell off the national patrimony of state enterprises, in some cases merely to meet payroll. Privatization in Latin America has been more far-reaching than in East Asia or in India (we remind the reader that South Korea was closed to FDI prior to the Asian crisis of 1997–1998). The frequency of political and economic crises in Latin America and the temptation of populist governments to deal with distributional conflict by printing money are ultimately due to the unresolved legacies of the origins of Latin American society. The recent political assertion of indigenous peoples of the Andean region constitute a break with the past and hold out the promise that the long suppressed cultural practices and institutions of indigenous peoples of the Americas may contribute to novel forms of democratic governance and organization of economic life.

Recommended reading: Petras and Veltmeyer (2001), Polanyi Levitt (2013).

The contradictions of financialization

Since the early 1980s, we have witnessed a reversion to accumulation by dispossession, reminiscent of the old days of the mercantilist era that preceded industrial capitalism. Transnational corporations (TNCs) have increasingly secured monopolistic control over markets on a global scale. In many respects, they are more powerful than governments. The largest of these companies, such as Monsanto, do indeed resemble the old chartered trading companies. Millions of farmers are in bondage to this and similar companies, and many thousands have been dispossessed of their land. In the industrialized world, transnational corporations have outsourced production to cheap labour countries, and millions of workers have been dispossessed of good jobs. This is reflected in the declining contribution of manufacturing, and the increasing contribution of finance, distribution and business services to GDP, most dramatically in the US and the UK. Progressive financialization of capital has substituted short-term market-based considerations of shareholder value for the long-term strategic planning horizon of corporations producing for mass markets. In this Anglo-American variety of capitalism, finance has become decoupled from production, and the capital market has lost its useful function of judging the long-term productive capabilities of different firms. Once the criterion of shareholder value became the objective of good management of a company, the capital market became a gigantic casino where people attempted to guess the market with confidence that it would maintain a secular rising trend. Of all the aspects of globalization, it is the financialization of capital that has had the most profound consequences in the West.

With increasing turbulence and uncertainty in financial markets, funds moved into commodities, including petroleum, copper and other minerals, and more recently into food and land. Whereas biofuels have contributed to a secular rising trend in prices of corn and soy, only speculative forward purchases can account for the spike in rice, wheat and many other food products since 2007. The financial crisis is impacting in the first instance on the value of personal and institutional savings and threatens recession in the North; the Global South appeared to be relatively insulated. However, speculative activity in commodity markets was directly responsible for the food crisis of 2008, which, according to the World Bank, plunged 100 million people into dire poverty. Food prices doubled and tripled, and poor people in developing countries, where food expenditures account for some 70 per cent of income, have been the victims of a crisis originating in the financialization of the major capitalist economies. Food riots erupted in 33 countries and the World Bank expressed concern regarding the social stability of the developing world. The FAO considered 37 countries in need of food aid, but the UN had difficulty in meeting its target of $500 million. Contrast this with Cargill's posted profit of $1.2 billion in the first quarter of 2008. Indeed, the dominance of transnational agribusiness in world markets is a manifestation of the subordinate position of producers to corporations, which control access to inputs of high-yielding seeds, pesticides and fertilizers, and access to markets including processing facilities. Their profits greatly exceed the incomes of agricultural producers.

But the disparity between agricultural incomes of farmers and the mega-profits of corporations are very much more extreme in developing countries, as are the disparities between capital and labour in their various forms. The food crisis of 2008 extinguished the gains of post-Washington Consensus poverty reduction programmes and it has put the entire free trade and globalization agenda into question. According to Fred Bergsten, trade liberalization has come to a 'screeching halt'. Developing countries blocked the FTAA; they suspended the WTO Doha round; and the objectives of food self-reliance will require some reversal of economic liberalization. India and many other developing countries suspended the export of food to meet domestic demand, and food sovereignty has become an important objective of many developing countries. Programmes to increase domestic production will require land reform and protection from the destructive effects of the imports of subsidized food and food products. The large increase in exports of agricultural products has failed to raise the net income of farmers, which has been stationary for the last 20 years.

The huge increase in incomes derived from financial services contributed significantly to GDP growth. Accounting conventions record incomes generated in finance, insurance and real estate as an addition to national production as measured by GDP. By these conventions, the services of the top hedge fund managers are now 40 times more valuable than those of the top corporate CEOs, and roughly 13,000 times more valuable than the highest paid members of US Congress, who earn just under $200,000. Thus, individuals and corporations engaged in financial services, who receive one-fifth of all incomes generated in the US, appear to have contributed one-fifth of the value of all goods and services of the national economy. But what useful goods or services have been produced by the financial sector to merit this reward?

The actual contribution of financialization has been the ability to sustain economic growth in the US, still the largest economy in the world, by an ever-increasing volume of debt, facilitated by easy money from the Federal Reserve. On 29 July 2016, the national debt had grown to $14 trillion, or about 76 per cent of the previous 12 months of GDP, and by 5 November it had grown to $19.8 trillion for a total debt to GDP ratio of approximately 106 per cent (www.usdebtclock.org).[1]

The near-doubling of GDP over the past three decades of the neoliberal era barely raised median family incomes, while the physical and social infrastructure of the country deteriorated and the industrial base of the economy was eroded, with a reduction in industrial employment and earnings. Manufacturing jobs, as President

Donald Trump was fond of trumpeting during his campaign, were exported while imports of manufactured goods (predominantly from China) exploded, leading to a trade deficit of enormous and growing proportions. An estimated 80 per cent of the wealth that was generated in the process, mostly in the form of financial assets, was appropriated by the financial elite, the purported '1%' (including Forbes' 1,200 or so multibillionaires). At the same time, the US's famed middle class, the backbone of the economy and the development process, was 'hollowed out' while earned incomes were reduced and the value of wages fell.

What sustained the economy through this financialization process was the willingness of the rest of the world to finance the US's external payments deficits of 6–7 per cent of GDP by purchasing US securities and holding increasing amounts of dollar reserves. But this situation is plainly unsustainable and is unravelling in the context of the ascendency of China and a major realignment of economic power in the world capitalist system.

According to George Soros, the 'current crisis is the culmination of a super-boom that has lasted for more than 60 years', and was aided by authorities who intervened to rescue the global financial system whenever it was at risk. However, the capacity to manage these risks and to maintain US hegemony in the world capitalist system has clearly reached its limits and is fast coming to an end, eroded by the contradictions of capitalist development and the fundamental structural fragility of the US economy, which is caused by the very process of globalization that had brought about its economic dominance (on these contradictions and dynamics, see Chapters 7–11 in this volume). The globalization and financialization of capital has come home to roost.

Recommended reading: Streeck (2014).

A reconfiguration of international power relations

It is evident that the economic crisis that was triggered by the implosion of financial institutions in 2008 will have transformative consequences for power relations within the world economic order. The US will continue to play an important but no longer a hegemonic role, and the US dollar will lose primacy as countries diversify their holdings of official reserves. It may prove difficult to revive the US economy because three decades of neoliberal policies have significantly reduced the share of wage and salary income in US GDP from levels of the 1960s and 1970s. The American economy is driven by the growth of consumption expenditure, but since the end of the 1990s, consumption expenditure has increased only by the annual increase in the volume of household debt, which has now reached levels of 140 per cent of household income. Consumption expenditure will now decline, as will domestic investment. As long as other economies remain in recession, the prospect for exports is dim. Only massive government expenditures can lift the economy out of the slump, but who is going to cover the fiscal deficit, which will now be very much larger? Will foreigners wish to continue to purchase US securities, whose value will decline with a weaker dollar?

For years, the US market has driven the export-led growth of developing Asia, Africa and Latin America, and access to this market has been the principal bargaining chip in negotiations for enhanced FTAs or EPAs. Will declining export earnings and a trade deficit in the order of more than half a trillion dollars ($531.5 billion in 2015) favour and encourage protectionist policies in the US and lead the US under the presidency of Donald Trump to renogiate or unilaterally abandon existing trade agreements such as NAFTA? This could have a major impact on the existing architecture governing international relations, and possibly on the configuration of economic power in the global economy. Will developing countries concerned with food security assist domestic agriculture to meet a larger share of the food bill? In this protectionist context, will developing countries engage in managed non-market trade? Will they now create regional institutions of mutual financial assistance? These are some of the possibilities arising from the persistence of economic crisis conditions generated by the dynamics of global capitalist development (see Section III in this volume for a critical discussion of these issues).

We do not know what the future holds, but it is clear that the world has become both more diverse and more interdependent, as well as a more dangerous place at the level of economic, environmental, political and personal security. We live on one planet that is seriously threatened by climate change and environmental degradation of the rivers, seas and earth that sustain our lives. There is agreement that the predatory mode of capitalism, which has dominated international trade and finance, has failed. But there is no agreement, indeed there cannot be, on any one alternative mode of economic organization. All modern economies are mixed economies, with some combination of state enterprise, at national, regional or municipal levels, private sector, cooperative, community or social economy, non-profit associations and work performed within the household. But all societies require an effective state with the authority and legitimacy to negotiate conflicting domestic interests. Just as there are many forms of organizing an economy, there are many forms of democratic governance, and representational government by political parties is not necessarily the most appropriate for any particular society. The economic crisis invites innovation in the regions of political and social organization in accordance with the specific historical and cultural heritage of the varied peoples of the world. This much more interesting approach to the study of international development challenges its students to explore the history and the culture of the diverse societies that make up the world today.

Recommended reading: Veltmeyer (2013).

Capitalism in the current conjuncture of neoliberal globalization

The current conjuncture in the evolution of the world capitalist system has revealed one of the fundamental features and veritable truths about capitalism, one that Thomas Piketty (2014), in his 700-page treatise on *Capital in the 21st Century*, describes as the fundamental contradiction of capitalism, *namely* its propensity towards crisis and the expansion of international and social inequalities in the distribution of global income. Another study by Jomo (2016), and a compilation of essays edited by Jomo and Baudot (2007), substantiates this proposition regarding capitalism when released from regulatory constraint.[2] Wealth and income inequalities among different regions across the world, he notes – with reference here to data provided by the economic historian Angus Maddison – began to increase around five centuries ago, before accelerating under conditions of the Industrial Revolution and the emergence of the capitalist system. After a brief reversal of this trend during the 'golden age' of capitalism a quarter-century after the World War II,[3] and despite protracted slowdowns in most rich countries following the 2008 financial crisis and reduced international disparities between North and South based largely on the China factor, the fundamental contradiction of capitalism has reasserted itself with a vengeance in the short history of what David Harvey has dubbed the 'neoliberal era'. Unequal distribution of wealth and income on both a global scale and in many regional contexts is a predominant feature of world capitalism today. And with it, we can see the beginnings, if not the end, of a global resistance movement. At the moment, the forces of resistance are evidently deeply divided. Should they become united in one form or another – most likely in very different ways – then the possibility of a systemic transition towards 'another world' arises. At the moment, however, the prospects for this development is nowhere on the horizon, except perhaps for the new frontier of extractive capital in Latin America.

Over the course of the last 150 years of industrial and then monopoly capitalism, the 'inequality predicament', as UNDESA (2005) terms it, has taken a different form. Before the Industrial Revolution, inequalities among regions were relatively small, while within-country inequalities accounted for most of overall global income inequality. But today, inter-country income inequalities account for about two-thirds of world inequality, with intra-country inequalities accounting for about one-third.

The 2016 UNCTAD Report, authored by Richard Kozul Wright (Head of the UNCTAD Division on Globalization and Development Strategies) together with his team of economists, presents a trenchant critique of the neoliberal policies of unfettered capital liberalization, which resulted in what Joseph Stiglitz, Chief Economist at the World Bank until 2000,[4] has described as the 'great divide', and also the conditions of a deep financial crisis and the 'greatest contraction since the Great Depression'. The report argues that 'enthusiasts for efficient markets promised that financial deregulation would boost productive investment, but this promise has not been met'. Rising profits coincide with increased dividends, stock buy-backs and mergers and acquisitions, but not with investment in new plants and equipment. Reliance on cheap credit to stimulate recovery has fuelled an explosion of corporate debt in emerging economies, now totalling $25 trillion, and UNCTAD warns that developing countries have become increasingly vulnerable to speculative and large capital flows: 'Financial markets are chastened but unreformed, debt levels are higher than ever and inequality continues to rise'. With specific reference to the US economy, where the contradictions of capitalism are particularly acute, the UNCTAD Report describes this conjuncture as a 'Polanyi period' in which 'the regulatory normative framework . . . having already warped, is beginning to buckle as the weight of Greenspan's mistake is felt in an ever-widening swathe of economic and social life – from precarious employment conditions to corporate tax inversions to undrinkable tap water'.

The comparison made by the authors of the report with the interwar period suggests that they believe something similar to Karl Polanyi's *The Great Transformation* is now in the works or required. The report notes that Western governments after the Second World War struck a balance between market efficiency, shared prosperity and economic security – between the market and the state. 'Managing such a transformation in our highly interconnected global economy', the report adds, 'is today's big political challenge, for countries and communities at all levels of development' (UNCTAD, 2016). The report might have added that this challenge is in fact not so much for these countries and communities as for the guardians of the system, who are naturally enough concerned to save capitalism from itself. But the challenge for these countries and communities that the report refers to, in the words of the Zapatistas (see Chapter 37), is rather different: how to confront the capitalist hydra.

Recommended reading: Jomo (2016), Stiglitz (2016), UNCTAD (2016).

Notes

1 Approximately 45 per cent of this debt is owned by foreign investors, the largest of which are China (which holds about 21 per cent of the debt) and Japan (www.bea.gov/national/index.htm#gdp).
2 Also very much worth reading are two reports on the inequality syndrome both released in 2010 by ECLAC and the Development Centre of the OECD.
3 On this 'golden age', see Marglin and Schor (1990).
4 The significance of Stiglitz's study is that he shows very clearly that the yawning inequalities of our time are not simply the result of the structural forces generated by the contradictions of capitalism, as Berberoglu seems to argue in this volume (Chapter 11), but the cumulative result of unjust policies and misguided priorities in the interest of the ruling class. As a point of fact (or theory, rather), both system dynamics and unjust policies are implicated in the emergence of the 'great divide'.

References

Bello, W. (2009). 'The global collapse: a non-orthodox view'. *Z Net*, 22 February.

Bienefeld, M. (2013). 'The new world order: echoes of a new imperialism'. In H. Veltmeyer (ed.), *Development in an Era of Neoliberal Globalization*. London/New York: Routledge, pp. 119–40.

Davis, M. (2002). *Late Victorian Holocausts*. London: Verso.

ECLAC (2010). *Time for Equality: Closing Gaps, Opening Trails*. Santiago: UN.

Jolly, R., Emmerij, L., Ghai, D. and Lapeyre, F. (2004). *UN Contributions to Development Thinking and Practice*. Bloomington, IN: Indiana University Press.

Jomo, K.S. (2016). 'Inequality and its discontents'. iCrowdNewswire and Global Geopolitics and Political Economy Net – IPS, Kuala Lumpur, Malaysia, 17 November.

Jomo, K.S. and Baudot, J. (2007). *Flat World, Big Gaps*. London: Zed Books.

Marglin, S. and Schor, J. (1990). *The Golden Age of Capitalism: Reinterpreting the Post-War Experience*. Oxford: Clarendon Press.

OECD (2010). *Perspectives on Global Development 2010: Shifting Wealth*. Paris: OECD.

Parpart, J. and Veltmeyer, H. (2004). 'The dynamics of development theory and practice: a review of its shifting dynamics'. *Canadian Journal of Development Studies*, 25(1), Special Issue.

Petras, J. and Veltmeyer, H. (2001). *Globalization Unmasked: Imperialism in the 21st Century*. Halifax: Fernwood.

Piketty, T. (2014). *Capital in the 21st Century*. Cambrige: Cambridge University Press.

Polanyi Levitt, K. (2013). 'Mercantilist origins of capitalism and its legacies: decline of the West and rise of the rest'. In H. Veltmeyer (ed.), *Development in an Era of Neoliberal Globalization*. London/New York: Routledge, pp. 9–51.

Stiglitz, J. (2016). *The Great Divide*. Harmondsworth: Penguin.

Streeck, W. (2014). *Buying Time: The Delayed Crisis of Democratic Capitalism*. London: Verso.

UNCTAD (2016). *Structural Transformation for Inclusive and Sustained Growth: Trade and Development Report, 2016*. Geneva: UNCTAD.

UNDESA (2005). *The Inequality Predicament: Report on the World Social Situation*. New York: United Nations.

Veltmeyer, H. (2005). 'Development and globalization as imperialism'. *Canadian Journal of Development Studies*, 26(1): 89–106.

Veltmeyer, H. (ed.) (2013). *Development in an Era of Neoliberal Globalization*. London and New York: Routledge.

World Bank (1995). *Workers in an Integrating World*. Washington, DC: World Bank.

PART II
Thinking critically about development

2

CRITICAL DEVELOPMENT THEORY

Results and prospects

Ronaldo Munck

This chapter carries out a genealogy of critical development theory in relation to Marxism, which has played a dominant role in the field. It traces the complex views of Karl Marx himself, the sharp turn taken by Leninism, and the practice of development in the socialist world to finally take up the challenge of post-development. Our emphasis is on tensions and contradictions, and we do not assume a linear development to a unified critical development theory.

Marx and development

For Marx, development and capitalism were almost synonymous. Marx's vision of development was also totally wrapped up with the era of modernity. Production was becoming increasingly internationalized and capital was being centralized. Capitalism advanced at an evermore frantic pace and development spread across the globe. This vision of what we might call 'Manifesto Marxism' is quite explicit: '[t]he bourgeoisie cannot exist without constantly revolutionizing the instruments of production, and thereby the relations of production, and with them the whole relations of society' (Marx and Engels, 1977: 71). For the Marx of the *Communist Manifesto*, 'everlasting uncertainty and agitation distinguish the bourgeois epoch from all earlier ones. All fixed, fast-frozen relations, with their train of ancient and venerable prejudices and opinions, are swept away, all new-formed ones become antiquated before they can ossify' (p. 70). This exhilarating rollercoaster of modernization is the essence of Marx's conception of development. As the bourgeois era mounted the world stage, it would sweep away all old orders and transform all in its own image. The more developed country was a mirror in which the less developed could glimpse its own future.

The bourgeois era, for 'Manifesto Marxism', is one of unprecedented development of the productive forces: 'The bourgeoisie, during its rule of scarce one hundred years, has created more massive and more colossal productive forces than have all previous generations together' (Marx and Engels, 1977: 72). Nature is subjected to humankind, chemistry is applied to industry and agriculture, the railway and the telegraph revolutionized communications. The insatiable drive of bourgeois development tears up all obstacles in its path. Markets are constantly expanding, capitalist social relations corrode all others, productivity increases by leaps and bounds. Manifesto Marxism is a thoroughly modernist discourse, but Marx did not stop at his paean of praise for the bourgeoisie and its revolutionary development role for human society. This capitalist development process was also creating its own 'gravedigger', the proletariat or working class. In proportion, as the bourgeoisie – that is to say capital – develops, so does that class of labourers who sell their labour, as a commodity, to this hungry new mode of production. The same process that revolutionizes society creates the revolutionary class that will overthrow the new order. Capitalism will be devoured by the product of its own incandescent energy in this vision. The development of modern capitalist society produces 'dialectically', as it were, the basis for its own surpassment.

The ambiguity of Marx's views on development can be illustrated through his (admittedly journalistic) writings on India. In these passages, Marx paid tribute to the progressive role of capitalist colonialism: 'England has to fulfil a double mission in India: one destructive, the other regenerating – the annihilation of old Asiatic society, and the laying of the material foundations of Western society in Asia' (Avineri, 1969: 132). Modern industry and the railway system would dissolve the old divisions of labour, break up the 'inertia' of the Indian villages and drag the country into the slipstream of global capitalist development. Of course:

> The Indians will not reap the fruits of the new elements of society scattered among them by the British bourgeoisie till in Great Britain itself the new ruling classes shall have been supplanted by the industrial proletariat, or till the Hindoos themselves shall have grown strong enough to throw off the English yoke altogether.
>
> *(Avineri, 1969: 137)*

While those passages can be read as a support for the civilizing effect of Western capitalism over Eastern barbarism, in fact Marx's writings on India, admittedly one-sided, dated and not too well informed, are consistent with the message of the Manifesto. Capitalism is a revolutionary force but it begets the cause of its own eventual downfall.

Where Marx began to break with his previously mechanistic/modernist views on development was in relation to Russia. In 1881, Marx spent some considerable time and effort drafting a reply to Vera Zasulich on the nature of the Russian peasant commune. Marx had been studying Russia since 1861, the year of the 'emancipation of the serfs'. The question was whether the commune was a symptom of all that was archaic in Russian society or whether it was a harbinger of a progressive 'communist' future. Marx's intervention in this debate was quite clear-cut. He foresaw two alternatives. The first would involve state capitalism penetrating and destroying the commune. The second option, however, was that the commune would become 'the fulcrum of social regeneration in Russia' (Shanin, 1983: 124). What Marx was arguing against, on the basis of the Russian case, was the tendency to make his analysis of mature capitalism in *Capital* into a schema of historical inevitability. This has major implications for any theory of development, and seemingly contradicts his earlier dictum that the backward country saw its future in the mirror of the advanced one. What Marx actually argued later, in a letter to another Russian follower, was that:

> to metamorphose my historical sketch of the genesis of capitalism in Western Europe into a historico-philosophic theory of the general path every people is fated to tread, whatever the historical circumstances it finds itself . . . is honouring and shaming me too much.
>
> *(cited in Shanin, 1983: 59)*

There is a refusal here of any deterministic, blanket application of 'laws' of historical development. Marx was engaging, in fact, with the combined and uneven nature of development in strikingly 'modern' terms.

Marx did not, either, have a particularly developed idea of what we would today call the Third World. He was certainly aware of the role of colonial plunder in oiling the wheels of the Industrial Revolution. However, in analysing the internal and external factors in the 'primitive accumulation' that gave rise to capitalism, Marx undoubtedly prioritized the first dimension. Subsequent Marxists, engaged in debates over imperialism and dependency, would reverse the order and prioritize the external dimension as the explanation of why capitalism emerged in some regions of the world and not others. Anthony Brewer correctly points out that '[a] stress on external factors is consistent with a picture of capitalism in which a centre-periphery division on a world scale is a defining feature, but such a definition of capitalism is not to be found in Marx' (Brewer, 1980: 44). While in his writings on Ireland Marx can be seen to be aware of the stunting effects of colonialism on development, his emphasis is on the internal development of capitalism as a mode of production and its appetite to create a whole world in its own image.

Leninism and development

It is ironic, given the subsequent history of Marxism-Leninism, that when Lenin engaged with the issue of the Russian commune in the mid-1890s, he was implicitly opposing Marx's views of the same phenomenon. Lenin's perceptions of the Russian peasantry were extremely negative, stressing their individualistic nature. Belief in the peasants' 'communist instincts' had naïvely infected many Russian socialists 'based on a purely mythical idea of the peasant economy as a special communal system' (cited in Bideleux, 1985: 71). Lenin developed the label of 'populism' to criticize those Russian socialists who sought in some way to bypass capitalism via the commune. For Lenin, only the industrial proletariat (however minuscule it might be) could lead a revolution: 'only the higher stage of capitalist development, large-scale machine industry, creates the material conditions and social forces necessary for . . . open political struggle towards *victorious communist revolution*' (cited in Bideleux, 1985: 73, emphasis in original). We have here a conception of development that is quite unilinear and mechanical.

Lenin developed his ideas further in his turn-of-the-century book *The Development of Capitalism in Russia* (Lenin, 1967), considered by many as one of the best Marxist studies of the emergence of capitalism from feudalism. Lenin's theme is the apparently technical one of how the home market of Russian capitalism was formed. His task was to demonstrate how the commodity economy became established in all branches of economic life, and how the division of labour became dominated by capitalism. Against the under-consumptionist arguments of the 'populists', Lenin showed convincingly that capitalism had created for itself a home market in Russia. Lenin's conception of capitalist development is centred on the question of social differentiation, which he examined in detail in relation to the rural population. It should be pointed out that he clearly exaggerates the role of capitalism at this stage, treating as capitalist 'economic structures which Marx explicitly described as *pre-capitalist*' (Harding, 1977: 87, emphasis in original). Lenin did admit that his earlier writings had led to an '*over-estimation*' of the degree of capitalist development in Russian agriculture, but the point is clear that Lenin's early conception of development was absolutely focused on the internal development of capitalism in Russia.

What Lenin, or Leninism, is better known for is his theory of imperialism. In terms of Marx's view of the progressive function of capitalism on a world scale, and Lenin's own analysis in *The Development of Capitalism in Russia*, this theory, elaborated during the First World War, was a watershed. It is only somewhat exaggerated to state, as Bill Warren did, that:

> In effectively overturning Marx and Engels's view of the character of imperialist expansion, Lenin set in motion an ideological process that erased from Marxism any trace of the view that capitalism would be an instrument of social progress even in precapitalist societies.
>
> *(Warren, 1980: 48)*

From now on, the Marxist tradition would begin to view the world system as centre-periphery, and imperialism as a block or impediment to development. Certainly, it was easy to understand that a political movement that was setting out to gather support among the poor and downtrodden worldwide would find it difficult to maintain Marx's stance on India, for example. Though Marx never ignored the negative effect of capitalist expansion worldwide, he undoubtedly stressed the positive effect it would have on the productive forces. In the period of crisis, expectation and uncertainty of the First World War, lofty, detached observation of this sort seemed out of place.

Lenin's work on imperialism is not, and was not intended to be, a major or innovative investigation. It was based largely on the works of others, such as the Marxist Bukharin and the non-Marxist Hobson. It outlined what it saw as certain key tendencies of the period, such as the concentration of capital, its export to 'underdeveloped' countries and the dominance of finance capital (a merger of industrial and banking capital). Lenin's political objective was to counter Kautsky's notion of 'ultraimperialism', which implied a fairly smooth and peaceful carve-up of the world by the major powers. Instead, Lenin tried to show the inevitable trend towards world war implicit in increased worldwide competition. He was not really concerned with the impact of capitalist imperialism in the colonial world. He did recognize that '[t]he export of capital affects and greatly accelerates the development of capitalism in these countries to which it is exported' (Lenin, 1970: 718). Yet, Lenin also moved towards the underconsumptionist positions he had criticized in *The Development of Capitalism in Russia*. In particular, he became the forerunner of the neo-Marxist underdevelopment school (Baran, Frank, etc.), with his argument that imperialism would become a fetter or a brake on development, referring to 'the tendency to stagnation and decay, which is characteristic of monopoly, continues to operate, and in certain branches of industry, in some countries, for certain periods of time, it gains the upper hand' (p. 745).

Gradually, the latter tendency, to view imperialism and monopoly capitalism as the highest or last stage of capitalism, prevailed. Not only that, but the view also prevailed that imperialism was becoming the major obstacle to development. In regard to the colonial world, the communist movement now began to prioritize its alliance with nationalist movements. It is this political imperative that explains the resolutions explicitly and unambiguously portraying imperialism as retrogressive economically, and foreign capital investment not only as an affront to national dignity, but also a simple drain on national resources. Development henceforth became synonymous with national development. Somehow, capital acquired political colouring so that the same social relations of production could be seen as healthy if under national bourgeois control, and exploitative if under international or imperialist control. The later school of 'development of underdevelopment' (Frank) has its intellectual/political origins here. Leninism became transmuted into a veritable ideology of development for what was soon to become the 'Third World'. The ideology of proletarian revolution in the West became the ideology of peasant mobilization in the East, and then the ideology of modernizing elites in the South. David Lane puts it bluntly that 'Leninism is the developmental ethic of Marxism' (Lane, 1974: 31). Lenin had inaugurated this productivist-economistic-developmentalist version of Marxism with his notorious definition of communism in 1920 as 'Soviet power plus the electrification of all the country'.

Recommended reading: Lane (1974), Lenin (1970), Warren (1980).

Socialism and underdevelopment

Marx expected socialism to flourish in the most advanced capitalist countries, but most socialist revolutions occurred in conditions of relative or absolute under development. Socialist practice seems to contradict socialist theory as socialism and development had become practically synonymous in many parts of the world. It is hardly surprising that, in conditions of underdevelopment, wide sections of the population might come to view socialism as potentially liberating. Furthermore, Lenin advanced within his account of imperialism the notion that the world capitalist system would break at its 'weakest link'. This points towards a realist interpretation of revolution, unencumbered by Marxist or any other teleology, where a whole range of political, strategic or ideological factors may create a situation 'ripe' for revolution. It is not a question of simply waiting for the development of the forces of production to reach the point where a country is ready for socialism.

Whether it is a paradox or a natural concomitant of uneven capitalist development, socialist regimes have almost always inherited the legacy of underdevelopment. The constraints on the fledgling socialist state are formidable. Not only must it seek a more even distribution of income, but it also needs to create a massive advance in terms of economic development. The 'gigantomania' of a Stalin is not just the product of his fevered imagination and lust for power. The country will, more than likely, be devastated by external or internal war. There will probably be a small industrial base and an underdeveloped internal market. Natural resources may exist but may well not be immediately available. Human resources will exist but will, on the whole, not be endowed with great training or education. These hardly add up to fertile conditions for the development of socialism. It is not surprising that Paul Baran once famously admitted that 'Socialism in backward and underdeveloped countries has a powerful tendency to become a backward and under-developed socialism' (Baran, 1968: viii).

To the legacy of underdevelopment, one must add the hostile international environment that socialist regimes faced from 1917 onwards. Being a 'weak link' in an imperialist chain may have facilitated a socialist revolution, but, for sure, imperialist aggression would ensue. This was the case for Russia, Cuba, Vietnam or Angola. Revolutionary nationalist self-determination had its place in the imperialist system. Wars, boycotts, external aggression and blockades have been a fact of most successful revolutions. The transition to socialism has thus been 'overdetermined' by the conditions prevailing in the international political system. This situation can only exacerbate the already difficult internal conditions for democratic, let alone socialist, development. The internal balance of forces between democratic transformation and restoration are, inevitably, tilted towards the latter. While in the short term external aggression may hasten the transformation of social relations after the revolution, in the longer term it needs only to be maintained to fatally weaken the transformation project or turn it in an authoritarian militarist direction, as happened in Nicaragua.

The twin constraints of economic underdevelopment and external aggression point many victorious revolutions towards self-reliance, if not outright autarky. The radical dependency theory of development, which built on Lenin's concept of imperialism, advocated some form of 'delinking' from the world economy as the remedy for underdevelopment. National liberation, however defined, became a central goal of socialist movements and regimes. This is understandable, but it does not lead to socialism in the way Marx understood it. Nor do we need to look at the experience of Burma or Kampuchea to see the terrible cost of autarky as a substitute for socialism.

It is clear by now that the socialist regimes of the 20th century existed more in the 'realm of necessity' than in the promised 'realm of freedom'. This meant that socialism, as it actually materialized, had to confront, above all, the problems of underdevelopment. As Ken Post and Phil Wright argue, the main characteristic of all socialist regimes was that they are 'resource-constrained economies', the principal characteristic of which 'is the continuous reproduction of shortages or, alternatively, continuous underproduction, in contrast to the overproduction of capitalism' (Post and Wright, 1989: 72). In this scenario, it is inevitable that there will be distributional conflicts between industry and agriculture, investment and consumption, or military and civilian expenditure, for example. There is no plenty to be socialized, no irrationality to be ironed out to everyone's benefit, no benign or virtuous circle waiting to be activated. It is certainly easy to see how, from the very start, there would be a tendency towards full reintegration into the world market in a bid to escape the critical resource constraints that the new socialist economies faced.

The balance sheet of socialism and underdevelopment or underdeveloped socialism is, inevitably, a mixed one. Adrian Leftwich argues that in the well-established socialist states such as China, Cuba and North Korea, 'the grossest forms of pre-revolutionary oppression, inequality, disease and poverty have been eliminated; industrialisation has progressed *some way*; and average life expectancy and perinatal infant mortality . . . compare well or begin to approach levels typical of industrialised societies' (Leftwich, 1992: 38, emphasis in original). Socialism was once seen as the best means to 'catch up' with advanced Western capitalist societies. In 1936, Jawaharlal Nehru spoke for many Third World nationalist leaders when he declared that 'I see no way of ending the poverty, the vast unemployment, the degradation and the subjection of the Indian people, except through socialism'. Yet, 50 years after Nehru's desperate leap of faith, it was abundantly clear that 'socialist development' was just a pale imitation of its capitalist progenitor, with its own undesirable features and inefficiencies thrown in.

Recommended reading: Baran (1968), Leftwich (1992), Post and Wright (1989).

Post-development

If until now we have largely taken for granted the concept of development itself, we must now question its meaning. We cannot simply assume, from a critical theoretical perspective, that development is a common human good. Recent attempts to deconstruct the development discourse have helped highlight its less than benign role. Gustavo Esteva points to the apparent contradiction that while 'development occupies the centre of an incredibly powerful semantic constellation . . . At the same time, very few words are as feeble, as fragile and as incapable of giving substance and meaning to thought and behaviour as this one' (Esteva, 1992: 8). Development acts as a truism and its open-ended significance renders it almost meaningless. Yet, its conceptual inflation has led it to dominate almost all treatments of the non-Western world. Development seems to act as a metaphor for the Western way; a word to represent a world to be built in its own image. Far from benign, a wholesome objective all political tendencies could agree to, development begins to appear as a disciplinary mechanism in the Foucaultian sense.

Marxism might seem to be above this type of critique. After all, Marxism has hardly been on a par with Western imperialism as an agent of development. Yet, Marxism is an integral part of the modernist paradigm, in many ways its epitome. Development can, indeed, be seen as a central axis of the whole of Marx's work. The Hegelian concept of history as an unfolding of the spirit; and Darwin's concept of evolution merge and intertwine in the classic Marxist notion of development. As seen above, Marxism exudes confidence in the onward march of history and the inexorable progress of development. The Marxist stages of human history – the sequence of modes of production – are imbued with a modernist conception of development. Thus, from a post-Marxist perspective, we need to establish some critical distance from this conception. Whatever contradictions Marxism may contain within its various theoretical and political manifestations, it is clearly imbued with the spirit of the Enlightenment and its concept of development. One way of illustrating this argument would be through a discussion of the radical, Marxist and otherwise dependency theory.

This is not the place to carry out a genealogy of the concept of dependency. The point is that the dependency approach emerged in the late 1960s as a supposedly radical critique of the orthodox, conservative theory of modernization. But in all its tenets, it simply reversed the arguments of the mainstream discourse. Where modernization theory saw the diffusion of progress across the globe, the dependency approach saw simply the 'development of underdevelopment'. Where one saw integration into the capitalist world economy as the only path to development, the other saw delinking from the world economy as the key to development. Where one saw capitalist development leading steadily towards democracy, the other saw only an inexorable slide into dictatorship or fascism. Thirty years later, it would seem that modernization had won the battle of ideas hands down with the rise of neoliberalism as uncontested development paradigm. Reform in development parlance had now become synonymous with neoliberal, free-market doctrines, where once it conjured up images of agrarian reform and income distribution.

If the modernization and dependency theories are, at one level, simply mirror images of each other, what could break this impasse in development theory? From a post-Marxist perspective, both feminism and ecology appeared to be attractive alternatives. The various attempts to carry out an 'engendering' of development theory – women in/and development, gender and development, and so on – have utterly transformed this area of study. In theoretical terms, however, some of the criticisms of development theory, such as its essentialism, can be applied equally to feminism, at least prior to the emergence of post-structuralist feminism. As to ecology, we now have a new radical/reformist orthodoxy of 'sustainable development', a blanket term covering various perspectives, but imbuing them all with the warm glow of 'motherhood and apple pie'. While these new critical approaches have taken over at the margins of development practice, the mainstream carries on being dominated by the technocratic/Western-centred/evolutionist perspectives of modernization theory, which has even brought under its sway many erstwhile dependency theorists.

We now see emerging a new post-Marxist synthesis on the question of development. From feminism, ecology and other 'new' social movements, we can take a critique of mainstream notions. From the emerging 'anti-development' school (see Sachs, 1992), we can take the sharp deconstruction of the developmentalist discourse and puncture its self-assuredness. Yet, this school's anti-modernism hardly takes us 'beyond' modernism or even a post-Marxist terrain. There is also something arrogant about talk of 'another' development that preaches non-material values and evades the basic problems of material needs. The postmodern tack is a different one and at the very least it has carried out an effective 'decentring' of the white European male who invented development to deal with the rest of the world when colonialism had had its day. A new era of scepticism towards metanarratives of progress is upon us, we stress self-reflexivity more, and we are much more open towards difference and local knowledge than in the heyday of development theory.

Recommended reading: McEwan (2008), Sachs (1992).

References

Avineri, S. (ed.) (1969). *Karl Marx on Colonialism and Modernization*. New York: Anchor.

Baran, P. (1968). *The Political Economy of Growth*. New York: Modern Reader Paperback.

Bideleux, R. (1985). *Communism and Development*. London: Methuen.

Brewer, A. (1980). *Marxist Theories of Imperialism: A Critical Study*. London: Routledge.

Esteva, G. (1992). 'Development'. In W. Sachs (ed.), *The Development Dictionary: A Guide to Knowledge and Power*. London: Zed Books, pp. 1–23.

Harding, N. (1977). *Lenin's Political Thought Volume 1: Theory and Practice in the Democratic Revolution*. Basingstoke: Macmillan.

Lane, D. (1974). 'Leninism as an ideology of Soviet development'. In E. de Kadt and G. Williams (eds), *Sociology and Development*. London: Tavistock.

Leftwich, A. (1992). 'Is there a socialist path to socialism?' *Third World Quarterly*, 13(1), Special Issue, 'Rethinking Socialism'.

Lenin (1967). *The Development of Capitalism in Russia*. Moscow: Progress Publishers.

Lenin (1970). 'Imperialism, the highest stage of capitalism'. In *Selected Works in Three Volumes, Vol. 1*. Moscow: Progress Publishers, pp. 265–75.

Marx, K. and Engels, F. (1977). 'Manifesto of the Communist Party'. In K. Marx, *The Revolutions of 1848: Political Writings, Vol. 1*. Harmondsworth: Penguin.

McEwan, C. (2008). *Postcolonialism and Development*. London: Routledge.
Post, K. and Wright, P. (1989). *Socialism and Underdevelopment*. London: Routledge.
Sachs, W. (1992). *The Development Dictionary: A Guide to Knowledge as Power*. London: Zed Books.
Shanin, T. (ed.) (1983). *Late Marx and the Russian Road*. London: Routledge.
Warren, B. (1980). *Imperialism: Pioneer of Capitalism*. London: Verso.

3

THINKING CAPITALIST DEVELOPMENT BEYOND EUROCENTRISM

Alf Gunvald Nilsen

Bringing capitalism back in – but how?

If there is an imperative challenge in critical development studies today, it is to restore a historical understanding of the political economy of global capitalism to our field of study. In many ways, this should be an uncontroversial statement. On the one hand, as Cowen and Shenton (1996: 110) reminded us some time ago, the modern idea of development arose as a response to the perceived need 'to ameliorate the social misery which arose out of the immanent process of capitalist growth' – in particular, the social misery of dispossession. On the other hand, capitalist dynamics and relations have arguably never been more entrenched in the world-system than they are today – indeed, capitalism is 'present throughout the globe, not simply in the abstract, but in institutions that people encounter in their daily lives' (Cooper, 2000: 241). Yet, to insist that the study of development is – in essence – the study of how populations, territories and resources are embedded in those dynamics and relations is nevertheless anathema to the mainstream of development research. Poverty is still predominantly understood as a question of individual lack of skills and resources and development is understood strictly in what Cowen and Shenton (1996) would refer to as 'immanent' terms – that is, as the technical management of institutional designs to improve populations, territories and resources (Ferguson, 1994; Harriss-White, 2006; Leys, 1996; Li, 2007; Mosse, 2010).

This is in no small part due to the enduring effect of the neoliberal counter-revolution in the field of development research. The rejection by neoliberal economists of the idea that a particular form of economic theory was required in order to make sense of the developmental predicaments of the Global South – the turn to 'monoeconomics' (see Hettne, 1995; Toye, 1987) – was accompanied by a wider turn away from perspectives oriented towards macrostructural analyses of the historical development of the capitalist world-system. The debate over the purported 'impasse' in radical development sociology was of signal importance in this respect – and in particular the work of David Booth (1985).[1] According to Booth, Marxian sociologies of development – dependency theory, Bill Warren's restatement of Marxist orthodoxy, and articulation theory in particular – failed to produce meaningful insights into developmental trajectories in the Global South. This, he submits, is a result of a 'metatheoretical commitment to demonstrating that what happens in societies in the era of capitalism is not only explicable, but also in a stronger sense necessary' (p. 773). Despite strong rebuttals – for example, from Jorge Larrain (1989) and Ray Kiely (1995) – that demonstrated the possibility of a Marxist understanding of historical capitalism that was premised neither on determinism nor teleology, perspectives grounded in macrostructural political economy gave way to middle-range theories that constituted development research as 'a branch of policy-oriented social science within the parameters of an unquestioned capitalist world order' (Leys, 1996: 56; see also Harriss, 2003, 2007; Hickey and Mohan, 2005; Robinson, 2002).

However, if we take a step back and look critically at the capitalist order that is currently present throughout the globe, and very tangibly so in the institutions that we encounter in our daily lives, there is no shortage of reasons why critical approaches to development studies should not be constituted as a 'field of inquiry about the contemporary dynamics of that order itself' (Leys, 1996: 56). Three and a half decades of neoliberal restructuring has generated a world-system ravaged by inequality and dispossession. As the richest 1 per cent of the world's population has come to amass as much wealth as the bottom half of humanity – that is, 3.6 billion people (Oxfam, 2016) – a relative surplus population has emerged that is relegated 'to irregular, insecure, temporary and precarious forms of employment' (Neilson and Stubbs, 2011: 436). A substantial part of this surplus population inhabits the Global South as dispossessed peasantries, for example, that often end up swelling the ranks of the informal working class that inhabits the urban peripheries of Africa, Asia and Latin America (see Araghi, 1995; Davis, 2006). As Mark Duffield (2007) has rightly noted, this surplus population is relegated to 'uninsured life' – and uninsured life more often than not entails enhanced vulnerability to premature death (McIntyre and Nast, 2011). And inequality and disposability are coupled with planetary ecological devastation – a devastation that is also rooted in the dynamic of dispossession and commodification that is at the very heart of neoliberalism (Castree, 2008a, 2008b; Smith, 2007). In other words, it is very clear that if the field of development studies is to have any relevance to the human condition in this millennium, it has to aspire to much more than simply devising policy prescriptions that will enable political elites to 'contain the circulatory and destabilizing effects of underdevelopment's non-insured surplus life' (Duffield, 2007: 19). Capitalism has to be brought back into the field of critical development studies.

But how do we do this? I pose this question because a particular current of radical critique has made it quite evident that a simple return to past approaches to the analysis of historical capitalism – be it Wallerstein's world-systems theory or Robert Brenner's focus on social property relations, for example – would be an inadequate response to the challenge at hand. The current of radical critique that I have in mind is postcolonialism, and in particular the postcolonial critique of Eurocentric historiographies – including Marxist historiographies. Take the example of Gurminder Bhambra's recent interventions into the historical sociology of modernity. Bhambra (2007) argues that regnant historical sociological approaches rest on a foundational conceptual deep structure that assumes two fundamental ruptures: a temporal rupture that divides a traditional agrarian past from a modern industrial present, and a spatial rupture that inscribes the traditional/modern dichotomy in a separation between Europe and the rest of the world. Modernity is portrayed as a social formation that initially emerged within a European space and then subsequently dispersed outwards to incorporate the non-Western world. What this does, Bhambra argues, is to erase from view 'the colonial relationship which has comprised a significant aspect of modernity from its inception' (p. 131) and to render invisible the many ways in which colonialism, the slave trade, and slave labour were constitutive of the emergence of capitalism (Chapter 6). This, I believe, is a critique that has to be taken seriously. I return, then, to the question with which this paragraph began: How do we bring capitalism back into the field of critical development research – without reproducing the blind spots and silences of the Eurocentric optic?

In the remainder of this essay, I attempt to formulate a response to this question from the point of view of Marxist historical sociology. My point of departure is another recent attempt to do just the same – namely Vivek Chibber's (2013) book *Postcolonial Theory and the Specter of Capital* (henceforth *PTSC*). For some, this text amounts to a significant argument for 'the ongoing indispensability of Marxian theory for explaining capitalism and social change in the postcolonial world' (Levien, 2014: 497).[2] I believe this to be a fundamentally mistaken assessment. Indeed, as I have argued elsewhere, Chibber's critique of the postcolonial turn – a critique that he attempts to carry out via an engagement with the work of Ranajit Guha, Partha Chatterjee and Dipesh Chakrabarty as representatives of the Subaltern Studies project – ends up reinscribing the Eurocentric erasure of 'connected histories' (Subrahmanyam, 1997) squarely at the centre of the conceptual optic (see Nilsen, 2015). In the following, I first engage Chibber's criticism of postcolonial theory before attempting to outline a possible Marxist approach to a non-Eurocentric conception of capitalist development.

Recommended reading: Bhambra (2007), Kiely (1995).

Chibber versus Chakrabarty

The key objective of Chibber's (2013: 5, 12–20) critique of postcolonial theory is to question the validity of the metatheoretical conclusion that he identifies at the core of the work of scholars such as Guha, Chatterjee and Chakrabarty – namely that classical social theory does not provide us with conceptual tools to understand the non-Western world. These metatheoretical conclusions, he argues, rest on the assumption that there is a fundamental historical difference between the colonial centre and the colonial periphery. This assumption reverses and simultaneously reproduces orientalist representations of the East, which results in an inability to adequately theorize and criticize capitalism (pp. 24–26).

It is arguably in Chibber's engagement with Chakrabarty's work that this critique is articulated most clearly. As is well known, Chakrabarty (2000) set out in *Provincializing Europe* to develop a strong critique of the universalism and historicism that he argues is inherent to the categories and concepts of Western social theory. A key part of this effort is centred on an engagement with Marxist approaches to capitalist development. Marxism, he argues, is marred by a historicism that conceives of 'capital in the image of a unity that arises in one part of the world at a particular period and then develops globally over historical time, encountering and negotiating historical differences in the process' (p. 47). In order to move beyond these assumptions, Chakrabarty suggests that we should think of the universalization of capital as something that is always incomplete. And this incompleteness, in turn, can be captured by making a distinction between 'History 1' – that is a set of structures, institutions and practices that contribute to the reproduction of capital – and 'History 2' – that is, those structures, institutions and practices that 'do not lend themselves to the reproduction of the logic of capital' (p. 64). History 2, he submits, is significant because it is a source of constant destabilization and interruption in capitalist development: 'What interrupts and defers capital's self-realization are the various History 2s that always modify History 1 and thus act as our grounds for claiming historical difference' (p. 71).

Chibber's engagement with *Provincializing Europe* and its central proposition about historical difference in capitalist development departs from a diametrically opposite assumption – namely that universal theoretical categories are both valid and necessary. This is because of how modernity has been shaped and animated by:

> the twin forces of, on the one side, capital's unrelenting drive to expand, to conquer new markets, and to impose its domination on labouring classes, and on the other side, the unceasing struggle by these classes to defend themselves, their well-being, against this onslaught.
>
> *(Chibber, 2013: 208)*

Whereas Chibber views the distinction between History 1 and History 2 as being in and of itself unproblematic, the key problem with Chakrabarty's formulation, he argues, is that there is no convincing evidence to suggest that History 2 causes 'the logic of capital to be modified in type-*transforming* way' (p. 227). Rather, it is History 1 that destabilizes capitalist development – above all due to the intrinsic systemic contradictions between capital's logic of reproduction and other universals – above all 'the universal interest that working people have to protect their well-being from capitalist authority and abuse' (p. 231).

Historicism, then, is not a problem according to Chibber. And what is more, post-Enlightenment theories such as Marxism would, according to him, recognize that 'a universalizing capitalism generates a diversity of social forms' (Chibber, 2013: 243) – and to understand the origin and nature of these social forms, it is necessary to draw on universal theoretical categories that can help illuminate 'whichever properties of capitalism are implicated in their reproduction' (p. 246). Towards this end – an end that revolves around understanding that both East and West are 'subject to *the same basic forces* and are therefore part of *the same basic history*' (p. 291) – Marxism remains indispensable, precisely because, throughout the 20th century it has attempted to develop a critical understanding of '*the specificity of the East*' (p. 291, emphasis added).

Recommended reading: Chakrabarty (2000), Chibber (2013), Kaiwar (2014).

Chibber in the Eurocentric tunnel of time?

Chibber's critique of Chakrabarty is in many regards highly apposite. Indeed, it echoes a central concern that has been articulated by Marxist scholars who have been embedded in the field of postcolonial studies for a long time – namely that by displacing 'the structuration of the modern world by capitalism', postcolonialism has rendered 'the structurality of the global system either arbitrary or unintelligible' (Lazarus, 2002: 45, 60; see also Kaiwar, 2004, 2014; Lazarus, 2011; Lazarus and Varma, 2010; San Juan, 2002). However, I am far from convinced that his proposition that in order to provincialize Europe we should start from the assertion that both East and West are subject to the same social forces and part of the same universal history, is supported by an ontology that is adequate to the task of conceptualizing 'the globality of capitalism as a historical formation' (Lazarus, 2002: 63).

As Julian Go (2013: 37) has argued, historical sociology is often marked by 'a methodological nationalism that occludes expansive relations across space' (see also Boatcă and Costa, 2012). This methodological nationalism is apparent in the tendency within historical sociological inquiry to 'analytically [separate] relations that might not have been separate at all' (Go, 2013: 36). This bifurcation, in turn, is moored in a substantialist understanding of the social world – that is, an ontology in which the units that are at the heart of sociological inquiry are thought of as self-contained substances, essences or systems (p. 41). If we are to move beyond this methodological nationalism, it will be necessary, at the most fundamental level, to develop a relational ontology that emphasizes 'the interactional constitution of social units, processes, and practices across space' (p. 28) – it is only then that we might be able to fully acknowledge 'the constitutiveness of the international both to the emergence and the expansion of capitalism' (Matin, 2013: 370; see also Anievas and Nisancioglu, 2013, 2015; Bhambra, 2010; Hobson, 2011; Tansel, 2014).

This line of critique also has consequences for Marxist historical sociology. As much as Chibber (2013: 291) is correct in arguing that Marxists have devoted much time and energy 'to understand the peculiar effects of capitalist development in the non-West', these interrogations have often proceeded from a vantage point in which capitalism is posited as a mode of production that emerges in and emanates from Europe. Moreover, within Marxist historical sociology, there is also a tendency to conceive of colonialism as something that is '*consequent* to capitalism' rather than '*constitutive* of it' (Bhambra, 2010: 674, emphasis in original). If we consider that elsewhere, Chibber (2007) has argued forcefully against a more globally oriented view of the origins of modernity, it becomes all to clear that his view of capitalism is marred by this particular shortcoming. Modern institutions, he argues, originated in Britain in the late 17th century. Agrarian capitalism was one such institution, and it enabled a restructuring of the state that in turn used its greatly enhanced powers to finance expansion: 'Britain was the epicenter from which the shockwave of the eighteenth century radiated outwards' (p. 136).

For Chibber, then, the universalization of capital is conceived of as a process that originates in the internal properties of the bounded entity that is the English economy. It then subsequently radiates outwards to incorporate the non-Western world in the orbit of capitalist accumulation (see Nilsen, 2015). This, I would argue, comes dangerously close to the historical 'tunnel vision' that James Blaut (1994: 351) detected in the work of Robert Brenner, in which the rise of capitalism is explained solely with reference to 'European facts' – and neglecting, therefore, 'the history of the world outside of Europe both as a cause of change within Europe and as the site of historically efficacious change in its own right'. What would it entail to critically question this view of the universalization of capitalism and its underlying ontological and historiographical assumptions – without letting go of the ambition of bringing back into analytical view a universal conception of historical capitalism in critical development studies?

Recommended reading: Blaut (1993), Go (2016), McEwan (2008).

A possible Marxist approach

Let me first answer that question in the negative: it does not entail a refusal to acknowledge that England witnessed the emergence of socioeconomic relations with a distinctive potential for wealth creation during the 16th and 17th centuries. Rather, it means that the genesis of capitalist development has to be understood in terms of how this transformation came to interlock with other processes of change occurring elsewhere through relations that stretch across a quintessentially global space. As Marx (1990) pointed out, the enclosure of the commons and the dispossession of the English peasantry were fundamentally interwoven with multiple forms of primitive accumulation in the emerging colonial periphery (see also Heller, 2011; Pradella, 2013, 2015). Furthermore, the coeval unfolding of primitive accumulation in core and periphery generated a globe-spanning division of labour that made it possible for substantial merchant groups to establish control over 'a variety of enterprises from putting out networks and peasant agriculture to slave plantations and factories in the modern sense' (Banaji, 2010: 273). The challenge, then, is to chart a path towards a way of conceptualizing the emergence and universalization of capitalism as a process that unfolded through and on the basis of a latticework of relations that cut across global space – that is, we need to develop a relational ontology for the study of capitalist development.

An important resource that can be mobilized in this process is Justin Rosenberg's (2006, 2010) reconstruction of Trotsky's theory of uneven and combined development (see also Barker, 2006; Matin, 2013). The point of departure for this reconstruction is the argument that historical sociology must develop a conception of historical causality that posits 'inter-societal coexistence and interaction' (Rosenberg, 2006: 311) as an ontological foundation. A sociological definition of the international, Rosenberg argues, can be crafted from the claim that unevenness and combination are intrinsic properties of sociohistorical development in general, and not just distinctive characteristics of capitalist development. Unevenness finds its manifestation in the spatio-temporal coexistence of social formations that have developed specific material capabilities and sociocultural forms in the context of distinct geographical environments (pp. 313–19). Simultaneously, the spatio-temporal coexistence of multiple and different social formations is profoundly interactive due to the fact that the constitution and reproduction of these social formations are intrinsically predicated upon the relations of material and ideational exchange that exist between them. In other words, unevenness is always already intertwined with combination in social development as a historical process (pp. 319–29).

If we acknowledge the developmental significance of inter-societal connections, we can move beyond the assumptions of 'ontological singularity', which posits development 'as the unfolding of characteristics internal to a given society' (Rosenberg, 2010: 179; see also Hobson, 2011: 151). This still leaves us with the challenge of outlining the particular social dynamics of historically determinate forms of combined and uneven development. Nevertheless, Rosenberg's reconstruction of uneven and combined development leaves us well equipped to do this in a way that transcends 'the conventional stereotype of capitalist history as the history of the first capitalist nation' (Banaji, 2010: 12).

As we begin this theoretical labour, however, we must first consider a possible objection to the capacity of notions of uneven and combined development to overcome Eurocentrism. In a recent article, Bhambra (2011) has pointed to what she perceives to be the persistent assumption in theories of combined and uneven development that development is, ultimately, linear and stadial. The problem with this, she submits, is that a theory of uneven and combined development will not have analytical space for the colonialism that is a part of the development of unevenness (p. 675). For Bhambra, this is expressive of an inherent limitation in the way that Marxist historical sociology theorizes capitalism as a mode of production that 'is said to rest on a singular relation between capital and labour that is argued to be its intrinsic form' (p. 676). Unfree forms of labour that were at the heart of the ascent of capitalism – chief among them, slavery – are thus erased from analytical view.

There is no doubt that Bhambra's objection holds true for specific Marxist approaches to the study of historical capitalism. But – and this is crucial, I believe – the problem that she has identified is not necessarily an absolute limit to the extent to which Marxism can overcome Eurocentric assumptions. On the contrary, it is quite possible to conceptualize the capitalist mode of production in a way that renders possible the analysis of developmental trajectories in far more complex ways.

One way of doing so is to draw on Jairus Banaji's (2010: 53) critique of 'formal abstractionism' in Marxist historiography. Formal abstractionism results in a tendency to deduce and define a mode of production according to 'the given forms of exploitation of labour' (p. 53) that prevail in a determinate social formation. So, an economic system in which serfdom prevails as the predominant way of exploiting labour will automatically be classified as a feudal mode of production, whereas an economic system in which free wage labour is predominant would automatically be classified as a capitalist mode of production. This way of reasoning, Banaji argues, conflates levels of abstraction by elevating a 'simple category' – that is, a category that is common and shared across different systems of production across historical time – to the status of a 'historically determinate category' (p. 55). This is problematic, because wage labour as a simple category can be found in many social formations and forms of production that precede capitalism. And conversely, capitalist accumulation can draw its sustenance from forms of labour exploitation that would generally be thought of as pre-capitalist (pp. 54–5).

Given that '*the deployment of labour is correlated with modes of production in complex ways*' (Banaji, 2010: 5, emphasis in original), we have to conceptualize modes of production from a different vantage point. For Banaji, that vantage point is 'the defining role of the laws of motion' (p. 58). On this view, modes of production are defined by specific developmental tendencies that are manifest in distinct economic rhythms. Consequently, whereas the feudal mode of production is animated by aristocratic consumption needs, the capitalist mode of production is animated by expanded reproduction through the production and accumulation of surplus value (p. 60). The fundamental point of this proposition is that the laws of motion of the capitalist mode of production can find their realization in a variety of forms of labour exploitation – slavery, bonded labour, sharecropping, or free wage labour. And this means, ultimately, that 'there is not one ostensibly unique configuration of capital but a series of *distinct configurations*, forms of the accumulation process, implying other combinations' (p. 9, emphasis in original).

What this approach enables us to do is to take a much longer view of the historical emergence of capitalism, which considers how capitalism as a mode of production characterized by distinct laws of motion emerged through 'determinations and conditions that arose from . . . social interactions between societies' (Anievas and Nisancioglu, 2013: 84). This process is not a linear one, in which modes of production based on distinct forms of labour control follow one after the other as historical time advances, but an uneven and combined process in which different forms of labour control are fused together across transnational space in specific configurations at particular conjunctures. Admittedly, these are only the bare bones of a Marxist historical sociology that would enable us to think capitalist development beyond Eurocentrism. Yet, to reiterate my opening point, capitalism in its current avatar – an avatar that consigns ever-larger segments of humanity to disposability and premature death – leaves those of us who are committed to a critical agenda in development research no choice but to take up this gauntlet. In doing so, we will have to depart from the concrete observation that capitalism – and modernity in a wider sense – emerged through relations between societies across global space. We will then have to move towards the more abstract recognition that this is expressive of the intrinsically uneven and combined nature of processes of social change, before we return, yet again, to the level of the concrete with a richer understanding of capitalism as a concrete historical entity – *and* with concrete proposals for how to transform the system that has generated the planetary crisis that humanity confronts in the early decades of the 21st century.

Recommended reading: Anievas and Nisancioglu (2015), Banaji (2010), Pradella (2015).

Notes

1 See also Booth (1994), Corbridge (1990), Mouzelis (1988), Schuurman (1993), Sklair (1988) and Van Der Geest and Buttel (1988) for key contributions to this debate.
2 Chibber's book has been widely reviewed. See, for example, Chatterjee (2013), Hitchcock (2015), Lazarus (2016), Murphet (2014), Purakayastha (2014) and Spivak (2014). See also Warren (2016).

References

Anievas, A. and Nisancioglu, K. (2013). 'What's at stake in the transition debate? Rethinking the origins of capitalism and the "rise of the West"'. *Millennium*, 42(1): 78–102.

Anievas, A. and Nisancioglu, K. (2015). *How the West Came to Rule: The Geopolitical Origins of Capitalism*. Chicago, IL: University of Chicago Press.

Araghi, F. (1995). 'Global depeasantization, 1945–1990'. *Sociological Quarterly*, 36(2): 337–68.

Banaji, J. (2010). *Theory as History: Essays on Modes of Production and Exploitation*. Leiden: Brill.

Barker, C. (2006). 'Beyond Trotsky: extending combined and uneven development'. In B. Dunn and H. Radice (eds), *100 Years of Permanent Revolution: Results and Prospects*. London: Pluto Press, pp. 72–87.

Bhambra, G. (2007). *Rethinking Modernity: Postcolonialism and the Sociological Imagination*. London: Palgrave.

Bhambra, G. (2010). 'Historical sociology, international relations, and connected histories'. *Cambridge Review of International Affairs*, 23(1): 127–43.

Bhambra, G. (2011). 'Talking among themselves? Weberian and Marxist historical sociologies as dialogues without others'. *Millennium*, 39(3): 667–81.

Blaut, J.M. (1993). *The Colonizer's Model of the World: Geographical Diffusionism and Eurocentric History*. Oxford: Guildford Press.

Blaut, J.M. (1994). 'Robert Brenner in the tunnel of time'. *Antipode*, 26(4): 351–74.

Boatcă, M. and Costa, S. (2012). 'Postcolonial sociology: a research agenda'. In M. Boatcă, S. Costa and E.G. Rodríguez (eds), *Decolonizing European Sociology: Transdisciplinary Approaches*. London: Routledge.

Booth, D. (1985). 'Marxism and development sociology: interpreting the impasse'. *World Development*, 13(7): 761–87.

Booth, D. (1994). *Rethinking Social Development: Theory, Research and Practice*. London: Longman.

Castree, N. (2008a). 'Neoliberalising nature: the logics of deregulation and reregulation'. *Environment and Planning A*, 40(1): 131–52.

Castree, N. (2008b). 'Neoliberalising nature: processes, effects, and evaluations'. *Environment and Planning A*, 40(1): 153–73.

Chakrabarty, D. (2000). *Provincializing Europe: Postcolonial Thought and Historical Difference*. Princeton, NJ: Princeton University Press.

Chatterjee, P. (2013). 'Subaltern studies and capital'. *Economic and Political Weekly*, 48(37): 69–75.

Chibber, V. (2007). 'Sidelining the West?' *New Left Review*, 47: 130–41.

Chibber, V. (2013). *Postcolonial Theory and the Specter of Capital*. London: Verso.

Cooper, F. (2000). 'Back to work: categories, boundaries and connections in the study of labour'. In P. Alexander and R. Halpern (eds), *Racializing Class, Classifying Race: Labour and Difference in Britain, the USA and Africa*. Basingstoke: Macmillan, pp. 213–35.

Corbridge, S. (1990). 'Post-Marxism and development studies: beyond the impasse'. *World Development*, 18(5): 623–39.

Cowen, M. and Shenton, R.W. (1996). *Doctrines of Development*. London: Routledge.

Davis, M. (2006). *Planet of Slums*. London: Verso.

Duffield, M. (2007). *Development, Security and Unending War: Governing the World of Peoples*. Cambridge: Polity.

Ferguson, J. (1994). *The Anti-Politics Machine: Development, Depoliticization and Bureaucratic Power in Lesotho*. New York: Cambridge University Press.

Go, J. (2013). 'For a postcolonial sociology'. *Theory and Society*, 42(1): 25–55.

Go, J. (2016). *Postcolonial Thought and Social Theory*. New York: Oxford University Press.

Harriss, J. (2003). 'Do political regimes matter? Poverty reduction and regime differences across India'. In P. Houtzager and M. Moore (eds), *Changing Paths: International Development and the New Politics of Inclusion*. Ann Arbor, MI: University of Michigan Press, pp. 204–32.

Harriss, J. (2007). 'Bringing politics back in to poverty analysis: why understanding of social relations matters more for policy on chronic poverty than measurement'. Available at: www.trentu.ca/ids/documents/Q2_WP34_Harriss.pdf.

Harriss-White, B. (2006). 'Poverty and capitalism'. *Economic and Political Weekly*, 41(13): 1241–6.

Heller, H. (2011). *The Birth of Capitalism: A 21st Century Perspective*. London: Pluto Press.

Hettne, B. (1995). *Development Theory and the Three Worlds*, 2nd edition. Essex: Longman Scientific and Technical.

Hickey, S. and Mohan, G. (2005). 'Relocating participation within a radical politics of development'. *Development and Change*, 36: 237–62.

Hitchcock, P. (2015). 'Postcolonial theory and the specter of capital by Vivek Chibber'. *The Comparatist*, 39: 355–64.

Hobson, J. (2011). 'What's at stake in the neo-Troskyist debate? Towards a non-Eurocentric historical sociology of uneven and combined development'. *Millennium*, 40(1): 147–66.

Kaiwar, V. (2004). 'Towards orientalism and nativism'. *Historical Materialism*, 12(2): 189–247.

Kaiwar, V. (2014). *The Postcolonial Orient: The Politics of Difference and the Project of Provincialising Europe*. Leiden: Brill.

Kiely, R. (1995). *The Sociology of Development: The Impasse and Beyond*. London: Routledge.

Larrain, J. (1989). *Theories of Development: Capitalism, Colonialism and Dependency*. Cambridge: Polity Press.

Lazarus, N. (2002). 'The fetish of the West in postcolonial theory'. In C. Bartolovich and N. Lazarus (eds), *Marxism, Modernity and Postcolonial Studies*. Cambridge: Cambridge University Press, pp. 43–64.

Lazarus, N. (2011). 'What postcolonial theory doesn't say'. *Race and Class*, 5(1): 3–27.

Lazarus, N. (2016). 'Vivek Chibber and the spectre of postcolonial theory'. *Race and Class*, 57(3): 88–106.

Lazarus, N. and Varma, R. (2010). 'Marxism and postcolonialism'. In J. Bidet and S. Kouvelakis (eds), *Critical Companion to Contemporary Marxism*. Leiden: Brill, pp. 309–32.

Levien, M. (2014). 'Subalternists scrutinized'. *European Journal of Sociology*, 54(3): 485–97.

Leys, C. (1996). *The Rise and Fall of Development Theory*. Nairobi: Bloomington.

Li, T.M. (2007). *The Will to Improve: Governmentality, Development, and the Practice of Politics*. Durham, NC: Duke University Press.

Marx, K. (1990). *Capital: A Critique of Political Economy – Volume 1*. London: Penguin Books.

Matin, K. (2013). 'Redeeming the universal: postcolonialism and the inner life of Eurocentrism'. *European Journal of International Relations*, 19(2): 353–77.

McEwan, C. (2008). *Postcolonialism and Development*. London: Routledge.

McIntyre, M. and Nast, H. (2011). 'Bio(necro)polis: surplus populations and the spatial dialectics of reproduction and race'. *Antipode*, 43(5): 1465–88.

Mosse, D. (2010). 'A relational approach to durable poverty, inequality and power'. *Journal of Development Studies*, 46(7): 1156–78.

Mouzelis, N.P. (1988). 'Sociology of development: reflections on the present crisis'. *Sociology*, 22(1): 23–44.

Murphet, J. (2014). 'No alternative'. *The Cambridge Journal of Postcolonial Literary Inquiry*, 1(1): 157–63.

Neilson, D. and Stubbs, T. (2011). 'Relative surplus population and uneven development in the neoliberal era: theory and empirical application'. *Capital and Class*, 35(3): 435–53.

Nilsen, A.G. (2015). 'Passages from Marxism to postcolonialism: a comment on Vivek Chibber's *Postcolonialism and the Specter of Capital*'. *Critical Sociology* (published online before print). doi: 10.1177/0896920515614982.

Oxfam (2016). 'An economy for the 1%: how privilege and power in the economy drive extreme inequality and how this can be stopped'. Available at: www.oxfam.org/sites/www.oxfam.org/files/file_attachments/bp210-economy-one-percent-tax-havens-180116-en_0.pdf.

Pradella, L. (2013). 'Imperialism and capitalist development'. *Historical Materialism*, 21(2): 117–47.

Pradella, L. (2015). *Globalization and the Critique of Political Economy: New Insights from Marx's Writings*. London: Routledge.

Purakayastha, A.S. (2014). 'Postcolonial theory and the specter of capital'. *Postcolonial Writing*, 50(3): 369–70.

Robinson, W. (2002). 'Remapping development in the light of globalization: from a territorial to a social cartography'. *Third World Quarterly*, 23(6): 1047–71.

Rosenberg, J. (2006). 'Why is there no international historical sociology?' *European Journal of International Relations*, 12(3): 307–40.

Rosenberg, J. (2010). 'Basic problems in the theory of uneven and combined development part 2: unevenness and political multiplicity'. *Cambridge Review of International Affairs*, 23(1): 165–89.

San Juan, E. (2002). 'Postcolonialism and the problematic of uneven development'. In C. Bartolovich and N. Lazarus (eds), *Marxism, Modernity and Postcolonial Studies*. Cambridge: Cambridge University Press, pp. 221–39.

Schuurman, F.J. (ed.) (1993). *Beyond the Impasse: New Directions in Development Theory*. London: Zed Books.

Sklair, L. (1988). 'Transcending the impasse: metatheory, theory and empirical research in the sociology of development and underdevelopment'. *World Development*, 16(6): 697–709.

Smith, N. (2007). 'Nature as accumulation strategy'. *Socialist Register 2007*, 43: 19–41.

Spivak, G.C. (2014). 'Postcolonial theory and the specter of capital'. *Cambridge Review of International Affairs*, 27(1): 184–98.

Subrahmanyam, S. (1997). 'Connected histories: notes towards a reconfiguration of early modern Eurasia'. *Modern Asian Studies*, 31(3): 735–62.

Tansel, C.B. (2014). 'Deafening silence? Marxism, international historical sociology and the spectre of Eurocentrism'. *European Journal of International Relations*, 21(1): 76–100.

Toye, J. (1987). *Dilemmas of Development: Reflections on the Counter-Revolution in Development Theory and Policy*. Oxford: Blackwell.

Van Der Geest, P. and Buttel, F. (1988). 'Marx, Weber and development sociology: beyond the impasse'. *World Development*, 16(6): 683–95.

Warren, R. (ed.) (2016). *The Debate on Postcolonial Theory and the Specter of Capital*. London: Verso.

4

DEVELOPMENT THEORY

The Latin American pivot

Cristóbal Kay

It could be argued that one of the origins of critical development studies in Latin America has been the writings of the Peruvian Marxist José Carlos Mariátegui (1971). His main writings were published in the late 1920s and early 1930, in which he argued that the feudal landlord class and the national bourgeoisie allied with imperialism continually reproduced the system of exploitation and domination. He did not believe that the national bourgeoisie were able to perform the progressive role it had achieved in Europe. Hence, he advocated a socialist revolution so as to achieve the liberation of the oppressed classes and in particular of the indigenous people. Contrary to many thinkers at the time, he foresaw the revolutionary potential of the indigenous peasantry. He was one of the early Marxists who tried to adapt Marxism to the Latin American reality as he understood it, and in general break with Eurocentric thinking (Quijano, 2000). In this sense, he foreshadowed structuralism and dependency theory, which I consider to be the main contributions to critical development theory to emanate from the region, as will be discussed in the second and third sections of this chapter. However, while structuralism in its critique of the orthodoxy of the times only sought to reform the capitalist system, the Marxist strand within dependency theory aimed at overthrowing it so as to achieve socialism.

While the debate on 'reform or revolution' already emerged in the first decades of the 20th century, it acquired particular intensity after the Cuban Revolution in 1959 (Petras and Zeitlin, 1968). Several governments in Latin America and the Caribbean followed some of the development policy recommendations of structuralism during the 1950s, 1960s and early 1970s, but only to a limited extent, while dependency theory had far less influence on government policy at the time, although it was very popular among students, left-wing political parties and revolutionary social movements. With the rise of the counter-revolution in development thinking (Toye, 1987) in the late 1970s and 1980s, neoliberal ideas gained prominence and shaped government policy not only in the developing world, but also in the developed countries. It was only in the early 1980s that structuralist thinkers were able to respond to the neoliberal challenge by proposing neostructuralist development strategies, as will be discussed in the third section. The chapter ends with some brief conclusions in the fourth section.

Recommended reading: Hettne (1995), Munck and O'Hearn (1999), Nederveen-Pieterse (2001).

Structuralist theory of development

The emergence of what came to be known as the structuralist school or theory of development was haphazard. It originated with the path-breaking and controversial publication of the Economic Survey of Latin America 1949, which was published by the United Nations Department of Economic Affairs in New York in 1951. The original Spanish text was already published in 1950 by the United Nations Economic Commission for Latin America (ECLA) in Santiago de Chile. CEPAL, to use its Spanish acronym for Comisión Económica para América Latina, was established in 1948. The renowned development economist Albert Hirschman (1961) referred to this publication as the 'ECLA manifesto' (which has echoes with another well-known manifesto), and not without reason. The publication was penned by Raúl Prebisch, who had become head of the ECLA in 1949. In his analysis, he challenged the economic orthodoxy at the time, which argued on the basis of the theory of comparative advantages that international trade was beneficial for the trading nations concerned, and particularly for the less developed countries. Instead of the income gap being reduced through trade, Prebisch argued that it actually increased. Such a conclusion had explosive consequences for the relations between the rich and the poor countries, and thus it is not surprising that Prebisch was attacked and vilified by the powerful, particularly in the centre countries (Dosman, 2008). But Prebisch knew how to defend himself and the institution he led. He had indeed assembled an extraordinarily gifted and transnational team of social scientists who he ably led and inspired (Kay, 2005).

Prebisch divided the world into centre countries and the periphery countries, which roughly correspond in the conventional terminology to the developed and less developed or developing countries respectively. By using this terminology, Prebisch already highlighted the power asymmetry between the nations of the world. Using historical statistics, he discovered that the long-term trend of terms of trade between Latin America (the periphery) with its main trading countries, largely the US and Europe (the centre) were deteriorating. Latin America was mainly or almost exclusively exporting primary products such as mineral and agricultural commodities to the centre countries, while it largely imported manufacturing commodities from them. While the terms of trade fluctuate over time, the trend was negative for the periphery, meaning that during the cyclical upswing the price index of the commodities exported by the periphery increases less than the price of the commodities imported by the periphery, meanwhile during the cyclical downswing the opposite happens. Hence, the terms of trade deteriorate against the periphery and in favour of the centre, which is contrary to what the conventional international trade theory sustained. Expressed more directly, this means that the periphery countries had to export an increasing amount of primary commodities to be able to import the same amount of industrial commodities from the centre countries. There was thus an unequal exchange between them. Prebisch did not necessarily argue that international trade was negative for the periphery, but that the fruits of international trade favoured more the centre than the periphery (Kay, 2006). This thesis is known in the literature as the 'Prebisch-Singer thesis on the deterioration of the terms of trade' and has generated much controversy ever since (Toye and Toye, 2004). More generally, given Prebisch's pioneering conceptual-ization of the centre-periphery relations, some authors refer to structuralism as the centre-periphery paradigm in development studies (Rodríguez, 1977).

The lesson that Prebisch and his team at ECLA drew from this finding is that the periphery should shift its development strategy from being 'outward-oriented' to one that is 'inward-oriented'. This was to be achieved by the state promoting the indus-trialization of the periphery country through various means such as protectionism, subsidies and infrastructure for the nascent industry, a process that became known as 'import substitution industrialization', or ISI for short. The aim was to reduce the dependence on exports of primary products and to shift the gravity of the economy to industry and the domestic economy. Many governments in Latin America, and elsewhere, followed such an ISI development strategy during the 1950s until the 1970s and gave rise to what has been termed 'state developmentalism' given the cen-trality the state assumed in this process. This statist development strategy was much criticized by orthodox economists and was largely overturned with the neoliberal shift of the 1980s, as will be discussed later.

Another important legacy of the structuralist school of development concerns the issue of inflation, which had plagued some countries in Latin America for decades. Again, their particular interpretation of the causes of inflation generated a fierce controversy as it challenged the orthodox view. This became known as the 'structuralist-monetarist debate' on inflation. Instead of just stressing mone-tary factors, the ECLA structuralists stressed what they called the structural factors underlying the inflationary phenomena, such as the inability of the agricultural sec-tor to sufficiently increase food supply to meet the rising demand, thereby causing food prices to rise, which in turn led to demands from workers for wage increases, and so on, leading to spiralling inflation. Structuralists blamed the unequal land tenure system and the rentier attitude of landlords for this lack of response from them to the higher price incentive (what economists refer to as supply inelasticity). Other structural factors arose from the continuing deficit in the balance of trade, which required periodic devaluations of the local currency, thereby increasing the price of imports. This imbalance in foreign trade resulted not only from the dete-rioration of the terms of trade, but also from the particular character of the ISI process, which demanded increasing imports of inputs, machinery and equipment while being unable to break into the export market. Also, agricultural exports did not rise fast enough. These various imbalances and bottlenecks were embedded in the structure of the developing countries. Hence, the inflationary spiral and curse could not be tackled merely through monetary means such as restricting the supply of money, but required structural reforms of the country such as land reform and making ISI more competitive and export-oriented. Thus, the structuralists argued that the monetarist prescription for dealing with inflation was merely tackling the 'propagating' factors and may do more harm than good by negatively affecting growth (Sunkel, 1960).

Furthermore, what I find remarkable is the particular interpretation of the structuralist economist Noyola, who also introduced a social and political dimension to the debate by stressing that inflationary pressures also arose as a consequence of the class struggle between workers and capitalists and landlords (Kay, 1989). While landlords were seeking to increase their appropriation of land and labour rents from peasants and of surplus value from rural workers, and the industrial capitalists were seeking to expand their profits by squeezing the wages of workers, those affected resisted and demanded lower rents and higher wages, respectively. Due to the economic power of landlords and capitalists, they passed on any concession they made to peasants and workers to the consumers by raising prices and thereby feeding the inflationary process. Hence, to tame inflation from the structuralist perspective also required a new social compact between the contending social forces. In short, a more equitable distribution of income is required. The issue of equity becomes an important component of the neostructuralist development thinkers, as will be discussed later.

Prebisch's analysis on the unequal centre-periphery relations led him to look beyond ECLA. He was the main driving force behind the creation of UNCTAD, the United Nations Conference on Trade and Development, which was established in 1964 in Geneva with the remit to negotiate fairer trade relations between the developed and the developing countries. Prebisch became its first secretary general, but resigned in 1969 as he was unable to make much progress in his aim of seeking to establish a new international economic order. It was indeed a very ambitious goal, which remains unfulfilled to this day (Toye and Toye, 2004). First, the rise of Taiwan and South Korea in the 1970s and 1980s, and the subsequent rise of China, as well as other former periphery countries, in the last decades has, and is, reshaping relations between centre and periphery, but not exactly in the way desired by Prebisch and the structuralists, as it is taking place within the context of neoliberal globalization.

Recommended reading: Furtado (1964), Kay (1989, 2009), Rodríguez (1977).

Dependency theory

A key critical perspective in development studies is dependency theory, which arose out of disenchantment with, and critique of, the ISI process. I am not referring to the critique by orthodox economists and neoliberals (of which more later), but to the critique arising from within structuralism, as well as by Marxists. Thus, within dependency theory, it is possible to distinguish at least two strands: structuralist and Marxist. Despite their differences, they share the basic premise that the process of development of the developing countries can only be understood in their relations with the developed countries. As formulated by Sunkel (1972: 520) from a structuralist perspective: 'Development and underdevelopment . . . are simultaneous processes: the two faces of the historical evolution of capitalism'. Similarly, for Frank (1966: 18) from a Marxist perspective: 'Contemporary underdevelopment is in large part the historical product of past and continuing economic and other relations between the satellite underdeveloped and the now developed metropolitan countries'. In this interdependent relationship, it is the developed countries that are dominant while the developing countries are in a dependent situation. This dependency has its historical origins in colonialism and imperialism but persists to this day for a variety of reasons. The two strands differ mainly in the analytical tools they deploy, and above all in the solution they propose for overcoming the dependent relationship. For obvious reasons, Marxists tend to use concepts derived from Marxist political economy. However, contrary to Marx, they argue that the development of capitalism in the dependent countries does not display the progressive features it has had in the dominant countries. Thus, some authors refer to this position as neo-Marxist. As for solutions, the structuralists believe it is possible to overcome dependence by radically reforming the capitalist system via creating a new international economic order, while the Marxists believe that this is only possible by overthrowing the capitalist system itself and creating a socialist world order (Sunkel, 1990).

Dependency authors are quite an eclectic group. For example, they stress different factors for explaining the dependency situation even within the two strands I propose. For example, within the structuralist strand, Sunkel (1969) argues that the rise of foreign transnational corporations as a consequence of ISI in the dependent countries is leading to a process of national disintegration and the marginalization of social groups, which are displaced by this process. Meanwhile, Furtado (1973) puts the emphasis on the 'dependent patterns of consumption' generated by these ISI transnational corporations, thereby creating an industrial structure not suited for underdeveloped countries as it is too diversified and too capital-intensive, thereby increasing the surplus population and perpetuating the high concentration of income, and hence the dependent pattern of consumption. And so the cycle of dependence continues. As my last example for an author within the structuralist strand, I refer to Cardoso, who coined the term 'associated dependent development'. Contrary to Frank and others, he argued that dependency does not mean stagnation, and, on the contrary, it can lead to economic growth, although with several undesirable features such as inequality and marginalization. Also contrary to Frank, Cardoso (1972) highlighted the 'diversity within unity' instead of the 'unity within diversity', as for him the dependency situation varies between dependent countries due to their specific historical, economic, social and political circumstances.

With reference to the Marxist strand, I can refer to Frank (1966), who I mentioned already. He coined the much-quoted phrase 'the development of under-development', by which he meant that the dependent relationship reproduces the underdevelopment of the developing countries instead of leading to a process of genuine development. Dos Santos (1973) argued that a key element in the depend-ent relationship arises due to the lack of a capital goods sector in the developing countries. The ISI process had not enabled the countries to produce their own tech-nology as transnational corporations wanted to keep control over it back in their headquarters in the developed countries. Hence, developing countries had become dependent on imports from the developed countries to access the productivity- and growth-enhancing machinery, equipment and other technological goods for sustaining their ISI and other economic sectors. Thus, 'technological dependence' is a key factor in the reproduction of the dependency relationship. As a final example within this dependency strand, I refer to Marini (1973), who focuses on the 'super-exploitation of labour' by capital that arises from the 'unequal exchange' between the developed and underdeveloped countries.

It is possible to speak also of a 'Caribbean' dependency strand, which emerged largely from a group of scholars and activists linked to the University of the West Indies. While they were influenced by structuralist and Marxist dependency theo-rists, they argued that these had to be adapted to the particular context of the Caribbean countries, which were small island economies that all had a recent colonial past (Girvan, 1973).

Dependency theory was particularly influential from the late 1960s to the 1970s. It provoked much debate and criticism. While the Marxist strand of dependency theory tended to morph into world-systems theory, particularly in the case of Frank (Kay, 2011), the structuralist strand of dependency morphed into neostruc-turalism, which will be discussed next. A world-systems perspective is discussed in Chapter 7 in this book.

Recommended reading: Kay (1989, 2011), Kay and Gwynne (2000), Munck (1999).

Neostructuralism and alternative development

The neoliberal counter-revolution in development studies (Krugman, 1992) that was brewing during the 1970s gathered momentum at the turn of the decade with the victory of the Conservative Party under the leadership of Margaret Thatcher in 1979 in the UK and the subsequent election of Ronald Reagan in 1981 to the US presidency. Both pushed forward the neoliberal agenda that aimed to dismantle many of the achievements of the welfare state and strengthened the forces pushing for neoliberal transformation in the developing countries. With the debt crisis of the 1980s, which was particularly acute in Latin America, the neoliberal forces seized the moment and used the international financial institutions (WB and IMF) and the aid programmes of the US and UK, among others, to impose certain conditions for the disbursement of the credits and aid to the recipient countries. This package of wide-ranging reform measures was labelled 'structural adjustment programmes' or

SAPs, which led to the 'Washington Consensus', so named as Washington, DC, is not only the seat of the US government and treasury, but also of the WB, IMF, IDB (Inter-American Development Bank) and OEA (Organization of American States), who all promoted neoliberalism. Among the required reforms were the dismantling of the developmentalist state and the protectionist measures of the ISI period so as to give free reign to the global market forces (Saad-Filho and Johnston, 2005). Chile under the dictatorship of General Pinochet (1973–1990) already pioneered neoliberalism (Valdés, 1995), which became the dominant policy discourse in many countries of the world.

Among the first development institutions to take up the challenge of the neo-liberal paradigm was ECLAC, previously known as ECLA, which now included the Caribbean in its name, hence the added C at the end of the acronym. As from 1990, they published a series of books in which they set out their new approach to development, which evolved from the earlier structuralism, seeking for its renewal, and thus referred to as 'neostructuralism'. The foundational text of neostructuralism is *Changing Production Patterns with Social Equity* (ECLAC, 1990), whose intellectual author was Fajnzylber (Torres, 2006). Neostructuralists tried to come to terms with the demise of structuralism and dependency theory, the rise of the Newly Industrializing Countries (NICs), and particularly the success of South Korea and Taiwan, the hegemony of neoliberalism and the challenges of globalization, as well as with the rise of poverty and inequality in Latin America as a consequence of neoliberal policies.

The key elements of neostructuralism can be summed up as follows. First, it shifts from the structuralist emphasis on inward-looking development to 'development from within' to selective domestic priorities, but increasingly to the world market in areas that offer the best opportunities for the strategic and long-term development of the country. Thus, foreign trade was to become a more important sector than in the past, as it was now seen as having a more dynamic potential than the domestic market. The whole issue of unequal exchange was given less priority, sidelined or not mentioned at all.

Second, this required transforming the production structure of the country by shifting from traditional raw material exports to exports with higher value added, and especially towards industrial exports. Instead of continuing with the country's comparative advantages, the state was now charged with developing its 'competitive advantages'. Hence, the state was to expand education, improve standards and promote technological skills and innovations.

Third, to achieve this aim, a more nimble, competent, pragmatic, enabling and catalyst state was required, as compared to the past clientelist, bureaucratic and over-sized state, so as to encourage the private sector to seek out the new opportunities of globalization, as well as being able to adapt its policies according to changing international and national circumstances. The state was no longer required to create state enterprises, but could establish public–private partnerships where this was the most appropriate way to stimulate investment, entrepreneurship and high-value economic activities. In short, a developmentalist state 'light' (Petras and Veltmeyer, 2007).

Fourth, a more flexible and open view of the market was taken. Thus, instead of using protectionist measures, price controls, exchange rate controls and so on, in a rather clientelist and indiscriminate manner as in the past, the purpose now was to 'govern the market', but in a purposeful manner so as to achieve certain developmental goals within a certain time frame so that market intervention did not become entrenched. Thus, an eye was always kept on market signals.

Fifth, so as to be in a better position to face the world, market neostructuralists proposed a policy of 'open regionalism' (i.e. trade and investment agreements between countries of the region), but with a view that the region would negotiate agreements with other countries or regions in the world. Thus, bilateral country agreements were to be avoided, as a single Latin American country, especially the smaller ones, would have a weak bargaining position when dealing with rich and large countries.

Sixth, last but not least, as markets tend to foster inequalities, especially those of a neoliberal kind, the state had to encourage measures that promote equity. One of the slogans was 'growth with equity', as without growth it would be difficult to finance equity measures. The achievement of social inclusion, cohesion and poverty reduction was thus an important part of the neostructuralist development agenda.

Neostructuralism was attacked by some neoliberals as well as by some of the more radical Left. Neoliberals view it as too statist, interventionist and too wedded to the worn out and discredited structuralism, while the radical Left view it as a new version, perhaps with a human face or a pragmatic kind, of neoliberalism and too close to what has been called the 'post-Washington Consensus' (see Chapter 11 in this book), in which specific social and poverty alleviation measures were introduced to the earlier 'Washington Consensus', which was seen as too harsh (Leiva, 2008).

While few governments in Latin America openly admit to being influenced by neostructuralist ideas or even trying to follow aspects of a neostructuralist development strategy, it is my view that it is far more influential than what can be gathered from reviewing the development literature, where it is rarely mentioned, except in the writings of ECLAC (Gwynne and Kay, 2004). I would argue that most centre-left and left-wing governments in Latin America, even those who proclaim to follow a *buen vivir* (Ecuador) or *vivir bien* (Bolivia) alternative post-development path, when it comes to implementation of macroeconomic policies are heavily influenced by neostructuralist thinking. What might be even more surprising is that, in some cases, their policies are even less radical than those proposed by neostructuralists, which are often dismissed by left-wing critics as being reformist and not going beyond neodevelopmentalism. While the left-wing governments have managed to substantially reduce poverty and promote social inclusion, they have not managed to change the production matrix, but instead have actively pursued and even reinforced an unsustainable neo-extractivist development agenda (Acosta, 2013; Veltmeyer and Petras, 2014).

Recommended reading: Bárcenas and Prado (2016), Leiva (2008), Sunkel (1993).

Conclusions

In this chapter, I have highlighted some contributions to critical development studies that have emanated from Latin America. I am aware I have not dealt with all of them, but I hope to have focused on some of the most important ones. What I find remarkable and wish to stress is the ability of some thinkers, scholars and activists to go beyond and even overturn the dominant orthodoxy of the times as they realized that those theories, largely emanating from the developed countries, were unable to explain the complexities of the Latin American reality and other developing countries. Mariátegui and the Marxist dependency thinkers went beyond certain dogmatic interpretations of Marxism, seeking to apply it creatively to the Latin American context. Meanwhile, Prebisch and the structuralist thinkers challenged the orthodox economic and development theories of the time and created an alternative interpretation of the dynamics of the world system. Both streams in Latin American critical development theory aimed at transforming the existing capitalist system either by reformist or revolutionary means so as to achieve their respective aims. These aims have yet to be achieved. Hence, the continuing relevance of critical development studies, the need to develop it further and promote its relevance to those social movements and organizations struggling for a better world (see Chapter 2 by Munck in this volume).

Recommended reading: Levitt (2005), Munck (2013), Petras and Veltmeyer (2009).

References

Acosta, A. (2013). 'Extractivism and neoextractivism: two sides of the same curse'. In M. Land and D. Mokrani (eds), *Beyond Development: Alternative Visions from Latin America*. Amsterdam/Quito: Transnational Institute/Fundación Rosa Luxemburg, pp. 61–86.

Bárcenas, A. and Prado, A. (eds) (2016). *Neostructuralism and Heterodox Thinking in Latin America and the Caribbean in the Early Twenty-First Century*. Santiago: ECLAC.

Cardoso, F.H. (1972). 'Dependency and development in Latin America'. *New Left Review*, 74: 83–95.

Dos Santos, T. (1973). 'The crisis of development theory and the problem of dependence in Latin America'. In H. Bernstein (ed.), *Underdevelopment & Development: The Third World Today*. Harmondsworth: Penguin, pp. 57–80.

Dosman, E.J. (2008). *The Life and Times of Raúl Prebisch 1901–1986*. Montreal/Kingston: McGill-Queen's University Press.

ECLAC (1990). *Changing Production Patterns with Social Equity*. Santiago: United Nations Economic Commission for Latin America and the Caribbean.

Frank, A. (1966). 'The development of underdevelopment'. *Monthly Review*, 18(4): 17–31.

Furtado, C. (1964). *Development and Underdevelopment: A Structural View of the Problems of Developed and Underdeveloped Countries*. Berkeley, CA: University of California Press.

Furtado, C. (1973). 'The concept of external dependence in the study of underdevelopment'. In C.K. Wilber (ed.), *The Political Economy of Development and Underdevelopment*. New York: Random House, pp. 118–23.

Girvan, N. (1973). 'The development of dependency economics in the Caribbean and Latin America: a review and comparison'. *Social and Economic Studies*, 22(1): 1–33.

Gwynne, R.N. and Kay, C. (eds) (2004). *Latin America Transformed: Globalization and Modernity*. London: Hodder Education.

Hettne, B. (1995). *Development Theory and the Three Worlds*, 2nd edition. London: Longman.

Hirschman, A.O. (1961). 'Ideologies of economic development in Latin America'. In A.O. Hirschman (ed.), *Latin American Issues: Essays and Comments*. London: George Allen & Unwin.

Kay, C. (1989). *Latin American Theories of Development and Underdevelopment*. Routledge: London.

Kay, C. (2005). 'Celso Furtado: pioneer of structuralist development theory'. *Development and Change*, 36(6): 1201–7.

Kay, C. (2006). 'Raúl Prebisch'. In D. Simon (ed.), *Fifty Key Thinkers on Development*. London: Routledge, pp. 199–205.

Kay, C. (2009). 'The Latin American structuralist school'. In R. Kitchin and N. Thrift (eds), *International Encyclopedia of Human Geography, Volume 6*. Oxford: Elsevier, pp. 159–64.

Kay, C. (2011). 'Andre Gunder Frank: "unity in diversity" from the development of underdevelopment to the world system'. *New Political Economy*, 16(4): 523–38.

Kay, C. and Gwynne, R.N. (2000). 'Relevance of structuralist and dependency theories in the neoliberal period: a Latin American perspective'. *Journal of Developing Societies*, 16(1): 49–69.

Krugman, P. (1992). 'Toward a counter-counterrevolution in development theory'. In *Proceedings of the World Bank Annual Conference on Development Economics, 1992*. Washington, DC: World Bank, pp. 15–38.

Leiva, F.I. (2008). *Latin American Neostructuralism: The Contradictions of Post-Neoliberal Development*. Minneapolis, MN: University of Minnesota Press.

Levitt, K. (2005). *Reclaiming Development: Independent Thought and Caribbean Community*. Kingston: Ian Randle.

Mariátegui, J.C. (1971). *Seven Interpretive Essays on Peruvian Reality*. Austin, TX: University of Texas Press.

Marini, R.M. (1973). *Dialéctica de la Dependencia*. Mexico City: Ediciones Era.

Munck, R. (1999). 'Dependency and imperialism in the new times: a Latin American perspective'. *European Journal of Development Research*, 11(1): 56–74.

Munck, R. (2013). *Rethinking Latin America: Development, Hegemony, and Social Transformation*. New York: Palgrave Macmillan.

Munck, R. and O'Hearn, D. (eds) (1999). *Critical Development Theory: Contributions to a New Paradigm*. London: Zed Books.

Nederveen-Pieterse, J. (2001). *Development Theory: Deconstructions/Reconstructions*. London: Sage.

Petras, J. and Veltmeyer, H. (2007). 'The development state in Latin America: whose development, whose state?' *Journal of Peasant Studies*, Special Issue, 34(3–4), July–October: 371–407.

Petras, J. and Veltmeyer, H. (2009). *What's Left in Latin America? Regime Change in New Times*. Farnham: Ashgate.

Petras, J. and Zeitlin, M. (eds) (1968). *Latin America: Reform or Revolution?* New York: Fawcett.

Quijano, A. (2000). 'Coloniality of power, Eurocentrism, and Latin America'. *Nepantla: Views from South*, 1(3): 533–80.

Rodríguez, O. (1977). 'On the conception of the centre-periphery system'. *CEPAL Review*, 3: 195–239.

Saad-Filho, A. and Johnston, D. (eds) (2005). *Neoliberalism: A Critical Reader*. London: Pluto Press.

Sunkel, O. (1960). 'Inflation in Chile: an unorthodox approach'. *International Economic Papers*, 10: 107–31.

Sunkel, O. (1969). 'National development policy and external dependence in Latin America'. *Journal of Development Studies*, 6(1): 23–48.

Sunkel, O. (1972). 'Big business and "dependencia": a Latin American view'. *Foreign Affairs*, 50(3): 517–31.

Sunkel, O. (1990). 'Structuralism, dependency, and institutionalism: an exploration of common ground and disparities'. In J.L. Dietz and D.D. James (eds), *Progress Toward Development in Latin America*. Boulder, CO: Lynne Rienner, pp. 29–39.

Sunkel, O. (ed.) (1993). *Development from Within: Toward a Neostructuralist Approach for Latin America*. Boulder, CO: Lynne Rienner.

Torres, M. (ed.) (2006). *Fernando Fajnzylber, Una Visión Renovadora del Desarrollo en América Latina*. Santiago: CEPAL.

Toye, J. (1987). *Dilemmas of Development: Reflections on the Counter-Revolution in Development Theory and Policy*. Oxford: Blackwell.

Toye, J. and Toye, R. (2004). *The UN and Global Political Economy*. Bloomington, IN: Indiana University Press.

UN Department of Economic Affairs (1951). *Economic Survey of Latin America 1949*. New York: UN DEA.

Valdés, J.G. (1995). *Pinochet's Economists: The Chicago School of Economics in Chile*. Cambridge: Cambridge University Press.

Veltmeyer, H. and Petras, J. (2014). *The New Extractivism: A Model for Latin America?* London: Zed Books.

5

POST-DEVELOPMENT AND OTHER CRITIQUES OF THE ROOTS OF DEVELOPMENT

Eduardo Gudynas

The 1980s not only saw a counter-revolution in development theory and practice – a neoliberal approach that highlighted the virtues of free-market capitalism and rejected the agency of the developmental state – but a wide-ranging search for 'another development', an alternative form of development that was human in scale and form, people-centred and participatory, equitable and inclusive (particularly as regards women and the poor), sustainable in terms of the environment and liveli-hoods, and, above all, initiated 'from below and within' rather than 'from above and the outside'. However, towards the end of the decade, this critique of mainstream development theory and practice was extended to the very notion of development, and in the early 1990s it was consolidated with at least four different emphases.

Some denounced the failure of development in any expression and the need to aban-don it (Esteva, 1992). Others argued that development is essentially a Western belief, myth or religion imposed on other cultures (Rist, 1997). Others questioned develop-ment, focusing on the role of economic growth as a central problem, and from there postulated the need for a need for degrowth (Latouche, 2009). Finally, another stream, known as post-development, in the formulation of its best-known promoter, Arturo Escobar, argued that development should be considered as a discourse that expressed premises such as the modernization or the appropriation of nature, but clothed them as universal truths, which had the effect of subordinating other cultures (Escobar, 1995).

A more detailed examination of post-development shows that at least two stages must be distinguished in Escobar's propositions: in the first, post-development was emphasized as a form of critical analysis; in the second, in addition to this criticism, more and more attention was given to different alternatives.

Post-development as critique

The initial formulation of post-development as a critique was inspired by post-structuralism, especially in the analysis of 'discourses' promoted by Michel

Foucault. Hence, a more correct term would be a 'post-structuralist critique' of development (an introduction to this current is found in Belsey, 2002; see also Gibson Graham, 2000). In this context, development 'discourse' includes not only statements of ideas, and how they are thought, expressed and felt, but also concrete actions, the institutions that promote them, and modes of legitimation. In this way, issues such as the basic ideas in a development plan, the state agencies by which they are implemented, the actions they promote, and the ways of legitimation should be analysed.

This type of criticism points to features that are common to many ways of thinking about development and to the idea that development had a universal meaning. The imposition of the idea of development in the image of the industrialized countries simultaneously relegated all others to the status of underdeveloped. Therefore, development is simultaneously both an imposition of specific knowledges and the exclusion of others.

A post-development perspective allows us to highlight concepts that are critical but nevertheless supportive of the development project – the idea that the social condition of people, or a targetted population, can be improved, changed in a progressive direction. This would be a universal, progressive, essentially positive, linear process. The main engine would be economic growth, which is conceived as perpetual, and which in turn generates the material well-being of people, social, cultural and political advances. Development, therefore, defends different versions of modernization.

Development in one way or another understands that society and nature are separate. Environmental and social impacts are denied or minimized, and scientific and technical optimism is defended. The economic emphasis of development generates a growing commodification of the environment and social relations, anchored in a Western lifestyle and consumption. Consumerism is reinforced, and even a Western aesthetic is imitated. Patriarchal positions of various kinds are maintained, subordinating and making women invisible.

In its more formal application, an analysis from the post-development considers the forms of knowledge (for example, the delimitation of disciplines, the conditions of validity, etc.), the subjectivities involved, the forms of representation of these discourses, and the dynamics of power that cross all these spheres, from the role of experts to local demands or resistance to development (Escobar, 1995, 2012). In this way, the criteria of truth and falsity are determined on what is development, the reasons for conceiving it as a positive process, acceptable conceptions of its constitutive ideas (such as welfare, efficiency, growth, etc.), and even forms by which we interpret our relationships with the social and natural environment.

As we can see, the idea of development is not restricted to economic issues, but spills over into social, cultural and political dimensions, and even personal sensibilities and aesthetics. This post-development critique shows that while development is not a unified field and does not have a precise meaning, basic attributes are repeated, and there are processes of organization, legitimation and action that are analogous. Development then appears as a certain type of relationalities, grouping some ideas and practices but excluding others. In its shadow have emerged concepts of enormous influence, such as human capital or natural capital, or have redefined others, such as efficiency or inequity, all of which can be thought of in a few ways.

Post-development as critique and a space for alternatives

Post-development in its initial stage made it possible to make a key distinction: on the one hand, there would be 'alternative developments' and, on the other, 'alternatives to development' (e.g. Escobar, 1995: 215). The first are debates about instrumental adjustments or different ways of organizing development; its conceptual foundations are not under discussion. Discussions, for example, are one of the best ways to feed economic growth, and the role of the market or the state.

The latter, as alternatives to any of the visions of development, became evident thanks to the criticisms of post-development. In its original formulations, post-development understood that these alternatives aimed, for example, at shaping a discourse of difference or to rescue the trials and resistances that started from the movements of the South. But from the mid-2000s, little by little, a certain confusion spread.

On the one hand, several interpreted that the prefix 'post' referred to a future development that would overcome the limitations of the present ones or would even include anti-development positions (such as those of G. Esteva). In this way, the direct link with post-structuralism was weakened and some alternative developments were mixed with alternatives to development. On the other hand, Escobar himself contributed to this confusion by adding to post-development the task of creating new discourses and representations, diversifying the agents of knowledge production or supporting resistances (Escobar, 2005). More recently, he added questions such as 'discourses of transition' (Escobar, 2012). Undoubtedly, in the initial work of Escobar, there was a certain overlap between the questioning of post-structuralist inspiration and the imagination of alternatives, but all this became more acute in this second stage (see also the essays in Ziai, 2007).

This expansion, still in progress, generated a greater adherence to the post-development label, especially from social militants, but at the cost of losing analytical specificity. In turn, while a post-developmental critique is powerful, it is not enough to generate alternatives, and in fact they need other instruments and reflections of their own (Gudynas, 2014b).

Reactions and constancy in relation to post-development

Post-development in its first stage was the subject of many questions. Among the objections was, for example, the inability to understand heterogeneity in development practices or the romanticization of social movements, and therefore some considered it to be only anti-modern rhetoric (see, for example, Nederveen Pieterse, 2000). According to several analysts the problem was not development itself, but its capitalist applications or the persistence of poverty.

Methodological problems were also pointed out, among them that the initial exercises were actually a partial or impoverished expression of post-structuralism (Ziai, 2004).

However, post-development remained a space of critical analysis and development response, including some new contributions that followed the post-structuralist perspective more rigorously. Simultaneously, from the field of development studies, initial rejection reactions gave way to more rigorous reflections that accepted some of the post-development warnings (see a summary of this situation in Ziai, 2015).

Some limitations and precisions must be pointed out anyway. The critique of post-development, although invoking direct links with certain social movements, was in fact primarily an academic exercise with weak connections with major political transformations.

This was evident in South America, from which emerged one of the most radical development critiques, known as *buen vivir*. This conception is as much a critic to development as the opening to post-capitalist and post-socialist alternatives. It is a position that emerged outside of academic exercises, and as a result of certain heterodox social and political practices and a remarkable diversity of actors (with a substantial contribution of some indigenous militants) (Gudynas, 2014b). Anyway, it is true that these criticisms show remarkable similarities with the initial post-development.

At the same time, the severe economic and financial crisis of 2007–2008, which for some announced the end of capitalism, did not in fact diminish the prevalence of development ideas, and only changed its components and expressions. Examples are the huge diversity of discussions around the Millennium Development Goals and the most recent Sustainable Development Goals. Post-development played a limited role in those discussions, but the persistence of the basic ideas of development shows that those components are so deeply rooted as to be reproduced again and again.

In the same way, an examination of the most recent development strategies since the beginning of the 21st century shows a remarkable diversity in its instrumental expressions, but a great constancy in the basic components. Regimes, such as the European administrations defending neoliberal adjustments or the development plans formulated by the Communist Party in China, are certainly different, but at the same time they show common basic elements.

A more detailed examination for the case of South America is even more striking, since in a very short period of time very diverse development strategies have been tested there. These range from conservative positions (for example, in Chile, Colombia and Peru) to heterodox trials invoking a new 21st-century socialism (in Bolivia, Ecuador and Venezuela), through market economies under some state regulation (in Brazil and Uruguay). The legitimations of these varieties of development in some cases allude to orthodox neoclassical conceptions, but in others Marx or Lenin are mentioned (as are the president of Ecuador, Rafael Correa, or vice president of Bolivia, Alvaro García Linera). These experiences, which are the subject of intense debate, show that they are certainly diverse, with successes in some areas, but it is shocking to observe that basic elements, such as the attachment to economic growth or the ambition of modernization, are repeated. Therefore, these conceptual bases are prior to the different ideological political currents in any of these countries. In fact, we are dealing with conceptions and sensibilities that are common to different political and philosophical ideologies of modernity. This is just another of the points pointed out by post-development in its original version.

Rethinking critical development studies

Faced with this paradoxical situation, given the diversity of instrumental expressions of development even in contexts of crisis and political change, while maintaining a basic core it is essential to take a critical approach from a post-development perspective.

We should recall that the term 'criticism' refers to different questions about the various manifestations of development. For some, this 'criticism' is based on normative commitments, such as analysing certain subjects (the effects of development on the poorest or the situation of the Third World) or certain issues (such as social justice or equity). For others, a critique of development is a means of challenging mainstream schools of economic and political thought (some question capitalism, others socialism). In recent years, it has become more commonly understood that critical development studies (CDS) provides a 'leftist' perspective on a broad range of issues, including political economy, Marxism, postcoloniality, ecology and feminism. For example, of this critical perspective on development, see the essays collected in Kothari (2005), Schuurman (2009) and Veltmeyer (2011). An appreciable number of CDS advocates are heirs to the critical theory of the Frankfurt School, rejecting positivism and defending socially and historically framed forms of knowledge that are oriented towards practices of transformation.

Another, perhaps more serious, problem is that well-known critical stances focus on capitalism, not development. These currents in many cases are very good at stripping the dark side and contradictions of capitalism, but as they fail to address the roots of development they fail to raise questions at that level or alternatives to overcome it (an example of this is Harvey, 2015). Even more problematic is the attempt to construct *buen vivir* as a new variety of socialist development (as promoted by actors linked to the governments of Ecuador and Bolivia) – stripping it of its radical criticism.

The key question is that several approaches end up being discussions between different forms or models of development, where some versions are attacked while others are postulated as alternatives that supposedly would be better. There is no doubt that capitalism and development overlap, but since the main issue is how to confront capitalism such studies are self-limiting in the field of development. For example, Munck argues that 'it is not possible to overcome the challenge of critical development theory by moving away or abandoning development. The challenge is to imagine development differently and put it into practice in a different way' (Munck, 2011: 76–7). Thus, this understanding of CDS questions the capitalist background in development and looks for alternatives in a non–capitalist form of development. This perspective, namely that criticism and alternatives must necessarily be within and not outside development, is precisely what post-development questions.

Of course, critical analyses of development with a left-wing sensibility are very useful in dealing with certain families of development issues – but they are insufficient. To complete the field of criticism, to make it as rigorous and comprehensive as possible, it is necessary to go deeper.

Levels of critical development studies

It is possible to identify at least four levels on which critical development assessments operate (identified as 3, 2, 1 and 0). Level 3 is the most common, and the most superficial. It corresponds to analyses of specific development actions, such as a rural credit programme or a housing development plan. Level 2 corresponds to sectoral development programmes; the actions indicated in the previous example correspond in turn to understandings about what is 'rural' or 'human' development. It is obvious that at the second level, from the sectoral programmes, different plans and actions are derived from the third stratum. At these two levels, the aim of analysis is to weigh the appropriateness of the instruments used in bringing about change and development, the differences between expected and obtained results, the degree to which these instruments promote economic growth, serve to generate employment and improve the social condition of a targetted population, or bring about progressive change, for example.

Level 1 corresponds to an evaluation within one of the great families of development, such as capitalist development. A good example of analysis at this first level is to question development as 'ideology', where criticism is made from philosophical–political stances (e.g. neoliberals attacking the premise of state planning in development, or socialists claiming control of the market). From this critical perspective, development is not so much about structural analysis of conditions that are objective in their effects on people, classes and nations according to their location in the system as it is about 'discourse', i.e. different ways by which people construct their own reality, allowing them to come to a shared understanding and to act collectively on the basis of this understanding. In other words, the issue is different and also common ways of understanding and acting in the world that people themselves have created by their own actions – by taking actions on ideas and their beliefs regardless of the ontological status of these ideas and beliefs (whether they truly 'represent' the real world as it is rather than as it is imagined). Also at this level are the well-known critical development studies that are actively engaged with or committed to the popular sectors of society or, as mentioned above, with themes such as social justice or bringing about 'another world'.

Finally, there is a level 0 that corresponds to the concepts and sensibilities that form the foundations of development thinking and practices, the 'roots' common to any of its varieties. This is the deepest stratum where the conceptual roots of development are located. No doubt there are links between the different levels, since some are embedded in the others. But the critical instruments that are applied at one level are not necessarily the best for another level. For example, critical studies at level 1 may be useful at levels 2 and 3, but they are not best for level 0.

Post-development in its initial understanding as poststructuralist criticism is appropriate for a critical evaluation of the zero level. It is clear that it is not the best tool to study, for example, the effectiveness of a particular development strategy, especially its known limitations in dealing with the heterogeneity of development. In turn, this type of analysis allows for appealing to other instruments that complement the critique on that zero level. Several complementary tools are required, given the intricacies and barriers in deeply rooted prejudgements, understandings and sensitivities.

A toolbox for the critical analysis of the roots of development

For the zero level of the analysis, which corresponds to what could be called 'roots' in the conceptions and sensibilities of development, it is possible to assemble a Critical Development Root Analysis toolbox. It would include the following instruments: post-development and other poststructuralist analyses of development discourses, deconstruction, certain ethnographies of development, various methodologies in ecological economics, environmental ethics in its treatment of the allocation of values, gender studies, critical epistemology, and some of the essays focused on so-called 'ontological openings'. This composition is the result of our work at CLAES (Latin American Centre for Social Ecology) in recent years. Some attributes of these tools are discussed below.

It is a critical root analysis in the sense that it points to the basis of these ideas, practices and sensibilities of development in all its expressions. It does not refer to a mere enumeration of errors, nor are they necessarily a means to develop alternatives to development, although the belief or need to think other options than the current ones remains one of the engines of these criticisms.

Under this classification, post-development in its strict sense would be an instrument among other possible in this toolbox. In fact, it is difficult to defend the idea that there is a single tool that is the most effective and complete in unravelling the zero level in all its aspects. In addition, each instrument has specificity, where the components that escape its consideration can be approached by other complementary tools. In this complementation, a more complete approach is achieved.

It is possible to mention the highlights of some of these instruments. Deconstruction allows us to identify the hierarchical and binary conditions that impose certain ideas and sensibilities, and that in turn excludes others. Performativity serves to identify repeated practices by means of which discourse produces the effects to which it gives its name (these two instruments appear in Gibson Graham, 2000). The development is full of circumstances where the action generates acts that are defended as development.

The new ethnographies of development address in all their details concrete practices in specific undertakings and sites, unravelling, for example, how local actors process them, the networks of relationships that are created, the resistances or reinterpretations that emerge, etc. (e.g. Mosse, 2005).

Ecological economics, a different perspective from mainstream environmental economics (see the chapter by David Barkin on this), provides essential instruments for addressing, inter alia, the impossibility of perpetual economic growth, the actual metabolisms of the links between society and nature, and the ecological and economic effects of environmental impacts (see, as an example of some contributions, Martínez Alier and Roca Jusmet, 2000). In addition, it helps us to rethink the valuation schemes by questioning the perfect commensurabilities.

Environmental ethics, especially those that address the values of non-humans themselves, whether living species or ecosystems, is fundamental to unravel the anthropocentric value base of modern development. In this field, there are heterodox approaches that incorporate the sensitivities of some indigenous peoples (Gudynas, 2014a), as more formal reflections inspired, among others, in Naess (e.g. Naess, 2016).

Many of the above instruments involve other ways of conceiving the generation of knowledge, and therefore are articulated with certain critical epistemologies. By way of example, Donna Haraway in her non-essentialist and feminist position, extends identities over others that are considered radically different (e.g. Haraway, 2004). Here, too, the contributions of the coloniality of power and of knowledge (inspired by, for example, Quijano, 2000) must be rescued. The foundations of development are a product of modernity, generating knowledge and sensibilities that have been built in a framework of power, subalternizing other knowledge and sensibilities.

Ontological openings allow us to approach other ways of understanding and feeling what is considered as the world in which we live (e.g. De la Cadena, 2014). This perspective permits us to make explicit the dynamics of the society–nature relation, a fundamental component of both conventional ways of thinking about development (which postulate a divide between society and nature) and alternative ways of thinking about development (which are not based on such a divide). Thus, the opening to other ontologies that lack this gap, such as the ones found in some indigenous cosmovisions, is a much-needed critical tool for zero-level analysis. For other understandings of the nature–society nexus, see the recent outstanding contributions from anthropology such as Descola (2012) and Viveiros de Castro (2004).

This toolkit for root analysis opens up enormous potential for a new generation of critical development studies. They are being applied in different places, and in several cases they are used directly from the social movements. All have the potential to promote alternatives that avoid falling back into the chiaroscuro of development.

Recommended reading: Escobar (2012), Gibson Graham (2000), Gudynas (2014b), Ziai (2007, 2015).

References

Belsey, C. (2002). *Post-Structuralism: A Very Short Introduction*. Oxford: Oxford University Press.

De la Cadena, M. (2014). *The Politics of Modern Politics Meets Ethnographies of Excess Through Ontological Openings*. 13 January. Available at: https://culanth.org/fieldsights/471-the-politics-of-modern-politics-meets-ethnographies-of-excess-through-ontological-openings.

Descola, P. (2012). *Más allá de naturaleza y cultura*. Buenos Aires: Amorrortu.

Escobar, A. (1995). *Encountering Development: The Making and Unmaking of the Third World*. Princeton, NJ: Princeton University Press.

Escobar. A. (2005). 'El "postdesarrollo" como concepto y práctica social'. In D. Mato (ed.), *Políticas de economía, ambiente y sociedad en tiempos de globalización*. Caracas: Universidad Central Venezuela, pp. 17–31.

Escobar, A. (2012). 'Preface to the 2012 edition'. In *Encountering Development: The Making and Unmaking of the Third World*. Princeton, NJ: Princeton University Press, pp. vi–xliii.

Esteva, G. (1992). 'Development'. In W. Sachs (ed.), *The Development Dictionary*. London: Zed Books, pp. 6–25.

Gibson Graham, J.K. (2000). 'Poststructural interventions'. In E. Sheppard and T.J. Barnes (eds), *A Companion to Economic Geography*. Oxford: Blackwell, pp. 95–110.

Gudynas, E. (2014a). *Derechos de la Naturaleza. Etica biocéntrica y políticas ambientales*. Lima: CooperAcción, RedGE & CLAES.

Gudynas, E. (2014b). 'El postdesarrollo como crítica y el Buen Vivir como alternativa'. In G.C. Delgado Ramos (ed.), *Buena Vida, Buen Vivir: imaginarios alternativos para el bien común de la humanidad*. Mexico City: UNAM-CEIICH, pp. 61–95.

Haraway, D. (2004). *The Haraway Reader*. New York: Routledge.

Harvey, D. (2015). *Seventeen Contradictions and the End of Capitalism*. London: Oxford University Press.

Kothari, U. (2005). 'A radical history of development studies: individuals, institutions and ideologies'. In U. Kothari (ed.), *A Radical History of Development Studies: Individuals, Institutions and Ideologies*. London: Zed Books, pp. 1–13.

Latouche, S. (2009). *La apuesta por el decrecimiento*. Barcelona: Icaria.

Martínez Alier, J. and Roca Jusmet, J. (2000). *Economía ecológica y política ambiental*. Mexico City: Fondo Cultura Económica.

Mosse, D. (2005). *Cultivating Development: An Ethnography of Aid Policy and Practice*. London: Pluto Press.

Munck, R. (2011). 'Teoría crítica del desarrollo'. In H. Veltmeyer, I. Farah and I. Ampuero (eds), *Herramientas para el cambio: manual para los estudios críticos del desarrollo*. La Paz: CIDES, pp. 73–7.

Naess, A. (2016). *Ecology of Wisdom*. London: Penguin.

Nederveen Pieterse, J. (2000). 'After post-development'. *Third World Quarterly*, 21(2): 175–91.

Quijano, A. (2000). 'Coloniality of power, Eurocentrism and Latin America'. *Nepantla: Views from the South*, 1(3): 533–80.

Rist, G. (1997). *The History of Development: From Western Origins to Global Faith*. London: Zed Books.

Schuurman, F.S. (2009). 'Critical development theory: moving out of the twilight zone'. *Third World Quarterly*, 30(5): 831–48.

Veltmeyer, H. (2011). 'Vías hacia el cambio progresivo y el desarrollo alternativo'. In H. Veltmeyer, I. Farah and I. Ampuero (eds), *Herramientas para el cambio: manual para los estudios críticos del desarrollo*. La Paz: CIDES, pp. 351–8.

Viveiros de Castro, E. (2004). 'Perspectivismo y multiculturalismo en la América indígena'. In A. Surralles and P. García Hierro (eds), *Tierra adentro: Territorio indígena y percepción del entorno*. Lima: Grupo Internacional de trabajo sobre Asuntos Indígenas (IWGIA), pp. 37–80.

Ziai, A. (2004). 'The ambivalence of post-development: between reactionary populism and radical democracy'. *Third World Quarterly*, 25(6): 1045–60.

Ziai, A. (ed.) (2007). *Exploring Post-Development: Theory and Practice, Problems and Perspectives*. London: Routledge.

Ziai, A. (2015). 'Post-development: premature burials and haunting ghosts'. *Development Change*, 46(4): 833–54.

6

DEVELOPMENT IN QUESTION

The feminist perspective

Fernanda Wanderley

Feminist thought has expressed forceful criticism of the economistic and reductionist idea of development that sidelines social equity and individual and collective well-being as the economy's ultimate objectives. One of feminism's main contributions is its analysis of the crisis in the social organization of care. This chapter follows the path of feminist thinking about the economy, work and gender equity that led to the concept of care as a social right and an issue of social development.

In empirical terms, care refers to a series of human interactions, including feeding, educating, nursing, parenting, supporting and protecting. These interactions lie at the heart of social life, and all human beings need care. Some groups, however, need more care than others, as a result of their life cycle stage. They include children, adolescents, people with a disability or illness and older people. These groups need full-time care if they are to develop their whole potential and lead a dignified life.

Feminism's contribution on care as a social right started from an anti-systemic position and because it implies the need for a radical democratization of every social sphere. Feminist thinking denounced the patriarchal order, the utopia of the free, self-regulating market and the centrally-organized economy, and proposed new ways to build another economy that would place human life at the centre of political decision-making. By revaluing the reproductive sphere and calling for the recognition of care as a social right, it challenged the hegemonic economy whose ways of working deepen inequality and poverty, perpetuate the exclusion of a large majority from exercising human rights and citizenship, and reproduce inequitable social relations.

The feminist political position consequently demands a radical reformulation of the concept of the economy that organizes power relations based on the sexual division of labour in the family and the market. By adhering to the view of the economy as a social and institutional sphere, constructed – quintessentially – by normalizing political practices and decisions, feminism helped to demystify the idea of the economy as supposedly natural and above society, while also contributing to a rethink of its meanings and potential transformations.

The feminist critique of neoclassical economics

During the 20th century, feminist thinkers identified women's public participation and the changing family, social and economic arrangements taking place in increasingly urban societies as an irreversible trend. A first group of studies showed that growing numbers of women were leaving the private sphere of the home and joining the world of work and the public sphere more generally (Arriagada, 1990; Anker and Hein, 1986; Benería and Roldán, 1987; Benería and Sen, 1982; Blau and Ferber, 1986; Borderías and Carrasco, 1994; Boserup, 1970; García Fanelli, 1989; Kabeer, 1998; López et al., 1992). These studies revealed the occupational segregation, the wage gap between men and women, and the discriminatory practices in the labour market. They questioned the neoclassical explanation for the continuing concentration of women in certain jobs and occupations (horizontal segregation), their majority presence at the lowest levels of each occupation (vertical segregation) and the aggregate wage gap.

In neoclassical economics, the market is an abstract mechanism for maximizing resources that tends towards efficiency; therefore, the place that women and men occupy in the labour market reflects their different levels of productivity. Feminist studies showed, in contrast, that the market is an institution established by social practices among agents embedded in social and cultural frameworks, who do not behave solely as atomized individuals seeking to maximize their gains. There was ample evidence to show that companies' decisions regarding hiring, training and promotion opportunities, and salary levels for men and women are influenced by socially constructed customs, prejudices and stereotypes. Gender constructions and discriminatory practices in the labour market explain much of the occupational segregation and wage gaps. This shows that the differences in labour market participation between men and women are not just the result of differing levels of productivity in a competitive, free and self-regulated market.

These studies also questioned the separation between the public and private sphere by demonstrating that differences in paid work and unpaid work tended to define the job opportunities of men and women. Thus, the unequal distribution of labour between men and women in the family is revealed as one of the main barriers preventing women from getting paid work and participating socially and politically on an equal footing. Men display a cultural and social resistance to sharing reproductive and care work in the family, even though women have been taking increasing responsibility for supporting the home financially (Anderson,

1992, 2011; Bielby and Baron, 1986; Bielby and Bielby, 1992; Farah and Sánchez, 2008; Glass and Camerigg, 1992; Tilly and Scott, 1978; Wanderley, 2003).

Feminist studies questioned the neoclassical explanations for the sexual division of labour within the family, and showed how it determines men and women's participation in the labour market. Until the 1960s, neoclassical economic theory was only concerned with market production and paid work. However, Gary Becker's study *A Treatise on the Family* (Becker, 1991) introduced a new line of thinking – new home economics (NHE) – into the neoclassical paradigm. It had the merit of situating the analysis of production within the home on the same conceptual level as paid work, changing the view of the home as solely a leisure and recreation space and seeing it as equally important as the market for the production of socially necessary goods and services. Thus, the home came to be defined by neoclassical economic theory as a space that combines the production of goods and services for consumption with leisure and recreation. Equally important was the idea that time is a limited factor and people have to allocate it between paid market-related activities, domestic non-market activities and rest and recreation activities. This proposal was a step forward from traditional neoclassical theory in the sense that time not devoted to paid work is not identified as leisure time. Furthermore, the idea of time as a scarce resource implies that it has to be allocated between different types of work. Therefore, the theory now places emphasis on the interrelationship between the domestic sphere and the labour market.

Following neoclassical axioms, NHE argued that the distribution of labour time within the family between household work and income-generating activities, together with how resources and goods are shared out between family members, is in keeping with the principle of efficiency as it seeks to meet the needs of the group as far as possible. Drawing on international trade theory's idea of comparative advantages, Becker argued that the production of goods and services, both inside and outside the home, is more efficient when one member of the family specializes in market production and the other specializes in household production. Therefore, the model of the two-parent family, where the man specialized in market production while the woman specialized in household production, would be the most efficient arrangement for maximizing the family's collective utility, as each partner would obtain higher monetary returns or benefits from their respective work.

Feminism's most radical criticism of NHE focused on the assumption underlying the neoclassical paradigm of the economic actor seeking to maximize utility, as it does not question the social and cultural factors that determine the differences in the behaviour of individuals, specifically men and women. Thus, NHE constructs male and female utility functions assuming that men's behaviour would be aimed at maximizing leisure and pay, while women's behaviour would be aimed at maximizing leisure, pay, household work and child-rearing. Thus, NHE naturalizes gender roles and does not question their inequitable effects on the way the production of goods and services is organized inside and outside the home. What feminist studies criticized in the neoclassical model was the explanatory principle of efficiency and the assumption of the instrumental rationality of individual actors aiming to maximize their own well-being. They argued that it failed to take into account the social and power relations within the home, or the normative mandates that determine different behaviours and the division of labour. Neither did it help us to understand that the continuation of women's inferior position is not the result of individual choices.

Recommended reading: Benería and Roldán (1987), Farah and Sánchez (2008), Kabeer (1998), Wanderley (2003).

Changes in the family and the household as the unit of production of goods and services

This scholarship also provided evidence of the changes taking place in the family, with the comparative loss of importance of the two-parent family composed of a father earning the income and a mother available full-time to provide care in the home. Instead, types of families were seen to be diversifying, with an increase in single-parent families and female-headed households, two-parent families where both partners shared the responsibility for earning the household income, and families with different sexual orientations (Abramo, 2006; Aguirre and Batthyány, 2007; Alberdi, 1999; Beck and Beck-Gernsheim, 1998; Farah, 2002; INEGI, 2000; Jelin, 2000; Paulson, 1996; Wanderley, 2003).

These studies revealed the limits of the view of the household as a homogenous unit where there was no place for diverse age-group and gender dynamics or differences in interests, expectations, responsibilities and well-being. By seeing households as diverse units, it was possible to understand, first, how sex, age and class structure the division of labour inside and outside the home and, second, the everyday interaction between cooperation and conflict. Furthermore, households are dynamic spaces that change over time. Their life cycles are marked by various happenings and situations (the birth of children, the joining of new members living in the same physical space, illness, separation and death, or external circumstances such as a fall in the demand for labour or natural disasters).

The social, economic and family changes that take place over time therefore influence and aggravate the tensions between working life in the labour market and family life, making it difficult for families to combine earning an income with care work, especially for those who need it most. Women are the ones who experience this conflict most intensely, due to the still-prevalent social and cultural mandate that assigns them the responsibility for caring for the dependent members of the household, naturalizing this as 'non-work'. This goes in the opposite direction to the socioeconomic and cultural changes that would contribute to emancipate women. It is why the ways in which women are able to participate in the labour market still depend on the limited social conditions for combining care and income-generating work.

Recommended reading: Abramo (2006), Aguirre and Batthyány (2007), Alberdi (1999), Beck and Beck-Gernsheim (1998), Farah (2002), INEGI (2000), Jelin (2000), Paulson (1996), Wanderley (2003).

The relationship between paid and unpaid work

Feminist economics changed the definition of the working realities of men and women as being divided into income-generating activities and reproductive tasks within the family. Both types of activity (paid and unpaid) were now seen as *work* because they require physical, emotional and psychological effort, as well as the availability of time. Thus, the concept of work ceased to be associated solely with income-generating activities. Although the work done in the home and the community may not add or generate monetary value, it is essential for the reproduction of individuals, families and society as a whole. Therefore, one of feminism's main contributions to economics was to explain the close relationship between unpaid work in the home or community and paid work. This made it possible to understand and explain the unequal opportunities men and women have to earn an income and achieve well-being for themselves and their families.

While feminist scholars started by revealing the unequal distribution of reproductive and care work within the family, the next step was to problematize the unequal division of care work in society. This second wave of feminist critique moved on to question the naturalization of care as belonging to the sphere of the family and the community, thus freeing the state and society as a whole from responsibility for the care required to reproduce life. Thus, the feminist critique named the problem of care as a public problem in the sphere of social rights and expanded the responsibility for organizing care to new institutional spheres: the state and the market, as well as the family and the community. From this broader perspective, the unequal position of families from different socioeconomic strata was revealed in terms of their ability to combine reproductive and productive work.

This literature has focused mainly on urban settings, looking at how socioeconomic inequalities do not allow all families to care for their dependents in the way they would wish. This represents a key mechanism through which inequalities are perpetuated not just between men and women within the family, but also from one generation to the next. High-income families have more options for reconciling working and family life by, for example, buying care services (either by hiring a domestic worker or by paying for institutional childcare or out-of-school-hours services). The majority of low-income families are unable to buy these services, and they do not have access to good-quality public childcare services either (Wanderley, 2003). Fewer studies have focused on the situation in rural areas; there is therefore much research still to be done to guide public policies in the different rural areas.

As these studies show, the fact that the family, society and the state do not share the responsibility for providing care in many countries leads to inequity between families. It is the poorest families who are unable to ensure that their children are well looked after while the adults are working outside the home. This situation obliges these families, and especially women, to adapt by 'choosing' paid jobs that allow them to keep their children with them, or part-time work. This restricts the employment opportunities of women with family responsibilities and limits their education, training or public participation possibilities (Aguirre, 2007; Carbonero Gamundí and Levín, 2007; Gutiérrez, 2007; ILO and UNDP, 2009; Montaño and Calderón Magaña, 2010; Wanderley, 2009b).

This scenario also has consequences for the children, because many families have no other option than to delegate care responsibilities to children and adolescents themselves. These precarious care and protection arrangements mean that the majority of children and adolescents are more exposed to all sorts of risks, including crime and drug use, joining the labour market at a young age to the detriment of their education, physical and emotional insecurity such as sexual violence within and outside the family, and health problems due to their presence in unsuitable public places. Other risks, both in the cities and in rural communities, include inadequate cognitive, physical and social stimulation, teenage pregnancy and family abandonment, which could be prevented by providing services in childcare centres or out-of-school activities to complement children's schooling while their parents are earning an income. As feminist studies show, those worst affected by these problems are the poorest families (Farah *et al.*, 2012; Marco Navarro, 2007; Ministerio de Justicia, 2007; Pautassi and Rico, 2011; Pautassi and Zibecchi, 2010; Soares Guimaraes, 2012).

As outlined by feminists and gender studies, this is clearly a public problem that enables us to understand the vicious circle whereby inequality and poverty are perpetuated from one generation to the next. It also leads us to question the cultural and social norm that assigns families/communities (read women) the responsibility for providing the care required to sustain life for 'living well' – *buen vivir* in social solidarity and harmony with nature (to give an Andean indigenous twist to the discourse on social development).

Care as a social right

The specific questions posed by feminists and gender studies as arising from this academic and political thinking are: Who should be responsible for providing care to dependents, especially children and adolescents, taking into account the changes that families, labour markets and society as a whole are experiencing? How can we get beyond the market-oriented, familist organization of care to prevent the gaps or inequalities in care and protection among citizens? How should care responsibilities and work be distributed, both within the family and in society, to avoid producing gender and generational inequalities? And, given that this problem is at the heart of a broad conceptualization of the economy and labour, how does shared responsibility for care and protection work relate to the 'other economy', an economy that needs to be constructed not within, but on, the margins and interstices (local spaces) of the broader capitalist system (Wanderley et al., 2015)?

The answer given by many feminists leaves no doubt: the responsibility for care should be shared between the state, society and families, with different sorts of arrangements depending on the characteristics of each particular setting. Although families and communities will continue to be the primary site of caregiving, they should have the conditions in place and the support of accessible, good-quality, state and non-state public services to enable them to do the work of providing care and protection to children and adolescents. This is the only way to ensure that citizens are able to exercise their right to care and protection without distinction as to socioeconomic status, ethnicity or age and/or their ability to pay for these services in the market (Farah et al., 2012).

It is this position that underpins the idea of care as a social right that should be recognized, named and made explicit in order to change current institutional and social conditions with the aim of enabling everyone to effectively exercise already established human and civil rights (the right to education, health, nutrition, work, equality, protection and physical, emotional and psychological integrity). This requires going beyond segmented social policies and moving towards coordinated policies to address problems of discrimination, social inequality and poverty in a comprehensive way and from a territorial approach.

Changing the social organization of care so that care becomes a social right entails many challenges. These include understanding the diversity of location-specific social and economic dynamics and the different types and thickness of the boundaries between reproductive and productive work. In many rural Andean contexts in particular, the household is the family's place of residence and the site of reproduction and economic production: it combines production (subsistence) and social reproduction in space and time. This situation is different from that of any family – whether urban or rural – for whom the household is only the space-time for reproduction. And this is true for any society whether on the margins or at the centre of the broader capitalist system – or, for that matter, beyond capitalism (after all, a sizeable part of the population across Latin America live and work on the margins or outside the confines of the capitalist system).

In addition to this, rural households in Andean contexts are not isolated from the community (or broader economic and social processes). Their framework for the distribution, allocation, access to and control of the resources required for subsistence – bound by community norms – means that the domestic setting transcends the home to encompass the community, thus reconfiguring the public–private distinction in this dimension too (Farah and Sostres, 2015). Likewise, the changes taking place in the economy and work in rural communities – including multiple residences, multiple activities and migration, alongside increasing links with urban areas and new arrangements for the division of labour between men and women – are posing new challenges for organizing the care of dependents.

Considering the important differences in the social organization of the economy across territories, the following dimensions of the right to care can be identified:

- *The right to receive care*: Depending on their life cycle stage, people need support, assistance, stimulation and the development of capacities and competencies under equal conditions.
- *The right to provide care*: Related to the availability of time and conditions for combining caring for the family members who require it with income-generating activities, education and training, and social and political participation. In other words, the right to provide care depends on the redistribution of care responsibilities within the family and society, with the active involvement of the state in providing services for children of pre-school age and out-of-school-hours services for children and adolescents to complement their schooling.
- *Workers' rights for paid carers*: Including rights for teachers, nursery workers, assistants and other employees working to provide care in institutional spaces, as well as paid domestic workers providing home care. This dimension requires ceasing to see care services as a form of charity and moving on to an idea of caregiving as professional work that requires knowledge and emotional and physical skills, and therefore recognizing it as a job with social and economic value that is protected by labour laws.

This concept of care links the rights of children with those of women, in order to rethink social welfare policies in the 21st century under the principles of solidarity, justice, cooperation and equity from a feminist (and *vivir bien*) perspective. The notion of solidarity draws on the important role of the state as a provider of social well-being to all citizens. It is an idea that re-emerges as a key value in building a new social order that ensures non-hierarchical and equitable coexistence among people and between people and nature. This will make it possible to overcome the injustices that weigh on women and children by reconfiguring the welfare system, and ensure that the four principles mentioned above are incorporated in the design and management of public policies in societies that do not yet have a welfare system (Arriagada, 2004, 2007; Esping-Andersen, 1996, 2002; Martínez, 2008; Orozco, 2010; Pautassi, 2007; Sunkel, 2006; Wanderley, 2009a). Care also opens up a new field of work in the 'other economy', where solidarity is a key value in its organization. On the nature of this 'other economy' – a social and solidarity economy that is being constructed 'from the bottom up' at the level of local development in Chiapas, Mexico, and across Latin America, see Coraggio (2008) and Wanderley *et al.* (2015).

Concluding remarks

Feminist thinking has contributed radical criticisms of the concept of the economy in neoclassical theory, by questioning: (i) its view of the economy as limited to the market and the invisibility of the reproductive sphere and care work as part of the economy; (ii) its confusion of the market with the utopia of the free, self-regulated market, thus denying the importance of regulatory frameworks, social roles and practices of power and discrimination at the heart of actual markets; (iii) the idea of work as limited to paid activities and the failure to recognize the social and economic contribution that unpaid activities make to the reproduction of life in society; (iv) the view of the home as a space for leisure and recreation, failing to recognize that goods and services necessary for the reproduction of human life are produced there; (v) the dominant notion of a single model of the family; (vi) the division between public and private spheres; and (vii) the assumption of instrumental rationality (*homo economicus*) as the only possible behaviour if the economy is to work properly.

In line with other critical standpoints, feminism's denaturalization of the economy as an abstract, ahistorical mechanism reveals the fallacy of the assumption that rational-instrumental behaviour seeking to maximize gains is sufficient, or the assumption that explains economic dynamics. The inclusion of economic activities in social, cultural and political structures makes it possible to get beyond essentialist views of the economy and reveal the social conventions and social and political structures that define the limits of what is possible and desirable.

The feminist critique has pointed out the challenges faced by movements seeking to make the economy and society more democratic and avoid perpetuating the status quo of the patriarchal gender order. With this aim in mind, it is essential to acknowledge the plurality of economic principles involved in the production and distribution of goods and services – commercial and non-commercial, familist and statist, individualist and collectivist, selfish and solidarity-based – in order to see the range of contradictions and power relations present in all socioeconomic structures.

From a plural perspective on the economy, the feminist viewpoint is faced with theoretical and political challenges in order to address local territorial dynamics where the boundaries between the public and the private are more blurred. It will therefore be necessary to update women's enquiry, thinking or debate on the real meaning of being inside or outside the home, autonomy or belonging to the realm of the community, and arrive at the real meaning of the community as a particular political sphere that blurs the distinction between public and private, the productive and the reproductive. In short, knowledge and theorizing on the public and the private in contexts of economic and social pluralism needs to be updated (Farah and Sostres, 2015).

In conclusion, adopting the feminist perspective has multiple consequences. These include a critique of the inadequacy of proposals to decommercialize the public goods and services needed to sustain life, unless they are accompanied by proposals to democratize the institution of the family and community as the key sites of patriarchal power in social practices and relations. Once again, rethinking the origins of patriarchal power and the set of mediations that project it into other institutional structures – including state structures – is a requirement for being able to think about dismantling patriarchy, together with decolonization.

Without such systematic thinking, there is a risk of reproducing discourses that tend to idealize the rural and indigenous community and family as spaces of harmonious, static relations governed by the principle of complementarity. In other words, including the objective of denaturalizing the sexual division of labour in the reproductive and productive sphere – by democratizing it – is key to preventing the direct and indirect negative effects on women that both conservative and progressive political positions may have. At the same time, it is also key for advancing towards laying the organizational foundations of an 'other economy'.

References

Abramo, L. (ed.) (2006). *Trabajo decente y equidad de género en América Latina*. Geneva: International Labour Office.

Aguirre, R. (2007). 'Trabajar y tener hijos: insumos para repensar las responsabilidades familiares y sociales'. In M.L. Gutiérrez (ed.), *Género, familias y trabajo: rupturas y continuidades. Desafíos para la investigación política*. Buenos Aires: CLACSO, Colección Grupos de Trabajo, pp. 99–136.

Aguirre, R. and Batthyány, K. (2007). 'Introducción'. In M.L. Gutiérrez (ed.), *Género, familias y trabajo: rupturas y continuidades – Desafíos para la investigación política*. Buenos Aires: CLACSO, Colección Grupos de Trabajo, pp. 19–21.

Alberdi, I. (1999). *La nueva familia española*. Madrid: Taurus.

Anderson, J. (1992). *Intereses o justicia: ¿A dónde va la discussion sobre la mujer y el desarrollo?* Lima: Flora Trístan Ediciones, entre Mujeres.

Anderson, J. (2011). *Responsabilidades por compartir: la conciliación trabajo-familia en Perú*. Santiago de Chile: ILO.

Anker, R. and Hein, C. (1986). *Sex Inequalities in Urban Employment in the Third World*. New York: St. Martin's Press.

Arriagada, I. (1990). *Participación desigual de la mujer en el mundo del trabajo*. Santiago de Chile: CEPAL.

Arriagada, I. (2004). 'Estructuras familiares, trabajo y bienestar en América Latina'. In I. Arriagada and V. Aranda (eds), *Cambio de familias en el marco de las transformaciones globales: necesidad de políticas públicas eficaces*. Santiago de Chile: CEPAL and UNFPA, pp. 43–73. Available at: http://repositorio.cepal.org/bitstream/handle/11362/6781/S0412955.pdf ?sequence=1.

Arriagada, I. (2007). 'Abriendo la caja negra del sector servicios en Chile y Uruguay'. In M.A. Gutiérrez (ed.), *Género, familias y trabajo: rupturas y continuidades. Desafíos para la investigación política*. Buenos Aires: CLACSO, Colección Grupos de Trabajo, pp. 23–47.

Arriagada, I. (2008). 'Futuro de las familias y desafíos para las políticas'. *Serie seminarios y conferencias*, 52, CEPAL.

Beck, U. and Beck-Gernsheim, E. (1998). *El normal caos del amor. Las nuevas formas de la relación amorosa*. Esplugues de Llobregat, Barcelona: El Roure Editorial.

Becker, G. (1991 [1981]). *A Treatise on the Family*. Harvard, MA: Harvard Press.

Benería, L. (2003). *Género, desarrollo y globalización*. Barcelona: Editorial Hacer.

Benería, L. and Roldán, M. (1987). *The Crossroads of Class and Gender: Industrial Homework, Subcontracting and Household Dynamics in Mexico City*. Chicago, IL: University of Chicago Press.

Benería, L. and Sen, G. (1982). 'Class and gender inequalities and women's role in economic development: theoretical and practical implications'. *Feminist Studies*, 1(8): 157–8.

Bielby, W. and Baron, J. (1986). 'Men and women at work'. *American Journal of Sociology*, 9: 759–99.

Bielby, D. and Bielby, W. (1992). 'I will follow him: family ties, gender role beliefs, and reluctance to relocate for a better job'. *American Journal of Sociology*, 97(5): 1241–67.

Blau, F.D. (1993). 'Gender and economic outcomes: the role of wage structure'. *Labour*, 7(1): 73–92.

Blau, F.D. and Ferber, M. (1986). *The Economics of Women, Men and Work*. Englewood Cliffs, NJ: Prentice Hall.

Borderías, C. and Carrasco, C. (1994). *Las mujeres y el trabajo: Rupturas conceptuales*. Madrid: Economía Crítica.

Boserup, E. (1970). *Woman's Role in Economic Development*. London/New York: Allen & Unwin.

Carbonero Gamundí, M.A. and Levín, S. (eds) (2007). *Entre familia y trabajo: Relaciones, conflictos y políticas de género en Europa y América Latina*. Sarmiento, Argentina: Homo Sapiens Ediciones.

Coraggio, J.L. (2008). 'La sostenibilidad de los emprendimientos de la economía social y solidaria'. *Revista Latinoamericana de Economía Social y Solidaria*, 2(3).

Esping-Anderson, G. (1996). *Welfare States in Transition: Social Security in the New Global Economy*. London: Sage.

Esping-Andersen, G. (2002). *Why We Need a New Welfare State*. Oxford: Oxford University Press.

Farah, I. (2002). *Hogares y Familias bolivianas: Trabajo de hombres y mujeres*. La Paz: CIDES-UMSA and INE.

Farah, I. and Sánchez, C. (eds) (2008). *Bolivia: Perfil de género*. La Paz: Viceministerio de Género y Asuntos Generacionales, CIDES/UMSA, ASDI and JICA.

Farah, I. and Sostres, F. (2015). 'Lineamientos para seguir dialogando'. Unpublished paper based on Carmen Sánchez García (coord.), *La politización en la diferencia: Experiencias y diálogos políticos de las mujeres en Bolivia*. La Paz: Conexión Fondo de Emacipación and ISET.

Farah, I. and Vasapollo, L. (2011). 'Introducción'. In I. Farah and L. Vasapollo (eds), *Vivir Bien: ¿Paradigma no capitalista?* La Paz: CIDES-UMSA, Sapienza Universitá di Roma and Oxfam.

Farah, I., Salazar, C., Sostres, F. and Wanderley, F. (2012). *Hacia una política municipal de cuidado: Integrando los derechos de las mujeres y la infancia*. La Paz: CIDES-UMSA and Conexión Fondo de Emancipación.

García Fanelli, A. (1989). 'Patrones de desigualdad social en la sociedad moderna: Una revisión de la literatura sobre discriminación ocupacional y salarial por género'. *Desarrollo Económico*, 29(114), June: 239–64.

Glass, J. and Camerigg, V. (1992). 'Gender, parenthood and job-family compatibility'. *American Journal of Sociology*, 98(1): 131–51.

Gutiérrez, M.A. (ed.) (2007). *Género, familias y trabajo: rupturas y continuidades. Desafíos para la investigación política*. Buenos Aires: CLACSO, Colección Grupos de Trabajo.

ILO and UNDP (2009). *Trabajo y familia: Hacia nuevas formas de conciliación con corresponsabilidad social*. Santiago de Chile: ILO and UNDP.

INEGI (2000). *Las familias mexicanas*. Mexico: INEGUI.

Jelin, E. (2000). *Pan y afectos. La transformación de las familias*. Mexico DF: Fondo de Cultura Económica, Colección Popular.

Kabeer, N. (1998). *Realidades trastocadas: Las jerarquías de género en el pensamiento del desarrollo*. Mexico DF: Paidós.

López, C., Pollack, M. and Villarreal, M. (1992). *Género y Mercado de Trabajo en América Latina*. Santiago de Chile: PREALC.

Marco Navarro, F. (2007). *El cuidado de la niñez en Bolivia y Ecuador: derecho de algunos, obligación de todas.* Santiago de Chile: CEPAL, Serie Mujer y Desarrollo.

Marco Navarro, F. (2011). 'Los derechos al cuidado y a su redistribución: temas ausentes en las estrategias de desarrollo de ayer y hoy'. In F. Wanderley (ed.), *El desarrollo en cuestión: Reflexiones desde América Latina.* La Paz: CIDES-UMSA and Oxfam, pp. 595–622.

Martínez, F. (2008). *¿Arañando bienestar? Trabajo remunerado, protección social y familias en América Central.* Buenos Aires: CLACSO, Colección CLACSO-CROP.

Ministerio de Justicia (2007). *Bolivia: informe de progreso. Un mundo apropiado para los niños.* La Paz: Viceministerio de Género y Asuntos Generacionales and UNICEF.

Montaño, S. and Calderón Magaña, C. (eds) (2010). *El cuidado en acción: Entre el derecho y el trabajo.* Santiago de Chile: CEPAL and UNIFEM. Available at: www.cepal.org/es/publicaciones/27845-cuidado-accion-derecho-trabajo.

Orozco, A. (2010). *Cadenas globales de cuidado: ¿Qué derechos para un régimen global de cuidados justos?* Santo Domingo: United Nations International Research and Training Institute for the Advancement of Women (UN-INSTRAW).

Pagliccia, N. (2011), 'Solidaridad: el renacimiento de un viejo concepto socialista'. In Farah and L. Vasapollo (eds), *Vivir Bien: ¿Paradigma no capitalista?* La Paz: CIDES-UMSA, Sapienza Universitá di Roma and Oxfam, pp. 145–58.

Paulson, S. (1996). 'Familias que no conyugan e identidades que no conjugan: la vida en Mizque desafía nuestras categorías'. In S. Rivera (ed.), *Ser mujer indígena, chola o birlocha en la Bolivia postcolonial de los años 90.* La Paz: Subsecretaría de Asuntos de Género – SAG.

Pautassi, L. (2007). *El cuidado como cuestión social desde un enfoque de derechos.* Santiago de Chile: CEPAL, Serie Mujer y Desarrollo.

Pautassi, L. and Rico, N. (2011). 'Licencias para el cuidado infantil. Derechos de hijos, padres y madres'. *Desafíos,* Boletín de la Infancia y la Adolescencia sobre el avance de los Objetivos de Desarrollo del Milenio – CEPAL and UNICEF, pp. 4–10.

Pautassi, L. and Zibecchi, C. (2010). *La provisión de cuidado y la superación de la pobreza infantil. Programa de transferencia condicionadas en Argentina y el papel de las organizaciones sociales y comunitarias.* Santiago de Chile: CEPAL, Serie Mujer y Desarrollo.

Rico, M. (2011). *El desafío de un sistema nacional de cuidados para el Uruguay.* Santiago de Chile: CEPAL and UNFPA.

SAG (1994). *Informe sobre el avance de las mujeres en Bolivia.* La Paz: Comité Nacional Preparatorio para la Cuarta Conferencia Mundial de la Mujer, SAG.

Salazar, C. (2011). 'Ética del cuidado y desarrollo para todos: desafíos desde la diferencia'. In F. Wanderley (ed.), *El desarrollo en cuestión: Reflexiones desde América Latina.* La Paz: CIDES-UMSA and Oxfam, pp. 575–94.

Salazar, C., Jiménez, E. and Wanderley, F. (2010). *Migración, cuidado y sostenibilidad de la vida.* La Paz: CIDES-UMSA and Plural Editores.

Soares Guimaraes, A. (2012). *Infancia, cuidado y género.* La Paz: CIDES-UMSA and Plural Editores.

Sunkel, G. (2006). *El papel de la familia en la protección social en América Latina.* Santiago de Chile: CEPAL, Serie Políticas Sociales, División de Desarrollo Social.

Tilly, L. and Scott, J. (1978). *Women, Work and Family.* New York/London: Hold, Rinehart & Winston.

Treiman, D. and Hartman, H. (eds) (1981). *Women, Work and Wages: Equal Pay for Jobs of Equal Value.* Washington, DC: National Academy.

Valenzuela, M.E. and Mora, C. (eds) (2009). *Trabajo doméstico: un largo camino hacia el trabajo decente.* Santiago de Chile: ILO.

Wanderley, F. (2003). *Inserción laboral y trabajo no mercantil – un abordaje de género desde los hogares.* La Paz: CIDES-UMSA and Plural Editores. Available at: https://cides.academia.edu/FernandaWanderley.

Wanderley, F. (2009a). 'Entre el cambio y la inercia – Régimen de empleo y de bienestar en los últimos 20 años'. *Revista Internacional del Trabajo*, 128(3): 2–17. Available at: https://cides.academia.edu/FernandaWanderley.

Wanderley, F. (2009b). *Crecimiento, empleo y bienestar social en Bolivia*. La Paz: CIDES-UMSA. Available at: https://cides.academia.edu/FernandaWanderley.

Wanderley, F. (2011). *El cuidado como derecho social: situación y desafíos del bienestar social en Bolivia*. Santiago de Chile: ILO. Available at: https://cides.academia.edu/FernandaWanderley.

Wanderley, F. (2015). *Desafíos teóricos y políticos de la economía solidaria. Lectura desde América Latina*. La Paz: CIDES, Hegoa and Plural Editores. Available at: https://cides.academia.edu/FernandaWanderley.

Wanderley, F., Farah, I. and Sostres, F. (eds) (2015). *La economía solidaria en la economía plural: discursos, prácticas y resultados en Bolivia*. La Paz: CIDES-UMSA and HEGOA. Plural Editores. Available at: https://cides.academia.edu/FernandaWanderley.

WFP (2006). *Evaluación estadística de Centros PAN y de Centros NDC*. La Paz: WFP.

PART III

Capitalism, imperialism and globalization

Implications for development

7

THE WORLD-SYSTEMS PERSPECTIVE

Salvatore Babones

The world-systems perspective is a structural-historical approach to critical development studies that focuses on processes that operate at the highest level of social organization, the world-system. World-systems are the largest-scale and most-encompassing forms of social organization. They constitute the social milieux in which societies are embedded. All societies are characterized by cultural, economic and political systems, but these systems can in principle span multiple societies. For example, China has remained an integrated cultural system even though for many centuries it was composed of many independent societies. Economic and political systems can also encompass and integrate multiple societies. Thus, societies can be embedded in larger 'worlds' – systems of interaction – that include other societies as well. A world-system is the overarching social system in which those societies are embedded.

Before the long 16th century (c. 1460–1640), multiple world-systems coexisted in the world, but during the long 16th century most of the world came to be integrated, directly or indirectly, into a single global market. Since the global social system that emerged in the 17th century incorporated all areas of the world into a single economic system, that social system is characterized as a world-economy. World-economies have existed in the past (e.g. the ancient Mediterranean before Rome) but never before on a global scale. Other possible types of world-systems are world-cultures (e.g. China in the age of Confucius; medieval Western Europe) and world-polities (e.g. dynastic China; imperial Rome). The 'modern world-system' that was born in the long 16th century was a world-economy with its historical core in Western Europe.

The world-systems perspective is inextricably linked to the life work of Immanuel Wallerstein, who is widely recognized as the father of world-systems analysis. Wallerstein's (1974) *The Modern World-System* – the first volume of a projected five-volume series (of which four have so far been published) – introduced world-systems analysis to a wide audience and laid down the basic parameters of the world-systems perspective. In a famous 'theoretical reprise' at the end of the book (pp. 346–57), Wallerstein clarified many concepts that were only implicit in the main text. This short (and not always clear) distillation of concepts has become a touchstone for much of the ensuing literature in and on world-systems analysis; many key concepts that Wallerstein and others introduced subsequently have failed to gain wide currency.

Drawing on Wallerstein's theoretical reprise and other key sources, Babones (2015) identifies five 'defining elements' of world-systems analysis, which can be summarized as:

1. The organization of societies into macro-level world-systems has important implications for those societies.
2. World-systems can productively be described in terms of their economic, political and cultural systems.
3. The modern world-system was created in the long 16th century as a world-economy.
4. Other types of world-systems have been based on the primacy of cultural systems (world-cultures) or political systems (world-polities).
5. World-systems are characterized by core-periphery hierarchies that arise from the ways societies have historically been incorporated into them.

Element 5 is the most relevant for critical development studies. Even before the emergence of world-systems analysis as a distinct perspective, Frank (1969) observed that the poverty-ridden northeastern states of Brazil were originally incorporated into the European-centred world-system as highly exploited agricultural export zones. This observation formed the basis of his famous theory of the 'development of underdevelopment': the idea that underdevelopment was not a pristine state (the mere lack of development), but an acquired status. Similarly, Wallerstein (1972) observed that the Mediterranean core of the previous medieval European world-system was incorporated into the modern world-system as a semiperiphery 'in the process of deindustrializing' (p. 96). Other areas that were formerly at the core of their own pre-existing world-systems were also incorporated as semiperipheries of the modern world-system, in particular China and the Ottoman Empire.

Wallerstein asserted in his 1974 theoretical reprise (and most world-systems analysts continue to assume) that the core-periphery structure of all world-systems is tripartite: all world-systems can be divided into core, semiperipheral and peripheral zones. This assumption has given rise to an entire industry of classification schemes (most famously that of Arrighi and Drangel, 1986), though others have asserted that there exists a continuum of world-system positions (Chase-Dunn, 1998). That all actually existing world-systems (like all social systems) have been hierarchical seems beyond dispute; whether core, semiperiphery and periphery are categorical or merely heuristic statuses in those hierarchies is more open to debate. The relevant fact for critical development studies is that modes of incorporation have very long-term consequences. The genocidal incorporation of the African, indigenous Australian and indigenous American world-systems into the modern world-system plunged their populations into a deep poverty from which they have never emerged. By contrast, China, which survived its incorporation into the modern world-system largely intact, is still part of the global semiperiphery (Babones, 2012).

Incorporation remains at the heart of world-systems analysis when considered as a *longue durée* approach to critical development studies. It is deeply embedded in the logic of the perspective. Modes of incorporation into historical world-systems seem to have been important for determining the conditions of life in societies throughout history. For example, the incorporation of Greece as a semiperiphery and Egypt as a periphery of ancient Rome set their developmental trajectories for the next millennium or more; the Roman indigenization of the Celtic peoples of France had similarly long-lasting consequences. These ancient events have close parallels in the history of the incorporation of societies into the modern world-system. Thus, this chapter focuses first on incorporation, peripheralization and indigenization. These processes are the ultimate basis for understanding such sophisticated economic concepts as the structure of exchange in global value chains.

The world-systems perspective, however, is not static. The historical multiplicity of world-systems and world-system forms suggests that other world-systems are possible, even today. The rise of East Asia – first Japan and now China – has led scholars to ask whether or not the world might be experiencing a transition to a new world-system configuration. Whether that new system is oriented around countries or perhaps around cities is an exciting research question. It is quite possible that a new world-system has already replaced the modern world-system but intellectual inertia has prevented scholars from noticing. Research on anti-systemic movements might prove the answer to this question by elucidating the structure of the system they are rebelling against. Here, the 'critical' in critical development studies comes to the fore. Globalization from below may prove to be the key to understanding, resisting, and ultimately redirecting the otherwise destructive forces of world-system incorporation.

Recommended reading: Babones and Chase-Dunn (2012), Wallerstein (1974).

Incorporation, peripheralization and indigenization

Historical patterns of the incorporation of the regions of the world into the modern world system in the long 16th century are clearly visible in the economic geography of the world today. Meaningful estimates of income per capita are not available for the 1500s, but the regional income patterns established by 1820 account for around 90 per cent of the variability in regional incomes per capita today. This is entirely consistent with A.G. Frank's (1969) 'development of underdevelopment' thesis, which continues to form the intellectual substratum for much of critical development studies. World-systems analysis grew from this soil as an attempt to understand contact and colonization as forms of incorporation.

From a historical perspective, it is important to keep in mind that Europeans had little or no military-industrial advantage over most of the rest of the world until very late in the life of the modern world-system. Spanish conquistadors were able to rapidly occupy what is now Latin America due to the accidental fact that Native Americans were highly susceptible to Eurasian diseases; had the reverse been true, history would have turned out very differently. Europeans only became major players in India in the 18th century and occupied no other significant territories on the Afro-Eurasian mainland until the 19th century. The disruption of non-European societies that occurred as a result of their incorporation into the modern world-system long predated formal European colonialism, except in the biologically determined case of what is now Latin America.

When underdevelopment is understood as resulting from peripheralization – from subaltern incorporation into a larger system – it becomes easier to understand why 20th-century decolonization did not result in major changes in the objective economic conditions of most of the newly independent countries. After all, most Latin American countries gained their independence in the 1820s but remained mired in the peripheries of the world-economy. Africa and (most of) India remain very poor. Galtung's (1971) early on elucidated one of the major reasons for this in his structural theory of imperialism: peripheral elites share the class interests of core elites while peripheral populations have class interests that are at odds with those of core populations. Structural imperialism is possible because all societies are subsumed within system-level class structures. World-systems analysis provides an overarching conceptual framework for understanding such transnational class relations.

World-system incorporation provides a similar overarching framework for understanding indigeneity. The indigenization of the native populations of North America and Australasia was accomplished through the genocidal incorporation of these territories into the core of the world-system. These were not 'accidental' biological genocides (as in Latin America), but intentional political ones that achieved the intended outcome of the territorial expansion of the world-system core into these new continents. Indigenous nations have thus become internal world-system peripheries in both North America and Australasia, with social indicators that resemble those of the populations of independent peripheral nations on other continents. The indigenous nations of Latin America by contrast were peripheralized inside the world-system semiperiphery through racialization under Spanish and post-independence governments. Indigenization is just a process of incorporation in which peripheralization is accompanied by racialization and genocide (Fenelon, 2016).

Global value chains

In the heyday of the modern world-system, global markets organized trade in all kinds of goods, from bulk commodities to sophisticated manufactures. Most international trade was trade in finished goods: final products to be consumed by their purchasers. Today, most trade is in intermediate goods: goods that are inputs into larger production processes. The wave of globalization that began in the 1970s and became highly visible in the 1990s has been characterized by the organization of production processes into strongly hierarchical global value chains (Gereffi *et al.*, 2005). The most profitable nodes in these chains are usually those that are closest to the consumer; the company that 'owns' the consumer tends to dominate the chain. These consumer-driven value chains disproportionately reward multinational (particularly American multinational) firms over local firms in both core and peripheral countries.

At first glance, it may seem like the structuration of hierarchy in global value chains has little to do with incorporation into the world-system, but the reorganization of the global economy from international markets into transnational value chains recapitulates earlier processes of the incorporation of non-European regions into the modern world-system. Whereas independent national economies connected by international trade might develop autonomous beginning-to-end production processes (as to some extent the Soviet Union did), interdependent national economies integrated into global value chains have little opportunity to develop high value-added activities inside their own borders. Incorporation into global value chains can thus be seen as a new form of incorporation and peripheralization. An economic system governed by global value chains is no longer a market system (Babones, 2016); the forms and loci of exploitation in this emerging system are not yet well understood, but are clearly determined at the global level.

Control over the governance of (non-market) global value chains offers at least the potential for peripheral producers to shift value in their direction through the use of ethical, organic, fair trade and other labels (Guthman, 2009). It is not clear, however, to what extent this is possible in practice. It may be that the use of labelling as an upgrading strategy is only effective in agricultural value chains due to the high salience for consumers of the sources of the food they literally put into their bodies (agro-exceptionalism). The use of fair trade and other labels may be growing rapidly but it still represents a tiny proportion of global consumption – and it still leaves the ultimate power in the hands of the (rich) consumer. The shift from market exchange to global value chains has changed the structure of the global economy but it has not overturned the basic logic of core-periphery hierarchy: the core consumer is still at the center of the system. The shift from markets to chains may even be reinforcing global power differentials.

Recommended reading: Babones (2016), Gereffi *et al.* (2005).

Global cities

The global world-system is changing in other ways, too. The long-standing division of the world into core and peripheral zones seems to be fracturing within each zone as urban areas pull away from their surrounding rural hinterlands. The increasing dominance of cities over the countryside is a global phenomenon but it is most pronounced in a small number of so-called 'global cities' (Sassen, 1991).

The first generation of global cities research focused on the globally dominant cities of New York and London (Sassen, writing at the peak of the Japan boom, included Tokyo as well) but second- and third-tier cities exhibit the same characteristics, only to a lesser extent. The newly emerging global cities of East Asia are perhaps even more fully rationalized as economic focal points than are the longer-established global cities of the West (Chiu and Lui, 2009). Cities increasingly serve as major facilitators of investment and trade flows, are magnets for skilled and unskilled immigration, and host high concentrations of business services firms. As economic growth shifts from agriculture and manufacturing to services, cities become wealthier relative to rural areas.

The major cities of all but the poorest countries now contain islands of glass office buildings and shopping malls that are, in many cases, deeply estranged from their surrounding populations. The rise of global cities seems to be part of the same process that has led to the rise of urban slums (large districts of dense informal settlement that lack city services). The connection is still poorly theorized, but it seems reasonable to assume that the rise of the global city is closely tied to the transition from market exchange to value chains. Lindsey (2012) refers to these new kinds of slums as 'embedded peripheries'. Another form of embedded periphery exists in global cities in which a large proportion of the population is composed of non-citizen immigrants who are permanently excluded from political participation. Dubai is the most extreme example of this phenomenon, but other Persian Gulf cities, Singapore, Hong Kong and in some ways even London, exhibit the same pattern. These global cities are recreating core-periphery citizenship hierarchies that parallel the global core-periphery hierarchy even more closely than do the embedded peripheries of poor countries' urban slums.

Recommended reading: Sassen (1991).

World-system futures

Innovations in the literatures on global value chains and global cities – two of the most exciting frontiers of world-systems analysis – suggest that the modern world-system in which countries are the basic units of an overarching world-economy may be in the process of changing to a new structural form. Wallerstein (2014) himself regularly points to a final structural crisis of capitalism that began in 1968 and argues that 'the system is absolutely certain to go out of existence entirely' (p. 168), although he refuses to be drawn on the timing or shape of world-system to come. Boswell and Chase-Dunn (2000) once offered an outline of a world making a peaceful transition to global democratic socialism, but as the 1990s recede into history this hope looks increasingly absurd. More in line with the 21st-century zeitgeist, but perhaps with even less credibility, Arrighi (2007) looked to China to offer a more humane form of capitalism to replace the modern world-system's harsh market discipline.

The hollowing out of countries as the main actors in global capitalism and their replacement by transnational cities and networks does, however, point to important changes in the structure of the global world-system. If the *longue durée* approach of the world-systems perspective has taught us anything, it is that world-systems have a lifespan. Much like a living animal, their structures are remarkably stable over the course of their lives, but also like a living animal they can change radically during their conception and birth. It took nearly 200 years for the modern world-system to take shape over the course of the long 16th century. If the postmodern world-system was born in the crises of the 1960s – as Wallerstein has repeatedly asserted – then historical precedent suggests that we may not know its final form until the 2140s.

Nonetheless, some outlines seem clear. By the late 1960s, the world-economy had been thoroughly endogenized under state control: levels of international trade were extraordinarily low and highly regulated; exchange controls bound nearly all the world's currencies in the Bretton Woods system; levels of state ownership were so high even in nominally capitalist countries that social scientists began to talk seriously about institutional convergence between capitalism and communism. After the 1960s, all of that began to change. Over the period 1972–2008, global exports measured as a proportion of global GDP more than doubled from 14 to 31 per cent. Other indicators of global integration expanded commensurately.

The new, globally integrated economy that has emerged is governed more by multinational corporations than by national governments, especially outside the high-capacity states of the developed West. Even in these states, the corporate capture of governing elites is routine. Because capital is now fully globalized, the ultimate governance of transnational political–economic networks of corporations, their employees, their contractors, and their (captive) political benefactors occurs at the global level. Hardt and Negri (2000) argue that this new global governance network is a shadowy denationalized 'Empire',[1] but a strong argument can be made that contemporary global governance networks are overwhelmingly focused around the United States, its four close Anglo-Saxon partners, and its wider system of allies (Babones, 2016). Wang (2013) goes so far as to suggest that the pervasive influence of American ways of thinking may constitute a global American *tianxia*, using the Chinese word to indicate an ideological system 'backed by unmatched military power and political influence' (p. 135). The world may increasingly be governed by multinational institutions, but those institutions (especially corporations) share a thoroughly American world view.

Recommended reading: Arrighi (2007), Hardt and Negri (2000), Wallerstein (2014).

Anti-systemic movements

Finally, the most active area of current research and writing in the world-systems tradition is the study of anti-systemic social movements. Today's anti-systemic movements have their roots in 500-year-old processes of incorporation, peripheralization and indigenization. This can be seen most clearly in the case indigenous rights movements. Indigenous nations are active in processes of globalization from below, forming transnational social networks in which to embed their local community struggles (Fenelon and Hall, 2008). Anti-globalization movements are also transnationally networked, forming global alliances to resist global processes of commodification and dispossession (Smith and Wiest, 2012). But what is the system that these anti-systemic movements are fighting? Fenelon and Hall (2008) recognize the importance of this question, calling for a 'return to an explicit examination of a world-system context' (p. 1895), but they do not answer it. Smith and Wiest (2012) similarly observe a transition from state-centred to transnational movement-centred transnational activism (p. 164) without addressing the character of the system to be mobilized against. They merely assume that American hegemony is giving way in the face of challenges from BRICS countries (Brazil, Russia, India, China, and South Africa), the European Union, and transnational terrorism.

But the BRICS countries themselves are more often targets than champions of anti-systemic social movements (Bond and Garcia, 2015), the European Union is chronically moribund, and no one expects transnational terrorism to become the basis for a new, postmodern world-system. Smith and Wiest (2012) point out that in the contemporary world-system, 'the bases of power, authority, influence, and legitimacy have shifted from territorial sovereignty claims . . . to normative ones' (p. 4). The 'American *tianxia*' thesis is at heart the thesis that the emerging postmodern world-system configuration is centered on an individualistic world cultural triptych of democracy, human rights, and the rule of law, all concepts that originated in and are promoted by the US, its allies and its acolytes. This might give rise to a positive vision for the future except for the fact that the three elements are not created equal: global rule of law is well developed, global human rights are widely asserted but poorly enforced, and global democracy is essentially non-existent. The challenge for critical development studies is figure out how to give global democracy the upper hand.

Recommended reading: Arrighi *et al.* (1997), Wallerstein (2014).

Note

1 *Editors' note*: For a critique of Hardt and Negri's conception of imperialism and their world capitalist system, see Petras and Veltmeyer (2005).

References

Arrighi, G. (2007). *Adam Smith in Beijing: Lineages of the Twenty-First Century*. New York: Verso.

Arrighi, G. and Drangel, J. (1986). 'The stratification of the world-economy: an exploration of the semiperipheral zone'. *Review*, 10: 9–74.

Arrighi, G., Hopkins, T. and Wallerstein, I. (1997). *Anti-Systemic Movements*. London: Verso.

Babones, S. (2012). 'Position and mobility in the contemporary world-economy: a structuralist perspective'. In S. Babones and C. Chase-Dunn (eds), *Routledge Handbook of World-Systems Analysis*. Oxford: Routledge, pp. 327–35.

Babones, S. (2015). 'What "is" world-systems analysis?' *Thesis Eleven*, 127: 3–20.

Babones, S. (2016). 'From world-market to world-empire: the political economy of the third millennium'. In H. Nolte, M. Boatca and A. Komlosy (eds), *Worldregions, Migration and Identity*. Zurich: Muster-Schmidt Verlag, pp. 145–57.

Babones, S. and Chase-Dunn, C. (eds) (2012). *Routledge Handbook of World-Systems Analysis*. Oxford: Routledge.

Bond, P. and Garcia, A. (2015). *BRICS: An Anticapitalist Critique*. Chicago, IL: Haymarket Books.

Boswell, T. and Chase-Dunn, C. (2000). *The Spiral of Capitalism and Socialism: Toward Global Democracy*. Boulder, CO: Lynne Rienner.

Chase-Dunn, C. (1998). *Global Formation: Structures of the World-Economy*, 2nd edition. Lanham, MD: Rowman & Littlefield.

Chiu, S. and Lui, T. (2009). *Hong Kong: Becoming a Chinese Global City*. Oxford: Routledge.

Fenelon, J. (2016). 'Genocide, race, capitalism: synopsis of formation within the modern world-system'. *Journal of World-Systems Research*, 22: 23–30.

Fenelon, J. and Hall, T. (2008). 'Revitalization and indigenous resistance to globalization and neoliberalism'. *American Behavioral Scientist*, 51: 1867–901.

Frank, A. (1969). 'The development of underdevelopment'. *Monthly Review*, 18(4): 17–31.

Galtung, J. (1971). 'A structural theory of imperialism'. *Journal of Peace Research*, 8: 81–117.

Gereffi, G., Humphrey, J. and Sturgeon, T. (2005). 'The governance of global value chains'. *Review of International Political Economy*, 12: 78–104.

Guthman J. (2009). 'Unveiling the unveiling: commodity chains, commodity fetishism, and the "value" of voluntary, ethical food labels'. In J. Bair (ed.), *Frontiers of Commodity Chain Research*. Stanford, CA: Stanford University Press, pp. 190–206.

Hardt, M. and Negri, A. (2000). *Empire*. Cambridge, MA: Harvard University Press.

Lindsey, D. (2012). 'Slums, favelas, shantytowns and a new regime of spatial inequality in the modern world-system'. In S. Babones and C. Chase-Dunn (eds), *Routledge Handbook of World-Systems Analysis*. Oxford: Routledge, pp. 345–52.

Petras, J. and Veltmeyer, H. (2005). *Empire with Imperialism*. Halifax/London: Fernwood/Zed Books.

Sassen, S. (1991). *The Global City: New York, London, Tokyo*. Princeton, NJ: Princeton University Press.

Smith, J. and Wiest, D. (2012). *Social Movements in the World-System: The Politics of Crisis and Transformation*. New York: Russel Sage.

Wallerstein, I. (1972). 'Three paths of national development in sixteenth-century Europe'. *Studies in Comparative International Development*, 7: 95–101.

Wallerstein, I. (1974). *The Modern World-System: Capitalist Agriculture and the Origins of the European World-Economy in the Sixteenth Century*. New York: Academic Press.

Wallerstein, I. (2014). 'Antisystemic movements, yesterday and today'. *Journal of World-Systems Research*, 20: 158–72.

Wang, G. (2013). *Renewal: The Chinese State and the New Global History*. Hong Kong: Chinese University Press.

8

THE CENTRAL CONTRADICTIONS OF CAPITALISM AND CAPITALIST CRISES

Berch Berberoglu

The origins and development of capitalism in Western Europe, and later North America and elsewhere in the world, is replete with contradictions and crises that have characterized the capitalist mode of production over the past several centuries. This chapter examines the central contradictions of capitalism that are the basis of capitalist crises originating from the exploitation of wage labour by capital – the basis of the private accumulation of capital – which is the fundamental contradiction of capitalism and capitalist relations of production throughout its turbulent history. After a brief historical background on its origins and development in the 18th century, the chapter focuses on the contemporary manifestations of capitalist development and its attendant crises in the age of imperialism and capitalist globalization, and provides an analysis of the continuing crisis of advanced capitalism in the early 21st century.

Historical background

Historically, a number of conditions set the stage and led to the emergence of capitalism and the capitalist state in Western Europe and elsewhere. These included the availability of free labourers, the generation of moneyed wealth, a sufficient level of skills and technology, markets and the protection provided by the state. In general, these conditions were the foundations on which a pre-capitalist feudal society transformed itself into a capitalist one until capitalism developed through its own dynamics (Marx, 1965). Once capitalism was established as a mode of production, it began to produce and reproduce the conditions for expanded commodity production and capital accumulation. From this point on, capitalism developed in accordance with its inherent dynamics and contradictions.

During the development of capitalism since the late 18th century, the commercial and industrial interests that merged into a single unified class, forming the rising bourgeoisie, increasingly viewed their interests as tied up with the nation in which they amassed their growing wealth and came to require the protection of the state to safeguard their increasingly privileged position in society. This led to the control of state power during the transition from feudalism to capitalism in order to advance the interests of capital as distinct from the interests of the overthrown landed aristocracy, on the one hand, and the emerging working class, on the other (Hilton, 1976).

With the main relation of production being wage labour versus capital (the owners of the means of production), capitalism established itself as a mode of production based on the exploitation of wage labour by the capitalists, whose political power and authority in society derived from their ownership and control of the means of production. Lacking ownership of the means necessary to gain a living, workers were forced to sell their labour power to the capitalists in order to survive. As a result, the surplus value produced by labour was appropriated by the capitalists in the form of profit. Thus, private profit (the accumulation of capital), generated through the exploitation of wage labour, became the motive force of capitalism and capitalist development through the 19th and 20th centuries (Perlo, 1988).

The contradictions imbedded in such antagonistic social relations in time led to the radicalization of workers and the formation of trade unions and other labour organizations that were to play an important role in the struggles between labour and capital. The history of the labour movement in Europe, the United States, and elsewhere in the world is chronicled with bloody confrontations between labour and capital, and the latter's repressive arm, the capitalist state. From the early battles of workers in Britain and on the continent in the late 18th and early 19th centuries, to the decisive role played by French workers in the uprising of 1848–1851, to the Paris Commune in 1871 and beyond, the working class put up a determined struggle in its fight against capital to overthrow the capitalist state – a struggle spanning over two centuries (Lenin, 1971 [1916]).

Established to protect and advance the interests of the capitalist class, the early capitalist state assumed a pivotal role that assured the class rule of capitalists over society, and thus became an institution of legitimization and brute force to maintain law and order in favour of capitalism. Sanctioning and enforcing laws to protect the rights of the new property owners and disciplining labour to maintain a wage system that generated profits for the wealthy few, the capitalist state became the instrument of capital and its political rule over society (Szymanski, 1978).

Among the major functions of the early capitalist state were guaranteeing private property at home and abroad; collecting taxes; recording income for purposes of taxation and raising armies; guaranteeing contracts; providing the infrastructure for the new industries; facilitating the growth of private industry; mediating among various wealthy interests; securing a cheap and disciplined labour-force for private enterprise; and preserving law and order to keep the masses under control.

The central task of the early capitalist state in Europe was that of disciplining the labour-force. Union activity, strikes or collective actions of any kind by workers against businesses were prohibited; demonstrations, agitation and propaganda initiated by workers against the employers and the system were systematically repressed. Thus, while state intervention in the economy was kept to a minimum to permit the capitalists to enrich themselves without regulation, the capitalist-controlled state became heavily involved in the conflict between labour and capital on behalf of the capitalist class, bringing to bear its repressive apparatus on labour and its allies who threatened the capitalist order (Lenin, 1971 [1916]). Law and order enforced by the state in early capitalism (and right up to the present) served to protect and preserve the capitalist system and prevent its transformation. In this sense, the state came to see itself as a legitimizing institution of the new social order and identified its survival directly with the capitalists who controlled it. This mutual relationship between state and capital in time set the conditions for the structural environment in which the state functioned to promote capitalist interests. Within this process of the state's development from early to mature capitalism, the structural imperatives of capital accumulation placed the state in the service of capital, thus transforming it into a capitalist state (Szymanski, 1978).

An analysis of the nature and dynamics of relations between labour and capital would provide us with the necessary insight to an understanding of the class nature of relations between labour and capital at the point of production. Such relations, which are at base manifestations of larger, capitalist relations of production, become evident in their social form as workers confront capital who extract from them an ever-growing sum of surplus value or profits. It is in this context of the struggle between labour and capital at the point of production that we begin to see the class nature of this struggle – a struggle that, in its broader *class* context, becomes a *political* struggle involving the state, hence a struggle for state power (Berberoglu, 2002, 2009). The balance of forces in this class struggle beyond point-of-production work relations translates into a political struggle for the preservation or transformation of the capitalist system itself. It is in this context of the nature of capitalist society in terms of both the economy and the state that the class nature of the contradictions of capitalism and capitalist crises must be viewed. And it is within this context of the broader economic, political and social forces at work that the impact of the global capitalist crisis must be analysed and understood.

Recommended reading: Berberoglu (2002, 2009), Harvey (2003), Perlo (1988), Szymanski (1978).

The contradictions and crises of global capitalism

The development of capitalism over the past few hundred years has formed and transformed capitalism in a crucial way, one that is characterized by periodic crises resulting from the capitalist business cycle, which is a product of the contradiction between the expanded forces of production and existing exploitative social relations of production (i.e. class relations), which manifest in a number of ways, including:

1. Intensification of the exploitation of labour through expanded production and reproduction of surplus value and profits that facilitate the further accumulation of capital and the reproduction of capitalist relations of production.
2. The problem of overproduction, resulting from the imbalance created between wages and prices of commodities, leading to periodic recessions and depressions.
3. Increasing unemployment resulting from continued application of high technology in production (i.e. automation).
4. The restructuring of the international division of labour through the export of capital and transfer of production to low-wage areas abroad, resulting in industrial decline and decay, hence greater unemployment, in the centre states.
5. Increased polarization of wealth and income at the national and global level between the capitalist and working classes and growth in numbers of the poor and marginalized segments of the population throughout the world. These and other related central contradictions of capitalism define the parameters of capitalist development through its various stages – now at global proportions as capitalism and capitalist crises unfold on a global scale.

Given the logic of global capital accumulation in late capitalist society, it is no accident that the decline of the domestic economy of advanced capitalist countries over the past several decades corresponds to the accelerated export of capital abroad in search of cheap labour, access to raw materials, new markets, and higher rates of profit. The resulting deindustrialization of the domestic economy has had a serious impact on workers and other affected segments of the labouring population and has brought about a major dislocation of the national economy (Berberoglu, 2003, 2010; Phillips, 1998). This has necessitated increased state intervention on behalf of the monopolies and has heightened the contradictions that led to the crisis of advanced capitalist society.

The widening gap between the accumulated wealth of the capitalist class and the declining incomes of workers (within a deteriorating national economy and the state's budgetary crisis) has led to the ensuing political crisis within the state apparatus and has sharpened the class struggle in a new political direction. As the crisis of the capitalist economy has brought the advanced-capitalist state to the centre stage of economic life and revealed its direct ties to the monopolies, thus exacerbating the state's legitimization crisis, the response of the working class and the masses in general have increasingly become directed against the state itself (Beams, 1998).

The global expansion of capital (i.e. capitalist globalization) has had a great impact on the national economies of advanced capitalist countries. This impact is the result of the capitalist globalization process that has destroyed national economies in the interests of transnational capital that profits from its global operations on a worldwide basis – a process that has generated contradictions on a dual level. At the global level, it has meant, first and foremost, the ever-growing exploitation of workers through the use of cheap labour. In addition, it has caused a depletion of resources that could be used for national development, as well as environmental pollution, and other health hazards, a growing national debt, tying many countries to the dictates of international financial institutions, and a growing militarization of society through the installation of brutal military and civilian dictatorships that violate basic human rights. The domination of Third World countries for transnational profits through the instrumentality of the advanced capitalist (imperialist) state has, at the same time, created various forms of control by centres of global capitalism that has become a defining characteristic of capitalist globalization in the age of imperialism (Sklair, 2002).

Domestically, the globalization of capital and imperialist expansion has had immense dislocations in the national economies of advanced capitalist countries. Expansion of the manufacturing industry abroad has meant a decline in local industry, as plant closings in the US and other advanced capitalist countries have worsened the unemployment situation. The massive expansion of capital abroad has resulted in hundreds of factory shutdowns with millions of workers losing their jobs, hence the surge in unemployment in the US and other centres of global capitalism (Bluestone and Harrison, 1982; Wagner, 2000). This has led to a decline in wages of workers in the advanced capitalist centres, as low wages abroad have played a competitive role in keeping wages down in the centre states. The drop in incomes among a growing section of the US working class has thus lowered the standard of living in general and led to further polarization between labour and capital in recent decades (Berberoglu, 1992, 2010, 2014).

The globalization of capital and the integration of national capitalist economies into the global capitalist system, a process that has been developing over the latter half of the 20th century, and its intensification under neoliberal policies over the past several decades, has had a direct impact on the extent and depth of the current continuing global capitalist crisis. Previously nationally based economies, now under the control of transnational corporations and international financial institutions, have become appendages of the global economy that operates under the logic of global capital accumulation for the benefit of the transnationals and their owners, while at a great cost to those who have become victims of this process.

Recommended reading: Beams (1998), Bello (2006), Berberoglu (2014), Harvey (2003), Jomo and Baudot (2007).

Capitalist globalization and the global capitalist crisis

After nearly a decade of the continuing global capitalist crisis that began with the September 2008 financial meltdown on Wall Street and other centres of global capitalism, the prospects for a rapid recovery of the economies of the United States and Europe, as well as those integrated into the global capitalist system, appear to be dim. While stock markets across the globe have made a big turnaround over the past decade, from their lows in late 2008 and early 2009 to their pre-recession highs and beyond by 2017, unemployment rates have continued to remain near double-digit levels in most advanced capitalist economies, with depression-level rates in countries suffering from the sovereign debt crisis, such as Greece,

Spain, Portugal and Italy. The grim economic situation, which has cast doubt over chances of a rapid recovery anytime soon, was made worse with the new wave of mortgage foreclosures that the banks unloaded in the past several years – a situation that has relegated the US and the global economy into greater uncertainty (Berberoglu, 2014).

Writing about the continuing capitalist crisis and its aftermath in my recent book *Beyond the Global Capitalist Crisis: The World Economy in Transition*, published in early 2012, and pointing out that 'Global capitalism is in serious crisis, and the current continuing severe global recession is the worst economic downturn since the Great Depression of the early twentieth century', I added, 'as the global capitalist crisis takes on depression–era characteristics', and 'as millions of unemployed working people look for a job to pay for their basic necessities, capitalist states throughout the world have spent hundreds of billions of taxpayer dollars to bail out failed commercial and financial institutions', with more than a trillion dollars spent by the US government alone 'to save the global capitalist system from total collapse' (Berberoglu, 2012: 1).

It turns out that the total bailout money that was spent to save the system from collapse was much more than officially reported at the time; in fact, according to a US Government Accountability Office (GAO) Report released in July 2011, the bailout money used to rescue dozens of corporations and banks across the globe was in excess of $16 trillion! (GAO, 2011: 131). Moreover, according to Sanjeev Ghotge, in 2009, while US economic output was $12 trillion and US savings was $2.4 trillion, the amount of debt accumulated from derivatives by the private sector was $473 trillion (Ghotge, 2009: 85–6) – an alarming situation that could lead to an economic catastrophe if this sector of finance capital was to unravel in another future financial meltdown (Bivens, 2011; Sherman, 2010).

Given the severity of the 2008–2009 global capitalist crisis and its magnitude, I argued boldly, and in no uncertain terms, that what we have been facing is 'a systemic crisis that is permanent and irreversible' (Berberoglu, 2012: 179). Thus, any attempt to rescue the system from total collapse, I insisted, would be a futile exercise that is palatable only to those who operate under the illusion that capitalism once again will be rescued and will survive – and this, despite the massive role of the capitalist state in intervening in the global economy to reverse its decline and fall. If a decade after the great catastrophe we continue to suffer from the effects of the crisis across the globe, it most certainly tells us that we are in fact at a major turning point in recent world history – an epochal transformation of world systemic proportions in the early 21st century, i.e. the impending transformation of global capitalism (Calhoun and Derluguian, 2011; Robinson, 2014).

A major global economic crisis, such as the one we have been experiencing for nearly a decade, greatly affects the economies of nations that have become part of the global capitalist system. Thus, all the known consequences of such severe economic downturn on working people (growing consumer debt, rising unemployment and underemployment, declining purchasing power, home mortgage foreclosures, bankruptcies and a host of other economic problems) are the very ingredients of a system-wide crisis that has affected not only working people in the advanced capitalist countries (where the most recent crisis originated), but all others integrated into the global capitalist system, especially workers in the periphery of the system around the world. And more so is the case with the latter, as they are more vulnerable to the forces of the global capitalist economy and its periodic crises (Petras and Veltmeyer, 2012).

The ongoing global capitalist crisis that we are experiencing today is a product of more than three decades of neoliberal capitalist policies of privatization, deregulation, tax cuts for the wealthy, speculative investments, financialization and profiteering of unimaginable proportions. Through these practices, many capitalists became very wealthy and amassed great fortunes during this period, while working people were super-exploited through extremely low wages in the sweatshops of the giant capitalist corporations that have spread their tentacles across the globe.

Global capitalism came very close in 2008 to destroying the very system that it had created not so long ago. Cyclical crises of recessions and depressions, economic rivalry, political and military conflict, war and other forms of disruptions and catastrophes have been the characteristic of global capitalism ever since its inception a few centuries ago. In my recent book *Beyond the Global Capitalist Crisis: The World Economy in Transition*, published by Ashgate in 2012, I pointed out that:

> [t]racing the evolution of the capitalist economy and the capitalist business cycle historically, it becomes clear that the ups and downs – *booms and busts* – of the capitalist economy is the result of the *normal* process of evolution of the capitalist system, and that economic crises (i.e. recessions and depressions) are a recurrent aspect of capitalism at the national and now the global level.
>
> *(Berberoglu, 2012: 179, emphasis in original)*

I went on to argue that, therefore:

> the crisis-ridden business cycle of capitalism – one that is to be found *only under capitalism* – is the life-blood of the capitalist system in that capitalism cannot grow and prosper without such a *correction* (crisis) in the economy every few years. And this can be seen as part of the process of capitalist expansion and contraction over its life course.
>
> *(Berberoglu, 2012: 179, emphasis in original)*

Recommended reading: Bello (2006, 2009), Berberoglu (2012, 2014), Harvey (2003).

Global capitalism: prospects for its transformation

The current continuing global capitalist crisis that originated in the Great Recession of 2008–2009 is but one serious crisis in a series of capitalist crises that have erupted over the past few centuries as capitalism developed and expanded from Europe to

North America and elsewhere across the globe over this period. The dynamics and contradictions of this process of recurrent crises of the capitalist system leading to the crisis of global capitalism have been documented very clearly and in great detail in a wide array of literature (Berberoglu, 2003, 2010, 2012, 2014; Bivens, 2011; Calhoun and Derluguian, 2011; Petras, 2009; Sherman, 2010). It has been shown that this most recent crisis of global capitalism is a manifestation of capitalism and capitalist globalization at this (imperialist) stage of the globalization process. Thus, to go beyond the crisis of global capitalism and imperialism, we need to address a variety of issues that emanate from the system itself – issues that are directly linked to the very nature of neoliberal capitalist globalization and the global capitalist crisis in the age of imperialism (Petras and Veltmeyer, 2001). This raises further questions as to the nature and sources of the changes that are necessary to take us beyond this epochal predicament: Who (which social class) shall lead the process of transformation, and in which direction? It is here that we benefit from analyses of capitalist imperialism that not only lay out the process at work that has taken us to the point where we are today, but help us move forward and go beyond the contradictions and crises of this exploitative and oppressive system.

The economic crisis brought by the 2008 financial meltdown is a direct outcome of the operations of the very same capitalist system that has dominated the global economy to this day. And the ramifications of this latest and deepest economic crisis since the Great Depression of the early 20th century will be felt for a long time to come. While this means the impact of the crisis on the working class will be significant, it is also the case that this may lead to greater class consciousness among workers, who will increasingly become aware of the system's fault lines, as its unequal and exploitative nature becomes visible and obvious for all to see. This process would surely assist in the development of sufficient class consciousness that would call into question the very premises and legitimacy of the capitalist system. It is this unfolding process that in time comes to inform the working class of the necessity to organize and engage in class struggle for state power. While this is a long process and requires much work and determination on the part of the workers to wage such a struggle, the dynamics of the class struggle under capitalism will of necessity force workers to take the required steps to achieve its transformation through organized collective political action (Berberoglu, 2009; Polet, 2007; Veltmeyer, 2012).

The contradictions of global capitalist expansion, which has caused so much exploitation, oppression and misery for the peoples of the world, both in the Third World and in the imperialist countries themselves, has in turn created the conditions for its own downfall. Economically, it has afflicted the system with recessions, depressions and associated realization crises; politically, it has set into motion an imperial interventionist state that through its presence in every corner of the world has incurred an enormous military expenditure to maintain an empire, while gaining the resentment of millions of people across the globe who are engaged in active struggle against it.

The imperial capitalist state, acting as the repressive arm of global capital and extending its rule across vast territories, has dwarfed the militaristic adventures of past empires many times over, and through its political and military supremacy it has come to exert its control over many countries and has thus facilitated the exploitation of labour on a world scale (Parenti, 2011). As a result, it has reinforced the domination of capital over labour and its rule on behalf of capital. This, in turn, has greatly politicized the struggle between labour and capital and called for the recognition of the importance of political organization that many find necessary to effect change in order to transform the global capitalist system.

The contradictions of the unfolding process of global expansion and accumulation have brought to the fore new political realities: renewed repression at home and abroad to control an increasingly frustrated working class in the imperial heartland, and a militant and revolutionary mass of workers and peasants in the Third World poised to resist capitalist globalization (Houtart and Polet, 2001). It is these inherent contradictions of modern global capitalism that are making it increasingly difficult for the imperial state to control and manage the global political economy, while at the same time preparing the conditions for international solidarity of workers in confronting global capital throughout the world.

Recommended reading: Harvey (2003), Petras and Veltmeyer (2001), Polet (2007), Sherman (2010).

References

Beams, N. (1998). *The Significance and Implications of Globalization: A Marxist Assessment*. Southfield, UK: Mehring.

Bello, W. (2006). 'The capitalist conjuncture: over-accumulation, financial crises and the retreat from globalisation'. *Third World Quarterly*, 27(8): 1345–67.

Bello, W. (2009). 'The global collapse: a non-orthodox view'. *Z Net*, 22 February.

Berberoglu, B. (1992). *The Legacy of Empire: Economic Decline and Class Polarization in the United States*. New York: Praeger.

Berberoglu, B. (ed.) (2002). *Labour and Capital in the Age of Globalization*. Lanham, MD: Rowman & Littlefield.

Berberoglu, B. (2003). *Globalization of Capital and the Nation-State: Imperialism, Class Struggle, and the State in the Age of Global Capitalism*. Lanham, MD: Rowman & Littlefield.

Berberoglu, B. (2009). *Class and Class Conflict in the Age of Globalization*. Lanham, MD: Lexington Books.

Berberoglu, B. (ed.) (2010). *Globalization in the 21st Century: Labor, Capital, and the State on a World Scale*. New York: Palgrave Macmillan.

Berberoglu, B. (2012). *Beyond the Global Capitalist Crisis: The World Economy in Transition*. Farnham, UK: Ashgate.

Berberoglu, B. (2014). *The Global Capitalist Crisis and Its Aftermath: The Causes and Consequences of the Great Recession of 2008–2009*. Farnham, UK: Ashgate.

Bivens, J. (2011). *Failure by Design: The Story Behind America's Broken Economy*. Ithaca, NY: ILR Press.

Bluestone, B. and Harrison, B. (1982). *The Deindustrialization of America*. New York: Basic Books.

Calhoun, C. and Derluguian, G. (eds) (2011). *Aftermath: A New Economic Order?* New York: New York University Press.

GAO (2011). *Report to Congressional Addressees. Federal Reserve System: Opportunities Exist to Strengthen Policies and Processes for Managing Emergency Assistance*. Washington, DC: GAO.

Ghotge, S. (2009) 'Financial meltdown: an intriguing silence at the core'. *Capitalism, Nature, Socialism*, 20(4), December: 85–8.

Harvey, D. (2003). *The New Imperialism*. New York: Oxford University Press.

Hilton, R. (ed.) (1976). *The Transition from Feudalism to Capitalism*. London: New Left Books.

Houtart, F. and Polet, F. (eds) (2001). *The Other Davos Summit: The Globalization of Resistance to the World Economic System*. London: Zed Books.

Jomo, K.S. and Baudot, J. (2007). *Flat World, Big Gaps*. London: Zed Books.

Lenin, V.I. (1971 [1916]). 'The state and revolution'. In *Selected Works in One Volume*. New York: International Publishers.

Marx, K. (1965). *Pre-Capitalist Formations*. New York: International Publishers.

Parenti, M. (2011). *The Face of Imperialism*. Boulder, CO: Paradigm.

Perlo, V. (1988). *Super-Profits and Crises*. New York: International Publishers.

Petras, J. (2009). *Global Depression and Regional Wars*. Atlanta, GA: Clarity Press.

Petras, J. and Veltmeyer, H. (2001). *Globalization Unmasked: Imperialism in the 21st Century*. London: Zed Books.

Petras, J. and Veltmeyer, H. (2012). *Beyond Neoliberalism: A World to Win*. New York: Routledge.

Phillips, B. (1998). *Global Production and Domestic Decay: Plant Closings in the US*. New York: Garland.

Polet, F. (2007). *The State of Resistance: Popular Struggles in the Global South*. London: Zed Books.

Robinson, W. (2014). 'The "great recession" of 2008 and the continuing global capitalist crisis'. In B. Berberoglu (ed.), *The Global Capitalist Crisis and Its Aftermath*. Farnham, UK: Ashgate, pp. 59–78.

Sherman, H. (2010). *The Roller Coaster Economy: Financial Crisis, Great Recession, and the Public Option*. Boston, MA: M.E. Sharpe.

Sklair, L. (2002). *Globalization: Capitalism and Its Alternatives*. New York: Oxford University Press.

Szymanski, A. (1978). *The Capitalist State and the Politics of Class*. Cambridge, MA: Winthrop.

Veltmeyer, H. (2012). *Imperialism, Crisis, and Class Struggle*. Chicago, IL: Haymarket Books.

Wagner, H. (ed.) (2000). *Globalization and Unemployment*. New York: Springer.

9

IMPERIALISM, CAPITALISM AND DEVELOPMENT

James Petras and Henry Veltmeyer

In this chapter we are concerned with unravelling the intimate relation of imperialism to capitalism and clearing away some of the confusion surrounding it. There are two major problems in the way these two concepts are understood and used in the literature. In the liberal tradition of political science, the projection of imperial power and associated dynamics are normally disconnected from capitalism and its economic dynamics, reducing imperialism to a quest for world domination based on a lust for power or purely geopolitical considerations by the guardians of the national interest in the most powerful countries. But in the Marxist tradition of political economy, we can find the opposite tendency in which the institutional specificity of the state as an instrument of class power is downplayed or ignored, and imperialism is reduced to a purely economic dynamic – essentially confusing imperialism with capitalism. In this chapter, it is argued that capitalism and imperialism are intimately connected but engage distinct dynamics in the geoeconomics and the geopolitics of capital that need to be clearly distinguished. We advance this argument with reference to the capitalist development process as it has unfolded in Latin America.

The debate on imperialism: points of dispute

Almost all theories of contemporary imperialism, both in its (neo)Marxist and (neo) liberal variants, lack any but the crudest sociological analyses of the class and political character of the governing groups that direct the imperial state and its policies (Amin, 2001; Foster, 2006; Hardt and Negri, 2000; Harvey, 2003; Magdoff, 2003; Panitch and Leys, 2004). The same is true for contemporary theorizing about the imperial state, which is devoid of both institutional and class analysis.

Many theorists of imperialism resort to a form of economic reductionism in which the political and ideological dimensions of imperial power are downplayed or ignored, and categories such as 'investments', 'trade' and 'markets' are decontextualized and presented as historically disembodied entities that are comparable across space and time. Changes in the configuration of class relations and associated dynamics are then accounted for in terms of general economic categories such as 'finance', 'manufacturing', 'banking' and 'services' without any analysis of the political economy of capitalist development or the nature and sources of financial wealth – illegal drug trade, money laundering, real estate speculation, etc. (Panitch and Leys, 2004).

Contemporary theorizing about imperialism generally ignores the sociopolitical and ideological power configurations of imperial policy, as well as the role of international financial institutions such as the World Bank in shaping the institutional and policy framework of the new world order, which not only provides a system of global governance, but the rules of engagement for the class war launched by the global capitalist class against labour in its different redoubts of organized resistance. The focus of theorists of the 'new imperialism' is on the transnational corporations that dominate the global economy viewed as the operational agency of imperial power in the world capitalist system, having displaced the powers of the state. While theorists and analysts in the liberal tradition continue their concern with the dynamics of US foreign policy in the projection of imperial power, and Marxists in the tradition of international political economy and critical development studies continue to concentrate their analysis on the dynamics of state power, the theorists of the 'new imperialism' focus almost entirely on the globalizing dynamics of monopoly capital.

The argument advanced by Hardt and Negri (2000) and other world-systems theorists is that the 'class relations of global capitalism are now so deeply internalized within every nation-state that the classical image of imperialism as a relation of external domination is outdated' (Robinson, 2007: 7). Although what these class relations might be is unclear, Robinson argues that 'national capitalist monopolies' no longer need to 'turn to the state for assistance'. In Robinson's formulation, 'the system of nation-states . . . is no longer the organizing principle of capitalist development, or the primary institutional framework that shapes social and class forces and political dynamics' (Robinson, 2007: 8). However, if, as Robinson contends, capital no longer needs the support of state power, does it mean that imperialism will wither away or, as argued by Klare (2003: 51–2), that it will take the form of 'geopolitical competition . . . the contention between great powers and aspiring great powers for control over territory, resources, and important geographical positions such as ports and harbours . . . and other sources of wealth and influence'?

Or does it mean what Robinson and some – including Amin (2001), Arrighi (2005), Foster (2003) and others in the torrent of 'new imperialism' literature that has appeared since 2001 – have suggested or contend, namely that imperialism today is advanced primarily in economic terms through the agency of transnational(ized) corporations that constitute an empire without imperialism – as Hardt and Negri would have it – or capitalism beyond imperialism, as Robinson has it?

In opposition to this rather reductionist view of imperialism, we hold that imperialism is shaped predominantly by the imperial state and its policies. Taking into consideration its political dynamics and its economic operations (investments, production, sales), imperialism is clearly designed and works to advance the project of capital accumulation in whatever and in as many ways as possible – to penetrate existing markets and open up new ones, exploit labour as humanely as possible but as inhumanely as needed, extract surplus value from the direct producers where possible, and access as needed or process raw materials and minerals. Insofar as the capitalist class is concerned, the aim and the agenda of its individual and institutional members is to accumulate capital. As for the imperial state and its agents and agencies, including the World Bank and the agencies of international cooperation for security and development, the agenda is merely to pave the way for capital and to create the conditions needed for economic and social development. In neither case is uneven development of the forces of production and its social conditions (social inequality, unemployment, poverty, social and environmental degradation, etc.) on the agenda. Rather, these conditions are the unintended or 'structural' consequences of capitalist development, and as such inevitable and acceptable costs of progress that need to be managed and, if and where possible, mitigated in the interest of security and development.

Under these strategic and structural conditions, it is not particularly useful to measure the impact of imperialism merely in economic terms of the volume of capital inflows (FDI, bank loans, portfolio investments, etc.) and outflows (profit, interest payments, etc.). This is because imperialism is a matter of class and state power, and as such an issue of politics and political economy – issues that are not brought into focus in an analysis of national accounts. At issue here are not only the structural dynamics of uneven capitalist development (the 'development of underdevelopment', in André Gunder Frank's formulation), but social and international relations of power and competition between imperial and domestic classes, between officials and representatives of the imperial state and the state in 'emerging economies' and 'developing societies'.

As for relations of 'domination' and 'dependence' among nations on the lines of a North–South divide, the structure of global production and international relations of domination and subordination are dynamic and change over time, in part because the geopolitical and economic concerns of the nation state subject to imperial power lead to a quest for relative autonomy by state officials and politicians in these countries, as well as protection of the national interest. Developments along these lines have resulted in qualitative changes in the relations between established imperial and emerging capitalist states. Therefore, theorizing that is focused only on an analysis of inflows and outflows of capital – as if the 'host' country was a 'blank factor' – or a focus on the structure of global production based on a fixed international division of labour cannot account for the dynamics of capitalist development in countries and regions on the periphery of the system and those at the centre. Nor can this type of economistic theorizing explain dynamic features of the world capitalist system, for example the shift in economic power from North America and Western Europe towards Asia – China and India, to be precise.

Recommended reading: Amin (2001), Arrighi (2005), Foster (2006), Harvey (2003), Magdoff (2003), Panitch and Leys (2004), Robinson (2007).

Capitalism, class struggle and imperialism

In outlining his conception of historical materialism, Marx argued that at each stage in the capitalist development process – the development of the forces of production – can be found a corresponding system of class relations and struggle. For Marx, this was a matter of fundamental principle arising out of a fundamental conflict between the forces and relations of production. But he could have added that at each stage of capitalist development can also be found both a corresponding and distinct form of class struggle based on the forces of resistance to this advance, as well as imperialism in one form or the other, and distinctly understood as the projection of state power in the service of capital – to facilitate its advance in the sphere of international relations and secure its evolution into and as a world system. That is, the projection of state power in the quest for world domination – to establish hegemony over the world system – is a necessary condition of capitalist development. Capitalism requires the state not only to establish the necessary conditions of a capital accumulation process, but to ensure its inevitable expansion – the extension of the capital–labour relation, and its mechanism of economic exploitation (the extraction of surplus value from the labour of the direct producers) – into a world system.

Lenin had theorized this projection of state power in the service of capital as the most advanced stage in the capitalist development process, which includes a phase of 'primitive accumulation' in which the direct producers are separated from the land and their means of production, and a process by which the small-landholding agricultural producers or peasant farmers are proletarianized, converted and made over into a working class. As Lenin saw it, imperialism so conceived (as the 'highest stage of capitalism') featured: (i) the fusion of industrial and financial capital; (ii) the export of capital in the search for profitable outlets overseas; (iii) the territorial division of the world by European capitalist powers within the institutional and policy framework of *Pax Britannica* (the hegemony and dominion of Great Britain over its colonies); and (iv) an international division of labour based on an international exchange of primary commodities for goods manufactured at the centre of the system. These features encompassed an economic dynamic of capital accumulation, but this dynamic and the economic structure of this system evidently required and was secured politically with the projection of state power, including military force.

Lenin astutely identified the fundamental structural features of the world capitalist system at this stage of development. However, it was misleading to characterize it as 'imperialism' in that the projection of imperial class-based state power was a distinct feature of capitalism in an earlier phase in the evolution of capitalism as a world system, namely mercantilism, a system in which merchant's capital was accumulated through the expropriation of natural resources as much as exploitation of labour as well as state-sanctioned and regulated international trade. And imperialism was also a distinct feature and an adjunct to the capital accumulation process in later periods of capitalist development.

Recommended reading: Petras and Veltmeyer (2001).

Imperialism and capitalism in an era of neoliberal globalization (1980–2000)

Neoliberalism as an ideology of free-market capitalism and a doctrine of policy reform in the direction of free-market capitalism was some four decades in the making, manufactured by a neoliberal thought collective put together by Van der Hayek (Mirowski and Plehwe, 2009). But it was not until the early 1980s that the necessary conditions for bringing these ideologues to state power (i.e. in a position to influence and dictate policy) were available or otherwise created. These conditions included an unresolved systemic crisis of overproduction, a fiscal crisis in the North and an impending debt crisis in the South, and the defeat of the popular movement in the class struggle over land and labour.

Under these conditions, the imperial state, via its international organizations and financial institutions, mobilized its diverse powers and forces so as to mobilize the forces needed to reactivate the capital accumulation process. The main problem here – from a capitalist and imperialist perspective – was how to liberate the 'forces of freedom' (to quote from George W. Bush's 2012 *National Security Report*) from the regulatory constraints of the welfare-development state. The solution: a programme of 'structural reform' in macroeconomic policy (the vaunted 'structural adjustment programme' constructed by economists at the World Bank and the IMF) within the framework of a Washington Consensus (Petras and Veltmeyer, 2001; Williamson, 1990).

By 1990, all but four major Latin American states had succumbed or joined the Washington Consensus in regard to the virtues of free-market capitalism and the need to liberate the 'forces of economic freedom' (private enterprise, capital, the market, etc.) from the regulatory constraints of the welfare-development state. What followed was what has been described as the 'golden age of US imperialism' (viz. the facilitated entry and productive operations of large-scale profit- and market-seeking investment capital), as well as the formation of powerful peasant and indigenous social movements that were formed in the resistance to the neoliberal policy offensive, in protest against the destructive impact of neoliberal policies on their livelihoods and communities (Petras and Veltmeyer, 2005, 2009, 2013).

By the end of the decade, these movements had successfully challenged the hegemony of neoliberalism in the region as an economic model and policy agenda. What resulted was a 'red' and 'pink' tide of regime change – a turn to the Left in national politics and the formation of regimes oriented towards the 'socialism of the 21st century' (Venezuela, Bolivia, Ecuador) or a post-Washington Consensus on the need for a more inclusive form of development – 'inclusionary state activism' (Argentina, Brazil, Chile, Uruguay). The regimes formed in this progressive cycle of regime change constituted a new anti-imperialist front in the struggle against US imperialist intervention – another front to the one formed by the social movements in their resistance to the neoliberal policy agenda and direct action. It was the activism of these movements that led to the delegitimation of neoliberalism as an economic doctrine and development model, and that opened the floodgates of inclusionary state activism and the formation of a number of post-neoliberal regimes in South America (Barrett *et al.*, 2008).

Recommended reading: Barrett *et al.* (2008), Mirowski and Plehwe (2009), Petras and Veltmeyer (2005, 2009, 2013).

Imperialism and anti-imperialism in an era of extractive capitalism

The neoliberal agenda of the Washington Consensus facilitated a massive inflow of capital in the form of foreign direct investments directed towards non-traditional manufacturing, financial and high-tech information-rich services and natural resource extraction. The 1990s saw a sixfold increase in the inflows of FDI in the first four years of the decade and then another sharp increase from 1996 to 2001. In fewer than 10 years, the foreign capital accumulated by the transnational corporations had tripled (ECLAC, 2012: 71) while profits soared. John Saxe-Fernandez, a well-known Mexico-based political economist, determined that over the course of the decade that the inflow of FDI had netted enormous profits, reflected in the net outflow of US$100 billion over the entire decade of (Saxe-Fernández and Núñez, 2001).

Another major inflow occurred in the first decade of the new millennium in the context of a major expansion in the worldwide demand for natural resources and a consequent primary commodities boom in South America (Ocampo, 2007). This boom in the export of primary commodities in the energy sector of fossil and biofuels (oil and gas), as well as minerals and metals and agrofood products, primarily affected South America, which led a worldwide trend towards the (re)primarization of exports from the periphery of the system and the expansion of extractive capitalism.

The main destination points for FDI in Latin America over the past two decades have been the service sector (particularly banking and finance) and the natural resources sector: the exploration, extraction and exploitation of fossil and biofuel sources of energy, precious metals and industrial minerals, and agrofood products. In the previous era of state-led development, FDI had predominantly served as a means of financing the capitalist development of industry and a process of 'productive transformation' (technological conversion and modernization). However, two cycles of neoliberal reforms dramatically improved conditions for capital, opening up the Latin American market to goods manufactured in the North (the US, Canada and Europe) and providing greater opportunities for resource-seeking capital – consolidating the role of Latin America as a supplier of natural resources and exporter of primary commodities.

At the turn into the new millennium, the service sector accounted for almost half of FDI inflows, but data presented by ECLAC (2012: 50) point towards a steady and increasing flow of capital towards the natural resources sector, especially in South America, where the share of 'resource-seeking' (extractive) capital in total FDI increased from 10 to 30 per cent. In 2006, the inflow of 'resource-seeking' investment capital grew by 49 per cent to reach US$59 billion, which exceeded the total FDI inflows of any year since economic liberalization began in the late 1980s (UNCTAD, 2007: 53).

Despite the global financial and economic crisis at the time, FDI flows towards Latin America and the Caribbean reached a record high in 2008 (US$128.3 billion), an extraordinary development considering that FDI flows worldwide at the time had shrunk by at least 15 per cent. This counter-cyclical trend signalled the continuation of the primary commodities boom and the steady expansion of resource-seeking capital in the region. This flow of productive capital into Latin America was fuelled by two factors: high prices for primary commodities, which attracted resource-seeking capital, and the economic growth of the South American subregion, which encouraged market-seeking investment. This flow of FDI was concentrated in four countries – Argentina, Brazil, Chile and Colombia – which accounted for 89 per cent of the subregion's total inflows. The extractive industry in these countries, particularly mining, absorbed the greatest share of these inflows. For example, in 2009, Latin America received 26 per cent of global investments in mineral exploration (Sena-Fobomade, 2011). Together with the expansion of oil and gas projects, mineral extraction constitutes the single most important source of export revenues for most countries in the region.

Recommended reading: ECLAC (2012), Ocampo (2007), Saxe-Fernández and Núñez (2001), UNCTAD (2007).

The geopolitics of capital and the dynamics of extractive imperialism

Several waves of resource-seeking FDI – the inflow of extractive capital – was a major feature of the political economy of global capitalist development at the turn into the new millennium. Another was the demise of neoliberalism as an economic model – at least in South America, where powerful social movements successfully challenged this model. Over the past decade, a number of governments in this subregion, in riding a wave of anti-neoliberal sentiment generated by these movements, experienced a process of regime change – a tilt towards the left and what has been described as 'progressive extractivism' (Gudynas, 2010).

Progressive extractivism – or 'neo-extractivism' in the discourse of critical development studies – makes reference to an economic model constructed on the basis of two pillars: the 'new developmentalism', an approach based on a neostructuralist conception of the (capitalist) development process and a post-Washington Consensus on the need for a more inclusive form of development (Bresser-Pereira, 2009; Sunkel and Infante, 2009); and progressive extractivism – the use of resource rents derived from the extraction of natural resource wealth and the export of these resources in primary commodity form (Cypher, 2012; Gudynas, 2010).

Recommended reading: Petras and Veltmeyer (2014a, 2014b).

Theses on the imperialism of the 21st century

The conclusions that we have drawn from our analysis of economic and political developments in Latin America over the past two decades can be summed up in the form of nine theses:

1. The dynamic forces of capitalist development are both global in their reach and uneven in their outcomes. Furthermore, the capital accumulation process engages both the advance of capital and the agency of the imperial state in facilitating this advance.
2. While in the 1980s imperialism – the diverse powers of the imperial state – was used to remove the obstacles to the advance of capital and to facilitate the flow of productive investment into the region, in the new millennium it has been called upon to assist capital in its relation of conflict with the communities directly affected by the operations of extractive capital.
3. The new geoeconomics of capital in the region has significant implications for US imperialism and US–Latin American relations, reducing both the scope of US state power and the capacity of Washington to dictate policy or dominate economic and political relations.
4. The new millennium, in conditions of a heightened global demand for natural resources, the demise of neoliberalism as an economic model, and a number of popular upheavals and mass mobilizations, has released new forces of resistance and a dynamic process of regime change.
5. The centre-left regimes that came to power under these conditions called for public ownership of society's wealth of natural resources, the stratification and renationalization of privatized firms, the regulation of extractive capital in regard to its negative impact on livelihoods and the environment (Mother Nature), and the inclusionary activism of the state in securing a progressive redistribution of wealth and income.
6. The forces of change and resistance that emerged did not lead to a break with capitalism. Benefiting from high commodity prices, the progressive regimes that assumed state power turned away from neoliberal policy agenda towards what has been described as 'inclusionary state activism' – the use of resource rents (revenues derived from the extraction of natural resources and the exportation of commodities) to reduce poverty and create a more inclusive form of national development.
7. The fluidity of US power relations with Latin America is a product of the continuities and changes that have unfolded in Latin America. Past hegemony continues to weigh heavily but the future augurs a continued decline. Barring

major regime breakdowns in Latin America, the probability is of greater divergences in policy and a sharpening of existing contradictions between the spouting of rhetoric and political practice on the political left.

8. The destructive operations of extractive capital, facilitated and supported by the imperial state have generated powerful forces of resistance in the form of social movements. These forces are changing the contours of the class struggle, which today is focused less on the land and the labour struggle than on the negative socioenvironmental impacts of extractive capital and the dynamics of imperialist plunder and natural resource-grabbing.

9. The correlation of forces in the anti-imperialist struggle is unclear and changing, but it is evident that the United States has lost both power and influence. Taken together, these historical continuities argue for greater caution in assuming a permanent shift in imperial power relations with Latin America. Nevertheless, there are powerful reasons to consider the decline in US power as a long-term and irreversible trend.

Recommended reading: Petras and Veltmeyer (2015).

References

Amin, S. (2001). 'Imperialism and globalization'. *Monthly Review*, 53(2). Available at: www. monthlyreview.org/601amin.htm.

Arrighi, G. (2005). 'Hegemony unraveling I'. *New Left Review*, 32: 23–80.

Barrett, P., Chávez, D. and Rodríguez Garavito, C.A. (eds) (2008). *The New Latin American Left: Utopia Reborn*. London: Pluto.

Bresser-Pereira, L.C. (2009). *Developing Brazil: Overcoming the Failure of the Washington Consensus*. Boulder, CO: Lynne Rienner.

Cypher, J. (2010). 'South America's commodities boom: developmental opportunity or path dependent reversion?' *Canadian Journal of Development Studies*, 30(3–4): 635–62.

ECLAC (Economic Commission for Latin America and the Caribbean) (2012). *Statistical Yearbook for Latin America and the Caribbean*. Santiago: ECLAC.

Foster, J.B. (2003). 'The new age of imperialism'. *Monthly Review*, 55(3): 1–14.

Foster, J.B. (2006). *Naked Imperialism*. New York: Monthly Review Press.

Gudynas, E. (2010). 'The new extractivism in South America: ten urgent theses about extractivism in relation to current South American progressivism'. 21 January. Available at: www.bicusa.org/en/Article.11769.aspx.

Hardt, M. and Negri, A. (2000). *Empire*. Cambridge, MA: Harvard University Press.

Harvey, D. (2003). *The New Imperialism*. Oxford: Oxford University Press.

Klare, M. (2003). 'The new geopolitics'. *Monthly Review*, 55(3): 51–6.

Lenin, V.I. (1965). *Imperialism, the Highest Stage of Capitalism*. Peking, Russia: Foreign Language Press.

Magdoff, H. (2003). *Imperialism without Colonies*. New York: Monthly Review Press.

Mirowski, P. and Plehwe, D. (eds) (2009). *The Road from Mont Pelerin: The Making of the Neoliberal Thought Collective*. Cambridge, MA: Harvard University Press.

Ocampo, J.A. (2007). 'The macroeconomics of the Latin American economic boom'. *CEPAL Review*, 93, December: 7–28.

Panitch, L. and Leys, C. (2004). *The New Imperial Challenge*. New York: Monthly Review Press.

Petras, J. and Veltmeyer, H. (2001). *Unmasking Globalization: The New Face of Imperialism.* Halifax/London: Fernwood/Zed Books.

Petras, J. and Veltmeyer, H. (2005). *Empire with Imperialism: The Globalizing Dynamics of Neoliberal Capitalism.* Halifax/London: Fernwood/Zed Books.

Petras, J. and Veltmeyer, H. (2009). *What's Left in Latin America.* Aldershot, UK: Ashgate.

Petras, J. and Veltmeyer, H. (2013). *Imperialism and Capitalism in the 21st Century.* London: Ashgate.

Petras, J. and Veltmeyer, H. (2014a). *Extractivist Imperialism in the Americas.* Leiden: Brill Books.

Petras, J. and Veltmeyer, H. (2014b). *The New Extractivism: A Model for Latin America?* London: Zed Books.

Petras, J. and Veltmeyer, H. (2015). *Power and Resistance: US Imperialism in Latin America.* Leiden: Brill Books.

Robinson, W. (2007). 'Beyond the theory of imperialism: global capitalism and the transnational state'. *Societies Without Borders,* 2: 5–26.

Saxe-Fernández, J. and Núñez, O. (2001). 'Globalización e Imperialismo: La transferencia de Excedentes de América Latina'. In J. Saxe-Fernández *et al.* (eds), *Globalización, Imperialismo y Clase Social.* Buenos Aires/México: Editorial Lúmen, pp. 87–186.

Sena-Fobomade (2011). 'Se intensifica el extractivismo minero en América Latina'. *Foro Boliviano sobre Medio Ambiente y Desarrollo,* 03-02. Available at: http://fobomade.org.bo/art-1109.

Sunkel, O. and Infante, R. (2009). *Chile: Hacia un desarrollo inclusivo: Caso de Chile.* Santiago: ECLAC.

UNCTAD (United Nations Conference on Trade and Development) (2007). *World Investment Report 2007.* New York/Geneva: UNCTAD.

Williamson, J. (ed.) (1990). *Latin American Adjustment: How Much Has Happened?* Washington, DC: Institute for International Economics.

10

CRITICAL GLOBALIZATION STUDIES AND DEVELOPMENT

S.A. Hamed Hosseini and Barry K. Gills

Understanding 'development' and 'globalization' as abstract organizing concepts

'Globalization' and 'development' are highly contested general organizing concepts, in both theory or praxis. The term 'development' emerged in English language usage in the 1840s, coinciding with rapid industrialization, radical social transformation and European imperialism. Its use spiked following the Second World War, coinciding with decolonization and *Pax Americana* (Escobar, 2012). Usage peaked circa 1980, on the threshold of a new period of neoliberal economic globalization (Gills, 2000). Notably, 'globalization' entered the English lexicon in the early 1980s, its usage rising steeply from that time onward, rapidly overtaking 'development' and even subsuming its meaning. The relationship between the ideas/ideologies/ discourses of development and globalization remains a matter of intense theoretical debate and empirical exploration.

Both 'development' and 'globalization' have widely functioned in the literature as abstract concepts for a set of complex (interacting) historical processes of social and environmental transformation, constantly contested and negotiated among contending social forces, in arenas between states, corporations (public and private, and financial), people (all categories) and 'nature' (the web-of-life). However, development is relevant to socially constructed understandings of what constitutes the betterment of the human condition, whereas globalization normally refers to the (new) social relations of 'global' dimensions transcending previously understood boundaries of space and time.

Contestations around the concept globalization stem from a number of sources, including: conflicting ideologies that underpin different interpretations, the complexity of phenomena to which the term refers, and a problematic 'global imaginary' shared between both affirmative and critical scholars that constitutes a world view socially constructed by theorists that are predominantly from the Global North.

Some have argued that globalization is a single, overarching or dominant process, while others contend that there are a plurality of processes, or 'globalizations' (e.g. see the journal *Globalizations* at: www.tandfonline.com/rglo). Globalization tends to imply all-inclusiveness, the compression of social spaces and time. In mainstream literature, it is widely used to signify 'connectivity' and mutual interconnectedness, or supra-territorialization (i.e. a post-national condition transcending established borders based on territorial sovereign authority). It may imply a belief in the integration of the human community and of 'the-world-as-a-single-space' established upon converging economic, cultural and political relations; a 'global' integration occurring at the expense of national and local autonomy, subsuming all into a new overarching historical structure, a nascent or future 'global society' or 'global state' formation (Alamuti, 2015; Patomäki, 2008; Shaw, 2000). Critical scholarship has been investigating the 'global politics of globalization' and 'global politics of justice' (Gills, 2008a, 2008b), and, more recently, the relationship between 'globalization, development and social justice' (El Khoury, 2015), 'globalization and global citizenship' (Langran and Birk, 2016), and new 'global political theory' (Held and Maffettone, 2016).

Globalization indicates profound social transformations (e.g. wherein rapid increase in the 'quantity' and speed of flows and interactions produces a new 'quality' wherein no 'sovereign entity' can operate independently of global forces and constraints nor solve major problems independently). Multiple transnational corporations, organizations and networks now act beyond the established territorial boundaries, often with little dependence on or accountability to any single nation state. Globalists or hyper-globalists celebrate such claims, while others oppose or reject aspects of these historical changes or cast doubt upon claims over the presumed extent or newness of such change (Hirst *et al.*, 2009), its direction (James, 2009), or even the credibility of the very idea (i.e. denouncing 'globalization' as an empirically baseless theory) (Rosenberg, 2000, 2005) with no conceptual utility for understanding the complexity of current global changes. Others critique the conventional ideas of globalization for teleological, essentialist and instrumental characteristics (Amoore *et al.*, 2000); as a political language serving the interests of 'new imperialism'; and as a political economic agenda (or an ideology) invented by American think thanks, widely propagated by corporate media, and regurgitated by elites in the global south, in order to justify the agenda of further extending capital(ism)'s reach across the world (Bond and Garcia, 2015; Fuchs, 2010).

There is a broad variety of conceptual framings and research approaches: ranging in perspective from considering globalization as a new period in world history; an inevitable process of human progress resulting from unprecedented acceleration in interconnectedness (a product of technological innovations); leading to greater economic openness among globalized societies (Huwart and Verdier, 2013; Stiglitz,

2002); to the view that globalization is only a new form of capitalist discourse orchestrated by a transnational class or cosmopolitan-oriented global elite, ideologically constructing a new global hegemony wherein state-centred discourses of 'development' lose their legitimacy (Friedman and Friedman, 2013); to a set of theories of 'late modernization' wherein space-time is compressed, creating new global risks (Giddens, 2000); to its consideration as a multi-century process of global stratification that can be traced back to the 16th-century 'discovery' of the Americas, the expansion of European colonialism, or even earlier, to the period when new world religions first extended their global reach (Arrighi, 2005; Sklair, 1999).

Sceptics have argued there is nothing new or surprising about today's (economic) globalization (Arestis *et al.*, 2012; Hirst *et al.*, 2009). Some divide the long world history of globalization patterns (Pieterse, 2017) into successive waves (e.g. cycles of expansion and contraction) (Frank and Gills, 1993) and consider the most recent wave (starting from the end of the Cold War) as highly distinctive (Chase-Dunn and Gills, 2005; Robertson, 1992). According to such historical interpretations, globalization has been multi-centric (and the 'centre' 'shifts' across space and time) and cyclical, for example via 'rise and demise' patterns (Chase-Dunn and Hall, 1997). Therefore, evidence of recent increasing global trade, financial and communications integration is potentially 'reversible', and may yet rise again from somewhere else (e.g. the 'Global East' where it had yet older 'oriental globalization' historical roots) (Abu-Lughod, 1989; Frank, 1998, 2014; Frank and Gills, 1993; Hodos, 2017; Pieterse, 2006).

Recommended reading: Ritzer (2012), Scholte (2008), Veltmeyer (2012).

Globalization studies

In the summer of 2014, *Globalizations* published a special issue on 'Globalization: the career of a concept', featuring interviews with 12 leading scholars in the field, and an introduction examining the lineages and processes, and the role of key scholars whereby the concept of globalization became so important (James and Steger, 2014). The idea of globalization has profoundly challenged pre-existing discourses, theories and practices of 'development'. There are, however, significant resonances and overlaps between globalization studies and development studies. McMichael (2005: 111) argues, however, that the separation between the two academic fields is ideologically constructed, and yet draws upon a widely shared but problematic dichotomization, i.e. that between transnational analyses and state-centred analyses of social change. State-centred political discourses of 'development' have, it is claimed, increasingly lost their legitimating power. A critical approach is necessary to problematize this foundational and yet deeply misleading dualism between development and globalization. This is particularly acute in the current context of what some call the 'post-globalization' era (Latham, 2016), characterized by the weakening of previous patterns of global and regional integration, and a seemingly endless economic weakening following the global financial crisis of 2008 and its aftermath (Roberts, 2016), and the widespread resurgence of nationalist/populist politics and ideologies.

There is now a large body of literature, structured around extensive studies addressing a broad range of global issues, including debates over theories, global structures, processes and transitions, which together constitute a major field of study (Ritzer, 2007). This field has evolved from initially dominant reductionist accounts of globalization that stressed structural standardization processes (e.g. economic rationalization, Americanization, McDonaldization or cultural imperialism) towards more diversified accounts of the complexities of global transitions, requiring more interdisciplinary approaches (Turner, 2010). There is almost no major social, environmental, economic, political or cultural issue that is currently left untouched by globalization studies. In its broadest sense, globalization studies interacts with not only development studies, but with numerous related fields, including international relations, (international) political economy, regional and global studies, political geography, political theory, communication and media studies, (cosmopolitan) political philosophy, (global) sociology and anthropology, and cultural studies, thus rendering contemporary globalization studies profoundly interdisciplinary (e.g. see the book series: *Rethinking Globalizations*, www.routledge.com/Rethinking-Globalizations/book-series/RG).

Social scientific studies of globalization may be characterized along five foci. These five foci of globalization studies are not mutually exclusive. Within each domain, there are multiple and sometimes conflicting perspectives.

In the first focus, globalization studies is concerned with the significance of the increase in the density of 'large-scale interaction networks', communications, mobilities and flows of capital, labour, knowledge, services, resources and goods, arguing for or against the idea that such an increasing density may have worked in favour of a greater 'global integration' (Appadurai, 1999; Castells, 1996; Held *et al.*, 1999; Hirst and Thompson, 1996; Negri and Zolo, 2003; Rodrik, 2011; Zolo, 1997). Although the multidimensional, processual, partial and nonlinear nature of globalization processes is now widely acknowledged, avoiding the exaggerations made by hyper-globalists (such as Dollar, 2005; Ohmae, 1990), the stress still uncritically remains on the convergent nature of multiple transformations towards the emergence of a new historical epoch (Held, 2006: 294; Scholte, 2008).

The second focus has attempted to explore the bifurcating or polarizing impacts of economic globalization, highlighting those processes that entail growing social inequalities, disparities or divergences within and/or between societal, spatial, gendered, racial, national or cultural groupings (Dicken, 2011; Galbraith, 2012; Lindio-McGovern and Wallimann, 2016; Mills, 2009; Saith, 2011; Wade, 2004). Much academic and public discussion has taken place concerning the so-called 'winners and losers' of globalization (Sassen, 2010). It is difficult to ignore the persistently high aggregate levels of global poverty and mounting evidence of rising inequality in wealth (Galbraith, 2012; Piketty and Goldhammer, 2014). While the Occupy movement highlighted the gap between the richest '1%' and all the rest (the '99%'), the beneficiaries of really existing globalization processes are estimated to be no more than one-fifth of the total world population (McMichael, 2008). Notwithstanding arguments and protestations to the contrary, neoliberal(izing) economic globalization policies promoting 'economic growth' do not necessarily promote either gender equality or 'pro-poor' outcomes (Held and Kaya, 2007; Schuerkens, 2010).

The third focus is on the webs of power relations (or 'governance') directed by the international financial institutions, powerful states, transnational corporations, 'transnational capitalist class' (or 'global corporate elite'), their associated hegemonic (political) cultures and ideologies, and the expansion of these throughout the world, especially since the end of the Cold War (Carroll and Carson, 2003; Hardt and Negri, 2000; Sklair, 2001). 'Global governance' in the post-2015 era must move humanity towards a more equitable, just and sustainable world, as McKeon (2017) argues. While the most powerful corporate and military elites and nation states in the current world (dis)order are still able to prominently shape the world's direction in response to climate change (Buxton and Hayes, 2015), new political forces are simultaneously arising within and across many nations, drawing on anti-globalization sentiments and lived experiences of (mal)development practices, towards re-constituting the global forces of resistance (Cox and Nilsen, 2014; de Sousa Santos, 2006).

The fourth focus, often assuming a logic of cause and effect, explores the impacts of globalization at all societal levels from the 'local' to 'global', including the development of (new) social risks, socio-ecological problems (including eco-destruction, climate change), food and energy crises, financial instability and uncertainties, health inequalities and crises ('epidemiologic' and 'pathological' profiles of global change), human insecurity, terrorism, violence, war, social disorders, crime, sex/drug/organs/human trafficking, migration, population mobility and displacements, identity crises (e.g. among youth), and social tensions (Beck, 1999; Birn et al., 2016; Curran, 2016; Dasgupta, 2004; George and Page, 2004; Gills, 2011; Glassman et al., 2004; Held and Kaya, 2007; Munck, 2010).

The fifth focus is that placed upon transformative potential and (new) forces of resistance, that oppose 'hegemonic globalization' processes constructed through such mechanisms as free trade regimes (Hopewell, 2016); official development projects and assistance (e.g. funded by governments or by the World Bank); the role of the IMF, TNCs' foreign investments and social and environmental practices; the changing nature of war and militarism; the new extractivism and the commodification of environmental resources (Veltmeyer and Petras, 2014) and indigenous knowledge; the postcolonialist enclosures of the commons through the privatization of public assets and corporatization of the public sector; and the adoption of austerity measures (della Porta, 2015; Gills, 2000; Goodman and James, 2007; Hosseini, 2010; Lemert et al., 2010; Reitan, 2007; Turner and Holton, 2015; Veltmeyer, 2008).

Critical Globalization Studies (CGS)

Although globalization studies is a very broad interdisciplinary field, we may speak of a widely shared interest among many researchers in taking a 'critical' approach. The vision is 'critical' in the sense of holding some of at least six features:

(i) epistemologically reflexive and methodologically skeptical of positivistic approaches; (ii) discursively deconstructionist; (iii) analytically counter-hegemonic; (iv) ontologically mindful of 'complexity', disorder and chaos; (v) culturally counter-orientalist; and (vi) normatively emancipatory or transformative in praxis. These six features are, respectively, elaborated upon briefly in the following subsections (Appelbaum and Robinson, 2005; Fuchs, 2010; Mittelman, 2005).

Epistemological reflexivity and methodological scepticism

Many sociological studies in the CGS have Lupon started to draw the legacy of 'critical social theory', mainly underpinned by the German idealism and abstract Kantian universalism, the critique of instrumental rationality and the rejection of positivism. This post-empiricist tradition has widened its scope by incorporating a broader range of analytical approaches, including historical materialist, dialogical, and post-structuralist analyses. The sufficiency of this tradition in dealing with non-Western experiences has, however, been questioned more recently (El-Ojeili and Hayden, 2006; O'Byrne, 2005; Roach, 2008).

Discursive deconstructionism

A group of CGS scholars have attempted not only to demystify and de-reify the mainstream (both affirmative and critical) notions of 'globalization' – as epistemes/discourses that are socially constructed by the mass media, political authorities, intellectual powerhouses and the dominating schools of economic and social sciences – but also question the discursive and cognitive binaries embedded in these notions, such as the global and the local, the national and the transnational, the cause and the effect, change and stability, system and its environment, process and structure, territoriality and supra-territoriality (see Hosseini, 2015a; Sassen, 2008b; Urry, 2003). Demystification starts from deconstructing the term 'globalization' and its associated ideologically constructed and simplistic dualisms, and then extends into discussions of the implications of such demystifications for understanding practical issues such as spatial disparities, solidarity networks and cosmopolitan interactions. New concepts such as 'glocalization', 'creolization' and 'transversalization' are coined in order to capture such movement beyond the old binaries (Cohen and Toninato, 2010; Hosseini, 2015b; Robertson, 1995).

Highlighting the questions of power and hegemony

Another element of CGS comprises attempts to highlight how old power structures are being restructured through globalization processes, in the forms of new colonialism, new imperialism or the new transnational capitalist class, as well as the intensifying democratic deficits at both national and international political levels. More importantly, these studies politicize the scholarly and non-scholarly discourses of globalization, by questioning the way the dominant globalist imaginaries and discourses in fact serve the interests of institutionalized power, create hegemony and depoliticize our understandings of social change. This criticism of embedded blindness to the question of power could be extended to the field of CGS itself as part of its own commitment to *self-reflexivity* (Buckley, 2013; Chomsky, 2016; Gills, 2008a).

Ontological mindfulness of complexity and disorder

Attempts are being made to theorize the complexities of global transformations such as the contradictory associations between global integrations and fragmentations, order and disorder, and how the multidimensionality and the multi-spatiality of global change should be grasped. These efforts can be differentiated between those who draw directly on complexity or chaos theory and those who use a broader theoretical framing (Marshall, 2013; Urry, 2003; Walby, 2009).

Rejecting Eurocentrism and Orientalism

More recent developments, however, strongly argue for going beyond the Euro-centric legacy and 'metropole-centred logic' that still exists even among many critical theorists, by incorporating Southern and subaltern perspectives (Connell, 2007; de Sousa Santos, 2007) and by reflecting on the experiences of the solidarity networks and internationalist coalitions in the so-called Global South. The wider implications of new approaches to studying Southern experiences globalization studies in certainty need to be discussed. However, many such promises have yet remained unfulfilled in the realm of mainstream CGS (Amar, 2012, 2014; de Sousa Santos, 2014; Gray and Gills, 2016).

Emancipatory orientation

CGS goes beyond mere criticism of corporate modes of production and repro-duction, and seeks to systematically and conscientiously pave the way for under-standing forces of resistance, transformative movements, and post-imperialist, post-globalist and post-capitalist futures. These studies range from those who have taken neo-Gramscian or neo-Polanyian approaches of theorizing resistances based on the binary of hegemony versus counter-hegemony (Gill, 2008; Munck, 2007; Olesen, 2011), to post-Gramscian approaches to dissident knowledge and praxis (Hosseini, 2010) that acknowledge the complex contextual specificity and historicity (Drainville, 2012), and the transversality of social forces involved in multiple forms of power struggles and contestations for radical social transformation (Buckley, 2013).

   Recommended reading: Hosseini *et al.* (2016), Patomäki and Teivainen (2004), Robinson and Tormey (2009), Veltmeyer (2011).

Beyond CGS: is it really all about globalization?

A special issue of *Globalizations* in 2013 hosted a debate on global studies between a number of leading scholars in this field. Jan Nederveen Pieterse (2013), in his extensive review of global studies, criticized the field for not being adequately and systematically interdisciplinary, multi-centric and recognizant of the multidimensionality of global change. He nevertheless recognizes a rather linear progress in the evaluation of the field, which itself indicates an emerging capacity for what he envisions as an analytically different approach to the existing trends. From their early stages, social scientific studies of globalization have been aware of the multiplicity of global transformations and of the serious structural contradictions promoted by globalization, as Steger (2013) reminds us in his response to Pieterse. One may, however, still agree with Pieterse that this trend is not satisfactorily mature and requires greater efforts to become more critical. What remains puzzling is the situation whereby the more these efforts have acknowledged the existing complexities, the more they have added to our confusion(s); mostly as the result of addressing so many contradictory processes under integrative framings.

Many studies show that processes through which social relations have crossed their traditionally established boundaries have actually been asymmetrical, partial and directed by sources of power (Held and Kaya, 2007; Scholte, 2000). These processes have resulted in responses such as the World Social Forum that attempt to connect transformative social forces from across the world, but also in fragmentations, e.g. in regional entities such as the EU (recently manifested by the Brexit referendum result in the UK) or mobilization of right-wing movements and national-populism, as well as a broad range of various reformist, hybridizing and radically transformative alternative movements across the globe.

The acknowledgement of the partiality of globalization processes is a step forward (Scholte, 2008). However, such a moderation by changing the 'G word' to a 'g word' still fails to recognize that there are similarly important processes that need to be analysed in their interactive relation to one another, rather than separately, as is the case today in much of existing global studies. This includes processes such as *localization, internationalization, polarization, Americanization, McDonaldization, creolization, hybridization* and *Balkanization* (O'Byrne and Hensby, 2011). These are multiple processes in interaction with one another, rather than simply being the multiform of one mega-phenomenon called globalization.

The more such processes infiltrate into our analysis, the more the analytical autonomy of 'globalization' weakens. Pieterse's (2013) proposed reformation, by maintaining commitment to the centrality of globalization in his ideal value-added global studies, however, leaves the current paradigm mainly unchallenged. CGS is no longer exclusively about globalization, since the notion itself, whether in the sense of time–space compression in all major aspects of life across the globe, or as an expansionist economic (neo)liberalization trend, has exhausted its capacity to play the role of the 'theory of everything', and in fact has already started to lose its conceptual centrality, reflecting the way recent major social transitions are now transpiring.

In today's world, cross-societal communications and connections have increased and there are greater capacities for various modes of convergences. Nevertheless, social and cultural divisions have also widened, while inequalities within and between countries are acute and becoming even more pronounced (Piketty and

Goldhammer, 2014). The planet's bio-capacity to sustain the present form of global 'development' is nearly exhausted. Much of 'development' around the world could be characterized as 'maldevelopment', in which long-term negative consequences tend to outweigh short-term positive benefits (Moore, 2015), thus prompting the rise of post-development theory, the call for 'alternatives to development', and the search for new roads to human empowerment and liberation (Dussel *et al.*, 2013; Escobar, 2008; Gibson-Graham, 2006; Gudynas, 2016; Ziai, 2015).

While many are the victims of globalizing changes and the dominant paradigm of 'economic development', they have also continuously shown their capacity to respond, to resist and to initiate 'bottom–up' social transformation (Selwyn, 2014), and still in many cases seeking to resiliently survive under intense pressures. All of these complex and fluidly changing social responses, movements and new patterns of transformative praxes cannot be theorized under one single umbrella term or a single theory of politics. We must be prepared to accept both the historicity and extreme complexity of globalization, while embracing the call to liberate our minds from imprisonment in the past and from the centrality of Eurocentric thinking. New forms of 'transversal cosmopolitanist' praxes may be one avenue of hope for the future (Gills *et al.*, 2016), with scope to radically transform both globalization and development in theory and practice.

The concept of globalization is not to be used to simply refer to many contradictory, uneven processes of 'transformation'. In Urry's words, '[n]either the global nor the local can exist without the other', or, as Sassen (2008a) puts it, '[p]art of the research task is, then, decode, and, more generally, discover and detect the global *inside* the national' (emphasis added). Steger (2013) reminds us that globalization is not just about 'the transcending of traditional boundaries – but also about process of reterritorialization'; 'that is, inscriptions and eruptions of the global *within* the national and the local' (emphasis added). We wish to conclude this chapter by emphasizing that this analytical move also requires an equal, if not greater, scrutiny of the upsurge of the local and the national (in the forms of resistance and sources of future transitions) from *within* the global (Hosseini, 2013). Therefore, we redefine 'globalization' as an 'orientation' in social change rather than a (single or singular) historical phenomenon exclusively worthy of holding an analytical autonomy in our theories. This move requires us to see globalization as part of a bigger picture, and to further critically explore the interactions between globalization processes and other ones, especially 'development' (i.e. moving towards a more genuinely critical programme in both 'global' and 'globalization' studies).

Recommended reading: Connell (2007), Gills *et al.* (2016).

References

Abu-Lughod, J.L. (1989). *Before European Hegemony: The World System A.D. 1250–1350*. New York/Oxford: Oxford University Press.

Alamuti, M.M. (2015). *Critical Rationalism and Globalisation: Towards the Sociology of the Open Global Society*. London: Routledge.

Amar, P. (2012). 'Global South to the rescue: emerging humanitarian superpowers and globalizing rescue industries'. *Globalizations*, 9(1): 1–13. doi:10.1080/14747731.2012. 657408.

Amar, P. (2014). *The Middle East and Brazil: Perspectives on the New Global South.* Bloomington, IN: Indiana University Press.

Amoore, L., Dodgson, R., Gills, B.K., Langley, P., Marshall, D. and Watson, I. (2000). 'Overturning "globalization": resisting teleology, reclaiming politics, new political economy'. In B.K. Gills (ed.), *Globalization and the Politics of Resistance.* Basingstoke: Palgrave, pp. 12–28.

Appadurai, A. (1999). Globalization and the research imagination. *International Social Science Journal*, 51(2): 229–38.

Appelbaum, R.P. and Robinson, W.I. (eds) (2005). *Critical Globalization Studies.* New York: Routledge.

Arestis, P., Chortareas, G., Desli, E. and Pelagidis, T. (2012). 'Trade flows revisited: further evidence on globalisation'. *Cambridge Journal of Economics*, 36(2): 481–93. doi:http://cje. oxfordjournals.org/content/by/year.

Arrighi, G. (2005) 'Globalization in world-systems perspectives'. In R.P. Appelbaum and W.I. Robinson (eds), *Critical Globalization Studies.* New York: Routledge, pp. 33–54.

Beck, U. (1999). *World Risk Society.* Malden, MA: Polity Press.

Birn, A.-E., Pillay, Y. and Holtz, T.H. (2016). *Textbook of Global Health.* Oxford: Oxford University Press.

Bond, P. and Garcia, A. (eds) (2015) *BRICS: An Anti-Capitalist Critique.* London: Pluto Press.

Buckley, K.M. (2013). *Global Civil Society and Transversal Hegemony: The Globalization-Contestation Nexus.* New York: Routledge.

Buxton, N. and Hayes, B. (2015). *The Secure and the Dispossessed: How the Military and Corporations Are Shaping a Climate-Changed World.* London: Pluto Press.

Carroll, W.K. and Carson, C. (2003). 'The network of global corporations and elite policy groups: a structure for transnational capitalist class formation?' *Global Networks: A Journal of Transnational Affairs*, 3(1): 29–57.

Castells, M. (1996). *The Rise of the Network Society.* Cambridge: Blackwell.

Chase-Dunn, C.K. and Gills, B.K. (2005). 'Waves of globalization and resistance in the capitalist world-system: social movements and critical global studies'. In R.P. Appelbaum and W.I. Robinson (eds), *Critical Globalization Studies.* New York: Routledge, pp. 45–54.

Chase-Dunn, C.K. and Hall, T.D. (1997). *Rise and Demise: Comparing World-Systems.* Boulder, CO: Westview Press.

Chomsky, N. (2016). *Who Rules the World?* London: Hamish Hamilton.

Cohen, R. and Toninato, P. (2010). *The Creolization Reader: Studies in Mixed Identities and Cultures.* London/New York: Routledge.

Connell, R. (2007). 'The Northern theory of globalization'. *Sociological Theory*, 25(4): 368–85.

Cox, L. and Nilsen, A.G. (2014). *We Make Our Own History: Marxism and Social Movements in the Twilight of Neoliberalism.* London: Pluto Press.

Curran, D. (2016). 'Risk society and Marxism: beyond simple antagonism'. *Journal of Classical Sociology*, 16(3): 280.

Dasgupta, S. (2004). *The Changing Face of Globalization.* Thousand Oaks, CA: Sage.

de Sousa Santos, B. (2006). *The Rise of the Global Left: The World Social Forum and Beyond.* London: Zed Books.

de Sousa Santos, B. (2007). *Another Knowledge Is Possible: Beyond Northern Epistemologies.* London/New York: Verso.

de Sousa Santos, B. (2014). *Epistemologies of the South: Justice Against Epistemicide*. London: Paradigm.

della Porta, D. (2015). *Social Movements in Times of Austerity: Bringing Capitalism Back into Protest Analysis*. Malden, MA: Polity.

Dicken, P. (2011). *Global Shift: Mapping the Changing Contours of the World Economy*. London: Sage.

Dollar, D. (2005). 'Globalization, poverty, and inequality since 1980'. *World Bank Research Observer*, 20(2): 145–75. doi:10.1093/wbro/lki008.

Drainville, A.C. (2012). *A History of World Order and Resistance: The Making and Unmaking of Global Subjects*. London: Routledge.

Dussel, E.D., Vallega, A.A. and Mendieta, E. (2013). *Ethics of Liberation in the Age of Globalization and Exclusion*. Durham, NC: Duke University Press.

El Khoury, A. (2015). *Globalization, Development and Social Justice: A Propositional Political Approach*. London: Routledge.

El-Ojeili, C. and Hayden, P. (2006). *Critical Theories of Globalization*. Basingstoke: Palgrave Macmillan.

Escobar, A. (2008). 'Development, trans/modernities, and the politics of theory'. *Focaal*, 2008(52): 127–35. doi:10.3167/fcl.2008.520109.

Escobar, A. (2012). *Encountering Development: The Making and Unmaking of the Third World* (with a new preface by the author). Princeton, NJ: Princeton University Press.

Frank, A.G. (1998). *ReOrient: Global Economy in the Asian Age*. Berkeley, CA: University of California Press.

Frank, A.G. (2014). *ReOrienting the 19th Century: Global Economy in the Continuing Asian Age* (edited and with an introduction by R.A. Denemark; afterword by B.K. Gills). Boulder, CO: Paradigm.

Frank, A.G. and Gills, B.K. (1993). *The World System: Five Hundred Years or Five Thousand?* London: Routledge.

Friedman, J. and Friedman, K.E. (2013). 'Globalization as a discourse of hegemonic crisis: a global systemic analysis'. *American Ethnologist*, 40(2): 244–57.

Fuchs, C. (2010). 'Critical globalization studies: an empirical and theoretical analysis of the new imperialism'. *Science & Society*, 74(2): 215–47.

Galbraith, J.K. (2012). *Inequality and Instability: A Study of the World Economy Just Before the Great Crisis*. New York: Oxford University Press.

George, V. and Page, R.M. (eds) (2004). *Global Social Problems*. Cambridge: Polity Press.

Gibson-Graham, J.K. (2006). *A Postcapitalist Politics*. Minneapolis, MN: University of Minnesota Press.

Giddens, A. (2000). *Runaway World: How Globalization is Reshaping our Lives*. New York: Routledge.

Gill, S. (2008). *Power and Resistance in the New World Order*. Basingstoke/New York: Palgrave Macmillan.

Gills, B.K. (2000). *Globalization and the Politics of Resistance*. Basingstoke: Palgrave.

Gills, B.K. (2008a). *The Global Politics of Globalization: 'Empire' vs 'Cosmopolis'*. London/New York: Routledge.

Gills, B.K. (2008b). *Globalization and the Global Politics of Justice*. London: Routledge.

Gills, B.K. (2011). *Globalization in Crisis*. London: Routledge.

Gills, B.K., Goodman, J. and Hosseini, S.H. (2016). 'Theorizing alternatives to capital: towards a critical cosmopolitanist framework'. *European Journal of Social Theory* (published online before print, 10 April 2016): 1–18. doi:10.1177/1368431016642609.

Glassman, R.M., Swatos, W.H. and Denison, B.J. (2004). *Social Problems in Global Perspective*. Lanham, MD: University Press of America.

Goodman, J. and James, P. (eds) (2007). *Nationalism and Global Solidarities: Alternative Projections to Neoliberal Globalisation*. London/New York: Routledge.

Gray, K. and Gills, B.K. (2016). 'South–South cooperation and the rise of the Global South'. *Third World Quarterly*, 37(4): 557–74. doi:10.1080/01436597.2015.1128817.

Gudynas, E. (2016). 'Beyond varieties of development: disputes and alternatives'. *Third World Quarterly*, 37(4): 721–32.

Hardt, M. and Negri, A. (2000). *Empire*. Cambridge, MA: Harvard University Press.

Held, D. (2006). *Models of Democracy*. Cambridge: Polity Press.

Held, D. and Kaya, A. (eds) (2007). *Global Inequality: Patterns and Explanations*. Cambridge: Polity Press.

Held, D. and Maffettone, P. (2016). *Global Political Theory*. Cambridge: Polity Press.

Held, D., McGrew, A., Goldblatt, D. and Perraton, J. (1999). 'Globalization'. *Global Governance*, 5(4): 483–96.

Hirst, P. and Thompson, G. (1996). *Globalization in Question*. Cambridge: Polity Press.

Hirst, P., Thompson, G. and Bromley, S. (2009). *Globalization in Question*. Cambridge: Polity.

Hodos, T. (ed.) (2017). *The Routledge Handbook of Archaeology and Globalization*. London/New York: Routledge.

Hopewell, K. (2016). *Breaking the WTO: How Emerging Powers Disrupted the Neoliberal Project*. Stanford, CA: Stanford University Press.

Hosseini, S.A.H. (2010). *Alternative Globalizations: An Integrative Approach to Studying Dissident Knowledge in the Global Justice Movement Milton Park*. New York: Routledge.

Hosseini, S.A.H. (2013). 'Occupy cosmopolitanism: ideological transversalization in the age of global economic uncertainties'. *Globalizations*, 10(3): 425–38.

Hosseini, S.A.H. (2015a). 'A transversalist justice: responses to the corporate globalization'. In S. Litz (ed.), *Globalization and Responsibility*. Champaign, IL: Common Ground Publishing, pp. 71–101.

Hosseini, S.A.H. (2015b). 'Transversality in diversity: experiencing networks of confusion and convergence in the world social forum'. *International and Multidisciplinary Journal of Social Sciences-Rimcis*, 4(1): 54–87.

Hosseini, S.A.H., Gills, B.K. and Goodman, J. (2016). 'Towards transversal cosmopolitanism: understanding alternative praxes in the global field of transformative movements'. *Globalizations* (published online before print, 16 August 2016): 1–18. doi:10.1080/147 47731.2016.1217619.

Huwart, J.-Y. and Verdier, L. (2013). *Economic Globalisation: Origins and Consequences*. *OECD Insights*. Paris: OECD.

James, H. (2009). *The Creation and Destruction of Value: The Globalization Cycle*. Cambridge, MA: Harvard University Press.

James, P. and Steger, M.B. (2014). 'A genealogy of "globalization": the career of a concept. *Globalizations*, 11(4): 417–34. doi:10.1080/14747731.2014.951186.

Langran, I.V. and Birk, T. (2016). *Globalization and Global Citizenship: Interdisciplinary Approaches*. London/New York: Routledge.

Latham, R. (2016). *The Politics of Evasion: A Post-Globalization Dialogue Along the Edge of the State*. London/New York: Routledge.

Lemert, C.C., Elliot, A., Chaffee, D. and Hsu, E. (eds) (2010). *Globalization: A Reader*. London/New York: Routledge.

Lindio-McGovern, L. and Wallimann, I. (2016). *Globalization and Third World Women: Exploitation, Coping and Resistance*. London: Routledge.

Marshall, J.P. (2013). 'The information society: permanent crisis through the (dis)ordering of networks'. *Global Networks: A Journal of Transnational Affairs*, 13(3): 290–309. doi:10.1111/Glob.12023.

McKeon, N. (2017). 'Global governance in the post-2015 era: transformative towards a more equitable and sustainable world?' *Globalizations*, forthcoming. doi:10.1080/1474 7731.2016.1244757.

McMichael, P. (2005). 'Globalization and development studies'. In R.P. Appelbaum and W.I. Robinson (eds), *Critical Globalization Studies*. New York: Routledge, pp. 111–20.

McMichael, P. (2008). *Development and Social Change: A Global Perspective*. Los Angeles, CA: Pine Forge Press.

Mills, M. (2009). 'Globalization and inequality'. *European Sociological Review*, 25(1): 1-8. doi:10.1093/Esr/Jcn046.

Mittelman, J.H. (2005). 'What is a critical globalization studies?' In R.P. Appelbaum and W.I. Robinson (eds), *Critical Globalization Studies*. New York: Routledge, pp. 19–29.

Moore, J.W. (2015). *Capitalism in the Web of Life: Ecology and the Accumulation of Capital*. New York: Verso.

Munck, R. (2007). *Globalization and Contestation: The New Great Counter-Movement*. London: Routledge.

Munck, R. (2010). 'Globalization, crisis and social transformation: a view from the South'. *Globalizations*, 7(1–2): 235–46.

Negri, A. and Zolo, D. (2003). 'Empire and the multitude: a dialogue on the new order of globalization'. *Radical Philosophy*, 120, July–August: 23–37.

O'Byrne, D.J. (2005). 'Toward a critical theory of globalization: a Habermasian approach'. In R.P. Appelbaum and W.I. Robinson (eds), *Critical Globalization Studies*. New York: Routledge, pp. 75–87.

O'Byrne, D.J. and Hensby, A. (2011). *Theorizing Global Studies*. Basingstoke/New York: Palgrave Macmillan.

Ohmae, K. (1990). *Borderless World: Power and Strategy in the Interlinked Economy*. London: Collins.

Olesen, T. (2011). *Power and Transnational Activism*. London/New York: Routledge.

Patomäki, H. (2008). *The Political Economy of Global Security: War, Future Crises and Changes in Global Governance*. London/New York: Routledge.

Patomäki, H. and Teivainen, T. (2004). *A Possible World: Democratic Transformation of Global Institutions Strategy*. London/New York: Zed Books.

Pieterse, J.N. (2006). 'Oriental globalization: past and present'. In G. Delanty (ed.), *Europe and Asia Beyond East and West*. London: Routledge, pp. 61–73.

Pieterse, J.N. (2013). 'What is global studies?' *Globalizations*, 10(4): 499–514. doi:10.1080/ 14747731.2013.806746.

Pieterse, J.N. (2017). 'Long histories of globalization'. In T. Hodos (ed.), *The Routledge Handbook of Archaeology and Globalization*. London/New York: Routledge, pp. 935–53.

Piketty, T. and Goldhammer, A. (2014). *Capital in the Twenty-First Century*. Cambridge, MA: The Belknap Press of Harvard University Press.

Reitan, R. (2007). *Global Activism*. London/New York: Routledge.

Ritzer, G. (2007). *The Blackwell Companion to Globalization*, Malden, MA: Blackwell.

Ritzer, G. (2012). *The Wiley-Blackwell Encyclopedia of Globalization*. Chichester, UK/Malden, MA: Wiley Blackwell.

Roach, S.C. (2008). *Critical Theory and International Relations: A Reader*. New York: Routledge.

Roberts, M. (2016). *The Long Depression: How It Happened, Why It Happened, and What Happens Next*. Chicago, IL: Haymarket Books.

Robertson, R. (1992). *Globalization: Social Theory and Global Culture*. London: Sage.

Robertson, R. (1995). 'Glocalization: time-space and homogeneity-heterogeneity'. In M. Featherstone, S.M. Lash and R. Robertson (eds), *Global Modernities*. London: Sage, pp. 25–47.

Robinson, A. and Tormey, S. (2009). 'Resisting "global justice": disrupting the colonial "emancipatory" logic of the West'. *Third World Quarterly*, 30(8): 1395–409. doi:10.1080/01436590903321836.

Rodrik, D. (2011). *The Globalization Paradox: Democracy and the Future of the World Economy*. New York: W.W. Norton & Co.

Rosenberg, J. (2000). *The Follies of Globalisation Theory: Polemical Essays*. London/New York: Verso.

Rosenberg, J. (2005). 'Globalization theory: a post mortem'. *International Politics*, 42(1): 2–74.

Saith, A. (2011). 'Inequality, imbalance, instability: reflections on a structural crisis'. *Development and Change*, 42(1): 70–86.

Sassen, S. (2008a). 'Neither global nor national: novel assemblages of territory, authority and rights'. *Ethics & Global Politics*, 1(1–2): 61–79. doi:10.3402/egp.v1i1.1814.

Sassen, S. (2008b). *Territory, Authority, Rights: From Medieval to Global Assemblages*. Princeton, NJ: Princeton University Press.

Sassen, S. (2010). 'A savage sorting of winners and losers: contemporary versions of primitive accumulation'. *Globalizations*, 7(1–2): 23–50. doi:10.1080/14747731003593091.

Scholte, J.A. (2000). *Globalization: a Critical Introduction*. New York: St. Martin's Press.

Scholte, J.A. (2008). 'Defining globalisation'. *The World Economy*, 31(11): 1471–502. doi:10.1111/j.1467-9701.2007.01019.x.

Schuerkens, U. (2010). *Globalization and Transformations of Social Inequality*. New York: Routledge.

Selwyn, B. (2014). *The Global Development Crisis*. Cambridge: Polity Press.

Shaw, M. (2000). *Theory of the Global State: Globality as Unfinished Revolution*. Cambridge: Cambridge University Press.

Sklair, L. (1999). 'Competing conceptions of globalization'. *Journal of World-Systems Research*, 2, Summer: 143–63.

Sklair, L. (2001). *The Transnational Capitalist Class*. Oxford: Blackwell.

Steger, M.B. (2013). 'It's about globalization, after all: four framings of global studies. A response to Jan Nederveen Pieterse's "What is global studies?"'. *Globalizations*, 10(6): 771–7. doi:10.1080/14747731.2013.845958.

Stiglitz, J.E. (2002). *Globalization and Its Discontents*. New York/London: W.W. Norton & Co.

Turner, B.S. (ed.) (2010). *The Routledge International Handbook of Globalization Studies*. London/New York: Routledge.

Turner, B.S. and Holton, R.J. (eds) (2015). *The Routledge International Handbook of Globalization Studies*. New York: Routledge.

Urry, J. (2003). *Global Complexity*. Malden, MA: Polity.

Veltmeyer, H. (2008). *New Perspectives on Globalization and Antiglobalization: Prospects for a New World Order?* Aldershot, UK: Ashgate.

Veltmeyer, H. (2011). 'Unrest and change: dispatches from the frontline of a class war in Egypt'. *Globalizations*, 8(5): 609–16. doi:10.1080/14747731.2011.625823.

Veltmeyer, H. (2012). 'Globalization: alternative perspectives'. In G. Ritzer (ed.), *The Wiley-Blackwell Encyclopedia of Globalization*. London: John Wiley & Sons.

Veltmeyer, H. and Petras, J.F. (2014). *The New Extractivism: A Post-Neoliberal Development Model or Imperialism of the Twenty-First Century?* London: Zed Books.

Wade, R.H. (2004). 'Is globalization reducing poverty and inequality?' *International Journal of Health Services*, 34(3): 381–414.

Walby, S. (2009). *Globalization and Inequalities: Complexity and Contested Modernities*. London: Sage.

Ziai, A. (2015). 'Post-development: premature burials and haunting ghosts'. *Development and Change*, 46(4): 833–54. doi:10.1111/dech.12177.

Zolo, D. (1997). *Cosmopolis: Prospects for World Government*. Cambridge: Polity Press.

11

THE END OF GLOBALIZATION

Walden Bello

The Great Recession (or the Great Financialization, as Kari Polanyi Levitt terms it) has lasted a decade. In the US and Europe, the heady years of globalization, when seemingly inexhaustible credit allowed the middle classes access to an unimaginable range of goods, are fast fading from the popular memory. With the economies of the US and Europe barely registering growth, the great engine of capitalism appears palpably to have downshifted. Indefinitely. With unemployment in the US failing to drop below 8 per cent and hitting 20–25 per cent in the worst affected European countries, we have what economist Paul Krugman sees as the greatest tragedy of what he unhesitatingly calls a depression: the tremendous waste of human resources represented by the masses of unemployed workers.

The situation is perhaps most alarming among youth. In 2012, some 16 per cent of them were unemployed in the US, 20 per cent in the UK, 35 per cent in Portugal, and 51 per cent in Spain and Greece. 'These people are delaying their advance into adulthood', asserted Sara Elder, an economist with the ILO. 'It's a very scary time for young people. They find the path that worked for their parents is not working for them'.[1]

The return of mass poverty

Mass poverty, which in the North had been regarded as a thing of the past during the late 20th century, one confined to a small section of the population, made its reappearance. Almost one in four people in the European Union (EU) was threatened with poverty or social deprivation in 2010, according to a December 2011 report of the European Commission. This meant that 115 million people, or 23 per cent of the EU population, were designated as poor or socially deprived. The main causes of poverty were unemployment, old age and low wages, with more than 8 per cent of all employees said to belong to the 'working poor'. Citing the latest census data at the time, the *Washington Post* reported in September 2011 that in the US, '[n]early one in six Americans was living in poverty last year . . . a development that is ensnaring growing numbers of children and offering vivid proof of the recession's devastating impact'. The article portrayed 'a nation where many people are slipping backward in the wake of a downturn that left 14 million people out of work and pushed unemployment rates to levels not seen in decades' (Fletcher, 2011).

Poverty, of course, is the lot of an even larger proportion of the population in our part of the world, among developing countries, but whereas material hardship is common to both the poor in the North and those in the South, the special quality of poverty in the North is the despair that has accompanied it, something that is less evident in the more flexible populations of the South that are used to coping with poverty. The sense that austerity was here to stay, that growth and prosperity was a distant dream, and that even in the best of circumstances, indebtedness far into the future was the common lot, to be paid with massive cuts in living standards into the indefinite future, has come so quickly and jarringly after years of stable prosperity that people have not been able to adjust to it psychologically. According to the *New York Times*:

> the economic downturn in Europe has . . . swept away the foundations of once sturdy lives. Especially in the most fragile nations like Greece, Ireland, and Italy, small business owners and entrepreneurs are increasingly taking their own lives in a phenomenon some European newspapers have started calling 'suicide by economic crisis'.[2]

In Greece, the suicide rate among men rose more than 24 per cent from 2007 to 2009. During the same period, in Ireland, suicides among men increased by more than 16 per cent. In Italy, suicides traced to economic difficulties increased 52 per cent. A Greek student summed it up to a newspaper reporter:

> There is a depression in the Greek people, in all of my friends . . . they keep saying: 'I can't take it.' There is depression about our jobs, depression on the news, depression about the economic situation, depression in our family, depression and fighting among friends.[3]

Recommended reading: Bello (2006).

The global economic conjuncture

This chapter will not go in detail into the causes and dynamics of the economic crisis, which has to do with the dynamics of capitalism's crisis of overproduction and the unravelling of finance. One might simply say in this regard that it is very hard to see growth returning soon to the US and Europe. President Donald Trump based his electoral campaign in part on the promise to reduce unemployment by obliging US corporations that had decamped to Mexico and other havens of cheap labour to return to the US and so bring back US jobs, but the jury is out, and not back soon, as to whether this strategy will or can work. As for Europe, the devastation of Germany's export markets in Southern Europe by austerity programmes promoted by the German government will make itself felt in a significant slowdown of growth in Germany itself, which in fact has already started.

It is perhaps only recently that we have come to realize that what we are going through is a crisis of globalization (i.e. one that has spelled the end of the so-called second era of globalization that began in the 1980s, and one that has ended the spell that globalization has had on the popular imagination).

What do I mean? In late 2008 and 2009, the recession in Europe and the US brought down growth rates in East Asia, but this was only for about a year. By 2010, East Asia and the big 'newly emerging economies' known as the BRICS (Brazil, Russia, India, China, South Africa) appeared to have recovered, although the extractivist strategy pursed by the government of Brazil over the past decade in 2012 brought Brazil's engine of growth to a virtual standstill (see Chapter 31 in this volume). The BRICS were regarded as bright spots in the global economy, exhibiting resiliency and growth even as the North stagnated. Indeed, to economists such as Nobel laureate Michael Spence, '[w]ith growth returning to pre-2008 levels, the breakout performance of China, India, and Brazil are important engines of expansion for today's global economy' (Spence, 2011: 187). In a decade, the share of global GDP by the emerging economies would pass the 50 per cent mark, he predicted. Much of this growth would stem from 'endogenous domestic-growth drivers in emerging economies, anchored by an expanding middle class' (p. 188). Moreover, as trade among the BRICS increases, the future of emerging economies is one of reduced dependence on industrial–country demand.

Recent trends, however, appear to show that the idea that the fate of the BRICS had become decoupled from that of the US and Europe was an illusion. Since 2012, it seems that the emerging economies have yielded to the turbulent waves emanating from the sinking economies of the North. Economies are slowing down, with India's growth rate in 2011 falling by close to 5 per cent relative to 2010, although recovering some of that fall since then. Brazil's growth rate was under 3 per cent lower than sickly Japan's, and by 2012 experienced zero to negative growth, a situation that persists into 2016. China's growth has now officially fallen to around 6.7 per cent per year, a figure that the leadership now acknowledges to be the 'new normal'. The main reason appears to be the continued great dependence of these economies on Northern markets and their inability to institutionalize domestic demand as the key engine of the economy. I do not usually agree with the *Economist*, but I find it hard to disagree with the assessment of India in its issue of 9 June 2012:

> In a world economy as troubled as today's, news that India's growth rate has fallen to 5.3 per cent may not seem important. But the rate is the lowest in several years, and the sputtering of India's economic miracle carries social costs that could surpass the pain in the eurozone. The near double-digit

pace of growth that India enjoyed in 2004–2008, if sustained promised to lift hundreds of millions of Indians out of poverty – and quickly. Jobs would be created for all the young people who will reach working age in the coming decades, one of the biggest, and potentially scariest, demographic bulges the world has seen . . . But now . . . the miracle feels like a mirage.[4]

We are, in short, entering the third stage of the global depression. The first was the collapse of Wall Street, which led to the crisis of the real economy of the US. The second was the so-called sovereign debt crisis of the European economies, which triggered the implosion of the real economy of Europe. The third and current phase is the less dramatic but very tangible unravelling of the real economy of the so-called emerging markets, the dynamic developing countries that escaped the first phase of the financial meltdown. Having indiscriminately integrated our economies in the last 25 years, we are now reaping the wages of corporate-driven globalization.

The dynamics of the economy of China illustrate this third phase. Being the world's second largest economy, China's downshifting is particularly alarming. In 2008, in response to the crisis, China launched a US$585 billion stimulus programme to enable the domestic market to make up for the loss of export demand. Achieving some success at first, China, however, reverted back to export-led growth oriented towards the US and European markets. The reason for the retreat was explained by the respected Chinese technocrat Yu Yongding:

> With China's trade-to-GDP ratio and exports-to-GDP ratio already respectively exceeding 60 per cent and 30 per cent, the economy cannot continue to depend on external demand to sustain growth. Unfortunately, with a large export sector that employs scores of millions of workers, this dependence has become structural. That means reducing China's trade dependency and trade surplus is much more than a matter of adjusting macroeconomic policy.
>
> *(Yongding, 2010)*

The retreat back to export-led growth, rather than merely a case of structural dependency, reflected a set of interests from the reform period that, as Yu put it, 'have morphed into vested interests, which are fighting hard to protect what they have'. The export lobby, which brings together private entrepreneurs, state enterprise managers, foreign investors and government technocrats, remains the strongest lobby in Beijing.

Indeed, according to Yu, only crisis beckoned in the future since China's 'growth pattern has now almost exhausted its potential'. The economy that most successfully rode the globalization wave, China 'has reached a crucial juncture: without painful structural adjustments, the momentum of its economic growth could suddenly be lost. China's rapid growth has been achieved at an extremely high cost. Only future generations will know the true price'.

Recommended reading: Bello (2013).

Crises of the infrastructure and superstructure

The current crisis of the global economy has spawned problems for both the infra-structure and superstructure of global capitalism, to use these terms in a broad, not mechanical, sense. With respect to the infrastructure, global trends have buffeted the favoured economic organization of capitalist production: the transnational corporation whose profitability is sustained by global supply chains. According to the *Economist,* the 'integration of the world economy is in retreat on almost every front'. Global supply chains, it said, 'like any chain they are only as strong as their weakest link. A danger will come if firms decide that this way of organizing production has had its day'.[5] It appears that, aside from the impact of the economic crisis, the multinational corporations have also been brought to question the viability of far-flung supply chains by the massive impact of the two disasters that ravaged Asia in 2011: the floods in Thailand and the earthquake in Japan, which closed down vital multinational corporation subsidiaries for long periods, resulting in great losses.

In terms of the superstructure or the political canopy of globalization, even before outbreak of the financial crisis in 2007, the multilateral system was already eroding. The WTO was in a stalemate while the World Bank was trying to rein-vent itself as the 'Climate Bank'. As for the IMF, it has not recovered from its debacle in 1997, when it prescribed the wrong medicine to East Asia during the Asian financial crisis, one that led to a worse situation. Its leaders, notably managing director Dominique Strauss Kahn and his successor Christine Legarde, have tried to shore up the Fund's position by rhetorically distancing themselves from the neoliberal approach of the past and putting a Keynesian gloss to the institution. The G20 has also brought the Fund in as a mechanism to channel funds to Ireland, Greece, Iceland and other European economies that were suffering from the financial crisis. However, its influence was very limited, as the European Commission, the European Central Bank and national governments such as Germany and France took the reins directly in dealing with the crisis, unlike during the Asian financial crisis, when the IMF played the central role.

By the beginning of 2012, with indefinite economic stagnation in both the US and Europe being a certainty, and with the BRICS slowing down, the retreat from globalization had become more of a certainty in many quarters. As Nader Mousavizadeh and George Kell wrote in the *International Herald Tribune,* 'we are entering a period of competitive sovereignty, replacing two decades of consensus around the universal benefits of globalization – however uneven and unequal its path' (Mousavizadeh and Kell, 2002: 8).

With the retreat from globalization being accompanied by the erosion of the system of multilateralism that served as its political canopy, the fear that haunted many pro-globalist sectors was what happened after 1914, when the first era of globalization that began in 1815, a period in which, in many ways, the global economy was more integrated than today, came to an end in war, national competition and depression. Let me just say here that I do not share this pessimistic view, being of the perspective that the end of globalization opens up new avenues for organizing the economy that would better serve the interests of people and the environment.

Responses to the crisis

There have been a number of strategic responses to the crisis, one associated with the neoliberals.

The neoliberal non-solution

In the immediate aftermath of the crisis, the neoliberal University of Chicago Nobel laureate Robert Lucas said, '[e]very economist is a Keynesian in the foxhole'. By 2010, however, the neoliberals had left the foxhole. But their solution was no solution inasmuch it did not address the issue of ending unemployment and restarting growth. From the neoliberal standpoint, a deepening of the crisis was, in fact, part of the natural order of things, whereby the 'excesses' and distortions created by government intervention were wrung out of the system.

What the neoliberals managed to do was to change the narrative or the discourse, playing on the American middle-class traditional distrust of government, deficit spending, and taxes. Here, they were supported by the propaganda machinery of Wall Street, which sought to move the public focus away from financial reform. Instead of unemployment and stagnation in the short and medium term, the real problem they pointed to was the debt and the deficit. Massive deficits financed by debt, they said, would ensure a future of debt slavery for future generations.

The limits of Keynesianism . . . and Marxism

Let me now turn to the Keynesians. They saw unemployment as the problem, and it was to be banished by massive deficit spending, low interest rates and loose money policies. Criticism of Keynesianism, however, not only came from the Right, but also from progressive quarters, who saw its focus on growth by stimulating consumption as simply a short-term solution bereft of a transformative vision for restructuring the economy along lines of greater equity and democracy. In the view of Marxists, Keynesianism's basic flaw was its adherence to the framework of monopoly capitalism, which rested fundamentally on deriving profit from the exploitative extraction of surplus value from labour, was driven from crisis to crisis by inherent tendencies towards overproduction, and tended to push the environment to its limits in its search for profitability.

At both the national and the global arena, the new Keynesianism promoted a new class compromise accompanied by new methods to contain or minimize capitalism's tendency towards crisis. Just as the old Keynesianism and the New Deal stabilized national capitalism, the historical function of the new Keynesianism was to iron out the contradictions of contemporary global capitalism and to re-legitimize it after the crisis and chaos left by neoliberalism. In the view of many progressives, the new Keynesianism old and new was, at root, about social management.

As for Marxists, while the analysis of capitalist crisis they offered was often very insightful, their alternative was often vague, being couched at times as 'post-capitalism', a defensive paradigm and terminology that was a legacy, no doubt, of the collapse of centralized bureaucratic socialism as an alternative during the latter half of the 20th century.

The 'End of Growth' school

Other quarters have seen the crisis as providing the opportunity to move from mere firefighting to proposing more fundamental economic restructuring. I am speaking about the 'End of Growth' school and the 'deglobalization' perspective, to which I myself have contributed.

Radical environmentalists have located the crisis in the much broader context of a growth-oriented, fossil-fuel-addicted mode of production. To analysts such as Richard Heinberg, the intersection of the financial collapse, economic stagnation, global warming, the steady depletion of fossil fuel reserves, and agriculture reaching its limits was a fatal one. It represents a far more profound crisis than a temporary setback on the road to growth. It portends not simply the end of a paradigm of global growth driven by the demand of the centre economies. It means the 'end of growth' as we knew it. It is, in short, the Malthusian trap, though Heinberg understandably avoids using the term.

The gyrations of the finance economy, he said, do not simply stem from the dynamics of capital accumulation, but from an all-encompassing ecological disequilibrium:

> Perhaps the meteoric rise of the finance economy in the past couple of decades resulted from semi-conscious strategy on the part of society's managerial elites to leverage the last possible increments of growth from a physical, resourced based economy that was nearing its capacity. In any case, the implications of the current economic crisis cannot be captured by unemployment statistics and real estate prices. Attempts to restart growth will inevitably collide with natural limits that simply don't respond to stimulus packages or bailouts . . . Burgeoning environmental problems require rapidly increasing amounts of efforts to fix them. In addition to facing limits on the amount of debt that can be accumulated in order to keep those problems at bay, we also face limits to the amounts of energy and materials we can devote to these purposes. Until now the dynamism of growth has enabled us to stay ahead of accumulating environmental costs. As growth ends, the environmental bills for the last two centuries of manic expansion may come due just as our bank account empties.
>
> (Heinberg, 2011: 152)

The next few decades, Heinberg asserts, will be marked by a transition from expansion to contraction, a process 'characterized by an overall contraction of society until we are living within Earth's replenishable budget of renewable resources, while continually recycling most of the minerals and metals we continue to use' (p. 284). The future points in the direction of decentralized eco-communities marked by more manageable participatory decision-making, powered by low-energy systems, reliant on cooperatives for production and other economic functions, dependent on organic farming for food, and using non-debt-based currencies for exchange.

Recommended reading: Bello (2013), Heinberg (2011).

Deglobalization

Some of the proposals advanced by the 'End of Growth' school have been shared by the 'deglobalization' perspective, although the latter does not endorse the former's view that radical economic contraction is inevitable nor desirable. Essentially, the deglobalization perspective, which has been associated with the Bangkok-based progressive think tank *Focus on the Global South*, aims at enhancing ecological equilibrium, democracy and equality while promoting the principle of subsidiarity or locating the locus of production and decision-making at the lowest level where it can be done with minimal economic cost.

The aim of the deglobalization paradigm is to move beyond the economics of narrow efficiency, in which the key criterion is the reduction of unit cost, never mind the social and ecological destabilization this process brings about. Rather, it promotes an 'effective economics', which strengthens social solidarity by subordinating the operations of the market to the values of equity, justice and community by enlarging the sphere of democratic decision-making. To use the language of the great Hungarian thinker Karl Polanyi in his book *The Great Transformation*, deglobalization is about 're-embedding' the economy in society, instead of having society driven by the economy (Polanyi, 1957: 68–76).

Acting to balance and guide the market must not only be the state, but also civil society. In this regard, it would be important to point out something that Pierre Rosanvallon makes eloquently: that the market is a political project, and that it competes with democracy. In the debate on neoliberalism:

> [I]t is not hard to see that the stakes and the problems are actually much deeper. It is, more profoundly, a whole model of society and its relationship to political will that have been under debate. If the market is seductive and worrisome by turns, it is, in fact, because more than a simple mechanism of management and regulation is at stake. The market appears as the agent of a far vaster ambition to organize civil society through decentralization and anonymity, presenting itself as the implicit competitor of the democratic project of artificially constituting the political realm.
>
> *(Rosenvallon, 2006: 147–8)*

In other words, in place of the invisible hand as the agent of the common good must be the visible hand of democratic choice.

The deglobalization paradigm also asserts that a 'one–size–fits–all' model such as neoliberalism or centralized bureaucratic socialism is dysfunctional and destabilizing. Instead, diversity should be expected and encouraged, as it is in nature. Having said this, we feel that shared principles of alternative economics do exist, and they have already substantially emerged in the struggle against and critical reflection over the failure of centralized socialism and neoliberal capitalism.

There are, in our view, 11 key prongs of the deglobalization paradigm, which we have arrived at mainly from a reflection of the conditions of developing economies:

1. Production for the domestic market must again become the centre of gravity of the economy rather than production for export markets.
2. The principle of subsidiarity should be enshrined in economic life by encouraging production of goods at the level of the community and at the national level if this can be done at reasonable cost in order to preserve community.
3. Trade policy (i.e. quotas and tariffs) should be used to protect the local economy from destruction by corporate-subsidized commodities with artificially low prices.
4. Industrial policy – including subsidies, tariffs and trade – should be used to revitalize and strengthen the manufacturing sector.
5. Long-postponed measures of equitable income redistribution and land redistribution (including urban land reform) can create a vibrant internal market that would serve as the anchor of the economy and produce local financial resources for investment.
6. De-emphasizing growth, emphasizing upgrading the quality of life, and maximizing equity will reduce environmental disequilibrium.
7. The development and diffusion of environmentally congenial technology in both agriculture and industry should be encouraged.
8. Strategic economic decisions cannot be left to the market or to technocrats. Instead, the scope of democratic decision-making in the economy should be expanded so that all vital questions – such as which industries to develop or phase out, what proportion of the government budget to devote to agriculture, etc. – become subject to democratic discussion and choice. In other words, the market and economics must be demystified, their workings made transparent to all subject to the democratic decision of all.
9. Civil society must constantly monitor and supervise the private sector and the state, a process that should be institutionalized. As Pierre Rosenvallon has noted, 'the growth of the self-generating capacity of civil society stands out as the truly remarkable phenomenon' of our era. It represents a real expansion and deepening of the democratic project (Rosenvallon, 2006: 226).
10. The property complex should be transformed into a 'mixed economy' that includes community cooperatives, private enterprises and state enterprises, and excludes transnational corporations.

11. Centralized global institutions such as the IMF and the World Bank should be replaced with regional institutions built not on free trade and capital mobility, but on principles of cooperation that, to use the words of Hugo Chávez in describing the Bolivarian Alternative for the Americas (ALBA), 'transcend the logic of capitalism'.

Although it may sound radical, the espousal of deglobalization is not really new. Deglobalization's pedigree includes the writings of Keynes, who, at the height of the Depression, bluntly stated 'We do not wish . . . to be at the mercy of world forces working out, or trying to work out, some uniform equilibrium, according to the principles of *laissez faire* capitalism'. Indeed, he continued, over:

> an increasingly wide range of industrial products, and perhaps agricultural products also, I become doubtful whether the economic cost of self-sufficiency is great enough to outweigh the other advantages of gradually bringing the producer and the consumer within the ambit of the same national, economic and financial organization. Experience accumulates to prove that most modern mass-production processes can be performed in most countries and climates with almost equal efficiency.
>
> *(Keynes, 1933)*

And with words that have a very contemporary ring, Keynes concluded:

> I sympathize . . . with those who would minimize rather than with those who would maximize economic entanglement between nations. Ideas, knowledge, art, hospitality, travel – these are the things which should of their nature be international. But let goods be homespun whenever it is reasonably and conveniently possible; and, above all, let finance be primarily national.
>
> *(Keynes, 1933)*

Recommended reading: Bello (2013).

Conclusion

Let me end by saying the old order is passing, but the contours of the new are not very clear. That the globalized world will be replaced by a multipolar, multispeed world – to use the description of Michael Spence – where the so-called emerging economies share hegemony with the old centres of Europe and the US is not at all certain.

In conclusion, things will definitely get worse before they get better, and this provides the opportunity to raise fundamental issues and proposals for the restructuring of economic organization to better serve the interests of people and the environment. We had better take this opportunity and get down to work. We have not talked about peoples' movements here, but though they seem weak and confused right now, they will become a central force in the years to come, a force that traditional parliamentary politics will not be able to control. Where these movements will head for, whether towards the Right or the Left, will depend to a great extent on how credible and viable the alternatives proposed by progressives such as us will be.

Notes

1 'Millions march in Spain and Greece as crisis spreads through Europe'. *Yorkshire Post*, 9 June 2012. Available at: www.yorkshirepost.co.uk/news/international/millions-march-in-spain-and-greece-as-crisis-spreads-through-europe-1-4628846.
2 'The return of mass poverty to Europe'. World Socialist Web Site, 5 January 2012. Available at: http://wsws.org/articles/2012/jan2012/pers-j05.shtml.
3 Quoted in 'Coming to terms with decline in Greece'. *International Herald Tribune*, 15 June 2012.
4 'Farewell to Incredible India'. *The Economist*, 9 June 2012, p. 14.
5 'Turning their backs on the world'. *The Economist*, 19 February 2009. Available at: www.economist.com/node/13145370?story_id=13145370.

References

Bello, W. (2006). 'The capitalist conjuncture: overaccumulation, financial crises, and the retreat from globalization'. *Third World Quarterly*, 27(8): 1345–69.

Bello, W. (2013). *Deglobalization II: The Global Crisis and How to Get Out of It*. London: Zed Books.

Fletcher, M. (2011). 'Nearly one in six in poverty in the U.S.; children hit hard, Census says'. *Washington Post*, 13 September. Available at: www.washingtonpost.com/business/economy/us-poverty-rate-hits-52-year-high-at-151percent/2011/09/13/gIQApnMePK_story.html?utm_term=.da9565a67a8c.

Heinberg, R. (2011). *The End of Growth*. British Columbia: New Society.

Keynes, J.M. (1933). 'National self-sufficiency'. *The Yale Review*, 22(4), June: 755–69. Available at: www.mtholyoke.edu/acad/intrel/interwar/keynes.htm.

Mousavizadeh, N. and Kell, G. (2002). 'Getting down to business in Rio'. *International Herald Tribune*, 15 June.

Polanyi, K. (1957). *The Great Transformation*. Boston, MA: Beacon.

Rosenvallon, P. (2006). *Democracy Past and Future*. New York: Columbia University Press.

Spence, M. (2011). *The Next Convergence: the Future of Economic Growth in a Multispeed World*. Crawley, Australia: University of Western Australia.

Yongding, Y. (2010). "A different road forward," *China Daily*, 23 December. Available at: www.chinadaily.com.cn/opinion/2010-12/23/content_11742757.htm.

PART IV

Poverty, inequalities and development dynamics

12

THE POVERTY AND DEVELOPMENT PROBLEMATIC

Joseph Tharamangalam

The paradox of our age, and its great scourge, is the dogged persistence of chronic and endemic poverty in a world of unprecedented opulence. And this is despite a half-century of a 'war on poverty' waged by the World Bank and other development agencies. In 1973, when the World Bank, a linchpin of the Bretton Woods system and the quarterback of the world capitalist system that called its major plays, described poverty reduction and alleviation as the main goal of development and its own central mandate, two-fifths of the world's population was unable to meet their basic human needs and thus the target of the Bank's interventions. But some three decades later, after the expenditure of untold resources and efforts, and various shifts in strategy and tactics in the war against global poverty, nearly one-half of the world's population – more than 3 billion people – still live on less than $2.50 a day, making them poor by the World Bank's definition. And more than 1.4 billion live in extreme poverty (on less than $1.25 a day), according to the latest update on global poverty facts and statistics (DoSomething.org).[1]

Poverty: a matter of definition or strategic action?

Extreme poverty, understood as a state of deprivation of vital resources and opportunities needed to sustain a reasonably healthy life, is the condition if not fate of a large part of the world's population today, anywhere from 896 million people to 1.3 billion, depending on the definition and measure used. By 2008, after numerous twists and turns in the war against global poverty, and just eight years upon the declaration by the United Nations of a New Millennium Goal of a 50 per cent reduction in the rate of global poverty, it was finally possible to report some progress on the poverty reduction front – that millions had been lifted out of poverty. By all accounts, these gains were not the result of actions taken by the World Bank, which continued to push for policies that the UN agency ECLAC and a number of economists held responsible for producing poverty or reproducing it on a global scale (Burkett, 1990; Chossudovsky, 1997). As the World Bank saw it, and continues to argue despite considerable evidence to the contrary, the best way to reduce poverty is for countries to open up their economies to the global economy and the forces of the free market. However, by many accounts, virtually all of the gains made in the war against global poverty over the past two decades can be attributed to three factors: (i) the extraordinarily high rate of economic growth achieved by China and sustained over several decades – as the result of market-friendly but state-led macroeconomic policy; (ii) the turn in recent years of many South American governments away from the free market towards a strategy of inclusive development – channelling export revenues into poverty reduction programmes; and (iii) actions taken by the poor themselves, including to migrate and remit some of their labour income to the communities and families that they were forced to abandon in the search for a better life.

As Chossudovsky argued, poverty is a social function of economic growth, i.e. the inevitable product of the normal functioning of the capitalist system and the result of the way and how the benefits or fruits of economic growth – i.e. the wealth of nations – are socially distributed. This is to say, the poverty that afflicts at least two-fifths of the world's population and close to one-half of the total population in developing countries where poverty is concentrated is intimately connected to the sprouting of billionaires and the concentration of the wealth of nations in the hands and banks of the top 1 per cent, the all-powerful super-rich who have managed to rig the system to their advantage. On the other hand, to some extent, poverty is a matter of definition and measurement The definition of poverty, and the various ways of measuring it, is highly contested, particularly in regard to the use of a standard measure of income poverty, such as the World Bank's poverty line currently (and over the past 10 years) set at US$2.50 a day (or $1.25 a day as a measure of extreme poverty).

The use of such a standard measure of income poverty is particularly problematic when used to make international comparisons and when income is calculated on the basis of the exchange rate of various currencies against a US dollar standard (Malhotra, 2014). To correct for the obvious distortions created in the measurement of poverty by use of an exchange rate measure, the UNDP introduced what is now standard in poverty studies: to adjust the income measure and poverty line for purchasing power parity (i.e. for the amount and value of the goods and services that this amount of income will allow a person in a particular country to actually buy). The result is a more realistic measure of the rate of poverty for a given population. For example, to use an exchange rate measure of per capita income for a country such as Cuba, for whose local currency there is no market, would mean that the average Cuban would be seen to only receive or earn $5 to $10 a month, and that most of the population would fall below the poverty line. Needless to say, this statistic is meaningless, particularly given the fact that whatever the country's average income might be, Cuba happens to be the only Latin American country where extreme or absolute poverty does not exist – the result of a socialist model that ensures that the social product is distributed equitably among all members of the population, and a system that makes public provision for basic needs such as nutritious food, education, health, shelter and decent housing, and access to water and sanitation, which in many capitalist societies, whether developed or under-developed, are viewed and treated as commodities to be accessed via the market (depending on available income) rather than as a fundamental human right.

Using its parsimonious measure of extreme poverty (living below the poverty line of $1.25 a day), the World Bank reported that in 2012, 896 million people (17 per cent of the population) lived in extreme poverty. This was down from 37 per cent or 1.99 billion people in 1990, indicating some progress in the war on global poverty launched by the World Bank in 1973 (World Bank, 2015). On the other hand, many poverty scholars argue that income is a poor or inadequate measure of poverty – that poverty is multidimensional and requires a multidimensional measure. To this end, several alternative multidimensional measures have been elaborated. The most widely used of these is the Multidimensional Poverty Index (MPI), developed by the Oxford Poverty and Human Development Initiative (Alkire and Santos, 2010) and used by UNDP's Human Development Reports (HDRs) since 2010. The MPI uses measures for education and health as well as income. According to the 2016 Multidimensional Poverty Index, which covered 102 countries and 75 per cent of the world's population, 1.6 billion people or 30 per cent of those covered were identified as MPI poor (World Bank, 2016).

Another multidimensional measure of poverty is the Global Hunger Index (GHI), produced annually by the International Food Policy Research Institute (IFPRI), using a composite index of four parameters: malnutrition, childhood wasting (the proportion of children under 5 with low weight for their age), stunting (the proportion of children under 5 with low height for their age) and under 5 child mortality rates. These reflect chronic malnutrition as well as unhealthy environments (IFPRI, 2008). According to the Global Hunger Index (GHI), 795 million people in 2015 were still chronically undernourished, about one in nine on the planet (IFPRI, 2015). More than one in four children are affected by stunting, and 9 per cent of children by wasting. Between 2000 and 2013, the most recent years for which data are available, the percentage of children dying before age 5 fell from 8.2 to 4.9 per cent. Finally, there is the widely used Human Development Index (HDI), available in the UNDP's annual Human Development Report (HDR) since 1990, which attempts to provide a composite index of 'human devel-opment', a measure of human and social well-being. Besides income (an indicator of standard of living), the HDI uses education and health as two additional param-eters. It provides such useful, but also shocking, measures as the very chance of survival on this planet, a measure of life expectancy (LE) that varies between over 80 in the rich countries and less than 40 in the poorest countries of Sub-Saharan Africa (World Bank, 2015). It also highlights the fact that a country's ranking by income does not necessarily correspond with its ranking in human development; some low-income countries such as Sri Lanka and Cuba ranking relatively high, and at the other end some high-income countries such as Qatar ranking relatively low in HD. It also includes a measure of this disparity, GNI per capita rank minus HDI rank; Sri Lanka's score is 29, Qatar's is −31, a substantial deficit in translating Qatar's high income into human development.

Recommended reading: Chossudovsky (1997), Green (2012), Melhotra (2014), Narayan *et al.* (2000).

The World Bank's long war on poverty

It is ironic, although no accident, that the fight against global poverty has been led not by the poor or even by the countries with the bulk of the poor, but by the World Bank, a Washington-based international financial institution committed to ensuring the welfare of the world capitalist system (Mendes Pereira, 2013, 2015). Established in 1944 to finance post-war reconstruction, the Bank became interested in the developing countries in the context of the Cold War and the rising tide of anti-colonial struggles that coalesced into the peasant and socialist movements of the time. Robert McNamara, a prominent World Bank president (1961–1981) who was moved from the prosecution of the Vietnam War as Secretary of Defence to the prosecution of the global war on poverty as President of the Bank, saw poverty in the developing countries not as a moral issue, but as a political and security issue. Social justice, he said famously, is a political imperative. Clearly, the Bank's interest was to turn these countries into client states within the orbit of the global capitalist block presided over by the US, and to mange their poverty within the framework of the global capitalist system. 'Development' would be the answer to the social movements and class struggles, 'rural development' the alternative to redistributive agrarian reform policies in addressing the appalling levels of rural poverty. Nevertheless, in contrast to the later neoliberals, McNamara advocated public investment and services in health and education, in addition to economic growth, as critical factors of poverty reduction.

Recommended reading: Chossudovsky (1997), Veltmeyer and Tetreault (2013).

Structural roots of poverty: global capitalism, inequality and uneven development

Poverty is a structural matter, something implicitly understood by the poor but purportedly a surprise to World Bank researchers involved in the Bank's 'Listen to the Voices of the Poor' project (Narayan *et al.*, 2000). These researchers found that in giving voice to the poor, they spoke less about their income and more about the way they felt 'powerless', trapped in a structure of unfreedoms and capability deprivations (Melhotra, 2014; Narayan *et al.*, 2000; World Bank, 2001). The structures of economic and political power at the regional, national and global levels determine access to the planet's resources and the social product, and the extent of deprivations that cause poverty and hunger.

It is no accident that the largest pockets of poverty in the world are found in the Global South – in the former colonies of the rich countries of the North that exploited them for centuries and created the North–South divide. The early postcolonial period saw several newly independent countries attempting to free themselves from the structures of 'dependency', initiating their own independent paths of development, launching state-led structural reforms (such as land reforms) developmental and redistributive policies – with vastly varied effectiveness and outcomes. The World Bank's 'war on poverty' promoted a path that eschewed such structural reforms and reversed some of these during the neoliberal era, promoting (imposing) a path of managing poverty, in consonance with neoliberal capitalism.

The neoliberal period saw an unprecedented increase in inequality within countries and across the world, placing a major roadblock in the path of poverty reduction efforts (Green, 2012; Piketty, 2014). Some figures are scandalous: 80 per cent of the world's people have just 6 per cent of global wealth, 20 per cent have 94 per cent. There has been a sharp increase at the top. In the US alone, the share of total income appropriated by the top 1 per cent rose from 9 to 20 per cent between 1996 and 2011. Globally, just 80 individuals control as much wealth as the world's poorest 3.5 billion. The richest 1 per cent held 48 per cent of the global wealth in 2014. In the developing countries, income inequality increased by 11 per cent between 1990 and 2010 (UNDP, 2015: 65). Some 10 per cent of the world's population now consumes 60 per cent of the world's social product (Green, 2012). The two ends of this distribution also defines the phenomenon of the 'stuffed and the starved', the rich becoming increasingly overfed and obese, while the marginalized and the poor become more malnourished and hungry (Patel, 2007). The global capitalist system that underlies such inequality is a complex and highly structured system, managed by the political leaders and technocrats of the rich countries (with the support of their clients and allies in the developing countries), who stand ready to deploy their military power when deemed necessary. The wonder is that such a fundamentally unjust and unfair system (global capitalism) is not causing greater moral outrage among world leaders and economists, forcing them to re-examine the claim that this system is driven by some amoral natural laws.

Recommended reading: Jomo (2007), Piketty (2014).

Poverty reduction programmes: a critical review

Despite widespread and increasing disillusionment with the Washington Consensus policies, the World Bank has continued to promote its 'growth first' strategy. The World Bank (2001) report devoted to the issue, titled *Attacking Poverty*, placed 'promoting opportunity by stimulating overall growth' as the first line of attack against poverty. This was reportedly an altered version of the draft prepared by the lead author, Ravi Kanbur, who resigned from the Bank refusing to revise his 'unorthodox' views. In preparation for his report, Kanbur had launched the Listen to the Voices of the Poor research initiative/project mentioned above, and subsequently organized a wider discussion of his first draft with 1523 people from over 80 countries across the world. Kanbur had reportedly advocated a reversal of the 'growth first' approach, emphasizing the need for empowerment of the poor and more pro-poor state intervention (GPF, 2000). The UNDP, in its 2000–2001 *Human Development Report*, did incorporate some of the dissenting ideas such as the need to empower the poor, but giving it a secondary role. It should be noted that to the World Bank ideologues, 'empowerment of the poor' means not organized exercise of political power to counter the overwhelming power of the economic and political elite and to influence state policies in their favour, but capacitating the poor for self-help in moving out of poverty by adapting to the changing economic system.

Does growth actually reduce poverty? How, and to what extent? The answers to these questions are controversial, but two facts are clear. First, growth does help to reduce poverty, but the degree to which growth translates into poverty reduction (the growth elasticity of poverty reduction or GEP) varies widely across countries and regions. There are very striking contrasts such as Uganda versus Bangladesh, the former far more effective in this respect (World Bank, 2001: Chapter 3). Interestingly, the report acknowledges that the difference must be explained by the levels of inequality (p. 53). It is noteworthy that there is a similar contrast between China and India (Sen, 2013) and in India between the states of Kerala and Bihar. It has been pointed out that the GEP varies four times between Kerala and Bihar; that is, $1 of growth in Kerala translates into as much poverty reduction as $4 of growth does in Bihar (Harriss, 2003; Thomas, 2006) Second, as will be discussed below, the main factors that determine such difference in the GEP are also of critical importance for successful poverty reduction.

Recommended readings: Harriss (2003), Sen (2013), Tharamangalam (2006).

Conditional Cash Transfers (CCTs)

Hailed as a success in recent years, even, in some development circles, a 'magic bullet' (Lomeli, 2013), Conditional Cash Transfer (CCT) refers to cash payments made to poor families under the condition that the parents send their children to school and make regular health visits. The strategy, launched in Brazil, and spreading quickly to all of Latin America, the Caribbean and beyond (18 countries by 2014 had adopted the new social policy), has two goals: (i) provide *social assistance* by putting cash into the hands of the poor to purchase food and other basic needs, thus reducing poverty in the short term, and (ii) *social investment*, capacitating the family members to invest in their children's future to achieve human development and the human capital needed to break the intergenerational cycle of poverty.

Evaluations have been largely positive as regards the programme's first goal. CCTs have been effective in reaching the poorest inhabitants directly, providing the needed cash for basic necessities, building human capital, lowering income inequality, and improving education, health and nutrition – all these achieved at a relatively low cost. But critics argue that the programme's effect on poverty reduction has been very modest; it has helped to reduce the intensity of poverty, not the head count ratio (i.e. reduced the gap between incomes of the poor and the poverty line, but not lifted them above the poverty line). As regards its second and long-term goal of capacitating the poor to move out of poverty by building human capital, the outcome is doubtful and the final verdict yet to come. Furthermore, CCT has not been integrated into the broader, rights-based security programmes that promote social citizenship and the robust institutions needed to sustain citizenship rights. Indeed, social security coverage declined in Latin America from 61.2 per cent in 1980 to 52.2 per cent in 2000 (Lomeli, 2013: 183–4).

Recommended reading: Veltmeyer and Tetreault (2013).

Poverty Reduction Strategy Papers (PRSPs)

The name of this programme signifies an innovation and a fundamental change in direction and approach by the World Bank. Instead of insisting on a one-size-fits-all neoliberal programme of 'structural reform' in public policy as a conditionality of aid and accessing the capital markets, the Bank, under this programme, holds developing countries seeking foreign aid responsible for preparing their own policy 'papers' (with the participation of all stakeholders), thus 'owning' their own policies. Other innovations include the apparent softening of conditionalities attached to loans, and a new focus on poverty reduction, the specific needs and strategies for this to be worked out and 'owned' by the aid-receiving country.

The UNDP, in its 2001 annual report, claimed that the programme 'helped to bring about the beginning of a fundamental culture change in the Bretton Woods Institutions and donors in terms of pro-poor thinking' (UNDP, 2001).

PRSP is seen as a 'post-Washington Consensus' strategy that integrated a neo-Keynesian paradigm elaborated by Joseph Stiglitz, among others, with a new form of Latin American structuralism, as advanced by Osvaldo Sunkel and others (Leiva, 2008). It presupposed a more effective working partnership between the donor agencies and developing country governments, which assumed responsibility to implement the strategy (subject, of course, to final approval by the former). The primary agency of economic development would still be the private sector, freed from the regulatory constraints of the welfare/developmental state (O'Malley, 2013). The poor are to be empowered to be able to act for themselves availing of the new opportunities created by a reformed and growing neoliberal economy, the government's role being to facilitate the new development. The rural poor (the bulk of the poor in most developing countries) who will be displaced by the agrarian transition that is envisaged will be capacitated to take advantage of the new opportunities that will be created in the non-agricultural sectors. Unsurprisingly, the strategy eschews land reforms or support systems for small farmers.

Predictably, the gains made under the PRSP strategy have been modest at best and none at worst. Indeed, an examination of three Latin American countries by O'Malley and Veltmeyer (2006) found greater rural distress, and little improvement in poverty in general.

Recommended reading: Leiva (2008), O'Malley (2013).

Microfinance[2]

Microfinance refers to a micro-banking system designed to help the poor to start their own small businesses (see Chapter 19 for a more extended discussion). The informal microenterprises and self-employment ventures operating in very basic product and service markets – basket-making, simple services such as shoe-shining, bicycle maintenance and so on – would create the 'bottom-up' economic and social development needed to reduce poverty in local communities (Bateman, 2013). First launched in Bangladesh by economist Mohammad Yunus in the 1970s, it soon captured the imagination of the international agencies and campaigners across the world, especially after Yunus was awarded the Nobel Prize, instantly achieving the status of an international icon. The economic philosophy underpinning the movement is simple: enable the poor to help themselves with small loans; governments should facilitate the process, but can then abdicate all responsibility to provide social support and social welfare.

Early enthusiasm has been replaced in recent years by disappointment and criticisms by observers and experts in the field. Limited local micro-success stories did not translate into significant poverty reduction anywhere. In addition to the limitations of the neoliberal projects described above, critics such as Bateman and Chan (2012) have added an economic reason to explain the failure, the fallacy of assuming that low-value products of the numerous microenterprises will find sufficient demand. The viability and success of *one* new informal microenterprise making baskets cannot be replicated endlessly.

Bateman draws especially on his research in Bolivia (which invested heavily in this policy) to argue that microfinance has been an 'anti-development model' that has contributed to a process of deindustrialization and informalization and the weakening of the local economy (Bateman, 2013).

Recommended reading: Bateman (2010, 2013), Bateman and Chan (2012), Veltmeyer (2013), Veltmeyer and Tereault (2013).

The war on poverty: what's new?

Why has the mountain of a war brought forth just a mouse? The answer is that the war has been as successful as possible within the limits of the framework within which it has been fought. The ideology behind this framework masks a fundamental contradiction: even as huge efforts are made to eradicate poverty, the model of development through neoliberal globalization is systematically accentuating the structures underpinning poverty and weakening the democratic and state institutions that have historically played a critical role in reducing poverty. It has attempted to define what is fundamentally a political issue (one rooted in the economic and political power structure) as a depoliticized technical issue to be addressed through technocratic management tools.

A quick look at successful models of poverty reduction through a historical and comparative lens will help to illustrate this point. Practically all countries or regions that have achieved significant poverty reduction have followed paths very different from those promoted by the international agencies. They have followed models of development that addressed the structural issues in varying degrees. This is the case with Scandinavian and other Western European democracies (or even the post-war US under the New Deal), as it is with East Asia, and especially China, and other recent success stories everywhere. Even some poor countries, such as Cuba and the Indian state of Kerala, have achieved success in this respect, but by following a radically different socialist path (Tharamangalam, 2006, 2010).

In the former case, it was the development of what Bateman (2013) calls 'collective capabilities' and state-coordinated institutional vehicles and policies that were historically decisive in promoting development, democracy and poverty reduction. Robust, rational-legal people's movements and organizations from below – trade unions and other people's organizations, pro-poor political parties – led to the development of 'vibrant democracies' (including adversarial politics) that put pressure on the state to pursue social reform and redistributive policies, as well as public provisioning of basic human and social security such as pensions and unemployment insurance and services (e.g. health and education). Broadly, this was the trajectory of the 'welfare state', in synergy with a mobilized and politically conscious society.

In the latter case, the path to poverty reduction has been similar, led and regulated by strong states and state institutions. The example of China,[3] the country responsible for the bulk of global poverty reduction in the past four decades,[4] is of particular interest from this perspective. Contrary to the myth propagated by the World Bank and neoliberal economists who attribute China's success solely to its recent high growth, China's exceptional success was, in fact, rooted in the establishment of a strong state that effected radical reforms (especially land reforms), dismantling the old structures of economic and political power, and establishing institutions for the extensive public provisioning of basic social security, and health and educational services. The result was rapid improvement in health and education indicators achieved well before the reforms and the high growth (Sen, 2013). When China launched its economic reforms around 1979, entering a period of sustained high growth, the Chinese state took charge of the process, selectively and at its own pace, largely sustaining its social welfare programmes and safety nests (though not without some setbacks in the early period). China had already prepared the ground, the structural preconditions, that made its high growth generally more inclusive than elsewhere, thus more effective in poverty reduction (Bardhan, 2009: 92; Fosu, 2010; Sen, 1999).

In conclusion, four interrelated factors have been critical in the achievement of poverty reduction in recent years: (i) rapid economic growth and an associated process of productive and social transformation (conversion of the peasantry into an urban-based working class) in China, and to a much lesser degree, in India – by themselves accounting for 36 per cent of the world's population; (ii) the nature and capacity of the state and state policy in effecting structural reforms by redistributing wealth and power and making public provisioning for basic services and social security; (iii) 'active citizens' – the activism of citizens and social movements of the poor, mobilized and empowered to confront and challenge the bastions and holders of economic and political power; and (iv) a degree of 'state–society synergy' through institutions that accommodate democratic participation and an adequate system of checks and balances.

Recommended reading: Green (2014), Mehrota and Delamonica (2007), Melhotra (2014), Veltmeyer and Tetreault (2013).

Notes

1 In recent years, the World Bank has observed a system-wide reduction in the rate of global poverty, but this was in part an artefact of how poverty is measured. In the World Bank's most recent estimation (see its website, updated in April 2016) over 2.1 billion people in the developing world (35 per cent of the population) were poor in that they lived on less than US$3.10 a day in 2012, compared with 2.9 billion in 1990 (66 per cent of the population in the developing world, www.worldbank.org/en/topic/poverty/overview). However, according to DoSomething.org, a nongovernmental organization for social change, nearly half of the world's population – more than 3 billion people – are poor in that they have to live on less than $2.50 a day. And more than 1.3 billion live in extreme poverty (on less than $1.25 a day).
2 See Chapter 18 by Bateman in this volume.
3 See Chapter 33 by So and Chu in this volume.
4 According to the World Bank, China by itself accounted for most of the decline in extreme poverty over the past three decades. Between 1981 and 2011, 753 million people moved or were elevated above the $1.90 a day threshold of extreme poverty. At the same time, the developing world as a whole saw a reduction in poverty of 1.1 billion.

References

Alkire, S. and Santos, M.E. (2010). 'Acute multidimensional poverty: a new index for developing countries'. *OPHI Working Paper 38*. Oxford Poverty and Human Development Initiative (OPHI).

Bardhan, P. (2009). 'Economic reforms, poverty and inequality in China and India'. In R. Kanbur and K. Basu (eds), *Arguments for a Better World: Essays in Honour of Amartya Sen: Volume II*. Available at: www.oxfordscholarship.com/view/10.1093/acprof:oso/9780199239979.001.0001/acprof-9780199239979.

Bateman, M. (2010). *Why Doesn't Microfinance Work? The Destructive Rise of Local Neoliberalism*. London: Zed Books.

Bateman, M. (2013). 'The age of microfinance: destroying Latin American economies from the bottom up'. *OFSE Working Paper 39*, Australian Foundation for Development Research.

Bateman, M. and Chang, H.-J. (2012). 'Microfinance and the illusion of development: from hubris to nemesis in thirty years'. *World Economic Review*, 1(1): 13–36. Available at: http://wer.worldeconomicsassociation.org/article/view/37.

Burkett, P. (1990). 'Poverty crisis in the Third World: the contradictions of World Bank policy'. *Monthly Review*, 42(7): 20–32.

Chossudovsky, M. (1997). *The Globalisation of Poverty: Impacts of IMF and World Bank Reforms*. London/New York: Zed Books.

Fosu, A. (2010). 'Growth, inequality and poverty reduction in developing countries: recent global evidence'. *CSAE Working Paper WPS/2011-07*. University of Oxford.

GPF (Global Policy Forum) (2000). 'Statement on Ravi Kanbur's resignation as World Development Report lead author'. 14 June. Available at: www.globalpolicy.org/component/content/article/209/42754.html.

Green, D. (2012). *From Poverty to Power: How Active Citizens and Effective States Can Change the World*, 2nd edition. London: Practical Action.

Harriss, J. (2003). 'Do political regimes matter? Poverty reduction and regime differences across India'. In P. Houtzager and M. Moore (eds), *Changing Paths: International Development and the New Politics of Inclusion*. Ann Arbor, MI: University of Michigan Press, pp. 204–32.

IFPRI (International Food Policy Research Institute) (2008). *Global Hunger Index: The Challenge of Hunger 2008*. Washington, DC: International Policy Research Institute.

IFPRI (International Food Policy Research Institute) (2015). *2015 Annual Report*. Available at: www.ifpri.org/publication/2015-annual-report.

Jomo, K.S. with Baudot, J. (2007). *Flat World, Big Gaps: Economic Liberalization, Globalization, Poverty and Inequality*. New York: Orient Longman, Zed Books and Third World Network.

Leiva, F.I. (2008). *Latin American Structuralism: The Contradictions of Post-Neoliberal Development*. Minneapolis, MN: University of Minnesota Press.

Lomeli, E. (2013). 'Conditional cash transfers asocial policy: limitations and illusions'. In H. Veltmeyer and D. Tetreault (eds), *Poverty and Development in Latin America*. Sterling, VA: Stylus, pp. 163–88.

Malhotra, R. (2014). *Tackling Poverty, Hunger and Malnutrition: India Public Policy Report 2014*. New Delhi: Oxford Univeristy Press.

Mehrota, S. and Delamonica, E. (2007). *Eliminating Human Poverty: Macroeconomic and Social Policies for Equitable Growth*. London: Zed Books.

Mendes Pereira, J.M. (2013). 'Banking on the poor: the World Bank and the assault on poverty'. In H. Veltmeyer and D. Tetreault (eds), *Poverty and Development in Latin America*. Sterling, VA: Stylus, pp. 33–58.

Mendes Pereira, J.M. (2015). 'Continuidade, Ruptura ou Reciclagem? Uma Análise do Programa Político do Banco Mundial após o Consenso de Washington'. *DADOS – Revista de Ciências Sociais, Rio de Janeiro*, 58(2): 461–98.

Narayan, D. *et al.* (2000). *Voices of the Poor: Crying Out for Change*. New York: World Bank and Oxford University Press.

O'Malley, A. (2013). 'Poverty reduction programs and rural poverty'. In H. Veltmeyer and D. Tetreault (eds), *Poverty and Development in Latin America*. Sterling, VA: Stylus, pp. 117–26.

O'Malley, A. and Veltmeyer, H. (2006). 'Banking on poverty'. *Canadian Journal of Development Studies*, 26(3): 287–307.

Patel, R. (2007). *Stuffed and Starved*. Toronto: HarperCollins.

Piketty, T. (2014). *Capital in the Twenty-First Century*. Cambridge, MA: Harvard University Press.

Sen, A. (1999). *Development as Freedom*. New York: Anchor Books.

Sen, A. (2013). 'Why India Trails China', *New York Times*, 19 June. Available at: www.nytimes.com/2013/06/20/opinion/why-india-trails-china.html?_r=0.

Tharamangalam, J. (ed.) (2006). *Kerala: The Paradoxes of Public Action and Development*. New Delhi: Orient Langman.

Tharamangalam, J. (2010). 'Human development as transformative practice: lessons from Kerala and Cuba'. *Critical Asian Studies*, 42(3): 363–402.

Thomas, V. (2006). 'Kerala: a paradox or incomplete agenda?' In J. Tharamangalam (ed.), *Kerala: The Paradoxes of Public Action and Development*. New Delhi: Orient Langman, pp. 69–93.

UNDP (United Nations Development Programme) (2001). *Annual Report 2001: Partnerships to Fight Poverty*. Available at: www.undp.org/content/undp/en/home/librarypage/corporate/undp_in_action_2001.html.

UNDP (United Nations Development Programme) (2015). *Human Development Report*. New York: UNDP.

Veltmeyer, H. (2013). 'Microfinance: crediting the poor'. In H. Veltmeyer and D. Tetreault (eds), *Poverty and Development in Latin America*. Sterling, VA: Stylus, pp. 124–42.

Veltmeyer, H. and Tetreault, D. (eds) (2013). *Poverty and Development in Latin America*. Sterling, VA: Stylus.

World Bank (2001). *World Development Report 2000/2001: Attacking Poverty*. Oxford: Oxford University Press.

World Bank (2015). *Global Monitoring Report*. Available at: www.worldbank.org/en/publication/global-monitoring-report.

World Bank (2016). *Global MPI 2016 | OPHI*. Available at: www.ophi.org.uk/multidimensional-poverty-index/global-mpi-2016.

13

POVERTY ANALYSIS THROUGH A GENDER LENS

A brief history of feminist contributions in international development[1]

Naila Kabeer

One approach to poverty analysis concerns itself with shortfalls in basic needs satisfaction at a particular point in time, or poverty as 'state'. An alternative approach, poverty as 'process', focuses on changes in the distribution of the means by which people meet their various needs. It thus deals with the underlying causes through which poverty is generated and reproduced over time (Fergany, 1981). The two are of course closely interrelated: basic needs deprivation at a particular point in time is both outcome of past processes of poverty and a determinant of the future. The aim of this chapter is to summarize feminist contributions to both these ways of thinking about poverty.

Poverty as state: money-metric measures

Mainstream concerns with poverty as state conceptualizes it in terms of the income needed by an average household to achieve some minimum level of basic needs. Early research assumed that households were internally unified and that their incomes were equitably distributed among their members. Consequently, all members of a poor household were likely to be equally poor.

This assumption was challenged by a growing body of evidence showing that household income was distributed in ways that systematically discriminated against women and girls in relation to health, nutrition, education and even survival chances. The need to deconstruct households and explore the distribution of basic needs satisfaction within it was an important step in bringing a gender lens to poverty analysis.

Another critique of conventional approaches focused on the gender of household heads. Micro-level studies had suggested that female-headed households constituted a special group among the poor. Unfortunately, census data did not collect the relevant information, making it impossible to determine the prevalence of this phenomenon. Buvinic and Yousseff (1978) developed a typology of categories of women who, as a result of marital dissolution, desertion, abandonment, absence of spouse or male marginality, were most likely to be primary breadwinners for their families. They then used census data on marital status to provide aggregated estimates of women in this category, confirming that female-headed households were indeed a significant percentage of the population in developing countries and that they were over-represented among the poor (Buvinic, 1993).

Over time, references to female-headed households as the 'poorest of the poor' became commonplace in the development literature, but unfortunately the earlier focus on those categories of female heads likely to be primary breadwinners was lost. The taken-for-granted equation between female headship and poverty gave rise to what became a widely repeated claim: that women made up 70 per cent of the world's poor. Marcoux (1998) challenged this claim. He pointed out that, given global estimates of people in poverty of 1.3 billion, the claim suggested the improbable ratio of 900 million women and girls to 400 million men and boys. To explain this excess by the existence of female-headed households would require the equally improbable additional assumption that male-headed households had a balanced sex composition but that female-headed ones were made up of an excess of female members.

What remains true nevertheless is that in certain regions of the world, women continue to be disproportionately represented among the poor. For instance, UN Women (2012) reports that in all but three of 25 countries in Sub-Saharan Africa (SSA), women outnumbered men in the poorest households by ratios that varied from 110 to 130 for every 100 men. Such a finding is best explained by the over-representation of female-headed households in the ranks of the poor.

Recommended reading: Buvinic (1993), Buvinic and Yousseff (1978), Marcoux (1998).

Poverty as state: qualitative insights

Qualitative assessments of poverty helped to move the 'money-metric' approach to 'poverty as state' to more multidimensional conceptualizations. Once again, gender emerged as a significant factor in this literature. For instance, women's greater time burdens were highlighted in a number of studies in the African context, adding the concept of 'time poverty' to the understanding of poverty (Hanmer et al., 1997). Differences in experiences gave rise to differences in priorities. Physical distance from drinking water sources, and seasonal variations in the quality of drinking water, was a concern almost exclusively voiced by women in participatory assessments in African countries, a reflection of their primary responsibility for ensuring its availability for household use and the distances they had to travel to obtain it.

While qualitative assessments of poverty had pointed to the harsh nature of the trade-offs faced by poor people, feminist researchers noted that these trade-offs often differed for men and women. For instance, while the poor were often prepared to accept their dependency status within patron–client relations as the necessary price to pay for some degree of security in times of crisis (Wood, 2003), women often accepted their subordinate status within marital relationships as the price they paid for male provision (Kabeer, 1991). Not all women accepted this trade-off: some opted out of such relationships to head up their own households because lack of income was preferable to lack of power (Chant, 2003).

Another overlooked gender dimension of poverty related to violence. The class-based nature of the violence experienced by poor people had been widely acknowledged in the literature (Beck, 1994), but not its patriarchal character. My own study in Bangladesh (Kabeer, 1991) offered insights into this. It suggested that class-based violence frequently took a sexual form when it came to women: many young women in my study spoke of their vulnerability to sexual harassment by employers or by young men from affluent families in their village.

My study also found that domestic violence in poor households was inflected by class through its link to shortfalls in basic needs. Conflicts revolving around food emerged as a frequent trigger for violence: women were beaten if there was not enough food, if it did not taste right or if they were found tasting it before their husbands had eaten. As Hartmann and Boyce (1981) were told by a share-cropper's wife: 'When my husband's stomach is empty, he beats me, but when it is full, there is peace'.

Recommended reading: Beck (1994), Kabeer (1991).

Poverty as process: causal inequalities

Processes of poverty can be divided into those that explain why poor people remain poor over extended periods of time, the so-called 'poverty trap', and those that explain processes of impoverishment. A focus on processes necessarily draws attention to the unequal distribution of the means through which people seek to meet their needs and make provision for the future. A gendered analysis of poverty processes goes deeper to examine gender inequalities in access and control to these means among households who were themselves disadvantaged in their distribution.

As the livelihoods literature has pointed out, households in poverty generally lacked the material means of production and had to rely on family labour as the primary, often sole, productive resource at their disposal. It also found marked asymmetries between men and women in their ability to dispose of their own labour, as well as in their ability to command the labour of others.

The first, and most widespread, asymmetry related to the fact that while house-holds everywhere had to divide the labour at their disposal between earning a living and caring for their families, women bore a disproportionate share of the unpaid work of caring for the family in much of the world. This 'reproductive tax' (Palmer, 1995) on women's time, from which men were largely exempt, gave women disproportionate responsibility for meeting the basic needs of the family but left them with less time for earning a living, and hence more or less dependent on male earnings.

Other asymmetries in women's control over labour related to the relations governing women's productive contributions. In areas of strict seclusion, such as South

Asia and the MENA region, most women either worked as unpaid family labour in male enterprises or in home-based activities of their own in which their returns were low and largely appropriated by male household members.

Gender asymmetries in control over labour were also evident in contexts where women had greater freedom to take up income-earning activity. In West Africa, for instance, husbands and senior males had prior and non-reciprocal rights over the labour of wives and female members for their own cultivation efforts. These obligations restricted the amount of time that women had for their independent economic activities and for their ability to purchase the labour of others.

Gender asymmetries were also evident in the ability to translate labour effort into income in the market place. These reflected gender inequalities in endowments, such as education and productive assets. They also reflected the gendered organization of economic opportunities. Labour markets across the world are organized along hierarchical lines: women from poor and socially marginalized groups (lower castes or minority ethnic groups, for instance) tend to be concentrated in activities at the bottom of the hierarchy, which are poorer paid and more likely to be characterized by risks, stigma and exploitative working conditions.

Finally, gender asymmetries in livelihood opportunities were reproduced through policy-related inequalities in access to credit, agricultural extension and other services (Hanmer et al., 1997). As Narayan et al. (2000) pointed out, the problem was not merely one of neglect by public providers, but also of arrogance and disdain of those, often male, from better-educated and higher-status households, towards those who occupied inferior positions by virtue of their class, gender, caste and other marginalized identities.

Recommended reading: Hanmer et al. (1997), Narayan et al. (2000).

Poverty as process: idiosyncratic shocks and natural disasters

While the idea of the 'poverty trap' captures the way in which multiple and reinforcing inequalities keep poor people in poverty, research into the way in which households cope with various forms of crisis provides useful insights into the processes through which they often slide into greater poverty. A first wave of studies focused on particular categories of 'shocks': idiosyncratic (such as illness in the household); generalized but recurring and hence anticipated (such as seasonal floods); and unanticipated (such as natural disasters) (Agarwal, 1990; Corbett, 1988; Dreze, 1988).

Analysis of household strategies to deal with such shocks suggested a systematic pattern to the sequence of responses. Priority was given in the early stages to responses characterized by greater reversibility, or which entailed less threat to the household productive assets. These included cutting back on number of meals, purchasing less nutritious foods, foraging for wild food, borrowing from neighbours, moneylenders or wealthy patrons, letting illness go untreated, depletion of household stores, selling off smaller consumer durables, taking children out of school, and temporary migration in search of work. Much later in the sequence came the distress sale of productive assets, which was likely to undermine the household's chances of recovery. The final stages included permanent migration and the breakdown of the family unit.

While the shocks in question were not confined to poor households, what distinguished poor from better-off households was their greater exposure to certain kinds of shocks (illness in the family; seasonal unemployment) and their lower likelihood of recovery from any kind of shock. With fewer options available to them, they arrived at the later, more irreversible stages of the sequence outlined with greater rapidity and their slide into greater poverty was more likely to be permanent.

Gender-disaggregated analyses of the ordering of these sequences, and the consequences associated with them, showed that they were rarely neutral between family members. For instance, efforts to cut back on consumption often bore more severely on female members than male. Thus, the mortality rates of girls peaked sharply relative to boys in times of drought in the Indian context (Rose, 1999). And a drought in Zimbabwe led to a decline in women's nutritional status, but not men's, with the negative impact stronger among women from poorer households (Hoddinott, 2006).

The gender of children taken out of school appeared to vary according to whether girls' education was seen less essential or whether boys' earning capacity was considered more necessary. At some point in the sequence, however, not only did education become unaffordable for all children, but it became essential to put as many of them to work as possible. Indeed, at some point in the sequence, members of the household who were not normally in employment – married women with young children, the very old and the very young – were forced to take on earning responsibilities.

Gender also differentiated the sequence of household divestment strategies. In South Asia, assets owned or controlled by women (stores of fodder, fuel, household utensils, jewellery) were generally sold off earlier in the sequence (Agarwal, 1990). As Jiggins (1986: 14) observed, 'whatever women's personal earnings or assets, these (were) consumed before the point of family breakdown'. This meant that further down the spiral into greater poverty, when family interdependencies began to break down, women had fewer resources to fall back on than men.

The final stages of impoverishment were characterized by more drastic measures: the wholesale migration of family members, the sale of children or abandonment of weaker members. Able-bodied male earners were generally the first to abandon the family unit, leaving women to look after the very young and the very old. At extreme levels of destitution, mothers abandoned their children to fend for themselves as best they could (Alamgir, 1980).

Recommended reading: Agarwal (1990), Alamgir (1980), Dreze (1988).

Poverty as process: policy-induced shocks

The onset of structural adjustment policies (SAPs) in the 1980s in the wake of the debt crisis experienced by various countries in SSA and Latin America signalled the beginning of a worldwide shift to market-led growth strategies. It was spearheaded by neoliberal governments in powerful donor countries and promoted across the world through the lending policies of the international financial institutions.

SAPs consisted of a number of key policy measures: downsizing the state's role in the economy, cutbacks in public expenditure, promotion of private enterprise, deregulation of labour and capital markets, and liberalization of trade and financial flows. The hypermobility of international capital and the exposure of countries to fluctuations in global markets inaugurated by these policies ushered in an era marked by a series of financial crises, of which the East Asian crisis in 1997–1998 and the global financial crisis of 2008 crisis were only the most dramatic.

SAPs introduced the concept of 'policy-induced shocks' into the development lexicon. Elson (1995) summarized a second wave of studies that sought to analyse how households coped with this new category of shocks. She distinguished between two sets of responses. Income-generating responses referred to the increase in labour-force participation by women and children and changes in household structure to increase ratio of earners to dependents. Consumption and expenditure responses included cutting down on meals, cheaper foods, borrowing in cash or kind, resort to borrowing and reliance on the community.

Heltberg *et al.* (2012) examined some of the responses associated with the 2008–2011 financial, food and fuel crises in developing and transitional economies. They divided coping mechanisms into three categories. 'Behaviour-based responses' referred to reducing quantity and quality of food and non-food expenditure, taking children out of school, intensifying work efforts, diversifying income sources, migration and resort to illicit activities, such as sex work, drug dealing and theft. 'Asset-based responses' included sale of assets, loans from moneylenders, microfinance organizations and relatives, and drawing on common property resources. Finally, 'assistance-based responses' included welfare assistance from governments, NGOs, religious organizations, mutual solidarity groups, relatives, friends and neighbours.

Some general points can be made about this second wave of studies. First of all, there is a remarkable continuity in the crisis-coping responses reported in both waves of literature. There are clearly a finite number of actions that households are able to take in order to protect themselves from the worst effects of crisis. At the same time, the fact that Heltberg *et al.* covered a wider range of countries in their study highlighted some of the variation in options between countries. For instance, formal government assistance was available to a greater extent in the former socialist countries than elsewhere, while reliance on common property resources for food and fuel was largely confined to low-income countries.

Second, the later studies made a distinction between the first- and second-order effects of shocks. In many countries, the first-order effect of structural adjustment policies was loss of male jobs because the public sector entrenchments central to these policies hit a sector in which men predominated. The first-order effects of financial crisis, on the other hand, varied considerably for countries because they depended on which sectors were first hit and who predominated in them (Aslanbeigui and Summerfield, 2000).

Regardless of first-order effects, women's time emerged as 'a crucial variable of adjustment' in second-order effects (Commonwealth Secretariat, 1989). This reflected women's role in meeting the family's basic needs through unpaid work as well as contributing to family earnings. Women's unpaid work responsibilities for family health and welfare increased to offset cutbacks in public expenditure and rising price of essentials. At the same time, as noted earlier, they increased their participation in the labour market to offset declining levels of male employment and earnings, giving rise to an 'added worker' effect in times of crisis. Women were often able to find jobs even when men were not, because they were willing to work for lower wages and to take up jobs wherever they could find them in order that household basic needs were met.

Second-order effects affected children. For instance, in the context of the Indonesian crisis, entry into school was deferred for young children, while older ones, particularly girls, were withdrawn in order to contribute to household livelihoods:

> Some wound up far away in cities where they could be easily exploited as domestic servants, factory labour, or street vendors. Those who became street children searching for food and money had little protection and became prey to pimps, policemen and gangs, who incorporated them in their criminal activities.
>
> *(Knowles et al., 1999: 44)*

Second-order effects also impacted on social relations within family and community. Reporting on the impact of SAPs in urban Ecuador, Moser (1989) noted that women who were dependent on their husbands to make ends meet were more likely to report a rise in domestic violence than those who had a reliable income of their own. In urban Zimbabwe as well, Kanji (1994) reported higher levels of domestic conflict in households struggling to meet household needs with very little support from husbands.

In their analysis of the impacts of the 2008 financial crisis, Heltberg *et al.* (2012) reported that reduced incomes and rising unemployment in certain sites had led to a rise in domestic violence – by men against women and by women against children. In others, domestic violence was exacerbated by high rates of unemployment and alcohol consumption by men. They also reported a rise in female-headed households as men migrated in search of jobs without necessarily sending remittances home or simply abandoning their families.

Third, while the second wave of studies did not refer explicitly to the sequencing pattern identified in the earlier literature, they did note that some coping mechanisms had longer-lasting – and less reversible – effects than others. As Heltberg *et al.* (2012) point out, 'coping came at significant costs to poor individuals, families and communities and . . . some of these costs may continue to be felt well after the crises subsides'. As examples, they mention the impact of reduced food consumption in the context of chronic malnutrition, the sale of productive assets, the foregone education and healthcare, and the rise in antisocial behaviours, which are likely to reverberate for a long time to come.

Fourth, the studies made it clear that responses that were possible in the face of idiosyncratic or localized crisis, for instance drawing on common property resources or seeking help from family and neighbours, were likely to dry up in situations when large numbers of people were simultaneously resorting to these measures. At the same time, the fact that large numbers of people were engaging at the same time in the other strategies meant that they influenced changes at the macro level.

For instance, the added worker effect shows up at the national level. Bhalotra and Umana-Aponte (2010) used national survey data from 63 developing countries for the period 1986–2006 to study the impact of fluctuations in per capita GDP on women's employment status at the time of the survey. They found a strong counter-cyclical pattern in Asia and Latin America, with less educated women dominating the 'added worker' effect, suggesting the effect was strongest among poorer households. In SSA, on the other hand, where many more women were already in paid work, women, particularly those from better-off households and presumably in formal sector jobs, lost their jobs along with men in times of recession.

The spread of informal work can be seen as one of the longer-term macro-level changes that both accompanied and resulted from economic liberalization. Workers laid off as part of public sector retrenchment or in times of crisis generally turned to the informal economy for 'last-resort' survival activities. The fact that men and women fared very differently in their search for informal work is evident in that fact that, in most developing country contexts, women are more likely than men to be in what the ILO terms 'vulnerable employment', viz. own account work and unpaid family labour. And of men and women in vulnerable employment, women are more likely than men to be in unpaid family labour, and hence without an income of their own.

Recommended reading: Kabeer (1991, 2003).

Conclusion

The analysis in this chapter suggests a number of broad generalizations about the gender dimensions of poverty. It suggests that men and women experience the state of poverty differently, and unequally, with women and girls more likely to report basic needs deficits than men and boys in most contexts. It also suggests that their poverty reflects different processes. Women are more likely than men to be engaged in unpaid work of looking after the family's basic needs and have less time to engage in paid work. And when they do engage in paid work, they generally earn less than men. While women's paid and unpaid contributions are likely to intensify in times of crisis, their subordinate position within the household means that they are also likely to bear the brunt of household coping strategies. In short, policies and projects that fail to acknowledge the critical gender dimensions of poverty in their design will not only fail to address the problem of poverty, but are likely to exacerbate gender inequalities.

Note

1 A longer version of this article was published in the 'Inequalities' issue of *Gender & Development*, 23(2), July 2015: 189–206.

References

Agarwal, B. (1990). 'Social security and the family in rural India coping with seasonality and calamity'. *Journal of Peasant Studies*, 17(3): 341–412.

Alamgir, M. (1980). *Famine in South Asia: The Political Economy of Mass Starvation*. Cambridge, MA: Oelgeschlager & Hain.

Aslanbeigui, N. and Summerfield, G. (2000). 'The Asian crisis, gender, and the international financial architecture'. *Feminist Economics*, 6(3): 81–103.

Beck, T. (1994). *The Experience of Poverty: Fighting for Respect and Resources in Village India*. London: Intermediate Technology.

Bhalotra, S. and Umana-Aponte, M. (2010). 'The dynamics of women's labor supply in developing countries'. *IZA Discussion Paper* No. 4879. Bonn: Institute for the Study of Labour.

Buvinic, M. (1993). 'The feminization of poverty? Research and policy needs'. Presentation to *Symposium on Poverty: New Approaches to Analysis and Policy*. 22–24 November. Geneva: International Institute for Labour Studies.

Buvinic, M. and Yousseff, N. (1978). *Woman-Headed Households: The Ignored Factor in Development Planning*. *Office of Women in Development*. Washington, DC: USAID.

Chant, S. (2003). *New Contributions to the Analysis of Poverty: Methodological and Conceptual Challenges to Understanding Poverty from a Gender Perspective*. Santiago: CEPA, Women and Development Unit.

Commonwealth Secretariat (1989). *Engendering Adjustment for the 1990s*. London: Commonwealth Secretariat.

Corbett, J. (1988). 'Famine and household coping strategies'. *World Development*, 16(9): 1099–112.

Dreze, J. (1988). 'Famine prevention in India'. *Development Economics Paper* No. 3, Suntory Toyota International Centre for Economics and Related Disciplines. London: School of Economics and Political Science.

Elson, D. (1995). 'Household responses to stabilization and structural adjustment: male bias at the micro level'. In D. Elson (ed.), *Male Bias in the Development Process*. Manchester: Manchester University Press, pp. 211–52.

Fergany, N. (1981). 'Monitoring the condition of the poor in the third world: some aspects of measurement'. *ILO/WEP Research Working Paper* WEP 10-6/WP52. Geneva: ILO.

Hanmer, L., Pyatt, G. and White, H. (1997). *Poverty in Sub-Saharan Africa: What Can We Learn About the World Bank's Poverty Assessments?* The Hague: Institute of Social Studies.

Hartmann, B. and Boyce, J. (1983). *A Quiet Violence: View from a Bangladesh Village*. London: Zed Books.

Heltberg, R., Hossain, N., Reva, A. and Turk, C. (2012). 'Anatomy of coping: evidence from people living through the crises of 2008–2011'. *Policy Research Working Paper* 5951. Washington, DC: World Bank.

Hoddinott, J. (2006). 'Shocks and their consequences across and within households in rural Zimbabwe'. *Journal of Development Studies*, 42(2): 301–21.

Jiggins, J. (1986). 'Women and seasonality: coping with crisis and calamity'. *IDS Bulletin*, 17(3): 9–18.

Kabeer, N. (1991). 'Gender dimensions of rural poverty: analysis from Bangladesh'. *Journal of Peasant Studies*, 18(2): 241–62.

Kabeer, N. (2003). 'Approaches in poverty analysis and its gender dimensions'. In *Mainstreaming Gender and Poverty Eradication in the Millennium Development Goals*. London: Commonwealth Secretariat, pp. 79–104.

Kanji, N. (1994). 'Structural adjustment in Zimbabwe: the way forward for low income urban women'. In F. Meer (ed.), *Poverty in the 1990s: The Responses of Urban Women*. Paris: UNESCO, pp. 41–64.

Knowles, J., Pernia, E. and Racelis, M. (1999). 'Social consequences of the financial crisis in Asia'. *Economic Staff Paper* No. 60. Manila, the Philippines: Asian Development Bank.

Marcoux, A. (1998). 'The feminization of poverty: claims, facts and data needs'. *Population and Development Review*, 24(1): 131–9.

Moser, C. (1989). 'The impact of recession and adjustment policies at the micro-level: low income women and their households in Guayquil, Ecuador'. In UNICEF (ed.), *Poor Women and the Economic Crisis: The Invisible Adjustment*. Santiago: UNICEF, pp. 137–62.

Narayan, D., Chambers, R., Shah, M. and Petesch, P. (2000). *Voices of the Poor: Crying Out for Change*. Oxford: Oxford University Press.

Palmer, I. (1995). 'Public finance from a gender perspective'. *World Development*, 23(11): 1981–6.

Rose, E. (1999). 'Consumption smoothing and excess female mortality in rural India'. *Review of Economics and Statistics*, 81(1): 41–9.

UN Women (2012). *The Millennium Development Goals Report: The Gender Chart*. New York: UN Women.

Wood, G. (2003). 'Staying poor, staying secure: the "Faustian bargain"'. *World Development*, 31(3): 455–71.

14

GENDER INEQUALITIES AT WORK

Explanations with examples from Cambodia, the Philippines and China

Fiona MacPhail

Economic development and globalization have contributed to increases in paid work, both waged and self-employment, and considerable evidence of the global feminization of labour exists. Feminization of labour refers to women's increased share of employment and also harmonizing downward of men's labour market outcomes (Standing, 1989), although feminization may pertain only to specific sectors such as manufacturing (or agriculture) rather than across the whole economy. Economic development is taken here to involve structural change, the shift of production away from the primary sector, towards the secondary and tertiary sectors with an associated transfer of labour out of agriculture. Further, economic development is viewed in terms of improved capabilities, meeting basic needs, and human development reflected in increased education, life expectancy and decent standard of living, among other indicators.

Globalization, and particularly increased trade furthered by national governments' export-oriented neoliberal development strategies, has led to the deepening of markets and increased employment in the manufacturing sector, as well as increased commercial agriculture, rise of subcontracting and precarious work. Such development strategies have increased the demand for labour in the manufacturing sector and pulled labour from rural areas, heightening rural–urban and international migration.

The main argument advanced here is that economic development and globalization have led to increased paid work opportunities for women but that pervasive gender inequalities exist, and in some locations inequalities have increased. In making this argument, key feminist economics concepts and approaches for analysing gender and work are outlined and empirical evidence is provided from three Asian countries at different levels of national income per capita, namely Cambodia, the Philippines, and China. In exploring the argument that continued gender inequality in paid work exists, five specific issues are addressed: meanings of gender equality in the labour market and women's economic empowerment; explanations of gender inequality in the labour market; gender and unpaid domestic and care work; gender and paid work; and gender, migration and work.

Recommended reading: Benería *et al.* (2016), Sen and Grown (1985).

Gender, gender equality and women's economic empowerment

The meaning of gender, gender equality and women's economic empowerment are outlined to inform the analysis of gender and work in subsequent sections. In addition, the importance of gender equality in development strategies at international and national levels is noted to further motivate the topic.

Gender refers to the socially constructed differences between women and men, although the notion of binary categorization is critically discussed. Values, norms, attitudes and expectations about femininity and masculinity shape female and male identities and give rise to gendered roles, behaviours, rights, resources and privileges. Gender difference is not only a matter of gender stereotypes, but a hierarchical system that confers greater resources, privilege and power to those with a male identity. Since gender is socially constructed, it is specific to a location and can change over time. Gender interacts with other social categories and markers, including race, ethnicity, class, caste and sexuality, and thus feminist analysis requires an intersectional analysis.

Gender equality in paid work requires both equality of opportunity in participation and employment and equality of treatment or benefit. As outlined in the ILO's fundamental Discrimination (Employment and Occupation) Convention (C111), equality of opportunity 'means having an equal chance to apply for a job, to attend education or training, to eligible to attain certain qualifications and to be considered as a worker or for a promotion in all occupations or positions, including those dominated by one sex or the other'. As for equality of treatment, it 'refers to equal entitlements in pay, working conditions, security of employment, reconciliation between work and family life, and social protection' (ILO, 2008: 20). There are 173 countries that have ratified C111 and 187 countries are signatories to CEDAW, and thus are legally obligated to uphold gender equality and progressively move towards achieving gender equality in the labour market.[1]

Gender equality in the labour market contributes to women's economic empowerment. While the meaning of economic empowerment continues to evolve and variation exists among definitions, a useful starting point is the definition provided by Eyben *et al.* (2008: 9–10):

> Economic empowerment is the capacity of poor women and men to participate in, contribute to and benefit from growth processes on terms which recognize the value of their contributions, respect their dignity and make it possible for them to negotiate a fairer distribution of the benefits of growth. Economic empowerment means people thinking beyond immediate survival needs and thus able to recognize and exercise agency and choice.

Thus, gender equality in paid work in terms of equality of opportunity and treatment is intrinsically linked to empowerment through the benefits from paid work and the opportunities provided for agency. Agency, captured in Kabeer's (1999) phrase, is the opportunity to 'make strategic life choices' at the household level where bargaining and negotiation of resource allocation occurs, as well as at higher community, nation and global levels, where women can collectively exert agency to transform economies and lives of marginalized people.[2]

Gender equality is widely recognized as a policy goal, as the UN Sustainable Development Goal 5 illustrates; however, the motivation for upholding the goal varies.[3] While gender equality as a human right is highlighted by UN Women (2015), other agencies focus on the instrumental value of promoting gender equality. The World Bank (2012) stresses that gender equality is 'smart economics' (although it does also recognize the intrinsic value) since it utilizes society's human capital resources to the full, and the regional development banks such as the Asian Development Bank and ILO (2012) have stressed the distributional benefits of gender equality as a contributor to 'inclusive growth'. While gender equality is a human right, and equality in law is important, achieving substantive gender equality requires actions at all levels, including changing the economic system (UN Women, 2015).[4]

At national levels, countries have expressed commitment to gender equality in constitutions and development plans, advanced legislation and policies, and created government machinery to promote gender equality. Nonetheless, despite commitments and actions, gaps remain between expressed goals of gender equality and the outcomes in practice, substantive equality. Explanations and evidence of gender inequality in work are analysed in this contribution.

Recommended reading: Chant and Sweetman (2012), Eyben *et al.* (2008), ILO (2008), special issue of *Feminist Economics* (2016, 22: 1).

Explanations of gender inequality in work

So how has gender been incorporated into feminist analysis of work, and why do women participate to a lesser extent and experience inferior outcomes in work compared to men?

Work is generally divided into paid work and unpaid domestic and care work. Paid work refers to any activity performed to produced goods or services for monetary or in-kind payment. Improvements in the conceptualization (and measurement) of paid work, ongoing since the 1960s, have broadened the definition of paid work beyond formal wage employment and as owner of a registered business, to include work related to subsistence production and informal employment which includes self-employment, work as an unpaid contributing household member in a household business, and wage labour on a causal or precarious basis. Unpaid domestic and care work, hereafter referred to as unpaid work, is defined as labour expended in the household, which is not remunerated monetarily, on physical tasks such as cooking, washing up, cleaning and washing clothes, as well as caring and emotional tasks such as teaching, care for children, the sick, disabled, elderly people, as well as care for able adults. The distinction between the physical and care tasks emerged in the 1990s with the work of Folbre (1995), Himmelweit (1995) and others.[5]

The enduring gendered division of labour in which women perform the majority of unpaid work is central to feminist economics analyses of gender inequality at work. Marxist-feminist analyses, particularly in the late 1970s and 1980s, attribute gender differences in paid work to the interaction of capitalism and patriarchy. Feminist researchers, such as Hartmann (1981), Folbre (1982) and Walby (1990), advance arguments regarding the role of men in sustaining a sex-segregated labour market that works to preserve their status and privilege in the market, as well as their ability to extract unpaid labour from women, and overall dependence of women on men. Such explanations differ strikingly from those of neoclassical human capital and new household economics (NHE) approaches, which take the gendered division of labour as exogenous and which attribute women's lower labour-force participation rate (LFPR) and wages as a result of choices made by women. A breakthrough in feminist economics was to shift conceptualization of the household away from the assumption of a unitary, harmonious household in both neoclassical NHE and Marxist theories, to take account of both cooperation and conflict within the household, as exemplified in the paper by Agarwal (1997).[6]

Feminist analyses of work from the 1990s onwards have emphasized the role of institutions in creating and maintaining gender difference in the labour market. Building upon Folbre's (1994) 'structures of constraint', Kabeer (2012), and in earlier work, distinguishes between intrinsic gender-specific constraints and imposed structures of constraints and argues that each constraint, along with the feedback loop between the two, underpin women's labour market disadvantage.

Intrinsic gender-specific structures refer to norms and beliefs that define masculinity and femininity at the level of the family, and imposed gender constraints operate at the level of the public domain, including the market, and include laws, rules, policies and discriminatory attitudes of actors.

In terms of intrinsic gender constraints, the notion that feminine characteristics are valued less highly than masculine characteristics at the household level is sharply indicated by the gross magnitude of missing girls and women and levels of gender-based violence. In China, the preference for sons results in abortion of female foetuses and female infanticide, and is starkly evident in the high number of males compared to females; among children aged 0–4 years, there are 117 boys for every 100 girls in 2014 (PRC, 2015: Table 2.8). In Cambodia, violence against women is widespread, with one in five ever partnered women reporting physical and/or sexual violence (RGC, n.d.). Likewise, in China, one-quarter of married women have experienced domestic violence, and this is likely an underestimate (PRC, 2012).

In terms of imposed gender constraints, gender continues to operate in the public sphere to women's disadvantage. In agriculture, women not only have less access to land through intrinsic gender constraints such as inheritance norms, but also through laws, land titling systems and their ability to purchase land and register it in their own name. In Cambodia, despite gender-aware land laws, women have difficulty registering land, which is attributed to lack of information, documents and literacy, as well as social norms that discourage them from owning land individually (RGC, 2008). Although women work in agriculture to the same extent as men, they receive only 10 per cent of the agricultural extension services, and female-headed household have less access to land, less access to credit and extension services, and participation in farmers' organizations (FAO and RGC, 2010). Likewise, in the Philippines, women comprised only 11 per cent of landowners and only 33 per cent of the beneficiaries when land was redistributed (FAO, n.d.). In China, land tenure reforms designed to increase agricultural productivity have reduced women's access to land. Women comprise 70 per cent of the landless and 44 per cent of women report losing land due marriage, typically as a result of moving from their natal village to their husband's village, and also after divorce. The lack of land property rights exacerbates gender equality in work but is also associated with violence against women in China (Song and Dong, 2016).

In the public realm, the actions of employers and government influence women's participation and benefit from paid work. Employers' stereotypes of who is an appropriate worker is evident in job advertisements and bias in hiring practices, with gender interacting with ethnicity. In China, for example, among women job applicants, the rates at which women were invited for a job interview based upon a written resume varied with ethnicity: applicants with a Han-sounding name were much more likely to receive an interview invitation compared to applicants with a minority-sounding name (Maurer-Fazio, 2012). Gender biases exist in laws, such as prohibited jobs, in services, such as thresholds on loans, and in fiscal expansionary policies, which are more likely to positively affect male employment.

Despite the gendered constraints, paid work has some liberating effects through increased decision-making and agency regarding marriage, children and self-esteem (see Heath and Mobarak, 2015, for a Bangladesh example). In rural China, wage employment opportunities are related to greater decision-making by women in the household, although not to reduced total work burden (MacPhail and Dong, 2007). Despite potential for improvements in gender equality, extensive gender inequalities prevail, in some parts of the world are inequalities are increasing, and new forms of gender inequalities develop: as Elson and Pearson (1981: 16) concluded, 'there are inherent limits to the extent to which the provision of wage work for women through capitalist accumulation can dissolve the subordination of women as a gender'. There is a tendency to 'intensify', 'decompose' and/or 'recompose' gender inequalities, resulting in ongoing subordination of women.

Recommended reading: Agarwal (1997), Elson and Pearson (1981), Kabeer (2012).

Gender and unpaid work

A central feature of feminist economics is the analysis of unpaid domestic and care work. The role of unpaid work in capitalist accumulation and reproducing the labour-force (Benería and Sen, 1981; Himmelweit and Mohun, 1977) drew attention to the economic importance of unpaid work, alongside its contribution to human well-being measured in terms of a percentage of GDP.

In general, women perform more unpaid work than men, consistent with the gender norms that assign women this responsibility, resulting in gender gaps in unpaid work. In Cambodia, married women aged 18–64 years provided on average 3.5 hours per day more unpaid work than married men in 2004, and women's total work burden (sum of paid and unpaid work) is greater than men, regardless of marital status, age, and rural or urban location (RGC, 2007). In China, the gender gap in unpaid work time was 2 hours 24 minutes per day in 2008 (Dong and An, 2015: see also Zhan and Montgomery, 2003).

The amount of unpaid work that women perform and the gender gap varies with economic conditions, government policies and changes in gendered norms. With technology, rising income and women's increased paid work, the amount of unpaid work provided by women has fallen in some countries. Gender gaps remain, however, even where men have increased their contributions, and women's total work burdens have often increased, indicating that the gendered division of labour is slow to change. Changing demographics and rise of the elderly population, combined with the reduced state support for care services, is increasing the unpaid work burden for women and is likely to increase work–family conflicts. Government fiscal and monetary policies have clearly gendered impacts on unpaid (and paid) work, as Elson's (1991) analysis of the impact of structural adjustment programmes on increased unpaid work for women clearly showed.

The amount of unpaid work and its gendered dimension have clear connections with gender inequality in paid work. First, girls and women's normative and actual responsibility for unpaid work has been linked to their lower levels of education. In Cambodia, girls are more likely than boys (among children aged 6–17 years) to be withdrawn from school to help with household chores and income generation (RGC, 2013a).

Second, among women, care responsibilities negatively impact paid work. For example, in China, caring for parents-in-law is associated with lower probability of the caregiver being employed and reduced numbers of paid work hours per year (Liu et al., 2010). In the Philippines, 29 per cent of working age women reported that they were not in the labour-force due to household or family duties, compared to only 3 per cent of men, in 2015 (RoP, 2016a).

Third, unpaid work clearly adds to the total work burden and greater work burden of women compared to men, resulting in less leisure, and greater potential stress in combining work and family life. This is particularly the case for low-income women who are less able to afford market substitutes (Floro and Pichetpongsa, 2010).

Recommended reading: Benería et al. (2016: Chapter 5), Floro and Pichetpongsa (2010).

Gender and paid work: continued and/or increased inequality

Structural change and globalization are generally associated with increased women's labour-force participation rates (LFPRs) and increased wage employment; however, a gender LFPR gap persists (World Bank, n.d.). The gender LFPR gap varies substantially by country indicative of gendered norms and inequality in opportunity. Among Southeast Asian countries, for example, the gender LFPR gap ranged from 32 percentage points in Indonesia to about 3 percentage points in Laos, in 2012 (ILO, n.d. a).

Rising women's LFPR and closing of a gender LFPR gap in some countries could be taken as indicative of movement towards equality of opportunity; however, several qualifying points are needed. First, in part, the increase in women's LFPR in some countries is a statistical artefact arising from the underestimation of women's productive work in subsistence agriculture, along with ongoing underreporting of women's work due to cultural norms regarding appropriate gender work roles, despite efforts by statistical agencies. Thus, women's movement into wage employment or self-employment away from subsistence agriculture may reflect only a change in sector of employment associated with structural change, and not an increase in their participation.

Second, while generally women's LFPR and wage employment have increased, resulting in feminization of the labour-force, in some countries defeminization is underway. Declines in women's LFPR have multiple causes, including technological upgrading in manufacturing and stereotyping of jobs as being male. In China, the decline in women's LFPR and rising gender LFPR gap is attributed to declining relative wages and gender wage discrimination and unpaid care burden of women (Cook and Dong, 2011; Hare, 2016).

Third, while structural change is associated with the transfer of labour out of agriculture and increased participation of women, nonetheless, in many countries, men access wage opportunities at a faster rate, resulting in a higher percentage of women remaining in agriculture. This is the case in both Cambodia and China: in China, 43 and 31 per cent of women and men, respectively, work as agriculture and water conservancy labourers in 2014 (a proxy for work in the agricultural sector) (PRC, 2014); in Cambodia, 66 per cent of women and 62 per cent of men work in the primary sector (agriculture, forestry and fishing) in 2013 (RGC, 2013b).

Even where women's LFPRs have risen, substantial industrial and occupation segregation by gender exists. With regard to industrial sex segregation, among employed people, women tend to be segregated in industries that pay lower wages. For example, in Cambodia, women comprise 68 per cent of total employment in manufacturing, a sector in which the average wage is 88 per cent of the average wage across the entire economy, and women earn only 71 per cent of men's earnings in this sector (RGC and ILO, 2012). In China, women are disproportionately employed in subsectors of manufacturing such as textiles, and in retail trade, and hotels and catering, where average wages are low compared to the national average (and specifically 73, 73 and 66 per cent of the national average wage, respectively) (PRC, 2014).

There are also high levels of vertical segregation with women concentrated in bottom of occupational hierarchies, contributing to low wages, poor working conditions, and little opportunities for voice and agency. An important aspect of this gender segregation is that men often have greater opportunities for work in the civil service, a sector that typically offers better opportunities for social security provisions such as pensions, and also opportunities for voice and agency in influencing development strategy. For example, in Cambodia, women's share of employment in the public administration, defence and social security category is only 13 per cent, resulting in more than six times as many men as women being employed as public civil servants, in 2008 (RGC and ILO, 2012). In business, there are substantially fewer women leaders. In China, less than 6 per cent of CEOs are women and only about 8 per cent of board members are women (DELL, 2015). Women are more likely to have unregistered and small businesses compared to men, and profits are generally lower.

Despite increasing or high levels of participation in paid work, women experience less benefit from their paid work, indicative of inequality of treatment in the labour market. Among people with wage employment, a gender wage gap generally exists, although the size of the gap varies among countries. Further, gender wage discrimination has actually increased in many countries, indicating that structural change and globalization have not reduced gender inequalities in treatment. In China, the gender wage gap in urban areas is 33 per cent, i.e. women earn 67 per cent of men's earnings (PRC, 2012). After controlling for gender differences in human capital, the gender wage gap persists, indicative of discrimination against women, and this discrimination appears to have increased (ILO, 2015). In Cambodia, women earn 81 per cent of men's wages on average, and there is evidence of increased gender wage gap after controlling for human capital characteristics (RGC and ILO, 2013; World Bank, 2013). Women are also less likely to have wage employment than men and therefore have fewer opportunities for decent work.[7]

Recommended reading: Benería et al. (2016: Chapters 3–4).

Gender, migration and paid work

Structural change, globalization and neoliberal development strategies underpin gendered migration patterns and its overall feminisation. Export-oriented manufacturing development strategies have increased the demand for women's labour, which has often been met through rural–urban migration. A combination of factors, including increased paid employment among women, neoliberal policies that shift care (back) to households, and demographic changes such as the ageing populations, have increased the demand for paid care services (Benería et al., 2012; Yeates, 2011). This demand has fuelled both internal and international migration of women for paid care work.

Migration flows are increasingly feminized. In China, there are over 270 million rural–urban migrants, accounting for 19 per cent of the total population; and women are over one-third of all migrants in China, and half of all young migrants (Chiang et al., 2015; PRC, 2016). While migration in Cambodia is obviously of smaller scale in absolute terms, at 4.2 million, nonetheless, this represents 29 per cent of the population and women comprise half of all migrants (RGC, 2012). Women represent 51 per cent of the 2.4 million international migrants from the Philippines, of which over half are women (RoP, 2016b). Gender interacts with other key markers such as religion and class to influence the gender composition of migration within a country and differences between countries. Within China, for example, migration among Han women is more prevalent than among some ethnic minorities (Gustafsson and Yang, 2015).

Neoclassical economic analyses of migration focuses on the determinants of migration in terms of relative wage differentials between the origin and destination sites, and, second, on the impact of migrant remittances on poverty alleviation in the site of origin. Rural–urban wage differentials are often substantial, as data for China illustrate, with the migrant workers estimating that, on average, they earn 2.4 times more than they would if they stayed in their home villages (Knight *et al.*, 2011: 587). Similarly, evidence on remittances attest to reduction in income and human poverty, although migration as longer-term development strategy remains controversial (see CDRI, 2007, for a Cambodian example).

Gendered analyses of migration, however, go beyond determinants proxied by relative rural–urban (or domestic–foreign) wages to consider how intrinsic gender constraints affect decisions to migrate and remittances, imposed gender constraints affect the nature of participation and benefit from migration, and development and globalization affect these flows and benefits.

Women's migration for paid work may suggest increased equality of opportunity; however, given strong gendered norms and hierarchies, the decision to migrate for work cannot be viewed purely as an individual choice with individual benefits. Often women's migration is influenced by gender norms regarding their responsibilities as daughters and mothers. In China, for example, women are more likely to explain their motivation to migrate in terms of altruistic/family reasons, whereas men refer to personal development and individual income gain as the main reasons for migration (Chiang *et al.*, 2015). Just as family reasons, such as the responsibility to pay for their brothers' tuition fees or family health services, leads to women's migration, family responsibilities such as care for children and family members contributes to women migrants returning home.

Imposed gender constraints, the gender norms, laws and practices operating through actions of employers and the state give rise to a gendered demand for labour, resulting in high levels of sex segregation of employment. In Cambodia, the degree of sex segregation among migrants is even more pronounced than among non-migrants. Among women migrants, 54 per cent are factory workers (49 per cent are in garments factories alone); among men migrants, 43 per cent are construction workers or labourers in non-construction fields (RGC, 2012); women's high concentration in the garment sector also means that their employment is highly vulnerable to economic shocks and a drop in global demand results in women being pushed into even more precarious forms of employment. Beyond the factory, women are increasingly migrating within countries and internationally for paid domestic and care work in private households as cleaners and caregivers, as well as for firms and the state sector.

Turning to equality of treatment, women migrants generally fare worse than men migrants, across a wide range of dimensions. In China, women migrants earn less than half their urban counterparts (Meng, 2012) and the gender wage gap for migrants is estimated to be 21 per cent (Cui *et al.*, 2013). Women migrants are more likely to have informal employment than men, and hence fewer opportunities for decent work offering access to social security provisions and voice: 64 per cent and 54 per cent of women and men migrants, respectively, have informal employment in China (Dong *et al.*, 2016).

Women migrants often work exceptionally long hours. Even in Cambodian factories involved in third-party monitoring of labour standards, less than 20 per cent of the factories are found to comply with working hour labour standards (ILO and IFC, 2013). In the case of China, as Pun (2007) argues, due to the residential permit system that constrains living in urban areas, people are more willing to work overtime since the window for working in the city is short, and this makes them more vulnerable to exploitation. Further, she argues, tying paid work of women in factories to the dormitory accommodation facilitates long working hours and close monitoring and control over their labour. Here, the patriarchal control of women's labour remains in place, but now exercised by factory managers rather than by fathers and brothers in the countryside. Women international migrants work long hours, often compounded by living with their employers, and suffer from further exploitation and abuse, including physical and sexual abuse, withholding of travel documents, and withholding and underpayment of wages. These outcomes again illustrate the changing form and/or increased gender inequality of treatment.

Despite lower earnings, women migrants often remit a greater proportion of their earnings to families in rural areas, compared to men. In Cambodia, more than three-quarters of women migrant workers sent money to their parents, compared with 68 per cent of men, and women also sent more money in absolute terms, despite their lower earnings (RGC, 2012).

The impacts of migration on the left-behind population are also gendered. Migrant women and men may need to leave their children behind in rural areas given the difficulty and cost of obtaining childcare in urban areas. About 20 per cent of migrants in Phnom Penh with children report that their children are not living in Phnom Penh and the majority live with their grandparents (RGC, 2012). One estimate for China indicates that there are over 61 million children living in rural areas without one or both parents (ACWF, n.d.). Given intrinsic gender constraints, elderly women are typically faced with increased unpaid domestic and care work related to the care of grandchildren (Chang *et al.*, 2011). Women migrants still perform unpaid care tasks for their left-behind children and family members, where such work is made more complicated by distance (see, for example, Parreñas, 2005).

Recommended reading: Benería *et al.* (2012), Pun (2007), Yeates (2011).

Conclusion

Despite widespread stated commitment to the goal of gender equality and women's economic empowerment, gender inequalities in work persist, and in many cases are increasing. Achieving gender equality at work, and more generally improvements in the well-being for women and marginalized groups, requires a shift away from neoclassical economics thinking and policies.

Notes

1 Cambodia, China and the Philippines ratified C111 in 1999, 2006 and 1960 respectively (ILO, n.d. b). Cambodia, China and the Philippines ratified CEDAW in 1992, 1980 and 1981, although China has ratified subject to reservation on Article 29 (UN Women, n.d.).
2 See the special issue of *Feminist Economics* 2016 22(1) on voice and agency.
3 For SDG5, see UN Women at: www.unwomen.org/en/news/in-focus/women-and-the-sdgs/sdg-5-gender-equality.
4 See Chant and Sweetman (2012) for a gendered critique of international development strategies.
5 Unpaid work is typically distinguished from leisure, using the third-party criterion. Based upon this criterion, tasks such as cooking, cleaning and childcare are classified as work because it is possible to pay someone to do the task, whereas activities such as eating, reading and socializing are classified as leisure since one cannot pay another person to provide these services.
6 Neoclassical game-theoretic bargaining models also critiqued the unitary household model and provided alternatives.
7 The concept of decent work refers to adequate earnings and productive work, decent working time, stability and security of work, equal opportunity and treatment in employment and social dialogue. For a complete list, together with definitions and indicators, see ILO (2012).

References

ACWF (n.d.). *The Research Report of the Status of Left-Behind Children in Rural China and Migrant Children in Urban Areas.* Available at: www.womenofchina.cn/womenofchina/html1/survey/1611/3666-1.htm.

Agarwal, B. (1997). 'Bargaining and gender relations: within and beyond the household'. *Feminist Economics*, 3(1): 1–51.

Asian Development Bank and ILO (2012). *Women and Labour Markets in Asia: Rebalancing for Gender Equality.* Bangkok: Asian Development Bank and ILO.

Benería, L. and Sen, G. (1981). 'Accumulation, reproduction, and women's role in economic development: Boserup revisited'. *Signs*, 7(2): 279–98.

Benería, L., Berik, G. and Floro, M.S. (2016). *Gender, Development, and Globalization: Economics as if All People Mattered*, 2nd edition. New York/London: Routledge.

Benería, L., Deere, C.D. and Kabeer, N. (2012). 'Gender and international migration: globalization, development and governance'. *Feminist Economics*, 18(2): 1–33.

CDRI (2007). 'Youth migration and urbanization in Cambodia'. *Working Paper* 36. Phnom Penh: CDRI.

Chang, H., Dong, X. and MacPhail, F. (2011). 'Labor migration and time use patterns of the left-behind children and elderly in rural China'. *World Development*, 39(12): 2199–210.

Chant, S. and Sweetman, C. (2012). 'Fixing women or fixing the world? "Smart economics", efficiency approaches and gender equality in development'. *Gender & Development*, 20(3): 517–29.

Chiang, Y.-L., Annum, E. and Kao, G. (2015). 'It's not just about the money: gender and youth migration from rural China'. *China Sociological Review*, 47(2): 177–201.

Cook, S. and Dong, X.-Y. (2011). 'Harsh choices: Chinese women's paid work and unpaid care responsibilities under economic reform'. *Development and Change*, 42(4): 947–65.

Cui, Y., Nahm, D. and Tani, M. (2013). 'Earnings differentials and returns to education in China, 1995–2008'. *IZA Discussion Paper* No. 7349, April.

DELL (2015). *2015 Global Women Entrepreneur Leaders Scorecard*. Available at: http://powermore.dell.com/gwelscorecard/.

Dong, X.-Y. and An, X. (2015). 'Gender patterns and value of unpaid care work: findings from China's first large-scale time use survey'. *Review of Income and Wealth*, 61(3): 540–60.

Dong, X.-Y., Li, S. and Yang, S. (2016). 'Trade liberalization, social policy development and labour market outcomes of Chinese women and men in the decade after China's accession to the World Trade Organization'. *Discussion Paper* No. 9, February. Available at: www.unwomen.org/-/media/headquarters/attachments/sections/library/publications/2016/china-labour-force-analysis.pdf?vs=1916.

Elson, D. (1991). *Male Bias in the Development Process*. Manchester: Manchester University Press.

Elson, D. and Pearson, R. (1981). 'Nimble fingers make cheap workers: an analysis of women's employment in Third World export manufacturing'. *Feminist Review*, 7(1): 87–107.

Eyben, R., Kabeer, N. and Cornwall, A. (2008). 'Conceptualising empowerment and the implications for pro-poor growth'. Paper for the DAC Poverty Network. Institute of Development Studies.

FAO (n.d.). *Gender and Land Rights Database*. Available at: www.fao.org/gender-landrights-database/en/.

FAO and RGC (2010). National Institute of Statistics and Ministry of Planning. 2010. *National Gender Profile of Agricultural Households, 2010, Report based on the 2008 Cambodia Socio-Economic Survey*. Phnom Penh: FAO and RGC.

Floro, M.S. and Pichetpongsa, A. (2010). 'Gender, work intensity, and well-being of Thai home-based workers'. *Feminist Economics*, 16(3): 5–44.

Folbre, N. (1982). 'Exploitation comes home: a critique of the Marxian theory of family labor'. *Cambridge Journal of Economics*, 6: 317–29.

Folbre, N. (1994). *Who Pays for the Kids? Gender and the Structure of Constraints*. London: Routledge.

Folbre, N. (1995). '"Holding hands at midnight": the paradox of caring labor'. *Feminist Economics*, 1(1): 73–92.

Gustafsson, B. and Yang, X. (2015). 'Are China's ethnic minorities less likely to move?' *Eurasian Geography and Economics*, 56(1): 44–69.

Hare, D. (2016). 'What accounts for the decline in labourforce participation among married women in urban China, 1991–2011?' *China Economic Review*, 38(C): 251–66.

Hartmann, H. (1981). 'The unhappy marriage of Marxism and feminism'. In L. Sargeant (ed.), *Women and Revolution: A Discussion of the Unhappy Marriage of Marxism and Feminism*. Boston, MA: South End Press, pp. 1–41.

Heath, R. and Mobarak, A.M. (2015). 'Manufacturing growth and lives of Bangladeshi women'. *Journal of Development Economics*, 115: 1–15.

Himmelweit, S. (1995). 'The discovery of "unpaid work": the social consequences of the expansion of "work"'. *Feminist Economics*, 1(2): 1–20.

Himmelweit, S. and Mohun, S. (1977). 'Domestic labour and capital'. *Cambridge Journal of Economics*, 1(1): 15–31.

ILO (n.d. a). *Key Indicators of the Labour Market (KILM)*. Available at: www.ilo.org/global/statistics-and-databases/research-and-databases/kilm/WCMS_498929/lang—en/index.htm.

ILO (n.d. b). *NORMLEX*. Available at: http://ilo.org/dyn/normlex/en/f?p=NORMLEXPUB:1:0::NO:::.

ILO (2008). *Work, Income and Gender Equality in East Asia: Action Guide*. Bangkok: ILO.

ILO (2012). *Decent Work Indicators: Concepts and Definitions*. Geneva: ILO.

ILO (2015). *Women in the Labor Market in China*. ILO Asia-Pacific Working Paper Series. Available at: www.ilo.org/public/libdoc/ilo/2015/487966.pdf.

ILO and IFC (2013). *Better Factories Cambodia: Thirtieth Synthesis Report on Working Conditions in Cambodia's Garment Sector*. Geneva: ILO.

Kabeer, N. (1999). 'Resources, agency, achievements: reflections on the measurement of women's empowerment'. *Development and Change*, 30(3): 435–64.

Kabeer, N. (2012). 'Women's economic empowerment and inclusive growth: labor markets and enterprise development'. *Social Innovation Generation Working Paper 2012/1*. IDRC and Department for International Development of the UK. Available at: www.idrc.ca/sites/default/files/sp/Documents%20EN/NK-WEE-Concept-Paper.pdf.

Knight, J., Deng, Q. and Li, S. (2011). 'The puzzle of migrant labour shortage and rural labour surplus in China'. *China Economic Review*, 22(4): 586–600.

Liu, L., Dong, X.-Y. and Zheng, X. (2010). 'Parental care and married women's labor supply in urban China'. *Feminist Economics*, 16(3): 169–92.

MacPhail, F. and Dong, X.Y. (2007). 'Market labor and women's status in the household in rural China: implications for gender equity under the WTO'. *Feminist Economics*, 13(3–4): 93–124.

Maurer-Fazio, M. (2012). 'Ethnic discrimination in China's Internet job board labor market'. *IZA Journal of Migration*, 1(12): 1–24.

Meng, X. (2012). 'Labor market outcomes and reform in China'. *Journal of Economic Perspectives*, 26(4): 75–101.

Parreñas, R. (2005). *Children of Global Migration: Transnational Families and Gendered Woes*. Palo Alto, CA: Stanford University Press.

PRC (2012). *Women and Men in China: Facts and Figures 2012*. Beijing: PRC.

PRC (2014). *China Labour Statistical Yearbook 2014*. Beijing: PRC.

PRC (2015). *China Statistical Yearbook 2015*. Beijing: PRC.

PRC (2016). *National Monitoring Report of Migrant Workers (in Chinese)*. Available at: www.stats.gov.cn/tjsj/zxfb/201604/t20160428_1349713.html.

Pun, N. (2007). 'Gendering the dormitory labor system: production, reproduction, and migrant labor in South China'. *Feminist Economics*, 13(3–4): 239–58.

RGC (n.d.). *National Survey on Women's Health and Life Experiences in Cambodia: Report*. Phnom Penh: RGC.

RGC (2007). *Cambodia Socio-Economic Survey 2004, Time Use in Cambodia*. Phnom Penh: RGC.

RGC (2008). *A Fair Share for Women: Cambodia Gender Assessment*. Phnom Penh: RGC.

RGC (2012). *Migration in Cambodia: Report of the Cambodian Rural Urban Migration Project (CRUMP)*. Phnom Penh: RGC.

RGC (2013a). *National Institute for Statistics*. Available at: www.nis.gov.kh/nis/CSES/Data/CSES_2013/CSES_Education.htm.

RGC (2013b). *Cambodia Inter-Censal Population Survey 2013. Final Report*. Phnom Penh: RGC.

RGC and ILO (2012). *Labour and Social Trends in Cambodia 2010*. Phnom Penh: RGC and ILO.

RGC and ILO (2013). *Cambodia Labourforce and Child Labour Survey 2012. Laborforce Report*. Phnom Penh/Geneva: RGC and ILO.

RoP (2016a). *Decent Work Statistics (DeWS): Philippines. Summary Tables 1995–2015*. Manila: Philippines Statistics Authority.

RoP (2016b). *2016 Gender Statistics on Labor and Employment*. Manila: Philippines Statistics Authority.

Sen, G. and Grown, C. (1985). *Development, Crises and Alternative Visions: Third World Women's Perspectives*. New Delhi: DAWN.

Song, Y. and Dong, X.-Y. (2016). 'Domestic violence and women's land rights in rural China: findings from a national survey in 2010'. *Journal of Development Studies*.

Standing, G. (1989). 'Global feminization through flexible labour'. *World Development*, 17(7): 1077–95.

UN Women (n.d.). *Declarations, Reservations and Objections to CEDAW*. Available at: www. un.org/womenwatch/daw/cedaw/reservations-country.htm.

UN Women (2015). *Progress on the World Women 2015–2016: Transforming Economies, Realizing Rights*. New York: UN Women.

Walby, S. (1990). *Theorizing Patriarchy*. Oxford: Basil Blackwell.

World Bank (n.d.). *World Development Indicators*. Available at: http://data.worldbank.org/ indicator/SL.TLF.CACT.FM.ZS.

World Bank (2012). *World Development Report 2012: Gender Equality and Development*. Washington, DC: World Bank.

World Bank (2013). *Where Have All the Poor Gone? Cambodia Poverty Assessment 2013*. Washington, DC: World Bank.

Yeates, N. (2011). 'Going global: the transnationalization of care'. *Development and Change*, 42(4): 1109–30.

Zhan, H.J. and Montgomery, R. (2003). 'Gender and elder care in China: the influence of filial piety and structural constraints'. *Gender and Society*, 17(2): 209–29.

PART V

Policy configurations for development

International, national and local

15

THE POST-WASHINGTON CONSENSUS

Elisa Van Waeyenberge

When we seek to reflect critically on policy configurations for development, the crucial role of an international financial institution (IFI) such as the World Bank assumes centre stage. The World Bank has aspired to a leadership role in development since the McNamara Presidency (1968–1980), but its capacity to do so has depended on the broader environment within which it operates. During the 1980s, a set of events, including the debt crisis, the political turn to the right in major OECD economies, the Volcker shock, etc., coincided to enable such a leadership role for the Bank. At the same time, its broader policy framework shifted from an earlier Keynesian or more structuralist orientation towards a neoliberal frame, most aptly captured through the emergence of the Washington Consensus.

Nearly two decades later, as the neoliberal policy experiment in developing countries failed to deliver on its projected benefits, attempts were made to move the policy paradigm towards a post-Washington Consensus. This shift sought to capture the persistence of market failure in developing countries and the need for policy prescriptions to reflect such realities. Where previously, under the Washington Consensus, the state and market had been presented as alternative economic governance mechanisms, with a strong bias against resource allocation through the state, a more comprehensive approach now sought to project a partnership between the two institutional settings. The recognition of persistent market failure called for more extensive state intervention with the main aim of making markets work better.

The primacy of both the market as a preferred resource allocation mechanism and the private sector as a preferred agent in development, however, remained unchallenged, and the shift from Washington to post-Washington Consensus is best understood as capturing a transition from one phase of neoliberalism to another. Where for the Washington Consensus 'rolling back' the state to promote markets dominated the agenda, with the post-Washington Consensus the state is recognized as indispensable to support market expansion and to manage the various contradictions that the initial phase of neoliberalism under the Washington Consensus engendered. Further, the transition from Washington to post-Washington Consensus took place against the backdrop of an unprecedented expansion of private sector flows to the developing world, which was only temporarily punctured by the dramatic events of the global financial crisis (GFC). Since at least a decade, whether through the post-Washington Consensus or not, development discourse has become entirely oriented towards the promotion of private sector (and financial) interests, and this is perhaps most blatant in the recently reinvigorated promotion by the donor community of public–private partnerships (PPPs) across *any* area of public service provision.

This short contribution seeks to situate the emergence of the post-Washington Consensus within development policy discourse and practices. It first charts the rise of the Washington Consensus. It proceeds by sketching the way in which notions such as good governance and ownership became promoted in development rhetoric, as the Washington Consensus was extended across a broader policy terrain. And, finally, it discusses the nature and significance of the post-Washington Consensus against the backdrop of changing global development financing realities. It undertakes this brief review with particular attention to the uneven and shifting relationship between the rhetoric, scholarship and policies in practice of the World Bank against the backdrop of a constantly evolving neoliberal world.

The Washington Consensus

The 1980s was characterized by the neoliberal turn in development, and the World Bank played a crucial role in effecting this transition. This was facilitated by the introduction in the early 1980s of a new lending modality by the Bank. Lending for adjustment programmes provided balance-of-payments support not linked to any specific investment project. It did so, however, in return for changes in policy through conditionalities. Policy-based lending bought the Bank a space at countries' policy table and provided the opportunity for a paradigm shift that would reflect the broader turn to the right taking place in the institutions' main shareholder countries. Policy-based lending indeed easily lent itself to ideological affiliation with the right-wing political sentiment in core Bank shareholders, tempering their initial hostility towards development cooperation as the substantive content of the new lending programmes came to reflect a new aid discourse focused on price incentives and perfectly working markets. Policy-based lending, of course, was not new, being enshrined in the constitution of the Bank's sister institution, the International Monetary Fund (IMF), and the Bank's venture into structural adjustment lending implied issues of overlap, which the institutions attempted to deal with through increased cooperation and collaboration.

At the Bank, the Berg Report (World Bank, 1981) was emblematic of the shift to the right, with its representation of Africa's deteriorating economic conditions entirely in terms of misguided government policies. The Report made a series of recommendations. These included: (i) to restore prices to 'market' levels; (ii) to devalue exchange rates; and (iii) to remove parastatals, subsidies and price controls. In short, the Report sought a 'restoration' of the 'superior' allocative role of the price system and a 're-establishment' of the incentives deriving from private ownership. These features would come to characterize the structural adjustment programmes promoted by the Bank during the 1980s.

The publication of the Berg Report indicated the rise of 'monoeconomics' in development economics (Hirschman, 1981). The idea came to prevail that 'economic rationality' characterized agents across time and regions, and that the economic logic of individual optimization leading to social optima characterized economic interactions in the developed as well as developing world. The appointment of Anne Krueger as the Bank's Chief Economist to replace Hollis Chenery in 1982 was emblematic of this shift. Hollis Chenery had made major contributions to structural development economics, while Anne Krueger was a trade economist of the most orthodox (and neoliberal) kind. In the first issue of the *World Bank Research Observer*, she left no doubt regarding her creed as she stated that: 'Once it is recognised that individuals respond to incentives, and that "market failure" is the result of inappropriate incentives rather than of non-responsiveness, the separateness of development economics as a field largely disappears' (Krueger, 1986: 62). For Williamson (1990: 19), as another spearhead of the neoliberal transformation of development scholarship, the rise of the monoeconomics during the 1980s exposed the previous development literature as a 'diversion from the harsh realities of the dismal science [of economics]'. None of the ideas that prevailed in previous development scholarship, such as the big push, balanced or unbalanced growth, surplus growth, surplus labour, mattered anymore in a monoeconomic understanding of development.

By the mid-1980s, the ideas about economic management underlying the structural adjustment and stabilisation programmes promoted by the Bretton Woods Institutions (BWIs) had become readily accepted orthodoxy in the official donor community. The policy conditions set by the World Bank and IMF sought to eliminate obstacles to a 'perfect market' as the presumed optimal path to growth. What came to be referred to as the 'Washington Consensus' (Williamson, 1990) – to reflect a policy consensus shared between three Washington-based institutions, the World Bank, IMF and US Treasury – embodied the twin imperatives of 'stabilization' and 'adjustment', where the former was to proceed through tight controls on money supply growth and the latter necessitated a set of supply-side measures aimed at boosting private sector activity.

In essence, this boiled down to the mantra of deregulation, privatization and liberalization. More specifically, the Washington Consensus included 10 policy recommendations. First was 'fiscal discipline' necessitating strict control on budget deficits (which were argued to cause inflation and capital flight). Second, government subsidies needed curtailing and government expenditures to be redirected towards education, health and infrastructure. Third, tax reform sought to broaden the tax base and cut marginal tax rates. Fourth, interest rates were to become market-determined (i.e. liberalized). Fifth, exchange rates were to be liberalized so as to become 'competitive' and stimulate exports. Sixth, tariffs were to replace quotas, and to be reduced as fast as possible ('trade liberalization'). Seventh, foreign direct investment was to be liberalized by dismantling barriers to entry. Eighth, state-owned enterprises were to be privatized. Ninth, the economy was to be deregulated (i.e. regulations that impede the entry of new firms or restrict competition are to be abolished). And tenth, property rights were to be established and enforced.

The Washington Consensus relied on the economic theory of perfectly working markets that derives from general equilibrium theory. According to this theory, the competitive market yields welfare-maximizing outcomes when a set of conditions are satisfied (no externalities, no public goods or natural monopolies, complete set of markets, given preferences, initial endowments and technology). The case for government intervention is limited to lump sum redistributions and the correction of a well-defined set of market failures listed above. The priority for government policy is to allow prices to be 'right' (reflecting scarcity and preferences) so that individual economic agents can allocate resources efficiently in response to these signals.

Mainstream economic theory has raised a set of objections regarding this framework as appropriate for the analysis of developing economies (see Van Waeyenberge, 2006). Fundamentally, however, the highly abstract assumptions upon which the policy prescriptions of the Washington Consensus proceed are incapable of accommodating real-world features as they fail to reflect the historic and context-specific characteristics of a developing country in favour of universal principles of rationality and optimization. This leads to fundamental misunderstandings of the interactions between private and public sectors and a persistent failure to understand economic and social outcomes, including those deriving from 'state' or 'market' dynamics, as anchored on and deriving from specific social-economic structures and relationships. The nature of the interests, including of private and foreign capital, served by the promotion of such a paradigm should not be treated as a moot point.

Recommended reading: Gould (2005), Van Waeyenberge (2006).

Good governance and ownership

The 1980s came to a close and the decade-long experience with Washington Consensus-inspired policies failed to deliver promised results. For the Bank, however, the problem did not originate with its programmes, but stemmed from the inadequate adoption of the policy prescriptions. It was the 'lack of local capacity, both private and public, in their design and execution' (World Bank, 1989: 62) that accounted for the lacklustre results of the adjustment programmes. Rather than revisit the flawed premise of the conditions imposed on countries through structural adjustment programmes, conditionalities were to be extended to areas responsible for the adoption of IFI-advocated policies. Attention shifted towards mechanisms of policy implementation. This was supported by a growing conservative literature on the 'political economy' of reform in developing countries (Haggard and Webb, 1993; Krueger, 1993).

For the IFIs, the implementation of macroeconomic reforms then necessitated 'governance' reforms, and the traditional (economic) reform agenda of the 1980s was extended to incorporate issues of a traditionally more political nature. These encompassed public sector management, accountability and transparency of the public sector, the legal framework, corruption, military expenditure, etc. These were all put in the service of a core set of neoliberal policies. At the same time, and without any intention of parody, recipient governments were urged to adopt a more 'participatory' approach to formulating the development agenda. While remaining strongly committed to its core economic reform programme, the donor community argued that 'effective change' could not be imposed from outside and sought to cast the donor–recipient relationship in a new light. In donor rhetoric, 'ownership' of the development agenda moved centre stage. Implementation of aid programmes involved 'partnerships' with recipient governments as well as nongovernmental organizations ('civil society'). Aid-dependent countries became caught between a dramatic narrowing of the policy space and an obligation to fulfil predetermined conditions of consultation and participation, apart from broader scrutiny of their public sector management in an attempt to satisfy the good governance agenda.

By the end of the 1990s, the participation and ownership agenda became formally enshrined in the Poverty Reduction Strategy initiative. The Poverty Reduction Strategy Papers (PRSPs) became a precondition for low-income countries to access loans from the BWIs. These sought to incorporate a commitment to poverty reduction and at the same to elevate the principles of consultation and ownership that had become celebrated by the BWIs in an attempt to improve the adoption of their policy conditionalities. The PRSPs combined with a more selective approach to the allocation of its aid funds on behalf of the World Bank, where the a priori assessment of a country's performance in a set of policy domains, including macroeconomic policy, trade policy, financial sector policy, and public sector management and governance increasingly guided aid allocation decisions (see Van Waeyenberge, 2009). The onus for low-income countries' access to aid resources dramatically worsened to include a priori tests of their capacity to comply with a broadened agenda of policy reform ranging from economic, administrative and governance issues, as well as testing their capacity to deliver on prescribed forms of consultation.

Recommended reading: Brown (2004), Van Waeyenberge (2009).

The post-Washington Consensus

The 1990s, however, had witnessed increased mobilizations against the BWI-dictated policy order. The fiftieth anniversary of the institutions was marked by vocal campaigns that 50 years had been enough. The economic performance of the adjusting countries failed to impress and the social impact of the IFI-promoted programmes had been deleterious. State provision across various sectors had collapsed, subsidy regimes of staple foods were eliminated with catastrophic impacts on standards of living, investment had failed to pick up, formal sector employment fell dramatically, real wages declined, and there was limited supply response across agricultural and manufacturing sectors.

The World Bank could not ignore the manifold critiques of its adjustment programmes. It also faced questions from its second largest shareholder, Japan, over the way in which the Washington Consensus-inspired policy reform programme sat with Japan's own development history. The East Asian Miracle (EAM) Report (World Bank, 1993) ensued, and within it the World Bank managed to reconcile a set of contradictory propositions. In the first instance, the Report admitted that there was a theoretical case for industrial policy. It then proceeded to refute its empirical importance for industrial performance in East Asia. And finally, the Report argued that there were practical objections on why the policy was not transferable to other countries (Chang, 1999; Wade, 1996). However, even if the EAM Report endorsed a continuing market-friendly approach, at the same time it facilitated a shift from a simple dichotomy of government versus market towards a more cooperative relationship between the two.

Next, the Bank was to find a way to move beyond both structural adjustment and the EAM Report. Joseph Stiglitz was to take up the challenge with his proposal for a post-Washington Consensus. This had become even more urgent against the backdrop of the disastrous results of IFI-led transitions in the Eastern European countries (see Florio, 2002), and the outbreak of a series of international financial crises during the mid to late 1990s (Mexico 1994, East Asia 1997–1998, Russia 1998, Brazil 1999). And so the post-Washington Consensus entered the policy stage, when, from the platform of the Annual United Nations WIDER Lecture, Stiglitz (1998a) openly denounced the failings of Washington Consensus with a talk entitled 'More instruments and broader goals: moving toward the post-Washington Consensus'.

For Stiglitz (1998a), the Washington Consensus was at best incomplete and at worst misguided. It had focused on a small set of instruments, including macroeconomic stability, liberalized trade and privatization, to achieve the narrow goal of economic growth. The singular focus on such policies as trade liberalization, deregulation and privatization had detracted from important conditions for stability and long-term development. These included the legal and regulatory framework, competition policy, technology policy, investments in education, etc. Further, development is not merely an interplay of economic variables, but has to be understood as a 'holistic' process. The post-Washington Consensus tried, at least in principle, to move beyond the reductionist conception of the development process implied by its predecessor. It also sought to project a different view of state–society interactions, and following the 1997 World Development Report (World Bank, 1997), development became understood as an inter-sectoral cooperation process. Such posturing was stronger on rhetoric than substance, and conveniently failed to extend its vision of past development thinking and policy to the *pre*-Washington Consensus. Nonetheless, the projected antagonism between state and society/market gave way to a notion of 'partnership': the private and public sector were now recognized to be intimately entwined (Stiglitz, 1998a).

With the post-Washington Consensus paradigm, market failure then acquired ontological status. The policy implications of such failure, however, were less clear-cut. Where previously in the pre-Washington Consensus era the recognition of the pervasive nature of market failure in a developing country setting provided strong arguments in favour of state interventions, with the post-Washington Consensus a more ambivalent set of prescriptions emerged. Market failures no longer necessitated 'old-style' government intervention where the state acted instead of the market. Instead, new mediations of state–market interactions had to be deployed. Furthermore, with different sources and degrees of market failure (and states with varying levels of 'capability'), the implications for the role of the state could differ significantly across countries (World Bank, 1997). The issue then became a quest for a particular institutional set-up (a 'partnership' between state and society across private profit and non-profit sectors) that would maximize benefits to society. Crucially, the state was to make sure that market failures are overcome without imposing 'unnecessary' costs on society. As a result, when state 'capability' was low, it was to rely, as much as possible, on the relative strengths of the private sector, the community, the family and the individual 'citizen' (Stiglitz, 1998b).

The new agenda reflected a set of propositions that had become increasingly popular in development economics. These drew on a collection of mainstream economic innovations and through these theoretical innovations traditionally non-economic issues became increasingly addressed within the discipline (see Fine, 1997, on economic imperialism). Hence, after a temporary retreat of development from economics during the reign of the Washington Consensus, a 'resurgence' of development economics seemed to be taking place. This new framework purportedly incorporated issues whose neglect had rendered the preceding analysis incomplete, and claimed to revisit important matters touched upon in the earlier debates on development of the post-war period. Furthermore, the new approach allegedly anchored the economic analysis of development in its broader social reality.

However, the extent to which the post-Washington Consensus provides us with improved insights into the processes of development remains questionable. First, the restatement of an analysis of development proposed by Stiglitz essentially proceeds on the same principles of optimization and choice as its predecessor. Its distinctiveness lays mainly in changes to the initial assumptions under which optimization takes place. A softening of the assumptions as proposed through the post-Washington Consensus, however, strengthens social (and development) theory on the basis of methodological individualism to the neglect of the social, the historical and the specific. Second, the extension of the analysis into traditionally non-economic domains (including, for instance, institutions) proceeds at the expense of substantive content and analytical power. The analysis remains hampered by its ahistorical, asocial and reductionist method. Accounts of economic and other social phenomena emerge as a result of individual choice and optimization. Development, with its complex and uneven processes of social and economic change through technological progress, productivity growth, structural change, industrialization, urbanization, the spread of markets and the various conflicts and struggles these engender, is ill-served by such a narrow and reductionist analytical prism.

Finally, in the context of its propositions regarding the role of the state, it is true that compared to the 'rolling back of the state' precept of the Washington Consensus, some progress seems to have been made through the shift towards a post-Washington Consensus, with its stronger recognition of the importance of the state for a sound working of the economy. The role of the latter, however, remains essentially confined to the creation of a conducive environment for the private sector to fulfil its allegedly dynamic role in development. The government is, in essence, to improve the institutional environment in which private agents steer their interaction in socially desirable directions. The abiding legacy of the new political economy, with its negative normative presumptions regarding the public sector, implies a persistent underlying bias against direct management of economic resources by the state: the market (but now also the non-market non-state) remain superior. Even in comparison with the pre-Washington Consensus, McNamara era, the post-Washington Consensus appears as a 'regression', contrasting with the former's tolerance (and support) for state-controlled development enterprises.

The post-Washington Consensus can then perhaps better be understood as a policy paradigm attached to a particular moment in neoliberalism, which necessitated a reorientation of state–market interactions to the benefit of private capital, as well as reflected the need to manage the contradictions engendered by the crude neoliberal policy prescriptions of the 1980s. It is indeed striking that as the post-Washington Consensus took hold, private international capital flows to the developing world moved onto an exponential trajectory, dramatically accelerating the financial integration of core parts of the developing world. This expansion was temporarily halted as a result of the GFC, but picked up again soon after. Accompanying this trend, we have seen a significant redefinition of the purpose of development cooperation, recrafted now almost exclusively in support of the expansion of private flows.

Since the early 2000s, the commitment to the public financing of development has indeed steadily eroded in favour of a view of development as spearheaded by mobile private capital (Van Waeyenberge, 2015). The position that attributes a pivotal role to the private sector in financing development was at the heart of the outcome document of the Third Financing for Development Summit held in Addis Ababa in 2015, which set out the framework through which the Sustainable Development Goals (SDGs) are to be financed. The official adoption by the international community of the principle that financing for development is increasingly to be provided through international capital markets has combined with strong statements in support of PPPs for infrastructure provision as a way to achieve the SDGs. The role of public sector flows has become redefined in support of private sector expansion, also to address basic needs in developing countries, rather than that public service provision is expanded through mobilization of taxes (and official development cooperation) and the sustained efforts to combat illicit capital flows. Instead, the enormous glut of private savings that has emerged over the last decade is celebrated as providing the possibilities to finance basic needs provision in developing countries. Such a position can easily be supported through the post-Washington Consensus, as long as there is sufficient attention to regulatory and other issues framed around improving incentives for private providers. This is to the detriment of any attempt to understand the distributional dynamics implied in these developments where the satisfaction of basic needs, including health, education and housing, and of poor people, becomes opened up for the extraction of revenues by private capital.

Recommended reading: Bayliss and Van Waeyenberge (2017), Bayliss *et al.* (2011), Fine (2001).

References

Bayliss, K. and Van Waeyenberge, E. (2017). 'Unpacking the Public Private Partnership Revival'. *The Journal of Development Studies*, doi: 10.1080/00220388.2017.1303671

Bayliss, K., Fine, B. and Van Waeyenberge, E. (eds) (2011). *The Political Economy of Development: The World Bank, Neoliberalism and Development Research*. London: Pluto.

Brown, D. (2004). 'Participation in poverty reduction strategies: democracy strengthened or democracy undermined?' In S. Hickey and M. Mohan (eds), *Participation: From Tyranny to Transformation?* London: Zed Books, pp. 56–98.

Chang, H.-J. (1999). 'Industrial policy and East Asia. The miracle, the crisis and the future'. Paper presented at the World Bank workshop on Re-thinking the East Asian Miracle, San Francisco, February.

Fine, B. (1997). 'The new revolution in economics'. *Capital and Class*, 61, Spring: 143–8.

Fine, B. (2001). 'Neither the Washington nor the post-Washington Consensus: an introduction'. In B. Fine, C. Lapavitsas and J. Pincus (eds), *Development Policy in the Twenty-First Century: Beyond the Post-Washington Consensus*. London: Routledge, pp. 1–27.

Florio, M. (2002). 'Economists, privatization in Russia and the waning of the "Washington Consensus"'. *Review of International Political Economy*, 9(2): 374–415.

Gould, J. (ed.) (2005). *The New Conditionality: The Politics of Poverty Reduction Strategies*. London: Zed Books.

Haggard, S. and Webb, S. (1993), 'What do we know about the political economy of economic policy reform?' *World Bank Research Observer*, 8(2): 143–68.

Hirschman, A. (1981). 'The rise and decline of development economics'. In *Essays in Trespassing*. Cambridge: Cambridge University Press, pp. 1–24.

Krueger, A. (1986). 'Aid in the development process'. *World Bank Research Observer*, 1(1): 57–78.

Krueger, A. (1993). *Political Economy of Policy Reform in Developing Countries*. Cambridge, MA/London: MIT Press.

Stiglitz, J. (1998a). 'More instruments and broader goals: moving toward the post-Washington Consensus'. Wider Annual Lecture, Helsinki, 7 January.

Stiglitz, J. (1998b). 'Towards a new paradigm for development strategies, policies and process'. 1998 Prebish Lecture at UNCTAD, Geneva, 19 October.

Van Waeyenberge, E. (2006). 'From Washington to post-Washington Consensus: illusions of development'. In K.S. Jomo and B. Fine (eds), *The New Development Economics: After the Washington Consensus*. London: Zed Books, pp. 21–45.

Van Waeyenberge, E. (2009). 'Selectivity at work: country policy and institutional assessments at the World Bank'. *European Journal of Development Research*, 21(5): 792–810.

Van Waeyenberge, E. (2015). 'The private turn in development finance'. *FESSUD Working Paper* 140.

Wade, R. (1996). 'Japan, the World Bank, and the art of paradigm maintenance: the East Asian miracle in political perspective'. *New Left Review*, 217: 3–37.

Williamson, J. (1990). 'What Washington means by policy reform'. In J. Williamson (ed.), *Latin American Adjustment: How Much Has Happened?* Washington, DC: Institute for International Economics, pp. 7–20.

World Bank (1981). *Accelerated Development in Sub-Saharan Africa: An Agenda for Action*. Washington, DC: World Bank.

World Bank (1989). *Sub-Saharan Africa: From Crisis to Sustainable Growth*. Washington, DC: World Bank.

World Bank (1993). *The East Asian Miracle: Economic Growth and Public Policy*. New York: Oxford University Press for the World Bank.

World Bank (1997). *World Development Report 1997: The State in a Changing World*. New York: Oxford University Press for the World Bank.

16

INTERNATIONAL COOPERATION FOR DEVELOPMENT

Peter Kragelund

Recently, international cooperation for development has undergone tectonic shifts. While overseas development assistance (ODA) was the cornerstone of planned inter-action between the Global North and the Global South during and after the Cold War, ODA is now, at best, facilitating this interaction, and is instead mainly used to accelerate other financial flows such as trade and foreign direct investment (FDI).

This change in international cooperation for development affects both aid donors and aid recipients in several interrelated ways. For instance, it is chang-ing how, and the extent to which, Northern donors shape policies in the Global South; it has undermined the hegemonic power of the Development Assistance Committee (DAC) in defining what development is and how to achieve it; and the degree to which governments in the Global South can define and fund their own development policies. These developments have prompted researchers to talk of 'Aid 2.0', 'beyond aid' and a 'post-aid world' (Janus *et al.*, 2015). In recipient countries, the effects of this post-aid world are uneven and depend on factors such as the possibility of attracting alternative forms of finance (e.g. remittances, FDI, trade and natural resources) (Kragelund, 2012), their perceived attractiveness to external financers (e.g. governance and conflicts) and their geographical location.

This chapter outlines this tectonic shift in international cooperation for devel-opment and analyses how it affects international cooperation for development 'as we know it'. It further seeks to crack open the black box of what these changes might mean for the Global South. In order to do this, I first summarize the field of international cooperation for development 'as we knew it' in the second sec-tion; then in the third section, I analyse the underlying reasons for this tectonic shift, focusing in particular on the role of new state and private sector actors. In the fourth section, I reflect on how this shift is affecting the donor landscape; and in the fifth section, I provide a preliminary assessment of its effects on the Global South.

International development cooperation 'as we knew it'

International development cooperation 'as we knew it' originated in the post-World War II restructuring of the global economy. The Bretton Woods Conference held in New Hampshire, USA, in 1944 is often referred to as the beginning of development assistance and, by extension, of the development cooperation era. This conference led to the establishment of the International Bank for Reconstruction and Development (the World Bank) and the International Monetary Fund (IMF). In the years that followed, the UN Charter was drawn up (1945), and organizations such as the International Labour Organization (1946), the United Nations International Children's Emergency Fund (1946) and the World Health Organization (1948) were established.

Equally important was the so-called Marshall Plan (i.e. the US-funded recovery programme for Europe under which approximately US$13 million were transferred from the US to war-torn European countries between 1948 and 1951). The Marshall Plan is frequently lauded as the most effective development aid programme ever, and as such it is often used to 'prove' that aid can indeed succeed in stimulating growth and creating stability and prosperity by alleviating resource shortages and (re-)establishing crucial institutions.

In terms of thinking, however, the most important event was the publication of President Truman's 'Point Four Program' in January 1949. In addition to the *usual suspects* of that epoch in international relations – i.e. support for the UN family, the continuation of the Marshall plan and the creation of NATO – it proposed a 'fair deal' for the world, to be achieved by deploying technical and financial assistance to help 'underdeveloped' countries to become 'developed'. Thereby, the Point Four Program '*evoked not only the idea of change in the direction of a final state but, above all, the possibility of bringing about such change*' (Rist, 2008: 73). This was the official birth of international development cooperation and the initiation of the 'development age'. It also became the cornerstone of orthodox development thinking that held that 'underdevelopment' could be eliminated through economic growth and modernisation, led by high savings rates facilitated by development aid (Escobar, 1995).

This thinking also informed the individual aid programmes established by bilateral donors in the 1950s and 1960s. The Marshall Plan had 'proven' that aid did indeed work, and the Point Four Program established the development-oriented thinking that was necessary in order to set widespread aid programmes in motion. Concurrently, while Europe was gradually recovering from World War II, Africa experienced a wave of decolonization. With increasing wealth and in order to maintain allies in the wake of the Cold War, Britain and France used aid to engage primarily with their former colonies while the US used aid to engage with the former colonies of Portugal, Spain and Belgium.

International development cooperation was maturing and new state actors were entering the field every year. To help them learn from each other, the Development Assistance Group was formed in 1960. It was originally made up of eight bilateral donors and the Commission of the European Economic Community, but in the years that followed more bilateral donors joined the group. In 1961, it was transformed into the Development Assistance Committee (DAC) of the OECD. From being an experience-sharing entity, it changed into a norm-making entity. In particular, DAC began a process of coordinating aid in order to improve standards of living for the inhabitants of less developed countries. Moreover, DAC worked to increase the amount of money available to finance development, and focused on long-term development issues.

Based on this work, DAC became *the* hegemonic power in international development cooperation. DAC defined the purpose of aid (to promote economic and social development in developing countries), its terms (concessional), and its rationale (for developing countries to engage in the global economy and for people to overcome poverty). In order to compel members to abide by these aims and rationales, DAC developed common objectives and guidelines (e.g. untying aid and spending 0.7 per cent of GNI on aid), established standards for monitoring and evaluation, and instituted recurrent peer aid reviews and high-level meetings.

Parallel to the increasing hegemonic power of the DAC donors, development aid began to play an increasingly prominent role in recipient countries' development strategies. While the Cold War era was characterized by the large degree of sovereignty enjoyed by recipient country governments – which was mainly due to the clear policy aims of the political elites in the decolonized states and competition between East and West, which meant that donors were willing to ignore almost any non-compliance or disobedience from the recipients – this changed radically at the beginning of the 1980s.

Aid to the newly established states in the 'Third World' did not produce results comparable to the Marshall Plan. As a result, Elliot Berg was asked to analyse the nature of the development problems facing African countries. The result was the Berg Report from 1981, which, in short, argued that investment projects fail when policies are bad. It thus provided the analytical justification for donor interventions in recipient countries' internal affairs. The economic justification for those interventions was, in turn, furnished by the debt crisis of 1982. The result was the structural adjustment and stabilisation programmes that turned the donor–recipient power game on its head. In a single move, donors were able to tie loans and grants to macroeconomic policies and conditions in recipient countries. By the end of the Cold War, the West had secured a monopoly on aid, which allowed donors to impose political as well as economic conditions, thus curbing recipient countries' sovereignty even further (Fraser, 2008; Stokke, 1995).

International development cooperation 'as we knew it' was thus characterized by a few dominant actors, including the World Bank, IMF, the UN family and the DAC donors. Over a 50-year period, their influence over policies and politics in the Global South increased steadily until all major policy documents were drafted by external donors, and bureaucrats in aid-dependent countries also began to think and act like donors (Fraser, 2008; Harrison, 2004).

Recommended reading: Escobar (1995), Rist (2008), Stokke (1995).

A tectonic shift in international development cooperation

This trend did not endure. The system did not sufficiently address global challenges such as climate change, epidemics, migration, and terrorism that span national boundaries. What is more, aid was fragmented and poorly coordinated despite DAC's efforts to direct and harmonize aid efforts (Janus *et al.*, 2015). Moreover, the spatiality of poverty has changed: according to conventional measures, there are now fewer poor countries in the world but many more poor people in middle-income countries (Sumner, 2012). This spatial change has taken place simultaneously with the rejuvenation of 'non-traditional' donors,[1] the growth of private development actors, and the exponential growth of other financial transfers from the Global North to the Global South (and within the Global South), creating what Gore describes as a '*more complex and diverse landscape of development cooperation*' (2013: 769).

Since the turn of the century, countries such as China, India and Brazil have gradually expanded their aid programmes and are now providing substantial amounts of 'development finance' (less ODA and more other official flows) to other countries in the Global South. These 'new' actors provide aid differently from the 'traditional' actors. Most notably, the aid modality, sectoral focus and the form of aid differ – resembling the 'traditional' aid of the 1970s–1980s more than current DAC aid (Kragelund, 2011). Importantly, they offer an alternative development trajectory to that proposed by the (post)-Washington Consensus and they insist on a policy of non-interference in recipient countries' internal affairs.

Likewise, the development arena has witnessed an explosion in the number and scope of non-state actors engaged directly or indirectly in international development cooperation. Chief among these are private foundations, celebrity organizations and private enterprises. Simultaneously, they bring in additional finance for development and introduce new ways of approaching development challenges (via vertical funds, innovative financing mechanisms, technicalisation, privatization and commercialization). Whether this is good or bad for development is an empirical question. In the literature, this trend is either perceived as a solution to global problems due to its innovativeness and perceived efficiency or as highly problematic due to lack of accountability, lack of transparency and its short-term focus (Fejerskov, 2015).

Importantly, other financial flows have grown tremendously relative to ODA over the past couple of decades. This is especially the case for FDI and remittances that are now much more important in aggregate terms than ODA for most developing countries. None of these, however, are as predictable and as evenly spread as ODA. Moreover, they do not necessarily target the needs of the poor and vulnerable.

Finally, the financial crisis also played a major role in transforming international development cooperation. First, the aid budgets of many 'traditional' donors were cut because of the crisis, recently (2014) amounting to a mere 0.29 per cent of GNI – a far cry from the target of 0.7 per cent. Second, the Global South managed to quickly recoup from the crisis due largely to financial flows from 'non-traditional' actors. Essentially, this showed that the Global South could manage without the assistance of the 'traditional donors'. Linked hereto, the financial crisis exposed shortcomings in the Global North. So far, the 'traditional' partners' credibility rested on a combination of their financial power to provide aid, the fact that they were the world's strongest and richest economies, and their hegemonic power to define the development agenda. The new providers of development finance are challenging all these erstwhile advantages. They provide assistance of great symbolic value: for instance, the financial crisis originated in the Global North, and the development path of a country such as China shows that the (post)-Washington Consensus is not the only road towards economic development. Rather, a plethora of routes exist that include aspects of gradualism and state-drivenness, combined with market-based learning, strong leadership and attentiveness to agriculture and infrastructure (Kragelund, 2015). The combination of these 'game-changing trends' led Mawdsley (2015) to suggest that 'traditional' donors are undergoing three interrelated crises: an ontological (donors no longer only come from the Global North), an ideational ('traditional' donors' normative power is challenged) and a material (economic growth is largely taking place in the Global South) crisis.

Whether this leads to more divergence and heterogeneity or a new equilibrium in international development cooperation based on processes of convergence and homogenising forces (cf. Fejerskov, 2015) remains to be seen. No doubt, DAC is losing its hegemonic power – largely because it has failed to persuade the majority of 'non-traditional' donors to join or to abide by its rules. New cooperation fora are therefore being established (Verschaeve and Orbie, 2016) and DAC donors are allowing themselves to be inspired by new actors. It is to these processes of convergence and divergence that we now turn.

Recommended reading: Mawdsley (2015), Whitfield (2008).

Effects on the donor landscape

The modus operandi of the 'non-traditional' donors is encouraging 'traditional' donors to reconsider their relations with partners in the Global South. The perceived efficiency and successfulness of 'non-traditional' donors' development cooperation have made major 'traditional' actors question the current development agenda and helped provoke a stronger focus on national interests among the main 'traditional' actors. In fact, we are currently witnessing a move towards a 'development effectiveness paradigm', where the focus in recipient countries is on economic growth and industrial productivity rather than on the social, and where the private sector in donor countries directly benefits from the transfers (Kragelund, 2015).

'Traditional' donors thereby replicate the 'new' development actors' approach, focusing on 'win–win' partnerships that involve companies directly in the execution of development interventions. The rise of 'new' donors is not the only factor that has triggered this process: neoliberalism, in general, and the rehabilitation of the private sector in development in the decades that followed the 1980s, in particular, have played a major role in this shift. However, what made 'traditional' donors describe the change openly was the rejuvenation of China, India and Brazil as donors. In so doing, 'traditional' donors have triggered a process of convergence in international development cooperation. This is already visible in the UK, where funding for 'economic growth' for the recipient country has doubled in three years and now makes up one-fifth of the total bilateral budget; new private sector partners have been engaged in developing future aid avenues; and civil society has also bought into the new reality of bilateral aid (Mawdsley, 2015). Likewise, the Netherlands, Denmark and the EU are moving in the same direction (i.e. focusing on economic growth in order to assist home country/region firms). The novel element here is not that business is part of development (via corporate social responsibility and/or cause-related marketing), but that 'traditional' development organizations are outsourcing development cooperation to private sector actors and that business is becoming responsible for development (Blowfield and Dolan, 2014).

The process of convergence is further reinforced by 'traditional' donors' efforts to establish dialogue fora with 'new' actors in order to persuade them to buy into the idea of international development cooperation 'as we knew it'. For example, the OECD has sought to include the 'emerging' donors in its own existing framework, through the DAC Working Party on Aid Effectiveness. Likewise, DAC has established a China–DAC Study Group to facilitate mutual learning, and in 2011 DAC invited 'emerging' donor representatives to its yearly senior-level meeting that charts the future direction of the DAC. Of late, a couple of 'emerging' donors have taken part in the DAC's internal peer reviews of DAC members, thereby easing future cooperation (Kragelund, 2015).

Changes are also taking place at the heart of international development cooperation 'as we knew it'. Internal voices in the DAC have proposed replacing the ODA with a new Official Development Effort measure, which in short returns to the core intention of the ODA (i.e. social and economic development in developing countries). It thereby excludes all the 'transfers' now included in the ODA that stay in donor countries, and instead only counts either grants or concessional elements of loans for development purposes in developing countries (Hynes and Scott, 2013).

Alongside these converging processes among state actors, homogenizing tendencies are also apparent between private foundations and the rest of the 'traditional' donor community. The Bill and Melinda Gates Foundation, for instance, not only influences other donors via its focus on cost-effectiveness and short-term benefits; it is also affected by the system's established norms such as gender norms (Fejerskov, 2015).

However, most of these developments have to do with processes set in motion by the 'traditional' donors to balance the competition initiated by the reintroduction of 'non-traditional' donors in the donor landscape. Presently, major differences still exist, for instance in relation to the modality, form and geographical coverage of aid. These differences are not offset by (also) including economic growth in donor countries as a critical allocation aspect, by establishing dialogue fora, or by promoting trilateral development cooperation, i.e. a development relationship in which a 'traditional' donor collabourates with a 'non-traditional' donor to work in a third country in the Global South (McEwan and Mawdsley, 2012). At present, the situation is therefore that countries of the Global South can, in theory, benefit from the destabilization of international development cooperation either to negotiate more favourable deals or to get away with non-implementation of agreed reforms.

Recommended reading: Fejerskov (2015), Kragelund (2015).

Effects on the Global South

The above-mentioned changes in international development cooperation are of relatively recent origin. Hence, studies of the effects of the rejuvenation of non-traditional state actors, for instance, are only just beginning to emerge. Despite this, the 'China-Africa literature' in particular is rich on examples of pre-established conclusions of the effects of the rejuvenation of China's interest in development. Most importantly, it is claimed that as China provides aid with 'no strings attached', it blindly supports rogue states. Related hereto, arguments such as no condition-alities lead to increased corruption, a bad allocation of scarce resources, and poor governance is widespread in this literature. Moreover, it is argued that China's use of loans (over grants) will re-indebt recipient countries (cf. Woods, 2008, for an excellent presentation and refutation of the arguments in the early literature on 'emerging' donors).

The most recent body of literature seeks to open the black box of the effects of the rejuvenation of 'emerging' donors. This literature reveals a mixed picture. On the one hand, some studies perceive the situation as an opportunity to provide recipient governments with a choice of development partners, which leads to a strengthening of their negotiation power and carves out policy space to define and implement policies that affect social and economic development. They argue that the competition that is introduced into the aid system increases bargaining power vis-à-vis 'traditional' donors and offers the opportunity to 'triangulate' between donors. Moreover, non-traditional state actors affect bargaining power in the international system, and thereby potentially affect the terms and conditions that apply to loans and grants from international financial institutions to recipient countries (Harman and Brown, 2013; Woods, 2008). On top of this, the mere fact that an alternative exists to the (post)-Washington Consensus provides recipients with leverage to negotiate new deals with 'traditional' donors. Among others, these studies have shown how Angolan elites have been able to extract favourable spot prices for 'their' oil when that oil is sold to China (Vickers, 2013); the Ethiopian government has been able to use China to finance investment in sectors not supported by the West (Feyissa, 2012); and the Rwandan political elite has been able to leverage its Western partners due to the negotiating power it gains from having more partners (Grimm, 2013). Not surprisingly, therefore, these studies have been complemented by a growing belief in the ability of recipient countries' political elites to challenge the existing power relations in the system.

On the other hand, some studies question the recipient country governments' ability to – in the short term – fundamentally alter the structural power relations between the Global North and Global South. In short, they argue that the new actors in international development cooperation do not radically alter the Global South's place in the global division of labour, since many countries of the Global South remain suppliers of raw materials to the Global North. They therefore argue that the power gains of recipient country elites are limited to bargaining rather than structural change (Carmody and Kragelund, 2016). Moreover, Kragelund (2015) showed that some of the cases most often highlighted as examples of changing power aid relations may indeed have to do with other factors. Angola, for instance, increased its policy space, but this may be more a consequence of rising commodity prices than interest shown by non-traditional state actors. In contrast, the Ethiopian case shows how different interpretations of a key concept, debt sustainability, may be used for developmental purposes.

Taken together, these studies inform us that the differences between 'new' and 'old' development cooperation actors may not be as great as first anticipated (Dreher *et al.*, 2011); that the group of 'new' development actors is extremely heterogeneous (Sato *et al.*, 2011); and that processes of homogenization are taking place between private and public actors (Fejerskov, 2015) and between 'traditional' and 'non-traditional' state actors (Kragelund, 2015). This new homogenized model increasingly focuses on the productive sector; it seeks to make sure that development interventions are of mutual benefit for both donors and recipients; it centres on short-term measurable (and easily communicable) results; and it is based on public–private partnerships.

Recommended reading: Carmody and Kragelund (2016), Woods (2008).

Conclusion

This chapter sought to outline the tectonic shifts in international development cooperation and examine their consequences for the donor landscape as well as for the Global South. Most importantly, it established the differences between international development cooperation 'as we knew it', i.e. a relatively stable system governed by the DAC with increasingly more power to influence recipient countries' internal affairs; and the current system of flux characterized by more state and non-state actors, a variety of modalities, growing donor competition, and hence potentially more policy space for the Global South.

But what is clear is that the tectonic shifts in international development cooperation have hitherto neither translated into a fundamentally different perception of what development aid is all about – it still aims to bring about 'development' – nor have they profoundly changed the power relations between donors and recipients. What is new is that the number of donors has increased dramatically compared to the post-Cold War era. Despite the major changes that we have witnessed lately, therefore, international development cooperation today bears many resemblances to international development cooperation 'as we knew it'.

Note

1 'Non-traditional' donors are often referred to as emerging donors/powers. In fact, they are neither non-traditional nor emerging. The most important ones, such as China and India, were already providing aid to other developing countries as early as the late 1950s.

References

Blowfield, M. and Dolan, C.S. (2014). 'Business as a development agent: evidence of possibility and improbability'. *Third World Quarterly*, 35: 22–42.

Carmody, P. and Kragelund, P. (2016). 'Who is in charge? State power and agency in Sino-African relations'. *Cornell International Law Journal*, 49: 1–23.

Dreher, A., Nunnenkamp, P. and Thiele, R. (2011). 'Are "new" donors different? Comparing the allocation of bilateral aid between nonDAC and DAC donor countries'. *World Development*, 39: 1950–68.

Escobar, A. (1995). *Encountering Development: The Making and Unmaking of the Third World*. Princeton, NJ: Princeton University Press.

Fejerskov, A.M. (2015). 'From unconventional to ordinary? The Bill and Melinda Gates Foundation and the homogenizing effects of international development cooperation'. *Journal of International Development*, 27: 1098–112.

Feyissa, D. (2012). 'Aid negotiation: the uneasy "partnership" between EPRDF and the donors'. *Journal of Eastern African Studies*, 5: 788–817.

Fraser, A. (2008). 'Aid-recipient sovereignty in historical context'. In L. Whitfield (ed.), *The Politics of Aid: African Strategies for Dealing with Donors*. Oxford: Oxford University Press, pp. 45–73.

Gore, C. (2013). 'The new development cooperation landscape: actors approaches, architecture'. *Journal of International Development*, 25: 769–86.

Grimm, S. (2013). 'Aid dependency as a limitation to national development policy? The case of Rwanda'. In W. Brown and S. Harman (eds), *African Agency in International Politics*. London: Routledge, pp. 81–96.

Harman, S. and Brown, W. (2013). 'In from the margins? The changing place of Africa in international relations'. *International Affairs*, 89: 69–87.

Harrison, G. (2004). *The World Bank and Africa: The Construction of Governance States*. London/New York: Routledge.

Hynes, W. and Scott, S. (2013). *The Evolution of Official Development Assistance*. Paris: OECD.

Janus, H., Klingebiel, S. and Paulo, S. (2015). 'Beyond aid: a conceptual perspective on the transformation of development cooperation'. *Journal of International Development*, 27: 155–69.

Kragelund, P. (2011). 'Back to BASICs? The rejuvenation of non-traditional donors' development cooperation with Africa'. *Development and Change*, 42: 585–607.

Kragelund, P. (2012). 'The revival of non-traditional state actors' interests in Africa: does it matter for policy autonomy?' *Development Policy Review*, 30: 703–18.

Kragelund, P. (2015). 'Towards convergence and cooperation in the global development finance regime: closing Africa's policy space?' *Cambridge Review of International Affairs*, 28: 246–62.

Mawdsley, E. (2015). 'DFID, the private sector and the re-centring of an economic growth agenda in international development'. *Global Society*, 29: 339–58.

McEwan, C. and Mawdsley, E. (2012). 'Trilateral development cooperation: power and politics in emerging aid relationships'. *Development and Change*, 43: 1185–209.

Rist, G. (2008). *The History of Development: From Western Origins to Global Faith*, 3rd edition. London: Zed Books.

Sato, J., Shiga, H., Kobayashi, T. and Kondoh, H. (2011). '"Emerging donors" from a recipient perspective: an institutional analysis of foreign aid in Cambodia'. *World Development*, 39: 2091–104.

Stokke, O. (1995). 'Aid and political conditionality: core issues and state of the art'. In O. Stokke (ed.), *Aid and Political Conditionality*. London: Frank Cass, pp. 1–87.

Sumner, A. (2012). 'Where do the poor live?' *World Development*, 40: 865–77.

Verschaeve, J. and Orbie, J. (2016). 'The DAC is dead, long live the DCF? A comparative analysis of the OECD Development Assistance Committee and the UN Development Cooperation Forum'. *European Journal of Development Research*, 28(4): 571–87.

Vickers, B. (2013). 'Africa and the rising powers: bargaining for the "marginalized many"'. *International Affairs*, 89: 673–93.

Whitfield, L. (ed.) (2008). *The Politics of Aid: African Strategies for Dealing with Donors*. Oxford: Oxford University Press.

Woods, N. (2008). 'Whose aid? Whose influence? China, emerging donors and the silent revolution in development assistance'. *International Affairs*, 84: 1205–21.

17

THE DEVELOPMENTAL STATE AND LATE INDUSTRIALIZATION

Still feasible? And desirable?

Paul Bowles

History shows that the now advanced countries (the 'developed' world) did not reach their current status by following the neoliberal policies that have been widely prescribed to developing countries over the past three decades. Neither did the few countries that have successfully closed the gap and reached developed country status over the past hundred years. Japan, South Korea, Taiwan, Hong Kong, Singapore and erstwhile challenger China have all relied heavily on state intervention – on a developmental state. While other chapters in this volume point to the particular contributions of Latin America to development theory, including dependency theory, Bello (2009) has described the developmental state as the East Asian contribution to development theory. It has proven to be the one development model capable of enabling countries to reach the same living standards as those which initially went through the Industrial Revolution and claimed their place at the top of the international hierarchy. Per capita GDP in Singapore is equal to that of the US, Hong Kong's is not far short of that in the UK and France, and South Korea's is higher than that of Portugal and Greece.[1] The theory of the developmental state is primarily a theory of industrialization and it takes the Industrial Revolution as its starting point (rather than, say, European colonization of the Americas in the 16th century and the formation of a 'world system', the *longue durée*, as Babones calls it in Chapter 7 in this volume).

The role of the state is, of course, one of the central issues in the study of development. The dominant neoliberal paradigm ascribes to the state the basic functions of establishing and protecting private property rights, providing infrastructure, and facilitating education and health services, as well as security in a military sense. All of this should be provided by a competent, transparent administrative arm adopting the principles of 'good governance'. In the economic sphere, the state is seen as advancing the development process by adopting 'market-friendly' policies, 'getting prices right', and allowing and ensuring that markets operate to mobilize and allocate those scarce resources available to developing countries. This policy orthodoxy reached its zenith with the 'Washington Concensus' (Williamson, 1989). This remains the main policy thrust today, even if some wrinkles, such as the need to better regulate financial markets and admission of justifiable capital controls, are more common. With 'Trumpism' as the reaction to US imperial decline, a new state interventionism will likely re-emerge; but it will not be aimed at providing a new development ladder, rather in preserving old hierarchies.

This chapter discusses three main issues. The first is what, analytically, constitutes a developmental state drawing upon East Asian country experience. The second concerns whether this is replicable in other countries and feasible given current configurations of power at the global level and the organization of global capitalist production. The third issue concerns the desirability of the model, given the oppression that has, historically, accompanied it.

Recommended reading: Bello (2009).

The analytics of the developmental state

In the 1960s, the post-independence developing states expected to make the most economic progress were typically identified as resource-rich countries such as Ghana and Brazil. Resource-poor, population-dense countries in East Asia were not expected to become the next industrializing countries. And yet they did. By the 1980s, it became clear that a select number of countries (or economies, depending on the view taken of the political status of Taiwan and Hong Kong) were making the transition from primarily agricultural to industrial countries at remarkable speed and with considerable success.

They achieved this in part by success in export markets. The rise of the so-called Newly Industrializing Countries (NICs) in the 1980s was initially interpreted by mainstream development economists as proof of the follies of import substituting industrialization strategies and the 'export pessimism' of dependency theory, which saw countries trapped into a neocolonial international division of labour with little prospect of escaping. The East Asian NICs proved this thinking wrong, it was argued, and the success of export-oriented industrialization was seamlessly translated into proof of the efficacy of trade openness and free-market policies in general.

This interpretation of the NIC experience was subject to detailed critique by a group of critical development scholars who convincingly demonstrated that the NICs' success posed a major challenge for free-market orthodoxy and provided definitive evidence of the possibility of an alternative development path based on state activism. Bienefeld (1981) argued that the position of the NICs in the international political economy demonstrated that some of the key propositions of dependency theory were still relevant in explaining the success of the NICs. To expand on this point, the external environment still played a crucial role in determining countries' development prospects, although in this case by providing a positive window of opportunity. The geography of the NICS – all in East Asia – was no coincidence.

This was the region of the world in which capitalism confronted communism in its most brutal form, war. This was not just the region of a 'cold war', fought at the ideological level, but of actual war fought on the ground in the Korean peninsula and in Vietnam. South Korea, Hong Kong, Taiwan and Singapore were all potential dominoes and central to the fight against communism. For this reason, they received unquestioned military support from the US and pursued economic policies with a degree of autonomy that was not afforded to other countries; access to the US markets for exports was not a problem either. Furthermore, land reforms were instituted in South Korea and Taiwan that led to relatively equal land holdings designed to remove the basis for peasant revolution. In all these respects, the East Asian NICs were unusual, a deviance from the more typical position of developing countries, resulting from their unique geopolitical location in the fight against communism (Stubbs, 2012).

This geopolitical position also had internal consequences. National survival was by no means guaranteed and economic development was imperative. National survival provided the state with the legitimacy to play a leading role in the economy and to shape the mobilization and allocation of resources to meet the economic development imperative. Critical development scholars argued that the starting point for analysing how this was done was not the free-market thinking of Adam Smith, as mainstream development economists would have us believe, but the state interventionism of theorists such as Frederich List (1841) and Alexander Gerschenkron (1962). These theorists argued that 'late industrialization' in Europe by Germany and France, for example, required a degree of state intervention much greater than the initial industrializer – Great Britain – because the obstacles that they faced in competing with the world's dominant industrial powerhouse of the time demanded it. The theory of 'late industrialization' was equally relevant, it was argued, for the analysis of the success of the 'late, late industrializers' of East Asia.

The pioneering work of Amsden (1992) on South Korea and Wade (1990) on (mainly) Taiwan showed how state policy was critical in shaping the development and, in Wade's famous phrase, 'governing the market'. Referencing Japan's earlier development trajectory (and analysed by Johnson, 1982), Amsden and Wade demonstrated that the state had played a central role in the economic development success story of the two countries, and that, furthermore, the suite of policies followed were consistent and coherent to the point that they could constitute an alternative model of development.

The basic pillars of what became known as the theory of the development state were as follows. First, the state was focused on and committed to national development as a security and survival requirement and was staffed by a relatively competent and relatively corruption-free bureaucracy that implemented policy decisions. Second, market interventions were necessary in the key areas of finance, trade, technology, industry and labour to ensure that markets were governed in ways that maximized resource mobilization and optimized long-term resource allocation; free markets with their short-termism could not be trusted to deliver this. In the area of finance, finance capital was subject to the needs of industrial capital. Bank-based systems dominated (as in Japan and Germany), with only a minor role for stock markets. Furthermore, the banks were subject to state-directed policy loans that supported key firms and key industries at subsidized interest rates. 'Financial repression', in the language of economists, was a deliberate policy choice designed to channel subsidized credit to key industries. By setting the interest rate on loans low in this way, this was one example of how these developmental states were, in Amsden's words, deliberately 'getting prices wrong' in contrast to the 'getting prices right' policy advice mantra of the Washington Consensus.

In the realm of trade, the state set companies and industries export growth targets. To avoid the balance of payments constrained growth that had plagued many developing countries (and which played a significant role in the adoption of ISI policies in developing countries, including previously in the East Asian NICs), state policy sought to expand exports and generate the foreign exchange necessary to pay for rising imports of technology and consumer goods. These export targets did not take the form of blank cheques, but rather were more akin to contracts between firms and governments. In an environment of competitive exchange rates and in return for access to policy loans and to technology, firms had to prove themselves and meet their export targets; if they did not, they risked governments closing their access to policy loans, merging firms, or supporting rival firms instead. South Korea and Taiwan had different industrial structures, with South Korea favouring the large conglomerate, *chaebol*, model and Taiwan characterized by more medium-sized and family firms, but they were similar in their approaches to export targeting. In short, firms were disciplined by their need to be competitive in export markets, but equally importantly they were disciplined by the state in their access to capital. This, of course, requires a particular configuration of class forces that provides the state with the relative autonomy to discipline capital in this way, even while broadly promoting capitalist industrialization.

The state also intervened in the field of technology, sponsoring domestic research and innovation, supporting key sectors and ensuring that imports of the latest technology were available to firms; technological acquisition and adoption was facilitated with the role of foreign direct investment assessed on its ability to contribute to this goal. This was particularly evident in ICT industries, and the global success of Taiwanese company Acer and South Korea's Samsung, for example, would not have happened without state support and intervention from the earliest stages. Listed as a separate policy area here, technology is sometimes subsumed within the broader category of 'industrial policy', that set of arrangements that might also include directed credit, procurement policies and tariff protection, which are used to support particular firms and industries; 'picking winners' as it sometimes called, but which, in practice, is much more than that, and is better seen as the many ways in which strategically important key sectors, whether defined on the basis of their role in being critical for other industrial activities (such as petrochemicals) or as areas for future growth (such as ICT industries), are supported.

As well as disciplining capital as described above, the developmental state also disciplined labour. Mobilizing and directing resources for investment left no room for organized labour to directly stake a claim for an increased share of the national income; the East Asia developmental state was authoritarian. To prevent wages rising, trade unions were initially banned and the fight for labour rights, as well as the wider transition to democracy, was often bloody and brutal. Industrialization may have been telescoped compared to the same process in the early industrializers, but it came with many of the same struggles. The East Asian path also had a clear gender dimension too, with 'export-led growth' also capable of being described as 'female-led growth' given the preponderance of young, unmarried women employed/exploited in export processing zones.

The success of the NICs in the last two decades of the 20th century therefore challenged conventional development thinking. The developmental state model, sometimes also known as the East Asian model, became a contentious point in the development debate. The World Bank, in its 1993 *East Asian Miracle* report, sought to again claim the NICs' success for its policy stance, an attempt that Wade (1996) termed 'paradigm maintenance'. Ironically, within a few years though, leading mainstream economists were all too pleased to attribute statism to the NICs and other Asian countries, and to blame it for the 1997 Asian financial crisis. The developmental state model, with its high levels of state-directed credit and 'crony capitalist' relations between states, banks and firms, was identified as the culprit and unfavourable contrasts made with the market-based Anglo-American system. But the proclamations of the vibrant health of the Anglo-American financial system proved ill-judged, as the global financial crisis in 2008 showed – and the reports of the death of the developmental state were exaggerated too.

Further reading: Amsden (1992), Bienefeld (1981), Stubbs (2012), Wade (1990, 1996).

Still feasible?

At one level, the continued feasibility of the developmental state model is clearly evident. The largest example of the developmental state model of them all – China – has had a spectacular 35-year-plus rise. It has followed a distinct path with nationalism and national revival (the 'Chinese dream') used as ideological underpinnings to state activism that has included the central pillars of the developmental state – a government-directed financial system, export orientation, technological advancement and labour repression. Many of the elements are there, although the size and scope of China's development has meant that there is still room to talk of multiple regional models, some more statist than others, in China today (Zhang and Peck, 2016). For all its growth, though, it is still a long way from joining the other NICs in breaking through into the ranks of the advanced industrial countries in terms of per capita incomes; its GDP per capita is still a little more than a quarter of Portugal's, a fifth of Spain's and an eighth of the US level. The possibilities for China joining the select club this depends on the sustainability – economically, technologically, socially, politically and environmentally – of the Chinese system with many critical development scholars highly skeptical of the prospects (see Chapter 33 by So and Chu in this volume), as well as those, including the Chinese leadership itself, wondering whether China will get caught in the 'Middle Income Trap' and fall at the final hurdle to industrial maturity.

The failure of the neoliberal model, confirmed by the global financial crisis in 2008, has led to a much wider acceptance of the role of the state, minimally in a regulatory sense, but also in broader terms that point to the continuing salience of the developmental state. The state interventionist paradigm, taking its lead from China's experience, the questions raised above notwithstanding, has become popularly known as the 'Beijing Consensus' (Ramo, 2004). This term signifies the recognition among developing countries of the role of the state and the opposition to the neoliberal Washington Consensus. Some have sought to root this alternative development paradigm in the broader East Asian experience and describe it as the 'BeST (Beijing-Seoul-Toyko) Consensus' (Lee and Matthews, 2010). Whatever the preferred term, the emergence of a general development paradigm based on the state interventionism central to East Asian late development has gained wide currency and has been seen as the basis for a development path for others beyond the region. It is now common to find the developmental state, as a term, being used to explain and assess policies in other countries in near neighbours such as Malaysia and Vietnam (Stubbs, 2012), but also further afield to Ethiopia (Fantini, 2013), Botswana (Taylor, 2005) and Brazil (Hochstetler and Montero, 2013), for example. While this may point to the feasibility and generalizability of the developmental state model, it should also be noted that in some ways the use of the term 'developmental state' has been reduced to an examination of particular features of the model, especially industrial policy. The East Asian NIC experience was based on a specific geo-political context, a particular constellation of state, capital and labour relations, and an integrated set of interventionist, market guiding policies; more recent applications of the developmental state term have a tendency to be much less comprehensive in their analysis and to highlight specific interventions. While the term developmental state can readily be found in the literature and applied to a wide range of countries, the use of the term has also expanded along with its geographical application.

While the developmental state paradigm has gained currency and wider applicability, therefore, its contemporary feasibility has been subject to debate on two grounds. The first is whether there is sufficient 'policy space' for interventionist strategies given the plethora of neoliberal trade agreements to which governments are now subject. The second is whether the changes in the structure of global capitalist production in the form of the rise of global value chains/global production networks means that 'national' policies are no longer viable.

WTO rules, as well as those embedded in regional and bilateral trade agreements, now significantly constrain governments in the sorts of interventions that they can make to support their industries and economies. The overarching aim of trade rules has been to ensure that all producers are treated 'equally', meaning that preferential treatment for domestic producers, local content procurement policies, 'subsidies' of any number of varieties, are seen as undesirable and violations of the rules. This places states in a 'straitjacket' and removes from them much of the policy space that is needed for developmentalist aims. Not only that, it removes from contemporary states the policies that the now industrialized countries used to reach their current status. This situation has been described by Chang (2002) as 'kicking away the ladder', the removal of the ability of countries to use the policy tools of trade protectionism, infant industry support and industrial policies, and credit policies, for example, which variously enabled Britain, Germany, France and the US to become the industrial powers that they are today. The 'myth of free trade' as the reason for the success of the now developed countries means that its status as orthodoxy for today's developing countries is seriously misplaced. Focus for some scholars has therefore been placed on the need to create the 'policy space' needed for developing countries in the global governance architecture (see Gallagher, 2005), an agenda that has also been taken up by the more critical parts of the UN system such as UNCTAD.

The second challenge to the feasibility of the developmental state model is the changes in the organization of global capitalist production over the past 30 years. The dispersion of production between different countries and the rise of intra-industry trade are symptomatic of a global reorganization of production in which global corporations locate different parts of the value chain in different countries and play the role of governing and integrating the resulting global production. Thus, a running shoe, for example, may be designed in the US, manufactured with low-cost labour in Vietnam, using imported leather from Australia, in a factory managed by a Taiwanese firm, with the accounting and trade functions undertaken by a Hong Kong firm, and marketed in North America and Europe by a German firm. This far from atypical description of global production poses significant challenges for a developmental state; how can policy interventions be made in the face of such a global value chain to promote national industrial development? The difficulties of doing this means that development policy in many countries has defaulted to a strategy of how best to integrate into the chains (Gereffi, 2014). Thus, governments aim to promote 'strategic coupling' whereby the 'local assets', such as low-cost labour, low tax regime, publically provided infrastructure and educated workforce, are used to attract global corporations seeking such a package. Industrial 'upgrading' then requires maximizing the linkages with the local economy that may occur from such arrangements in efforts to move up the 'value chain ladder'. This is a far cry from the conditions necessary to promote genuine national industrial development and technological capacity in the way that the NICs were able to. Some countries, especially large ones such as China, may still be able to develop and promote their own 'national champions', but for many developing countries the global value chain world is one where global corporations are major agents governing the chain and where the possibilities for development based on the nation state are severely constrained.

Recommended reading: Chang (2002), Gallagher (2005), Gereffi (2014).

A desirable developmental state?

The developmental state paradigm is primarily a model of industrialization. For some, this may be an aim that is no longer appropriate or desirable given the environmental costs, locally, nationally and globally, of industrialization. An alternative development paradigm, such as that articulated by *vivir bien*, for example, suggests a post-industrial vision of development. Whether such a vision can provide the standards of living, the longer life expectancy, the gradual escape from debilitating manual labour that industrialization has provided over the past two and half centuries is, however, an important question that must be asked. Others might argue that services are the future and that a focus on growing this sector should be the goal of government. However, this is a proposition requiring a 'sectoral leapfrogging' that is surely at least as daunting as late industrialization.

If industrialization is still deemed desirable as a goal for developing countries, a further problem arises in that in all countries, industrialization has, historically, been the cause of great social upheaval and brutality. The mobilization of resources for investment, the creation and transfer of a surplus to industry, and the creation of an industrial proletariat have been wrenching, destructive and brutal processes in both the capitalist and state socialist countries that have embarked upon them over the past two and half centuries. Some of these countries have been more successful – economically – in this process than others, as measured by per capita GNP growth. The East Asian developmental states fall into this latter category. But they were subject to many of the same brutalities of industrialization that occurred in the early industrializers, and which are being heaped upon the Chinese industrial working class today. Could it be different?

Selwyn (2016) has argued that what is needed is a 'labour-centred' development paradigm in which the agency of labour to collectively organize, design and promulgate development for their individual and communities' benefit is the central benchmark by which strategies should be judged. On this criterion, the developmental state model undoubtedly fails the test. Might the developmental state be capable of being democratized? The possibility of a specifically 'democratic developmental state' was raised by White (1998). He argued that such a state would need to have broad control over three functions: regulatory, infrastructure and redistributive. But for such a state simultaneously to achieve both developmental and democratic objectives would require a specific constellation of institutional design of the state, political society and civil society. It is no surprise that he concluded that 'given the particular characteristics of the democratic developmental state . . . it would be reasonable to be skeptical about their feasibility' (p. 42). This question, however, has remained very much alive and has been taken up more recently in other contexts. For example, the possibilities for a democratic developmental state in South Africa have been examined based on the ANC's explicit endorsement of this strategy (Edigheji, 2010), but scepticism is still warranted in this case too.

Recommended reading: Edigheji (2010).

Conclusion

The developmental state, in its East Asian incarnation, has shown that late industrialization is possible. The development divide that opened as a result of the first Industrial Revolution has been overcome by a handful of states using interventionist and market-guiding policies. There are no other examples of states that have managed to overcome this gap by other means and, as such, the developmental state model offers an important potential reference point for other countries, even though the environment that they now face is more unfavourable given differences in initial conditions, including global trading rules and the organization of global capitalist production. A 21st-century developmental state will look quite different from previous examples as a result. Whether it can also be quite different in terms of being democratic as well as developmental remains an unanswered question; the search for a humane industrialization path continues.

Note

1 These statements, and the other comparisons made in this chapter, are based on 2015 GDP per capita (constant 2010 US$) figures available from the World Bank's *World Development Indicators* database. Using the purchasing power parity (PPP) method would further increase the relative standing of the East Asian economies.

References

Amsden, A. (1992). *Asia's Next Giant: South Korea and Late Industrialization*. Oxford: Oxford University Press.

Bello, W. (2009). 'States and markets, states versus markets: the developmental state debate as the distinctive East Asian contribution to international political economy'. In M. Blyth (ed.), *Routledge Handbook of International Political Economy (IPE): IPE as a Global Conversation*. London: Routledge, pp. 180–200.

Bienefeld, M. (1981). 'Dependency and the newly industrialising countries (NICs): towards a reappraisal'. In D. Seers (ed.), *Dependency Theory: A Critical Assessment*. London: Frances Pinter, pp. 76–96.

Chang, H.-J. (2002). *Kicking Away the Ladder: Development Strategy in Historical Perspective*. London: Anthem Press.

Edigheji, O. (ed.) (2010). *Constructing a Democratic Developmental State in South Africa: Potentials and Challenges*. Cape Town: HSRC Press.

Fantini, E. (2013). 'Developmental state, economic transformation and social diversification in Ethiopia'. *ISPI Analysis*, 163: 1–7.

Gallagher, K. (2005). *Putting Development First: The Importance of Policy Space in the WTO and the International Financial Institutions*. London: Zed Books.

Gereffi, G. (2014). 'Global value chains in a post-Washington Consensus world'. *Review of International Political Economy*, 21(1): 9–37.

Gerschenkron, A. (1962). *Economic Backwardness in Historical Perspective: A Book of Essays*. Cambridge, MA: Harvard University Press.

Hochstetler, K. and Montero, A. (2013). 'The renewed developmental state: the national development bank and the Brazil model'. *Journal of Development Studies*, 49(11): 1484–99.

Johnson, C. (1982). *MITI and the Japanese Miracle: The Growth of Industrial Policy 1925–75*. Stanford, CA: Stanford University Press.

Lee, K. and Matthews, J.A. (2010). 'From Washington Consensus to BeST Consensus for world development'. *Asia Pacific Economic Literature*, 24(1): 86–103.

List, F. (1841). *The National System of Political Economy* (translated by S. Lloyd). London: Longmans, Green & Co.

Ramo, J.C. (2004). *The Beijing Consensus*. London: The Foreign Policy Centre.

Selwyn, B. (2016). 'Theory and practice of labour-centred development'. *Third World Quarterly*, 37(6): 1035–52.

Stubbs, R. (2012). 'The developmental state and Asian regionalism'. In M. Beeson and R. Stubbs (eds), *Routledge Handbook of Asian Regionalism*. London: Routledge, pp. 90–9.

Taylor, I. (2005). 'The developmental state in Africa: the case of Botswana'. In P. Mbabazi and I. Taylor (eds), *The Potentiality of Developmental States in Africa: Botswana and Uganda Compared*. Dakar: CODESRIA, pp. 44–65.

Wade, R. (1990). *Governing the Market: Economic Theory and the Role of Government in East Asian Industrialization*. Princeton NJ: Princeton University Press.

Wade, R. (1996). 'Japan, the World Bank, and the art of paradigm maintenance: *The East Asian Miracle* in political perspective'. *New Left Review*, 1(217): 3–36.

White, G. (1998). 'Constructing a democratic developmental state'. In M. Robinson and G. White (eds), *The Democratic Developmental State: Politics and Institutional Design*. Oxford: Oxford University Press, pp. 17–50.

Williamson, J. (1989). 'What Washington means by policy reform'. In J. Williamson (ed.), *Latin American Adjustment: How Much Has Happened?* Washington, DC: Institute for International Economics, pp. 7–20.

World Bank (1993). *The East Asian Miracle: Economic Growth and Public Policy*. Washington, DC: World Bank.

Zhang, J. and Peck, J. (2016). 'Variegated capitalism, Chinese style: regional models, multi-scalar constructions'. *Regional Studies*, 50(1): 52–78.

18

LOCAL ECONOMIC DEVELOPMENT AND MICROCREDIT

Milford Bateman

Every so often in the field of development policy, an idea or concept comes along that is simple, it seems to work very quickly, it 'feels good', and it receives a boundless amount of financial and other forms of support from the global community – yet it is a fundamentally misconceived concept and time inevitably shows that it does not actually work in practice.[1] The once universally celebrated concept of microcredit is now seen as one of the most important recent examples of this phenomenon.

First making an appearance in Latin America in the 1960s, but essentially popularized in the 1980s by the Bangladeshi economist and future Nobel Peace Prize winner (in 2006), Muhammad Yunus, the microcredit model perfectly reflected the free-market zeitgeist of the time. The new neoliberal era had been ushered in by the election of Margaret Thatcher in the UK in 1979 and Ronald Reagan in the US in 1980, with its central claim that private entrepreneurship and free markets should be the dominant drivers of development and economic growth. Since the microcredit model provided the tiny loan sums – microloans – that could assist the poor in the Global South to move into petty entrepreneurship projects and self-employment, it could hardly fail to be a popular intervention among the new generation of neoliberal policymakers. Sure enough, almost right away the microcredit model was being very widely described as the key to poverty reduction in the Global South. Yunus famously went on record as saying that the microcredit model would 'eradicate poverty in a generation' and that our children would have to go to what he called a 'poverty museum' to see what all the fuss was about. From the mid-1990s onwards, the microcredit model began to receive massive amounts of financial, technical and political support, and by the mid-2000s it was being widely described as the most effective international development policy of all time.

Yet almost immediately after such heady rhetoric reached its peak in 2006, coinciding with the huge Microcredit Summit event held in Halifax, Canada, in November of that year, the case in favour of the microcredit model began to implode with astonishing rapidity. The beginning of this reversal in fortunes can be very accurately timed to April 2007, when the now giant Banco Compartamos, Mexico's largest microcredit bank, underwent an initial public offering (IPO). Long self-described as making massive inroads into poverty in Mexico, the reality exposed by the IPO process turned out to be something completely different. Thanks to very high interest rates (from 98 per cent to as much as 195 percent per year at times), its senior staff became multimillionaires and its outside shareholders made hundreds of millions of dollars in gains, while no evidence was produced then (or since) to show that this egregious private enrichment had been of any meaningful benefit to Mexico's poor. In the wake of the IPO, there was understandable astonishment and anger within the microcredit community. But this only lasted a short while. Very quickly, in fact, the Compartamos IPO was reborn as the 'role model' that wised-up managers and shareholders attached to other microcredit institutions realized they had to learn from in order to also become spectacularly rich. The global microcredit sector had been 'Wall Street-ized' and turned into a money-making machine designed to benefit its CEOs, senior managers, shareholders, external investors, so-called 'social entrepreneurs', advisors and others also hoping to get rich by ostensibly 'helping the poor'.

A further hammer blow was then inflicted from 2010 onwards, thanks to the introduction of much more accurate evaluation methodologies. This important development was to reveal that it was not just in Mexico where there was no evidence to confirm that microcredit imparted a positive impact on poverty and local economic development. The positive results of even the most trusted studies and impact evaluations were soon being overturned and debunked all across the Global South.

Another central problem that emerged was that, in their desperate drive to maximize their short-term financial returns, far too many microcredit institutions were willing to push out levels of microcredit that were ultimately way beyond the capacity of the local economy to productively absorb. As on Wall Street in the run-up to the 2008 financial crash that was driven by greedy bank CEOs sanctioning the over-supply of sub-prime mortgages to the poor in the US, many unscrupulous microcredit institutions realized that they too could make huge profits by sanctioning the over-supply of sub-prime microloans right across the Global South. Spectacular levels of individual over-indebtedness thus began to arise across the world's poorest communities, which naturally greatly contributed to their poverty, insecurity and deprivation. When over-indebtedness finally began to peak and inevitably turn into default, this precipitated a rapid growth in the number of destructive 'microcredit meltdowns'. Again as on Wall Street, however, the savviest CEOs, managers and shareholders of the main microcredit institutions took steps to ensure that most of their profits were 'taken off the table' well before things turned really sour. In some cases, investors in microcredit institutions that did lose out were bailed out by the state or by the international development community. The poor, meanwhile, were all too often left stranded with petty businesses that did not generate a positive return. Not least because prior to the meltdown they had paid out so much of their meager earnings in order to cover the high risk-adjusted interest rates attached to their microcredit, the poor generally had very little to show for having gotten involved in the microcredit revolution.

The first of these 'microcredit meltdown' events took place in Bolivia in 1999, but from around 2007 further 'microcredit meltdowns' broke out one after the other in Bosnia, Nicaragua, Morocco and Pakistan. And then in 2010, there was the largest and most destructive meltdown to date in the state of Andhra Pradesh in India, a collapse very clearly precipitated by the reckless growth strategies pursued by the CEOs of the 'big six' microcredit institutions, all of whom hoped to get very rich very quickly (Arunachalam, 2011).[2] Many other developing countries remain today poised for a meltdown at some point in the near future, a list that includes Peru, Mexico, Cambodia and India (once again, but this time in Uttar Pradesh, Bihar and West Bengal).

Worst of all for the microcredit movement, the evidence began to suggest that microcredit was *destroying* those poor communities that had placed their trust in it as a way of developing the local economy and reducing poverty. With financial support for all manner of informal microenterprises rising dramatically in recent years, and much more productive and transformational formal small and medium enterprises (SMEs) increasingly starved of financial support as a direct result, far too many local communities in the Global South soon found themselves trapped in a deindustrializing, primitivizing and informalizing 'poverty trap' of their own making.

Not surprisingly, the original purveyors of the microcredit model were forced on to the defensive. This was no more so than in the case of Muhammad Yunus, whose role was increasingly likened to that of a 'faith healer' exposed by the lack of promised divine intervention. However, while the microcredit model was widely pronounced dead in the water in terms of its local economic development and poverty reduction effectiveness, it was nowhere near finished as an international development community intervention. Within neoliberal policymaking circles, any criticism of microcredit, and the central role that individual entrepreneurship supposedly plays in the development process, was seen as criticism of capitalism itself. No matter what the evidence suggests, all criticisms of capitalism are reflexively dismissed by the main international development institutions, especially by those located in Washington, DC. Accordingly, the World Bank was selected to mount a rescue plan to save the microcredit model. The way found to do this was to redefine microcredit as but one component of a much wider set of microfinancial interventions, known collectively as 'financial inclusion'. Imbued with a new (false) aura of humanitarian concern, legitimacy and effectiveness, the failed microcredit model lives on within the architecture of the new financial inclusion movement.

Four key claims to consider

Microcredit reduces poverty through the creation of informal microenterprises and additional incomes

The basic idea propounded by Muhammad Yunus (1989) was that microcredit would provide the crucial wherewithal – a microloan – that the poor would be able to creatively use in order to begin a range of informal income-generating business activities. This, it was assumed, would create an income for that individual, and thereby a gradual exit from poverty. A number of other benefits were also envisaged, notably gender empowerment. When, in the 1990s, the global microcredit sector was commercialized and privatized, and the supply of microcredit began to increase quite dramatically, the excitement grew even further. Microcredit advocates such as Otero and Rhyne (1994) were now convinced that the developing world was on the cusp of a 'new world' of massive poverty reduction.

By the early 2010s, however, the evidence began to turn against the microcredit model in a very big way. Duvendack *et al.*'s (2011) systematic review of virtually all the impact evaluation evidence to date proved to be one of the most devastating studies, finding almost no real evidence to confirm that there was a positive impact. Indeed, such was the categorically negative nature of their findings that the authors were forced to conclude that the microcredit concept had effectively been 'built on foundations of sand' (p. 76). Many of the one-time leading advocates of the microcredit model grudgingly began to accept the rather awkward reality that experience and the deployment of more accurate evaluation methodologies[3] were both very clearly pointing to.

What had gone wrong? One of the most important explanations for the microcredit model's failure to reduce poverty is actually quite simple. The basic idea was to use microcredit to help the poor to produce a simple item or provide a basic service that, it was assumed, would always generate an income. The heroic assumption was made here, however, that there would never be any problems profitably selling these outputs in the local community. Importantly, it was held to be a valid assumption, even in the very poorest communities, where by definition the poor are engaged in a life-or-death struggle to afford the simple items and services conducive to their day-to-day survival, and which were quite readily available to them – if they just had the cash. Muhammad Yunus (1989: 156) made perfectly clear his personal belief in this crucial assumption, noting that 'A Grameen-type credit programme opens up the door for limitless self-employment, and it can effectively do it in a pocket of poverty amidst prosperity, or in a massive poverty situation'.

However, this fundamental assumption was wrong. Those who constructed the microcredit model, above all Muhammad Yunus, had overlooked or simply misunderstood one of the most famous fallacies in economics – Say's law, the mistaken idea that supply creates its own demand. As Amsden (2010) argued, the core poverty problem in the Global South this last 30 or so years has *not* been an insufficient supply of the basic goods and services needed by the poor to survive, which would conceivably justify the role of the microcredit model in upping this supply, but the poor's sheer lack of purchasing power (effective demand) necessary to actually obtain these things. This very simple fact, as Bateman (2010, 2014) shows, very largely accounts for why Yunus's microcredit model essentially failed to resolve poverty: to unproblematically absorb the microcredit-induced increase in the supply of simple items and services in a local community required an automatic uptick in local demand, *but this was by no means an automatic conjuncture.*[4]

In poor communities in the Global South, where almost everyone is both a consumer *and* a basic producer in their own microenterprise, changes in local supply that are not matched by changes in local demand very often have negative effects on the poor. Turnover per individual microenterprise falls, as the prevailing level of demand is shared out among a larger number of microenterprises, while local prices also decline thanks to the increased competition.[5] The microcredit model, and the ultra-competition within the community that it induces, thus tends to have the ultimate effect of competing average incomes down to the bare subsistence level, thus undermining the poverty reduction objective that it was established to resolve. In addition, this deleterious situation is further exacerbated by an adverse employment effect. As Nightingale and Coad (2014) usefully point out, high levels of new entry in poor communities are typically followed by high levels of job displacement, where existing jobs are immediately destroyed by the entry of new microenterprises, followed by exit, where other microenterprises are eventually forced to close down. This combination of entry and exit results in the unproductive phenomenon known as 'job churn'.[6] Thanks to these and other effects, the microcredit model has largely succeeded in creating nothing more than hyper-competitive local markets wherein average incomes are subject to powerful downward pressures and where few secure jobs have been created.

An important illustration of these debilitating income and employment trajectories in practice comes from South Africa, in the early 1990s one of the test beds for the global microcredit movement. In the post-apartheid era after 1994, some additional jobs were created by the microcredit-induced entry of informal microenterprises in the poorest townships and rural communities. This was largely thanks to newly established retail outlets (spazas), house shops (selling from an open window), hairdressers, fast food outlets and informal bars (shabeens). These types of business were most unlikely to evolve into larger formal enterprises, and still less give rise to the crucial innovation and technology-driven dynamics found in a growth-oriented local economy. Moreover, the limited employment gains registered in these areas of activity were later completely swamped by the rapid overall decline in average informal sector self-employment incomes that began to transpire as a result (among other factors) of the increased competition within the informal economy. If some estimates put the decline in informal sector incomes over the period 1997 to 2003 at an astonishing 11 percent per year (see Bateman 2015), one can readily see why, in the post-apartheid era, poverty actually rose very significantly in the black South African community. Middle-class consumers, however, who were overwhelmingly from the white South African community, did fine, as the prices of many informal services they traditionally tapped into – gardeners, cooks, cleaners – softened on account of the price-dampening effect of a great many more poor individuals and informal microenterprises supplying these services. Inequality was thus exacerbated considerably, helping turn South Africa into one of the world's most unequal societies.

Recommended reading: Amsden (2010), Bateman (2010, 2014, 2015), Duvendack et al. (2011), Nightingale and Coad (2014), Yunus (1989).

Microcredit promotes local economic development in the longer term

With virtually no evidence to show that microcredit was making a short-term impact on poverty, microcredit advocates were forced to shift their position. A fallback argument was deployed that took a new line – the most important impacts of microcredit were actually to be found in the longer term. The main argument developed here was to partially concede that new microcredit-assisted informal microenterprises would always meet demand constraints, and that there may also be market fluctuations, declining average incomes and 'job churn' (of the type noted above) that actually disadvantaged the poor in the short term but the microcredit model would nevertheless *eventually* create a thriving local economy because it would gradually expand, consolidate, formalize and interconnect the local economy. Among other things, at least *some* of the many more informal microenterprises created would evolve into formally registered small and medium-sized enterprises, which economic history shows form the dynamic core of most successful local economies. This 'look to the long term' argument was actually first deployed by Hernando de Soto (1989) in the late 1980s when arguing that the programmed expansion of the informal microenterprise sector in Latin America, including with the help of microcredit, would eventually result in a decisively positive long-term development and poverty reduction outcome through the emergence of formal enterprises out of their informal roots.

Critics would argue that, just as with regard to the short-term impact, the longer-term impact of microcredit is also absent, if not the exact opposite to that proposed by the leading advocates of the microcredit model. Most notably, this negative view applies to Latin America under two decades of neoliberalism (the 1980s and 1990s). Thanks to so much economic activity shifting over to informal microenterprises and self-employment ventures during this period, not least because of the stimulation provided by the super-abundance of microcredit, the result was rapidly declining levels of innovation, technology adoption, scale and (so also) productivity. Bateman (2013) argues that this change very much helps explain the economic and social calamity that took place in these turbulent years. Importantly, this negative view was indirectly backed up by a group of researchers based at the Inter-American Development Bank (IBD) in a major book publication (Pagés, 2010: 6). The co-authors saw this programmed shift of economic activity into the informal microenterprise sector and self-employment ventures to be the *single* most important cause of the continent's rapidly rising levels of poverty and deprivation during the neoliberal era. They emphasize the downsides to what they call the '*pulverization of economic activity into millions of tiny enterprises with low productivity*', which they claimed demonstrated that '*the overwhelming presence of small companies and self-employed workers (in Latin America) is a sign of failure, not of success*' (p. 6, emphasis added). While for political and ideological reasons not explicitly or directly blaming it, these researchers nevertheless blew the local economic development case for microcredit right out of the water.

All across Africa, too, the microcredit-supported expansion of the informal microenterprise sector has been found wanting. Largely, this is because it has also come at the expense of the formal small and medium enterprise (SME) sector, which has been starved of credit on affordable terms and maturities. Moyo is a leading proponent of microcredit in Africa, and she has described her native Zambia as a nation where one must '*Think of a woman selling tomatoes on a side street . . . [T]his group – the real entrepreneurs, the backbone of Zambia's economic future – need capital just as much as the mining company*' (2009: 129, emphasis added). Moyo's misunderstanding of development is palpable. As Chang (2010: 157–67) points out, Africa effectively remains trapped in its poverty *precisely* because its increasingly microcredit-dominated financial structure has in the last 30 years or so patently helped to evolve a huge, *and hugely unproductive*, microenterprise-dominated economic structure right across the continent. Economic history and current practice show that such an economic structure simply does not possess the requirements for evolving sustainable development, which is largely based on reaping crucial economies of scale, introducing new technologies, promoting innovation, and developing new organizational routines and capabilities. Thus, channelling even *more* microcredit to tomato sellers in Zambia, as Moyo recommends, or to petty retailers in South Africa's poor townships (see section above), is most likely to undermine the development and poverty reduction process across Africa, according to Chang, not resolve it.

Given the enormous amount of time, financial resources and attention given over to the microcredit sector this last 30 years, the lack of evidence of long-term impact is, to say the least, disturbing. But the bad news goes even further than this. The fact is that the unstoppable growth of the unproductive informal sector has created huge problems in the Global South. As Davis (2006) argues, the international development community's fixation with microcredit, and the creation of as many informal microenterprises and self-employment jobs as possible, is one of the most important reasons why life for the poor in the Global South has become intolerable. The poor are increasingly condemned to a day-to-day life of ultra-low pay, 'turf-wars', exploitation, massive inequality, increased vulnerability and insecurity. Artificially stimulating hyper-competition in the local markets of the Global South is thus not the way out of poverty and human suffering, but is best described as an increasingly ugly manifestation of it.

Recommended reading: Bateman (2013), Chang (2010), Davis (2006), de Soto (1989), Moyo (2009), Pagés (2010).

Microcredit is all about helping the poor

It is an object of faith that the pioneers of microcredit in Bangladesh – Muhammad Yunus in particular – were overwhelmingly motivated by nothing other than their burning desire to help the global poor escape their poverty. Even when under US government and World Bank pressure in the 1990s to convert the microcredit model into a financially self-sustaining for-profit business model, the feeling was that this important development would allow the microcredit model to even *better* serve the global poor (Otero and Rhyne, 1994).

Critics would argue, however, that the microcredit movement was actually given its wings in the 1980s because of anything but genuine concern for the plight of the global poor. Rather, the microcredit model was supported because of its obvious serviceability to the neoliberal project. While the global microcredit movement is unequivocally associated with the work of Muhammad Yunus in Bangladesh in the 1980s, its actual genesis as a policy intervention is located in the extreme concern permeating the US government and US business establishment in the 1960s, which was that increasingly restive poor populations around the globe were evolving the potential and capacity to challenge the established US-led global political and economic order. Above all else, the US government feared the prospect of the global poor organizing collectively through trade unions, pro-poor leftist political parties and elected governments, social movements and, worst of all, Cuba-style revolutions, and thus evolving a successful and equitable non-capitalist development model outside of US government control. However, it was hoped that with the help of microcredit and a major PR effort in all corners of the Global South, the poor could instead be seduced into believing that the most realistic way of escaping their poverty was through engaging in individual entrepreneurship. By 'bringing capitalism down to the poor' in such a way, the US was attempting to avoid real structural change taking place. Real change that would be of benefit to the poor would undoubtedly jeopardize the model of US-led capitalism and the freedom of the largest US corporations to do whatever they wished to maximize profits, and this could not be tolerated.

With leftist political parties, trade union movements, 'liberation theology' informed church-based pro-poor movements and many other pro-poor social mobilization movements taking off in the 1950s and 1960s in the US's 'backyard' – Latin America – this accounts for why the microcredit movement essentially found its legs here in the late 1960s; first in Brazil, and then in Peru, Bolivia and elsewhere (Bateman, 2013). Latin America's poor majority simply could not be allowed to develop their 'collective capabilities', since this would inevitably precipitate a challenge to US dominance on the continent. Instead, the poor in Latin America, and then elsewhere around the Global South, were increasingly to be held responsible for individually resolving their own poverty predicament. With a microcredit easily to hand, the thinking ran, there was no excuse for not getting involved and facilitating one's own way out of poverty. This presented an historic opportunity for the US government and the international development community to effectively disempower the global poor. By denying the poor the choice of their own tools to resolve their poverty collectively, and thus shutting down the opportunity to follow in the path of the richest countries that had earlier used exactly such tools in the course of escaping their own poverty and underdevelopment (Chang, 2007), the poor could be 'contained'.

A second reason why microcredit was perfectly attuned to the neoliberal agenda was because it was discovered to be a fantastic way not just of disempowering the poor organizationally and politically, but financially too. As Mader (2015) shows, poor communities around the globe have been programmatically drained of their remaining wealth under cover of 'promoting poverty reduction'. Savvy investors everywhere began to see the earnings of informal microenterprises as a flow of funds that they could tap into in order to repay high interest rate micro-credit, thereby generating profits. This would result in the capture of a larger and larger part of the economic surplus of poor communities to the extent that they engaged with the microcredit model, and thus impoverish these communities even further into the longer term, just as those poor communities in the US that hap-lessly engaged with the sub-prime mortgage companies prior to 2008 found to their cost. But no matter: microcredit held out the possibility for the global invest-ment community (much of which was based in the US) to generate a high and growing source of profits, and that was what *really* counted.

Managers working within the main microcredit institutions, and even the CEOs employed in supposedly selfless microcredit advocacy bodies (famously in the case of such high-profile global microfinance advocacy bodies as FINCA and ACCION – see Sinclair, 2012), all began to demand and receive multimillion-dollar salaries, massive pension payments and ultra-generous bonus packages. Foreign investors and private commercial banks, many of them registered in tax havens, increasingly began to seek out struggling microcredit institutions to buy out and turn into 'cash cows' that could coldly extract value from the poor as never before. A more recent trend is to convert or buy out a microcredit institution and turn it into a 'payday' lending operation, a form of institution that everywhere has proved relentless in its exploitation of the most vulnerable of the poor. As a result, value and wealth began to flow up and out of the poorest communities and into the hands of a narrow domestic financial elite, and then also abroad into the hands of an even richer financial elite. In 2013 alone, for example, Banco Compartamos in Mexico (total assets in 2016 US$1.5 billion) paid out a massive €154 million in dividends to its mainly foreign shareholders, a sum that Rozas (2015) points out was way in excess of many much bigger banks, such as one of Europe's top four largest banks, Credit Agricole (total assets in 2016 US$1.9 trillion), which paid €301 million in dividend in that same year).

In truth, by the end of the 2000s, all pretense of a social mission had been abandoned in the world of microcredit. As clearly intended by some, the commer-cialization of the microcredit industry has resulted in a global scramble for profit.

What followed was the creation of a massive flow of financial resources moving up from poor individuals and communities in the Global South, and into the hands of a small number of global banks, hedge funds, pension funds and special micro-finance investment vehicles (MIVs) all located in the main global financial centres or offshore tax havens. Microcredit in the neoliberal era was thus turned into one of the purest, and most exploitative, subcategories of what has been termed the 'financialization' of the global economy.

Recommended reading: Bateman (2013), Chang (2007), Mader (2015), Otero and Rhyne (1994), Rozas (2015).

The new financial inclusion movement represents a bold new move that will help the poor even more than before

With no genuine evidence to confirm its effectiveness as an anti-poverty intervention in either the short or the longer term, the international development community ended up with a serious problem on its hands: microcredit did not work. Yet, it was impossible for the international development community to simply ditch the failed microcredit model, since that would also mean invalidating the central role of informal microenterprises and self-help. These were the absolutely key ideological foundations of the local neoliberal model preferred by the international development community, and they simply could not be challenged. Accordingly, the microcredit model was subsumed within what became known as the 'financial inclusion' movement. Defined as the drive to endow the poor in developing countries with the most basic financial tools routinely used in developed countries (credit, savings accounts, payment cards, mobile money systems, etc.), the financial inclusion movement was set up to act as a sort of witness protection programme for the failed microcredit model. It provided the microcredit model with a new life, a new name, and it was no longer visible to outsiders. Effectively led by the World Bank (2014), the financial inclusion movement was launched in the mid-2000s and it quickly went on to become the new darling of the international development community.

Legitimation for the financial inclusion movement was provided by a number of long-time advocates of the microcredit model. One very important early contribution on the theme of financial inclusion, which was especially influential in the African context (see Bateman, 2015), was provided by Porteous and Hazelhurst (2004). They argued that the concept of financial inclusion was a way of 'democratizing finance' to the immense benefit of the poor. Merely getting the poor 'included' in the local financial system, and given equal access to a range of suitably scaled-down financial instruments, they argued, would generate a major positive impact on poverty. Arguing along similar uplifting lines were Collins et al. (2009) in their best-selling book *Portfolios of the Poor*. This work centrally argued that the poor will greatly benefit from having access to a range of financial services, including micro-credit, which they could combine in such a way as to build resilience and enhance their survival chances on a day-to-day basis in difficult financial and economic times. Importantly, as in the work by Porteous and Hazelhurst, the co-authors refuse to go into the rather central issue of how and why the poor find themselves in such a desperate situation in the first place, and who might be benefiting from the prevailing social arrangements.

Critics argue that the mass of evidence from the field, as well as the supporting academic contributions just noted, do not offer any support whatsoever for the financial inclusion movement's main contentions. As Mader (2016) pointedly shows, the central claims of the financial inclusion narrative are all based on not much more than mere assumption. Notably, Mader shows, while financial sector deepening per se may indeed be positively related to economic development, as King and Levine (1993) reported many years back, there is absolutely nothing in this important literature that suggests that this applies in the special case of financial sector deepening with regard to the poor. This is not least because the data used in this literature all refer to the important rise in credit allocated to the enterprise sector *as a whole*, and not to how much the informal microenterprise sector received compared to small, medium and large enterprises. Conceivably, if the bulk of the increase in financial deepening detected by King and Levine also meant more financial support going into small, medium and large enterprises as opposed to informal microenterprises, as Mader goes on to speculate, then the positive poverty impact could even be interpreted the other way around entirely: financial sector deepening that involves channelling financial resources *away* from informal microenterprises, and *towards* small, medium and large enterprises, could be the very best development strategy for a country to adopt.

And, in fact, economic history *does* show that those countries that have managed to channel their financial resources into small, medium and, especially, large enterprises in exactly this manner have all developed much faster, and reduced poverty much faster, than those countries where the available financial resources were channelled into the informal microenterprise sector (Bateman and Chang, 2012). Thus, widespread claims that financial inclusion *causes* poverty reduction actually amount to nothing more than mere *correlation*, such as when better-off individuals choose to use more financial services as their income grows.

In addition, it is important to point out that effectively bankrolling the financial inclusion movement are the major Wall Street and European banks and two of the world's three largest credit card companies (Visa and Mastercard). Not least because of so much unethical behaviour on their part in the lead-up to the 2008 global financial crisis (Taibbi, 2010), which appears to have continued,[7] we must surely be extremely suspicious, like Da Costa (2016), of the motives behind the growing involvement in financial inclusion measures of such a high-profile set of global institutions. Like the tobacco companies in earlier times, the Global South represents a new virgin market, largely unregulated, where new 'inclusive' micro-financial relationships can be proliferated as the first step towards the generation and eventual repatriation of vast amounts of wealth back to head office, even if this undermines and destroys local communities in the Global South. Rhetoric and PR by the financial inclusion industry aside, this is what the evidence suggests financial inclusion is all about.

Recommended reading: Bateman and Chang (2012), Collins *et al.* (2009), Da Costa (2016), *Fortune* (2016), King and Levine (1993), Mader (2016), Porteous and Hazelhurst (2004), Sinclair (2012), Taibbi (2010), World Bank (2014).

Notes

1 An example would be the once mainstream idea that developing countries would do well to import much, if not most, of their food from the developed countries because it can often be produced much cheaper there thanks to better technologies and scale economies. It was later realized that becoming dependent upon food imports destroyed a country's own agricultural sector.
2 At the end of the day, the spectacular collapse of the microcredit sector in Andhra Pradesh in 2010 left only one CEO lavishly enriched – Dr Vikram Akula, the founder and CEO of SKS Microfinance. Akula was able to become rich, first by earning a very large salary indeed, for which his tax payment alone was of the order of $500,000 per year, and then by selling off in 2010 around 20 per cent of his self-awarded shares in SKS for just under $13 million (see Bateman, 2012: 1397).
3 These include the randomized control trial (RCT) methodology that supporters have long claimed is the 'gold standard' in terms of the accurate evaluation of policy interventions.
4 One might also usefully view the fundamental problem here as akin to the error made by those who long argued that famines were caused by 'a lack of food' and that 'more food availability' would quickly remedy the problem, when in fact, as Amartya Sen (1981) famously showed, the core problem was actually the limited purchasing power of the poor that prevented them from buying the food that was often quite widely available in a famine region.
5 Note that any price decline tends not to stimulate additional demand for most of the goods and services produced by the poor. That is, they supply outputs that are price-inelastic.
6 This dynamic should not be mistaken for the more familiar and productivity-raising process of Schumpeterian 'creative destruction', which is mainly associated with the entry and exit of somewhat more sophisticated, technology-based and innovative small and medium enterprises.
7 The US bank Wells Fargo, one of the world's largest banks, has recently been fined a total of US$185 million because until very recently (that is, after 2008), its employees were found to have secretly opened more than two million new accounts for existing clients without their knowledge or consent, thereby meeting aggressive performance targets that triggered bonus payments. More than 5,300 mid-level employees were dismissed (*Fortune*, 2016). The overall manager in charge of the entire operation during which the fraud took place, as well as the CEO, however, were only later forced out of the bank.

References

Amsden, A.H. (2010). 'Say's law, poverty persistence, and employment neglect'. *Journal of Human Development and Capabilities*, 1(1): 57–66.
Arunachalam, R. (2011). *The Journey of Indian Micro-Finance: Lessons for the Future*. Chennai: Aapti.

Bateman, M. (2010). *Why Doesn't Microfinance Work? The Destructive Rise of Local Neoliberalism*. London: Zed Books.

Bateman, M. (2012). 'How lending to the poor began, grew, and almost destroyed a generation in India'. *Development and Change*, 43: 1385–402.

Bateman, M. (2013). 'The age of microfinance: destroying Latin American economies from the bottom up'. *Working Papers*, No. 39. Austrian Research Foundation for International Development, Vienna, Austria.

Bateman, M. (2014). 'The rise and fall of Muhammad Yunus and the microcredit model'. *International Development Studies Working Papers*, No. 1, January. St Mary's University, Halifax, Canada. Available at: http://papers.ssrn.com/sol3/papers.cfm?abstract_id1/42385190.

Bateman, M. (2015). 'South Africa's post-apartheid microcredit experiment: moving from state-enforced to market-enforced exploitation'. *Forum for Social Economics*. doi: 10.1080/07360932.2015.1056202.

Bateman, M. and Chang, H.-J. (2012). 'Microfinance and the illusion of development: from hubris to nemesis in thirty years'. *World Economic Review*, 1: 13–36.

Chang, H.-J. (2007). *Bad Samaritans: Rich Nations, Poor Policies and the Threat to the Developing World*. London: Random House.

Chang, H.-J. (2010). *23 Things They Don't Tell You About Capitalism*. London: Allen Lane.

Collins, D., Morduch, J., Rutherford, S. and Ruthven, O. (2009). *Portfolios of the Poor: How the World's Poor Live on $2 a Day*. Princeton, NJ/Oxford: Princeton University Press.

Da Costa, P.N. (2016). 'Big banks and the White House are teaming up to fleece poor people'. *Foreign Policy*, 23 February. Available at: http://foreignpolicy.com/2016/02/23/big-banks-and-the-white-house-are-teaming-up-to-fleece-poor-people/.

Davis, M. (2006). *Planet of Slums*. London: Verso.

de Soto, H. (1989). *The Other Path*. New York: Basic Books.

Duvendack, M., Palmer-Jones, R., Copestake, J., Hooper, L., Loke, Y. and Rao, N. (2011). *What Is the Evidence of the Impact of Microfinance on the Well-Being of Poor People?*. London: EPPI-Centre, Social Science Research Unit, Institute of Education, University of London.

Fortune (2016). 'Wells Fargo exec who headed phony accounts unit collected $125 million'. *Fortune*, 12 September. Available at: http://fortune.com/2016/09/12/wells-fargo-cfpb-carrie-tolstedt/.

King, R. and Levine, R. (1993). 'Finance, entrepreneurship, and growth: theory and evidence'. *Journal of Monetary Economics*, 32(3): 513–42.

Mader, P. (2015). *The Political Economy of Microfinance: Financialising Poverty*. London: Palgrave MacMillan.

Mader, P. (2016). *Questioning Three Fundamental Assumptions in Financial Inclusion*. IDS Evidence Report 176. Brighton: IDS.

Moyo, D. (2009). *Dead Aid: Why Aid Is Not Working and How There Is a Better Way for Africa*. New York: Farrar, Straus & Giroux.

Nightingale, P. and Coad, A. (2014). 'Muppets and gazelles: political and methodological biases in entrepreneurship research'. *Industrial and Corporate Change*, 23: 113–43.

Otero, M. and Rhyne, E. (eds) (1994). *The New World of Microenterprise Finance: Building Healthy Institutions for the Poor*. London: Intermediate Technology.

Pagés C. (ed.) (2010). *The Age of Productivity: Transforming Economies from the Bottom Up*. Washington, DC: IDB.

Porteous, D. and Hazelhurst, E. (2004). *Banking on Change: Democratising Finance in South Africa 1994–2004 and Beyond*. Cape Town: Double Storey.

Rozas, D. (2015). 'Microfinance in Mexico: beyond the brink'. *European Microfinance Platform*, 19 June. Available at: www.e-mfp.eu/blog/microfinance-mexico-beyond-brink.

Sen, A. (1981). 'Ingredients of famine analysis: availability and entitlements'. *The Quarterly Journal of Economics*, 96(3), August: 433–64.

Sinclair, H. (2012). *Confessions of a Microfinance Heretic: How Microlending Lost Its Way and Betrayed the Poor*. San Francisco, CA: Berrett-Koehler.

Taibbi, M. (2010). *Griftopia: A Story of Bankers, Politicians, and the Most Audacious Power Grab in American History*. New York: Random House.

World Bank (2014). *Global Financial Development Report 2014: Financial Inclusion*. Washington, DC: World Bank.

Yunus, M. (1989). 'Grameen Bank: organization and operation'. In J. Levitsky (ed.), *Microenterprises in Developing Countries*. London: Intermediate Technology.

PART VI
Class and development

19

CLASS ANALYSIS AND DEVELOPMENT

Henry Veltmeyer

There are three different ways of understanding 'society' – either as a collection of individuals, each motivated to better themselves or to seek self-advantage; as a system of institutionalized practices that sets rules and limits to the action of individuals; or as a system of overlapping and interconnected social groups with shared experiences, able to act collectively on the basis of these experiences. The first relates to conception of the relation between individuals and society that is widely shared by economists and political scientists in the liberal tradition. For the sake of analysis, they see the individuals as rational calculators of self-interest, or as citizens who are equal in their opportunities for self-advancement, and as the fundamental agents of social change.

The second and third ways of understanding society accord with what could be described as the 'sociological perspective', which is the view that the problems, experiences and actions both of individuals and nations can and must be related to the position that they occupy in the broader system, and understood in terms of the way society or the economy is organized and structured. That is, the response to and actions of individuals – and, for that matter, nations – to some extent is a function of their status, their position or location in the system, which is to say that they are not free to choose and act in any way they please; the structure in which they are enmeshed limits or conditions, or to some degree 'determines', the choices and opportunities available to them and their actions. In this 'structural' context, individuals – and, at a different level, nations – are not 'free to act and choose', but are constrained by forces that arise from the structure of the system – from conditions that are objective in their effects according to the position or location in the system.

This does not mean that 'structures' are determinant and that the choices and actions of individuals do not matter – that they do not have a role to play in explaining the course of events, or the dynamics of the development process. As Marx noted, individuals are not free to act; they are a product of their circumstances, but it is people who make history, although not under conditions of their choosing. What this means is that individuals do indeed have a degree of freedom or the ability to act, but that their actions are constrained and limited by forces over which they do not control, but to which they can respond with collective consciousness and purpose. What Marx means is expressed in the notion of 'class in itself'.

As Marx saw it, and argued as a matter of principle, people enter society under conditions not of their choosing and that affect them – and shape their response – according to their class location within the capitalist system, i.e. their relationship to production. Under these conditions, the behaviour and actions of people can be analysed in structural, i.e. scientific, terms. And the same applies to international relations among entire nations in the world capitalist system. However, a structural analysis of class is but the first step in the method that he proposed of class analysis. The second step is to analyse the actions taken by individuals when they become class conscious, i.e. aware of their class position (the relation of labour to capital, or the exploitation), and the collective actions taken on the basis of this awareness. As Marx expressed it, individuals are only fully constituted or formed when they become class conscious – when they are transformed from a 'class in itself' (as determined by scientific analysis of their class position) into a 'class for itself'. We have here the fundamental precepts of what we might term critical development studies, critical sociology or political economy in the critical tradition.

Forms of class analysis

The distribution of socioeconomic conditions in society, and their association with different social groups and classes, is never haphazard, but the result of how society is organized and the institutionalized practices associated with relations of production and power in society. Notwithstanding significant differences in the social structure of different societies, there is nevertheless a surprising consistency in the pattern displayed by these practices – in the limits of variation in the social condition of the people, in what we might well define as the social structure of advanced capitalist societies and the typical class structure of societies on the periphery of the world capitalist system.

Social class per relations of production

An analysis of this 'structure' has been represented by sociologists and development theorists in four different ways. One is in terms of the dominant social relations of production, which defines two basic classes: the bourgeoisie, or the owners of the means of production; and the working class, those who, dispossessed from their means of production, are compelled to exchange their labour power for a living wage. In addition, the class structure of Latin American capitalist societies typically includes the petit-bourgeoisie, a class of small property owners that might well be conceived of as the traditional 'middle class', and a managerial-professional class of service providers, conceived of by sociologists as the 'new middle class' (Portes and Hoffman, 2003). Societies on the periphery of world capitalism also typically include a class of small-scale independent commodity or subsistence producers, whose relations of production are pre-capitalist in form, who do not have an identifiable 'position' vis-à-vis the capital–labour relation, and who are generally viewed, or view themselves, in traditional terms as 'peasants' (Bernstein, 2010).

With the capitalist development of agriculture and industry over the past five decades, the forces of which have brought about a structural transformation of rural society, well over one-half of the so-called 'peasantry' has been effectively or partially proletarianized, converted into a rural semi-proletariat and a peri-urban proletariat of self-employed street workers (Delgado Wise and Veltmeyer, 2016; Tokman, 1992). As a result, close to one-half of the Latin American working class today work for themselves rather than for wages in the so-called 'informal sector' of the burgeoning urban centres and cities (Davis, 2006).

Classes as occupational groups

A second way of understanding the social structure of Latin American societies is in terms of the division of labour formed through the capitalist development process. The process, as it has unfolded in different parts of the world over the past century and a half, implies the transformation of an agriculture-based society, characterized by pre-capitalist relations of production and a traditional culture of social solidarity, into a modern urban-centred capitalist system based on industry and a culture of individualism. In these terms, the social structure is generally defined in terms of major occupational groups, relations among which are understood in functional terms (i.e. in a relation of complementarity, structural interdependence and social solidarity). In contrast, when the social structure is defined in terms of the dominant social relations of production, they are typically understood in Marxist terms as relations of economic exploitation and class conflict.

Conceptualized and theorized in these terms, the social structure of occupational groupings is conceived as a status hierarchy in which each class of human functionary, according to its location in the social structure, is allocated a certain 'coefficient of well-being' – income, and other 'rewards for effort, talent and skills, commensurate with their occupational status. In these terms, the distribution of income and wealth in society is viewed as a function of the importance that society attaches to certain functions within a scale of assigned modern values.

Social class by grouping an individual's life chances

A third way of viewing the social structure is in terms not of an individual's relation to production, but his or her relation to consumption, or the market – what Max Weber conceived of as an individual's life's chances. In these terms, often combined (by theorists of social stratification) with the notion of occupational class, the categories of social class analysis are: upper, upper-middle, middle, lower-middle, and lower. In the mainstream of development studies, the central focus is on policies and practices that result in lifting the poor, those deprived of the resources, opportunity and income needed to meet their basic human needs, out of poverty and into the middle class (i.e. those individuals with the resources and income to not only meet their basic needs, but secure a decent standard of living).

Income class as a statistical grouping of the population

Another form of class analysis is associated with many economists in the mainstream of development. In this approach, 'class' is understood in terms of income – the distribution of national income per deciles or quintiles of the population. In this approach, which is based on class defined by share of national income, classes are statistical constructs rather than social groups defined by their location in the social structure and a corresponding identity or class consciousness. This is a critical issue in that classes can only be viewed as 'actors' to the degree that they act. What this means is that income class serves as a useful construct in a structural analysis – always the first step in the method of class analysis.

Recommended reading: Bernstein (2010), Davis (2006), Delgado Wise and Veltmeyer (2016), Portes and Hoffman (2003), Tokman (2007).

Class as a social relation of development

No matter how the social structure is conceptualized – and often these four different forms of class analysis are haphazardly or even systematically combined (see, for example, Portes and Hoffman, 2003) – Latin American societies are characterized by structured relations and conditions of social inequality – what ECLAC terms 'the structure of social inequality', a structure that underpins and gives form to, if not determines, the social distribution of wealth and income. However, because of the limited form in which statistics are collected and available, the social structure of this distribution is constructed on the basis of a statistical rather than a social grouping of the population. Thus, the methodological procedure is to break the population into declines or quintiles of income earners, and to determine the share of each in national income; and also, via the Gini index or a ratio of top to bottom groupings, to compare countries according to the deviation from a statistical average and the degree of social inequality. For example, Table 19.1 presents in statistical terms the structure of social income distribution for major countries in the region, with several reference points for international comparison. The table points to a structure of social inequality that has exhibited remarkable persistence over time, relatively immune to fluctuations in the rate of growth, and also resisting diverse albeit halting efforts over the past five decades of development to change this distribution in the direction of equity.

TABLE 19.1 Income distribution, % share; Gini coefficient, for selected Latin American countries, 1989–2009

	(Poorest 40%)			(Richest 10%)			Gini coefficient[1]	
	1989/90	2009	Change	1989/90	2009	Change	1989/90	2009
Argentina	15.0	15.5	+0.5	34.6	32.1	−2.5	0.50	0.51
Bolivia	12.1	11.2	−0.9	38.1	35.4	−2.7	0.54	0.57
Brazil	18.5	20.3	+1.8	43.9	41.0	−2.9	0.63	0.58
Chile	20.8	21.2	+0.4	40.7	38.4	−2.3	0.55	0.52
Ecuador	25.4	24.6	−0.8	30.6	32.7	+2.3	0.46	0.50
Mexico	22.6	24.0	+1.4	36.6	34.4	−1.8	0.54	0.52
Venezuela	25.7	27.9	+2.2	28.7	24.8	−3.9	0.47	0.41

Source: ECLAC (2010: 75–8)

The middle-class conundrum: what is it and where is it?

In practice, in the mainstream of development studies, improvements in the social condition of the people are measured in terms of income distribution – to determine the income shares of different social groups and classes. It is evident that such distribution is not random, but that it is 'structured' (i.e. associated with the position that individuals and groups occupy in the social structure). The social structure in capitalist societies assumes a hierarchical form, with each 'class of human functionary' (to use Durkheim's expression) assigned a 'certain coefficient of well-being' (a share of the wealth, a quota of income to reward effort and talent). The problem is how to identify the basic elements of this structure, and to connect the pattern of social distribution to these elements.

Above, we identified two sociological theories of an analysis of the social structure: (i) a Marxist theory of social class; and (ii) a theory of social stratification that combines a Weberian focus on an individual's 'life chances' (relation to the market) with a functionalist focus on the occupational class structure. However, the main way of analysing the distribution of income both within and among diverse societies and nation states is in terms of the methodology favoured by economists, which is to group people statistically in terms of average income earned or received by people in each group. In these terms, the share of different statistical groups (deciles or quintiles) can be compared and calculated. For example, the share of total income that accrues to the poorest 10–40 per cent can be compared to the share received or appropriated by the richest 10 or even 1 per cent. In this analysis, the 'middle class' is constructed not as a social group, but as a statistical artefact: all individuals in the middle range of income distribution – from the 40th to the 90th percentile of income distribution, or 50 per cent of the population.

Of course, the pattern of income distribution will vary by country, with a more solid 'middle class' of relatively high mass consumption in the advanced capitalist societies characterized by 'mass consumption'. Societies on the South of the global development divide, on the periphery of the world capitalist system, are assumed and shown to have a smaller middle class, much smaller in many cases, with correspondingly lower levels of consumption and thus a lower level of market-led development. In this regard, World Bank economists Branco Milanovic and Shlomo Yitzhaki (2002: 175) estimate that the world middle class encompasses barely 11 per cent of the economically active population.

The methodology used by these economists is problematic at a number of levels. First, if the middle class is defined as all those who are neither rich nor poor, then – depending on the defined poverty line – up to 50 per cent of the population in many developing societies would automatically fall into the middle class, a dubious and rather meaningless proposition. It would of necessity include, and lump together, a large category of low-income earners with a very restricted capacity to consume, with individuals in an upper-income bracket and a high level of consumption.

Another problem is to extend the definition of the middle class downwards to the poverty line. For example, *The Economist* (12 May 2011: 58) cites a report commissioned and prepared by the African Development Bank in which one-third of all Africans are placed in the 'middle class', defined as all those who are in a position to spend from $2 to $20 a day. The Bank notes that ten years ago only 25 per cent of Africans were in this middle-class position, an advance of 8 percentage points. But what does this possibly mean? A large swathe of low-income earners, and even some of the poor, by statistical fiat, materialize as the 'middle class' – a rather nonsensical procedure that requires no further comment.

A more sensible and analytically useful approach would be to use a Marxist conception of class in which the population can be categorized and divided into four classes, two formed around the capital–labour relation and two with a more indirect connection to this relation: (i) *the capitalist class*, in its dominant forms (financial, industrial); (ii) *the working class*, in its multitudinous and changing forms; (iii) *the petit-bourgeoisie* – an old middle class of small proprietors, independent farmers and business owners, artisans, and a new middle class of professionals and functionaries, providers of diverse 'business and corporate services', who, like all members of this 'upper-middle class' trade on their knowledge and other forms of intangible means of production; and (iv) *the peasantry*, a class of small landowning farmers who do not work and live to accumulate capital, but respond to a different development logic.

In this method of class analysis, the middle class is also viewed in structural terms, but not in terms of the relation of individuals to production; rather, social class is defined in terms of the capacity of individuals to consume, which defines its fundamental role in the capitalist development process: to constitute the market on which capitalism depends for its expansion and normal functioning – 'to create a group of consumers large enough to sustain broad economic spurts in the services and manufacturing sectors' (*The Economist*, 12 May 2011). In the current conjuncture of globalizing capital, the middle class is expanding most rapidly in the 'emerging markets' of Asia, particularly China and India. As for the US, at the epicentre of the system, three decades of capitalist development in its neoliberal mould has not only resulted in a serious deterioration in the condition of the American working class, but it has led to a dramatic increase in the level of social inequalities, and also a 'hollowing out' of the middle class, reducing the consumption capacity of millions of Americans rather than poverty.

According to Milanovick and Yitzhaki (2002: 175), '76 per cent of the world population lives in poor countries, eight per cent lives in middle income countries and 16 per cent lives in rich countries'. However, they add, 'if we . . . look at *true* distribution of people according to their income (regardless of where they live) we find [that]: 78 per cent of world population is poor, 11 per cent belong to the middle class, and 11 per cent are rich' (p. 175, emphasis in original). Thus, 'any way we consider it . . . the world lacks a middle class . . . It looks like a proverbial hourglass: thick on the bottom, and very thin in the middle. Why,' Milanovic asks, 'does the world not have a middle class?' First, he answers, it is because 'world equality is extremely high'. However, he conjectures, a more 'substantive cause' for the absence of a global middle class is 'because there is no agency whose mandate would be to care about it'. His thinking is not spelt out, but the implication, elaborated on by the OECD's Kharas (2010), is that the development community has been overly focused on poverty reduction, ignoring in the process the fundamental role of the middle class in advancing capitalist development.

The rich and the rest

The concern for the excessive inequalities generated by free-market capitalism was already in the minds of the social liberal critics of the Washington Consensus in the 1980s in the concern that the volume of debt repayments in such a short period (1983–1987) might be excessive and premature. Shortly thereafter, a number of development theorists and practitioners went back to the drawing board to design new policies, and create a new institutional framework for a more equitable and socially inclusive form of development – for the Washington Consensus policies were not only generating excessive inequalities in the distribution of wealth and income, but the development model was by all accounts evidently highly exclusive, benefiting but a small segment of the population. By the mid-1990s, other voices were raised in concert about the growing development divide based on an exceedingly unequal distribution of wealth and incomes. The UNDP noted that by the mid-decade, a small room full of individuals – some 365 to be exact – possessed the equivalent of the wealth and income of all of the world's poor, some 1.5 billion people, most of whom are found in the Global South.

This concern about excessive social inequalities was expressed by Ethan Kapstein, Senior Fellow at the Centre for a New American Security and Vice President of the Council on Foreign Relations (Kapstein, 1996). The concern was that the increase of social inequalities in the distribution of wealth and income, and the poverty generated at one extreme of this distribution, was such as to render a country ungovernable, leading to social discontent that likely enough would be mobilized against the capitalist democracies in the region. And the forces of resistance in the

1990s were indeed so mobilized. In some contexts (South America, for example), the response of the guardians of the new world order was not to regulate profit and wealth in the 'private sector' but to compel governments to adopt policies of 'good governance' – to engage diverse 'stakeholders' and 'civil society' in the responsibility for social development and political order – to create a more participatory form of politics and development. Thus, 'good governance' was added to the conditions attached to 'foreign aid' and accessing capital markets.

A full decade into the new millennium, what *The Economist* (22 January 2011: 13) defines as the Davos Consensus – the need to boost growth with free-market capitalism (pro-growth policies) and to reduce the incidence of extreme poverty – was given a new impetus as a new development model and poverty reduction strategy: macroeconomic structural reform (to boost growth) combined with obliging governments to write a PRSP with social participation. However, by the end of the first decade, despite a series of positive reports on progress made vis-à-vis MDG #1 (reducing by a half the rate of extreme poverty by 2015), it became clear that economic growth/poverty reduction was not enough – that there was a growing need to address the problem of growing and possibly excessive income disparities; that, as ECLAC would have it, 'it was time for equality'.

The most often expressed concern by officials in the development community regarding the inequality predicament (excessive disparities in income distribution) is ethical, with reference to equity as a principle of social justice and development. However, the underlying albeit normally unexpressed concern is for politically stability or governability. In this connection, a study and report commissioned by the UK Ministry of Defence (2007: 3) is eloquent in pointing out the profound political implications of the global divide in wealth and development that continue to breed 'forces of resistance' and will likely lead to a 'resurgence of not only anti-capitalist ideologies . . . but also to populism and the revival of Marxism'.

This concern has been echoed in voices as diverse as those of China's president (Hu Jintao), Britain's prime minister (David Cameron), America's second richest man (Warren Buffett), and Dominique Strauss-Kahn, the former IMF head and a 2007 socialist candidate for the presidency in France. Each has worried loudly and publicly about the dangers of the 'rising gap between the rich and the rest', as *The Economist* puts it. For Hu Jintao, the reduction of income inequalities, particularly between China's urban elites and the rural poor, is at the centre of his pledge to create a 'harmonious society'. Cameron, for his part, declared – what is now a truism among development theorists and practitioners – that more unequal societies do worse 'according to almost every quality-of-life indicator'.

As for Buffett, he became a crusader in the US context for a higher inheritance tax, arguing that without it, America risked the formation of an entrenched plutocracy and a dictatorship of money, with grave consequences for American democracy. Strauss-Kahn, accommodated for a while in a New York jail with a charge of rape, began to push for a new global growth model, arguing that gaping income gaps threaten social and economic stability. Thus, he has picked up a concern expressed earlier by Michel Camdessus, one of his predecessors, who, in 1996, on a visit to Mexico, declared that the policy of the IMF was no longer neoliberalism (free-market capitalism), but that IMF policy was now based on three pillars: the invisible hand of the market; the visible hand of the state; and 'solidarity between the rich and the poor'. It would take the IMF many years to come to the conclusion that this 'solidarity' would only be possible – and thus social and political stability – by dealing more effectively with the gaping inequalities in wealth and incomes.

We conclude that what *The Economist* terms the Davos Consensus (unregulated economic growth plus extreme poverty eradication) is no longer viable. Indeed, a recent survey conducted by the organizers of the World Economic Forum in Davos concludes that in addition to failings in global governance (the failure of a strategic response to the global financial crisis), the main global risk over the next decade is widening global economic disparities. The response to this 'inequality predicament' by the guardians of the capitalist world order and the architects of the post-Washington Consensus – many of whom have a Keynesian rather than a neoliberal conception of the capitalist development process – will most likely result in a new form of global governance, and a mixed economy that combines elements of both socialism and capitalism with the added soft touch of imperialism.

Class as the politics of class struggle and resistance

From a CDS perspective, class analysis has two dimensions – structural and political. The first step in class analysis is to determine an individual's class location – to locate individuals in the social structure, no matter how this structure is conceptualized and theorized. At this level, we can conceive of a class in itself, with reference to conditions that are given and 'objective' in their effects on the individual. This is to determine the impact of forces that operate on people according to their class location. The next step is to determine the strategic or political response of different class groupings to these conditions and forces, on the basis of their class or political consciousness, i.e. awareness of their objective situation, an awareness that, according to Marx, is only or best achieved in the process of class struggle. It is in these terms that Marxists generally do their analysis and politics (i.e. based on the assumption that to each advance of capital in the development process, there corresponds a certain form of collective action and resistance based on this consciousness).

For example, in the 1950s and 1960s, the class struggle was advanced and primarily took the form of the land struggle and the labour movement. This was in response to the dynamics of capitalist development at the time – the proletarianization of the direct producers, their transformation from peasants into a working class.

In the subsequent period of capitalist development, dubbed by David Harvey and others as the neoliberal era, the class struggle took the predominant form of resistance to the neoliberal policy agenda, which was used by governments to liberate the forces of economic freedom from the regulatory constraints of the welfare-development state and to facilitate and effect the advance of capital. The resistance took the form of opposition to the neoliberal policy agenda rather than a land struggle or labour movement. The agency of this struggle were new social movements based on the peasantry and the semiproletarianized rural landless workers. This resistance paved the way for the return of the Left to state power in the form of a post-neoliberal political and policy regime (Barrett *et al.*, 2008; Gudynas, 2013; Macdonald and Ruckert, 2009; Petras and Veltmeyer, 2009).

In the new millennium, in conditions of a transition towards a new phase in the capitalist development process and a progressive cycle in Latin American politics, the class struggle has taken diverse forms, including organized resistance against the destructive operations of extractive capital, the enclosure of the commons (land, water, territorial resources) and a struggle to reclaim the right of access to the commons. The agency of this resistance, which some analysts view as the new proletariat (or, in more philosophical language, the identical subject-object of history), are various class- and community-based social movements, the political dynamics of which have subjected to close study and given diverse interpretations, primarily as localised, anti-extractive and subterranean in form rather than as class-based anticapitalist organizations (Bebbington and Bury, 2013; Giarracca and Teubal, 2014; Zibechi, 2003, 2007).

Recommended reading: Barrett *et al.* (2008), Gudynas (2013), Macdonald and Ruckert (2009), Petras and Veltmeyer (2009).

Note

1 To put these statistics into perspective, the Gini index for the US rose from 39 in 1970 to 43 in 1990, and 46 in 2000 to 47 in 2010. The most recent Gini index constructed by ECLAC and the CIA shows the following: 25 (Japan), 34 (UK), 23 (Sweden), 25 (Norway), 29 (Denmark) (Sweden), 28 (Germany), 33 (France), 42 (Russia), 31 (South Korea), 33 (Pakistan), 33 (Canada), 33.3 (Pakistan), 58 (South Africa), 70.7 (Namibia). In this comparison, it is evident that Latin America contains the countries with the highest level of social inequality in the world and is the region of greatest inequality, averaging a Gini coefficient well over 50 per cent. As for China, according to the CIA Factbook, the Gini coefficient for China in 2000 was 40, rising to 42 in 2007, with an increase in the rate of social inequality even greater than the US, where income inequality has steadily increased from 1980 on, reaching new extremes in recent years, reflected in the rapid growth in the number of billionaires and the share of the richest 1 per cent and the spread and deepening of poverty.

References

Barrett, P.S., Chávez, D. and Rodríguez Garavito, C.A. (eds) (2008). *The New Latin American Left: Utopia Reborn*. London: Pluto.

Bebbington, A. and Bury, J. (eds) (2013). *Subterranean Struggles: New Dynamics of Mining, Oil and Gas in Latin America*. Austin, TX: University of Texas Press.

Bernstein, H. (2010). *Class Dynamics of Agrarian Change*. Halifax: Fernwood.

Davis, M. (2006). *A Planet of Slums*. London: Verso.

Delgado Wise, R. and Veltmeyer, H. (2016). *Agrarian Change, Migration and Development*. Halifax: Fernwood.

ECLAC (Economic Commission for Latin America and the Caribbean) (2010). *Time for Equality: Closing Gaps, Opening Trails.* Santiago, Chile: ECLAC.

Giarracca, N. and Teubal, M. (2014). 'Argentina: extractivist dynamics of soy production and open-pit mining'. In H. Veltmeyer and J. Petras (eds), *El neoextractivismo: ¿Un modelo posneoliberal de desarrollo o el imperialism del siglo XXI.* México DF: Editorial Crítica/ Ediciones Culturales Paidós.

Gudynas, E. (2013). 'Postextractivismo y alternativas al desarrollo desde la sociedad civil'. In *Alternativas al capitalismo. Colonialismo del Siglo XXI.* Quito: Ediciones Abya Yala, pp. 189–224.

Kapstein, E. (1996). 'Workers and the world economy'. *Foreign Affairs*, 75(3): 179–81.

Kharas, H. (2010). 'The emerging middle class in developing countries'. *Working Paper* 285, OECD Development Centre.

Macdonald, L. and Ruckert, A. (2009). *Post-Neoliberalism in the Americas.* Basingstoke, UK: Palgrave Macmillan.

Milanovic, B. and Yitzhaki, S. (2002). 'Decomposing world income distribution: does the world have a middle class?' *Review of Income and Wealth*, 48(2), June: 155–78.

Petras, J. and Veltmeyer, H. (2009). *What's Left in Latin America?* Farnham: Ashgate.

Portes, A. and Hoffman, K. (2003). 'Latin American class structures: their composition and change during the neoliberal era'. *Latin American Research Review*, 38(1): 41–82.

Tokman, V.E. (1992). *Beyond Regulation: The Informal Sector in Latin America.* Boulder, CO: Lynne Rienner.

UK Ministry of Defence (2007). *Global Strategic Trends 2007–2036.* London: DCDC Global Strategic Trends Programme.

Zibechi, R. (2003). 'Los movimientos sociales latinoamericanos: tendencias y desafíos'. *OSAL: Observatorio Social de América Latina*, No. 9, January. Buenos Aires: CLACSO. Available at: http://bibliotecavirtual.clacso.org.ar/ar/libros/osal/osal9/zibechi.pdf.

Zibechi, R. (2007). *Autonomías y emancipaciones: América Latina en movimiento.* Lima: UNMSM-Programa Democracia y Transformación Global.

20

CLASS DYNAMICS OF THE GLOBAL CAPITALIST SYSTEM

Berch Berberoglu

Global capitalism is an extension of capitalism from the national to the transnational and global level. Thus, in the era of neoliberal globalization, the class dynamics of the world capitalist system operate at the global level. The central class contradiction of capitalism, as it developed from its origins in Europe and subsequently spread throughout the world, is the labour–capital relation based on the exploitation of wage labour. And it is this inherent contradiction of the global capitalist system that translates into class struggle and social transformation at global proportions.

Global capital and its class dynamics

The global expansion of capital across the world, while beneficial to a handful of global monopolies and the capitalist class in general, has brought about a shift in the domestic economy of the advanced capitalist states – from industrial produc- tion to finance and the service sectors – resulting in an overall economic decline within the advanced capitalist centres. The ensuing changes in the material condi- tion of workers in the advanced capitalist countries have brought to the fore a new set of contradictions that are increasingly becoming problematic for the advanced capitalist/imperialist state. The global capitalist crisis and the declining standard of living of the working class in the US and other advanced capitalist countries is thus a direct reflection of the globalization of capital whose reach extends to vast ter- ritories across the world (Berberoglu, 2003, 2012, 2014).

The development of capitalism over the past hundred years formed and trans- formed capitalist society on a global scale. This transformation came about through the restructuring of the international division of labour prompted by the export of capital and transfer of production to cheap labour areas abroad. This, in turn, led to the intensification of the exploitation of labour through expanded produc- tion and reproduction of surplus value and profits by further accumulation of capital and the reproduction of capitalist relations of production on a world scale. A major consequence of this process is the increased polarization of wealth and income between labour and capital at the national and global levels, and growth in numbers of the poor and marginalized segments of the population throughout the world. These and other related contradictions of global capitalism define the parameters of modern, capitalist globalization and provide us the framework for discussion on the nature and dynamics of neoliberal globalization today.

The widening gap between the accumulated wealth of the capitalist class and the declining incomes of workers has sharpened the class struggle in a new political direction, which has brought the advanced capitalist state to the centre stage of the conflict between labour and capital and revealed its ties to the monopolies. This has undermined the legitimacy of the capitalist state, such that the struggles of the working class and the masses in general are becoming directed not merely against capital, but against the state itself (Beams, 1998; Petras and Veltmeyer, 2015; Pradella, 2016). This transformation of the workers' struggle from the economic to the political sphere is bound to set the stage for protracted struggles in the period ahead – struggles that would facilitate the development of a much more politicized international labour movement. The globalization of capital is thus bound to accelerate the politicization of the working class and lead to the building of a solid foundation for international solidarity of workers on a world scale that is directed against global capitalism and the advanced capitalist state on a world scale (Bina and Davis, 2002; Stevis and Boswell, 2008).

The relationship between the owners of the transnational corporations – the global capitalist class – and the imperial state, and the role and functions of this state, including the use of military force to advance the interests of this capitalist class, thus reveals the class nature of the imperial state and the class logic of globalization in the world today (Berberoglu, 1987; Warren, 1980). But this logic is more pervasive and is based on a more fundamental class relation between labour and capital that now operates on a global level – that is, a relation based on exploitation. Thus, in the age of neoliberal capitalist globalization, social classes and class struggles are a product of the logic of the global capitalist system based on the exploitation of labour worldwide (Berberoglu, 2009; Petras, 1978).

Capitalist expansion on a world scale at this stage of the globalization of capital and capitalist production has brought with it the globalization of the production process and the exploitation of wage labour on a world scale. With the intensified exploitation of the working class at super-low wages in repressive neocolonial societies throughout the world, the transnational corporations of the leading capitalist countries have come to amass great fortunes that they have used to build up a global empire through the powers of the imperial state, which has not hesitated to use its military force to protect and advance the interests of capital in every corner of the globe.

The globalization of capital and imperialist domination of the world political economy have thus led to the intensification of the global contradictions of capital, which continues to have a great impact on class relations throughout the world. The central contradiction of this global expansionary process and the spread of capitalist relations of production throughout the world is the exploitation of wage labour on a worldwide basis. And this, in turn, has led to the emergence of class conflict and class struggles in many countries around the world (Petras and Veltmeyer, 2003; Veltmeyer, 2012).

Looking at globalization in class terms, we see that a complex web of class relations has developed at the global level that is both complementary and contradictory. Thus, while the capitalist classes of the dominant imperialist states cooperate in their collective exploitation of labour and plunder of resources at the global level (as manifested in control of cheap labour, new markets and vital sources of raw materials, such as oil, and the intervention of the capitalist state to protect these when their continued supply to the imperial centre are threatened), the underlying contradictions of global competition and conflict among these states lead at the same time to inter-imperialist rivalries and confrontation throughout the world. Just as each imperialist power exploits its own as well as its rivals' working classes for global supremacy, so too one observes the potential unity of the working classes of these rival imperialist states as they come together in forging a protracted struggle against the entire global capitalist system. It is here that the capitalist/imperialist state comes to play a critical role in facilitating the exploitation of global labour by transnational capital, but in doing so also risks its demise through the unfolding contradictions of this very same process that it is increasingly unable to control and regulate.

The problems that the imperial state has come to tackle at both the global and national levels are such that it is no longer able to manage its affairs with any degree of certainty. At the global level, the imperial state has been unable to deal with the consequences of ever-growing super-exploitation of labour in Third World sweatshops that has led to immense poverty and inequality worldwide; nor has it been able to take measures to reverse the depletion of resources, environmental pollution and other health hazards, a growing national debt tying many countries to the World Bank, the International Monetary Fund and other global financial institutions, and a growing militarization of society through the institution of brutal military and civilian dictatorships that violate basic human rights. The domination and control of Third World countries for transnational profits through the instrumentality of the imperial state has, at the same time, created various forms of dependence on the centre that has become a defining characteristic of globalization and imperialism (Amaladoss, 1999; Sklair, 2002).

Domestically, the globalization of capital and imperialist expansion has had immense dislocations in the national economies of imperialist states. Expansion of manufacturing industry abroad has meant a decline in local industry, as plant closings in the US and other advanced capitalist countries have worsened the unemployment situation. The massive expansion of capital abroad has resulted in hundreds of factory shutdowns with millions of workers losing their jobs, hence the surge in unemployment in the US and other imperialist states (Wagner, 2000). This has led to a decline in wages of workers in the advanced capitalist centres, as low wages abroad have played a competitive role in keeping wages down in the imperialist heartlands. The drop in incomes among a growing section of the working class has thus lowered the standard of living in general and led to a further polarization between labour and capital (Berberoglu, 1992, 2002).

Globalization of capital, class conflict and class struggle on a global scale

The dialectics of global capitalist expansion, which has caused so much exploitation, oppression and misery for the peoples of the world, both in the Third World and in the imperialist countries themselves, has in turn created the conditions for its own destruction. Economically, it has afflicted the system with recessions, depressions, and an associated realization crisis; politically, it has set into motion an imperial interventionist state that, through its presence in every corner of the world, has incurred an enormous military expenditure to maintain an empire, while gaining the resentment of millions of people across the globe who are engaged in active struggle against it. While one consequence of imperialism and globalization has been economic contraction and an associated class polarization, a more costly and dangerous outcome of this process has been increased military intervention abroad. However, such aggressive military posture has created (and continues to create) major problems for the imperialist state and is increasingly threatening its effectiveness and, in the long run, its very existence (Petras, 2009).

The imperialist/capitalist state, acting as the repressive arm of global capital and extending its rule across vast territories, has dwarfed the militaristic adventures of past empires many times over. Through its political and military supremacy, it has come to exert its control over many countries and facilitate the exploitation of labour on a world scale, which in turn has generated a response from those affected by it to transform the entire capitalist/imperialist system. As a result, imperialism today represents a dual, contradictory process whose dialectical resolution is an outcome of its very nature – a product of its growth and expansion across time and space within the confines of a structure that promotes its own destruction and demise.

In our time, in the age of globalization, that is, the era of global capitalism, class and class conflict have become more, not less, pronounced, and their prevalence everywhere around the world made it a visible feature of the global capitalist system. Today, as class divisions widen and as classes become increasingly polarized and in continual conflict, class struggles are becoming more and more part of the social landscape of global capitalist society across the world.

With the worldwide spread of capitalism as the primary source of the globalization of capitalist class relations on a world scale, capital has effected transformations in the class structure of societies with which it has come into contact. As a result, the class contradictions of global capitalism have become the primary source of class conflict and class struggle throughout the world.

This in turn has greatly politicized the struggle between labour and capital and called for the recognition of the importance of political organization that many find it necessary to effect change in order to transform the capitalist–imperialist system.

Understanding the necessity of organizing labour and the importance of political leadership in this struggle, radical labour organizations have in fact taken steps emphasizing the necessity for the working class to mobilize its ranks and take united action to wage battle against capitalist imperialism globally (Beams, 1998).

It is important to understand that the critical factor that tips the balance of class forces in favour of the proletariat to win state power is political organization, the building of class alliances among the oppressed and exploited classes, the development of strong and theoretically well-informed revolutionary leadership that is organically linked to the working class, and a clear understanding of the forces at work in the class struggle, including especially the role of the state and its military and police apparatus – the focal point of the struggle for state power (Berberoglu, 2013; Knapp and Spector, 2011; Szymanski, 1978).

The global domination of capital and the advanced capitalist/imperial state during the 20th century did not proceed without a fight, as a protracted struggle of the working class against capital and the capitalist state unfolded throughout this period of capitalist globalization. The labour movement, the anti-imperialist national liberation movements, and the civil rights, women's, student, environmental, anti-war and peace movements all contributed to the development of the emerging anti-globalization movement in the late 20th and early 21st centuries. These and related contradictions of late 20th-century capitalist globalization led to the crisis of the imperial state and the entire globalization project, which increasingly came under attack by the mass movements of the global era that came to challenge the rule of capital and the capitalist state throughout the world.

The global expansion of capital and transnational capitalist domination of the Third World has led to the growth of anti-imperialist, anti-globalization movements, which have come to challenge the global capitalist system through revolutions across the world (Sanderson, 2005). These movements have often become part of the worldwide struggle against globalization and imperialism led by the working class through cross-border labour organizing and international labour solidarity through labour internationalism (Howard, 2005; Moody, 1997). This, in turn, has led to the development of broader international alliances made up of a multitude of movement organizations that bring together various oppressed peoples to wage a wider struggle against global capitalism through transnational activism (Brecher et al., 2000; Della Porta and Tarrow, 2005; Flesher Fominaya, 2014; Tabb, 2004).

The political mobilization of oppressed groups that have come together to effect change have sometimes succeeded in bringing about new non-exploitative social relations. The degree of success in constructing a new society along egalitarian lines has been an outcome of a variety of factors, above all the degree to which these experiments have been successful in thwarting imperialist attempts to undermine such efforts. Regardless of the varied experiences of one or another society or social movement to secure such change, however, social revolution and the revolutionary transformation of society in the epoch of global capitalism has more and more become the only viable option available to oppressed groups and classes to bring about fundamental social change.

The transformation of global capitalism

The global capitalist state, through its political and military supremacy, has come to exert its control over many countries and facilitated the exploitation of labour on a world scale. As a result, it has reinforced the domination of capital over labour and its rule on behalf of capital. This, in turn, has greatly politicized the struggle between labour and capital and called for the recognition of the importance of political organization that is necessary to transform the global capitalist system. In considering the emerging class struggles throughout the globe, the question that one now confronts is thus a *political* one. Given what we know of neoliberal globalization and its class contradictions on a world scale, how will the peoples' movements respond to it *politically* worldwide? What strategy and tactics will be adopted to confront this colossal force? It is important to think about these questions concretely, in a practical way – one that involves a concrete scientific analysis and organized political action.

Understanding the necessity of mobilizing labour and the importance of political leadership in this struggle, radical labour organizations have in fact taken steps emphasizing the importance for the working class to mobilize its ranks and take united action to wage battle against capitalist globalization (Munck, 2002; Waterman, 1998).

Strikes, demonstrations and mass protests initiated by workers and other popular forces have become frequent in a growing number of countries controlled by the transnationals in recent years. Working people are rising up against the local ruling classes, the state, and the transnational monopolies that have together effected the super-exploitation of labour for decades. Various forms of struggle are now underway in many countries under the grip of transnational capital.

The logic of transnational capitalist expansion on a global scale is such that it leads to the emergence and development of forces in conflict with this expansion. The working class has been in the forefront of these forces. Armed insurrection, civil war and revolutionary upheavals are all a response to the repression imposed on working people by global capitalism and its client states throughout the world. Together, these struggles have been effective in frustrating the efforts of global capital to expand and dominate the world, while at the same time building the basis of an international working-class movement that finally overcomes national, ethnic, cultural and linguistic boundaries that artificially separate the workers in their fight against global capitalism. The worldwide working-class struggle against global capital has led to several successful revolutions during the 20th century. Throughout this period, workers' organizations have focused on building international labour solidarity for worldwide efforts to wage a successful battle against global capitalism. In this sense, labour internationalism (or the political alliance of workers across national boundaries in their struggle against global capitalism) is increasingly being seen as a political weapon that would serve as a unifying force in labour's frontal attack on capital in the early 21st century (Beams, 1998).

The solidarity achieved through this process has helped expand the strength of the international working class and increased its determination to defeat all vestiges of global capitalism throughout the world, and build a new egalitarian social order that advances the interests of working people, and ultimately all of humanity.

Global capitalism today represents a dual, contradictory development whose dialectical resolution will be an outcome of its very nature – a product of its growth and expansion across time and space within the confines of a structure that promotes its own destruction and demise. It is important to understand that the critical factor that tips the balance of class forces in favour of the working class to win state power is *political organization*, the building of *class alliances* among the oppressed and exploited classes, the development of strong and theoretically well-informed *revolutionary leadership* that is organically linked to the working class, and a clear understanding of the forces at work in the class struggle, including especially the *role of the state* and its military and police apparatus – the focal point of the struggle for state power (Stevis and Boswell, 2008; Szymanski, 1978). The success of the working class and its revolutionary leadership in confronting the power of the capitalist state thus becomes the critical element ensuring that, once captured, the state can become an instrument that the workers can use to establish their rule, and in the process transform society and the state itself to promote labour's interests in line with its vision for a new society free of exploitation and oppression, one based on the rule of the working class and the labouring masses in general.

Our understanding of the necessity for the transformation of global capitalism, which is political in nature, demands a clear, scientific understanding of its contradictions in late 20th- and early 21st-century form, so that this knowledge can be put to use to facilitate the class struggle in a revolutionary direction. In this context, one will want to know not only the extent and depth of global capitalist expansion, but also its base of support, its linkage to the major institutions of capitalist society (above all, the state, but also other religious, cultural and social institutions), the extent of its ideological hegemony and control over mass consciousness, and other aspects of social, economic, political and ideological domination. Moreover – and this is the most important point – one must study its weaknesses, its problem areas, its vulnerabilities, its weak links and the various dimensions of its crisis – especially those that affect its continued reproduction and survival (Petras, 2016). Armed with this knowledge, one would be better equipped to confront capital and the capitalist/imperialist state in the struggle for the transformation of global capitalism in this century.

References

Amaladoss, M. (ed.) (1999). *Globalization and Its Victims as Seen by Its Victims*. Delhi: Vidyajyoti Education and Welfare Society.

Beams, N. (1998). *The Significance and Implications of Globalization: A Marxist Assessment*. Southfield, MI: Mehring Books.

Berberoglu, B. (1987). *The Internationalization of Capital: Imperialism and Capitalist Development on a World Scale*. New York: Praeger.

Berberoglu, B. (1992). *The Legacy of Empire: Economic Decline and Class Polarization in the United States*. New York: Praeger.

Berberoglu, B. (ed.) (2002). *Labour and Capital in the Age of Globalization: The Labour Process and the Changing Nature of Work in the Global Economy*. Boulder, CO: Rowman & Littlefield.

Berberoglu, B. (2003). *Globalization of Capital and the Nation State*. Boulder, CO: Rowman & Littlefield.

Berberoglu, B. (2009). *Class and Class Conflict in the Age of Globalization*. Lanham, MD: Lexington.

Berberoglu, B. (ed.) (2012). *Beyond the Global Capitalist Crisis: The World Economy in Transition*. Burlington, VT: Ashgate.

Berberoglu, B. (2013). *Political Sociology in a Global Era*. Boulder, CO: Paradigm.

Berberoglu, B. (ed.) (2014). *The Global Capitalist Crisis and Its Aftermath*. Burlington, VT: Ashgate.

Bina, C. and Davis, C. (2002). 'Dynamics of globalization: transnational capital and the international labour movement'. In B. Berberoglu (ed.), *Labour and Capital in the Age of Globalization*. Boulder, CO: Rowman & Littlefield.

Brecher, J., Costello, T. and Smith, B. (2000). *Globalization from Below: The Power of Solidarity*. Cambridge, MA: South End Press.

Della Porta, D. and Tarrow, S. (eds) (2005). *Transnational Protest and Global Activism*. Lanham, MD: Rowman & Littlefield.

Flesher Fominaya, C. (2014). *Social Movements and Globalization: How Protests, Occupations, and Uprisings Are Changing the World*. New York: Palgrave Macmillan.

Howard, A. (2005). 'Global capital and labour internationalism: workers' response to global capitalism'. In B. Berberoglu (ed.), *Globalization and Change: The Transformation of Global Capitalism*. Lanham, MD: Lexington, pp. 85–104.

Knapp, P. and Spector, A. (2011). *Crisis and Change Today: Basic Questions of Marxist Sociology*. Boulder, CO: Rowman & Littlefield.

Moody, K. (1997). *Workers in a Lean World: Unions in the International Economy*. London: Verso.

Munck, R. (2002). *Globalization and Labour: The New Great Transformation*. London: Zed Books.

Petras, J. (1978). *Critical Perspectives on Imperialism and Social Class in the Third World*. New York: Monthly Review Press.

Petras, J. (2009). *Global Depression and Regional Wars*. Atlanta, GA: Clarity Press.

Petras, J. (2016). *The End of the Republic and the Delusion of Empire*. Atlanta, GA: Clarity Press.

Petras, J. and Veltmeyer, H. (2003). *System in Crisis: The Dynamics of Free Market Capitalism*. London: Zed Books.

Petras, J. and Veltmeyer, H. (2015). *Beyond Neoliberalism: A World to Win*. Burlington, VT: Ashgate.

Pradella, L. (2016). *Globalization and Critique of Political Economy*. New York: Routledge.

Sanderson, S. (2005). *Revolutions: A Worldwide Introduction to Political and Social Change*. Boulder, CO: Paradigm.

Sklair, L. (2002). *Globalization: Capitalism and Its Alternatives*. New York: Oxford University Press.

Stevis, D. and Boswell, T. (2008). *Globalization and Labour: Democratizing Global Governance*. Boulder, CO: Rowman & Littlefield.

Szymanski, A. (1978). *The Capitalist State and the Politics of Class*. Cambridge, MA: Winthrop.

Tabb, W. (2004). 'Neoliberalism and anticorporate globalization as class struggle'. In M. Zweig (ed.), *What's Class Got to Do with It? American Society in the Twenty-First Century*. Ithaca, NY: ILR Press, pp. 63–76.

Veltmeyer, H. (ed.) (2012). *Imperialism, Crisis, and Class Struggle: The Enduring Verities and Contemporary Face of Capitalism*. Leiden: E.J. Brill.

Wagner, H. (ed.) (2000). *Globalization and Unemployment*. New York: Springer.

Warren, B. (1980). *Imperialism, Pioneer of Capitalism*. London: Verso.

Waterman, P. (1998). *Globalization, Social Movements, and the New Internationalisms*. London: Mansell.

21

THE MAKING OF THE MIGRANT WORKING CLASS IN CHINA

Pun Ngai

China as a world workshop

An astonishing change in China is the advent of the world's workshop on socialist soil during the last three decades. Thirty years of reform have completely transformed China and hooked it up to the neoliberal world. A socialist nation that was once viewed as a developing country now shapes and poses a challenge to the global economy. The rise of China as the 'world's workshop', accompanied by a new working class comprising of migrant labourers, allows us to understand the making of this class in the context of the transformed space of global capitalism. We are compelled to make sense of the making of a new working class comprising more than 270 million rural migrant workers who have now joined the workforce in all sorts of enterprises. In the new millennium, China's 'world workshop', constituted by this new migrant working class, is structurally embodied with capital's control and workers' resistance.

In recent years, the term 'world's workshop' has been commonly used to describe the export-led model of development and the capacity of China for global production (Pun and Koo, 2014). The concept of a world workshop can be understood only in the context of the extended reproduction of global capitalism to subsume the social life of non-capitalist nations. Global capitalism has won a victory in incorporating socialist regimes into its process of capital accumulation over the last century. With the opening of China and the arrival of global and private capital into export processing zones in the early 1980s, socialist China was already being transformed into a market economy under the wave of industrial relocation from advanced capitalist countries to the Global South. The Chinese state had also taken a lead in introducing pro-market initiatives and put huge effort into bringing the country into the World Trade Organization (WTO) and other world bodies. Due to the state efforts, China is able to attract transnational corporations (TNCs) to China from all over the world, especially from Hong Kong, Taiwan, Japan, Korea, the US and Western Europe.

Very often, we have heard that Western governments from the political left to the political right admire China's economic achievements, as well as the stunning financial figures reported by the media. For instance, China has passed the US and become the world's largest foreign direct investment (FDI) destination country since 2003. In 2005, China became the world's third largest trading country, surpassed only by the US and Germany. In 2010, China surpassed Japan as the second largest economy in the world. Alongside the dramatic economic growth in the quantity of output, the manufacturing structure was also moving into high-value and high-end goods in information and communicative technology industries. Today, China has become the world's top producer of more than 200 products, including garments, colour TVs, washing machines, DVD players, cameras, refrigerators, air conditioners, motorcycles, microwave ovens, PC monitors, tractors, and bicycles, not to mention iPhones and iPads.[1]

With 29 per cent of the world's workforce, labour costs in this giant 'world's workshop', however, are only one-sixth that of Mexico and one-fortieth that of the US. China's GDP per capita (US$6,807) was ranked as low as 84th in the world in 2013 (World Bank, 2014). This contradiction of rapid growth and cheap labour cost has led to criticism for China's role in driving a 'race to the bottom' in globalization from labour researchers, labour activists and journalists. However, instead of paying sympathy to the Chinese working class, China is one of the targets in Western campaigns against 'sweatshops'. 'Chinese workers steal our jobs' is one of the common myths for many. This is the backdrop to the 'China Threat'.

Due to severe competition in the course of capital accumulation on a global scale, as a 'world factory', China is now facing challenges from other developing countries such as India, Bangladesh and Vietnam. It has been widely recognized that workers around the world are pitted against each other in the game of 'race to the bottom' production over who will accept the lowest wages and benefits, and the most miserable working and living conditions. In this game, China appears to have an impact on the wage level for the world's workers in labour-intensive exports. The rapid flight of global capital to China is nevertheless not only looking for cheap labour and low land prices, but also diligent, skilled and well-educated Chinese workers who are willing to work in appalling conditions, who are suitable for just-in-time production, and who are potential consumers for global products.

Recommended reading: Pun and Koo (2014), Pun *et al.* (2016).

Misleading 'Made in China' label

As a world workshop, the labelling of the products as 'Made in China' is often presented as the 'China Threat', and harmfully creates an unfriendly approach to the Chinese working class. This label creates a misleading understanding, as it masks the reality of transnational corporate power that produces high profits and subsumes the phenomenon of labour exploitation through a global supply and production chain (Ross, 2006).

For instance, if we look at the distribution of the value for an iPhone, which Chinese workers toil day and night to produce, we find that Apple is able to capture an extraordinary 58.5 per cent of the value of the iPhone despite the fact that the manufacture of the product is entirely outsourced. Particularly notable is that labour costs in China account for the smallest share, only 1.8 per cent, or nearly US$10, of the US$549 retail price of the iPhone in 2010 (Kraemer *et al.*, 2011: 5). Other major component providers, mainly Japanese and South Korean firms that produce the most sophisticated components, captured slightly over 14 per cent of the value of the iPhone. In fact, the 'China price' of export goods as being globally competitive was fundamentally built upon the creation of a massive migrant class, which until recent years has been paid at the local minimum wage levels by the transnational corporations. The extraordinary amount of surplus value produced by this new working class was claimed by transnational corporations and their suppliers.

However, the label 'Made in China' is often manipulated to misrepresent a global capital war with nation state competition when, for example, US politicians come out to criticize China and create a Chinese Threat. The threat from China is usually augmented by the mass media at times when Chinese elites have sought to promote a 'big' country excelling in global politics such as the 'one belt, one road' policy. In fact, if we look at per capita GDP, Chinese income did not rank among the world's lowest, but it was a small fraction of that of the developed countries. As noted above, China's per capita GDP was ranked 84th, comparable to the Dominican Republic and Jamaica. The modest per capita incomes and their corollary, large portions of the new working class living in dire poverty, are indicative of the limits of the economic growth that has been so widely celebrated. 'Made in China', a label that misrepresented the wealth distribution in the global production chain, placed China in an astonishing position in the global economy.

The label 'Made in China' was misleading as it also disguised huge class cleavages and social inequalities in society at large. Throughout the 1990s and 2000s, the statutory minimum wage standards were often also the maximum pay rates for rural migrant workers. With rising food prices and general living costs between 2006 and 2010, provincial-level governments raised local minimum wages by an average of 12.5 per cent annually, except for a wage freeze in 2009 during the economic recession.[2] In 2015, the minimum wage for migrant workers in Shenzhen was 2,030 yuan (US$301.16) per month, the highest level of any city in China. Yet, when we turn to the high end of the social ladder, in 2010, China had 960,000 millionaires (one person in every 1,400) with more than 10 million yuan (US$1.5 million) in personal wealth, a 9.7 per cent increase over the previous year. In 2014, there were 152 Chinese billionaires by Forbes' reckoning.[3]

Recommended reading: Pun (2016), Ross (2006).

Neoliberalism in China: capital meets the state

The rise of China as a major centre for capital is not, however, a natural consequence of the 'free' market under the age of globalization. In fact, this transformation is ironically state-driven and has been achieved with the collusion of the interests of transnational capital in its search for offshore production relocation in the new age of the neoliberal expansion of global capitalism. The defeat of the Cultural Revolution left a reformist party-state that drove forward the process of 'reform and open' policies, bringing globalization into the country and shattering socialist production relations. This state-led process of economic globalization has been accompanied by a state withdrawal process in the areas of social reproduction and social protection for the peasantry and working class.

Globalization and market reform have brought profound changes to the mode of production and labour relations in China. First of all, the dismantling of the collective rural economy and the 'liberation of labour power' from the collective economy is the prerequisite for the return of capital. Since the 1970s, reformist leaders and business elites have called for the dismantling of the rural collective economy and greater labour flexibility and mobility to reshape China's rural and urban economy under the dictate of a commodity market. Following 30 years of huge efforts of socialist transformation in alleviating capitalistic labour relations after the founding of the People's Republic in 1949, labour became reconsidered as a kind of 'commodity' that could be freely exchanged in a nascent market. The free choice for individuals to turn themselves into wage labour was highly promoted. This paved the way for re-proletarianization in Marx's sense as the new labouring subjects now had to turn themselves into 'free' subjects, liberated from the collective economy, gradually losing means of production, having nothing but their labour to sell in a newly recreated labour market. In a sense, everything that could fit into the market economy had to be rebuilt from the scratch of socialist soil.

The process of reform and opening up in China took place under an ideology of globalizing China and competing in the neoliberal world market. Neoliberal economists, most of them educated in the West, acted as a social elite providing theoretical guidance and specific policy proposals for reform, proposals that were ultimately enacted as actual policies, and were elevated to become the will of the state. In the process of globalizing China, the social elite rejected China's former socialist path to development. They were of the view that the socialist system of public ownership could only lead to collective penury and was incapable of achieving economic development and popular prosperity. Guided by neoliberalism, China chose an imbalanced development strategy that would give priority to the development of a certain section of the population and certain regions. One concrete manifestation of this was in the industrial structure, with priority given to the development of light industries and the service sector. In terms of regions, it was the coastal provinces of the east that were given priority. In ownership models, growth in the private sector was vigorously promoted; priority was given to urban development rather than rural, in particular the cities in the coastal regions.

During the 'reform and opening up' period, guided by the neoliberal economists, a realignment was made in China's path to economic development, adopting an export-oriented economic model and turning China into the workshop of the world. This type of development required a massive amount of labour; the labour requirements of the export-oriented economy, combined with the low demand for labour in the small peasant economy, created mutually complementary push and pull factors that set millions upon millions of young rural workers on the one-way road to working as migrants in the cities.

The triumph of a neoliberal world has signalled the opportunity for capital to invade socialist China in the form of large-scale investment and offshore production. Starting at the end of the 1970s, global capital reached the stage of rapid expansion, destroying all potential barriers erected by non-capitalist or socialist nation states for capital flows, technology transfer, expropriation of production materials and markets, and, last but not least, the use of abundant labour. The strategy of capital concentration or monopoly was achieved by penetrating into non-capitalist countries via a multiplication of global supply and production chain. The best example is Apple and Foxconn, the top 5th and 31st companies on the Global 500 list in 2015, respectively.

In short, over the past 30 years, China has created an economic miracle that has caught the attention of the world, especially in the area of the alleviation of poverty. Yet, this development has come at a heavy price. The dismantling of the collective economy and the state retreat from the countryside meant that agriculture did not develop, rural China remained relatively poor, and large numbers of rural people were forced to out-migrate to allow an ample supply of labour for export-oriented industries.

In the face of this phenomenon, we are forced to ask, 'Who is paying the price? Who is development for?' A top-down application of state power determined the direction of China's social development and also had a direct impact on the individual members of society in general, and the new working class in particular.

Recommended reading: Li (2016), Pun *et al.* (2010).

A farewell to class

A fundamental error of Western hegemony is the proclamation of the end of the 'working class' and class conflicts. This hegemony shapes Western academia in almost all areas, as well as through cultural colonization, and penetrates into the intellectual circles of the rest of the world. A farewell to 'class' colludes with the 'end of history'. The trends of post-structuralism and postmodernism in academic circles further shifted the focus from the sphere of relations of production to the sphere of civil society and consumption, at best, a study of the middle classes and consumption. It is an obvious misunderstanding that post-structuralist studies could not enhance our understanding of class and labour, especially regarding the issues of agency and subjectivity. The death of 'class analysis' was, however, prevalent everywhere in the West (Lichtenstein, 2006).

Yet, a 'farewell to class' by Western academics and mainstream media did not make class relations obsolete in Western societies, which are now confronting deep class conflicts characterized by great social inequalities, high rates of unemployment and life precariousness. Instead, the issues of class and class conflicts were carried by global capital flight into Third World societies, putting China at the forefront of the struggle. The turn to neoliberal capitalism has created an impact on the world, defeating the attempts of communist revolutions of the 20th century and the golden age of welfare capitalist systems in the West. It has attempted to destroy the fruits of the socialist goals of promoting economic equality, human emancipation and people's democracy. This global creative destruction continued until a neoliberal world finally arrived, and reformed China is now part of it (Pun, 2016).

Today, if China is a dreamland for global capital looking for new forms of capital accumulation on an unimaginable pace and scale, we argue that it simultaneously creates a new working class comprised of rural migrants and urban poor, and they now constitute new political subjects for potential resistance, and shape the future of the labour movement in China, as well as providing a quest for world labour internationalism. The struggle to be a part of this new working class, however, is replete with blood, sweat and tears. Notwithstanding the predominant structural factor that has shaped the Chinese working class, the 'delinking' between class structure and class identity, between class consciousness and class action still largely exist. The reform hegemony, the neoliberal policies and the Western discourse on class all contribute to constituting this 'delinking' of class. The reform hegemony coincided with a Western 'farewell to class' discourse that firmly denounced the existence of the class issue in post-socialist China. Just like the argument on 'the end of history' that contributed to the birth of neoliberalism in post-socialist countries, a discourse on 'farewell to class' directly led to a death of 'class' analysis in China. Nowhere could we see a displacement of class conflicts from the West to the East so successfully achieved and have this displacement subsumed as a 'postmodern play' of class language.

The 'death' of class in the West hence imagined its second death in China, resisting fiercely recognizing that its death in fact represents an incarnation of the new working class in the Third World. Placing China squarely at the heart of global capitalist accumulation and the new international division of labour, we see not only offshore capital flight, but also that class conflicts were rapidly exported to developing countries.

Recommended reading: Li (2016), Pun (2016).

Radicalization of the working class

A spectre is haunting China – not global capital, but a new working class embodied with great forces of suppression and of resistance. In spite of the elusive class hegemonic discourse, class opposition from capital, institutional barriers from state and lack of support from society, this new working class is fighting for its own class formation through a vignette of actions, defiance, and resistance in daily life in both its working and living spaces. Notwithstanding the neoliberal project's attempt in China and elsewhere to render obsolete the concept of class, the new generation of the working class, with its class experience rooted from below, is now increasingly conscious of, and participating in, various forms of collective action. Working to remake its class rooted in its lifeworld, spontaneous strikes by migrant workers in South China have been multiplying since the mid-1990s (Pringle, 2013).

In the 1990s and 2000s, mass protests occurred and increased due to social conflicts. Official statistics reveal that between 1993 and 2005, the number of mass protests rose nationwide from about 10,000 to 87,000 cases – a nearly 20 per cent annual average increase. Also, the number of participants in these protests increased from 730,000 to more than 3 million, and 75 per cent of these protests were initiated by workers and peasants (Leung and Pun, 2009). These protests have not only increased in number, but also in average size, social scope, and degree of organization. The upward trend continued in the first 10 years of the 2000s, reflecting the widespread incidences of rights violations as the private sector expanded. Labour cases skyrocketed to 693,465, involving more than 1.2 million labourers nationwide during the economic crisis of 2008 (Pun, 2016). These were mainly disputes over wage and insurance payments, illegal lay-offs, and inadequate compensation payments.

Although systematic information on production days lost and picket line damages are not available in China, there is ample evidence that migrant workers are becoming more proactive in defending their rights, with their mobilization actions taking various forms, including individual and collective action, especially direct action (Pun and Lu, 2010a). The collective actions are not restricted to using established institutional or legal means to advance interests. They are also undergoing a process of 'radicalization', a process in which strikes, street actions and demonstrations are often used. These labour actions, though mostly interest-based, are accompanied by a strong anti-foreign capital sentiment and a discourse of workers' rights, and hence they are political. In many cases, they are not only organized on bases of locality, ethnicity, gender and peer alliance in a single workplace, but also attempt to nurture workers' solidarity in the broader sense of a labour oppositional force moving beyond exclusive networks and strong ties. Cross-factory strike tactics are sometimes used to invite workers from the same industrial region to participate in marches, street protests or highway blockages (Pringle, 2013; Pun and Lu, 2010b).

As a result of 30 years of reform, the repositioning of China as a 'world workshop' in the age of globalization has provided the bedrock for nurturing a new Chinese working class. The current intensified labour conflicts and proliferating labour activism reflect the further polarization of class relations in China. Collective struggles, such as demonstrations demanding pensions, road blockages by unpaid angry workers, and collective action against illegal compensations are no longer exotic news for Chinese workers, no matter in private, foreign or state enterprises. The struggle to create this new working class by itself and for itself is reshaping the future of class relations and class struggles not only in China, but also in the world. We call for a return of class from a Third World perspective to look at the making of the migrant working class in Chinese society. Instead of declaring an 'end of history', we see the creation of a new migrant working class that attempts to challenge neoliberal history.

Recommended reading: Butollo and Brink (2012), Chan and Selden (2016), Pringle (2013).

Notes

1 General Administration of Customs of the People's Republic of China, 8 November 2014. See www.customs.gov.cn/publish/portal0/tab49667/info691897.htm and www.customs.gov.cn/publish/portal0/tab49667/info721618.htm.
2 'China releases plan to create 45 million jobs'. *Xinhua*, 8 February 2012. Available at: http://english.gov.cn/2012-02/08/content_2061449.htm.
3 'Leading authority on China's wealthy counts 960,000 "millionaires", up 9.7 percent, with Beijing home to most'. *Forbes*, 7 March 2012. Available at: www.forbes.com/sites/russellflannery/2014/03/03/2014-forbes-billionaires-list-growing-chinas-10-richest/.

References

Butollo, F. and Brink, T.T. (2012). 'Challenging the atomization of discontent: patterns of migrant-worker protest in China during the series of strikes in 2010'. *Critical Asian Studies*, 44(3): 419–40.

Chan, J. and Selden, M. (2016). 'The labour politics of China's rural migrant workers'. *Globalizations*. doi:10.1080/14747731.2016.1200263.

Kraemer, K.L., Linden, G. and Dedrick, J. (2011). 'Capturing value in global networks: Apple's iPad and iPhone'. Available at: http://econ.sciences-po.fr/sites/default/files/file/Value_iPad_iPhone.pdf.

Leung, P.-N. and Pun, N. (2009). 'The radicalization of the new Chinese working class: a case study of collective action in the gemstone industry'. *Third World Quarterly*, 30(3): 551–65.

Li, M. (2016). *China and the 21st Century Crisis*. London: Pluto Press.

Lichtenstein, N. (ed.) (2006). *American Capitalism: Social Thought and Political Economy in the Twentieth Century*. Philadelphia, PA: University of Pennsylvania Press.

Pringle, T. (2013). 'Reflections on labour in China: from a moment to a movement'. *The South Atlantic Quarterly*, 112(1): 191–202.

Pun, N. (2016). *Migrant Labour in China: Post-Socialist Transformations*. New York/London: Polity Press.

Pun, N. and Koo, A. (2014). 'A "world-class" (labour) camp/us: Foxconn and China's new generation of labour migrants'. *Positions*, 23(3): 411–35.

Pun, N. and Lu, H. (2010a). 'Unfinished proletarianization: self, anger and class action of the second generation of peasant-workers in reform China'. *Modern China*, 36(5): 493–519.

Pun, N. and Lu, H. (2010b). 'A culture of violence: the labour subcontracting system and collective actions by construction workers in post-socialist China'. *The China Journal*, 64: 143–58.

Pun, N., Chan, C. and Chan, J. (2010). 'The role of the state, labour policy and migrant workers' struggles in globalized China'. *Global Labour Journal*, 1(1): 132–51.

Pun, N. *et al.* (2016). 'Apple, Foxconn, and Chinese workers' struggles from a global labour perspective'. *InterAsia Cultural Studies*, 17(2): 166–85.

Ross, A. (2006). *Fast Boat to China: Corporate Flight and the Consequences of Free Trade – Lessons from Shanghai*. New York: Pantheon Books.

World Bank (2014). *World Development Indicators*. 1 July. Available at: http://data.worldbank.org/indicator/NY.GDP. PCAP.CD.

22

CLASS STRUGGLE AND RESISTANCE IN LATIN AMERICA

Susan Spronk

The class struggle and development

For critical development theorists from various schools of thought on the Left, class struggle is at the root of the development process. Class struggle is a broad concept, but at its base tries to describe the conflict between opposing groups in a community resulting from different social or economic positions and reflecting different interests. One of the eminent founders of modern sociology, Max Weber, was more concerned with how control over productive assets shaped life chances rather than with how they 'structure patterns of exploitation and domination'. For Marx, however, class conflict is the driver of history (see Chapter 6 by Wanderley in this volume). In the pamphlet that he co-wrote with Engels, *The Communist Manifesto*, Marx pays particular attention to the role that industrial workers play in overthrowing capitalism, calling upon all working peoples of the world (he refers only to men as Marx was not yet a feminist) to 'throw off our chains' and join the international labour movement to advocate for socialist revolution.

As a result of high rates of worker militancy throughout the 19th and 20th centuries, workers' unions (or trade unions) have been given pride of place in analysis of historical processes of development for most of the modern era. As industrial forms of capitalism spread from Europe to other places in the world, workers formed trade unions to protect themselves from the worst excesses of exploitation by their employers. And as Silver and Arrighi (2000) argue in their analysis of workers in the context of neoliberal globalization, the relocation of industrial activities from richer to poorer countries has often led to the emergence of strong new labour movements in the low-wage sites of investment, rather than an unambiguous race to the bottom.

Although corporations were initially attracted to particular sites in the developing world because they appeared to offer cheap and docile workers (e.g. Brazil,

South Africa, South Korea), the subsequent expansion of capital-intensive mass-production industries created new and militant working classes with significant disruptive power. These labour movements not only succeeded in raising wages, improving working conditions and strengthening workers' rights, but they also often played a leading role in democracy movements.

Yet, with the neoliberal turn in contemporary studies of 'development' at the end of the 1990s, trade unions fell out of view. Today, they are only rarely thought to be important actors in the development process; most development studies textbooks make little mention of trade unions. Following the financial crisis of 2007–2008 that rocked the core centre of capitalism, however, trade unions have been depicted in a more positive light. For example, in July 2015, the IMF published a study entitled *Inequality and Labour Market Institutions* that argued that the decline in unionization and erosion of minimum wages are related to the rising social inequality, which is the first positive mention of trade unions in many years (see Jaumotte and Osorio Buiton, 2015).

Latin America is a particularly suitable region in which to study the role of unions and class struggle in the development process due to its relatively early and high rate of industrialization (compared to, for example, Sub-Saharan Africa). Despite a long history of union and revolutionary history, Latin America has been no exception to the above-noted trends. As James Petras (1990) has argued, there was a notable 'retreat of the intellectuals' in the wake of neoliberal restructuring that devastated working-class movements throughout the continent, and research on trade unions and development in the less developed Latin American countries (e.g. Bolivia and Ecuador) can be hard to find.

The situation of labour in Latin America during the neoliberal era parallels that of other Anglo-American countries, which also experienced declining union density, interest in joining labour unions and loss of labour's political influence. The roots of labour's decline in these regions can be attributed to both economic and political factors, from the increase in flexible and part-time labour and a shift from manufacturing to service sector employment to the deregulation and anti-union policies that are characteristic of neoliberalism. Latin America's recent turn to the left following the elections of Chávez in Venezuela (1999) and Lula in Brazil (2002) has reactivated some scholarly interest in working-class movements and the labour movement more particularly, although most scholars have focused on 'new' social movements such as the indigenous and women's movements that have gained institutional recognition throughout the continent over the course of the neoliberal period.

Recommended reading: Petras and Veltmeyer (2017).

Trade unions and development

The reasons for the absence of trade unions from development studies are complex. For neoclassical and neoliberal economists, trade unions are viewed as a kind of job cartel organized by workers who conspire to raise the price of labour through collective bargaining. For such thinkers, unions create lazy workers who are a drag on productivity since they provide too many protections for workers and exaggerate the segmentation of the labour market. Neoliberals argue that declining union density is a good thing, and that remaining unions should drop their demands for higher salaries and benefits, because then employers will have more money to hire even more workers, thus supposedly helping to solve the problems of unemployment. Public sector workers are often singled out for attack since they are seen as part of the problem of the 'rent-seeking state,' protecting lazy bureaucrats who make it difficult for governments to adjust their budgets due to rigidities created by collective agreements (see, for example, the World Bank's 2013 *World Development Report: Jobs*).

This pessimistic view of the role of trade unions, however, is not unique to neoclassical and neoliberal economists, but also pervades Marxian-inspired analyses of the dependency and world-systems variety, as evidenced by Emmanuel's and Amin's theories on unequal exchange. For Emmanuel, the problem of unequal exchange is rooted in different wage rates between developed and underdeveloped countries, and is at the base of the supposed transfer of surplus value from backward to developed countries; the implication is that high rates of unionization in the North are part of the problem. He further surmises that antagonism between classes in Europe has been progressively displaced by the antagonism between rich and poor nations, which explains the lack of revolutionary consciousness among the masses in the former. While Amin dismisses Emmanuel's suggestion that different wage levels are the 'independent variable' that explains why some countries are rich and others are poor, he embraces the view that unequal exchange occurs when wage differentials are bigger than the differentials in productivity, which are due to higher levels of technological development in the core compared to the periphery. Again, trade unions are partly to blame for such wage differentials between North and South (see Larrain, 1989).

By contrast, Marxist historians such as Robert Brenner criticize theorists of unequal exchange for locating their analysis of the uneven dynamics in the sphere of circulation rather than production, and as a result coming to the mistaken conclusion that the development of capitalism has fundamentally different dynamics in the periphery than in the core. An alternative view, rooted in an analysis of the combined and uneven development of capitalism, understands the processes of capitalist development in both North and South as sharing the same fundamental dynamics (with considerable room for variation), but that 'underdevelopment' reflects a lack of capitalist development rather than its overexposure to it. More recently, Selwyn's (2016) call for 'labour-centred development' theory has advanced this view, calling upon researchers in development studies to embrace a class-relational political economy that understands the 'development process' as one that subjects labouring classes to particular forms of (exploitative) work relations based upon Marx's labour theory of value.

In this labour-centred development paradigm, trade unions again take pride of place in the analysis of development and underdevelopment. Despite the decline of labour union strength and influence, such scholars argue that unionization remains important in guaranteeing workers good wages and benefits, a voice in their workplace, and protection from arbitrary and unfair management decisions. Returning unions to the centre of the analysis is also justified by empirical evidence that high levels of union density have been shown to contribute to stronger economic indicators across the board. More research is needed, however, to understand the variety of experiences of trade unions in the developing world, such as their role in resisting neoliberalism in Latin America.

Recommended reading: Larrain (1989), Selwyn (2016).

Trade unions: 'old' versus 'new' social movements

Dramatic changes in the world economy in the past quarter-century have posed major challenges to trade unions in Latin America. Labour markets throughout the region have been made more flexible, and patterns of production and employment in Latin America have also been transformed by economic integration, a process known as neoliberal globalization. Most notably, there has been a shift away from standard full-time regular employment (the traditional trade union base) to part-time, contract and unprotected, informal types of work. The labourforce has become increasingly scattered and fragmented, rendering collective organization at the workplace more and more difficult. More women have also joined the paid workforce in order to try to bolster the family wage and due to changing patterns of employment.

In the private sector, workers' organizations have been weakened with the threat of relocation to new zones of capital accumulation, such as the move of some factories from the Mexican maquiladoras to even lower wage zones in China or Honduras. In the public sector, trade union strength has declined significantly due to privatization, which includes the dual processes of the selling of state-owned firms and subcontracting service provision to private suppliers. Given the significant erosion of trade union strength over the past 30 years, there is wide agreement among scholars and activists that innovative strategies are needed to revive the labour movement (e.g. union revitalization and the inclusion of women and minorities, as noted above), but disagreement on what this means for working-class movements.

For scholars who embrace 'new social movement' analysis, the New Left in Latin America differs from the Old Left in several respects, including the prevalence of coalition-building among different social sectors and the predominance of civil society over the working class. While trade unions and socialist political parties still participate in these broad coalitions, such scholars observe, they are no longer the leaders of these initiatives, as was often the case during the middle decades of the 20th century. The most radical position in this debate was articulated by Laclau and Mouffe (2001), who argued that 'socialism' should be abandoned for a more fluid conception of 'radical democracy'. Other scholars such as Holloway (2002) argued that old socialist strategies of trying to elect revolutionary parties to office ought to be abandoned; since the capitalist state cannot be reformed, it is better to work outside of the state based upon strategies pursued by armed revolutionary and indigenous struggles such as the Zapatistas.

While the debates initiated by these scholarly interventions generated more heat than light, it is useful to recall that in many ways, their emphasis on the importance of more horizontal forms of decision-making to build popular power resemble the tactics embraced by the anarcho-syndicalist movements of the turn of the 20th century, which emphasized the centrality of building workplace democracy. While the anarcho-syndicalist movements were eventually defeated with the growing corporatization and institutionalization of the labour movement in the early 20th century, it is important to remember that there are some cyclical elements in social movement dynamics. More recently, the emphasis on internal democracy has been promoted by scholars working on 'social movement unionism' and 'union revitalization' (see Brickner, 2013).

Neoliberalization is a deeply contradictory process that has produced imperatives but also opportunities for creative resistance strategies. Continental integration under trade and investment deals such as the North American Free Trade Agreement and the Mercosur Agreement and the increasing globalization of capital have also increased transnational ties along global commodity chains. In the wake of economic crisis in countries in which the New Left came to office, such as Venezuela and Argentina, workers have recovered abandoned factories and experimented with more horizontal forms of work organization such as cooperatives. There have also been signs of labour revitalization at the national level with new union centrals emerging in Argentina, Brazil and Mexico as the leaders of the old (often corrupt) unions find it more difficult to control their members as clientelist ties break down between these unions, political parties and state officials. Public sector workers have employed creative strategies to defend against the privatization of essential services, defending these services as human rights in contexts such as Central America and Colombia.

Rather than making a strict division between 'new' and 'old' social movements, a more accurate and historically informed narrative observes that the rise and fall of workers' organizations follows the rhythms of capital accumulation, such that it may be erroneous to make a strict divide between 'old' and 'new' (Spronk, 2012). When capital accumulation is expanding, workers have more of what Wright calls 'structural power' – which refers to the position of workers in the production process and their ability to disrupt it – and are better able to win gains for their members and for the working class as a whole. When capital accumulation declines, workers' organizations such as trade unions also enter into crisis since their members depend on the salaries paid by employers. As noted in the examples above, however, sometimes workers in zones of declining capital can still exercise their 'associational power' – referring to workers' collective organization – by forming new workers' centrals and recuperated factory movements. In short, some workers manage to collectively organize in new ways to turn crisis into opportunity. As Polanyi's (2001 [1944]) thesis of the double movement suggests, working-class peoples will find ways to resist when capital's attempts to 'dis-embed the market' go too far.

Recommended reading: Brickner (2013), Spronk (2012), Wright (2000).

Trade unions and political and economic development in Latin America

Given its early industrialization and relatively high rates of union density, Latin American development studies has had a rich history of research on trade unions and their role in political and economic development. One of the central questions that has been debated by scholars of class struggle and resistance in Latin America is the important role that trade unions play in shaping class consciousness, and how they have influenced and interacted with political parties and social movements more generally.

One of the challenges in social formations such as those found in Latin America is the dominance of the informal sector. Industrial workers have always been a smaller minority of the economically active population in Latin American countries than in the advanced capitalist countries of the North. The relative size of the informal sector has also shaped class consciousness. Parodi's (2000) masterful study of industrial workers in Peru in the context of neoliberal restructuring in the 1980s shows how workers desperate to support themselves and their families were increasingly forced to seek opportunities outside the industrial sector. In the process, he shows how they began to question their very identities as workers.

In the context of the Cold War (1947–1991), the labour movement was a fundamental part of the 'multi-class' coalitions that brought these revolutionary governments in Bolivia (1952), Cuba (1959) and Nicaragua (1979) to office, but trade unions did not play the major role as expected by orthodox Marxist theory, challenging the common (mis)conception within Marxist thought and practice at the time: industrial workers are the privileged subject of history and therefore should play a 'vanguard' role in revolutionary struggles. Nonetheless, there are many points in history in which revolutionary industrial unions have played a leading role in working-class struggles across Latin America. Scholars such as Nash (1979) and Klubock (1998) have observed that unions that represent workers in particularly dangerous workplaces, such as mines in Bolivia and Chile, have tended to be more revolutionary than other workers' unions, because of the way that they can construct militant identities on the basis of a hyper-masculinity, often privileging their class identities over other forms of identity such as indigenous identity. In his study of workers in Chile's largest cotton textile mill, Winn (1986) provides a 'history from below', documenting the crucial role that these workers played in the movement that brought socialist president Salvador Allende to office in 1970 and in constructing his vision of socialism. Seidman (1994) similarly demonstrates how movements led by industrial workers in the contexts of apartheid in South Africa and non-constitutional rule in Brazil in the 1970s to the 1990s enjoyed broad public support as they fought for improved social services, land reform, expanding

electoral participation and racial integration in the context of rapid industrialization sponsored by authoritarian states.

One of the most innovative studies of the role of trade unions in 'shaping the
political arena' in Latin America is Collier and Collier's (1991) classic comparative
study of the way that trade unions and political parties shaped the political and
economic institutions that emerged in the context of rapid (state-sponsored) industrialization in the 1960s and 1970s. They find that the process by which the political
arena has been shaped provides the best clues as to why democracy collapsed in
Argentina and Brazil, and later Chile and Uruguay, and gave way to military
regimes in the 1960s and 1970s, while other cases such as Venezuela, Colombia
and Mexico did not experience similar patterns of regime change. The main thesis
is that the 'type of incorporation' of labour in the formal sector, whereby the state
engages in its first sustained attempt to provide a legitimate and institutionalized
role for the labour movement, has an important long-term impact in determining
the shape of the political arena, signifying nothing less than a 'critical juncture' in
a country's historical development, which crucially affects future regime dynamics
and the prospects of political stability. This study provides crucial insights to help
explain the 'second incorporation' of civil society organizations such as women's
groups within Latin America's New Left regimes.

Recommended reading: Collier and Collier (1991), Nash (1979), Winn (1986).

Women and trade unions in Latin America

Women in Latin American trade unions have experienced misogyny not only by
their employers, but also within their own unions. As the chair of the Women's
Committee of the Trade Union Confederation of the Americas reported in a
recent interview for IPS press, 'the participation of Latin American women workers in trade union leadership posts is not in line with the percentage of women who
are in the labourforce' (cited in Gutiérrez, 2013). There have been few exceptions
to this rule. Some unions have pursued strategies to democratize their internal
structures as a response to neoliberal restructuring and to respond to pressures facing workers in an increasingly competitive world market in a process described as
'union revitalization'.

In her study of trade unions in Mexico, Brickner (2013) observes that civil
society associations (such as labour-focused NGOs) have played an important role
in raising awareness among women workers as their fundamental rights by creating spaces within which union women engage in dialogue, training and education
about women workers' rights and gender equity and how these can be promoted
by their unions. She argues that the greater participation of women in unions has
opened up the possibility of building stronger links within civil society – among
women of different unions, and between those women and various civil society
groups. Her work provides a contrast to Bickam Mendez's (2005) work on women
workers in the maquiladoras in Nicaragua, in which she explains that women have
found the leadership of trade union centrals to be so patriarchal and impenetrable

that they opted to form an NGO named the Maria Elena Cuadra Organization, which the organizers define as an 'alternative' to a trade union.

Frank's (2005) book on the transformation of banana workers' unions in Central America highlights how women's rising participation was an unintended consequence of other democratic reforms. In 1975, a left-affiliated male leadership overthrew the conservative leadership that was affiliated with the Cold War AFL-CIO, and the new leadership changed the union's internal structure. They established two rank-and-file committees – one for the male-dominated agricultural division, and one for the female-dominated packing house. Although empowering women was not necessarily the intention of these men at the time, as Frank argues, the establishment of two rank-and-file committees 'finally opened the door for women to fully enter the union' (p. 24). Women's union organizing blossomed from there.

Selwyn's (2012) study of unionized women workers in the grape export sector in northeastern Brazil has similarly pointed to the vital role in pushing for maternity leave and childcare facilities. In keeping with other scholars, he emphasizes that women's participation in production has advantages and disadvantages for female workers. While it leads to greater self-esteem and more opportunities for women to play an active role in decision-making, a rigid gendered division of labour within the home creates a 'double burden': women's home workload does not decrease despite their work outside the home. This is not a surprising revelation to many feminist thinkers, but Selwyn's contribution lies in providing insights into the process of how women workers can win gender-specific concessions from employers by increasing their participation in their unions and orienting it towards their needs, a strategy that may prove useful to the cause of rural women workers in other countries.

Recommended reading: Frank (2005), Selwyn (2012).

References

Bickham Mendez, J. (2005). *From the Revolution to the Maquiladoras: Gender, Labor, and Globalization in Nicaragua*. Durham, NC: Duke University Press.

Brickner R. (2013). 'Gender conscientization, social movement unionism, and labour revitalization: a perspective from Mexico'. *Labour History*, 54(1): 21–41.

Collier, R.B. and Collier, D. (1991). *Shaping the Political Arena: Critical Junctures, the Labour Movement, and Regime Dynamics in Latin America*. Notre Dame, IN: University of Notre Dame Press.

Frank, D. (2005). *Bananeras: Women Transforming Banana Unions in Latin America*. Cambridge, MA: South End Press.

Gutiérrez, E. (2013). *Women Forge a Space for Themselves in Latin American Labour Movement*. Inter Press Service News Agency, 30 April.

Holloway, J. (2002). *Change the World Without Taking Power*. London: Pluto Press.

Jaumotte, F. and Osorio Buiton, C. (2015). 'Inequality and labour market institutions'. IMF Staff Discussion Note SDN/15/14, July. Washington, DC: International Monetary Fund.

Klubock, T. (1998). *Contested Communities: Class, Gender and Politics in Chile's El Teniente Copper Mine, 1904–1951*. Durham, NC: Duke University Press.

Laclau, E. and Moufe, C. (2001). *Hegemony and Socialist Strategy: Towards a Radical Democratic Politics*, 2nd edition. London: Verso.

Larrain, J. (1989). *Theories of Development: Capitalism, Colonialism and Dependency*. Cambridge: Polity Press.

Marx, K. and Engels, F. (1848). *Manifesto of the Communist Party*. Available at: www.marxists. org/archive/marx/works/download/pdf/Manifesto.pdf.

Nash, J. (1979). *We Eat the Mines and the Mines Eat Us: Dependency and Exploitation in Bolivian Tin Mines*. New York: Columbia University Press.

Parodi, J. (2000). *To Be a Worker: Identity and Politics in Peru*. Chapel Hill, NC: University of North Carolina Press.

Petras, J. (1990). 'Retreat of the intellectuals'. *Economic and Political Weekly*, 25(38), September: 2143–56.

Petras, J. and Veltmeyer, H. (2017). *The Class Struggle in Latin America*. London: Routledge.

Polanyi, K. (2001 [1944]). *The Great Transformation*. Boston, MA: Beacon Press.

Seidman, G. (1994). *Manufacturing Militance: Workers' Movement in Brazil and South Africa, 1970–1985*. Berkeley, CA: University of California Press.

Selwyn, B. (2012). *Workers, State and Development in Brazil: Powers of Labour, Chains of Value*. Manchester/New York: Manchester University Press.

Selwyn, B. (2016). 'Elite development theory: a labour-centred critique'. *Third World Quarterly*, 37(5): 781–99.

Silver, B. and Arrighi G. (2001). 'Workers North and South'. In L. Panitch and C. Leys (eds), *The Socialist Register 2001*. New York: Monthly Review Press, pp. 53–76.

Spronk, S. (2012). 'Neoliberal class formation(s): the informal proletariat and "new" workers' organizations in Latin America'. In J.R. Webber and B. Carr (eds), *The Resurgence of Latin American Radicalism: Between Cracks in the Empire and an Izquierda Permitida*. Lanham, MD: Rowman & Littlefield, pp. 75–93.

Winn, P. (1986). *Weavers of the Revolution: The Yarur Workers and Chile's Road to Socialism*. New York: Oxford University Press.

World Bank (2013). *World Development Report: Jobs*. Washington, DC: World Bank.

Wright, E.O. (2000). 'Working-class power, capitalist-class interests, and class compromise'. *American Journal of Sociology*, 105(4): 957–1002.

PART VII

Agrarian change and spatial reconfigurations

23

CONTEMPORARY DYNAMICS OF AGRARIAN CHANGE

Cristóbal Kay

The contemporary dynamics of agrarian change are being shaped by the neoliberal corporate food regime dominated by the agro-industrial system. A general insight into 'the global food regime' is provided in Chapter 24 by Akram-Lodhi in this volume. In this chapter, I focus on the following key interlinked issues: land grabbing, the crisis of the peasant economy and the emergence of a rural precariat, and the financialization of agriculture. While the contradictions between capital and labour have intensified, it has, paradoxically, become more difficult for labour to confront capital. Related issues such as the ecological impact of the current food regime, its contestation by peasant movements and the search for an alternative food regime are discussed by other contributors in this book.

Land concentration, land grabbing and agro-industrial capital

The period after the Second World War to the 1970s witnessed the implementation of land reforms in several developing countries, initiated either from below due to peasant revolts and social revolutions, or from above by the state to forestall any future revolts, or a combination of both so as to contain any further radicalization of the peasantry. These land reforms varied greatly in their reach; while in some countries almost the whole landlord class lost their land, such as in South Korea, Taiwan, China and Cuba, in others only a minority were expropriated, such as in the Philippines, Brazil and Ecuador.

During the 1980s, many developing countries, as well as several developed countries, liberalized their economies. In the countries of the South, the trigger for this shift was the debt crisis, which forced governments to request financial support from the World Bank and other financial institutions. These institutions demanded the implementation of a series of 'structural adjustment programmes' that focused on liberalizing the economy and opening it to world markets so as to encourage exports and thereby facilitate debt repayments. To facilitate the development of a land market, the World Bank and other international aid and government donor agencies encouraged governments to launch a land registration programme as many farmers, especially peasant farmers, either had no land titles or these were doubtful, by providing financial and technical support.

With the spectacular rise of China, together with the rapid growth rates of other large developing countries, the world demand for agricultural commodities rose significantly. Furthermore, the food crisis of 2007–2008, during which food prices doubled or trebled, led various governments to find ways to improve their food security as well as making agriculture profitable for private investors. Governments such as China and the Gulf States started to negotiate large-scale land deals with mainly African governments that gave the investing country the right to cultivate the acquired land and export the harvests back to their country. It was reported at the time that China had signed contracts in several countries for a total of 2.8 million hectares, and some sources even quoted that in Africa 134 million hectares had been acquired through these types of land deals, either through purchase or long-term land rental.

Those in favour of these types of land deals argued that they provide much needed investment in agriculture, incorporate new lands to cultivation, increase production and productivity, create jobs, provide an income to the local government and in general modernize agriculture (Deininger and Byerlee, 2011). In some cases, conflicts erupted as the lands that the government had provided were either not vacant lands and led to evictions, or these large-scale land deals began to negatively affect some peasant communities. As protest mounted against this 'fever for land' and 'foreignization', interest by researchers and activists in these large-scale land deals led to a growing literature on 'land grabbing', as critics labelled these land deals.

The critics argued that in several cases, these land deals led to the displacement of the local population, who, although they may not have had legal titles to the land, had been obtaining their livelihoods on those lands for decades or even generations. Furthermore, many of the promises of the foreign investors, such as providing decent and abundant employment opportunities, did not materialize. It often also led to a foreign enclave with few, if any, linkages to the rest of the local economy. Furthermore, it tended to lead to monoculture and the use of genetically modified seeds, pesticides and insecticides, with negative effects on the environment and the health of the local population. The investor, by using more water, drained the local supply of water, reducing the flow to other users and sometimes even polluting it.

Initially, these large-scale land deals focused on Africa, but with the shift to a wider and more critical analysis of land transactions indicated by the increasingly widely used term 'land grabbing', it was discovered that capitalists had progressively gained more and more control over natural resources, either through outright purchase of land, mining concessions and various kinds of rental agreements. A useful 'work-in-progress' definition of land grabbing is provided by Borras et al. (2012: 851):

land grabbing is the capturing of control of relatively vast tracts of land and other natural resources through a variety of mechanisms and forms that involve large-scale capital that often shifts resource use orientation into extractive character, whether for international or domestic purposes, as capital's response to the convergence of food, energy and financial crises, climate change mitigation imperative, and demands of resources from newer hubs of global capital.

Using this expanded view about land deals, it was discovered that land grabbing was a far more common phenomena than initially assumed, involving almost all developing regions of the world, including Eastern Europe (Borras *et al.*, 2012; Franco and Borras, 2013). This definition indicates the various factors (i.e. 'capital's response') that led to land grabbing, such as the food crisis of 2007–2008, the energy crisis when oil prices where sky-high before they fell sharply in 2014, the financial crisis of 2008–2009 (which led to the search for new investment opportunities by capitalists, and thereby intensified the financialization of nature, 'green grabbing') and the increasing demand for food by the rising developing countries such as China and India. This definition also refers to control and not necessarily ownership over resources, which could include, besides agricultural land, minerals, forest plantations, water and natural reserves. This control could be used for a variety of purposes, but often for a production process of an extractive character, especially in the case of mining and monocrop cultivation of 'flex crops' for either exports or the domestic market. Flex crops refers to crops such as soy, sugar cane, palm oil and maize, which can be put to various final uses according to what is most profitable at the time of the harvest. For example, soy, sugar cane and maize can be used for food, animal feed or biofuels, and as the price varies for each of these final uses to varying degrees, so does their profitability. This flexibility makes these crops particularly attractive to financial investors and speculators seeking to maximize profits.

While the term 'extractivism' is usually used for a production and economic growth process that relies on the extraction of minerals, oil and gas, which generates a rent income to those who own the resource but sooner or later depletes this natural resources, it is now also being used to refer to some agricultural products, hence the term 'agro-extractivism' (Petras and Veltmeyer, 2014). For example, the dramatic expansion of soy cultivation in Argentina, Brazil, Bolivia, Uruguay and Paraguay has led to deforestation, loss of biodiversity and 'green deserts' due to monocropping, with damaging consequences for the environment.

As for 'green grabbing', this refers to land deals with an environmental purpose such as biocarbon sequestration, setting up natural reserves, biodiversity conservation, and so on. These land deals might restrict the customary access that local communities used to have to these ecosystems, thereby having a negative impact on their livelihoods, for which they are not always compensated, thereby leading sometimes to conflicts. In some instances, a market is developing for these environmental services, such as carbon credits, thereby attracting private capital to finance these land deals, furthering the commodification of nature through 'green commodities' (Büscher and Fletcherb, 2015; Fairhead *et al.*, 2012).

While land grabbing tended to further land concentration, it was not the main driver, as it was the shift to neoliberalism and globalization that spurred the development of agro-industries that took advantage of the rapid growth in agro-exports. Although it attracted foreign capital, in the case of Latin America it was mainly domestic capital that financed this expansion, and it even invested in other countries of the region, largely in neighbouring countries. Hence, the term 'translatino' capital can be used to highlight this special characteristic of the Latin American case as compared to other developing regions (Borras *et al.*, 2012). For example, an Argentinian family enterprise cultivated around 250,000 hectares of wheat and soy in Argentina, Uruguay, Brazil and Paraguay (Murmis and Murmis, 2012). Meanwhile, a Chilean forestry company had access to 1.6 million hectares, of which almost 1 million hectares were forest plantations distributed in four countries of the region. A notable case is Paraguay, where two-thirds of the land cultivated with soy, which is the country's principal crop, is cultivated by mainly Brazilian and Argentinian capitalists (Galeano, 2011). However, foreign capital was also involved as a Belgian company whose shares were traded in Buenos Aires and New York controlled around 900,000 hectares in Argentina, Brazil, Paraguay and Bolivia. The magnitude of some of these land deals is indeed most striking.

Neoliberal globalization has given a boost to agro-industrial capital, which not only expanded their reach within their home country, but also beyond its frontier. In some developing regions, these agro-industries are part of a conglomerate linking commercial, financial, mining and industrial capital to farming. For example, some companies who own or rent land for the cultivation of soy try to extend their control over the soy commodity chain by investing in processing plants and establishing their own distribution and marketing networks, thereby capturing a larger share of the value generated by the commodity chain. The extent of penetration of agro-industrial capital varies between different countries depending on the degree of liberalization of the country concerned and the profitability and potential of its agriculture, among others.

The greater the dominance of agro-industrial capital within a country, the more difficult it becomes for social movements to succeed in their campaigns for land reform and food sovereignty. Some of these agro-industrial corporations have become too powerful, and some countries have become too dependent on the foreign exchange and rent income they generate for governments to go against their main interests, although they may be able to regulate and control some of their more harmful and contentious practices. While in Latin America during the period of land reforms the degree of land concentration tended to diminish, with the neoliberal turn it increased again, reaching in some countries a similar level as before the land reform. Unwittingly, some land reforms facilitated this process by breaking the control over land of the traditional landlords, and thereby easing with the neoliberal turn the development of a lively land market.

In sum, the neoliberal turn has led not only to increasing land concentration, but more significantly to a major concentration of capital and power in the agrarian sector and beyond, creating a new global food regime in which the state is subordinate to corporate capital, contrary to the previous food regimes in which the state played a key role in shaping it and had more control over capital. This is what McMichael (2013) has conceptualized as the 'corporate food regime'.

Recommended reading: Borras *et al.* (2012, 2012), Fairhead *et al.* (2012), Petras and Veltmeyer (2014).

The crisis of the peasant economy, de-agrarianization, and the precariousness and feminization of rural wage labour

Neoliberal globalization has intensified the crisis of the peasant economy or agricultural petty commodity producers (i.e. small-scale family household farmers producing agricultural goods for subsistence as well as for the market). Agro-industrial capitalist farmers are increasingly appropriating resources through a variety of means that further strengthen it while weakening the peasant farmers. Land grabbing is just one of those ways. Various governments have privatized state farms, collectives and several state enterprises and public utilities that it sold at often below-market value to private capitalists. These state enterprises often provided services such as technical assistance, credit, agro-processing and marketing facilities to peasant farmers at subsidized rates. With privatization, peasant farmers lost either access to these resources or were unable to pay the high charges now demanded by their new capitalist owners. Through the neoliberal land titling projects, some governments also introduced legislation that allowed the dissolution of indigenous communities and the granting of individual property rights. Only in a few countries were communal property rights strengthened as a consequence of the mobilization by indigenous peoples. Land titling in general was aimed at enhancing the land market, and many beneficiaries of land parcels from agrarian reforms, as well as existing peasant farmers, were unable to compete in the market for agricultural commodities being exposed to the full force of the neoliberal 'market compulsion'. They no longer had the protection of the developmentalist state (Borras *et al.*, 2008).

This wave of privatization of natural resources, the enclosure of the commons, the depletion of the 'global environmental commons', biopiracy and the various forms of land grabbing are referred to by Harvey (2003) as 'accumulation by dispossession', arguing that some of these phenomena are new forms of appropriations by capital, which, on the one hand, were not included in Marx's concept of 'original' or 'primitive' capital accumulation, and, on the other hand, are still ongoing processes, and hence the need for using a new concept.

As a consequence of the increasing pressures and vulnerabilities facing peasant farming, which is weakening their access to productive resources, their members are forced to engage in a greater variety of activities so as to be able to secure a livelihood (Scoones, 2015). A process of 'de-agrarianization' takes hold whereby the members of peasant farm households need to find other income opportunities beyond farming through engaging in 'pluriactivity' (Bryceson, 2000).

These other activities and income opportunities are largely confined to seeking different forms of wage employment such as agricultural wage workers in capitalist farms in the locality, as non-agricultural wage workers in nearby rural or urban areas maintaining their residence in the peasant household, or in wage employment of different kinds that require seasonal or longer-term migration beyond the household, within the country or internationally (Oya and Pontara, 2015). In areas where fruit, flower and vegetable production is intensive in the use of labour, producers tend to draw labour as much as possible from the local area, including nearby urban towns or cities. In some countries, there has been an export boom of these commodities that was much facilitated by drawing women into the wage labour market, at times with some resistance from men. Fruit cultivation generally only offers seasonal employment for the harvest and in the processing plants, while flower and vegetable cultivation, if undertaken in greenhouses, can offer longer-term employment. However, most jobs tend to be of a precarious, casual and temporary nature as it allows employers to avoid issuing contracts or only issue contracts that allow them to bypass social security payments and other benefits to their workers. This has been characterized by some authors as 'primitive' or 'savage' flexibilization. While in the past few wage employment opportunities existed for women in the countryside, they now constitute over half of the workers employed in these labour-intensive non-traditional agricultural activities and about two-thirds of those employed in the agro-industrial processing plants (Kay, 2008).

To illustrate the magnitude of these changes to off-farm employment and sources of income by the peasant households, I draw on data for Latin America: while in 1980 roughly one-fifth of the rural population worked in activities outside the farm, by 1990 this had increased to two-fifths, and by 2010 to an estimated three-fifths. This trend is reflected in the changing income composition of the rural household. While in 1980 the income derived from non-agricultural activities constituted about one-quarter of the rural household income, by 1990 it had reached about one-half, and by 2010 about two-thirds of their income. In some countries remittances from migrant workers accounted for a substantial proportion of the family household income. Remittances also became a major source of foreign exchange income for some countries and helped to reduce poverty.

Many countries have weak labour legislations that give few rights to workers, such as minimum wages, and do not offer much protection against unfair dismissal or abusive labour conditions. Increasingly, capitalist farmers and agro-industries are using the services of labour contractors so as to minimize their obligations to workers. These labour contractors take advantage of the vulnerabilities of workers, especially if they can draw on a large pool of unemployed workers, due to their gender, ethnicity or dubious legal status in cases of migrant workers. Instead of receiving a daily wage, workers are often paid by piecework (i.e. by result), leading to a working day beyond eight hours, as well as an intensification of the work rhythm so as to maximize their daily wage income. Work is also precarious in the sense that it tends to be monotonous and repetitive, leading in some instances to a high turnover of workers as they try to find better employment conditions whenever possible (Riella and Mascheroni, 2015).

Araghi (2009) argues that the process of neoliberal globalization is creating 'the great global enclosures of our times' and an 'enclosure food regime', whereby corporate agrofood capital intensifies 'depeasantization via displacement'. As a consequence, a massive global reserve army of labour is formed, which, by migrating nationally and internationally, is readily available for capital to employ as wage labour whenever it is required in urban and rural areas. With better transport infrastructure, cheaper fares and the spread of cell phones and other means of communication, workers are better informed of employment opportunities and able to grasp them. During the harvest season, workers living in the urban peripheries also engage in agricultural wage work, sometimes commuting on a daily basis with transport provided by labour contractors. Rural labour has become footloose on a massive scale, migrating to wherever they are able to find employment, allowing capitalists to increase their exploitation of wage workers, thereby achieving higher profits and sustaining the process of capital accumulation on a global scale. This surplus labour has put a downward pressure on wages and led to evermore degrading employment conditions (Delgado Wise and Veltmeyer, 2016). The greater mobility of labour is also eroding the rural–urban divide, with the peripheral areas in cities and towns forming a transmission belt between them, leading to expressions such as 'cities of peasants', 'the countryside in the city', 'the urbanization of the countryside' and 'rurbanization'.

These processes of de-agrarianization, depeasantization, proletarianization, fragmentation and precariousness lead Bernstein (2010) to prefer to use the term 'classes of labour', as the term peasant no longer captures contemporary reality dominated by neoliberal globalization. Hence, the key agrarian question of our times is the problematic of labour as it faces a crisis of reproduction. However, in some parts of the world, processes of peasantization and repeasantization have been occurring in recent decades, such as in China, Cuba and Brazil. And in many areas of the world, the peasant family farm household is still holding their own, although not always necessarily striving, particularly in the interstices of capitalism, generally marginal areas of poor-quality soils and with limited infrastructure making it little attractive for capital. In some areas, it is the fierce resistance of social movements, such as those of indigenous peoples, that has limited, if not necessarily stopped, the onward march of capitalist relations. Hence, the debate between 'peasantists' or 'neopopulists' (inspired by Chayanov) and 'depeasantists' or 'proletarianists' (inspired by Marx and Lenin) continues (Van der Ploeg, 2012).

Recommended reading: Araghi (2009), Bernstein (2010), Bryceson (2000), Harvey (2003), Kay (2008), Oya and Pontara (2015), Riella and Mascheroni (2015), Van der Ploeg (2012), Vergara-Camus (2014).

The financialization of agriculture and food

The food crisis of 2007–2008 drew attention to the influence of finance on the agri-food sector that had hitherto been neglected. Some authors charged the financial sector for being a major contributory factor to the food price spikes of 2007–2008, when prices of key staples doubled. They also blamed it for the increasing volatility of food prices. Financial deregulation in the 1990s and early 2000s gave a significant boost to the entry of new financial players, such as hedge funds, pension funds, sovereign wealth funds and investment banks, into the agricultural commodity exchanges to trade commodity futures contracts and other agriculture-related financial products. The financial sector had increasingly become involved in the agricultural sector through the creation of derivates and other financial instruments, such as agricultural commodity index funds. The financial system had also increasingly facilitated the purchase of farmland, food companies and the financing of parts of the agricultural commodity chain (Breger Bush, 2012).

A debate ensued trying to ascertain to what extent financial markets had contributed to the food crisis and what their specific impact had been (Clapp, 2012). For some authors, trade in agricultural derivates insures buyers and sellers against price volatility trade; other authors argued that they promoted speculative activity, resulting in higher price volatility, thus undermining the purported aim of stability. While in the past, producers and consumers used the highly regulated financial markets for hedging purposes, thereby stabilizing farm incomes, under the neoliberal regime financial firms increasingly entered the market for speculative purposes by trying to profit from food price volatility, thereby exacerbating volatility (Ghosh, 2010).

Financialization has also fostered land grabbing by facilitating large-scale land deals and helping to finance the rapid expansion of flex crops. In the period of high fuel prices, flex crops (soy beans, palm oil and sugar cane) were increasingly destined for biofuels instead of food. Land became gradually more attractive as an investment and became a financial asset through farmland securitization that enhanced land liquidity.

According to Isakson (2014: 749), 'financialization has reinforced the position of food retailers as the dominant actors within the agrofood system'. He also points out the deleterious consequences of financialization as it 'has intensified the exploitation of food workers, increasing their workload while pushing down their real wages and heightening the precarity of their positions'. Furthermore, he argues that:

> small-scale farmers have been especially hard hit by financialization, as their livelihoods have become even more uncertain due to increasing volatility in agricultural markets, they have become weaker vis-à-vis other actors in the agrofood supply chain, and they face growing competition for their farmland.

It is difficult for those negatively affected by financialization to organize and demand greater regulation by governments and protective measures due to the complexity and opaqueness of the financial world. It is often challenging to trace a direct link between a particular financial instrument and the actual physical agricultural commodity, especially in some speculative activities. Hence, Clapp (2012) argues that financialization, by fostering what she terms 'distancing' in the food system, obfuscates the resistance and struggle against the growing power of those institutions responsible for the damaging impacts of financialization. Governments may also be reluctant to intervene and mediate between finance and agriculture as they set up the basic building blocks of this new financial system by withdrawing the various regulatory and protective measures so as to make it attractive to private capital. Furthermore, the increasingly mobility, flexibility and power of finance capital make it today also more difficult to regulate and control (Visser *et al.*, 2015).

Recommended reading: Breger Bush (2012), Clapp (2012), Visser *et al.* (2015).

Conclusion

To understand the contemporary dynamics of agrarian change, we have focused on three issues that are closely interlinked. They all point to the dominant power of global capital in the shape of the agro-industrial corporate food complex and the concomitant rise of a global rural precariat that enables capital to intensify its exploitation of labour. This neoliberal food regime is being contested by national and transnational social movements, as analysed in other chapters of this book.

References

Araghi, F. (2009). 'The invisible hand and the visible foot: peasants, dispossession and globalization'. In A.H. Akram-Lodhi and C. Kay (eds), *Peasants and Globalization: Political Economy, Rural Transformation and the Agrarian Question*. London: Routledge, pp. 111–47.

Bernstein, H. (2010). *Class Dynamics of Agrarian Change*. Halifax: Fernwood.

Borras Jr., S.M., Kay, C. and Lahiff, E. (eds) (2008). *Market-Led Agrarian Reform: Trajectories and Contestations*. Routledge: London.

Borras Jr., S.M., Franco, J.C., Gómez, S., Kay, C. and Spoor, M. (2012). 'Land grabbing in Latin America and the Caribbean'. *Journal of Peasant Studies*, 39(3–4): 845–72.

Breger Bush, S. (2012). *Derivatives and Development: A Political Economy of Global Finance, Farming and Poverty*. New York: Palgrave Macmillan.

Bryceson, D. (2000). 'Peasant theories and smallholder policies: past and present'. In D. Bryceson, C. Kay and J. Mooij (eds), *Disappearing Peasantries? Rural Labour in Africa, Asia and Latin America*. Bourton-on-Dunsmore: ITDG-Practical Action, pp. 1–36.

Büscher, B. and Fletcherb, R. (2015). 'Accumulation by conservation'. *New Political Economy*, 20(2): 273–98.

Clapp, J. (2012). *Food*. Cambridge: Polity Press.

Deininger, K. and Byerlee, D. (2011). *Rising Global Interest in Farmland: Can It Yield Sustainable and Equitable Benefits?* Washington, DC: World Bank.

Delgado Wise, R. and Veltmeyer, H. (2016). *Agrarian Change, Migration and Development*. Halifax: Fernwood.

Fairhead, J., Leach, M. and Scoones, I. (2012). 'Green grabbing: a new appropriation of nature?' *The Journal of Peasant Studies*, 39(2): 237–61.

Franco, J.C. and Borras Jr., S.M. (eds) (2013). *Land Concentration, Land Grabbing and People's Struggles in Europe*. Amsterdam: Transnational Institute.

Galeano, L. (2011). *Dinámica del mercado de la tierra en América Latina y el Caribe: El caso de Paraguay*. Santiago: FAO.

Ghosh, J. (2010). 'The unnatural coupling: food and global finance'. *Journal of Agrarian Change*, 10(1): 72–86.

Harvey, D. (2003). 'Accumulation by dispossession'. In D. Harvey (ed.), *The New Imperialism*. Oxford: Oxford University Press, pp. 137–82.

Isakson, S.R. (2014). 'Food and finance: the financial transformation of agro-food supply chains'. *The Journal of Peasant Studies*, 41(5): 749–75.

Kay, C. (2008). 'Reflections on Latin American rural studies in the neoliberal globalization period: a new rurality?' *Development and Change*, 39(6): 915–43.

McMichael, P. (2013). *Food Regimes and Agrarian Questions*. Halifax: Fernwood.

Murmis, M. and Murmis, M.R. (2012). 'Land concentration and foreign land ownership in Argentina in the context of global land grabbing'. *Canadian Journal of Development Studies*, 33(4): 490–508.

Oya, C. and Pontara, N. (eds) (2015). *Rural Wage Employment in Developing Countries*. London: Routledge.

Petras, J. and Veltmeyer, H. (2014). 'Agro-extractivism: the agrarian question of the 21st century'. In J. Petras and H. Veltmeyer (eds), *Extractive Imperialism in the Americas: Capitalism's New Frontier*. Leiden: Brill, pp. 62–100.

Riella, A. and Mascheroni, P. (eds) (2015). *Asalariados Rurales en América Latina*. Buenos Aires: CLACSO.

Scoones, I. (2015). *Sustainable Livelihoods and Rural Development*. Halifax: Fernwood.

Van der Ploeg, J.D. (2013). *Peasants and the Art of Farming: A Chayanovian Manifesto*. Halifax: Fernwood.

Vergara-Camus, L. (2014). *Land and Freedom: The MST, the Zapatistas and Peasant Alternatives to Neoliberalism*. London: Zed Books.

Visser, O., Clapp, J. and Isakson, S.R. (2015). 'Introduction to a symposium on global finance and the agri-food sector: risk and regulation'. *Journal of Agrarian Change*, 15(4): 541–8.

24

THE GLOBAL FOOD REGIME

A. Haroon Akram-Lodhi

Capitalism, farming and the agrarian question in the 21st century

Since the late 1970s capitalism has been reconfiguring farming systems around the world in order to increase the production of food and cash crops. These sustain low-priced wage goods and industrial inputs, and can thus boost the profitability of capital. These processes have resulted in increases in the scale of on-farm production because of the need to meet market imperatives. Market imperatives are defined as the requirement, in commodity economies, that output must be sold at competitive market prices if it is to sell, and that this requires continually lowering costs of production by investing in efficiency-enhancing techniques and technologies (Wood, 2009); this process increases in the scale of farm production because it increases the capital-intensity of farming systems. The livelihood outcomes of this process are, for many in the countryside of the developing world, extraordinarily negative, as market imperatives and profitability requirements undermine the capacities of many small-scale petty commodity-producing peasant farmers to compete on domestic markets, and hence survive as viable farm operations, resulting in land sales. Such sales can be of private property that is freely entered into between buyers and sellers in land markets. However, the extent of the 'freedom' to enter into or exit from a transaction can be so severely circumscribed by the market imperative, and particularly by the accrual of debt as a result of the market imperative (Graeber, 2011), as to render the idea of freedom a fiction. As a result, an increase in the capital-intensity of farming systems is consistent with increases in land holdings; indeed, capturing scale economies from farm equipment and machinery may require larger farms (World Bank, 2007). Increases in the scale and scope of farming can thus come about as an outcome of the market imperatives that drive accumulation. It can also be the result of politically-driven forced displacement, that is, the so-called 'primitive accumulation' of the enclosures – or, in contemporary discourse, 'accumulation by dispossession' (Harvey, 2003). In this way, market imperatives and enclosures are a routine and predictable part of the process of capitalist development in the countryside (Akram-Lodhi, 2007; see also Hall, 2013). So ongoing rural restructuring in the 21st century is wholly consistent with the problematic of the 'agrarian question': whether and, if so, how capital is transforming farm production systems and the agricultural sector in the developing world (Delgado Wise and Veltmeyer, 2016; see also Chapter 11 by Bello in this volume). Capital transforms farming by enforcing market imperatives on farmers, and in so doing facilitates the emergence of capitalist social–property relations of production, in which the means of production are under the control of a socially dominant hegemonic class, labour is 'free' from significant shares of the means of production and free to sell its capacity to work, and the purpose of commodity production is the seeking of profit (Akram-Lodhi and Kay, 2016).

This is the context within which the debate over the importance of contemporary 'land grabbing' has emerged (Akram-Lodhi, 2015a; Cotula et al., 2014). Since the onset of the 2007 food price crisis (Akram-Lodhi, 2012), many argue that global capital has been seeking to 'resolve' context- and place-specific agrarian questions by facilitating the establishment of larger-scale, larger-sized farms organized under increasingly capitalist relations of production. However, as capital transcends state boundaries, the terms and conditions by which it transforms farming systems and the agricultural sector is subject to huge, highly uneven and contingent variations, what Byres (1996) calls 'historical puzzles'. This variation can be witnessed in terms of the social–property relations in the countryside within which capital does or does not insinuate itself, the upstream and downstream agricultural activities over which capital is hegemonic, the breadth and depth of the financialization of farming and agriculture, the spatial landscapes over which capital operates, and the temporal frame in which processes of agrarian change are played out. As a consequence, it is necessary to situate agrarian questions within the world-historical context of the dominant food regime (McMichael, 2013). In a classic formulation, a food regime can be defined as the 'international relations of food production and consumption' that can be directly linked 'to forms of accumulation' (Friedmann and McMichael, 1989: 95). The current food regime is widely labelled as 'corporate' (Akram-Lodhi, 2012; Bernstein, 2016; Holt-Giménez and Shattuck, 2011).

Recommended reading: Akram-Lodhi (2012), Bernstein (2016), Friedmann and McMichael (1989).

The corporate food regime

The corporate food regime is dominated by global agrofood transnational corporations, driven by world market prices and the financial imperatives of short-run profitability, and characterized by the relentless food commodification processes that underpin 'supermarketization'. This regime forges global animal protein commodity chains while at the same time spreading transgenic organisms, which together broaden and deepen the temperate 'industrial grain-oilseed-livestock' agrofood complex (Weis, 2013). At the point of production, the dominant producer model of the corporate food regime is the fossil-fuel-driven, large-scale, capital-intensive industrial agriculture megafarm, which in turn requires, through enclosures and market imperatives, deepening the simple reproduction squeeze facing small-scale peasant petty commodity producers around the developing world as world market prices for farm products fail to cover the actual costs of production at the farm gate (Akram-Lodhi and Kay, 2010).

A core market for the agrofood transnational corporations of the corporate food regime are relatively affluent global consumers in the North and South, whose food preferences in the last quarter-century have been shifted towards 'healthier', 'organic' and 'green' products that have large profit margins. At the same time, though, for the global middle class, the corporate food regime sustains the mass production of very durable highly processed food manufactures that are heavily reliant on soya, high fructose corn syrup and sodium, and whose lower profit margins mean that significantly higher volumes of product must be shifted. Thus, the corporate food regime simultaneously fosters the ongoing diffusion of industrial agriculture – Fordist food such as McDonald's – as well as standardized differentiation – post-Fordist food such as sushi (Akram-Lodhi, 2013).

The corporate food regime is sustained by capitalist states, the international financial and development organizations that govern the global economy, and the big philanthropy that can sustain the expansion of capitalism (Fridell and Konings, 2013). Notably missing from the profit-driven logic of the corporate food regime, however, are those that lack the money needed to access commodified food in markets and who are thus bypassed by the regime. This is a 'relative surplus population' (Marx, 1976) that is denied entitlements to food as a result of the normal and routine working of the food markets of the corporate food regime, and who are thus subject to food-based social exclusion (Akram-Lodhi and Kay, 2010). For this relative surplus population, the only answer to the agrarian question lies in waged labour, whether it be on the farms of others that have successfully navigated the complex and dynamic intricacies necessary for relative success in the corporate food regime, or whether it be off-farm, in rural or urban waged labour.

Recommended reading: Akram-Lodhi and Kay (2010), Weis (2013).

Five critical issues

This is the global agrarian context within which peasants in the developing world – and small-scale farmers in the developed world – find themselves. Arising from this context are five central issues in critical rural development studies.

Rural poverty and inequality

According to the World Bank (2014), some 800 million people around the developing world live in rural areas and rely on farming, livestock, aquaculture and other agricultural work to produce a livelihood. This represents some 78 per cent of the world's poor people. Thus, the epicentre of world poverty lies in the countryside. Almost 45 per cent of the rural poor are found in South Asia; around a quarter of the rural poor are found in Sub-Saharan Africa and East Asia; and just under 7 per cent of the rural poor are found in Latin America and the Caribbean (IFAD, 2010). The rural poor are diverse: farmers, fisherfolk and pastoralists, landless waged labourers, indigenous peoples and female-headed households, and displaced people. Most of the rural poor are driven by their poverty into diverse and precarious livelihoods, of which farming is a very significant component, and although they grow a significant proportion of their food requirements, they have narrow diets and must supplement their own production with purchases on food markets, for which money is required, which may be scarce.

Uniting the rural poor around the world is a lack of access to the single most important agrarian asset: land. Land holdings tend to be small. Moreover, the rural poor are far more likely to operate 'less favoured' or marginal land: land where the terrain, soil quality and lack of access to water results in lower levels of agricultural productivity. The rural poor are also likely to farm in 'less favoured' areas: areas with less favourable lands or areas where land has agricultural potential, but which is remote, often because of a lack of infrastructure, which limits access to markets (Pender and Hazell, 2000).

With access to land being the single most important determinant of household welfare, Table 24.1 presents somewhat dated comparative estimates of land Gini coefficients. It is clear from Table 24.1 that land-based inequality was remarkably high in the early years of the 2000s. Moreover, estimates by the International Monetary Fund indicate that, based upon a restricted sample of developing countries, land Gini coefficients globally rose by 7 per cent between 1960 and 1990 (Erikson and Vollrath, 2004: Table 2), prior to the most recent period of globalization, which is strongly correlated around the world with rising inequality.

TABLE 24.1 Land Gini coefficients for selected Latin American and African countries, various years

Latin America	
Venezuela	0.917
Argentina	0.856
Colombia	0.829
Bolivia	0.768
Africa	
Madagascar	0.804
Tanzania	0.790
Kenya	0.711
Uganda	0.549

Source: World Bank (2009: 104)

There is clear evidence of an inverse relationship between land Gini coefficients and agricultural productivity, indicating that the more unequal the land distribution, the lower the level of agricultural productivity, which has clear implications for rural livelihoods, incomes and welfare (Vollrath, 2007) because low productivity depresses agricultural growth and 'GDP growth originating in agriculture is at least twice as effective in reducing poverty as GDP growth originating outside agriculture' (World Bank, 2007: 6). Moreover, this is strongly gendered, as women's land holdings are systematically lower than men's, and less productive (World Bank, 2011). At the same time, a lack of land drives other sources of disadvantage: a lack of non-land assets such as tools, equipment and livestock; a lack of access to education and healthcare; a lack of access to adequate, remunerative, safe and secure waged work; oligopolistic or monopolistic product and services markets; and a lack of access to social protection. The result is a cumulative reinforcement of disadvantage that is particularly borne by women. In this light, it seems reasonably clear that while addressing rural poverty requires improving agrarian productivity in ways that are gender-responsive and pro-poor, the lack of attention paid to understanding specifically agrarian inequalities might significantly compromise efforts at tackling rural poverty.

Recommended reading: IFAD (2010).

Pro-poor gender-responsive redistributive agrarian reform

Therefore, agrarian inequality must be tackled simultaneously with rural poverty. In this regard, a stylized fact of development is that, at a global level, the distribution of land and other rural resources is the result of either imperialist theft or the glaring inequalities produced by market imperatives, as capitalism was introduced into the countryside of colonized countries by imperialist powers (Akram-Lodhi *et al.*, 2007). Granted, this stylized fact does not hold in all places and all spaces, but as a general statement it holds true in 2016. Agrarian inequalities were thus created, as a consequence of which there is a prima facie case for restitution. Pro-poor gender-responsive redistributive agrarian reform is defined as a redistribution of land and other rural resources from the resource-rich to the resource-poor such that the resource-poor are net beneficiaries of the reform and the resource-rich are net losers from the reform (Borras, 2005). Pro-poor gender-responsive redistributive agrarian reform directly addresses the historical injustices by which farmers lost their access to land over the last 150 years (Borras, 2003), fundamentally tempers some of the glaring inequalities generated by market imperatives, meets a basic precondition of how the rurally marginalized can begin to improve their livelihoods, and thus address global poverty, and creates the basis by which human rights can be realized and social and economic conditions transformed in a pro-poor direction (James, 2007). Moreover, pro-poor gender-responsive redistributive agrarian reform can involve a plurality of social–property relations, including private and collective forms of property.

Indeed, a glaring aspect of the structural transformation in East Asia since the 1950s was a pro-poor redistributive agrarian reform that brought forth the incentives to maximize agricultural production among the very poorest strata of society, who did so in order to create the preconditions of a better life for their families (Studwell, 2013). At the same time, it is important to stress that in East Asia, pro-poor redistributive agrarian reform was about far more than land. Land reform, in the absence of a raft of additional measures that facilitate the capacity of petty commodity producers to increase their production, productivity and incomes, will not be beneficial to them because they also need access to inputs at prices they can afford, access to farm machinery, electricity and water at prices that are reasonable for them, credit at the right time and at the right price, and access to markets that pay prices that reflect their costs of production, and not the prices that are set in global markets. Thus, pro-poor gender-responsive redistributive agrarian reform requires a number of supportive measures that shape the operation of markets for farmers to improve the well-being of their families.

Recommended reading: Akram-Lodhi *et al.* (2007).

Making markets work for the rural poor

Neoclassical economists have a strong view of how the world should work, and have sought, through neoliberal policy reforms that have redefined the role of the state into one that enables markets, to make the world more closely mirror that view. Thus, since the early 1980s it has been a fundamental tenet of development policy among global institutions that freer markets produce the best possible outcome for both the producer and the consumer, and that this applies to rural areas just as much as it does urban ones. However, for the rural poor, living in a system of commodity-based production, neoclassical arguments are problematic, for four reasons (Akram-Lodhi, 2000). First, in many markets, the social identity of those conducting an exchange is essential to its terms and conditions, including the price (Evans, 1991). As a consequence, exchange is often not anonymous. A lack of anonymity may, however, limit the degree to which market transactions are voluntary; commerce may be forced (Bhaduri, 1986). Second, it is common for commodities and wider market conditions to not be as well understood by the buyer as they are by the seller. As a result, prices may fail to give adequate information to the buyer because of an asymmetrical distribution of information regarding the qualities of the product and its place within specific market conditions (Gerrard, 1989). Third, in light of asymmetrical information, it follows that in order for markets to operate, there is a need for non-market institutions to compensate for the uncertainty and bounded rationality arising out of asymmetrical information. Non-market institutions include the household, the community, the farm, the firm and the state, which thus become a necessary precondition of markets (Fourie, 1989). Finally, buying and selling in markets must be logically and temporally preceded by the production of the commodity (Sawyer, 1993). This also implies a role for non-market institutions – the firm or the farm, for example – that coordinate resource allocation in production. In short, markets are built upon non-market institutions that structure resource control and allocation. Thus, markets are embedded within wider social processes and relations (Polanyi, 1944).

The prevailing set of wider social processes and relations within which farming is embedded in Asia, Africa and Latin America are, of course, capitalist, as defined above. Thus, peasant petty commodity production is subordinated, through a range of mechanisms under the corporate food regime, to capitalist social–property relations (Akram-Lodhi and Kay, 2010). This effects how markets work because markets in capitalism are politically constructed institutions that support the interests of dominant classes at the expense of subordinate peasants and workers; markets do not 'work' for the poor. The operation of markets in capitalism is shaped by four factors (Mackintosh, 1990). The first factor is differences in wealth. Members of dominant classes, controlling disproportionately large shares of the means of production, use markets because it is in their material advantage to do so (Bernstein, 1996). The corollary of this is that when members of subordinate classes use markets, such markets will be organized to the material advantage of the dominant classes. Second, then, it is necessary to examine the ways in which dominant classes influence the operation of markets. In particular, members of dominant classes may use principal–agent relations to shape the available information, bounded rationality and uncertainty that is witnessed in markets, to their own advantage. Third, it is necessary to understand the central role played by merchant capital in markets, as it plays a critical intermediary role linking a structure of production relations with a structure of consumption relations, and in so doing is a central aspect of the food regime. Indeed, it is important to stress that merchant capital makes its money on the basis of the extent to which it controls markets, and this explains tendencies to concentration and centralization within markets (Kay, 1975). Finally, in that markets require non-market institutions to work, it is necessary to understand when the direct actions of non-market institutions such as firms or the state replace markets.

That rural markets are politically constructed in ways that disproportionately benefit the powerful in order to sustain and indeed enhance privilege is what results in, as a by-product of the process of accumulation, market imperatives facilitating the appropriation of land and other assets by dominant classes from peasants in the countryside. This process is not one that reduces inequality. Nor is it one that simply perpetuates inequality. It is one that creates and deepens inequality. Thus, for rural petty commodity-producing peasants in Asia, Africa and Latin America, markets are not the solution to their disadvantage; they are part of the problem.

Recommended reading: Mackintosh (1990).

Increasing agricultural productivity through agroecology

Farming has the potential capacity to produce food and non-food output and financial resources above its consumption, reproductive, rental and cultural requirements, and this 'agricultural surplus' is the foundation of improvements in well-being (Ghatak and Ingersent, 1984). A key need in addressing rural poverty and agrarian inequality is therefore sustained increases in agricultural surpluses. During the latter half of the 20th century, the development framework that sought to sustain increases in agricultural surpluses were the technological traps of the green and gene revolutions (Buckland, 2004), which facilitated the industrialization of agriculture (Weis, 2013). In the quest for sustained increases in agricultural surpluses, these must be forsaken, in favour of sustainable pro-poor gender-responsive biotechnological change.

Sustainable pro-poor gender-responsive biotechnological change is predicated upon maintaining rural environmental and natural resources. The sustenance of soil integrity, the use of appropriate quantities of water at the appropriate time, local seed varieties, sustainable cropping choices and patterns, and local and appropriate fertilizer, pest management and farm equipment technologies – all are central to sustainable biotechnological change in order to boost production, productivity, agricultural surpluses and incomes (Pretty, 2002). Where resources are degraded, sustainable pro-poor gender-responsive biotechnological change requires the restoration of those environmental and natural resources. In order to do this, indigenous knowledge needs to be shared, particularly through farmer-to-farmer networks, as has been done across Central America, East Africa and Brazil (Holt-Giménez, 2006). A necessary correlate of sustainable pro-poor gender-responsive biotechnological change in agriculture is the reassertion of agricultural research and extension as a public (not private) good, an end to the privatization of agricultural research and extension, and the re-establishment of publicly funded and disseminated agricultural research and extension that is not directed towards the rurally prosperous, as was the case in the past, but is instead directed towards meeting the livelihood challenges of the rurally marginalized (Akram-Lodhi, 2013).

A critical component of meeting the livelihood challenges of the rurally marginalized by enhancing their productivity and their production of surpluses is to facilitate the deepening and widening of farming practices rooted in agroecology (Altieri, 2009). This requires optimizing the sustainable use of low-impact local resources and minimizing the use of high-impact external farm technologies (Altieri, 1995). A correlate of such an agrarian strategy is that farm input and output choices, as well as local diets, need to be based, as they were for all but the last century or so, far more on local ecologies, landscapes and ecosystems, and not on the needs of distant external markets (Davis, 2000).

The benefits of agroecology for addressing issues of poverty and inequality are several. First, agroecological practices are far more employment-intensive than industrial agricultural practices, and as such meet a key challenge of the 21st century: creating jobs (McKay, 2012). These may not be the kinds of jobs that people would prefer to take, but for the underemployed relative surplus population such jobs are a vital part of the process by which their livelihoods are improved. As the East Asian case demonstrates, labour-intensive farming can increase rural incomes as structural transformation occurs (Studwell, 2013). Second, agroecological practices sustain soils and micronutrients, and in so doing not only maintain the integrity of the soil, but also sustain and indeed improve its productive potential. This is of critical importance, because built into agroecology must be the ongoing effort to not only sustain, but in fact increase crop yields by paying far closer attention to ecological requirements, input requirements, output choices, labour needs and the efficiency of energy production. One of the foundational myths of the corporate food regime is that industrial agriculture is required to feed the ever-growing population of the world (Conway, 2012). However, this is a myth. Granted, agro-ecological practices as they are currently constituted are not the dominant form of farm production around the world. However, copious scientific research from around the world indicates that agroecological production has the capacity to be as productive and profitable as industrial agriculture, and indeed once intertemporal environmental impacts are included in the assessment of the costs and benefits of alternative farm production systems, agroecological production has the capacity to be more productive and profitable than industrial agriculture while at the same time being both more labour-intensive and more climate-attentive (IAASTAD, 2009). For example, it has been recently estimated that if world consumption of meat were halved, the caloric 'savings' to food balance sheets would allow 2 billion more people to be fed (Cassidy et al., 2013). Agroecology is far more attuned to a nutrition-led farm production system than a market-led farm production system, and as such has the potential to supply the world, including those that are currently systemically food-insecure, with a nutritious diet that not only generates jobs, but also has far less impact on climate than the current industrial agriculture model. In other words, from the perspective of sustainable human well-being, labour-intensive high-productivity agroecological production is a necessary component of a 21st-century agriculture.

Recommended reading: IAASTAD (2009).

Building food sovereignty

A livelihood-enhancing, climate-friendly food system that does not exclude anyone from food requires the construction of a new food system: a system based upon food sovereignty (Akram-Lodhi, 2015b). As developed initially by Vía Campesina and further elaborated at the 2007 Nyéléni Forum for Food Sovereignty (Declaration of Nyéléni, 2007), food sovereignty is based on the right of peoples and coun-tries to define their own agricultural and food policy, and has five interlinked and inseparable components:

1. A focus on food for people: food sovereignty puts the right to sufficient, healthy and culturally-appropriate food for all individuals, peoples and com-munities at the center of food, agriculture, livestock and fisheries policies and rejects the proposition that food is just another commodity.
2. The valuing of food providers: food sovereignty values and supports the con-tributions, and respects the rights, of women and men who grow, harvest and process food and rejects those policies, actions and programmes that undervalue them and threaten their livelihoods.

3. Localizes food systems: food sovereignty puts food providers and food consumers at the centre of decision-making on food issues; protects providers from the dumping of food in local markets; protects consumers from poor quality and unhealthy food, including food tainted with transgenic organisms; and rejects governance structures that depend on inequitable international trade and gives power to corporations. It places control over territory, land, grazing, water, seeds, livestock and fish populations with local food providers and respects their rights to use and share them in socially and environmentally sustainable ways; it promotes positive interaction between food providers in different territories and from different sectors that helps resolve conflicts; and rejects the privatization of natural resources through laws, commercial contracts and intellectual property rights regimes.

4. Builds knowledge and skills: food sovereignty builds on the skills and local knowledge of food providers and their local organizations that conserve, develop and manage localized food production and harvesting systems, developing appropriate research systems to support this, and rejects technologies that undermine these.

5. Works with nature: food sovereignty uses the contributions of nature in diverse, low external input agroecological production and harvesting methods that maximize the contribution of ecosystems and improve resilience, and rejects methods that harm ecosystem functions, that depend on energy-intensive monocultures and livestock factories, and other industrialised production methods.

Food sovereignty thus offers a practice that is an alternative to the corporate food regime, with its proponents arguing that the food system needs to be predicated upon a decentralized agriculture, where production, processing, distribution and consumption are controlled by communities. In order to do this, food sovereignty requires challenging the class power that is expressed in and through the corporate food regime by constructing a broad democratic alliance of peasants, smallholders, fishers, indigenous peoples, urban workers and underserved food communities that are prepared to confront the power of capital in the food system by fostering alternative modes of organizing production and consumption in ways that contain elements of de-commodification and the re-regulation of markets on the basis of public need. The movement for food sovereignty is thus one that seeks to resolve the agrarian question through an agrarian transition to a new food regime.

Recommended reading: Akram-Lodhi (2015b).

Towards agrarian citizenship

This contribution has situated contemporary agrarian questions within the corporate food regime, and has suggested that for critical rural development studies, there are five key issues that need to addressed. These issues are: the reality of rural poverty and inequality; the need for a pro-poor gender-responsive redistributive agrarian reform; a recognition that markets, as institutions in which power and privilege can be expressed and reinforced, do not meet the needs of the poor; that the basis by which agricultural productivity can be increased is surplus-generating agroecological farming directed towards localized food systems; and that, cumulatively, these represent movements towards food sovereignty.

Food sovereignty challenges the corporate food regime by offering an alternative that resolves the agrarian question through the construction of a new 'common sense' around food production and food consumption, which would elaborate shared identities and common interests, and thus achieve what Hannah Wittman (2009) calls 'agrarian citizenship'. Agrarian citizenship is where the political and material rights and practices of rural dwellers are not solely based on issues of rural political representation, but also on their relationship with the socioecological metabolism between society and nature, defining society to include not only female and male food providers, but also food consumers. Agrarian citizenship recognizes nature's role in the continuing political, economic and cultural evolution of a broadly defined and evolving agrarian society, being predicated upon transcending the metabolic rift between humans and nature, and thus allowing agrarian and non-agrarian citizens to fully claim their individual and collective rights by establishing notions of democracy rooted in democratic economies, social and ecological justice, and the need for harmony between humans and nature.

References

Akram-Lodhi, A.H. (2000). 'A bitter pill? Peasants and sugarcane markets in northern Pakistan'. *European Journal of Development Research*, 12(1): 206–28.

Akram-Lodhi, A.H. (2007). 'Land, markets and neoliberal enclosure: an agrarian political economy perspective'. *Third World Quarterly*, 28(8): 1437–56.

Akram-Lodhi, A.H. (2012). 'Contextualising land grabbing: contemporary land deals, the global subsistence crisis and the world food system'. *Canadian Journal of Development Studies*, 33(2): 119–42.

Akram-Lodhi, A.H. (2013). *Hungry for Change: Farmers, Food Justice and the Agrarian Question*. Halifax: Fernwood.

Akram-Lodhi, A.H. (2015a). 'Land grabs, the agrarian question and the corporate food regime'. *Canadian Food Studies*, 2(2): 233–41.

Akram-Lodhi, A.H. (2015b). 'Accelerating towards food sovereignty'. *Third World Quarterly*, 36(3): 563–83.

Akram-Lodhi, A.H. and Kay, C. (2010). 'Surveying the agrarian question (part 2): current debates and beyond'. *Journal of Peasant Studies*, 37(2): 255–84.

Akram-Lodhi, A.H. and Kay, C. (2016). 'Back to the future? Marx, modes of production and the agrarian question'. In B.B. Mohanty (ed.), *Critical Perspectives on Agrarian Transition: India in the Global Debate*. London: Routledge, pp. 43–66.

Akram-Lodhi, A.H., Borras, S.M. and Kay, C. (eds) (2007). *Land, Labour and Livelihoods in an Era of Globalization: Perspectives from Developing and Transition Countries*. London: Routledge.

Altieri, M. (1995). *Agroecology: The Science of Sustainable Agriculture*, 2nd edition. Boulder, CO: Westview Press.

Altieri, M. (2009). 'Agroecology, small farms and food sovereignty'. *Monthly Review*, 61(3): 102–13.

Bernstein, H. (1996). 'The political economy of the maize *filière*'. In H. Bernstein (ed.), *The Agrarian Question in South Africa*. London: Frank Cass, pp. 120–45.

Bernstein, H. (2016). 'Agrarian political economy and modern world capitalism: the contributions of food regime analysis'. *Journal of Peasant Studies*, 43(3): 611–47.

Bhaduri, A. (1986). 'Forced commerce and agrarian growth'. *World Development*, 14(2): 267–72.

Borras, S.M. (2003). 'Questioning market-led agrarian reform: experiences from Brazil, Colombia and South Africa'. *Journal of Agrarian Change*, 3(3): 367–94.

Borras, S.M. (2005). 'Can redistributive reform be achieved via market-based voluntary land transfer schemes? Evidence and lessons from the Philippines'. *Journal of Development Studies*, 41(1): 90–134.

Buckland, J. (2004). *Ploughing Up The Farm: Neoliberalism, Modern Technology and the State of the World's Farmers*. Halifax: Fernwood.

Byres, T.J. (1996). *Capitalism from Above and Capitalism from Below*. London: Macmillan.

Cassidy, E.S., West, P.C., Gerber, J.S. and Foley, J.A. (2013). 'Redefining agricultural yields: from tonnes to people nourished per hectare'. *Environmental Research Letters*, 8(3): 1–9.

Conway, G. (2012). *One Billion Hungry: Can We Feed The World?* Ithaca, NY: Cornell University Press.

Cotula, L., Oya, C., Codjoe, E.A., Eid, A., Kakraba-Ampeh, M. and Keeley, J. (2014). 'Testing claims about large land deals in Africa: findings from a multi-country study'. *Journal of Development Studies*, 50(7): 903–25.

Davis, M. (2000). *Late Victorian Holocausts: El Niño Famines and the Making of the Third World*. London: Verso.

Declaration of Nyéléni (2007). 'Declaration of the Forum for Food Sovereignty, Nyéléni 2007'. Available at: http://nyeleni.org/spip.php?article290.

Delgado Wise, R. and Veltmeyer, H. (2016). *Agrarian Change, Migration and Development*. Halifax: Fernwood.

Erikson, L. and Vollrath, D. (2004). 'Dimensions of land inequality and economic development'. *IMF Working Papers* WP/04/158. Available at: www.imf.org/external/pubs/ft/wp/2004/wp04158.pdf.

Evans, A. (1991). 'Gender issues in rural household economics'. *Institute of Development Studies Bulletin*, 22: 51–9.

Fourie, F.C.V.N. (1989). 'The nature of firms and markets: do transactions approaches help?' *South African Journal of Economics*, 57(2): 142–60.

Fridell, G. and Konings, M. (eds) (2013). *Age of Icons: Exploring Philanthrocapitalism in the Contemporary World*. Toronto: University of Toronto Press.

Friedmann, H. and McMichael, P. (1989). 'Agriculture and the state system: the rise and fall of national agricultures 1870 to the present'. *Sociologia Ruralis*, 29(2): 93–117.

Gerrard, W. (1989). *Theory of the Capitalist Economy: Towards a Post-Classical Synthesis*. Oxford: Basil Blackwell.

Ghatak, S. and Ingersent, K. (1984). *Agriculture and Economic Development*. London: Wheatsheaf.

Graeber, D. (2011). *Debt: The First 5,000 Years*. Brooklyn, NY: Melville House.

Hall, D. (2013). 'Primitive accumulation, accumulation by dispossession and the global land grab'. *Third World Quarterly*, 34(9): 1582–604.

Harvey, D. (2003). *The New Imperialism*. New York: Oxford University.

Holt-Giménez, E. (2006). *Campesino a Campesino: Voices from Latin America's Farmer to Farmer Movement*. Oakland, CA: Food First.

Holt-Giménez, E. and Shattuck, A. (2011). 'Food crises, food regimes and food movements: rumblings of reform or tides of transformation?' *Journal of Peasant Studies*, 38(1): 109–44.

IAASTAD (2009). *Agriculture at a Crossroads: Synthesis Report*. Available at: www.unep. org/dewa/agassessment/reports/IAASTD/EN/Agriculture%20at%20a%20Crossroads_ Synthesis%20Report%20(English).pdf.

IFAD (2010). *Rural Poverty Report 2011*. Available at: www.ifad.org/documents/10180/ c47f2607-3fb9-4736-8e6a-a7ccf3dc7c5b.

James, D. (2007). *Gaining Ground? Rights and Property in South African Land Reform*. New York: Routledge.

Kay, G. (1975). *Development and Underdevelopment: A Marxist Analysis*. London: Macmillan.

Mackintosh, M. (1990). 'Abstract markets and real needs'. In H. Bernstein, B. Crow, M. Mackintosh and C. Martin (eds) (1990). *The Food Question: Profits versus People?* London: Earthscan, pp. 45–53.

Marx, K. (1976 [1867]). *Capital, Vol. 1*. Harmondsworth, UK: Penguin Books.

McKay, B. (2012). 'A socially-inclusive pathway to food security: the agroecological alternative'. International Policy Center for Inclusive Growth Policy Research Brief No. 23. Available at: www.ipc-undp.org/pub/IPCPolicyResearchBrief23.pdf.

McMichael, P. (2013). *Food Regimes and Agrarian Questions*. Halifax: Fernwood.

Pender, J. and Hazell, P. (2000). 'Promoting sustainable development in less-favored areas: overview'. In J. Pender and P. Hazell (eds), *Promoting Sustainable Development in Less-Favored Areas*. Washington, DC: International Food Policy Research Institute.

Polanyi, K. (1944). *The Great Transformation: The Political and Economic Origins of Our Times*. Boston, MA: Beacon Hill Press.

Pretty, J. (2002). *Agri-Culture: Reconnecting People, Land and Nature*. London: Earthscan.

Sawyer, M. (1993). 'The nature and role of the market'. In C. Pitelis (ed.), *Transactions Costs, Markets and Hierarchies*. Oxford: Basil Blackwell, pp. 20–40.

Studwell, J. (2013). *How Asia Works: Success and Failure in the World's Most Dynamic Region*. New York: Grove Press.

Vollrath, D. (2007). 'Land distribution and international agricultural productivity'. *American Journal of Agricultural Economics*, 89(1): 202–16.

Weis, T. (2013). *The Ecological Hoofprint: The Global Burden of Industrial Livestock*. London: Zed Books.

Wittman, H. (2009). 'Reworking the metabolic rift: La Vía Campesina, agrarian citizenship and food sovereignty'. *Journal of Peasant Studies*, 36(4): 805–26.

Wood, E.M. (2009). 'Peasants and the market imperative: the origins of capitalism'. In A.H. Akram-Lodhi and C. Kay (eds), *Peasants and Globalization: Political Economy, Rural Transformation and the Agrarian Question*. London: Routledge, pp. 37–56.

World Bank (2007). *World Development Report 2008: Agriculture for Development*. New York: Oxford University Press.

World Bank (2009). *Kenya Poverty and Inequality Assessment Volume I: Synthesis Report*. Africa Region Poverty Reduction and Economic Management Unit Report No 44190-KE. Available at: http://documents.worldbank.org/curated/en/2009/04/10842664/kenya-poverty-inequality-assessment-executive-summary-synthesis-report.

World Bank (2011). *World Development Report 2012: Gender Equality and Development*. Washington, DC: World Bank.

World Bank (2014). 'For up to 800 million rural poor, a strong World Bank commitment to agriculture'. Available at: www.worldbank.org/en/news/feature/2014/11/12/for-up-to-800-million-rural-poor-a-strong-world-bank-commitment-to-agriculture.

25

THE MIGRATION–DEVELOPMENT NEXUS

Raúl Delgado Wise

Between 1970 and 2012, the number of international migrants worldwide more than doubled from 84 million to 232 million. In 1970, about one out of every 29 people worldwide lived in a country where international migrants composed a tenth or more of the total population. Four decades later, the ratio was nearly one in nine (Terrazas, 2011: 1). Much of this growth took the form of mass migration from poor countries in the Global South on the periphery of the world capitalist system to the wealthier countries in the Global North. While in earlier periods of capitalist development people migrated for economic reasons, motivated by a desire for a better life and a search for more opportunity, the largest flow of migrant labour was from the European centre of world capitalism to European 'white' settlements in the North American outposts of the British Empire. But in the most recent current conjuncture of capitalist development (the neoliberal era), most migration has been in a South–North and South–South direction. Within the migrant-receiving countries in the North, these migrants generally settled in the larger cities, urban gateways to an apparently modern style of life and hoped-for economic opportunity.

Types of migrants

The literature places migrants into three basic categories: *economic* – including a large stream of individuals in search for a better way of life and greater economic opportunities, and those seeking refuge from poverty or oppressive socioeconomic conditions; *environmental refugees* – those seeking to escape environmental degradation and natural disaster: drought, floods, climate change, etc.; and *political refugees* – those seeking to escape conditions of political conflict, insecurity, persecution or oppression.

In contrast with the vast literature on international migration, studies on internal migration have been relegated to second place, particularly in the realm of contemporary capitalism, namely neoliberal globalization. But it should be understood that in this context, there are close links between internal and international migration. The number of internal (mostly rural–urban) migrants have been estimated at 750 million (IOM, 2014), which, together with international migrants, add up to nearly 1 billion. Considering that most migrants are labour migrants, nearly one of every three workers in the world lives in a place different from where they were born. In most cases, they constitute a highly vulnerable segment of the working class, often subjected to discrimination and conditions of super-exploitation.

As for the economic category of migrants, the literature divides them into two groups or streams: those who choose to migrate in the search for better economic conditions and those who we might term 'economic refugees', driven to migrate from their communities and way of life by extreme poverty, conditions such as deprivation, social exclusion and lack of economic opportunity that they need or seek to escape. In this context, the decision to migrate, often at great personal cost to the migrant, requiring or leading to the break-up of the family as a social unit, is explained in terms of some hierarchical combination of push and pull factors relating to either the economic structure of society or the development process. However, while the search for economic opportunities exert a powerful pull, there is little question that the vast majority of economic migrants and migrant workers migrate not by choice, but in response to and the search to escape limiting or oppressive conditions created by the workings of the capitalism, and particularly, in their home countries, as a result of the upsurge of uneven development.

Migration from a political economy perspective

While a majority of migration scholars might cite the desire and intent to escape poverty, or relative disparities in the economic development of migrant-sending and -receiving countries, as an explanation of the motivation or drive to migrate they do not blame capitalism (the forces of capitalist development) for this poverty. In fact, they see capitalism as the solution.

In this regard, we note that there is little question and few studies about the system dynamics of migrant labour – the dominant role of capitalism in generating the forces that lead to, and therefore can be used to explain, the massive flows of international migrants in the world today. But you would not know this in reading the vast volume of writings in the mainstream tradition of migration studies. In these studies, conducted predominantly by economists, anthropologists and sociologists in the liberal tradition of neoclassical economics, the concern is almost entirely with the motivations of migrants who are assumed to freely choose to migrate. The structural conditions and system dynamics underlying these decisions that, in a very real sense, condition and even in a sense force these individuals, and sometimes entire families, to migrate are left unexplored. The issue here is free choice or forced migration. Do these migrants have a choice? What are their options?

Regardless of one's perspective on this issue, the fundamental concern in the social scientific study of migration is to explain the strategic and structural conditions that drive the decisions of individuals and families to migrate – namely, its root causes – and the consequences of these decisions for the migrants themselves, as well as the societies of origin, transit and destination.

From a political economy (or Marxist) perspective, the focus of migration and development analysis is on what might be described as the labour migration dynamics of the capitalist development process, or the migration–development nexus. At issue in this development process – the development of society's forces of production and corresponding social relations – is the capital–labour relation, which constitutes the economic base of the social structure in all capitalist societies, as well as the structure formed by a global division in the wealth of nations. The first has to do with two basic social classes: the capitalist class, membership in which can be defined in terms of a relation of property in the means of production; and the working class, whose labour power is the fundamental source of value – the value of commodities that are bought and sold on the market, and which can be measured in terms of hours of work under given social and technological conditions – and surplus value or profit, the driving force of capitalist development.

Marx's theory of capitalist development, which remains a most useful tool for decoding the structural dynamics of the capitalist system in its evolution and development of the forces of production, is constructed around four fundamental propositions: (i) that labour is the source of value (the labour theory of value); (ii) that wage labour is a hidden mechanism of economic exploitation (extraction of surplus value from the direct producer or worker, by paying workers less than the actual or total value produced); (iii) that capitalism has an inherent propensity towards crisis; and (iv) what Marx described as 'the general law of capital accumulation', which specifies a twofold tendency: on the one hand, towards the centralization and concentration of capital, and, on the other, towards the 'multiplication of the proletariat' – the transformation of a class of small landholding agricultural producers (family or peasant farmers) into a proletariat of wage labourers and an industrial reserve army of surplus rural and urban labour.

Recommended reading: Delgado Wise and Veltmeyer (2016).

Rethinking migration in the neoliberal era

There are five basic theoretical and methodological approaches to understanding the migration–development nexus, each associated with a theory regarding the development dynamics of migration: (i) Positivism, used by many migration economists, but can be traced back to the sociologist Emile Durkheim. It is to search for and establish a correlation between the decisions made and actions taken by individual migrants and the objectively given conditions of these decisions and actions. (ii) Constructivism, used by many sociologists, seeks to incorporate and take into account subjective factors such as motivation and social awareness (subjective interpretations by individuals of their own reality), which is manifest not in theoretical or political discourse, but in the migrant's own words and thoughts in the discourse of migrants given or speaking in their own voice. (iii) Orthodox neoclassical theory of international trade, concerned about and focused on the free or (regulated) movement of capital and labour, as well as goods and services, across national boundaries. (iv) A women-centred or gendered approach to understanding and analysing the dynamics of migration is focused on the gender dimensions of migration.[1] (v) A Marxist political economy approach, concerned with the structural dynamics of labour migration in the capitalist development process (i.e. the evolution of capitalism as an economic and social system).

Recommended reading: Delgado Wise and Veltmeyer (2016).

Internal migration dynamics

In structural terms, the development process of long-term change in the evolution of large-scale societies has been conceptualized and periodized in terms of three alternative metatheories, each with its own historical narrative. One of these metatheories/narratives concerns the transformation of an agriculture-based economy and agrarian society into a modern industrial system via a process of industrialization. In the process of this transformation, it is possible to place countries in three categories of evolutionary development: pre-industrial, industrializing and industrialized. In this categorization, it is assumed that progress or improvements in the human or social condition achieved by a society can be measured in terms of 'economic growth' or the rate of annual increases in the country's total output of goods and services (the GDP), and that this progress is commensurate with an evolutionary process of productive transformation (i.e. change in the structure of economic production).

A second metatheory of long-term social change views the process in terms of a transformation in the structure of the values that underpin the institutional structure of the social system. In these terms, the evolution of the system, or the transformation of one into another, is viewed as a transition from a traditional type of social system (oriented towards traditional values such as communalism in which individuals are subordinated to the community of which they are a part at the level of mutual obligation) towards a modern system in which individuals are free to choose and 'achieve' their position rather than have it ascribed to them by 'society'. In this evolutionary process, societies can be characterized as traditional, modernizing or modern.

The third metatheory of long-term change, which provides another window into the process of long-term progressive change, is that of capitalist development (the transformation of a pre-capitalist society and economy into a capitalist system). In this conception, the fundamental change in the structure of society is the consequence of a process of social change – transformation of a society of small-scale agricultural producers ('peasants' in the lexicon of agrarian studies) into a proletariat, a class defined by its situation of being dispossessed from the land and their means of production, and thereby compelled to exchange labour power for a living wage.

These three metatheories of long-term social change and development – *industrialization*, *modernization* and *proletarianization* – might well be understood as three different facets or dimensions of the same process – the transformation of a pre-capitalist, traditional and agrarian society into a modern industrial capitalist system, a process that has taken several centuries to unfold and is still unfolding in different parts of the Global South. In the Global North, according to this theory, the process has been virtually completed or was completed sometime in the 1980s, if not before, leading to the formation or construction of a postmodern, post-industrial and post-capitalist society. In the Global South, it is argued, societies for the most part are either underdeveloped or undeveloped, in need of 'assistance' in making or completing the transition towards a modern economy and society.

However, there are other scholars who see the process of productive and social transformation not as a continuum or in linear evolutionary terms, but as discontinuous and dependent on the position of a country in an international division of labour or the structure of international relations within the global economy.

From a modernization theory perspective, the level of economic development achieved by a country, and its rate of economic growth, depends on the ability of the country to overcome obstacles such as an orientation towards traditional values, the absence or weakness of an appropriate institutional framework, or the lack of individuals with an entrepreneurial bent and access to both capital and modern technology. The economists behind the 2008 *World Development Report*, which focuses on the role of agriculture in the economic development process, take this view, as do the agrarian economists who have argued (and continue to argue) the inevitable passing of the small landholding 'peasant' or family farmer – the 'peasantry' in a underdeveloped country context – as an agent and agency of economic production.

The agrarian question: farewell to the peasantry?

The forces of change – primarily industrialization, modernization and proletarianization – that operated on underdeveloped societies in the 1960s and 1970s, by a number of accounts and diverse theoretical perspectives brought about the partial transformation of a society of small-landholding agricultural producers or peasant farmers into a working class. This process was theorized in various ways. Marxist scholars theoretically reconstructed capitalist development as an initial process of 'primitive accumulation' (the separation of the direct producer from the land and other means of production) followed by a process of 'proletarianization' (the conversion of the resulting surplus population into a working class). However, non-Marxist scholars, operating with an alternative theory of capitalist modernization, analysed the same dynamics using a different discourse and different lens, but in a not altogether different way, by making reference to a process that would lead to the disappearance of the peasantry as an economic agent, and thus as a category of analysis.

In the 1970s, this view of structural change, shared by both Marxist and non-Marxist scholars, gave way to a heated debate between 'proletarianists', adherents of Marx's thesis regarding the transformation of the direct agricultural producers into a working class, and the 'peasantists' or populists who argued that the forces of capitalist development and social change were not immutable, and that the resilience and resistance of peasants could defuse or derail these forces, allowing for the survival of the peasantry and the sustainability of their rural livelihoods.[2]

After a hiatus of some years – a decade and a half of neoliberal reform – this debate was renewed in a study of the 'new rurality' (conditions in rural society in an era of globalization), as well as the dynamic forces of resistance against the neoliberal agenda mounted by the landless workers, the indigenous communities and peasant or small producer organizations in the 1990s. Although according to several accounts this wave of active resistance has abated, the debate continues, with some arguing the inevitability of a trend towards the disappearance of the peasantry, and others arguing very much the contrary.

Recommended reading: Delgado Wise and Veltmeyer (2016), Otero (1999).

Development pathways out of rural poverty

As already mentioned, the World Bank (2008) reformulated the modernization theory that had dominated mainstream development and development studies from the 1950s on. This report, the first of its annual report on the state of development that was dedicated to 'agriculture for development', elaborated on the development strategy that it used to guide development practice since the mid-1970s when it described the war on global poverty. The strategy basically was to encourage the 'rural poor' (its conception of the peasants separated from the land) to take one or both of the development pathways out of rural poverty, namely migration and labour. As the economists at the Bank conceived of it, development entails a protracted but incessant process of structural change (modernization and industrialization) that brings about conditions for economic growth and an improvement in the social condition of the population. At issue is a process of productive and social transformation (modernization and urbanization, rather than industrialization), which paves the way out of poverty for the rural poor.

In a more nuanced and sociological variation on this way of thinking and strategy, in their study on rural poverty in Latin America, De Janvry and Sadoulet (2000) identified four strategies for getting out of poverty: (i) an exit strategy; (ii) an agricultural strategy; (iii) a pluriactive strategy (a mix of agriculture and wage labour); and (iv) a development assistance strategy. They conclude that approaches and programmes that are participatory in form seek to identify the needs of the rural poor in order to better target development programmes that assist the poor in their strategy of choice (p. 408). According to the WDR-08, for which De Janvry served as the lead author, there are three fundamental development pathways out of rural poverty, each involving an adjustment to the forces of change operating on the poor: *farming, labour* and *migration*.

As for farming or agriculture, it turns out that it provides an avenue of mobility or pathway out of poverty for very few, in that it requires peasants to become other than they are, a major transformation of the peasantry or small landowning family farmers into agro-capitalists, or entrepreneurs or capitalists, in order to access credit, markets and technology, and to mobilize the available productive resources. The driving force behind this social transformation is capitalist development of agriculture, which entails both a concentration of landholding and a technological conversion of production based on a significant increase in the rate of productive investment (in modernizing or upgrading production technology). The pressures on farming to increase the productivity of agricultural labour via technological upgrading or modernization (increasing the capital intensity of production) are immense.

Agricultural activity or farming under these conditions is clearly not an option for the vast majority of peasants, who are therefore encouraged, if not compelled, to abandon agriculture, and for many also the countryside, in order to migrate in the search for better opportunities for self-advancement or more productive economic activity. In this situation, there are essentially two pathways out of poverty (excluding resistance). One of them is through labour (to work off farm for wages) – a strategy that by many accounts large numbers of the rural poor are already pursuing. If the statistics on rural household incomes are any indication, over 50 per cent of rural householders acquire over half of their income from non-farming activities, i.e. off-farm wage labour (Kay, 2009).

The other pathway out of poverty is migration, one that by numerous other accounts many of the rural poor have opted for by migrating either to the urban centre or cities in the country or further abroad. The theory behind this development is that the countryside constitutes a massive reservoir of surplus labour, pushing the rural poor off the farms, and that the greater opportunity for wage-remunerated labour in the cities would attract and pull the displaced rural proletariat into the cities, absorbing them into the labour-force of an expanding capitalist nucleus of urban-based industry.

The theory behind this development took various forms but was constructed as a development model by Sir Arthur Lewis. However, research into the dynamics of this rural-to-urban migratory process suggests – and later studies have confirmed – that the outcome of the forces of change and development did not confirm this theory. For one thing, in the 1980s, the nucleus of capitalist industry did not expand, thus generating an enormous supply of migrant labour surplus to the absorptive capacity of the urban labour market, leading to the growth instead of a burgeoning informal sector of unregulated or unstructured economic activity – essentially, work not for wages in industrial plants, factories and offices, but working on one's own account in the streets. It has been estimated (Klein and Tokman, 2000) that in the 1980s and into the 1990s, at least 80 per cent of new employment opportunities and jobs created in the growing urban economies were generated in the 'informal sector', which in many underdeveloped countries in Latin America and Asia by the 1990s constituted around 40 per cent of the urban economic population (Davis, 2006).

Recommended reading: Bernstein (2012), Davis (2006), Otero (1999).

The migration–development nexus: dynamics of international migration

There are three principal themes of this chapter. First, as had been noted by Robin Cohen (1987) in his study of *The New Helots*, many migrant workers today are still locked into forms of labour exploitation that marked the birth of global capitalism. Second, also emphasized by Cohen, employer demand for cheap and often illegal forms of labour has not abated despite the spread of a fundamentalist and rather dogmatic utopian belief in capitalism with unregulated market forces – that under free-market capitalism, economic opportunities for self-advancement are available to everyone. Whether manufacturing is exported to low-wage areas or migrants are imported to work in metropolitan service sectors, the distinctions between established workers, privileged foreigners and helot labourers have remained and by some accounts have even deepened (see Cohen, 1987: Chapter 6). Third, politicians in migrant-importing states have been zealous in trying to police or militarize their frontiers in the name of 'national security' as a strategy not only to prevent economic migrants from flooding the labour market and legal migrants from 'masquerading' as political refugees in order to take advantage of social welfare programmes and free public education, but mainly to 'justify' the permanent violation of migrants' human and labour rights, the diminishment of labour costs, and the implementation of policies designed to regulate the flow of labour migrants as per the requirements of the labour market. This strategy has been labelled in the literature as 'migration management' (Delgado Wise *et al.*, 2013). In the case of the United States, the destination point of millions of migrants from Mexico, Central and South America, the migration management approach has been quite successful in jumping the queue ahead of legal migrants in order to gain increased profits and fiscal gains for both employers and the host local and federal government. Moreover, as Geiger and Pecoud argue:

> Many measures to stop unauthorized migration or to prevent refugees to claim asylum are . . . presented as *necessary* to fight human smuggling and trafficking . . . This victimhood approach seems to have replaced any kind of binding commitments to safeguard migrants' rights
>
> *(Geiger and Pécoud, 2010: 13)*

Recommended reading: Delgado Wise *et al.* (2013).

Dynamics of the international migrant labour market

One of the main engines of capitalist development is cheap labour. The cost of labour, reflected in variable yet 'structured' wage rates in different countries, can be affected by government intervention and tax policies, but in the global economy to an important degree it reflects the impact of a corporate-driven strategy regarding the global supply and demand of labour. Thus, capitalist employers are often in a position to take full advantage of the massive oversupply of labour relative to demand, which is reflected in growing levels of unemployment the world over. But given the role assigned to global labour arbitrage, expansion of the global reserve army of labour has occurred most dramatically in the Global South, where 73 per cent of this 'reserve army' for the global labour market or workforce can be found (Ghose *et al.*, 2008).

Migrant workers are useful as part of the reserve army of labour because they can be easily expelled when no longer needed. And the use of migrant workers also allows the receiver country to externalize the costs of renewing the labour-force. The state uses migrant workers to fill gaps in the labour market and create pressures for downloading wages but did not have to pay for the production and reproduction costs of this labour.

The size of this global reserve army of labour is dialectically related to the prevalence of low wages, a long-term trend towards the relative reduction in the value of labour power (the purchasing power of the wage) and a chronic undersupply of 'decent' employment that characterizes contemporary capitalism. Under these conditions, a global oversupply of labour has resulted in a scaling down of the global wage structure and an increase in the overall labour and job insecurity. For example, according to ILO estimates, the number of workers in conditions of labour insecurity rose to 1.5 billion in 2010 – encompassing more than half of the world's labour-force – with 630 million receiving a wage of less than US$2 per day, and nearly half of those finding themselves in situations of extreme poverty (ILO, 2011). At the same time, the number of unemployed both in the North and South continues to rise, leading to class conflict over austerity measures in the North and growing pressures to emigrate in the South.

Under the Washington Consensus regarding the virtues of free-market capitalism (neoliberal 'structural reform' in public policy), labour markets have been restructured and the working class reconfigured in the following ways: (i) the transformation of the small-scale agricultural producers and peasant farmers into a global proletariat and working class available to global networks of monopoly capital as an industrial reserve army and a supply of abundant cheap labour; and (ii) the covert proletarianization of the highly qualified scientific and technological worker, and a consequent South–North brain drain.

Recommended reading: Delgado Wise *et al.* (2013).

The neoliberal policy dynamics of the migration–development nexus

The great paradox of the migration–development agenda is that it leaves the principles that underpin neoliberal globalization intact and does not affect the specific way in which neoliberal policies are applied in migrant-sending countries, and does not address the fundamental issues of development such as the need to address: (i) the negative impacts of migration on the migrants and their families – the human rights and human security concerns underlying contemporary migration – and, more importantly, (ii) the root causes of forced migration, i.e. the urgent necessity to reduce the growing asymmetries that exist between sending and receiving countries that are at the core of the capitalist trend towards uneven development; (iii) the development implications of migrant remittances; and (iv) the development implications of a North–South 'brain drain'.

Migrant remittances and development

In the 1980s, several empirical studies in the central-west region of Mexico argued that migrant remittances had a negative effect in communities of origin, leading to social differentiation, land price inflation and the accumulation of local resources into the hands of a given few (see, for example, Stuart and Kearney, 1981). Subsequent studies in the 1990s, however, argued that the remittances did indeed have a productive role. The results of these studies indicated that remittances were invested in agricultural and human capital, and that the circulation of money not only provided families with subsistence funds, but the provision of investment funds had played a positive role in the development of local, municipal and regional economies. Some authors (e.g. Durand, 1994) argued that these investments had a substantial impact on specific sectors and localities, while others (Massey and Parrado, 1998: 18) argued that international migration via collective remittances had a broader development impact as a 'source of production capital' (the financing of productive investments and social infrastructure) and as a 'dynamic force that promotes entrepreneurial activity, the founding of businesses and economic expansion' in high-migration areas where public and private investment are negligible (Goldring, 1996). On the other hand, Canales (2011) among others argues that the economic impact attributed to remittances is totally disproportionate: the growth of the GDP through the multiplying effect of remittances is only 0.47 per cent and the elasticity of the GDP with regard to remittances is 0.036. As for the presumed impact of remittances on the poverty rate, according to Caneles, it is in the order of 1.3 percentage points, the same as the impact of remittances in reducing inequality (regarding the Gini index).

Development dynamics of the South–North 'brain drain'

Many scholars in the mainstream of migration studies agree that emigration modestly raises the wages of workers who remain behind in the countries of origin, but since it turns out that many migrants originate from the better-educated social strata of their home countries, it may also raise the cost of the goods and services produced by these workers. As a result, some researchers argue that migration results in a loss of workers whose skills and expertise are already scarce in their countries of origin – popularly known as a 'brain drain' (Bhagwati and Dellalfar, 1973). Most of the discussion on this issue, from as early as the late 1960s by researchers associated with or commissioned by UNCTAD, have focused on technically skilled workers such as medical professionals, engineers and computer programmers – and, of course, university researchers and faculty.

More recently, the earlier interest in the issue of a 'brain drain', which implies a benefit to the North and a cost to the South has been rekindled by a research programme initiated by the World Bank focused on the dynamics of international migration and development. The programme had its first major publication in 2006 – a study that examined the determinants and impact of migration and remittances in several underdeveloped countries, but also explored various aspects of the 'brain drain'. Indeed, the study 'has provided the most extensive brain drain database ever produced and has since become the reference in this area' (Bourguignon, 2007). However, what Bourguignon fails to note is that the research generated on the basis of this data has been predominantly to negate the 'brain drain' literature and provide a more optimistic perspective on the issue by viewing through the lens of a two-way development process and the notion of a 'brain gain' – that underdeveloped countries in the Global South benefit from a process of 'brain circulation'. However, most studies and recent literature on this question have led to the opposite conclusion. In cases where migrants have been educated at public cost in their country of origin – and this would seem to be in almost all cases – concerns have arisen that emigration of highly skilled and qualified labour represents a serious loss for the migrant-sending country – a massive 'brain drain' (Albo and Ordaz Díaz, 2011).

Some idea of the scale and magnitude of this problem for underdeveloped countries can be gleaned from the data provided by FLACSO Ecuador for different countries not only in the Andes, but the Caribbean, which continues to experience the highest rates of outmigration for all countries by migrants with a tertiary level of education – over 50 per cent in many cases (Carrington and Detragiache, 1998).

According to this migration database, 25 per cent of all Colombian migrants to the US from 2006 to 2010 possessed a university degree – up from 22.4 per cent in 2000 (*Andina Migrante*, 2012). This migration pattern is reflected in OECD data that show that up to 72 per cent of Colombian migrants living in the US had either secondary or tertiary education, and of these 28 per cent had completed a programme of university or advanced technical studies. Colombia in this respect is not typical, but nor is it unique. For example, in 2010, over 80 per cent of Peruvian immigrants to the US possessed some level of secondary or university education, and 15.3 per cent were university-educated. Studies by Lozano and Gandini (2012) show a similar pattern for Mexico.

In the Caribbean, the situation is worse – even dire. For example, according to World Bank data, 77 per cent of emigrants from Guyana possessed a university education, while nine other countries in the English-speaking Caribbean had a similar proportion of university-educated emigrants – 89.9 per cent in the case of Surinam, 82.5 per cent in Jamaica, 78.4 per cent in Trinidad and Tobago, and, in the case of the poorest country in the entire hemisphere, Haiti, up to 81.6 per cent of emigrants are university-educated (*Andina Migrante*, 2012: 7). What makes the situation in these countries so dire is that in some cases – Guyana, for example – well over

50 per cent of the country's stock of university-educated workers has migrated and can be found abroad in the Global North, mostly the US and Canada. The scale of exported brainpower from this region is nothing less than astounding, with an inestimably negative impact on the productive capacity and development prospects of the countries in the region (Canterbury, 2010).

Recommended reading: Albo and Ordaz Díaz (2011), Canterbury (2010), Delgado Wise and Marquez (2013).

Conclusion

A critical development perspective on the migration–development nexus is reflected in the conclusion that the fundamental patterns of both domestic and international migration are best understood in terms of the structural dynamics of capitalist development – the evolution of capitalism as a world system. A fundamental feature of this evolution in its latest phase and current era, that of neoliberal globalization, is the transnationalization of a dynamic and trends that can be traced out in diverse national and historic contexts throughout the 20th century, and indeed for several centuries. The neoliberal era of capitalist development has not only accelerated a century-long process of proletarianization and capitalist development – the conversion of traditional societies and communities of small-scale agricultural producers ('peasants' or 'rural landless workers' in the lexicon of critical agrarian change) into a working class, a class available for hire – but has created a global divide between societies and economies at the centre of the system and those on the periphery, between the Global North and the Global South, between the super-rich who have fed on the avails of labour and the masses condemned to a life of poverty and misery.

A critical development studies perspective on the migration–development nexus serves to dispel the following widely propagated myths: that (i) North–South regional integration based on free-market principles leads to economic convergence and reduced migration; (ii) neoliberal restructuring promotes progress and social well-being; (iii) emigration is a free and voluntary act; (iv) the management of the flow of migrant labour migration via public policies designed to regulate labour markets is beneficial for all stakeholders; and (v) immigrants are a burden for 'receiving countries' in the North and a benefit to 'sending countries' in the Global South.

Notes

1 By 1960, female migrants accounted for nearly 47 out of every 100 migrants living outside their countries of birth. Since then, the share of female emigrants among all international migrants has been rising steadily, to reach 48 per cent in 1990 and nearly 49 per cent in 2000. By 2000, female migrants constituted nearly 51 per cent of all migrants in the developed world and about 46 per cent of all migrants in developing countries (ILO, 2003: 9).
2 On this debate, see Otero (1999), as well as Bernstein (2012) and Van der Ploeg (2015), who represent polar positions in this debate: Marxism and economic populism.

References

Albo, A. and Ordaz Díaz, J.L. (2011). 'La Migración Mexicana hacia los Estados Unidos: Una breve radiografía'. BBVA Mexico, *Documentos de Trabajo*, núm. 11/05, February.

Andina Migrante (2012). No. 13, July.

Bernstein, H. (2012). *Class Dynamics of Agrarian Change*. Halifax: Fernwood.

Bhagwati, J. and Dellalfar, W. (1973). 'The brain drain and income taxation'. *World Development*, 1(1–2), February: 94–101.

Bourguignon, F. (2007). 'Dynamics of institutions, development and elites'. In F. Bourguignon and B. Pleskovic (eds), *Beyond Transition*. Washington, DC: World Bank, pp. 11–24.

Canales, A. (2011). 'Hacia una visión comprehensiva del nexo entre migración, desarrollo y derechos humanos'. *Migración y Desarrollo*, 9(16): 43–79.

Canterbury, D. (2010). 'The development impact of migration under neoliberal capitalism'. *Migración y Desarrollo*, 8(15): 5–42.

Carrington, W. and Detraglache, E. (1998). 'How big is the brain drain?' *IMF Working Paper* No. 98/102.

Cohen, R. (1987). *The New Helots: Migrants in the International Division of Labour*. Aldershot, UK: Gower.

Davis, M. (2006). *A Planet of Slums*. London: Verso.

De Janvry, A. and Sadoulet, E. (2000). 'Rural poverty in Latin America: determinants and exit paths'. *Food Policy*, 25: 389–409.

Delgado Wise, R. and Marquez, H. (2013). 'The migration and labour question today: imperialism, unequal development, and forced migration'. *Monthly Review*, 65(2): 25–38.

Delgado Wise, R. and Veltmeyer, H. (2016). *Agrarian Change, Migration and Development*. Halifax: Fernwood.

Delgado Wise, R., Marquez Covarrubias, H. and Puentes, R. (2013). 'Reframing the debate on migration, development and human rights'. *Population, Space and Place*, 19: 430–43.

Durand, J. (1994). *Más allá de la línea: patrones migratorios entre México y Estados Unidos*. Mexico City: CNCA.

Geiger, M. and Pécoud, A. (eds) (2010). *The Politics of International Migration Management: Migration, Minorities and Citizenship*. Basingstoke: Palgrave Macmillan.

Ghose, A., Nomaan, M. and Christoph, E. (2008). *The Global Employment Challenge*. Geneva: ILO.

Goldring, L. (1996). 'Blurring borders: constructing transnational community in the process of Mexico–U.S. migration'. *Research in Community Sociology*, 6: 69–104.

Kay, C. (2009). 'Estudios rurales en América Latina en el periodo de globalización neoliberal: ¿una nueva ruralidad?' *Revista Mexicana de Sociología*, 71(4), October–December.

Klein, E. and Tokman, V. (2000). 'La estratificación social bajo tension en la era de la globalización'. *Revista de CEPAL*, 72, December: 7–30.

Lozano, F. and Gandini, L. (2012). 'La migración calificada de México a Estados Unidos: tendencias de la década 2000–2010'. *Coyuntura demográfica*, 2: 51–5.

ILO (2011). *Global Employment Trends 2011: The Challenge of a Jobs Recovery*. Geneva: International Labour Organization.

ILO (2003). *Migration Survey 2003: Country Summaries*. Geneva: International Labour Organization.

IOM (2014). *Global Migration Trends: An Overview*. Geneva: International Organization for Migration.

Massey, D. and Parrado, E. (1998). 'International migration and business formation in Mexico'. *Social Science Quarterly*, 79(1): 1–19.

Nayyar, D. (1994). 'International labour movements, trade flows and migration transitions: a theoretical perspective', *Asian and Pacific Migration Journal*, 3(1): 7–30.

Otero, G. (1999). *Farewell to the Peasantry? Political Class Formation in Rural Mexico*. Boulder CO: Westview.

Stuart, J. and Kearney, M. (1981). 'Causes and effects of agricultural labor migration from the Mixteca of Oaxaca to California'. Working Papers in U.S.-Mexican Studies, No. 28, Program in United States-Mexican Studies, University of California, San Diego.

Terrazas, A. (2011). 'Migration and development: policy perspectives from the United States'. *MPI Report*, June. Migration Policy Institute.

Van der Ploeg, J. (2015). *Peasants and the Art of Agriculture: A Chayanov Manifesto*. Halifax: Fernwood.

World Bank (2008). *World Development Report 2008: Agriculture for Development*. Washington, DC: World Bank.

26

URBAN DEVELOPMENT IN THE GLOBAL SOUTH

Charmain Levy

In post-World War II classic modernization development theory, urbanization was considered a critical feature of the transition from traditional agrarian to modern industrial society. Capitalist development in the countryside pushed the peasant population off the land into the cities, where labour was required for urban industrial complexes. Rapid urbanization took place in most of the Global South, especially Latin America and Asia, where a significant part of the rural population migrated to the cities from 1960 to the 1980s. Urbanization in Africa took place at different rates in the postcolonial period, and since the 1990s has accelerated. Like development, urbanization took place at a more rapid and intense rate in the South compared to most Western countries, even though it was meant to follow in Western footsteps. It took New York approximately 150 years to grow to 8 million people, while Mexico and São Paulo generated the same interval of population growth in less than 15 years. In 2009, the world's urban population exceed the rural population for the first time in history.

Urbanization is still considered central to the development process, and historically urban development requires major public investments. Despite the importance of urbanization to modernization, practically no state-supported infrastructure was provided to this population in urban centres in the South. Where they were, public services were often skewed towards the upper- and middle-class neighbourhoods. To make thing worse, salaries for the large majority of the urban population were insufficient to cover the cost of living. As the low-income population were left to their own devices to survive in the city, in many countries and regions we find a collective 'self-help' reaction to the problems around the lack of urban infrastructure (transportation, housing, sanitation, electricity, streets, waste removal, schools, daycare, health services, etc.) and tenure regulation of the state. Neighbourhood and community associations became the basis of urban social movements and nongovernmental associations; a burgeoning 'civil society' in some cases formed to contest the urban space and demand political action as well as public services from local governments.

In many metropolises, one way for the working classes to survive has been to illegally squat on land either individually or collectively. This led to the formation of slums and shanty towns, which have become an integral and permanent part of the urban landscape in the Global South. This modern urban phenomenon is in fact a solution for the state as well as a reason not to provide low-income housing on a universal scale. Structural adjustment programmes, neoliberal macroeconomic policies and the integration of national markets into the global economy since the mid-1980s have exacerbated the spread and expansion of shanty towns and led to what geographers term 'spatial segregation'. However, if the golden years of economic industrial development meant stable jobs for semi-skilled workers, from the 1980s on we have witnessed what can be called urbanization without industrialization, and in many cases urbanization without development. New generations of workers and migrants now feed the (legal and illegal) informal economy, much of which takes place in large shanty towns (Davis, 2006).

In order to understand the dynamics of diverse urbanization processes in the South, we must first of all place and study them in the context of the global economy based on a new international division of labour and new forms of governance. We also need to take account of the diverse but relevant development theories, the macroeconomic and social policies implemented by successive governments, the political regimes and changing forms of the state in terms of how open they are to urban popular movements and their claims. We must also understand the dynamics of a growing civil society of nongovernmental organizations, an uncivil society and the role played by multilateral agencies and their policies aimed at the urban poor.

The readings in this chapter are intended to deepen reflection on the historical, economic, social and political factors that condition the different forms and patterns of urbanization in the South. Special attention is given to three key issues in a critical development studies approach: (i) urban production in terms of capital[1] and labour;[2] (ii) urban development in terms of the dynamics involved in reproducing the workforce and the social conditions of these dynamics – social exclusion, inequality and poverty; and (iii) forms of urban governance and politics. Studying these issues entails identifying in different periods of contemporary history, social and political structures, social actors, their interaction, and the results of their relations in terms of social and political continuity and change. This requires analysing how different levels of government, as well as international organizations (World Bank, UN-Habitat), deal with issues of unequal urban development and urban management in terms of maintaining order through social reform and the selective inclusion of civil society actors in governance and through the repression of what is designated as uncivil society. Attention is also given to social movements, political contention and collective action around urban issues such as access to land, public goods and services, as well as to decisions involving urban governance.

Recommended reading: Davis (2006).

Neoliberal globalization and urbanization: theoretical perspectives on the city and urban development

Urban development in the Global South over the past three decades has taken place in the context of what can be viewed as epoch-defining changes in social and economic organization and a process of globalization impelled by neo-liberalism, a programme of 'structural reforms' in macroeconomic policy that includes the privatization of public enterprises, financial and trade liberalization, deregulation of markets and the decentralization of government administration (Harvey, 2005). The retrenchment of national welfare state regimes and national intergovernmental systems imposed powerful new fiscal constraints upon cities, leading to major budgetary cuts during periods of intense local social problems and conflicts in conjunction with rapid economic restructuring (Brenner and Theodore, 2002).

Studies differ sharply as to how to theoretically represent the dynamics of neo-liberal policies, but they more or less agree that they relate to various cycles of 'structural' market-friendly 'reforms' designed during the Washington Consensus and then in the 1990s: (i) a new set of policies based on an emerging Post-Washington Consensus (see Chapter 11 in this volume) to establish a 'better balance' between the state and the market (Ocampo, 2007); (ii) a 'new social policy' protective of the most vulnerable groups of the poor; (iii) a decentralized form of local governance and development; and (iv) an overarching comprehensive development framework (CDF), and within it a new policy tool – the Poverty Reduction Strategy (PRSP).

During this period, the concept of global cities emerged, encouraging competition among urban centres to attract capital, markets, transnational offices and direct foreign investment (Sassen, 2001, 2006) in order to become 'hubs of knowledge, innovation, and entrepreneurship'. With this goal in mind, the local state must invest large sums of public funds in infrastructure for the rich and enterprises. It must also adapt local zoning and municipal laws in order to accommodate markets and the private sector. The city is conceived as the 'agglomeration economy', driver of economic growth and its purpose is to transform urban spaces to be as attractive as possible to financial investors. This often involves the expansion of downtown areas into attractive upscale service centres, the implementation of large-scale projects to attract big expositions, conventions and 'mega-events' such as the Olympics or World Cup, and the makeover of city centres to befit them as 'world-class' conference and hospitality destinations (Mayer, 2007).

Within the context of this development, theoretical perspectives and policy action prescriptions diverge. Salient among these are permutations of 'structural Marxism' (Davis, 2006; Harvey, 2005), structural and post-structural forms of urban sociology (Castells, 1983), international political economy and urban development economics, a largely untheorized approach shared by economists at the World Bank (Glaeser and Joshi-Ghani, 2015) and related organizations in the United Nations system. The authors of *The Urban Imperative: Towards Competitive Cities* illustrate this tradition of urban development theory and practice. This perspective leads to the 'urban fallacy': the notion that the problem is with the city itself, and not with the social relations that govern society (Angotti, 2013). What defines these studies is an approach that is supportive rather than critical of the neoliberal policy and institutional framework elaborated on the basis of the post-Washington Consensus. Others within the UN system highlight cities as the drivers of global environmental change.

Recommended reading: Harvey (2005), Sassen (2008, 2010).

The urban revolution, the informal sector and the urban labour market

This theme raises the questions of how economic factors are tied to production conditions in the cities and how changes in the world economy impact on capital and labour, as well as on the social–spatial organization of cities. Cities offer higher income levels than the average in the countryside. They are the sites of capitalist production, accumulation and consumption. They concentrate capital, manufacturing, distribution, labour and customer markets. A major aspect of capitalist development is the process of productive and social transformation in which a traditional, pre-capitalist and agrarian society is transformed into a modern industrial capitalist society (Delgado Wise and Veltmeyer, 2016). Typically, in the periphery of the world capitalist system under conditions that prevailed from the 1950s to the 1970s, this process of structural change and urbanization took a different form than it did in countries at the centre of the system. The most notable feature of peripheral capitalist development regarding rural–urban migration, urbanization and the growth of cities is the emergence of a dual-sector economy, each with its own labour market: a formal sector in which economic activities are 'structured' and the capital–labour relation is regulated by the state; and an unstructured 'informal sector', in which economic activities revolve around self-employment and family based microenterprises rather than the traditional capital–labour relation. In other words, in the developed capitalist economies, rural migrants, dispossessed of land or otherwise forced to abandon the countryside, were absorbed into the urban economy at the level of modern industry as an industrial proletariat or working class.

In the Global South, the social transformation from peasant to wage worker and productive transformation from agriculture to industry stalled and remains incomplete. For example, growth of urban manufacturing actually increases the demand for less-skilled workers. Urban and suburban industrial enclaves in 'free-trade' zones and maquiladoras have become giant labour reserves for both global and local capital (Angotti, 2013). Today, most of the jobs accessible to semi-skilled and non-skilled workers are in the manufacturing and service sectors and involve outsourced work. Most working arrangements can be described as temporary, short-term and/or part-time. This situation has create what can be call an urban 'precariat' class[3] (Standing, 2011), and in many cases has weakened unions. This context is the result of the new international division of labour, where industries of all types outsource different parts of the productive chain to the South in order to increase production and consumption in the West. This process accelerated during the 2000s in countries such as Bangladesh, Mexico, India and Cambodia, contributing to rapid urbanization.

Recommended reading: Portes (1989), Portes *et al.* (1989).

Urban poverty in a neoliberal context: social and class dynamics of income distribution and urban poverty

In all of the cities of the Global South, despite the diversity of the workforce, ethnic and racial differences, what the working class has in common are the living conditions of social exclusion and socio-spatial segregation. According to UN-Habitat (2013), 33 per cent of the urban population in the Global South in 2012 lived in slums. The proportion of urban population living in slums was highest in Sub-Saharan Africa (62 per cent), followed by South Asia (35 per cent), Southeast Asia (31 per cent), East Asia (28 per cent), West Asia (24 per cent), Oceania (24 per cent), Latin America and the Caribbean (23 per cent) and North Africa (13 per cent).

Urban costs of reproduction such as housing, transportation, childcare, food, etc. falls upon the workers whose wages most often fall short of covering these costs. This is especially the case in regard to women (see the discussion below). 'Poverty' in most cities is conditioned by low wages and a relative access to collective goods and services. The distribution and concentration of these goods and services affect the level of urban inequality and poverty, as well as individual and collective behaviour and attitudes towards urban development. Subsequently, an important number of urban dwellers in the Global South suffer to a greater or lesser extent from severe environmental health problems associated with insufficient access to clean drinking water, inadequate sewerage facilities, polluted air and insufficient solid waste disposal (Cohen, 2006).

In most cities in the South, the new economic model of pro-growth neoliberal policies, even when modified by pro-poor programmes in the 1990s and 2000s, resulted in increased inequalities in the distribution of income, socioeconomic conditions and access to essential services. The social inequalities have led to extreme wealth at one social pole and the growth of poverty on the other. In times of economic crises, we witness a downward social mobility of the middle class, as seen in the cases of Argentina, Tunisia and Egypt. The result is what some sociologists term a 'new dualism' and others 'urban poverty in a context of structural adjustment' (Moser *et al.*, 1993).

An understanding of inequality also requires consideration of the implications for low-income groups of the existence of a growing, wealthier urban elite – for example, how their demands and influences restructure cities and city planning to serve their own interests. In many metropolises, urban development projects aim at separating them from 'the poor' through gated communities and highways that connect their homes, workplaces and spaces for leisure, thus reproducing urban segregation.

Recommended reading: Davis (2006), Portes *et al.* (1989).

Social and spatial dynamics of exclusion, segregation and urban inequality

Despite the increase in the number of democratically elected regimes and the strengthening of civil society in Asia, Africa and Latin America, the urban masses have not experienced better material living conditions. In fact, in many countries, the opposite is true. It is evident that the neoliberal pro-growth policies promoted by international organizations under the 'new economic model' have not been 'pro-poor'. The overall result appears to be increasing social inequalities and associated socioeconomic conditions. While some groups among the poor, as well as the middle class, benefit from these pro-growth policies, a larger number have borne the brunt of the social costs – urban poverty is evidently on the increase in many development contexts.

Conditions of this poverty include inadequate and subpar housing, precarious low-wage employment, informal labour markets, high levels of unemployment, violence, crime and insecurity, affecting the middle class as well as the urban underclass and the working poor. Most sociological studies into these conditions point to the need for more socially inclusive policies, as well as specific policies designed to protect the most vulnerable groups from the competitive environment of pro-growth government policies (Lopez, 2004). This is especially true in the case of gender urban policy to address the needs of women head of households that in some metropolises represent up to 40 per cent of all households (Levy et al., 2016). According to Chant (2011), urban poverty has a distinctive gendered dimension. Although women make a crucial contribution to the prosperity of cities through their paid and unpaid labour, they remain at a disadvantage in terms of equitable access to work and living conditions, health and education, assets and representation in formal institutions and urban governance.

Studies suggest that the vast majority of the urban poor rely on self-help for housing and access to food and water; they do not have 'decent jobs' with adequate working conditions and suffer from a high incidence of social exclusion. In many of the megalopolis, especially in Latin America and South Asia, they engage in poorly remunerated economic activities in the informal sector (Portes, 1989) and live in what Davis (2006) terms a 'planet of slums'. Davis' study provides both a sociological portrait of the urban poor and an indictment of government policy – and of the economic model used by governments to make policy.

Angotti (2013) recognizes the development of enclave urbanism as the design and development of fragmented cites and metropolitan regions that contributes to the fragmentation of urban space into exclusive, elite residential enclaves and ghettos, malls, and business districts. Harvey (2005) points out that there is separation between social classes both in spatial contexts and in vertical segregations. Important features of the ongoing process of segregated urbanization include: the expansion and consolidation of gated and exclusive residential areas; a weakening of public space;[4] public insecurity mainly linked to police brutality, crime and drug trafficking in major urban centres; and growth of peripheries or peri-urban territories.

Recommended reading: Angotti (2013), Harvey (2005), Portes (1989).

Forms of urban governance, development policy and politics in the South

Over the last 30 years, economic growth has led to economic and social inequalities, as well as urban violence affecting the middle and working classes. In most countries, the reaction of the state to this problem is to strengthen law enforcement or to offer palliative social programmes aimed at certain areas of the cities. The readings in this theme discuss how urban policy is constructed in practice, as well as which strategies and policies are designed to alleviate and reduce the incidence of urban poverty – to bring about a development process in the urban areas of the Global South.

From the 1990s on, multilateral institutions have introduced local governance as a central element of political modernization in the South where the local could better serve the global. This was the World Bank's answer to the collapse of public services that characterized the condition of urban centres from the mid-1980s on in many Global South cities. With this goal, governance limits the role of government to a facilitator among market and civil society actors and the state becomes another actor among many. Governance thus encourages citizen participation, but it simultaneously allows for powerful corporations and real estate interests to engage in these same public spaces and to compete with the organized poor in shaping urban initiatives (Holston, 2008).

Under the free-market development paradigm, basic needs such as clean water, sanitation, healthcare and education are not considered a human right, but a privilege of the fee-paying user, even in the poorest low-income communities. The role of the state is not to be directly responsible for addressing society's needs and problems, but to facilitate and regulate the business sector in undertaking social functions and economic development. In the process of privatization, public goods are effectively transferred into private hands, and the government acts on behalf of corporations in operating (or building new and large-scale) infrastructures and realizing their profit potential. There is a prominent place given to public–private partnerships (PPPs) as a mode of governance, as in the case of Bolivian water management.

In most cities, local governance has been a top-down process, although in some places, such as Brazil, it was seen by civil society as bringing the state and political decision-making closer to citizens. For example, experiences in participatory budgeting in Brazil and other Latin American cities have led not only to better citizenship participation and substantive democracy, but also to a better quality of life of the working classes thanks to targeted investments in public infrastructure and social spending in poorer neighbourhoods (Abers, 2000).

Recommended reading: Abers (2000), Holston (2008).

Urban social movements: grassroots, civil society and popular responses

Until the 1980s, the most important social movements were based on organized labour in urban centres or the struggle for land waged in the countryside.

However, since the 1980s, urban centres in Latin America and Southeast Asia were the staging ground of a new type of urban social movement, which gave rise to a debate about 'new social movements' that were not class-based and that were more heterogeneous in their protests and claims – including, for example, issues such as environmental degradation, gender inequality, the violation of human rights and social exclusions of all sorts. In the 2000s and 2010s, new waves of urban protest emerged around the privatization of public goods and services (Bolivia), massive displacements (Kenya and South Africa) and state-promoted removals of low-income populations from city centres in the name of urban renewal. What is specific to many urban social movements is their practice of squatting, land occupation and street blockades. If we understand territory to embody not only physical space, but a set of social relations – between individuals, classes, social groups and the state – the struggles for urban land are fundamentally community and class struggles (Angotti, 2013).

Within the context of new class-based struggles, cities of the Global South are developing at the intersection of two major forces. One is the imposition of dominant projects articulated both globally and locally by recognized agents of development, such as state governments, world organizations, NGOs and national and transnational corporations. The other comprises the insurgent practices of the urban poor through which these development projects are lived and, typically, transformed, derailed and/or reconstituted. Insurgent citizenship describes a process that engages a counter-politics and destabilizes the present and renders it fragile. It disrupts established formulas of rule, conceptions of right and domination and deference (Holston, 2008).

At a local level, not only are these social movements resisting displacement and neoliberal urban management, but they are proposing and promoting a city that reflects their culture, networks, needs and rights. Insurgent practices include the occupation of urban peripheries, illegal housing, social and cultural movements, gender politics, immigration and new urban citizenships. This happens through protest and also alliances with political society actors, leading to innovative urban policy. At the international level, social movements and progressive urban NGOs in major Southern nations led by Brazil and other Latin American nations present the claim to 'the right to the city' within the UN system (Parnell, 2016) in order to guarantee it as a universal socioeconomic human right.

Recommended reading: Holsten (2008), Sassen (2010).

Notes

1 'Capital' can be understood and is normally used to mean the 'sum total of a society's wealth', or, more specifically, the source and means of generating this wealth, an investment in society's productive resources: income- or wealth-generating assets. In these terms, capital can take different forms: basically, *financial* (money invested in production), *physical* (technology embodied in machinery, equipment, computers, etc.), *natural* (land and its resources), *human* (education, knowledge) and *social* (norms of reciprocity embodied in a culture of social solidarity).

2 'Labour' is understood in abstract terms as 'labour power', or the capacity to labour, and more concretely as the act of producing something, transforming a nature resource into a product for use or exchange. In the context of capitalist development, labour power is viewed as a commodity, what the worker exchanges with capital for a living wage.
3 This is a Marxist conception of class that defines an individual's relation to production. This concept of social class can be distinguished from a structural functionalist concept of class as defining an individual's relationship to work, used to identify occupational groupings. It is also distinguished from a concept introduced by Max Weber, who used social class to define an individual's 'life chances', determined by an individual's relationship to the market (capacity to consume) rather than production. The categories of analysis in this conception are: upper, upper-middle, middle, lower-middle, lower (see Chapter 15).
4 Understood as spaces of meeting and exchange between the different groups and of the exercise of urban sociability.

References

Abers, R.N. (2000). *Inventing Local Democracy: Grassroots Politics in Brazil*. Boulder, CO: Lynne Rienner.

Angotti, T. (2013). *The New Century of the Metropolis: Urban Enclaves and Orientalism*. London: Routledge.

Brenner, N. and Theodore, N. (2002). 'Cities and the geographies of "actually existing neoliberalism"'. *Antipode*, 34(3): 349–79.

Castells, M. (1983). *The City and the Grassroots*. Berkeley, CA: University of California Press.

Chant, S. (2011). 'Introduction'. *UN-HABITAT State of Women in Cities 2012/13*, UNHABITAT, Nairobi.

Cohen, B. (2006). 'Urbanization in developing countries: current trends, future projections, and key challenges for sustainability'. *Technology in Society*, 28: 63–80.

Davis, M. (2006). *Planet of the Slums*. New York: Verso.

Delgado Wise, R. and Veltmeyer, H. (2016). *Agrarian Change, Migration and Development*. Halifax: Fernwood.

Glaeser, E. and Joshi-Ghani, A. (eds) (2015). *The Urban Imperative: Towards Competitive Cities*. Oxford: Oxford University Press.

Harvey, D. (2005). *A Brief History of Neoliberalism*. Oxford: Oxford University Press.

Holston, J. (2008). *Insurgent Citizenship: Disjunctions of Democracy and Modernity in Brazil*. Princeton, NJ: Princeton University Press.

Levy, C., Latendresse, A. and Carle-Marsan, M. (2016). 'Gendering the urban social movement and public housing policy in São Paulo'. *Latin America Perspectives*. doi:10.1177/0094582X16668317.

Lopez, H. (2004). 'Pro-growth, pro-poor: is there a trade-off?' The World Bank Policy Research Working Paper No. 3378.

Mayer, M. (2007). 'Contesting the neoliberalization of urban governance'. In H. Leitner *et al.* (eds), *Contesting Neoliberalism: Urban Frontiers*. Oxford: Guildford Press, pp. 92–4.

Moser, C., Herbert, A. and Makonnen, R. (1993). 'Urban poverty in the context of structural adjustment: recent evidence and policy responses'. *Discussion Paper*. Washington, DC: World Bank.

Ocampo, J.A. (2007). 'Markets: social cohesion and democracy'. In J.A. Ocampo, K.S. Jomo and S. Kahn (eds), *Policy Matters: Economic and Social Policies to Sustain Equitable Development*. London: Zed Books, pp. 1–31.

Parnell, S. (2016). 'Defining a global urban development agenda'. *World Development*, 78: 529–40.

Portes, A. (ed.) (1989). *The Informal Economy: Studies in Advanced and Less Developed Countries.* Baltimore, MD: Johns Hopkins University Press.

Portes, A., Castells, M. and Lauren, B. (1989). *The Informal Economy in Industrialized and Less Developed Countries.* Baltimore, MD: Johns Hopkins University Press.

Sassen, S. (2001). *The Global City: New York, London, Tokyo.* Princeton, NJ: Princeton University Press.

Sassen, S. (2006). *A Sociology of Globalization.* New York: W.W. Norton.

Sassen, S. (2008). 'Neither global nor national: novel assemblages of territory, authority and rights'. *Ethics & Global Politics,* 1(1–2): 61–79.

Sassen, S. (2010). 'A savage sorting of winners and losers: contemporary versions of primitive accumulation'. *Globalizations,* 7(1–2): 23–50.

Standing, G. (2011). *The Precariat: The Dangerous New Class.* London: Bloomsbury.

UN-Habitat (2013). *State of the World's Cities 2012/2013.* New York: Routledge.

Resources, energy and the environment

Part VIII

Resources, energy and the environment

27

CAPITALISM VERSUS THE ENVIRONMENT

Darcy Tetreault

Is sustainable capitalism possible? According to O'Connor (1998), who poses this question in what has now become a classic text for eco-socialists, the short answer is 'no' and the longer answer is 'probably not'. In his analysis, there are two basic contradictions to capitalist development that make it prone to crisis. The first is between capital and labour, tending towards overproduction crises (otherwise known as 'realization' crises), 'when individual capitals attempt to defend or restore profits by increasing labour productivity, speeding up work, cutting wages and using other time-honored ways of getting more production from fewer workers' (p. 240). The unintended result is to reduce the demand for consumer commodities. The second strikes from the side of costs, when capital undermines what Marx called the 'conditions of production', including natural, communal and human labour conditions. This can be done in two ways: 'when individual capitals defend or restore profits by strategies that degrade or fail to maintain over time the material conditions of their own production', and/or 'when social movements demand that capital better provide for the maintenance and restoration for these conditions of life' (p. 242). The possibility of capital internalizing environmental costs and reconstructing the conditions of production through state regulation in order to restore or increase its productivity in the long run is remote, O'Connor argues, since it would require coordinating huge investments and forsaking profits in the short run, something that is contrary to the self-expanding and anti-environmental logic of capital (p. 246).

According to Foster (2002), the appeal of O'Connor's theoretical explanation rests in that it provides a logically coherent argument that links ecological scarcity and economic crisis to the growth of new social movements, particularly the environmental movement. In O'Connor's scheme, labour movements stem from the first contradiction, and new social movements from the second. However, Foster sees some limitations to this explanation:

The whole thrust of the 'second contradiction' conception is that once ecological damage is translated into an economic crisis for capitalism a feedback mechanism is set into play, both directly through capital's attempt to hold down the growing costs of production associated with the undermining of its conditions of production, and indirectly through attempts by social movements to force the system to internalize the externalities.

(Foster, 2002: 10)

His contention is that there are no such feedback mechanisms for capitalism as a whole, and that we should not underestimate capitalism's capacity to accumulate in the midst of widespread ecological degradation. Moreover, instead of theorizing environmental problems in an economistic and functionalist way, Foster argues that a more fruitful path would be to follow Marx's dialectical approach, based on a deep materialist conception of human and natural history. Foster (2000) undertakes this task by building on Marx's metabolic-rift theory, which posits that the growth of industry and large-scale agriculture under capitalism has created an 'irreparable rift' in the 'metabolic interaction' between human beings and the natural environment.

In a more recent book with Brett Clark and Richard York, Foster makes reference to nine planetary boundaries or 'rifts' analysed by a group of researchers led by Johan Rockström at the Stockholm Resilience Centre: climate change, ocean acidification, stratospheric ozone depletion, the nitrogen and phosphorus cycles, freshwater use, change in land use, biodiversity loss, atmospheric aerosol loading and chemical pollution (Foster *et al.*, 2010: 13–19). According to said group of scientists, the first three boundaries are at their tipping points and the other six signify the onset of irreversible environmental degradation. This suggests that the current course of capitalist development is indeed ecologically unsustainable. Using this as a working hypothesis, this module reviews the limits-to-growth debate and analyses recent trends in global capitalist development that have a high impact on the environment, including neo-extractivism, land and water grabs, and growing greenhouse gas emissions. The last session of this module broaches social environmental conflicts and considers development alternatives – or 'alternatives to development' – that reflect the theme of defending, reclaiming and/or creating 'the commons'.

Recommended reading: Forester (2000), Foster *et al.* (2010), O'Connor (1998).

The limits-to-growth debate

The limits-to-growth debate can be traced back to Malthus' 1789 publication, *An Essay on the Principle of Population*, which claimed that food production would be unable to keep pace in the long run with population growth, since the former tends to grow linearly and the latter exponentially. Marx took issue with this claim, arguing that overpopulation was not determined by abstract numbers, but rather historically, with limits posited by specific conditions of production. For a review of this debate that sympathizes with Marx, see Foster (2000), and for one that seeks to reclaim elements of Malthus' preoccupation for critical political ecology, see Martínez Alier (2002).

In the late 1960s and early 1970s, a barrage of publications used Malthusian logic to raise public awareness about the environmental consequences of rapid population growth and industrialization (for example, Ehrlich, 1968; Hardin, 1968; Meadows *et al.*, 1972). These texts and others informed the emergence of new social movements that put environmental concerns on the development agenda. In this conjuncture, the UN Conference on the Human Environment, held in Stockholm in 1972, marked the beginning of the construction of a mainstream sustainable development model. The Conference's declaration acknowledged that 'the natural growth of population continuously presents problems for the preservation of the environment'. The mainstream sustainable development model was sketched out in the 1987 Brundtland Report, which does not recognize absolute limits to growth, only temporary ones imposed by the state of technology and social organization (WCED, 1987: 43). In this vision, economic growth is a necessary condition to alleviate poverty, which in turn is considered to be both a major cause and consequence of environmental degradation.

The mainstream sustainable development model places emphasis on market-based solutions for overcoming environmental problems, for example cap-and-trade carbon schemes. The profit motive is meant to stimulate technological innovation, as well as the search for additional reserves of non-renewable resources and for substitutes. From this perspective, the Earth's capacity to provide low-entropy materials and to absorb wastes can be extended indefinitely by increasing the ecological efficiency of productive activities and consumption. Martínez Alier (2002) refers to this as the 'gospel of eco-efficiency'. It ignores what has become known as the Jevons paradox, which postulates that increments in the efficiency with which a resource is used lead to increasing demand and consumption, ultimately eclipsing efficiency gains (Foster *et al.*, 2010; Martínez Alier, 2002).

In this debate, radical reformists advocate for a transition towards a steady-state economy, defined by constant stocks of physical wealth and people, and a low rate of energy and material throughput (Daly, 1996), or even for 'de-growth' in the Global North (Latouche, 2009), combined with redistributive policies in order to satisfy the basic needs of marginalized sectors of the population. However, as O'Connor (1998), Foster (2011) and other Marxist scholars point out, the *sine qua non* of capitalism is economic growth, or more precisely capital accumulation, implying that a transition to a steady-state economy must necessarily be a transition to some form of post-capitalist society.

Recommended reading: Daly (1996), Foster (2011), Latouche (2009).

Global warming

One of the researchers working at the Stockholm Resilience Center is Nobel Prize-winning atmospheric chemist Paul Crutzen, who coined the term *Anthropocene* to define the beginning of a new geological epoch characterized by human dominance of biological, chemical and geological processes on Earth. The *Anthropocene* is said to have begun roughly around the end of the 18th century, at the start of the Industrial Revolution. One of the features that distinguishes this new planetary epoch from the preceding one – the *Holocene*, which began at the end of the last Ice Age, roughly 12,000 years ago – is anthropogenic global climate change.

There is now widespread scientific consensus that global warming is happening, that it is caused by the build-up of greenhouse gases in the atmosphere, that human activity is the main driver, and that the consequences are likely to be devastating for humans and other species. According to the Fifth Assessment Report of the Intergovernmental Panel on Climate Change (IPCC, 2014), warming of the climate system is 'unequivocal'; the globally averaged combined land and ocean surface temperature show a warming of somewhere between 0.65 and 1.06°C over the period 1880 to 2012. It goes on to say that '[h]uman influence on the climate system is clear' and that 'recent anthropogenic emissions of green-house gases are the highest in history'. Even the World Bank, which was instrumental in applying and consolidating neoliberal structural reforms, acknowledges: 'The science is unequivocal that humans are the cause of global warming, and major changes are already being observed' (World Bank, 2012: iv). These changes include the acidification of oceans, a rise in sea levels, an exceptional number of extreme heat waves, and drought increasingly affecting major food crop growing areas (IPCC, 2014; World Bank, 2012).

To be sure, climate change deniers are alive and well. Right-wing think tanks such as the Heartlands Institute use corporate financing to spin discourses meant to cast doubt on anthropogenic global warming and its consequences (Klein, 2015). Moreover, a recent investigation details how, 'for nearly three decades, major fossil fuel companies have knowingly worked to distort climate science findings, deceive the public, and block policies designed to hasten our needed transition to a clean energy economy' (Mulvey and Shulman, 2015: 1). Their tactics include 'the use of front groups to hide companies' influence and avoid accountability, and the secret funding of purportedly independent scientists' (p. 1). Along these lines, it is noteworthy that just 90 fossil fuel and cement companies are responsible for emitting almost two-thirds of cumulative worldwide emissions of industrial CO_2 and methane between 1751 and 2010 (Heede, 2014). This suggests that analysing emissions produced by incorporated entities would be a more practical alternative to the nation state approach that currently dominates the UN-orchestrated agenda for dealing with climate change.

Since the United Nations Framework Convention on Climate Change (UNFCCC) was negotiated at the first Earth Summit, which took place in Rio de Janeiro in 1992, the only legally binding international treaty to curb greenhouse gas (GHG) emissions has been the Kyoto Protocol, which was brought into force in February 2005 with a commitment period between 2008 and 2012. Based on the principle of 'common by differentiated responsibilities', which recognizes the historic responsibility of developed countries for having emitted the bulk of GHG emissions in the past, only the industrialized countries that signed the Protocol were legally obliged to reduce their GHG emissions during the commitment period. To help countries meet their emission targets and to encourage the private sector to participate, the Protocol included three market-based mechanisms: emissions trading, the clean development mechanism and joint implementation. The United States did not ratify the agreement and the Kyoto Protocol fell far short of its overall objective of reducing GHG emissions by at least 5 per cent below 1990. As it turns out, global CO_2 emissions were 61 per cent higher in 2013 than in 1990 (Klein, 2015: 11).

Over the past few years, the annual UNFCCC Conferences of Parties (COPs) have been unable to move forward on establishing a legally binding follow-up treaty. COP15, held in Copenhagen in 2009, only resulted in a non-binding pledge to keep global temperatures from increasing more than 2°C. As Naomi Klein (2015: 12) observes, this was 'a highly political choice that has more to do with minimizing economic disruption than protecting the greatest number of people', since a 2°C temperature increase from pre-industrial times is expected to cause major flooding and drought, especially in the Global South. At COP16, held the next year in Cancun, there was talk of creating a $100 billion per annum Green Climate Fund; however, the sources of funding could not be agreed upon, and so far no country has stepped up to make their contribution known.

In sum, the market-based approaches that are at the centre of the UN's strategy for combating global warming have proven to be utterly ineffective. The global carbon market 'remains in the throes of a devastating crisis, earning carbon the distinction of 2011s worst performing global commodity' (Ervine, 2014: 723). The World Bank (2012: ix) observes: 'Scientists agree that countries' current United Nations Framework Convention on Climate Change emission pledges and commitments would most likely result in 3.5 to 4°C warming'. The full range of consequences of a temperature rise of this magnitude are impossible to predict, since the risk of crossing thresholds of nonlinear tipping elements increases as global warming approaches and exceeds 2°C.

Recommended reading: Heede (2014), IPCC (2014), Klein (2015).

Neo-extractivism

The 21st century began with a primary commodities boom, largely driven by rapid economic growth and industrialization in China, and to a lesser extent India. High international prices for a wide range of primary commodities stimulated a wave of foreign investments in developing countries to extract natural resources, ranging from fossil fuels and minerals, to agrofood products and biofuels. The catchword for this phenomenon is 'neo-extractivism', where 'neo' signals a certain degree of continuity with historic trends that began with the conquest and colonization of Latin America and Africa 500 years ago (Acosta, 2013). The scale and rhythm of extractive activities have reached unprecedented levels since the turn of the century, as capital scours the planet in search of speculative and productive investments in the context of overlapping crises: economic, financial, food, environmental, etc.

In Latin America, the neo-extractivist trend is manifest not just in countries that have adhered closely to the (post-)Washington Consensus (Mexico, Colombia and Peru), but also in countries with so-called 'progressive' or 'post-neoliberal' governments, including Bolivia and Ecuador, where the rights of Mother Earth have been enshrined in their respective constitutions. Svampa (2012) proposes that this has to do with the 'commodities consensus', which sees that all Latin American governments have promoted the expansion of extractive activities as a measure for stimulating economic growth and sustaining public finances, irrespective of their political-ideological orientation. For the progressive governments in South America, the 'new' extractivism (Gudynas, 2010) has boiled down to the state receiving a greater share of the rent, to be used for financing the expansion of social policies, especially anti-poverty programmes (Petras and Veltmeyer, 2014).

As easy-access mineral, oil and gas reserves are depleted, new technologies have been developed to exploit marginal or 'non-conventional' reserves, often with devastating environmental and social impacts. For example, open-pit mining of increasingly lower-grade ores involves the removal of massive amounts of material and the use of large quantities of water and highly toxic substances to extract and process minerals (Earthworks and Oxfam America, 2004). Tailing-pond spills and acid rock drainage contaminate surface and underground water supplies. In the oil and gas sector, deep-sea drilling, fracking and the exploitation of bituminous sands have increased the risks of water, air and land contamination (Heinrich Böll Stiftung *et al.*, 2011). These technologies are energy-intensive, emitting higher amounts of GHG per unit of production. Fracking consumes and contaminates enormous amounts of water and causes seismic activities (Earthworks, 2014). Among the people most adversely affected by these extractive activities are small-scale farmers and indigenous communities in the Global South. For these groups, the arrival of mining or petroleum companies constitutes a mortal threat to their health, livelihoods and culturally significant territories.

Recommended reading: Acosta (2013), Gudynas (2010), Petras and Veltmeyer (2014).

Land and water grabbing

Land and water grabs overlap with neo-extractivism, especially in the area of food and biofuel production. Land grabs have been defined as 'the explosion of (trans) national commercial land transactions and land speculation in recent years mainly, but not solely, around the large-scale production and export of food and biofuels' (Borras and Franco, 2012: 34). Water is an integral part of land grabs, since it is indispensable for agricultural production. However, as Mehta *et al.* (2012: 194) argue, 'water grabbing can be seen in relation to a much wider range of activity that spans food, water, energy, climate and mineral domains'. Water itself is often the object of grabbing, not just for agricultural purposes, but also for the production of hydroelectricity, mining, the corporate take over of public water systems, and as a sink for industrial waste.

Like neo-extractivism, the grabbing of land and water is not new. The term is meant to evoke a sense of social injustice in relation to an historic process that can be traced back to the enclosure of the commons in Europe during the transition from feudalism to capitalism, and to similar processes around the globe associated with the expansion of market relations via colonialism and imperialism. The contemporary wave of land grabs – or what the World Bank refers to as 'large-scale land acquisitions' – began in the 1990s and has gained momentum since the onset of the 2008 global food crisis (Borras *et al.*, 2012).

Rising food costs have underlined the importance of food security for countries that are lacking in sufficient land and water to feed their populations (for example, China, South Korea and the Gulf States). Since the crisis, these countries have intensified their quest to shore up access to natural resources by buying huge tracts of land in Africa, South America and elsewhere, where customary land tenure is weak. At the same time, speculative investment – mainly from the United States and Europe – has added impetus to this process, in its search for short-term profits in the production of 'flex crops', mainly soy, sugar cane, palm oil and corn, which can be easily interchanged as inputs for food, feed or biofuels. These crops are often genetically modified, producing 'green deserts' that displace small-scale farmers who produce for local consumption. They also use relatively large quantities of water (Kay and Franco, 2014).

Borras *et al.* (2012) have identified three interlinked features of contemporary land grabbing: first, it is essentially about controlling natural resources for capital accumulation; second, it entails large-scale transactions, both with regard to the scale of land acquisitions and to the scale of capital involved; and third, it occurs in response to the convergence of multiple crises on the global level. Land grabbing does not necessarily entail the 'foreignization' of land and associated natural resources; in fact, in some circumstances, it is carried out by domestic capital, in alliance with the state.

While much land grabbing results in ecologically destructive land use changes, some is paradoxically being carried out for environmental ends, for example biodiversity conservation, bio-carbon sequestration, and the creation of parks and nature reserves. Dubbed 'green grabbing', the appropriation of natural resources for environmental ends 'implies the transfer of ownership, use rights and control over resources that were once publicly or privately owned – or not even the subject of ownership – from the poor (or everyone including the poor) into the hands of the powerful' (Fairhead *et al.*, 2012: 238).

Recommended reading: Borras and Franco (2012), Borras *et al.* (2012), Fairhead *et al.* (2012), Mehta *et al.* (2012).

Social environmental conflicts and the commons

In the context of neo-extractivism and natural resources grabbing, social environmental conflicts have multiplied around the world during the first decade and a half of the new millennium. These conflicts revolve around mega-mining projects, dam building, oil and gas extraction, and the construction of infrastructure for the transportation of energy, water, goods and people. There are also conflicts around tourist developments, wind farms, urban sprawl, garbage dumps, genetically modified seeds and diverse forms of industrial contamination. Typically, large national and transnational companies, backed by federal governments, are pitted against local opposition groups, who build alliances with progressive and radical elements of civil society and deploy collective action through nested scales of social networks. In many cases, it is the state itself that spearheads controversial large-scale development projects, especially for dams, highways and oil exploitation, with private sector participation. These projects are promoted by capital and the state through appeals to the notions of 'progress', 'economic growth' and 'modernization'; while the discourse of resistance speaks to the defence of the livelihoods of small-scale rural producers, healthy living environments, territories, culturally significant landscapes and alternative cosmologies.

Of the 1,354 cases of 'ecological distribution conflicts' registered in 2015 by the Atlas of Environmental Justice around the world (Ejatlas, www.ejatlas.org), 21 per cent were about mining, 10 per cent dealt with industrial extraction of fossil fuels, 17 per cent were land conflicts and 14 per cent were water management conflicts (Martínez Alier *et al.*, 2016: 735). 'Hence, the majority of reported conflicts are located in the extraction phase of resources which are central to maintaining the current society's metabolism' (p. 735). Involved in these conflicts, on the side of capital, are giant transnational corporations in the mining sector, the fossil fuels sector, construction, water infrastructure and agro-industries. On the side of the affected and mobilized populations, there are indigenous groups, small-scale farmers, pastoralists, fisherfolk, concerned citizens, social activists, local scientists, students, artists and environmental justice organizations that operate on the local, national and international levels. The alternatives associated with these resistance movements in Latin America are based on the construction of 'social and solidarity societies' whose guiding principles are 'autonomy, social solidarity, self-sufficiency, productive diversification, and sustainable regional resource management' (Barkin and Lemus, 2014: 262).

How can social environmental conflicts and related alternatives be theorized? A critical approach that has gained currency in recent years takes as a point of departure Marx's theory of 'original accumulation', illustrated in the first volume of *Capital* through his analysis of the classic case of England, where peasants were separated from their means of production between the 15th and 18th centuries through a violent process of land enclosures. Luxemburg (2003 [1913]) argued that similar processes can be observed, not just during the birth of the capitalist system in Europe, but throughout its long history, as capitalism spread around the globe feeding on elements outside of itself (i.e. the commons). Building on this, Harvey (2003) has popularized the notion of 'accumulation by dispossession' to explain the depredatory expansion of market relations during the neoliberal era. The related but more specific metaphor of 'enclosing the commons' is used to refer not only to the commodification and privatization of land and environmental services, but also to that of knowledge, culture and other non-material goods (Bollier and Hilfrich, 2012). Correspondingly, resistance movements to dispossession and alternatives that look beyond the state and the market have been conceptualized in terms of reclaiming, defending or creating the commons. As Linebaugh (2008: 279) and others warn, it is misleading at best and dangerous at worst to speak of the commons as if it were a natural resource with certain intrinsic properties; better to speak of the commons as an activity, 'commoning', which can guide collective action.

Recommended reading: Barkin and Lemus (2014), Bollier and Hilfrich (2012), Martínez Alier *et al.* (2016).

References

Acosta, A. (2013). 'Extractivism and neoextractism: two sides of the same curse'. In M. Lang and D. Mokrani (eds), *Beyond Development: Alternative Visions from Latin America*. Quito: Fundación Rosa Luxemburg, pp. 87–104.

Barkin, D. and Lemus, B. (2014). 'Rethinking the social and solidarity society in light of community practice'. *Sustainability*, 6: 6432–45.

Bollier, D. and Helfrich, S. (eds) (2012). *The Wealth of the Commons: A World Beyond Market & State*. Amherst, MA: Levellers Press.

Borras, S. and Franco, J. (2012). 'Global land grabbing and trajectories of agrarian change: a preliminary analysis'. *Journal of Agrarian Change*, 12(1): 34–59.

Borras, S., Kay, C., Gómez, S. and Wilkinson, J. (2012). 'Land grabbing and global capitalist accumulation: key features in Latin America'. *Canadian Journal of Development Studies*, 33(4): 402–16.

Daly, H. (1996). *Beyond Growth*. Boston, MA: Beacon Press.

Earthworks (2014). 'Hydraulic fracturing 101'. Available at: www.earthworksaction.org/issues/detail/hydraulicfracturing101#.Uf5bP-Dnvap.

Earthworks and Oxfam America (2004). *Dirty Metals: Mining, Communities and the Environment*. Washington, DC: Earthworks and Oxfam America.

Ehrlich, P. (1968). *The Population Bomb*. New York: Ballantine.

Ervine, K. (2014). 'Diminishing returns: carbon market crisis and the future of market-dependent climate change finance'. *New Political Economy*, 19(5): 723–47.

Fairhead, J., Leach, M. and Scoones, I. (2012). 'Green grabbing: a new appropriation of nature?' *Journal of Peasant Studies*, 39(2): 237–61.

Foster, J.B. (2000). *Marx's Ecology: Materialism and Nature*. New York: Monthly Review Press.

Foster, J.B. (2002). 'II. Capitalism and ecology: the nature of the contradiction'. *Monthly Review*, 54(4): 6–16.

Foster, J.B. (2011). 'Capitalism and degrowth: an impossibility theorem'. *Monthly Review*, 62(8): 26–33.

Foster, J.B., Clark, B. and York, R. (2010). *The Ecological Rift. Capitalism's War on the Earth*. New York: Monthly Review Press.

Gudynas, E. (2010). 'The new extractivism of the 21st century: ten urgent theses about extractivism in relation to current South American progressivism'. Available at: https://ambiental.academia.edu/EduardoGudynas.

Hardin, G. (1968). 'The tragedy of the commons'. *Science*, 162: 1243–8.

Harvey, D. (2003). *The New Imperialism*. New York: Oxford University Press.

Heede, R. (2014). 'Tracing anthropogenic carbon dioxide and methane emissions to fossil fuel and cement producers, 1854–2010'. *Climatic Change*, 122: 229–41.

Heinrich Böll Stiftung, Oil Change International and Friends of the Earth Europe (2011). *Marginal Oil: What is Driving Oil Companies Dirtier and Deeper?* Available at: www.boell. de/sites/default/files/Marginal_Oil_Layout_13.pdf.

IPCC (Intergovernmental Panel on Climate Change) (2014). *Climate Change 2014. Synthesis Report: Summary for Policymakers.* Available at: www.ipcc.ch/pdf/assessment-report/ar5/ syr/AR5_SYR_FINAL_SPM.pdf.

Kay, S. and Franco, J. (2014). *The Global Water Grab: A Primer.* Available at: www.tni.org/ files/download/watergrabbingprimer-altcover2.pdf.

Klein, N. (2015). *This Changes Everything: Capitalism vs the Climate.* New York: Simon & Schuster.

Latouche, S. (2009). *Farewell to Growth.* Cambridge: Polity Press.

Linebaugh, P. (2008). *Magna Carta Manifesto: Liberties and Commons for All.* Berkeley, CA: University of California Press.

Luxemburg, R. (2003 [1913]). *The Accumulation of Capital.* London/New York: Routledge.

Martínez Alier, J. (2002). *The Environmentalism of the Poor. A Study of Ecological Conflicts and Valuation.* Cheltenham/Northhampton: Edward Elgar.

Martinez Alier, J., Temper, L., Del Bene, D. and Scheidel, A. (2016). 'Is there a global environmental justice movement?' *Journal of Peasant Studies*, 43(3): 731–55.

Meadows, D., Meadows, D., Randers, J. and Behrens, W. (1972). *The Limits to Growth: A Report for the Club of Rome's Project on the Predicament of Mankind.* New York: Universe Books.

Mehta, L., Veldwisch, G.J. and Franco, J. (2012). 'Introduction to the special issue: water grabbing? Focus on the (re)appropriation of finite water resources'. *Water Alternatives*, 5(2): 193–207.

Mulvey, K. and Shulman, S. (2015). *The Climate Deception Dossiers: Internal Fossil Fuel Industry Memos Reveal Decades of Corporate Disinformation.* Available at: www.ucsusa.org/ sites/default/files/attach/2015/07/The-Climate-Deception-Dossiers.pdf.

O'Connor, J. (1998). *Natural Causes: Essays in Ecological Marxism.* New York/London: Guilford Press.

Petras, J. and Veltmeyer, H. (2014). *Extractive Imperialism in the Americas: Capitalism's New Frontier.* Leiden/Boston, MA: Brill.

Svampa, M. (2012). 'Consenso de los commodities y megaminería'. *América Latina en movimiento. Extractivismo: contradicciones y conflictividad*, 473(36): 5–8.

World Bank (2012). *Turn Down the Heat: Why a 4°C Warmer World Must Be Avoided.* Washington, DC: World Bank.

WCED (World Commission on Environment and Development – Bruntland Commision) (1987). *Our Common Future.* Oxford: Oxford University Press.

28

CLIMATE CHANGE AND DEVELOPMENT

Marcus Taylor

Climate change is fast becoming the defining development issue of the 21st century. The United Nations Development Programme (UNDP), for example, claims that failure to recognize and deal with climate change impacts will consign the poorest 40 per cent of the world's population to a future of diminished opportunity and will sharpen the already acute divisions between the 'haves' and 'have-nots' (UNDP, 2007). These troubling impacts are envisaged to result from a series of shocks and stresses that impact upon livelihoods and human well-being. Climate shocks refer to the potential for increased incidences of extreme weather, specifically a growing occurrence and intensity of storms, floods, heatwaves and other potential hazards that threaten lives and damage physical infrastructure. Climate stresses are the longer-term impacts of rising temperatures and changing hydro-climatic patterns upon ecosystems, with important ramifications for agriculture, water systems and food security. Pivotally, both types of impacts are estimated to fall most severely on the developing world, where they are amplified by a relative lack of resources, capacity and infrastructure to effectively respond.

For critical development studies, climate change raises pressing analytical, ethical and practical questions. By engaging with mainstream thinking, critical approaches have sought to shift climate change debates from a narrow focus on technical issues towards broader ethical questions around the interface of climate change and development. To do so, they often use the term 'climate justice' as a way to highlight the inequities surrounding who benefits most from carbon intensive development and who bears the brunt of climatic shifts. Two key questions emerge. First, given the universally acknowledged need to reduce greenhouse gas emissions, critical scholars ask how the responsibility for cutting emissions should be distributed between countries and how equitable low-carbon development pathways can be formed. Second, given that climate change impacts are projected to fall most severely on countries in the Global South, critical scholars have questioned who is most vulnerable to climate change and how public policies might prioritize these groups. In this chapter, we examine these questions through four interrelated sections on mitigation, green development, adaptation and resilience respectively.

Mitigation

To limit future global warming to under the 2 degrees that scientists argue represents a pivotal threshold, most fossil fuels will need to stay buried under the ground. This, of course, raises pivotal questions regarding the future of development. Oil and coal are the mainstays of powering development: they provide the primary means of electricity generation for both industrial and consumption purposes. Equally, oil underscores contemporary transportation for both people and goods on local and global scales. As such, a sharp contradiction emerges between mitigation goals – that is, the reduction of greenhouse gas emissions – and existing development strategies that are carbon intensive. At the 2015 Paris Climate Summit, for example, India caused considerable disquiet by insisting on the right to increase its consumption of coal for development purposes, including meeting its target of providing electricity to its entire citizenry. At the core of India's argument was the notion of historical responsibility for climate change, in which already developed countries had developed in carbon-intensive manners, and therefore should carry the brunt of mitigation efforts.

This political question over responsibility has been in play since the first United Nations climate change summit in 1992, and the tentative agreement reached at the most recent 2015 Paris Climate Summit does not fully resolve this issue. Instead, it sets out a principle of common but differentiated responsibility. Under this principle, countries set out mitigation targets known as Intended Nationally Determined Commitments (INDCs) that in theory balance their responsibility to reduce emissions with their ability to do so given their level of development. This, of course, is a somewhat fuzzy compromise that leaves any firm mitigation commitments and financing pledges vague and to be resolved. Developing countries have repeatedly tried to formalize the differentiated responsibility facet of the negotiations, but this has been fiercely resisted by many Western countries. The United States in particular has steadfastly rejected any wording that implies the liability of past emitters for future damage to lives and livelihoods driven by climate change. As a result, both the specific mitigation commitments that countries will attempt to meet and the means of financing decarbonization remains unclear despite a common agreement in principle to limit global warming to 1.5 degrees above pre-industrial levels. Given that per capita emissions are still heavily uneven between developed and developing countries – those in the US are around 12 to 13 times higher than those in India, for example – the issue of responsibility for reducing emissions and providing financing for this transition remains intensely politicised and will remain a central point of conflict moving forward.

Green development

In terms of a practical process for promoting low-carbon development, current international agreements remain hinged to two key policy measures first introduced with the 1997 Kyoto Protocol. First, carbon markets have been repeatedly asserted as a core mechanism for delivering mitigation goals. A carbon market is where the government sets an overall limit on carbon emissions from industry and requires companies to purchase the right to make emissions in the form of carbon credits that it produces and regulates. In theory, high-polluting companies will buy extra credits from more environmentally efficient producers, creating a flexible and effective way of managing emissions. At the same time, overall economic and environmental efficiency will be incentivized because industries can minimize the amount of credits they need by upgrading towards clean production technologies. To be effective, however, carbon markets rely on their surrounding institutional infrastructures to establish and enforce a suitable cap to emissions. In the EU case, concerted industry pressures led to regulators providing a glut of carbon credits causing their price to collapse. In conjunction with the 2008 economic slowdown, carbon credits bottomed out at €3 per ton in 2013, before recovering to €6 in January 2016. This remains a fraction of the €30 price that is a minimum threshold for effectiveness. As a result, within the EU, the price of pollution is unimaginably low while its costs globally are frighteningly high.

Regardless of the lack of proven success in facilitating a transition to a low-carbon future, the World Bank and other key institutional actors continue to promote carbon markets as a primary means for reducing emissions in both developed and developing countries. They have recently sought to provide a framework to link such markets across borders, creating a more globalized market for carbon. This continued political support, however, is attributable primarily to the acceptance of carbon markets as a less intrusive form of regulation within the corporate sector. Without enforcing a more exacting price for carbon, it is difficult to see how carbon markets can be effective tools to leverage the degree of societal transformation necessary to meet mitigation targets. To do so, however, rests not upon fine-tuning market mechanisms, but upon overcoming vested political–economic interests that keep the price of carbon artificially low at the expense of those most threatened by climate change impacts (Lohmann, 2006).

A second key tool advanced within existing development infrastructures is the clean development mechanism (CDM). Under the CDM, a development project in the developing world that actively reduces or sequesters greenhouse gases in a demonstrable and measurable way can be certified, turned into a commodity, and then traded on Western carbon markets. In theory, the CDM is an effective means of promoting green development, with corporations in the West able to offset their emissions by purchasing CDM generated credits that provide a source of financing for green development in the Global South. Critical development scholars, however, have drawn attention to several problematic elements of this process. First, local CDM projects have often been controversial in their own terms, involving conflicts between local communities and states and corporations over the use of lands, forests and water resources (Leach and Scoones, 2015). Second, CDM projects are meant to represent entirely new reductions in greenhouse gas emissions, yet many CDM projects are argued to be existing projects that are given a green gloss, therein producing marginal or poor-quality offsets. Third, and perhaps most pivotally, financial flows for green development promoted under the CDM remain a fraction of the amount of investment flowing into carbon-intensive sectors. Whereas some countries have invested heavily in clean energy projects and have benefited greatly from the CDM, they have nonetheless continued to develop on a carbon-intensive trajectory. China, for instance, is now the world's largest single emitter of greenhouse gasses, a rank that represents both its role as an industrial mass producer of export commodities as well as the dramatic transformation of its own society towards urbanization and mass consumption.

In this respect, many critical development scholars are less enamoured with the large-scale CDM type projects that are typically unresponsive to the needs of the poor who exert little influence over the institutional structures and political alliances that promote them. Instead, they tend to value the potential embedded in smaller-scale grassroots initiatives that might directly address issues of equitable access alongside sustainability questions. In much the same way that many farmers in South Asia now have cell phones without ever having had landlines, some authors project that new forms of low-carbon technology might be rapidly introduced at a grassroots level by simply skipping the step of carbon-intensive energy forms. From solar-based rural electrification to sustainable smallholder agriculture that sequesters carbon in the soil, there are a range of grassroots projects that have mitigation and development potential outside of the formal institutional process (Abramsky, 2010).

Recommended reading: Newell and Paterson (2010), Urban and Nordensvard (2013).

Adaptation

With the recognition that mitigation policies would not be sufficient to avoid a considerable degree of global warming, policy attention in the mid-2000s increasingly shifted towards the idea of climate change adaptation. According to the Intergovernmental Panel on Climate Change (IPCC), adaptation is a process of transformation in social and environmental systems that can safeguard against the present and the future adverse impacts of climatic change while taking advantage of any new opportunities (IPCC, 2007). Although the idea of adaptation appears to be a self-evident good, there are a number of issues in its conceptualization and implementation that are of central concern for critical development studies.

First, much of the institutional and governmental literature on adaptation adopts a strongly technocratic and managerial approach. Here, climate threats are seen as external shocks requiring simple technological solutions to preserve the status quo. Whether it is building stronger flood defences, drilling deeper wells for water, or developing new drought-resistant crops, these kinds of projects tend to be top-down and seek to preserve the existing contours of society through defensive fixes to newly envisaged physical hazards. Rarely, however, do these perspectives consider how present social inequalities shape how different social groups are unequally exposed to climate threats while also making them unevenly positioned to take advantage of any benefits provided by adaptation processes. A key concern is that adaptation projects of this nature may come at the expense of marginalised groups, who may be ignored or displaced in the name of fighting climate change. Such an outcome represents a case of 'maladaptation' wherein, for marginalized groups, the 'cure' of adaptation may well prove to be worse than the curse of climate change exposure (Marino and Ribot, 2012).

In response, a second branch of the adaptation literature has been far more attuned to social inequalities as the starting point for analysis. Often framed within a human security perspective, this literature emphasizes that engrained social inequalities are the root cause of vulnerability to environmental change (Wisner *et al.*, 2004). Once seen from this perspective, vulnerability to climate change is seen less in terms of the magnitude of potential climatic shocks, and more as a function of overlapping social inequalities and marginalization. For example, in many contexts, women can be systematically excluded from decision-making processes, land ownership, reproductive healthcare education and information networks. These exclusions can accentuate their vulnerability to climatic shocks, such as storms or floods, while also hampering their ability to recover from them. For human security perspectives, adaptation policies therefore require a close examination of unequal exposure to climate hazards and must build upon proactive social policies to tackle the root causes of these extant vulnerabilities (Eriksen and O'Brien, 2007; Eriksen *et al.*, 2011).

Human security perspectives have clearly moved the dial forward on progressive approaches to adaptation. That said, a more critical perspective takes this focus on inequality further by adopting an explicitly relational approach. These authors argue that very often the relative security of affluent social groups is often directly linked to the relative vulnerability of others (Collins, 2010; Mustafa, 2005; Taylor, 2013). This makes thinking about adaptation more complex because it points out that climate change recalibrates the power relations between social groups. For example, if climate change impacts upon water availability in an agricultural region of rural India, then it consolidates the power to those who control wells, irrigation and water flows. This typically advantages social elites, meaning that climate change opens up accumulation strategies predicated upon new forms of domination and exploitation within a changing environment (Taylor, 2015). For these perspectives, it is the power relations between social groups, not simply inequality, that must be placed at the heart of the discussion. Politically, a strong and deliberate emphasis on empowering marginalized groups alongside rethinking ways of redistributing assets arises as key components of successful adaptation.

Recommended reading: Pelling (2011), Taylor (2015).

Resilience

One term that has increasingly colonized the development literature on climate change is 'resilience'. It is little exaggeration to say that a majority of institutional approaches to climate change pivot on this common yet ill-defined concept. Consider, for example, the World Bank's ambitious *Africa Climate Business Plan*, which seeks to set an agenda for $15 billion of government, NGO and private sector investment into a low-carbon development future for the continent. Pertinently, the World Bank frames and justifies each item of its agenda in terms of building resilience. Specifically, it talks of three components of a climate-adapted future for Africa that are composed of: (i) 'strengthening resilience' by improving infrastructure; (ii) 'powering resilience', by investing in clean energy; and (iii) 'enabling resilience' by sharing knowledge (World Bank, 2015). Problematically, however, the Bank never defines this core term despite it being the presumed linchpin of the entire agenda. The idea of resilience is apparently too self-evident to require close elaboration.

In this type of literature, the idea of resilience is typically deployed to express the capacity for a social or ecological system to 'bounce back' from external shocks, therein recovering to its original state and functions. Frequently, resilience is used in this way as a positive quality that can be possessed by vastly different units of analysis. From a city to a community, a region to an economic sector, all can be discussed in terms of having or lacking 'resilience'. Problematically, however, what it means for a city to be resilient would be very different from an economic sector or an ecosystem. Moreover, there may be sharply divided winners and losers within such resilience. It is because of this conceptual looseness that many authors have become sharply critical of the concept. Some call resilience an 'empty signifier', by which they mean it is a term that can be filled with almost any content according to the needs of the agency using it (Felli, 2016; Watts, 2014). For instance, in the above *Africa Climate Business Plan*, the World Bank projects a series of reforms to agricultural policies across the African continent that closely resemble its long-standing agenda of market liberalization accompanied by the incorporation of smallholders into global value chains and the entry of Western biotech corporations as primary suppliers of inputs and other technologies. Previously, this very same agenda was advanced under the idea of market efficiency and poverty reduction (World Bank, 2007). Now the project is argued to be necessary as a means to build resilience to climate change (World Bank, 2015).

That said, not all conceptualizations of resilience are quite so vacuous. Influenced by the literature on adaptive systems from ecological sciences, socioecological resilience theorists present more interesting ways of thinking about sustainability that can inform critical development studies (Brown, 2015; Leach *et al.*, 2011). Socioecological resilience theorists argue that the incredible complexity of environmental change means that appropriate governance forms for ecosystem management must be decentralized, participatory and adaptable. Contrary to standard ideas of resource development, these perspectives argue that we must value a diversity of landscapes, knowledge forms and in human ways of living with nature and seek to foster those qualities (Biggs *et al.*, 2015). Many of these norms can resonate with critical thinking within development studies because they share a deep suspicion of managerial, technocratic approaches to organizing society–nature relations. Whether such perspectives can adequately incorporate questions of power and inequality that animate critical development studies, however, is an open question.

Recommended reading: Biggs *et al.* (2015), Brown (2015).

Development and growth

Outside of engaging critically with realm official policies and practices, it is important to note that climate change creates a significant challenge for development thinking. For much of the 20th century, critical scholars and activists tended to accept the core development goals of increasing consumption as a means to improve human well-being. Marx, for example, was enamoured with the way that capitalism developed society's productive forces, creating the basis on which all human needs could be met through a surge in productivity (Marx and Engels, 1998). The problem, as he made very clear, was that capitalism would create and distribute this immense social wealth in a fundamentally unequal and polarizing manner. Socialism, he retorted, could do modernity better in a fundamentally egalitarian and democratic fashion. Climate change, however, opens the possibility that the very idea of development – whether capitalist or socialist – may be increasingly untenable. The rapid advances in our ability to produce ever-greater quantities of consumption goods appear to choke on the polluting emissions their creation requires. This has led to significant questions being raised about whether development itself has a future and whether critical thinking must position itself as 'anti-development'.

In the West, for example, there has been a growing interest in the concept of 'degrowth', which broadly refers to a planned shrinking of the economy. The idea here is not simply to do less with less, but to transform the very fundamentals of how societies operate. Degrowth would require a profound localization of work, production and consumption, with a strong redistributionist component to ensure substantive equality in a less materially affluent future (D'Alisa *et al.*, 2015). In the postcolonial world, similar ideas are frequently related to religious tenets or indigenous world views. Mahatma Gandhi, for example, famously argued that the pursuit of 'Western civilization' would bring ruin to India and put forward an alternative path based on locally networked rural economies in which work had a spiritual, not simply material, purpose. Activist-scholar Vandana Shiva has reworked such thinking, adding a critical feminist slant, and emphasized Gandhi's ideas about egalitarian community self-determination in opposition to a destructive and exploitative globalized economy (Shiva, 2010). In Latin America, the idea of *buen vivir*, or *Sumak Kawsay* in Quechua, has been mobilized to emphasize an alternative to development: rejecting materialism and economic growth and advocating for indigenous rights, community autonomy and the rights of nature (Lalander, 2014).

The latter is in stark contrast to the neodevelopmentalist tendencies of progressive governments that have staked their socialist projects of delivering development to the poor on further hydrocarbon resource extraction.

Critical modernist thinking, however, may not be entirely dead in the water. A different brand of authors argues that the scale of transformation required to deal with climate change requires the tools of modernity and development like never before (Mazzucato, 2015). From this perspective, the role of the state will be pivotal to effectively address the demands of climate change adaptation and a clean energy revolution, yet it is only by democratizing the state that such transformations can be effected (Parenti, 2015). Without socializing the means of production, the task of decarbonizing the economy will fall foul of entrenched interests that seek to continue existing patterns of capital accumulation and expansive growth. The continued influence of oil companies over energy policy, despite their activities to obscure the evidence of anthropogenic climate change and to frustrate adequate regulatory measures, represents a prime example (Ashton, 2015). In facilitating a thorough democratization of the state, the hope is that excess consumption, particularly among elite classes, can be curbed, and financing delivered quickly, efficiently and in sufficient quantities to effect a thorough decarbonization of the economy.

Recommended reading: D'Alisa *et al.* (2015), Sachs (2015).

References

Abramsky, K. (ed.) (2010). *Sparking a Worldwide Energy Revolution: Social Struggles in the Transition to a Post-Petrol World*. Chico, CA: AK Press.

Ashton, J. (2015). 'Open letter to Shell's Ben van Beurden from John Ashton'. *The Guardian*, Monday 30 March.

Biggs, R., Schluter, M. and Schoon, M. (2015). *Principles for Building Resilience: Sustaining Ecosystem Services in Social-Ecological Systems*. Cambridge: Cambridge University Press.

Brown, K. (2015). *Resilience, Development and Social Change*. London: Routledge.

Collins, T. (2010). 'Marginalization, facilitation and the production of unequal risk: the 2006 Paso del Norte floods'. *Antipode*, 42(2): 258–88.

D'Alisa, G., Demaria, F. and Kallis, G. (2015). *Degrowth: A Vocabulary for a New Era*. London: Routledge.

Eriksen, S. and O'Brien, K. (2007). 'Vulnerability, poverty and the need for sustainable adaptation measures'. *Climate Policy*, 7(4): 337–52.

Eriksen, S., Aldunce, P., Bahinipati, C.S., D'Almeida Martins, R., Molefe, J.I., Nhemachena, C. *et al.* (2011). 'When not every response to climate change is a good one: identifying principles for sustainable adaptation'. *Climate and Development*, 3(1): 7–20.

Felli, R. (2016). 'The World Bank's neoliberal language of resilience'. In S. Soederberg (ed.), *Risking Capitalism (Research in Political Economy, Volume 31)*. Bingley, UK: Emerald Group, pp. 267–95.

IPCC (2007). *Climate Change 2007: The Scientific Basis. Wg I Contribution to IPCC 4th Assessment Report*. Cambridge: Cambridge University Press.

Lalander, R. (2014). 'Rights of nature and the indigenous peoples in Bolivia and Ecuador: a straitjacket for progressive development politics?' *Iberoamerican Journal of Development Studies*, 3(2): 148–73.

Leach, M. and Scoones, I. (eds) (2015). *Carbon Conflicts and Forest Landscapes in Africa*. London: Routledge.

Leach, M., Scoones, I. and Stirling, A. (2011). *Dynamic Sustainabilities: Technology, Environment, Social Justice*. London: Earthscan.

Lohmann, L. (2006). *Carbon Trading: A Critical Conversation on Climate Change, Privatisation and Power*. Uppsala: Development Dialogue.

Marino, E. and Ribot, J. (2012). 'Adding insult to injury: climate change and the inequities of climate intervention'. *Global Environmental Change*, 22(3): 323–8.

Marx, K. and Engels, F. (1998). *The Communist Manifesto*. New York: Monthly Review Press.

Mazzucato, M. (2015). 'The green entrepreneurial state'. In I. Scoones, M. Leach and P. Newell (eds), *The Politics of Green Transformations*. London: Routledge, pp. 113–50.

Mustafa, D. (2005). 'The production of an urban hazardscape in Pakistan: modernity, vulnerability, and the range of choice'. *Annals of the Association of American Geographers*, 95(3): 566–86.

Newell, P. and Paterson, M. (2010). *Climate Capitalism: Global Warning and the Transformation of the Global Economy*. Cambridge: Cambridge University Press.

Parenti, C. (2015). 'Shadow socialism in the age of environmental crisis'. *Green Social Thought*, 66, Winter, 26–9.

Pelling, M. (2011). *Adaptation to Climate Change*. London: Routledge Press.

Sachs, W. (2015). *Planet Dialectics: Explorations in Environment and Development*, 2nd edition. London: Zed Books.

Shiva, V. (2010). *Earth Democracy: Justice, Sustainability, and Peace*. London: South End Press.

Taylor, M. (2013). 'Climate change, relational vulnerability and human security: rethinking sustainable adaptation in agrarian environments'. *Climate and Development*, 5(4): 318–27.

Taylor, M. (2015). *The Political Ecology of Climate Change Adaptation: Livelihoods, Agrarian Change and the Conflicts of Development*. London: Routledge.

UNDP (2007). *Human Development Report 2007/2008: Fighting Climate Change – Human Solidarity in a Divided World*. Geneva: United Nations.

Urban, F. and Nordensvard, J. (eds) (2013). *Low Carbon Development: Key Issues*. London: Routledge.

Watts, M. (2014). 'Resilience as a way of life: biopolitical security, catastrophism, and the food-climate change question'. In N. Chen and L. Sharp (eds), *Bioinsecurity and Vulnerability*. Santa Fe, NM: SAR Press, pp. 145–72.

Wisner, B., Blaikie, P., Cannon, T. and Davis, I. (2004). *At Risk: Natural Hazards, People's Vulnerability and Disasters*. London: Routledge.

World Bank (2007). *World Development Report 2008: Agriculture for Development*. Oxford: Oxford University Press.

World Bank (2015). *Accelerating Climate-Resilient and Low-Carbon Development: The Africa Climate Business Plan*. Washington, DC: World Bank.

29

EXTRACTIVE CAPITALISM AND SUBTERRANEAN RESISTANCES

Raúl Zibechi[1]

The new geoeconomics of capital

Although global flows of capital over the past three decades of neoliberal globalization have become increasingly speculative and disconnected from the production process, it is revealing to trace out the changing pattern of capital flows, especially in regard to North–South flows of FDI and 'resource-seeking' capital, which have increased dramatically in recent years. A review of data on these flows shows that over the past decade, and especially since 2005, they have moved away from manufacturing and high-tech information-rich services towards the extraction of natural resources, both renewable and non-renewable, including fossil and biofuels for energy, precious metals and industrial minerals, as well as agrofood products and the 'large-scale acquisition of land' ('land grabbing', in the lexicon of critical development studies)[2] for the purpose of accessing these resources directly (as opposed to trading them) – or, in regard to some of the governments involved in this global land grab (China, Japan, etc.), the food and energy security needs of some countries.

A close look at these flows of resource-seeking capital also points towards a major shift in their destination – in the geoeconomics of their global distribution. Not only has Latin America, especially Brazil, been the recipient or destination for much of this capital, but the changing pattern of capital flows reveals a major reconfiguration in the structure of global production, a structure modified by the continuous but changing flows of capital.

The so-called 'global financial crisis' triggered by the 2007 sub-prime debacle in the US served as a sort of watershed in this regard, but the process can be traced back to the turn into the new millennium and the 'primary commodities boom' provoked by the growing demand for precious metals, and by China and other 'emerging markets' for energy, industrial minerals and agrofood products (Cypher, 2010).

In 2010, for the first time since UNCTAD kept records (i.e. since 1970), the developed countries in the Global North received less than half of global FDI flows (until the late 1980s, they attracted 97 per cent of investments). In 2005, developing and emerging economies in the Global South attracted only 12 per cent of global flows of productive capital (FDI), but in 2010, against a background of a sharp decline in capital flows in the world, these economies in the aggregate overcame the 50 per cent barrier (ECLAC, 2010). Looking more closely at the geopolitics of these capital flows, it is evident that South America was the destination of choice, and this because FDI was evidently attracted to the huge reserves of natural resources (metals and industrial minerals, hydrocarbons or fossil fuels, soy and other forms of biofuels, and agrofood products) that the governments of the day were anxious to open up for exploitation by foreign investors in order to take maximum advantage of the economic opportunities provided in the form of additional fiscal revenues.

Under these conditions, Latin America changed from being a relatively marginal location for North–South capital flows (about 5 per cent of the world total) into an important and dynamic destination. Between 2000 and 2005, Latin America received an annual average of US$66 billion that grew exponentially up to US$216 billion in 2011, which meant that it was able to attract 15 per cent of all global flows of productive capital over this period (ECLAC, 2010: 45).

The main datum here is the pattern of continued growth of investment flows to the region, which in the case of South America reached US$150 billion in 2011, 15 times greater in absolute figures than in the early 1990s. But not all countries participated equally in these flows, a function of geopolitics as much as geoeconomics. Indeed it would seem that some countries – Venezuela, Argentina and Ecuador, in particular, but also, and less understandably, Mexico – have been 'punished' by capital. In the case of Venezuela, the explanation is very simple: Hugo Chávez's nationalization policy provoked a massive flight of capital that has not been offset by the relatively large investments originating in China and the much lower investments of Brazilian capital. As for Argentina, capital changed from euphoria under the Menem regime in the 1990s to substantial caution in the wake of the Kirchner regime's default in 2002 and its reluctance to heed the dictates of the IMF regarding debt repayment and restructuring in the context of the worst crisis in the country's history.

At the beginning of a sharp turn towards neoliberalism in the early 1990s, Argentina received twice the investments that Brazil received, and in the second half of the 1990s FDI inflows equaled those of Mexico, even though both economies are much larger than Argentina. After the 2001 crisis, foreign investors began to beat a retreat, although not to the same scale and speed as in Venezuela, and Brazilian capital – and to a lesser degree Chinese and Canadian capital – entered into the vacuum left by the retreating US and European investors.

The case of Mexico is very curious in that the government is closely aligned with both the neoliberal policy agenda and the US – and it has one of the most *entreguista* regimes in all Latin America, particularly as regards mining capital (no royalties, and an effective tax rate of 1.2 per cent) (Bárcenas, 2012). At the time of the inception of NAFTA in January 1994, Mexico received up to 60 per cent of FDI destined for Latin America. The subsequent withdrawal of capital from Mexico, or the evident reluctance to invest in a highly liberalized economy vis-à-vis US capital, evidently relates to the changing pattern of investment capital – for example, the dominance of 'resource-seeking' rather than efficiency- or market-seeking capital – as well as political instability in that the withdrawal of capital quickened as of 2008 when the state began its dirty war against drug trafficking.

The Latin American countries that today are the most attractive to capital include Brazil, the biggest economy in the region and very much open to business as far as foreign investments go, particularly as regards to what we term 'agro-extractivism'. Other countries favoured by extractive capital include Colombia, the linchpin of US imperialism in the region and long a supporter of extractive capitalism, and Chile, which continued to hoe the line of extractivism and neoliberalism when a number of other countries in the region turned towards inclusionary state activism and adopted a regulatory regime.

Brazil illustrates the success of the government's geopolitical project to convert the country into a global power (see Chapter 30), and the interest of foreign investors in an economy that has been able in just a decade to incorporate close to 40 million people into the market. Receiving only half of the investments that Mexico attracted two decades ago, the volume of FDI inflows today is four times that of Mexico, even though the two economies are comparable in size. But what distinguishes the Brazilian case is not the growth of FDI, which currently positions it as the fourth largest destination point for FDI in the world after the US, China, Hong Kong and the UK, but the quality of those investments. Before 2005, capital inflows went in three directions: industry, which absorbed from 30 to 50 per cent of total FDI inflows; services, which absorbed 50–60 per cent; and mining and agriculture, which accounted for less than 10 per cent of total FDI inflows (SOBEET, 2011). But several trends and 'developments' in recent years have dramatically changed this pattern. The strong demand for primary commodities on the world market, the expansion of large-scale foreign investments in land for the purpose of agrofood extraction and the production of biofuels, and the rampant speculation in food and minerals, as well as land, have wrought a profound change in the structure of capital inflows: FDI in services have fallen from around half of total investments to 30 per cent; the share of industry, where exports have lagged in recent years (partly as a result of the so-called 'Dutch disease'), has fallen to 35 per cent; while mining and agribusiness tripled their share of FDI inflows to 30 per cent (Zibechi, 2012).

Recommended reading: Cypher (2010), ECLAC (2010), Zibechi (2012).

Dynamics of extractivism and neo-extractivism

Speculation on commodity and capital markets is one way to advance capital accumulation (make a lot of money in a capitalist economy), and another is production based on the exploitation of labour (extracting some of the valued added to production in the labour process). Speculation is death, it is robbery, it is destruction, it is capital, it is capitalism, it is extractivism, it is mining, it is mono-culture, it is commodity production and poverty production – and militarization, genocide. Finally, we are what we bet on life, the need to create our food every day, our survival strategies, but also our dreams and our hopes. We do it collec-tively in community and in *minga* (collective struggle).

The first thing we need to address is why we have an extractivist model today? Why open-pit mining? Why today the widespread land grabbing and pillage of natural resources, and the associated conditions of dispossession and exclusion, the poisoning and damage to the health of those living in close proximity to the sites of extraction, and the degradation of the environment and rural livelihoods based on a more balanced and nurturing relationship with nature?

One answer to these questions can be found in the form taken by capitalism at this most advanced stage of its development – neoliberal globalization. We are now in a second period of neoliberalism based on the advance of extractive capital – 'resource-seeking' foreign private investment – and the multinational corporations seeking to accumulate capital by extracting natural resources from the land for which there is a strong demand and high prices on the world market. The first part of the neoliberal era was in the 1990s. It took the predominant form of privatization, a neoliberal policy designed to undermine the collective or communal rights to the land enjoyed for millennia by the aboriginal and indigenous peoples and com-munities in the region, and to commodify both land and the natural wealth of 'the commons' – the land, water and the resources for subsistence provided by the land.

Neoliberalism arrived in Latin America with the project to commodify and pri-vatize everything – surrender to the 'private sector', i.e. the capitalist multinational corporations that dominate the world market – the land and the major means of social production, public goods and even water, which is not only an important element of the global commons (not subject to a private property regime), but a fundamental source of life itself. In the process, neoliberalism – i.e. the neoliberal policy agenda of governments forced to submit to the Washington Consensus on the virtues of free-market capitalism – weakened the state, destroying its capacity to pursue an industrial policy and allowing foreign 'investors' and the multinational corporations to appropriate the public assets that had been built up by the people via the agency of state enterprises.

This second phase of neoliberal capitalist development was more or less com-pleted by the year 2000, although in a number of countries (Ecuador, for example), the neoliberal policy agenda was halted in its tracks by the activism and several uprisings of the indigenous people in the region, as well as the peasant social movements (see Chapter 35 by Vergara-Camus in this volume; see also Petras and Veltmeyer, 2005, 2013). The neoliberal agenda was unfinished because of the organized resistance of dozens of popular uprisings throughout Latin America, from Mexico to southern Patagonia. But in the new millennium (the 21st century), the forces pushing the advance of capital launched another assault, a new campaign, in the class war against labour, the direct producers on the land, the indigenous people and the rural communities, and nature. This second phase of the war and the project of neoliberal globalization in the advance of capital has taken form as extractive capitalism, reversion to a type of capitalism that predominated before the era of industrial capitalism, functioning not so much on the basis of labour exploitation (exploiting the apparently unlimited supply of surplus agricultural labour) as the exploitation of nature, extracting its wealth of natural resources for the purpose of exporting them in primary commodity form (see, for example, Veltmeyer, 2013; Veltmeyer and Petras, 2014).

Today, the world has fundamentally changed. What we now have is a system in crisis (on this, see Chapter 20). The world system formed in the wake of the Second World War has a centre (the rich countries in the Global North where most of the multinational corporations are based) and a number of peripheries in the so-called Global South. Prior to the changes ushered in with the new millennium, the working class and the producers on the periphery were exploited for their labour power, and the wealth that was generated in the process was transferred to the centre of the system, providing a major source of capital accumulation and 'development' there. But today that has changed. Today the countries in the centre of the system are experiencing a major financial and economic crisis – arguably the result of inherent structural contradictions, as well as a process of over-accumulation at the level of global finance (see Chapter 1 by Polanyi Levitt in this volume) – that has penetrated to the very foundation of the system (see Chapter 19 by Veltmeyer in this volume).

Today, capital is not interested in agriculture or industry as a source of accumulation. Production is agriculture, the peasantry, the rural community, industry and urban space; production means human beings, people, men and women. And in that space and place, people have learned to resist, to organize from below, to make it difficult for capital to exploit labour and nature, to appropriate surplus value and all the wealth of nature bequeathed to humankind. So today capitalists and foreign investors in land and resources have, to some extent, abandoned production and seek to accumulate capital by alternative means, for example by speculating on day-to-day changes in the exchange rate of different currencies or on the future price of different commodities and also the prices that consumers are willing to or forced to pay for these commodities. This too is extractivism – extractive capitalism.

People in the grassroots of the economy and society on the periphery of the system over the years did not abandon their rural communities and their livelihoods because they preferred the life in the cities over that on the farm and in their communities. No, their movements across space and time, and their migration to the cities and other countries, can be seen as a series of responses to the dynamic forces of capitalist development – forces generated by the advance of capital and the penetration of economy after economy (on this, see Chapter 24).

For several centuries, and then again after an interregnum of some 50 years, the advances made by capital in the countryside were speculative ventures, seeking to accumulate capital by extracting precious metals (gold and silver) and industrial minerals, food products and animal feed, and various forms of fossil fuel used to fuel the development of industry and provide energy to millions of consumers in both the North and South. In this extraction process, capital advanced step by step from commodity to commodity, squeezing from each as much profit as it could, betting on and seeking to gain from the changing values attached by the market to these commodities. But nowadays, the products that are most highly valued include precious minerals and metals – and food, the object of intense, at times frenzied, speculation on future commodity markets, generating from time to time a 'food crisis' (a condition in which people cannot afford the price attached by the market to food) (Bello, 2008).

The global food crisis, which is a fundamental assault on the natural right of all people to life and health, is only one of a number of major consequences of the relentless dynamics of extractive capital in its exploitation of people and nature.

First, there is no extractivism, no mining, no soy complex and no monoculture without militarization, without the deployment of the state of its repressive apparatus to settle the inevitable conflict over accessing and the social distribution of the most highly valued natural resources and forms of wealth. This is not just a mistaken policy; militarization is part of the model of capitalist development. Similarly, there is no open-pit or mega-mining without militarism. You may not see it in the city you live in – if you live in the city. But if you take a closer look in the subterranean spaces of the system, you will see an increasingly militarized environment. And accompanying militarization is a criminalization of the protests – even in countries such as Ecuador with a 'progressive' post-neoliberal regime, where not a few nongovernmental organizations and hundreds of people have been criminalized for defending their rights to the land and defending their community.

Second, extractive capital inevitably leads to acute social and economic polarization. This is in part because extractive capital tends to be highly concentrated, generating conditions under which most of the surplus (the value of the exported commodities) is exported, appropriated by different groups such as commodity traders and the capitalists that operate the corporations in the extractive sector, while the working class and people in the popular sector receive few of the benefits but all of the heavy social and environmental costs (on this, see the various studies collected in Veltmeyer and Petras, 2014). Needless to say, this is very perverse because open-pit mining or soy monoculture, as the current face of the model in a number of South American countries where extractive capital is concentrated, always generates this social polarization, which in turn inevitably breeds resistance.

The rich are getting richer and the poor are getting poorer. So what else is new (although not inevitable)? And this is very perverse and terrible enough. Latin American governments, especially those pursuing a so-called 'progressive' policy regime, following the post-Washington Consensus on the need for a more inclusive development, have attempted to reduce this polarization or reduce it with a new social policy focused on poverty reduction (on this see, inter alia, Veltmeyer and Tetreault, 2013). It is no coincidence that in Brazil, where the 'new social policy' was devised, there are 50 million people who currently receive a direct cash transfer under the *Bolsa Família* programme, or the *Zero Hunger* plan. Why is this?

It is because there is no extractivism without social policies that give crumbs to the poor in order to avoid or contain a social outbreak. The underlying motivation of this new social policy is not an interest in social justice or redressing or lessening social inequalities; only enough money in the form of cash is transferred to poor households so as to alleviate the worst effects of poverty and to extinguish any fires of social protest.

Third, often the indigenous peoples over the years – the peasants and the indigenous nationalities – have been forced to live in the worst places, environmentally and geographically speaking, in the cities on the banks of polluted streams, in the countryside in the worst places of land, in the heights or in places where they can barely survive. And to the extent that they manage to appropriate common goods such as water, they are condemned not to live, but to survive under increasingly worse conditions.

Fourth, we have the project of capital, which is nothing less than a genocidal project, a project to exterminate those people who refuse to migrate and occupy land from which the extractive companies need and seek to extract vital natural resources for the purpose of capital accumulation, but to which the indigenous and peasant communities claim territorial rights. The point is that these indigenous people and this population are an obstacle to the accumulation of wealth by the oligarchic classes and global capital. In an earlier time, workers in the factories and mines, and peasants in the field and on the haciendas of the agrarian oligarchs, generated profits for the owners of the land and employers of labour by being forced to work many hours longer than necessary to cover the cost of subsistence and reproduction of the labour power of these workers and peasants. But nowadays, this is no longer working, and the oligarchs and capitalists are not enriched by our sweat; they enrich themselves by speculating, and this journey made by capital, this strategic change, is what condemns us to death. So we have to assume that this is their project – to eradicate or force the displacement of those who they cannot exploit and stand in the way of their profits, their capital accumulation project.

Recommended reading: Veltmeyer (2013), Veltmeyer and Petras (2014).

Extractive capital and the resistance

Each advance of capital in its assault on labour and nature, it might be argued, activates the impulse to resist, and, by the same token, each particular form of capitalism generates particular forms of resistance. Developments on the new frontier of extractive capital in Latin America lends support to this idea in that the economic and political developments over the past two decades undoubtedly generated new forms of resistance and struggle. Throughout the 20th century, the resistance predominantly took the form of the land struggle and the labour movement. The first engaged the resistance of small-scale agricultural producers and peasant farmers against forces that worked to separate them from the land and their means of production. The second engaged the working class in a struggle to resist the workings of a system based on the exploitation of labour power.

This resistance led to a protracted struggle for higher wages and improved working conditions, a struggle that resulted in an ultimate defeat in the 1980s under conditions that weakened and then destroyed the capacity of organized labour to confront capital and even to negotiate collective agreements. While the indigenous communities and the dispossessed peasantry would recover from the defeat that they suffered in their land struggle, the labour movement in the region was never able to recover its former power. The obstacles to their successful resistance were simply too great to overcome. On the other hand, the semiproletarianized peasants and rural landless workers – the rural poor, in the development discourse of the World Bank – successfully mobilized powerful forces of resistance against the neoliberal agenda of those governments that were holding to the Washington Consensus. The 1990s saw the emergence of powerful indigenous uprisings and the formation of new social movements that managed to hold the neoliberal policy agenda at bay, resulting in a widespread discontent with and the rejection of neoliberalism – creating conditions of a new progressive cycle in Latin American politics (Barrett *et al.*, 2008).

In the new millennium, under conditions of extractive capitalism, the resistance took a number of new and different forms. The struggle for land or improved wages and working conditions were no longer the major forms of struggle. The struggle now was to resist and oppose the policies and efforts designed to privatize and deny them access to water and other elements of the global commons, and to protest the negative impacts of extractive operations on the environment, their rural livelihoods and health. The social movements and localized resistances formed under these conditions included the struggles of those forced to abandon their livelihoods and rural communities because they were deprived of their customary use of land for agriculture, or their right of access to potable water and the commons had been violated, and the environment on which their livelihoods depended had been degraded.

Resistance and struggle on the new frontier of extractive capital

Throughout Latin America, there are conflicts over the resistance to a model that is destructive of the environment and limits the possibility of communities to continue to cultivate the land, sustain their livelihoods and live as they would wish. As for the political conflicts in the mining sector, fumigations and transgenic crops stand out. According to the Observatory of Mining Conflicts of Latin America (OCMAL), there are more than 195 active conflicts for the *megaminería* (megamine sector) in the region. Peru and Chile top the list with 34 and 33 conflicts, respectively, followed by Mexico with 28, Argentina with 26, Brazil with 20 and Colombia with 12. Those with the least number of mining conflicts are Trinidad and Tobago, Paraguay and Uruguay, each with one.

The *megaminería* is affecting at least 290 communities across the region. In some countries such as Peru, where 25 per cent of the territory has been ceded to multinational mining companies, the resistance and the resulting conflict led to the collapse of two cabinets of Ollanta Humala's government and the militarization of several provinces. Between 2006 and 2011, socioenvironmental conflicts in this context led to the death of 195 activists.

Resistance to the production of soybeans, the main transgenic crop in the region, is particularly strong in Argentina, where over 20.3 million hectares of farmland is dedicated to growing soybeans, more than half of the country's farmland, much of it in the hands of foreigners,[3] for the purpose of supplying the world demand for energy in the form of agrofuels. One of these 'foreigners' is the multinational Monsanto, which intends to instal a plant in the locality of Malvinas Argentinas, near Córdoba, for the purpose of producing corn seeds. In this city, the Mothers of Ituzaingó, a working-class neighbourhood of 6,000 inhabitants in the south of Cordoba surrounded by soy fields, recently managed to win a battle against the fumigation of the crop. However, this is but one battle in an ongoing class war, and in many cases – as in Peru under Ollanta and even in Ecuador in the case of one of the region's most 'progressive' post-neoliberal regimes – the local communities have discovered that more often than not in their resistance and opposition to the destructive operations and negative impacts of extractive capital, they have to confront the opposition of their own government, which, in many cases, in a coincidence of economic interest, is on the side of capital (Veltmeyer, 2013).

Recommended reading: Veltmeyer (2013), Veltmeyer and Petras (2014).

Mining as a source of conflict and crisis

The countries with the most mining conflicts in the subregion are Peru and Chile. Jaime Borda of Peru's Muqui Sur Network warned that mining exploration spending in the world has increased 10-fold since 2002. He shows a map showing 'how entrepreneurs see Peru', a country covered with squares representing mining concessions (Borda, 2013). In 2002, there were only 7.5 million hectares granted to mining companies, a figure that jumped to almost 26 million in 2012, 20 per cent of the country's land area. Some Andean provinces such as Apurímac have 57 per cent of the surface ceded to the mining companies. Borda said that the high level of conflict in the country is motivated by the fact that 'the population understood that protest is the only way for the government to hear and listen to the communities'. He wondered if a new and different relationship with mining were possible.

The answer was not simple. Large mining companies such as the newly merged Glencore and Xstrata monopolize the markets in which they operate: 70 per cent of the world zinc market, 55 per cent copper, 45 per cent lead. 'The bases of extractive growth have been exhausted in democratic terms and it becomes an increasingly aggressive, vertical, authoritarian and deeply centralist growth', Borda said. That is why he defended 'greater institutionality regarding the issue of the environment, strengthening decentralization and land management', as it is not clear who plans the growth of mining that is turning the southern region into a mining corridor.

Chilean Lucio Cuenca of the Latin American Observatory of Environmental Conflicts (OLCA) said that despite being the world's largest producer of copper, the government has refused to regulate the market and prices to the point that 'transnationals decide where and at what rate to exploit' (Cuenca, 2013). Mining is the main export product but accounts for less than 1 per cent of employment, but 70 per cent is precarious by subcontracting. In 2010, 25 per cent of the territory was in exploration or exploitation. In Chile, mining consumes 37 per cent of the electricity produced by the country, and this will reach 50 per cent in a few years, compared to 28 per cent in industry and 16 per cent in the residential sector. This imposes on the state the permanent construction of new sources of energy, which accelerates the displacement of affected communities and the conversion of agricultural land to other uses.

Apart from the communities contiguous to the mines and negatively impacted by their operations, the state is also a major loser with the expansion of these operations. In 1990, the state-owned Codelco controlled 75 per cent of mining production, a percentage that fell to 28 per cent in 2007 due to a major expansion of private concessions. However, tax revenues are inversely proportional: with this small percentage of production, Codelco contributed US$8.3 billion in 2008 to the state's coffers; notwithstanding the fact that their production is double the volume of the state enterprise, the private and foreign-owned mining companies contributed only US$3.4 billion.

Anti-mining activists and the communities downstream from one of the largest gold mines in the world operated by Canadian-owned Barrick Gold garnered a major victory in 2013. They had been fighting since 2000 the operations of the Pascua Lama mine that Barrick Gold operates on the Chilean-Argentine border. The court stayed all mining operations until the company managed to work out how to mitigate the destructive impact of the contaminated water resulting from its mining operations on the communities downstream from the mine. The project, in which Barrick Gold had invested some US$8.5 billion, was halted by a local court at the request of indigenous communities in the area and downstream. Some five months later, the supreme court confirmed the order to suspend operations of the mine (Lopez, 2013). As a result, Barrick reported losses of US$8,560 million in the second quarter (40 per cent of its equity), and shareholders filed a lawsuit against management for hiding and misrepresenting information since October 2009. It may be the beginning of more mining problems in Chile. The north of the country suffers from a major water crisis, the responsibility for which lies with the *megaminería*.

Recommended reading: Bebbington and Bury (2013), Giarracca and Teubal (2014).

Notes

1 In constructing this chapter, the co-editors have pieced together and edited four of Raúl Zibechi's essays published in various periodicals.
2 On this, see Borras *et al.* (2012).
3 A map constructed by La Angostura Digital maps (http://laangosturadigital.com.ar) shows the spread and degree of foreign control of Argentine national territory. According to the map, almost 30 million hectares of the best land and fertile soil, watersheds and nature reserves – and reserves of strategic minerals – in 23 provinces are already foreign-owned, and another 13 million hectares are currently up for sale.

References

Bárcenas, F.L. (2012). 'Detener el saqueo minero en México'. *La Jornada*, 28, February: 31.

Barrett, P., Chávez, D. and Rodríguez Garavito, C. (2008). *The New Latin American Left: Utopia Reborn*. London: Pluto Press.

Bebbington, A. and Bury, J. (eds) (2013). *Subterranean Struggles: New Dynamics of Mining, Oil, and Gas in Latin America*. Austin, TX: University of Texas Press.

Bello, W. (2008). *Globalization, Development and Democracy: A Reflection on the Global Food Crisis*. Keynote Address, Canadian Association for the Study of International Development, University of British Colombia, Vancouver, 6 June.

Borda, J. (2013). Intervention in the seminar 'Desde el extractivismo a la re-construcción de alternativas' organized by BEPE (Bienaventurados los Pobres), the network Agroforestal del Chaco and the network Asistencia Jurídica contra la Megaminería, Buenos Aires, 29 August.

Borras Jr., S., Franco, J., Gomez, S., Kay, C. and Spoor, M. (2012). 'Land grabbing in Latin America and the Caribbean'. *Journal of Peasant Studies*, 39(3–4): 845–72.

Cuenca, L. (2013). Intervention in the seminar 'Desde el extractivismo a la reconstrucción de alternativas' organized by BEPE (Bienaventurados los Pobres), the network Agroforestal del Chaco and the netork Asistencia Jurídica contra la Megaminería, Buenos Aires, 29 August.

Cypher, J. (2010). 'South America's commodities boom: developmental opportunity or path dependent reversion?' *Canadian Journal of Development Studies*, 30(3–4): 635–62.

ECLAC (2010). *Foreign Investment in Latin America and the Caribbean*. Santiago: United Nations.

Giarracca, N. and Teubal, M. (2014). 'Argentina: extractivist dynamics of soy production and open-pit mining'. In H. Veltmeyer and J. Petras (eds), *The New Extractivism: A Post-Neoliberal Development Model or Imperialism of the Twenty-First Century?* London: Zed Books, pp. 47–79.

Lopez, E. (2013). 'UPDATE 2: in relief for Barrick, Chile court doesn't nix mine permit'. *Reuters*, 25 September.

Petras, J. and Veltmeyer, H. (2005). *Social Movements and the State: Argentina, Bolivia, Brazil, Ecuador*. London: Pluto Press.

Petras, J. and Veltmeyer, H. (2013). *Social Movements in Latin America: Neoliberalism and Popular Resistance*. New York: Palgrave Macmillan.

SOBEET (2011). Boletim No. 77, Sociedade Brasileira de Estudos de Empresas Transnacionais e da Globalização Econômica, São Paulo, 25 de enero.

Veltmeyer, H. (2013). 'The political economy of natural resource extraction: a new model or extractive imperialism?' *Canadian Journal of Development Studies*, 34(1), March: 79–95.

Veltmeyer, H. and Petras, J. (2014). *The New Extractivism in Latin America*. London: Zed Books.

Veltmeyer, H. and Tetreault, D. (eds) (2013). *Poverty in Latin America: Public Policies and Development Pathways*. West Hartford, CT: Kumarian Press.

Zibechi, R. (2012). 'La nueva geopolítica del capital'. ALAI, América Latina en Movimiento, Abril 19, *Le Monde Diplomatique*, Colombia.

30

POPULAR SUSTAINABLE DEVELOPMENT, OR ECOLOGICAL ECONOMICS FROM BELOW

David Barkin

Many people in Mexico and Latin America are organizing alternative ways of assuring their livelihood and that of their communities. There are numerous examples of people in urban areas promoting local activities, small workshops and organizing cooperative and markets for local exchanges (through barter or use of local currencies or national monies) within and among communities. However, in most of Latin America, these alternatives are emerging among peasants and indigenous groups, organized collectively in rural areas, forging evolving models of social economics that reflect their commitments to a variety of models of social, solidarity and ecological economies (SSEEs). The proliferation of these initiatives reflects the recognition of their importance for human development and the relationship of socioeconomic processes with the environment.[1]

In this chapter, we examine a number of experiences, joining them in an initial conceptualization of the SSEE. The chapter presents an integrated paradigm that highlights the ethical character of exchange, production and consumption processes. These alternatives are widely recognized as contributing to transforming the conception of individuals and their integration into social (collective) organizations, a dynamic that also transform their very essence. They are also changing the logic of production, deepening and extending communal processes, and contributing to improve synergies between the communities and their environments.

Many theoretical approaches have contributed to our work. Among these, we might include: (i) the anti–utilitarian movement in the social sciences (MAUSS), created in France on the basis of the initial legacy of Marcel Mauss, an anthropologist who is widely recognized for his early insights (at the beginning of the 20th century) as to the importance of reciprocity and 'gifts' in human society; (ii) *The Great Transformation* by Karl Polanyi (2001), whose understanding of the problem of markets continues to be fundamental; (iii) ecological economics, a relatively new school of economics (ca. 1990), building on the contributions of the Club of

Rome (Meadows *et al.*, 1972, 2004) and of Nicolás Georgescu-Roegen (1971), who reintroduced the second law of thermodynamics into social analysis, obliging us to reconsider the problem of energy, introduced long before the current realization of impacts of climate change; (iv) the diverse forms for implementing other structures of communities based on alternative cosmologies and systems of social construction, one of which has become well known as *buen vivir*, or living well, a principle that has been incorporated into the constitutions of Bolivia and Ecuador (Acosta, 2013; Barkin, 2012; Gonzales and Gonzalez, 2015; Lang, 2013); and (v) the doctrine of 'degrowth', emerging as a critique of today's dominant consumer-based growth model (Bonaiuti, 2012; Escobar, 2015; Kallis *et al.*, 2012; Latouche, 1991; Muraca, 2013). These approaches are complementary and their insights contribute to evaluate proposals for the regional management of natural resources in sustainable way. We argue that the SSEE represents a significant contribution for the development of a new theory for social reproduction.

Numerous peoples[2] around the world are finding alternatives that offer more opportunities and a better quality of life than offered by today's capitalist economy, while also contributing to environmental conservation. They are realizing that alternatives are necessary to create spaces – political, economic and social, within the territories they occupy – in which they can effectively resist the destructive impacts of the spread of capitalist organization of production on the quality of life, social organization and the planet. This process is of great significance globally, as communities are collectively searching for means to: (i) appreciate and enhance the significance of diversity within and among themselves; (ii) accept the necessity of coordination and cooperation emerging within the diversity that their projects offer; (iii) develop new means for concerted political action for socioeconomic and environmental governance on a supranational scale; (iv) recognize the need to compensate for the asymmetries that exist on a global scale, accepting responsibilities for assuring the well-being of those unable to undertake significant initiatives on their own; and finally, (v) strengthen or (re)construct their own sense of identity.

This is the broader context within which 'social and solidarity economies' (SSEs) are emerging locally while also creating regional and international networks. Underlying this dynamic is an understanding – oftentimes implicit – that their full insertion into the world market has been and continues to be a mechanism of impoverishment. Their experiences in the market economy – be it as wage labourers in their own countries or as migrants, as independent workers, or even as small-scale business people – have clearly demonstrated the difficulty of assuring a reasonable quality of life for their families, much less improve their lot, create opportunities for the future, and attend the needs of the planet. In this framework, it is clear that the search for SSE involves more than attempts to produce goods; that is, it requires moving beyond the market dynamics that depend on private accumulation and generates profound inequalities. The point of departure for an SSE must be a commitment to the ethical organization of a society and all of its activities: ethical in the sense that the needs of all people in the community are attended to, while also making provision for the well-being of future generations.

This alternative approach is based on the proposals of diverse indigenous and peasant groups for their own organization of the rural production process as part of their diagnosis of the functioning of the market economy. Their collective commitments to an alternative framework for production and social integration is grounded in the basic principles that shape their social and political organization, and offer a realistic but challenging strategy for local progress. These principles (Barkin, 2000, 2005), widely agreed upon in broad-based consultations among the communities, are:

- autonomy;
- solidarity;
- self-sufficiency;
- productive diversification; and
- sustainable management of regional resources.

The emphasis on local (regional) economies, the use of traditional and agroecological approaches in production, and the integrated management of ecosystems are the basis for their guarantee of a minimum standard of living for all their members and for a corresponding responsibility to participate, thus eliminating the phenomenon of unemployment. An integral part of this approach is the explicit rejection of the notion that people in rural communities conceive of themselves exclusively as farmers, or even as resource managers; rather, in these societies, it is more revealing to understand their decisions as the result of a *complex* allocation of their time among numerous activities of individual and collective benefit.

Recommended reading: Acosta (2013), Barkin (2012), Escobar (2015), Gonzales and Gonzalez (2015), Kallis *et al.* (2012), Muraca (2013), Polanyi (2001).

Development from a grassroots and indigenous perspective: the search for a sustainable model and a new path

This raises a fundamental question: How and why do our societies appear to perpetuate the poverty prevailing in most rural communities? In addition, why do so many societies continue to persist in their stubborn ties to the land and to their traditional structures for production and reproduction? In response, we suggest that what appears as poverty in many rural societies is the result of deliberate choices made by their members to shape or reshape their communities on the basis of different values, focusing on satisfying their own basic needs and assuring an ever more effective ability to govern themselves and negotiate their autonomy in the face of intensifying efforts to integrate them into global markets and the logic of rationalities based on individual benefit and monetary valuations of social relations and natural resources.[3]

Some evidence for this change in direction can be found in the concerted efforts made by societies throughout the Americas to forge solutions on their own, or in alliance with others, sometimes in collaboration with outside agents. Throughout the world, there are numerous social movements defending their territory and proposing alternatives that lead to a better quality of life, although not necessarily more consumption. What is striking is the volume of literature documenting these efforts, a literature so blithely ignored in most development thinking. Many of the peoples involved in this process are 'bringing up to date' the long-held traditions of many groups who tenaciously defend their ideological and cultural heritages (Toledo and Barrera Bassols, 2008), while others are searching out new paths, controlled by themselves (see, for example, Zermeño, 2010).

The movement to reassert indigenous identities in Mexico was strengthened in the aftermath of the 1994 uprising in Chiapas by the Zapatista Army of National Liberation (EZLN) (Muñoz, 2008).[4] The local *Caracoles* in Chiapas are contributing to this objective, directly improving the lives of their members while also portraying a model of social organization and change that continues to have a powerful effect on other communities, as well as in other countries.[5] There is ample evidence that their activities are contributing to diversifying the economy and increasing productivity in a region where perhaps as many as 500,000 people are participating; they have achieved a very high level of self-sufficiency in food while assuring health and education services for all (Baronnet *et al.*, 2011).

Since then, the activity and visibility of indigenous peoples throughout Mexico has increased along with a gradual recognition of their importance in the population. This renewed consciousness of their worth has come about because of *and* in spite of the growing intensity of repressive actions by the state and other actors, including private corporations given concessions in these territories and organized groups in various parts of the society.[6] While a recounting of the initiatives being implemented in these communities would be too lengthy for inclusion here, suffice it to say that the discussion of many of them within the framework of the National Indigenous Congress, and the increased circulation of information and meetings among members, is contributing to strengthen the resolve and ability of members to carry their projects forward.

Recommended reading: Toledo and Barrera Bassols (2008), Zermeño (2010).

Community-based development from below: the battle over the commons

In connection with their efforts to gain recognition and elaborate local management strategies, control of water resources has been particularly contentious as communities try to assert their rights to adequate supplies and protect their natural sources. We are accompanying a number of communities in their efforts to reinforce control in their territories by developing systems for managing water resources and organizing to impede encroachment by national and state-level authorities trying to limit their historical access (Barkin, 2001). These movements are inextricably combined with others in opposition to large-scale construction projects for dams designed to harness waters for electricity generation, to support mining operations, or for long-distance transfer between water basins to supply urban areas where ageing infrastructure and excessive growth in consumption are causing shortages due to lack of administrative and technical capabilities of dominant bureaucracies. As a result, many communities that have historically been able to satisfy their own needs and even share surpluses with neighbouring communities are now finding themselves involved in forming coalitions to defend their water resources, along with ecologists who argue that the engineering and public works ('tubes and pumps') approach of the public sector is inappropriate and simply postponing the day of reckoning with regard to the need for a more ecologically informed approach to water management.

Our collaborations with communities involved with protecting water sources has demonstrated the value of combing traditional and leading-edge technologies to protect their natural sources – the aquifer streams and springs on which they depend. This combination of technologies with direct community involvement in water management contrasts sharply with the national water authorities' approach that eschews local diversity, preferring a homogenous administrative model conducive to centralized management and engineering solutions. In response to the great differences in local conditions, there are many examples of water-saving technologies being implemented by the communities, such as installing composting toilets and separating grey from black water flows to allow for low-cost and passive biological processing conducive to restorative environmental practices.

A particularly noteworthy project, 'Water Forever', mobilized more than 100,000 people organized in many local cooperatives to transform a million hectares of barren plateau and steep slopes, using 'appropriate' technologies, to construct a large number of low-impact landscaping projects, including rock dams and ponds to channel surface flows and collect run-off, recreating underground aquifers and structures found in some of the oldest irrigation projects in the western hemisphere from the 11th century. This project, which began in the 1980s, is noteworthy because it combines community managed agroecological and agro-industrial activities and enterprises belonging to the participants, creating jobs and products that are proving attractive to consumers for their social, ecological and nutritional qualities (Hernández Garciadiego and Herrerías, 2008).[7] In Bolivia, the experience of the 'Water War' of 2000 in Cochabamba is still vivid in people's memories as local water committees continue to organize actively while resisting the state's effort to manage the commons (Dwinell and Olivera, 2014; Fogelberg, 2013).

Recommended reading: Barkin (2001, 2005), Dwinell and Olivera (2014), Fogelberg (2013).

Community-based resource management

Forestry is another important activity that many communities value. They waged an unrelenting and difficult battle during the last half of the 20th century to assert their rights to control the lands over which they were able to retain or regain control after the Revolution. They were particularly effective in wresting exploitative lumber contracts for their communal forests from private firms that had been given concessions to (mis)manage them (Bray, 2013). Today, there is a variety of management plans in effect, testimony to skills that the communities have acquired as they attempt to reconcile pressures for ensuring conservation with the need to create jobs and generate incomes. The literature offers rich accounts of these strategies, and many studies explore the relationship between these approaches and the cosmologies of the participating communities, particularly in community-managed forests, which comprise 71 per cent of the nation's forests (e.g. Barkin and Fuente, 2013; Bray *et al.*, 2003; Cronkleton *et al.*, 2011; Stevens *et al.*, 2014).[8]

Accompanying these initiatives, other communities are promoting collaboration with university and civil society researchers who are contributing to explaining the value of the work, while contributing to diversifying economies and improving production in sustainable ways (Toledo and Ortiz-Espejel, 2014; Toledo *et al.*, 2013). One application that has proved particularly illustrative involves the inclusion of waste avocados that were contributing to environmental damage in diets to fatten hogs in backyard settings, resulting in metabolic changes to produce low-cholesterol meat, improving incomes as they were marketed at a premium in local markets. In this case, as in others based on a similar paradigm, indigenous women were especially benefited, as they implemented the projects and were soon recognized for their leadership capabilities (Barkin, 2012; Fuente and Morales Ramos, 2013).

In a different approach, scholar-activists are working with producers in diverse regions to protect and enhance production of a traditional Mexican alcoholic drink, mezcal, modifying the traditional planting and harvesting techniques of agaves, taking care of the forest, and enriching community life by promoting cooperative production that is contributing to raising incomes and rehabilitating ecosystems (Delgado Lemus, 2014). In Guerrero, this work is part of an ambitious programme of the Grupo de Estudios Ambientales (Illsley *et al.*, 2007) for collaborative promotion of local forms of '*buen vivir*' and ecosystem restoration that was awarded the 'Equator Prize' in 2012 by the UNDP.

In another region of Oaxaca, four communities continue to care for their mulberry trees, raising silkworms to produce the traditional thread that they then weave into highly attractive and fairly priced garments, displayed and marketed locally and through a well-curated textile museum; elsewhere, others are experimenting with new plantings of perennial indigenous cotton varieties (cultivated before the Spanish conquest) that are woven into handicrafts and garments as an alternative to using genetically modified cotton that currently dominates the global industry. In Peru, and more recently Bolivia, a well-established technical promotion and development organization, Pratec, is deploying effective approaches for community-based learning, improving production in the multiple ecologies of the Andean world, focusing on potatoes, but carefully balancing its work to support broad-based, diversified progress (Gonzales, 2014).[9] Ecotourism is yet another more controversial activity, because it involves an explicit opening of the community to outsiders who are frequently unable to comprehend the magnitude of the cultural and economic chasm that separates them from their hosts (Barkin, 2002).

Recommended reading: Barkin (2002, 2012), Fuente and Morales Ramos (2013), Toledo and Ortiz-Espejel (2014), Toledo *et al.* (2013).

Agroecology and the peasant way (Vía Campesina)

The process is not limited to ethnic communities. It is interesting to note the significance for many peasant communities of the consolidation of one of the largest peasant organizations in the world, La Vía Campesina. This group comprises about 200 million members organized in groups in more than 80 countries around the world; small-scale farmer organizations are promoting local capacities for self-sufficiency based on technologies that combine the benefits of organic cultivation, where appropriate, with the intensive use of the producer's own equipment and knowledge to increase production. This approach, known as agroecology, is widely acknowledged to be appropriate for overcoming many of the considerable obstacles that impede the successful expansion of small-scale farming in the Third World (Altieri and Toledo, 2011; Holt-Giménez, 2010). Evaluations of the implementation of these strategies reflect the benefits not just of the productive gains from a system reoriented to local needs and distribution, but also of their contribution to strengthening local communities and environmental balance (Rosset and Martínez Torres, 2012). Its achievements are best reflected in the somewhat controversial decision of the FAO to declare 2014 the International Year of Family Farming (www.fao.org/family-farming-2014/home/structure-partnerships/en), where the organizations declare rather wistfully: 'Countries look to family farming as the key to food security and rural well-being'. La Vía Campesina also noted that this was the first time in its almost 60-year history that the organization made reference to the theme of agroecology, one of the principal strategies that can assure farmer control of agriculture and an appropriate response to the need for assuring food security for societies.

Recommended reading: Altieri and Toledo (2011), Holt-Giménez (2010), Rosset and Martínez Torres (2012).

Collective action and a global alliance against capitalist modernity

There is no space here to delve into the details of these innovative strategies, many of which do not offer material solutions to poverty when measured by ownership or access to a certain package of commodities. Instead, they address a much more thoroughgoing reconceptualization of the possibilities for a different meaning of the 'quality of life', and therefore of the social and material significance of poverty. In this different context, then, much of the poverty to which most of the literature is addressed has its origins in the individualism and alienation of the masses whose behaviour is embedded in the Western model of modernity, a model of concentrated accumulation based on a system of deliberate dispossession of the majority by a small elite.

The collectivism implicit in the alternatives offered by communities implementing their own areas of conservation is accompanied by the social concomitant of solidarity, which pervades the processes inherent in these strategies. The realization of the importance of people becoming involved in identifying and protecting their territories is an integral part of a complex dynamic that examines the significance of the place-based nature of cultures and their survival. As a result, peoples around the world are being accompanied in their efforts to protect these areas by a global alliance of such communities and organizations that seek to promote these efforts; the Indigenous Peoples' and Community Conserved Territories and Areas forum (www.iccaconsortium.org) is promoting and documenting the practice in dozens of countries and in hundreds of initiatives in which people are able to improve measurably their living conditions as part of processes that enable them to govern themselves more effectively while also contributing to ecosystem protection and rehabilitation (Borrini-Feyerabend, 2010; Ibarra *et al.*, 2011).

Recommended reading: Borrini-Feyerabend (2010), Ibarra *et al.* (2011).

Ecological economics from below: sustainable management of regional resources

In this context, then, we reiterate the underlying principles of this construction – distilled from the practice of many recent experiences – that help avoid the 'syndrome' of poverty: autonomy and communality; solidarity; self-sufficiency; productive and commercial diversification; and sustainable management of regional resources (Barkin, 2009). In the parts of the world where these alternatives are under construction, the collective commitment to ensure that there are no individuals without access to their socially defined basic needs implies a corresponding obligation of every single person to contribute to the strengthening of the community's productive capacity, to improve its infrastructures (physical, social and environmental), and to enrich its cultural and scientific capabilities. As a result, then, unemployment, as it is understood in the global marketplace, becomes a scourge of the past. Poverty, in this light, is an individual tragedy – created by the dynamics of a society based on individualism and its isolation – that is structurally anchored in the very fabric of society. To escape from this dynamic, the collective subject – popular sustainability – that is emerging offers a meaningful path to overcoming the persistence of poverty in our times.

Recommended reading: Barkin (2009).

Notes

1 The large literature that is now available is a reflection of the importance of this approach and the growing community of people involved. An early and widely read text throughout Latin America is Max-Neef *et al.* (1991). The continuing success of the journals *Otra Economía*, *Community Development Journal* and the *International Journal of the Commons*, to mention just three, offers testimony to the quality and volume of work being done in this area; they offer a valuable font of materials for students interested in exploring alternative approaches being implemented in the SSEE.
2 I use the expression 'peoples' to indicate that I am referring to social groups or classes rather than individuals.

3 The significance of the rejection of a monetary valuation of social and natural phenomena is enormous; for example, the widespread acceptance of apparently value-free concepts such as 'social capital' and 'natural capital', which offers a justification for placing prices and values on elements outside the market by asserting the need to assign them 'relevance', also facilitates their transformation into a new category of quasi-'commodities' that contributes to other mechanisms for personal and collective alienation. Fine (2010) offers an excellent introduction to this problem.

4 Cf. http://enlacezapatista.ezln.org.mx.

5 Five Caracoles, or 'Good Government Councils', were established in 2003 to implement a local governance structure in Zapatista territory.

6 The very definition of indigenous in the Census was modified in 2010 as a result of the inadequacy of the previous categorization, based on fluency in a native language. While Bonfil Batalla (1996 [1987]) mentioned there being about 8 million in his path-breaking book, the Census reported only 6 million in 1990. Today, however, there are about 18 or 20 million people who consider themselves indigenous (Toledo, 2014). The Mexican indigenous population is the largest of any country in the hemisphere; Bolivia, Ecuador, and Guatemala have larger proportions.

7 This project continues to mobilize the participation of more than 100,000 people in a region that has been in operation for more than a quarter of a century. By focusing on a broad range of activities that create numerous opportunities, requiring an ever-increasing range of skills, the region is encouraging people to remain, strengthening communities and improving people's welfare.

8 The efforts to assume collective control of the forests began in the 1970s (Simonian, 1995). Today, Mexico's community forest movement is recognized as one of the most effective and sustainable in the world, encompassing more than one-quarter of the nation's land area with differing management strategies that are cited as exemplary. The MOCAF and the Mexican Civil Society Organization for Sustainable Forestry (www.mocaf.org.mx and www.ccmss.org.mx) continues to play an important role in coordinating their activities and providing information about their history and achievements.

9 The breadth of this creativity can hardly be captured in this discussion. For more details about the projects mentioned in this paragraph, consult the following pages online: http://geaac.org, www.equatorinitiative.org/index.php?option=com_winners&view=winner_detail&id=67&Itemid=683&lang=es, www.museodetexitoaxaca.org, and www.pratec.org. Among the groups participating in our project, peasant and indigenous communities are engaged in urban agriculture, waste separation for reutilization and rainwater harvesting; near the center of Oaxaca's capital city, one of these initiatives received a national prize for 'Local Management and Governance' in 2012 (http://oaxaca.me/recibe-san-bartolo-coyotepec-premio-nacional-por-el-cuidado-ecologico).

References

Acosta, A. (2013). *El Buen Vivir: Sumak Kawsay, una Oportunidad para imaginar Otro Mundo.* Barcelona: Icaria-Antrazyt.

Altieri, M. and Toledo, V. (2011). 'The agroecological revolution in Latin America: rescuing nature, ensuring food sovereignty and empowering peasants'. *Journal of Peasant Studies*, 38(3): 587–612.

Barkin, D. (2000). 'Overcoming the neoliberal paradigm: sustainable popular development'. *Journal of Developing Societies*, 16(1): 163–80.

Barkin, D. (2001). *Innovaciones Mexicanas en el Manejo del Agua.* México: Universidad Autónoma Metropolitana.

Barkin, D. (2002). 'Indigenous ecotourism in Mexico: an opportunity under construction'. In D. McLaren (ed.), *Rethinking Tourism and Ecotravel.* Westport, CT: Kumarian Press, pp. 125–35.

Barkin, D. (2005). 'Reconsiderando las alternativas sociales en México rural: Estrategias campesinas e indígenas'. *Polis*, 5(15): 7.

Barkin, D. (2009). 'Principles for constructing alternative socio-economic organizations: lessons learned from working outside institutional structures'. *Review of Radical Political Economics*, 41(3): 372–9.

Barkin, D. (2012). 'Communities constructing their own alternatives in the face of crisis'. *Mountain Research and Development*, 32(S1): S12–S22.

Barkin, D. and Fuente, M. (2013). 'Community forest management: can the green economy contribute to environmental justice?' *Natural Resources Forum*, 37(3): 200–10.

Baronnet, B., Mora Bayo, M. and Stahler-Sholk, R. (2011). *Luchas muy otras: Zapatismo y autonomía en las comunidades indígenas de Chiapas*. Mexico: UAM-X-Ciesas-UNACH.

Bonaiuti, M. (2012). 'Degrowth: tools for a complex analysis of the multidimensional crisis'. *Capitalism, Nature, Socialism*, 23(1): 30–50.

Bonfil Batalla, G. (1996 [1987]). *Mexico Profundo: Reclaiming a Civilization*. Austin, TX: University of Texas Press.

Borrini-Feyerabend, G. (2010). *Bio-cultural Diversity Conserved by Indigenous Peoples & Local Communities: Examples & analysis*. Tehran: Indigenous Peoples and Community Conserved Territories and Areas (ICCA) and Consortium and Centre for Sustainable Development (CENESTA).

Bray, D.B. (2013). 'From Mexico, global lessons for forest governance'. *Solutions*, 4(3): 51–8.

Bray, D.B., Merino Pérez, L., Negreros Castillo, P., Segura Warnholtz, G., Torres Rojo, J.M. and Vester, H.F.M. (2003). 'Mexico's community-managed forests as a global model for sustainable landscapes'. *Conservation Biology*, 17(3): 672–7.

Cronkleton, P., Bray, D.B. and Medina, G. (2011). 'Community forest management and the emergence of multi-scale governance institutions: lessons for REDD+ development from Mexico, Brazil and Bolivia'. *Forests*, 2(2): 451–73.

Delgado Lemus, A. (2014). 'Ampliando Gustos Históricos'. *Mural*, Suplemento Negocios, 31 August. Available at: www.mural.com.

Dwinell, A. and Olivera, O. (2014). 'The water is ours damn it! Water commoning in Bolivia'. *Community Development Journal*, 49(S1): 144–52.

Escobar, A. (2015). 'Degrowth, postdevelopment, and transitions: a preliminary conversation'. *Sustainability Science*, 19(3): 451–62.

Fine, B. (2010). *Theories of Social Capital: Researchers Behaving Badly*. London: Pluto.

Fogelberg, K. (2013). 'From adopt-a-project to permanent services: the evolution of water for people's approach to rural water supply in Bolivia'. *Water Alternatives*, 6(2): Article 6.

Fuente, M. and Morales Ramos, F. (2013). 'El Ecoturismo Comunitario en la Sierra Juárez-Oaxaca, México: Entre el Patrimonio y la Mercancía'. *Otra Economía. Revista Latinoamericana de Economía Social y Solidaria*, 7(12): 66–79.

Georgescu-Roegen, N. (1971). *The Entropy Law and the Economic Process*. Cambridge, MA: Harvard University Press.

Gonzales, T. (2014). 'Kawsay (Buen Vivir) y Afirmación Cultural: Pratec-Naca, un Paradigma Alternativo en los Andes'. In B. Marañon (ed.), *El Buen Vivir y Descolonialidad: Critica al Desarrollo y la Racionalidad Instrumentales*. México: UNAM-Instituto de Investigaciones Económicas.

Gonzales, T. and Gonzalez, M. (2015). 'From colonial encounter to decolonizing encounters. Culture and nature seen from the Andean cosmovision of ever: the nurturance of life as whole'. In J. Pretty and S. Pilgrim (eds), *Nature and Culture*. London: Earthscan.

Hernández Garciadiego, R. and Herrerías, G. (2008). 'El Programa Agua para Siempre: 25 Años de Experiencia en la Obtención de Agua mediante la Regeneración de

Cuencas'. In L. Paré, D. Robinson and M. González Ortiz (eds), *Gestión de Cuencas y Servicios Ambientales. Perspectivas Comunitarias y Ciudadanas*. México: Instituto Nacional de Ecología.

Holt-Giménez, E. (2010). 'Linking farmers' movements for advocacy and practice'. *Journal of Peasant Studies*, 37(1): 203–36.

Ibarra, J.T., Barreau, A., Del Campo, C., Camacho, C.I., Martin, G.J. and McCandless, S. (2011). 'When formal and market-based conservation mechanisms disrupt food sovereignty: impacts of community conservation and payments for environmental services on an indigenous community of Oaxaca, Mexico'. *International Forestry Review*, 13(3): 318–37.

Illsley, C. *et al*. (2007). 'El Grupo de Estudios Ambientales, AC: Entre la Acción Social y la Consolidación Institucional'. In A.J. Bebbington *et al*. (eds), *Investigación y Cambio Social. Desafíos para las ONG en Centroamérica y México*. Guatemala: School of Environment and Development, pp. 175–208.

Kallis, G., Kerschner, C., Martinez Alier, J. and Douthwaite, R. (2012). 'The economics of degrowth'. *Ecological Economics*, 84: 172–269.

Lang, M. (ed.) (2013). *Beyond Development: Alternative Visions from Latin America*. Quito: Rosa Luxemburg Stiftung.

Latouche, S. (1991). *In the Wake of the Affluent Society: An Exploration of Post-Development*. London: Zed Books.

Max-Neef, M., Elizalde, A. and Hopenhaven, M. (1991). *Human Scale Development*. New York: Apex Press.

Meadows, D.H., Randers, J. and Meadows, D.L. (2004). *Limits to Growth: The 30-Year Update*. London: Earthscan.

Meadows, D.H., Meadows, D.L., Randers, J. and Beherns, W.W. (1972). *The Limits to Growth: A Report to the Club of Rome*. New York: Universe Books.

Muñoz, G. (2008). *The Fire and the Word: A History of the Zapatista Movement*. San Francisco, CA: City Lights Press.

Muraca, B. (2013). 'Decroissance: a project for a radical transformation of society'. *Environmental Values*, 22(2): 147–69.

Polanyi, K. (2001). *The Great Transformation: The Political and Economic Origins of Our Time*. Boston, MA: Beacon Press.

Rosset, P.M. and Martínez Torres, M.E. (2012). 'Rural social movements and agroecology: context, theory and process'. *Ecology and Society*, 17(1). doi:10.5751/ES-05000-170317.

Simonian, L. (1995). *Defending the Land of the Jaguar: A History of Conservation in Mexico*. Austin, TX: University of Texas Press.

Stevens, C., Winterbottom, R., Reytar, K. and Springer, J. (2014). *Securing Rights, Combating Climate Change: How Strengthening Community Forest Rights Mitigates Climate Change*. Washington, DC: World Resources Institute.

Toledo, V. (2014). 'México: La Batalla Final es Civilizatoria'. Series of four articles on 22 July, 5 August, 2 September and 30 September, *La Jornada*, México.

Toledo, V. and Barrera Bassols, N. (2008). *La memoria biocultural: La importancia ecológica de las sabidurías tradicionales*. Barcelona: Icaria.

Toledo, V. and Ortiz-Espejel, B. (2014). *México, Regiones que Caminan Hacia la Sustentabilidad: Una Geopolítica de las Resistencias Bioculturales*. Puebla: Universidad Iberoamericana, Campus Puebla.

Toledo, V., Garrido, D. and Barrera Bassols, N. (2013). 'Conflictos Socio-Ambientales, Resistencias Ciudadanas y Violencia Neo-Liberal en México'. *Ecología Política*, 46: 115–24.

Zermeño, S. (2010). *Reconstruir a México en el Siglo XXI: Estrategias para mejorar la calidad de vida y enfrentar la destrucción del medio ambiente*. Mexico: Océano.

PART IX

The BRICS as the new 'development giants'

31

BRAZIL

From the margins to the centre?

Ana Garcia and Miguel Borba de Sá

Since the middle of the 19th century onwards, debates about the forms of insertion of the Brazilian economy into the world market were already present. The condition of exporters of raw materials to the industrial centres of Europe, especially Britain, was not seen as desirable by the entirety of the intellectual and political elite of the country. The applicability of liberal theory to Brazil was questioned. However, even if part of the Brazilian decision-making elite lamented the dependence on primary exports, material conditions and external pressures would end up imposing until the 1930s the primary export model and its political counterpart – the oligarchic state – as hegemonic in Brazil and throughout the Latin American continent. Such hegemony, it should be noted, has always been contested.

Thus, for a century (ca. 1850–1950), there was a history of alternations, both theoretical and practical, between unequivocally free-market proposals, on the one hand, and diverse individual industrializing initiatives or even national developmentalist models, on the other. The result of this nonlinear trajectory was that the Brazilian economy gradually, yet erratically, transformed itself. At each disruption in the international division of labour caused by wars or economic 'depressions' in Europe and the United States (as in the years 1873, 1914, 1929 and 1939), Brazilian businessmen tended to respond with the 'import substitution' of industrial goods of low organic composition of capital (i.e. labour-intensive) as business became more oriented towards the domestic market. In this process, the old agrarian-exporting and mercantile bourgeoisies gradually became more complex as they were transformed into industrial and financial bourgeoisies as well.[1]

ECLAC and the struggle against the primary export model

The economic debate carried out within the framework of the United Nations Economic Commission for Latin America and the Caribbean (ECLAC), since its creation in 1947, is an inheritor and tributary of this long trajectory. By the time (1949) that Raúl Prebisch wrote his famous *Latin American Manifesto* – 'The economic development of Latin America and its main problems' – the crucial issue for the main economies of the continent such as Brazil was not overcoming for the first time the primary-export model, but rather resisting the desire to return to it. His text, originally published in Portuguese by the *Brazilian Journal of Economics*, enjoyed rapid diffusion and had a great influence in Brazil. For Prebisch (1949), the great risk of the 1950s was the temptation to reprimarize the economy as the window of opportunity opened by the intra-European and North American crises began to close with the establishment and consolidation of the post-Second World War order. According to him, the core-periphery structure of the world economy led to a trend towards the 'decline in the terms of trade' between agriculture-based countries on the periphery and the industrialized countries at the centre.[2]

Unlike the populist, national developmentalism of earlier years (1930–1940s), Prebisch's formulations did not advocate industrialization as a panacea for all the ills of underdevelopment, nor did he advocate endogenous or 'autarchic' growth for peripheral economies. For Prebisch, and to a certain extent the whole ECLAC tradition of thought that succeeded him, the solution was not for Latin America to delink from the international economy, but to know under what conditions more dividends – and no more debts – could be gained from participating in it. His argument was more cosmopolitan than nationalistic; designed to convince the elites and centres of power, rather than confronting them with popular mobilization.

What is innovative in Prebisch, therefore, is not his critique of Latin America's 'agrarian vocation' imposed on it by the international division of labour, nor his defense of industrialization as one of the ways of 'retaining some of the fruits of technical progress' (Prebisch, 1949: 48). This debate had already been going on for a hundred years. What distinguishes Prebisch and makes ECLAC a milestone in the history of Latin American economic thought is precisely that of representing the climax of this trajectory of polemics about the primary export model. In their historical context, Prebisch and ECLAC were able to formulate a critique of David Ricardo's theory of comparative advantages in a manner that was palatable for broad sectors of the Latin American, European and North American elites. His critique was intended to make peripheral capitalism work in Latin America, not to overcome it. In Cold War-times this gesture was not of minor value.

The concern about income distribution was a central feature of ECLAC, taken as a *sine qua non* condition for achieving genuine economic development. It is therefore a crucial factor that distinguishes the ECLAC tradition from orthodox economists who were generally spectical about the possibilities of redistributive and interventionist policies of the magnitude proposed by Prebisch. The rejection of methodological individualism, typical of orthodox theories, for the sake of historical and structural analysis led to ECLAC being given the nickname of 'Latin American structuralism' in terms of practitioners of economic science in the continent ever since.

Economists Celso Furtado and Maria da Conceição Tavares are the most prominent names when it comes to ECLAC thinking in Brazil. Both started from the formulations of Prebisch and expanded it in order to establish their respective criticisms of the directions that Brazil's economic development had taken. They sought to warn of the deleterious role played by the Brazilian elite's patterns of consumption, which, by emulating the European and American lifestyles, ended up wasting the precious (and scarce) foreign currency that their country needed to reinvest in diversifying its economy. This preoccupation with capital flight, reinforced by the peculiarities that US hegemony posed for Latin America, marked the apogee of ECLAC thinking during the 1950s and 1960s.

Finally, dualism is another hallmark of the ECLAC tradition, and refers to a notion according to which a great heterogeneity in the productive apparatus would give rise to 'two worlds' and 'historical times' coexisting simultaneously – the modernized elite, on the one hand, and the backward masses, especially the rural ones, on the other, without, however, merging into an integrated market, nor indeed constituting *one* society proper. The closure of this social gap – the major goal of ECLAC development policies – would ultimately depend on a broad reform of the world economy as a whole that would end the core-periphery structure, and thus enable capitalism to flourish in countries, such as Brazil, that were historically underprivileged by the international division of labour.

Recommended reading: Furtado (1974, 1979 [1954]), Prebisch (1949), Tavares (1973).

Marxist dependency theory and the question of sub-imperialism

The emergence of Marxist dependency theory was not a mere theoretical innovation detached from concrete reality. Rather, on the contrary, it was largely the result of the atmosphere of political polarization that erupted throughout the continent during the 1960s. In Brazil, with the military coup of April 1964, class struggles became more open (and violent) than before, demanding new political formulations from both the Left and the Right (Aarão Reis and Ferreira de Sá, 1985).

The Marxist Revolutionary Organization-Workers Politics (POLOP, in Portuguese) symbolized the watershed of this new wave of leftist organizations, when it published in 1961 the 'Socialist Program for Brazil', where the first formulation of the Brazilian Revolution as immediately socialist can be found, breaking decisively with the 'stages' schemes and the strategies of class conciliation with supposedly nationalist sectors of the national bourgeoisie advocated by the Communist Party.[3] Among the leaders of POLOP were intellectuals who would shortly afterwards become references in the literature of Marxist dependency theory, such as Ruy Mauro Marini. Sent into exile and writing in Spanish and English, Marini (1965) drew attention to the effects that 'imperialist integration' was promoting throughout the hemisphere, especially in regard to the changes in the Brazilian economy and its position vis-à-vis the United States.

Contrary to the 'stagnationist' theses propagated by Furtado (1965) and other exponents of ECLAC thought after the 1964 coup, Marini already realized that this new arrangement promoted by the military regime was not aimed at deterring Brazil's industrial development, but rather stimulating its rapid growth and modernization, concluding the cycle of Brazilian industrialization. But according to Marini, capitalist industrialization on the periphery had as a characteristic feature a 'super-exploitation' of the labour-force as a mechanism of compensation for the terms of trade in the world market being unfavourable to peripheral countries. One effect of this overexploitation is the rupture between the sphere of production and that of circulation, since what is produced is far detached from the consumption capacity and needs of the working masses. While in the core capitalist countries there is a consumer market and constant demand for manufactured goods, in Latin American production the individual consumption of the worker did not interfere as much in the commodity-value realization process. Internal demand was thus sacrificed in favour of foreign markets purchasing power of industrialization products assembled in Brazil.

Marini (1965) already envisaged ways that could support this arrangement for a longer time, such as the promotion of industrial exports, government purchases and military spending. He saw before others the emergence of an 'industrial–military complex' in Brazil. Integrated industrialization into the world capitalist economy meant that the internal productive structure converged with industry in the United States. From this resulted a new hierarchy of the capitalist countries in pyramidal form, with middle-size centres of accumulation, and the related emergence of middle capitalist powers. The export of manufactures advanced towards the export of capital, a process that Marini (1965, 1972, 1977) called 'sub-imperialism'. Sub-imperialism is the form taken by a dependent economy when it reaches the stage of monopoly and financial capital, with a high degree of concentration and centralization of capital, accentuated by foreign investment in associated with domestic enterprises. Its main components are a medium organic composition of the productive apparatus and a relatively autonomous external expansionist foreign policy, but with its integration in the market determined by the central capitalist countries. For Marini, only Brazil in Latin America fully expressed these conditions.

Brazilian sub-imperialism is the result of an economic phenomenon (i.e. a result of the financial boom since 1970) and of a political project, beginning with the civil–military dictatorship, with governments that have set up the legal and institutional framework for capturing external resources and securing investments from abroad through the operations of state-owned companies, intergovernmental credits or guarantees to private operations, and expanding investments in Latin America and Africa. Thus, Brazil embarked on the orbit of financial capital, attracting monetary flows without being able to assimilate them integrally as productive capital, and therefore reintegrating them into the movement of international capital. According to Marini (1977), Brazil hereinafter enters in 'associated and dependent' form, the stage of capital exports and the pillaging of raw materials and sources of energy abroad, such as oil, iron and gas.

Theotônio Dos Santos (1970) was another theorist known for his contributions to the dissemination of Marxist dependency theories in Brazil and abroad. He argued that there would be a succession of forms of dependence over time, beginning with 'colonial dependence' passing through 'financial–industrial dependence' until we arrive at the current 'industrial–technological dependence' in which large monopoly corporations transfer obsolete but not yet amortized technology to the peripheral countries in order to produce and sell into the domestic market of the dependent countries, even though they were composed of only small but wealthy 'buying' (comprador) elites (Dos Santos, 1970: 232). All these forms of dependence would produce situations of 'underdevelopment' and thus aggravate class struggles.

Dos Santos (1970) also recognized the condition of 'overexploitation of the labour-force' in dependent economies, but he did not believe that intermediate solutions could long delay the contradictions of 'dependent development', such as reformist and developmentalist stances stemming from ECLAC. The only solutions that presented themselves as feasible in the face of strong political radicalization were represented by the dilemma between 'strong governments that open the road to fascism' or 'popular-revolutionary governments that open the way to socialism' (Dos Santos 1970: 236). For more than a decade, the struggle between increasingly brutal military regimes versus clandestine left-wing organizations that opted for armed struggle seemed to confirm his prognosis.

Although there were variations in the analysis and tactical recommendations proposed by each, the pioneering authors linked to Marxist dependency theory shared the conviction that only a decisive, revolutionary break with capitalism could allow true Latin American development to take place. The task of the intellectual and political left was to convince the working classes of the need to break with a system that relegated them to a condition of political oppression and economic overexploitation. Other less radical, non-Marxist versions of dependency theory that advocated for the acceptance of the limits of dependent development as insurmountable also emerged. From this reformist perspective, the political task was reduced to negotiating the terms of dependency rather than trying to overcome it (Cardoso and Falleto, 1970). Neither formulation of dependency theory, however, survived over the 1980s. That is, dependency-orientated theorizing gradually lost its pre-eminent purchase within the field of development studies after its peak in the late 1970s.[4]

Recommended reading: Dos Santos (1970), Fernandes (1975), Marini (1965, 1972, 1977).

Neoliberalism and social crisis

Not only Brazil, but countries such as Argentina and Mexico, also suffered from the 'debt crisis' throughout the 1980s. These economies were virtually excluded from international capital markets until the turn of the 1990s inaugurated a new step. The 'solution' presented to crises generated by excessive orthodox economic policies was even more orthodox ones. It was the so-called 'Washington Consensus,' a set of measures agreed to by private lenders, multilateral financial institutions and US Treasury representatives. If followed, such measures would allow the return of countries such as Brazil to international credit markets, which in fact occurred in the Brazilian case in 1995, when US interest rates fell again and the supply of dollars in search of outflow destinations became great again.

The apparent success of the solutions presented by the 'Washington Consensus' was crucial for the establishment of neoliberalism as the new dominant economic paradigm in Brazil. Unlike other times, the 1990s were marked by a virtual suppression of the country's economic debate. For this reason, the decade was known for the supremacy of the neoliberal 'single thought', which sought to narrow the limits of the debate as to *how* to implement policies which were transmitted as the only viable model (Fiori, 1996, 1998).

At the domestic level, the neoliberal agenda in Brazil consisted of a vast privatization programme, which included the sale of public companies in strategic areas, such as energy and telecommunications, at prices below their market value. On the international relations front, the government of Fernando Henrique Cardoso (1994–2002), which coincided with the Clinton administration in the US, sought to join the international regimes of liberal fashion, on the assumption that participation in the new world order would allow Brazil the possibility of having greater influence in international forums (Vigevani and Cepaluni, 2007). This resulted in involvement in the neoliberal trade regime, with the accession (in 1994) to the World Trade Organization, together with the consolidation of the Common External Tariff in Mercosur, and the participation in the Miami Summit of 1994, which kicked off negotiations around a Free Trade Area for the Americas (FTAA). The negotiations for the creation of the FTAA reignited deep and extensive debates in Brazil and in the Latin American continent as to which development model to pursue. The FTAA was seen by many as an asymmetric agreement between unequal partners that would lead to increased US political, economic and military domination over the continent. If it had been consolidated, Brazil's regional integration initiatives, especially Mercosur, would have lost, some argue, one of their main pillars in the form of an endogenous strategy of productive integration with a more progressive trade regime from which countries in the region could derive mutual benefits (Guimarães, 2000).

However, 'globalization as a fable', which sought to convince us that Brazil was part of a global village with markets and persons integrated by the digital age, an almost homogenous world in which the state would be powerless in the face of the power of finance and large corporations, was unveiled as a 'globalization as perversity' (Santos, 2000). High unemployment, precarious labour conditions, the scrapping of public policies and the loss of the purchasing power of wages boosted the formation of anti-neoliberal social movements in the countryside and in the city (Soares, 2002).

Recommended reading: Fiori (1998), Guimarães (2000), Santos (2000).

Neodevelopmentism and Brazil's new international insertion

Faced with the social failures of neoliberal policies and the growing gap between the expectations it had generated and the few promises of improvement that it was able to deliver, a strong social opposition was formed in Brazil against the regining model. After the economic collapse of neighbouring Argentina in 2001, until then considered the best disciple of the IMF's teachings, the Brazilians chose to change course and in 2002 elected for the first time a government of the Workers Party (PT). Since then, the economic debates were given a breath of fresh air.

The PT governments sought to combine an orthodox economic policy involving very high interest rates, with credit policies for large, nationally based companies, and expanded social programmes, along with a progressive increase of the minimum wage. Some have classified this model as 'social liberalism' (Antunes, 2013), while others have presented it as decidedly 'post-neoliberal' (Sader, 2003). However, both advocates and detractors chose the term 'neodevelopmentalism' to characterize the economic policies pursued by the PT. This new developmentalism would be exemplified, among other things, by the resumption of the state's role in economic planning. Unlike the so-called 'old developmentalism' the state should now refrain from protectionist policies and meddling with finance or industrial activities. Rather, the government should be concerned with maintaining competition between both state and private enterprises capable of exporting high value-added products, establishing criteria for controlling the movement of capital, and be an investment inducer – not necessarily a direct producer – within the framework of a national development strategy (Bresser-Pereira, 2009). From this perspective, it would be necessary to consolidate an endogenous 'corporate core' for development to take place, 'with business groups able to participate on an equal playing field with two heavy weights of international trade and investment competition'. Hence, it was argued that what was required was a 'strong capitalism' with a 'strong national business sector' (Sicsu *et al.*, 2005).

In this context, the National Bank for Economic and Social Development (BNDES) played a central role by granting credit to large infrastructure projects as well as to the extractive and agribusiness sectors in Brazil and to Brazilian contractors operating abroad. BNDES also became a shareholder in many firms through the BNDESPar holding company. With this, it began to boost mega-projects and foster the consolidation of private Brazilian monopoly companies capable of competing in international markets. During the Lula da Silva and Dilma Rousseff PT governments, liberal economists criticized the actions of the BNDES on the grounds that these actions were unwarranted interventions in the economy (benefiting some groups over others), created deficits in times of financial crisis, and diverted investment.[5]

This policy of BNDES in facilitating the business of Brazilian companies abroad was in line with the foreign policy of the governments of Lula da Silva (2003–2010) and Dilma Rousseff (2011–2016), who shifted foreign policy towards relations with other 'Global South' countries and regions. South American regional integration was given priority, and the country strengthened relations with Africa, Asia and the Middle East (Soares de Lima and Hirst, 2006). With the diversification of trade and investment relations, Brazil sought to affirm itself as an 'emerging power' in global capitalism. Some see the increase in 'South–South' policies and the alignment with other developing countries as indications of Brazil's distancing itself from the orbit of Washington. However, others say that Brazil's international projection, combining diplomacy, investment and cooperation for development, is by no means dissociated from bourgeois interests. From this critical perspective, new multilateral spaces of the 'Global South', such as BRICS, are predominantly capitalist (Bond and Garcia, 2015). In this connection, some have even turned towards and updated the contributions of Ruy Mauro Marini to the current situation, resulting in a renewal of the debate on the sub-imperialist role of Brazil in South America (Luce, 2013). Still others have characterized Brazil's position in the 'capitalist–imperialist' spiral as a comprehensive process that began in the post-war period as a structure for the expanded reproduction of capital. In this view, although dependent on foreign capital, Brazil would no longer occupy a subordinate position (Fontes, 2010).

The debate on economic development in the present day is thus characterized by a fragmentation and multiplicity of analyses. Nevertheless, (neo)liberalism remains the dominant paradigm both in the Brazilian state and civil society. There is no consensus even as to the general course of the Brazilian economy today. While there are research agendas focused on reprimarization and deindustrialization (see, for example, Gonçalves, 2012) there are also analyses (for example, Zibechi, 2013) that depart from the opposite premise, namely that industrial capital has already reached its finance and imperialist phase in Brazil, and it is therefore unlikely that the country will regress to peripheral status or, even less likely, to the old primary export model.

Amid this diffuse controversy, a series of post-development paradigms that reject the traditional notion of economic development itself were constructed (Escobar, 1995; Quijano, 2000b). This post-development perspective is reflected in the *Buen Vivir* ('Living Well').[6] Originally proposed at the margins of Western modernity/ coloniality (Quijano, 2000a) by the indigenous movements from the Andean countries, this notion has been gaining ground in Brazil recently, both in academic work and in the language of social movements. Although it does not represent for the Left of today the same force that the idea of 'socialism' had throughout the 20th century, the concept of *buen vivir* (as opposed to the capitalist logic of 'living better' via accumulation and consumption) opens a new perspective for liberating Brazilian economic thought from its Eurocentric shackles and thus helps advance a debate as to what kind of civilizational paradigm would be more appropriate today for the country and its Latin American neighbours.

Recommended reading: Bresser-Pereira (2009), Fontes (2010), Sader (2003), Quijano (2000a, 2000b).

Notes

1 An emblematic case of this dynamic was that of the agrarian bourgeoisie of São Paulo, responsible for the largest portion of the wealth created by the export coffee economy, which gradually became the country's most powerful industrial and financial bourgeoisie. At each crisis in international coffee prices, the capital accumulated in this activity sought flows into other economic sectors, such as manufacturing, which were encouraged by

protectionist government policies, serving as an investment option at times of uncertainty or crisis in the primary sector (Furtado, 1979 [1954]: 195–203; Prado Jr., 1979 [1945]: 257–69).

2 This meant that, due to the incorporation of less technical progress, producer prices of products exported from the periphery were always lower than the prices of goods exported by the core – to the advantage of the latter and the disadvantage of the former. The core did not pass the advances of technical progress to the periphery, while the periphery continued to provide cheap inputs for the industry at the core, indirectly financing this technical progress. In turn, the consolidation of strong workers' organizations in the central countries prevented the fall in wages, which could lead to a fall in the rate of profit. Thus, capitalists in the more advanced capitalist countries in the core of the system countered this trend through unequal exchange in the world market (on this theory, see Chapter 4 by Kay in this volume).

3 Hegemony in the socialist movements was exercised by the 'official' version coming from Moscow, which schematically considered Latin America to be in a 'semi-feudal stage', necessitating therefore a national (and bourgeois) revolution first of all, so that the development of the capitalist productive forces could in the future seriously put the question of socialism (Werneck Sodré, 1963). Until then, alliances with the respective national bourgeoisie against imperialism in favour of autonomous 'national development' were the guidelines that prevailed in the most influential tactical formulations that gravitated around the local communist parties. In the case of Brazil, for example, it was believed that the Brazilian Revolution should take a bourgeois–democratic form with an anti-feudal and anti-imperialist content, as stated by its top leader Luiz Carlos Prestes. Out of this came the favorable preaching of the union between the communists and the nationalist forces, including the 'progressive' sectors of the domestic business class (Prado Jr., 1966).

4 See Chapter 4 by Kay in this volume for a review of dependency theory.

5 See, for example, Marcos Mendes in 'Financiamento do BNDES para obras no exterior' (*Valor Econômico*, 3/6/2014), and the response of João Carlos Ferraz in 'O que lhe parece o BNDES?' (*Valor Econômico*, 30/5/2014).

6 See Chapter 5 by Gudynas in this volume.

References

Aarão Reis, D. and Ferreira de Sá, J. (eds) (1985). *Imagens da Revolução: Documentos políticos das organizações clandestinas de esquerda dos anos 1961 a 1971*. Rio de Janeiro: Editora Marco Zero.

Antunes, R. (2013). 'Inglaterra e Brasil: duas rotas do social-liberalismo em duas notas'. *Currículo Sem Fronteiras*, 13(2): 204–12.

Bond, P. and Garcia, A. (ed.) (2015). *BRICS: An Anti-Capitalist Critique*. Johannesburg: Jacana Media.

Bresser-Pereira, L.C. (2009). *Developing Brazil: Overcoming the Failure of the Washington Consensus*. Boulder, CO: Lynne Rienner.

Cardoso, F.H. and Faletto, E. (1970). *Dependencia y desarrollo en América Latina: ensayos de interpretación sociológica*, 2nd edition. México: Siglo XXI.

Carvalho, J.M. (2014). *A construção da ordem: a elite política imperial/Teatro de sombras: a política imperial*, 9th edition. Rio de Janeiro: Editora Civilização Brasileira.

Dos Santos, T. (1970). 'The structure of dependence'. *The American Economic Review*, 60(2): 231–6.

Escobar, A. (1995). *Encountering Development: the Making and Unmaking of the Third Word*. New Jersey: Princeton University Press.

Fernandes, F. (1975). *Capitalismo dependente e classes sociais na América Latina*. Rio de Janeiro: Zahar Editores.

Fiori, J.L. (1996). *O Consenso de Washington*. Rio de Janeiro: Federação Brasileira de Associações de Engenheiros/Centro Cultural Banco do Brasil.

Fiori, J.L. (1998). 'Globalização, hegemonia e império'. In J.L. Fiori and M.C. Tavares (eds), *Poder e Dinheiro: Uma economia política da globalização*. Petrópolis: Editora Vozes.

Fontes, V. (2010). *O Brasil e o capital-imperialismo: teoria e história*. Rio de Janeiro: EPSJV/UFRJ.

Furtado, C. (1965). 'Development and stagnation in Latin America: a structuralist approach'. *Studies in Comparative International Development*, 1(11): 159–75.

Furtado, C. (1974). *O mito do desenvolvimento econômico*. Rio de Janeiro: Paz e Terra.

Furtado, C. (1979 [1954]). *Formação econômica do Brasil*, 16th edition. Rio de Janeiro: Companhia Editora Nacional.

Gonçalves, R. (2012). 'Governo Lula e o nacional-desenvolvimentismo às avessas'. *Revista Sociedade Brasileira Economia e Política*, 31, February: 5–30.

Guimarães, S.P. (2000). *Quinhentos Anos de Periferia: Uma contribuição ao estudo da política internacional*. Rio de Janeiro: Editora Contraponto.

Luce, M. (2013). 'O subimperialismo, etapa superior do capitalismo dependente'. *Crítica Marxista*, 36: 129–41.

Marini, R.M. (1965). 'Brazilian "interdependence" and imperialist integration'. *Monthly Review*, 17(7): 10–29.

Marini, R.M. (1972). 'Brazilian subimperialism'. *Monthly Review*, 23(9): 14–24.

Marini, R.M. (1977). 'La acumulacion capitalista mundial y el subimperialismo'. *Cuadernos Políticos*, 12. Mexico: Ediciones Era.

Prado Jr., C. (1966). *A Revolução Brasileira*. São Paulo: Editora Brasiliense.

Prado Jr., C. (1979 [1945]). *História Econômica do Brasil*. São Paulo: Editora Brasiliense.

Prebisch, R. (1949). 'O desenvolvimento econômico da América Latina e seus principais problemas'. *Revista Brasileira de Economia*, 3(3).

Quijano, A. (2000a). 'Colonialty of Power, Eurocentrism and Latin America'. *Nepantla: Views from South*, 1(3): 533–580.

Quijano, A. (2000b). 'El fantasma del desarrollo en América Latina'. *Revista Venezoelana de Economía y Ciencias Sociales*, No. 2, Caracas.

Sader, E. (2003). *A vigança da história*. São Paulo: Boitempo Editorial.

Santos, M. (2000). *Por uma outra globalização: Do pensamento único à consciência universal*. Rio de Janeiro: Editora Record.

Sicsu, J., De Paula, L.F. and Michel, R. (2005). 'Por que um novo desenvolvimentismo'. *Jornal dos Economistas*, 186, January: 3–5.

Soares, L. (2002). *Os custos sociais do ajuste neoliberal na América Latina*, 2nd edition. São Paulo: Cortez.

Soares de Lima, M.R. and Hirst, M. (2006). 'Brazil as an intermediate state and regional power: action, choice and responsibilities'. *International Affairs*, 82(1): 21–40.

Tavares, M.C. (1973). *Da substituição de importações ao capitalismo financeiro: Ensaios sobre Economia Brasileira*. Rio de Janeiro: Zahar Editores.

Vigevani, T. and Cepaluni, G. (2007). 'A política externa de Lula da Silva: a estratégia da autonomia pela diversificação'. *Contexto Internacional*, 29(2): 273–325.

Werneck Sodré, N. (1963). *Formação Histórica do Brasil*. São Paulo: Editora Brasiliense.

Zibechi, R. (2013). *Brasil Potencia: entre la integración regional y un nuevo imperialismo*. Lima: Fórum Solidariedad Peru/Programa Democracia y Transformación Global.

32

INDIA

Critical issues of a 'tortuous transition'

John Harriss

In January 1947, speaking before the Constituent Assembly that had the task of drawing up the Constitution for independent India, Jawaharlal Nehru – who was to become the first prime minister of the country – said: 'The first task of this Assembly is to free India through a new constitution, to feed the starving people, and to clothe the naked masses, and to give every Indian the fullest opportunity to develop himself according to his capacity'. It was a remarkable statement, anticipating Amartya Sen's definition of what development should mean – the enhancement of the capabilities of everyone to lead lives that they have reason to value. Nehru clearly argued that the *raison d'être* of government in modern and independent India was to liberate the minds and bodies of ordinary Indians by purposeful acts of economic and social transformation. In the years that followed, India, then still an overwhelmingly agrarian economy and society – in 1951, agriculture accounted for two-thirds of GDP and three-quarters of employment – became the archetypal 'developing economy'. The history of India's development is partially reflected in the data shown in Tables 32.1 and 32.2.

In practice, in spite of Nehru's brave words, promising an approach to development that would be more than the pursuit of economic growth, the governments that he led, and those that have followed them, have given absolute priority to growth – with varying degrees of success (Table 32.2). The redistributive measures that are required if every Indian is to have the fullest opportunity to develop herself according to her capacity have never been tackled. Perhaps the most egregious failure of Indian governments during Nehru's lifetime (he died in 1964) was in regard to redistributive land reform, such as was necessary for the country to have resolved its agrarian question – and so to have created a more dynamic and productive agricultural economy, while also improving the livelihoods of the mass of rural people (such as happened over the same period, in China). The unwillingness to tackle this redistributive measure followed from the political power of landlords and rich peasants in the ruling Congress Party. And though there were powerful voices in India at the time of independence favouring socialism – as a social democratic path of development – the Constitution of the country guaranteed the rights of private property. Big business was rather looked down upon at first by political leaders, but anti-capitalist rhetoric was never translated into practice, and by the 21st century the promise of 'socialism' in the Preamble to the Constitution was clearly disappointed. The political influence of big companies and of particular individual capitalists was increasingly evident in the course of the election of Narendra Modi as prime minister in 2014, on a platform of '*vikas*', meaning development as economic growth.

Successive Indian governments have in effect offered charity to the poor people of the country, through a whole plethora of measures intended to alleviate poverty, and not social development. This remains true, even in the early 21st century, following striking legislative interventions that have given rural households a right to employment (with the National Rural Employment Guarantee Act of 2005), that promise food security (with the Food Security Act of 2013), and that have at last provided for the right to eight years of elementary education (with the Right to Education Act of 2009). Yet, in the years since the passage of the Right to Education, the proportion of Indian children attending private schools has increased, a trend that at least in part reflects the failures of public education (with evidence showing declining educational outcomes over this period, especially in public schools). Public expenditure on education, and health – the most vital elements in a programme of social development – as a share of GDP remain low by international standards, and the share of private spending in all health expenditure rivals that in the United States. Having decent nutrition and health is fundamental to human capability, and the extent to which they are lacking in India is shown up in the fact that about half of all Indian children are undernourished.

One way of understanding the central problem of Indian development is explained by the economist Pranab Bardhan in his argument that India is experiencing a 'tortuous transition'. The members of the National Commission on Enterprises in the Unorganised Sector – all of them radical economists – made much the same point with the idea of a 'lopsided transition'. What these scholars were getting at is that the structural transformation of the Indian economy has not taken place, in spite of years of high rates of growth, and that India's 'transition to an enlarged and dominating sphere of capital in the economy' (Bardhan, 2009: 31) is correspondingly constrained. In India, the declining share of income from the agricultural sector has not been accompanied by an equivalent decline in employment in that sector. Agriculture now contributes less than 15 per cent of GDP (averaging 13 per cent during 2006–2007 to 2013–2014) but still employs about 50 per cent of the labour-force (see Table 32.2, but note that National Sample Survey [NSS] data for 2007–2008 show the share of agricultural employment as 55.4 per cent).

TABLE 32.1 Employment structure in India – daily status (per cent)

Year	Agr	Mfg	CTT	G&P	Total
2004–2005	53.9	12.8	21.8	9.00	97.5
1999–2000	58.0	12.1	18.9	8.90	97.9
1993–1994	61.1	11.4	14.8	10.80	98.1
1983	63.4	11.8	13.3	9.90	98.4

Agr = agriculture; Mfg = manufacturing; CTT = construction, trade and hotels, transport, storage and communications; G&P = government services, education, health, community services, personal services. Total less than 100 per cent because employment shares of mining and of real estate and finance are not included.

Source: After Eswaran *et al.* (2009): Table 6

Over the later part of the period to which the data shown in the table refer (from 1999 to 2005), the labour-force was increasing by about 1 million people *every month*. Some were absorbed into agriculture, even though agricultural output was growing only slowly – underlining the low productivity of the sector; relatively few were absorbed into manufacturing; and most found employment in construction and the 'old' service industries – trade and transport. The great majority of the new jobs were not 'good jobs' in the organized or formal sector, or in the most dynamic and productive sectors of the economy, but were in forms of informal employment, outside the purview of most employment legislation, often not very productive, usually low-paid, with work and incomes commonly irregular, though also involving long hours and hazardous workplaces. It is reliably estimated that about two-thirds of India's GDP comes from such unregistered, informal activity, and that it accounts for more than 90 per cent of jobs – more than half of them being generated from self-employment.

While a classic theory holds that those employed (or often self-employed) in informal activities constitute a 'reserve army of labour', necessary for the development of industrial capitalism over the longer run, it has been suggested that in India now a large share of the labour-force as a whole is better described as 'excluded', being unnecessary for the growth of the economy as a whole, and surviving in a wide range of activities that are of only marginal significance for the dynamic, corporate sector (Sanyal and Bhattacharyya, 2009). Whatever one makes of this argument, it is clear that the narrative of structural transformation and societal transition breaks down in regard to modern India.

The failure of the structural change in employment that, historically, has accompanied the change in output between sectors of the economy in the course of development, reflects critical issues of India's development: the pattern and the dynamics of economic growth; employment, or what has come to be described as 'jobless growth', and the possibility that much of the labourforce is 'excluded'; the problem of agriculture; and the persistence of poverty and the continuing limitations of 'human development'. We consider each of these in this chapter.

Recommended reading: Bardhan (2009), Corbridge *et al.* (2013), Eswaran *et al.* (2009), Sanyal and Bhattacharyya (2009).

Economic growth: scale, pattern and process

In 2015, amid much fanfare, it was declared that India's rate of economic growth had at last overtaken that of China, and that the country now was the fastest growing of all the major economies. It was a great moment for those political leaders and bureaucrats for whom this had long been the target. Scepticism was expressed about this by some economists, however. It was noted that the way in which the official measurement of growth is carried out had been revised in the previous year, with the result that the Indian economy was found to be growing much faster than had previously been calculated. Later, the respected Indian journal *Economic and Political Weekly* published an editorial under the title 'Lies, damned lies, and statistics' (11 June 2016), noting 'glaring anomalies in the GDP data', and pointing out, for example, that the old series of growth numbers for manufacturing showed 1.1 per cent growth in 2012–2013, while the new method reported 6.2 per cent. Defining and measuring the size of an economy, and then assessing change over time, are of course matters that involve many assumptions, and it is to be expected – although it is not always recognized – that there may be radical differences between estimations.

There are questions, therefore, about the size and the rate of growth of the Indian economy, and questions, too, about economic strategy and the historical pattern and process of growth. These are partly summed up in the following table, which compares data from the ways in which the economist Arvind Panagariya, a keen advocate of liberalization, on the one hand, and Atul Kohli, a sceptic, on the other, have defined different periods of India's growth history. Growth rates have varied widely even from year to year, so there is significant scope for different ways of understanding the historical pattern.

Both scholars identify the early years after India's independence, in the time of the first three five-year plans, as a period of successful growth, and Kohli's data show how very effectively India industrialized during this time. But industrial development depended upon public investment, for which governments found it increasingly difficult to sustain the funding. Development was driven from the supply side, and there was little of a demand-side stimulus, at least partly because of the failure of agrarian reform – that might have delivered higher incomes and more

TABLE 32.2 Two analyses of phases of India's economic growth

Panagariya	Four phases of growth	Kohli			
	Total GDP growth		Total	Agr	Ind
1951–1965	4.1	1950–1964	3.7	3.1	7.4
1965–1981	3.2 (the 'Hindu rate of growth')	1965–1979	2.9	2.3	3.8
1981–1988	4.8	1980–1990	5.8	3.9	6.5
1988–2006	6.3 (Pro-market or pro-capital?)	1991–2004	5.6	3.0	5.8

consumer demand in the rural economy. This continues to be a factor in India's path of economic development. Protection and the system of licensing allowed for inefficient industrial development that was nonetheless very profitable. The early approach to planning became fiscally unsustainable by the mid-1960s. Thereafter, growth slumped, and the later 1960s and 1970s saw what was described as 'the Hindu rate of growth', of around 3 per cent, barely ahead of the rate of growth of the population.

The 1980s saw a resurgence of growth. Kohli argues that this came about in part because of the coming together of government and private capital. Government became 'pro-capital'. India took off onto a higher rate of growth in this period, and according to Kohli's analysis the growth rate was higher in the 1980s than in the first decade or so following India's adoption of liberalizing economic reforms in 1991. He questions, therefore, whether the 'pro-market' reforms have been decisive. The way in which Panagariya views the data, on the other hand, leads him to argue that these reforms that were indeed decisive, and that they have put India onto a much higher growth trajectory. There remains considerable debate about the determinants of India's economic growth; about the reasons for the step up in growth rates from 2003 (since which time growth has averaged around 7.3 per cent annum); and also about how far growth is constrained by what is supposed to be the 'inflexibility' of labour markets, and by the still only limited privatization of public sector enterprises. For liberal reformers such as Panagariya, the reforms are never sufficient. What is clear is that India's growth has been driven by services, which now account for two-thirds of GDP, while manufacturing has remained stuck at about 16 per cent, with manufacturing growth generally lagging behind the growth of GDP. This has come to be regarded as a major problem for India. It seems that the country has probably missed the boat with regard to employment-intensive industrialization of the kind that drove China's very rapid economic growth.

Recommended reading: Chandrasekhar *et al.* (2015), Kohli (2012), Panagariya (2008).

'Inclusive growth' or jobless growth and excluded labour?

'Inclusive growth' was the theme of India's Eleventh Five Year Plan, for the period 2007–2012. Manmohan Singh, then the prime minister, in his Foreword to the Plan, spoke of the need to ensure that 'income and employment are adequately shared by the poor and weaker sections of our society'. Seventy million new 'work opportunities' were projected, but subsequent findings of the National Sample Survey showed that productive jobs were not created at anything like the rate that was required for 'inclusive growth'. It appeared that India experienced, instead, 'jobless growth'.

Some scholars argued that there was an acceleration of employment growth after 2000, and that much of this growth was of 'good-quality employment'. The argument depended in part upon the view that increasing self-employment is a positive trend, reflecting entrepreneurship; but it seems that much of it was rather a reflection of distress, causing many people to move into occupations of last resort. After 2004–2005, the rate of growth of the labour-force declined quite sharply, and this has been put down to the effects of increasing enrolments in elementary and secondary education, a reduction in child labour and the withdrawal of women from the labour-force. In this period, labour at last started leaving agriculture, but it was pulled out principally by jobs in construction, and even though the generation of non-agricultural jobs did accelerate – it was still not at a rate that was sufficient to absorb the increasing supply of workers.

The promise of creating better employment opportunities for India's youthful population – supposed to give India a 'demographic dividend' (because of the numbers of new entrants to the labourforce outweighing the increase in numbers of dependents) – played an important part in bringing Narendra Modi into power in 2014. And shortly after he took up office as prime minister, Modi launched a 'Make in India' campaign, intended to make India a second China. As he has said, 'We launched the Make in India campaign to create employment and self-employment opportunities for our youth . . . we want the share of manufacturing in our GDP to go up to 25 per cent in the near future' (in a speech of 13 February 2016). Such a step-up in manufacturing is expected to generate 100 million new jobs. The question of whether or not these objectives can be attained is one of the crucial issues of Indian development. Mr Modi has made much of the so-called 'Gujarat model' of development, referring to the success of economic growth in his home state during the period in which he was chief minister there. But this does not augur well for the country, given that Gujarat's growth has not been employment-intensive. The argument that there is extensive 'excluded labour' in India carries some conviction.

Recommended reading: Himanshu (2011), Lerche (2010), Mehrotra *et al.* (2014), Roy (2016).

The problems of agriculture

Even though, given the declining share of agriculture in its GDP, India is no longer an 'agrarian economy', agriculture remains a vitally important industry. Village studies show the increasing diversification of employment, and very large numbers of rural people are engaged in multiple forms of work, sometimes involving commuting from village homes, and often short- or long-term migration, much of it circular (when people move to and fro between village homes and distant work sites, both urban and rural). One recent estimate is that the numbers of such circulating migrants have reached 100 million, though the National Commission on Enterprises in the Unorganised Sector estimated that the number of seasonal migrants is of the order 'only' of 30 million. Yet, agricultural work, both wage labour and in the cultivation of the small farms (of one hectare and less) that account for 70 per cent of the total numbers of operated holdings in the country, remain the basis of very many livelihoods. So, as the London *Economist* put it (13 March 2010: 15), 'the [Indian] government cannot achieve the "inclusive" growth it aspires to without robust progress in agriculture'. The point was made at the same time also by key Indian policymakers, who expressed regret that agriculture had been growing at a rate of only about 2 per cent per annum, as against the target of 4 per cent set in the Eleventh Plan, and who spoke of the need to raise the growth rate.

The rate of agricultural growth is actually hard to calculate, because it is so volatile, but as Pranab Bardhan (2009) has argued, agriculture is in bad shape. This is the result of the very high incidence, now, of marginal holdings, of the costs of inputs, the degradation of the natural resource base, declining public investment, and decreased access to public sector credit. One tragic but powerful marker of the fact that many cultivators have not been doing at all well in recent times is the apparently high rate of suicides among them, that began to be reported in the later 1990s. Neither liberalization policies nor the earlier mode of state intervention in agriculture effectively addresses fundamental problems having to do with the inefficient and often wasteful use of agricultural resources – including the failure to use irrigation water efficiently, partly because of neglect of the maintenance of irrigation structures and limitations of their design; excessive use of chemical fertilizers; and degradation of soils. There is a long history of poor use of key agricultural resources in India, by comparison with China and elsewhere in East Asia.

What to do about these problems remains a critical question. One answer, favoured by liberal reformers, is that land markets should be opened up and contract farming encouraged. But it is clear supermarkets and other corporates are not interested in transacting with large numbers of small farmers. So what is the future for the vast majority of Indian farmers? The sequencing here is all-important – and there are very good reasons for fearing that in the absence of employment opportunities outside of agriculture, then their exclusion from contract farming, and even more the displacement of small farmers by the corporate takeover of agricultural land, will lead to further impoverishment.

Recommended reading: Ramachandran and Rawal (2010), Vaidyanathan (2006).

Poverty and social development

It is widely known that India is home to more of the world's poorest people than any other country. Yet, early in the 21st century, different official bodies in India have come up with widely divergent estimates of the incidence of poverty in the country, ranging between about 25 and as much as 80 per cent of the (rural) population. This very wide gap should be a reminder that poverty, understood in terms of income deprivation, is only a construct, depending upon more or less arbitrary judgements. One eminent economist, A. Vaidyanathan, who has devoted much of his long professional life to these matters, has argued that 'it is not possible to arrive at a definitive estimate of poverty incidence that can be used as a reasonably robust benchmark' (Vaidyanathan, 2013: 41). It is very confidently argued, however, that income poverty has been greatly reduced over the last quarter-century, as a result of the trickle-down effects of growth.

The evidence referred to above, about employment trends and the state of the agricultural economy, leads to questioning of such confident claims. In any event deprivation in terms of income is only one, limited way of conceptualizing poverty. As Vaidyanathan also says, the disabilities of the poor have to be assessed in regard to minimum desirable levels of the components of living standards 'such as food intake, unemployment and underemployment, housing, connectivity and indicators of health and education status' (p. 41). In regard to the latter – indicators of health and education – there is every reason to doubt the claims that are being made about improvements in the quality of life of the mass of the people of India. What can be done to improve education and healthcare are among the most crucial questions of Indian development.

Yet, as noted in the introduction to this chapter, India has seen some remarkable legislation in recent years, which has established what has been described as a 'new welfare architecture'. The implementation of the Mahatma Gandhi National Rural Employment Guarantee (as it is now called), which is supposed to provide up to 100 days of employment each year for every rural household, matters a great deal for the livelihoods of very many people, as does the implementation of the Food Security Act that should provide subsidized foodgrains for about two-thirds of the population. Now there is debate over whether it may not be more efficient and effective to replace these programmes with cash transfers, or even to provide a universal basic income. Such measures, however, will not reduce the vital need for the improvement of healthcare and education.

Recommended reading: Dreze and Sen (2014), Vaidyanathan (2013).

Conclusion

This chapter has sought to highlight the continuing tension of Indian development, between the achievement of high rates of economic growth and the realization of well-being for the mass of the people. The failure of the latter – the failure of the objective of 'inclusive growth' – and the manifest evidence of deepening inequality, have deeply worrying political implications, not least for the relations between different ethnic groups within India's diverse society.

References

Bardhan, P. (2009). 'Notes on the political economy of India's tortuous transition'. *Economic and Political Weekly*, 44(49), December: 31–6.

Chandrasekhar, C.P., Ghosh, J. and Patnaik, P. (2015). *ICSSR Research Surveys and Explorations: Economics*. Delhi: Oxford University Press.

Corbridge, S., Harriss, J. and Jeffrey, C. (2013). *India Today: Economy, Politics and Society*. Cambridge: Polity Press.

Dreze, J. and Sen, A. (2014). *An Uncertain Glory: India and its Contradictions*. Princeton, NJ: Princeton University Press.

Economic and Political Weekly (2016). 'Editorial: lies, damn lies and statistics'. *Economic and Political Weekly*, 51(24), 11 June.

Eswaran, M., Kotwal, A., Ramaswami, B., and Wilima, W. (2009). 'Sectoral labour flows and agricultural wages in India, 1983–2004: has growth trickled down?' *Economic and Political Weekly*, 44(2): 46–55.

Himanshu (2011). 'Employment trends in India: a re-examination'. *Economic and Political Weekly*, 46(37): 43–59.

Kohli, A. (2012). *Poverty Amid Plenty in the New India*. New York: Cambridge University Press.

Lerche, J. (2010). 'From "rural labour" to "classes of labour": class fragmentation, caste and class struggle at the bottom of the Indian labour hierarchy'. In B. Harriss-White and J. Heyer (eds), *The Comparative Political Economy of Development*. London: Routledge, pp. 64–85.

Mehrotra, S., Parida, J., Sinha, S. and Gandhi, A. (2014). 'Explaining employment trends in the Indian economy: 1993–94 to 2011–12'. *Economic and Political Weekly*, 49(32): 49–57.

Modhi, N. (2016). 'Make in India: PM promises stable tax regime, says more reforms to come'. *Deccan Chronicle*, 13 February.

Panagariya, A. (2008). *India: The Emerging Giant*. New York: Oxford University Press.

Ramachandran, V.K. and Rawal, V. (2010). 'The impact of liberalisation and globalisation on India's agrarian economy'. *Global Labour Journal*, 1(1): 56–91.

Roy, S. (2016). 'Faltering manufacturing growth and employment: is "making" the answer?' *Economic and Political Weekly*, 51(13): 35–42.

Sanyal, K. and Bhattacharyya, R. (2009). 'Beyond the factory: globalisation, informalisation of production and the new locations of labour'. *Economic and Political Weekly*, 44(22), May: 35–44.

Vaidyanathan, A. (2006). 'Farmers' suicides and the agrarian crisis'. *Economic and Political Weekly*, 41(38): 4009–13.

Vaidyanathan, A. (2013). 'Use and abuse of the poverty line'. *Economic and Political Weekly*, 48(44): 37–42.

33

INTERROGATING THE CHINA MODEL OF DEVELOPMENT

Alvin Y. So and Yin-Wah Chu

Since the turn of this century, the mass media have been buzzing regularly about China's remarkable development. China has become the largest exporter and second largest importer of goods in the world. In 2010, China – the world's fifth largest economy in 2006 – overtook Japan as the second largest economy in the world. If China grows at the same rate as it has done over the past three decades, it will overtake the size of the US economy by 2020.

China had a US$59.6 billion trade surplus with the US in 2015 and its foreign reserves were US$3.33 trillion – the largest in the world. As a result, there has been a dramatic change in China's status in the global economy. In 1980, China barely registered on the global economic scale, commanding a mere 1 per cent of global GDP. In 2015, China captured 15.49 per cent of global GDP due to its grasp of advanced technology, enhanced competitiveness and expansion of foreign direct investment flows.

Influenced by these impressive economic indicators, both the mass media and policy circles have coined terms such as 'The Rise of China' or the 'China Model' of development to describe China's fast-speed economic growth. Since 2004, we have also seen reference to 'The Beijing Consensus', representing the alternative development model to the North's 'Washington Consensus' (a US-led plan for reforming and developing the economies of Third World countries).

The China Model is said to have the following three distinctive features: *state-led*, *investment-driven* and *export-oriented*. The China Model is based on massive state-led investment in infrastructure – roads, ports, electricity, railways, harbours, airports – that facilitates industrial development to export manufactured goods for the global market.

It is argued that the China Model has influenced developing countries in the South. For example, the BBC reported that after the 2008 Olympic Games, the success of China's model of development was increasingly apparent. The China

Model was very well-received at the China–Africa Business Summit in Cape Town in 2009, and is likely to inspire both Islamic and African countries. In the 2010s, China is seeking to export its development model to other countries through the China-led Asian Infrastructure Investment Bank to finance the 'One Belt, One Road' initiative, which is designed to support massive infrastructure construction to link China and Central Asia and then to Europe, the Middle East and South Asia through railway and seaborne traffic.

How should we think about China? Mainstream development studies are so impressed by China's fast-speed economic growth that they fail to look at the negative side of China's development. Once researchers start to problematize the nature of the China Model, however, they will find that the features of the China Model are highly contested and the celebration of China's fast-speed economic growth is premature. This chapter identifies six critical issues for interpreting the origins, nature, impact and global implications of the China Model of development.

Recommended reading: BBC Monitoring Asia Pacific (2009), Fukuyama (2016), Lin (2011), Ramo (2004), Zhang (2011).

The legacy of the communist era: an impediment or a facilitator?

The China Model denotes that China's fast-speed economic growth started only since 1978, after China had discarded the harmful revolutionary heritage of the communist era (1949–1976). In this interpretation, the communist experiment under Mao was a disaster. The Great Leap Forward in the late 1950s led to famine and the death of tens of millions of Chinese. The 10 years of Cultural Revolution (1966–1976) turned Chinese society upside down and resulted in political anarchy. In this scenario, China's march to modernization began only in 1978, after the rise of Deng Xiaoping, a pragmatist, who paid little attention to the revolutionary ideology of Mao. Hence, Deng became the hero of Chinese modernization, whereas Mao was held responsible for the economic backwardness and political turmoil of the first 30 years of Chinese communist rule.

What is missing in the above account, however, is that it fails to recognize the fact that China did achieve rapid economic growth and significant structural transformation during the three-decade socialist experiment. For example, China's GDP grew annually at an average rate of 7 per cent between 1952 and 1978, and at 5 per cent between 1960 and 1981, which compared most favourably with the 1 per cent achieved by all the 'low-income countries excluding China and India' (Nolan and Ash, 1995: 981). Furthermore, Chinese industry grew at about 11 per cent per year between 1952 and 1976.

China's fast-speed economic growth over the past 30 years actually owed much to the historical heritage of the Maoist era (1949–1976). Despite many shortcomings, China during the communist era was dominated by a strong Leninist party-state that commanded a high degree of legitimacy, autonomy and capacity. The party-state was able to build a strong organizational framework capable of mobilizing popular energies for large-scale infrastructure projects. In turn, rural infrastructure and related local institutions were instrumental for carrying out the post-1978 economic reforms.

Specifically, it was during the Maoist era, the Great Leap Forward in particular, that the state mobilized millions of peasants to construct and improve dams, reservoirs, drainage networks and irrigation systems. It was also during the socialist experiments that rural industries and enterprises were set up in the communes, local officials accumulated managerial experience and human capital through running the commune and brigade enterprises, and local governments were asked to promote development in the community. The Maoist commune model and its decentralization policy provided the medium to tap local resources, to train local leaders and to stimulate local initiatives.

Without the infrastructure and institutional foundations built in the communist era, it is doubtful whether agricultural productivity could increase so rapidly in the early 1980s, whether rural entrepreneurs could emerge so quickly from the local official stratum, whether local township and village enterprises could play the leading role in China's industrialization during the critical transition in the late 1970s and the early 1980s, and whether local forces could occupy such an important role in China's remarkable economic development.

Recommended reading: Bramall (1993), Lippit (1982), So and Chu (2016).

Autonomous development or head servant of the US?

The China Model emphasizes that China has a highly autonomous, independent form of development. Proponents of the model argue that China shows how to fit into the international order in a way that allows the South true independence, to protect their ways of life and political choices in a world with a single powerful centre of gravity. In short, the China Model contains a theory of self-determination, one that stresses using leverage to move big, hegemonic powers that may be tempted to tread on your toes.

From a critical development studies perspective, however, China has lost its autonomy in developing its economy in ways not too different from other countries in the South. China is now dependent on the investment of multinational corporations and the foreign technology they bring. It is also dependent on the expansion of exports to the international market in order to maintain its high GDP growth rates.

How important are these multinational corporations to China's development? Roughly two-thirds of the increase in Chinese exports in the first decade of the 21st century can be attributed to non-Chinese-owned global companies and their joint ventures. Foreign-owned global corporations account for 60 per cent of Chinese exports to the US. In 2004, US retail giant Wal-Mart was China's eighth largest trading partner ahead of Russia, Australia and Canada. As argued by Hung Ho-fung (2009), China is merely 'the head servant' of the US and transnational corporations, leading other countries in the South in providing cheap exports to the US and using its hard-earned savings to finance American purchase of those exports.

Furthermore, since the China Model is export-driven, it is highly vulnerable to fluctuations in the capitalist world economy. With the onset of the economic crisis in fall 2008, China's exports suffered a sharp decline, dropping by more than 20 per cent from the previous year. In China's Pearl River Delta, many toy export-processing companies closed their doors or went bankrupt because of order reductions from the US and Europe. The country experienced a rapid deceleration of economic growth, expenditure on consumer durables fell sharply, home sales plummeted, and construction activity declined.

As the global economic crisis dragged into the 2010s, the China Model seemed to have reached its limit and outlived its usefulness. Facing slowing demand in the global market, China suddenly realized that its manufacturing industries had massive excess capacity, as shown by its idle factories, empty residential apartments and ghost towns. The excess capacity results directly from the investment-driven China Model, or the ways the communist party-state, local governments and state enterprises keep throwing resources into the Chinese economy – mountains of cash to build factories, roads and bridges, apartment towers and shopping malls, etc. New investment projects prop up GNP growth to make China look good in some development indicators, but only at the expense of the health of the overall economy.

The resultant large trade surplus may inflate China's global financial power, but the long-term suppression of manufacturing wages restrains the growth of China's consumption power, making it very difficult for China to reorient its development model to achieve a balance between domestic consumption and exports. Trapped by export-led and investment-driven industrialization, China could not free itself from dependence on the collapsing US consumer market and addiction to risky US debt, nor could it be transformed into a high-waged, sustainable economy to improve the quality of life for the Chinese grassroots population. In short, the crisis exposed China's external economic dependence and the recent deceleration of China's economic growth rate from 10 per cent to 6–7 per cent (the so-called 'new normal') gave further support to Hung's 'head servant' argument.

Recommended reading: Dirlik (2004), Hart-Landsberg and Burkett (2004), Hung (2009), Lee and Mathews (2009), Roach (2006), So (2012).

Technological upgrading or technological dependence?

The China Model stresses that China has modernized its educational system, upgraded its science and research capabilities, and participated in high-tech production. From the 1990s on, foreign corporations began to transfer a significant amount of their research and development activity into China. Microsoft, Oracle, Motorola, Siemens, IBM and Intel have all set up research laboratories in China because of its growing importance and sophistication as a market for technology and its large reservoir of skilled but inexperienced scientists, and its consumers, still relatively poor but growing richer and eager for new technology. In the 2010s, China began to move up the value added ladder of production and to compete with South Korea, Japan, Taiwan and Singapore in spheres such as electronics and machine tools.

However, despite the above assertion, a critical development studies perspective points out that the export-oriented growth model cultivates strong inertia, locking China in at the lower end of the value chain. China's world factory status only denotes that Chinese firms have successfully hooked into the global commodity chain: becoming assembly lines for foreign-branded transnationals, with the lion's share of the profits going to foreign investors. These kind of ties have not led to any significant technological upgrading or forward-and-backward linkages that characterize the shift to developed country status, or indeed to the form of upgrading that characterizes the first tier of East Asian Newly Industrializing Countries. In turn, transnationals have not exported their most current technology to China. Whatever technology is exported to China is often placed under strict control to prevent dissemination, and the US government has more than once accused Chinese firms of engaging in corporate espionage to steal high-tech inventions from US corporations.

Recommended reading: Buckley (2004), Kiely (2008), Sataline (2016), Wang (2008).

Poverty reduction or rising social inequality/rising class conflict

The China Model stresses that the investment-driven and export-led industrialization has led to fast-speed economic growth in China. This is evident from the first deades of the reform process. For example, from 1978 to 2001, China's annual average growth rate was 8.1 per cent and its annual rate of industrial growth was 11.5 per cent. China's exports grew from US$18.1 billion in 1978 to US$266 billion in 2001, reflecting an annual average growth rate of 12 per cent. By the early 2000s, China had become the global factory and the workshop of the world. In a short span of just over 20 years, China was transformed from a poor, backward country in the South to an economic powerhouse of the world.

For proponents of the China Model, this rapid economic growth allowed the country to reduce the share of its population living on less than US$1 per day from 64 per cent in 1981 to 16 per cent by 2004, effectively lifting 600 million people out of absolute poverty. The China Model worked more effectively than the IMF designated Structural Adjustment Program in the Washington Consensus model for Sub-Saharan Africa and the 'shock therapy' for Russia. Above all, success in poverty alleviation is said to have endowed widespread legitimacy in the Chinese communist party-state so that, unlike its communist counterparts in the Soviet Union and Eastern Europe, the Chinese state is not under any threat of revolution.

Critical researchers contest the above assertions. Instead of the highly celebrated poverty reduction in the China Model, they point to China's worsening income inequality. The Gini coefficient for household income in China rose from 0.33 in 1980, to 0.40 in 1994 and to 0.46 in 2000. The last figure surpasses the degree of inequality in Thailand, India and Indonesia. By 2004, observers suspect that China's Gini coefficient had exceeded 0.50, placing its income inequality near the levels of Brazil and South Africa. Within a short span of less than 30 years, therefore, China transformed itself from one of the most egalitarian to one of the most unequal societies in the world (So, 2013).

For critical researchers, China's stark income inequality was caused by the party-state's resolve to pursue fast-speed export-led industrialization, even at the expense of bankrupting the countryside and prolonging the unlimited supply of low-cost migrant labour to coastal export industries. Indeed, to stifle labour costs, keep the exports of Chinese factories competitive in the world economy, maintain a favourable environment to attract foreign investment, and encourage transnational corporations to relocate their labour-intensive production lines, the Chinese communist party-state has gone so far as to adopt authoritarian policies so as to discipline workers, suppress labour protests and pacify civil labour. It seems authoritarianism is unavoidable in export-led industrialization because labour subordination is an important means to cheapen labour and to make the working class docile. It is ironic that the Chinese state, with its tightly organized party-state machinery, has proven to be very effective in co-opting labour activists, dividing the working class, and silencing labour protests.

Despite this, there are limits to the success of these policies. By the 2010s, the 'unlimited' supply of low-cost migrant labour had dried up. China's demographic surplus is vanishing. China's population is ageing at a very fast rate due to the one-child policy. As a result, the supply of young labourers will gradually decrease in the near future, and the transfer of rural labourers to urban areas will be completed in the next 10 to 20 years.

At the same time, widening social inequality has caused many social problems, which, contrary to the sanguine picture painted by proponents of the China Model, threaten to undermine social stability and the long-term survival of the communist party-state. In the face of deteriorating social equality and the scaling back of social benefits by the Chinese state, the Chinese working class has become restless (see also Chapter 21 by Pun Ngai in this volume). According to official statistics, in 1998 there were 6,767 collective actions (usually strikes or go-slows with a minimum of three people taking part) involving 251,268 people. This represented an increase in collective actions of 900 per cent from the 1990s. In 2000, this figure further jumped to 8,247 collective actions involving 259,445 workers (China Labour Bulletin, 2002: 2). In 2008, China set up a New Labour Contract Law with an aim to cut down this wave of collective action. However, the number of strikes and worker protests in China continued to escalate dramatically towards the end of 2015 as the economy continued to decelerate, with manufacturing, construction and mining all seeing a massive upsurge in disputes. On 4 December 2015, Guangdong police detained seven prominent labour activists who had been instrumental in promoting China's labour movement. The police crackdown, however, has done little to stem the tide of labour unrest in the province, with another 56 strikes recorded in the province in December alone (China Labour Bulletin, 2016). Given such widespread labour protests, it is no wonder that the Chinese government has identified the labour problem as the biggest threat to social and political stability.

Taken together, high-speed economic growth has not done China much good: the development of the past 30 years has thrown tens of millions of workers out of the state factories into an exploitative private sector and has also ruined the foundation for long-term development of China's countryside. Capitalist development in the past 30 years has deprived a large portion of the Chinese population their security to the basic necessities of life (So, 2007, 2013).

Recommended reading: China Labour Bulletin (2002), Hart-Landsberg and Burkett (2004), So (2007, 2013), UNDP (2006).

Rapid growth versus environmental sustainability

Proponents of the China Model have as a rule turned a blind eye to problems of environmental degradation. Critical researchers, however, have drawn attention to the widespread disregard for environmental sustainability in the country's rush to entice foreign investment and promote exports. Hence, in the 1980s and 1990s, China embraced the relocation of many heavily polluting industries, such as fabric dyeing, paper manufacturing, leather processing and petrochemicals, without requiring them to instal proper waste disposal mechanisms. By the 2010s, China still handled much of the e-waste generated globally by using primitive and highly polluting methods. Just as important, the need for an enormous and inexpensive electricity supply for industry made room for the survival of power plants that used inferior and unwashed coals, as well as relied on inefficient burning practices. Similarly, the need for raw materials such as wood and pulp led to considerable deforestation.

As a result of the above and similar practices, water pollution is estimated to affect 90 per cent of China's urban groundwater and 75 per cent of rivers and lakes. In 2012, the country's Ministry of Water Resources ranked some 21.2 per cent of water flow in China's 10 water systems in category V or below, which meant that they were dangerous even for industrial use. Similarly, Judith Shapiro (2016) reported that the level of total suspended particulates (TSPs) and sulfur dioxide (SO_2) in most Chinese cities far exceeded the World Health Organization guidelines. In 2009, China surpassed the US to become the world's biggest emitter of carbon dioxide and, by extension, contributor to global warming.

Environmental problems have exacted heavy social and economic costs. Among other things, it is believed that some 300 million people in China do not have access to safe drinking water. Among the world's 30 most polluted cities, 20 are in China. In 2010, 459 villages in China were called 'cancer villages' owing to the prevalence of deaths induced by air and water pollution. Annual losses due to water and air pollution were estimated at the value of US$54 billion, whereas annual direct losses attributable to desertification totaled $7 billion. All these were ignored in the discussion of the China Model.

Recommended reading: Liu and Diamond (2005), So and Chu (2016), Wang *et al.* (2013).

A model or a culprit to pull down global wages?

Despite the fact that China is constructed as the model to emulate, many countries still see it as a competitor for foreign investments and jobs. An *Economist* report (*Economist*, 2001) noted the 'alarm and despair' with which China's neighbours reacted to its rise: 'Japan, South Korea and Taiwan fear a hollowing out of their industries, as factories move to low-cost China . . . Southeast Asia worries about 'dislocation' in trade and investment flows [to China]'. In addition, Global Labour Strategies (2008) reported that workers, communities and countries throughout the world are confronting the challenges posed by China's emergent role in the global economy. About 25 per cent of the global workforce is now Chinese. The 'China price' increasingly sets the global norm for wages and working standards at both the high and low ends of the production chain. As a result, the hard-won gains of workers in the Global North are being rapidly undermined while the aspirations of workers in the Global South are being dashed as China becomes the wage-setting country in many industries. Therefore, China celebrated as an export powerhouse in fact only intensifies economic tensions and contradictions throughout the South – to the detriment of workers everywhere.

In sum, although the mainstream literature wants to highlight the positive features of the China Model – such as fast-speed economic growth, export-led industrialization, an independent nation state and poverty reduction – a critical development studies perspective is quick to point to the harmful consequences of the China Model, such as rural bankruptcy, dependency on the US market, rising social inequality, social conflict and the downward pull on global wages. A critical perspective tends to see the China Model as an exercise in ideology to justify the global reach of the Chinese party-state and transnational corporations.

Recommended reading: Economist (2001), Global Labour Strategies (2008), Hart-Landsberg and Burkett (2004).

References

BBC Monitoring Asia Pacific (2009). 'China–Africa Business Summit Held in South Africa'. *BBC Monitoring Asia Pacific*, 24 October.

Bramall, C. (1993). *In Praise of Maoist Economic Planning: Living Standards and Economic Development in Sichuan Since 1931*. Oxford: Clarendon Press.

Buckley, C. (2004). 'Let a thousand ideas flower: China is a new hotbed of research'. *New York Times*, 13 September. Available at: www.nytimes.com/2004/09/13/technology/13china.html.

China Labour Bulletin (2002). 'Hong Kong: Han Dongfang (January 31)'. Available at: www.china-labour.org.hk/public/main.

China Labour Bulletin (2016). 'Strikes and protests by China's workers soar to record heights in 2015 (July 1)'. Available at: www.clb.org.hk/en/content/strikes-and-protests-china%E2%80%99s-workers-soar-record-heights-2015.

Dirlik, A. (2004). 'Beijing Consensus: Beijing 'gongshi': who recognizes whom and to what end?' Available at: www.ids-uva.nl/wordpress/wp-content/uploads/2011/07/9_Dirlik1.pdf.

Economist (2001). 'A panda breaks the formation'. *Economist*, 25 August.

Fukuyama, F. (2016). 'China's road or the Western way: whose economic development model will prevail?' *South China Morning Post*, 14 January.

Global Labour Strategies (2008). 'Why China matters: labour rights in the era of globalization'. Available at: http://labourstrategies.blogs.com/global_labour_strategies/files/why_china_matters_gls_report.pdf.

Hart-Landsberg, M. and Burkett, P. (2004). 'China and socialism: market reforms and class struggle'. *Monthly Review*, 56(3): 1–116.

Hung, H.-F. (2009). 'America's head servant? The PRC dilemma in the global crisis'. *New Left Review*, 60, November–December: 5–25.

Kiely, R. (2008). 'Poverty's fall/China's rise: global convergence or new forms of uneven development'. *Journal of Contemporary Asia*, 38(3): 353–72.

Lee, K. and Mathews, J.A. (2009). 'From Washington Consensus to BEST consensus for world development'. Paper presented to the Annual Convention of the Korean Economic Association at Seoul.

Lin, J.-Y. (2011). 'China and the global economy'. *China Economic Journal*, 4(1): 1–14.

Lippit, V. (1982). 'Socialist development in China'. In M. Selden and V. Lippit (eds), *The Transition to Socialism in China*. Armonk, NY: M.E. Sharpe, pp. 116–58.

Liu, J. and Diamond, J. (2005). 'China's environment in a globalizing world'. *Nature*, 435, June: 1179–86.

Nolan, P. and Ash, R.F. (1995). 'China's economy on the eve of reform'. *The China Quarterly*, 144: 980–98.

Ramo, J.C. (2004). 'The Beijing Consensus'. *The Foreign Policy Center*. Available at: http://fpc.org.uk/fsblob/244.pdf.

Roach, S. (2006). 'Doha doesn't matter any more: despite stiff resistance to the Doha agenda for five years, there have been powerful gains in world trade in the same period'. *Business Times Singapore*, 8 August.

Sataline, S. (2016). 'China slowdown'. *Sage Business Researcher*. Available at: http://businessresearcher.sagepub.com/sbr-1775-101044-2756201/20161010/chinas-slowdown.

Shapiro, J. (2016). *China's Environmental Challenges*, 2nd edition. Cambridge: Polity.

So, A.Y. (2007). 'The state and labour insurgency in post-socialist China: implication for development'. In Y.S. Cheng (ed.), *Challenges and Policy Programmes of China's New Leadership*. Hong Kong: City University of Hong Kong Press, pp. 133–51.

So, A.Y. (2012). 'The global capitalist crisis and the rise of China to the world scene'. In B. Berberoglu (ed.), *Beyond the Global Capitalist Crisis: The World Economy in Transition*. Burlington: Ashgate, pp. 123–44.

So, A.Y. (2013). *Class and Class Conflict in Post-Socialist China*. Singapore: World Scientific.

So, A.Y. and Chu, Y.-W. (2016). *The Global Rise of China*. Cambridge: Polity.

UNDP (2006). 'UNDP China wins 2006 poverty eradication awards'. Available at: www.undp.org/poverty/stories/pov-award06-China.htm.

Wang, F., Kuehr, R., Ahlquist, D. and Li, J. (2013). *E-Waste in China: A Country Report*. Available at: http://isp.unu.edu/publications/scycle/files/ewaste-in-china.pdf.

Wang, Y. (2008). 'Domestic demand and continued reform: China's search for a new model'. *Global Asia*, 3(4): 24-8.

Zhang, M. (2011). 'The transition of China's development model'. In W. Hofmelster (ed.), *G20 Perceptions and Perspectives for Global Governance*. Singapore: Konrad-Adenauer-Stitfung, pp. 51-6.

PART X

The search for a new model

Rethinking development in Latin
America

34

RETHINKING LATIN AMERICA

Towards new development paradigms

Ronaldo Munck

To 'rethink' Latin America, we first need to place the region in theoretical terms, and in particular in terms of development theory. We thus advance a critique of dominant modernization-type theories and the idea of a dual traditional/modern society. Then we reconsider the radical Latin American 'dependency' approach to development, arguing that, to some extent, it did not break radically from the modernization approach because it shared its nation state frame of reference. Now in the era of globalization, this approach might need to be modified to have the purchase it could have. Finally, we consider the post-neoliberal era we now, arguably, live in after the collapse of the Washington Consensus and the Latin American dictatorships. In particular, we explore the possibility that there may be a more radical development theory to be built, based on the Amerindian imaginary pointing towards a sustainable and human-centred mode of development.

Recommended reading: Munck (2012).

Situating Latin America

To 'rethink' Latin America, we first have to explore the debates around 'placing' Latin America in a conceptual rather than geographical sense. Is Latin America part of the so-called Global South? Or is it just a backward outpost of Europe or the West located elsewhere? Is it a 'developing' society heading towards modernity eventually, or is it condemned by its colonial origins to always be 'dependent' on the advances of industrial societies? We will also explore options beyond these ultimately debilitating binary oppositions so that we might better place, and thus understand, Latin America in terms of its social hybridity or, put another way, its liminality, which places it betwixt and between different worlds. Some analysts characterize Latin America by what it lacks – a democratic culture, entrepreneurialism, respect for the law and so on – and not according to what it is. Another current of thought reacts to these imperialist perspectives by stressing difference, a current sometimes known as Macondismo, after the mythical land Macondo created by Colombian magical realist writer Gabriel García Márquez. While I would be sympathetic towards the postcolonial critique of orthodoxy and recognize its value in our rethinking mission, it does run the risk of depoliticizing the analysis and ending up with a purely culturalist approach.

Most approaches, including some radical ones, have a shared understanding of Latin America as a dual system with traditional and modern worlds existing in their own time and space. Now, to carry out an effective critique of dualism, we do not need to see Latin America as always-already capitalist as Andre Gunder Frank, who popularized the dependency approach in the North, did. Brazilian political economist Francisco Oliveira has developed what is probably the most sophisticated 'critique of dualist reason', as he calls it (De Oliveira, 1973). The separation between the so-called backward and modern sectors of the economy simply did not exist as such. There was, in fact, a close complementarity between the agricultural and emerging industrial sectors, with the first providing much-needed food inputs and a ready supply of labour. A dialectical interdependence meant that 'the expansion of capitalism in Brazil occurred through the introduction of new relations in the archaic [sector] and by reproducing archaic relation in the new [sector]' (De Oliveira, 1973: 32). The first process freed up labour to work in the industrial sector, while the second process created a complex process of labour control and its subordination to the oligarchic capital accumulation process.

If we start instead from the premise that Latin America is characterized by contradictions, we need to understand that it experienced mixed temporalities, leading to multiple modernities. Modernization was never a smooth, linear process as we see when deconstructing the traditional dualist model. The most up-to-date modern technologies could be introduced in rural areas, while traditional small-scale production and various forms of coerced labour played a key role in the industrialization process. The new in the old, and the old in the new, was a socio-economic process, but it inevitably impacted on politics and culture as well. Too often, Western or North American political analysis assumes a modern democratic model that simply does not apply. Cultural formations in Latin America are most dramatically mixed and hybrid. In short, there are multiple paths to modernity, and even, as in Latin America's case, there can be modernity without modernization.

So, Latin America could perhaps be seen as betwixt tradition and modernity, in a liminal position so to say. Homi Bhabha (1994) identifies a liminal space where the hybrid emerges, a translational space or a 'third space'. Identity and culture is neither fixed nor homogenous from this perspective. This certainly is a flexible lens through which to analyse the encounters between the indigenous peoples and the European invaders, in the course of which neither remained unchanged. It was in this third (neither-or, thus liminal) space where the negotiations between different cultural systems of signification occurred. It is not necessarily a subversive concept because it was the *mestizo* (mixed indigenous-European) identity that played a key role in stabilizing the conservative order of postcolonialism based on the new *criollo* elite.

In recent years it is the concept of hybridity that has gained most purchase within Latin America as an analytical category seeking to explain its specificity. For others, the Manichean world of the dependency theorists – with its First and Third Worlds – misses out on the more flexible, hybrid world we now live in. For example, '[i]t does not explain the planetary functioning of an industrial, technological, financial, and cultural system whose headquarters is not in a single nation but in a dense network of economic and ideological structures' (García Canclini, 1995: 229). The transnational cultural political economy that holds sway today, the flows of migrants and money, and the dense network of images and information that shapes our understanding is not amenable to a simplistic explanation around geographical or political belonging to a mythical Third World.

Interestingly, the way García Canclini phrases the central tension of Latin America today is that we are between the promise of global cosmopolitanism and the failure of national projects (García Canclini, 2002: 50). Nation building in the traditional sense is no longer seen as viable in the era of global development. But globalism, in turn, seems somewhat of an empty promise when it reproduces hierarchies and inequalities, thus appearing to be just the new face of imperialism. Certainly, globalization as we know it does not produce a racism-free, sexism-free and sustainable oriented world, whatever its self-image might be. What it does create is a vastly speeded up world where the interconnections between the local and the global are much denser than they ever have been. We see everywhere in this new world 'examples of hybridization that do not reconcile the diverse and intercultural fusions which explode every day in the big cities' (García Canclini, 2002: 50). The story of this hybrid globalization has only just begun, and we can surmise that the Great Recession of 2008–2009 might have reined in some of its excesses, but that the greater internationalization of social, economic and cultural relations is an ongoing process.

Recommended reading: Bhabha (1994), De Oliveira (1973), García Canclini (1995).

Latin American dependency

Countering the dominant 'made in US' modernization theory of the 1960s was Latin America's own indigenous development theory, known as the dependency approach or paradigm. While in its more grounded variants, such as the F.H. Cardoso and Enzo Faletto classic *Dependency and Development in Latin America* (1969, 1979), it was a nuanced, structural and historical take on development and its relationship to social classes, but also had a much cruder manifestation. The later trend, best exemplified by the work of Andre Gunder Frank (1970) – elevated outside Latin America to *the* dependency theorist – often seemed to just reverse the modernization discourse to create its binary opposite. Where one saw the diffusion of capital into backward areas as the key to development, the other saw it as simply developing underdevelopment. Diffusion of innovation would develop the traditional areas for one theory but simply create stagnation and de-capitalization for the other. Creating a mirror image of a theory is probably not the best way to move critical analysis forward.

The main issue was that modernization and dependency theory both took for granted and saw as natural the nation state framework. National economic development was the objective and the state would play a crucial role in that process. Inevitably, the diversity of social interests – and the capital/wage labour conflict in particular – was somewhat subsumed under this paradigm. A social transformation perspective on the development process in Latin America would stress, rather, the emergence and development of social classes and class conflict. From the colonial period onwards, different social groupings were vying for hegemony and to impose their particular interests as the general interest. Landowners, industrialists, urban workers, rural smallholders, artisans and others all had diverse social interests. It was the struggle for hegemony that set a particular development path and determined the modalities of social transformation in each country. National development choices were really the outcome of class development and struggle, not something emerging spontaneously.

Ultimately, the modernization and simple dependency approaches shared a methodological nationalism that took the nation state to be a natural and self-sufficient envelope for the development process. They also shared a strong economism that led them to ignore or at least downplay the political process, not to mention the cultural dimension. They were also equally teleological in assuming a given end-station for the development process. For modernization theory, the end of the journey was to be a consumer-based modernity à la the United States, while for the dependency approach it was socialism à la Cuba, based on an ill-defined delinking from the global system. Both thus rejected the complexity of history, the contradictions of the accumulation process in a context of class struggle, and that the future is open to different outcomes, and not present in some original DNA pattern of development or underdevelopment.

We could go further in relation to a critique of the dependency approach from a postcolonial stance. In a way, dependency shares with modernization theory a strong attachment to modernity as an overarching perspective and a commitment to the *logos* of development. It is very much centred on the nation state that it takes as the unproblematized unit of analysis and the sovereign subject of development as it were. But some authors have gone further and accused the dependency approach of ignoring culture and the politics of representation, thus leading to a general ethnocentrism bordering on orientalism (Kapoor, 2008: 10). Europe is still seen as the universal model against which development on the periphery is judged and deemed (in)adequate. For their part, the broad brush visions of capital accumulation on a world scale run the risk of submerging the local and creating a totalizing narrative, which itself may disable alternative accounts of and strategies for development. We should maybe direct ourselves instead to the more complex cultural and political boundaries that shape the subaltern consciousness in the world of the majority.

A post-dependency approach would need to break out of its binary opposition with regards to modernization theory. We might still question, of course, whether the structures of domination located by the dependency theorists in Latin America have simply been superseded in the era of 'interdependent' globalization. Few progressive or critical analysts would argue today that the problems of development, as conventionally defined, have been overcome in Latin America. What is being challenged is more to do with the totalizing vision of dependency, one it shares with other modernist epistemologies. The challenge of a transformationalist approach would be to decolonize development knowledge and to adopt a more critical or deconstructionist approach towards the received terminology of development/dependency. We might thus consider more insecure forms of knowledge, a greater receptivity towards bottom-up or indigenous forms of knowledge, and less assurance in presenting a polished alternative to the status quo developed solely at the level of social and political theory.

Recommended reading: Kay (1989).

Post-neoliberal development

The neoliberal restructuring of socioeconomic relations and absolute prioritization of the free market in the 1990s led inevitably to a popular reaction. Sometimes muted and covert, at other times quite open, this reaction began to build from the mid-1990s, and, as Evelina Dagnino recounts, '[t]he work of Gramsci offered the Latin American Left an appropriate framework with which to examine the historical specificity of their own focuses, especially the particular kinds of relations between state and society' (Dagnino, 1998: 87). The Gramscian political categories helped open up previously static and Manichean approaches to social transformation. Above all, it allowed for the recentring of democracy as a political category, replacing previous simplistic oppositions between socialism and fascism. The democratic terrain was rediscovered and the notion that socialism could be nothing other than democratic was re-established (see Castañeda, 1993).

This reactivation of civil society saw the emergence of old and new social actors. The 1990s saw the emergence of a vast contentious cycle as diverse movements began to seek representation and to have their needs addressed. In particular, the indigenist or neo-indigenist movements saw the 36 million descendants of the original Amerindian peoples articulating their collective rights with considerable impact on the political system, most notably in the Andean countries. As Leo Zamosc reports for Ecuador, but more broadly applicable:

> The participatory breakthrough came on two fronts. Practicing the politics of influence, the movement forced new issues on to the public agenda, wrested concessions from governments, and led alliances that repeatedly hindered the imposition of neoliberal reforms. Engaging in the politics of power, it contested the control of the state's indigenous agencies and spawned a party that made strides in the electoral representation of the Indian groups, the procurement of their collective rights and their progress towards self-government.
>
> *(Zamosc, 2007: 26)*

In terms of the development of democracy in Latin America, these movements played an absolutely pivotal role.

Latin America, since the year 2000, has lived through a political spring that is quite unprecedented in terms of the depth and breadth of progressive social transformation. New paradigms of social change and political experimentation emerged that are, perhaps, of global significance. What the dependency approach meant to the 1970s in terms of overarching development paradigm, so today the concept of *Sumak Kawsay* (*buen vivir*) – only imperfectly rendered as 'living well' in English – captures the radical edge of current thinking (Acosta, 2012; Acosta and Martínez, 2009; Choquehuanca, 2010; Farah and Vasapollo, 2011; Gudynas, 2011; Gudynas and Acosta, 2011; Houtart, 2011). It essentially speaks to the extended reproduction of life rather than of capital. It advocates a different civilizational model to that of individualistic capital where community values and respect for nature take priority. It is a development paradigm now enshrined in the constitutions of Ecuador and Bolivia and causing ripples across the region (Acosta, 2012).

The concept of *buen vivir* or *Sumak Kawsay* departs from the premise that there are two transitions underway in Latin America: a relatively recent transition towards socialism barely 100 years old and a longer-term transition out of colonialism that goes back to the 15th century. An end to all forms of racism and greater self-determination form part of that longer-term struggle. It does not deny at all the relevance of Western forms of representative democracy, but adds as well the need for participative and communal forms of democracy. While this new cosmovision does not simply rearticulate ancient indigenous practices and is characterized by a profound hybridity, it does represent a challenge to Eurocentrism. It articulates new principles of production and property (Acosta and Martínez, 2009; Gudynas, 2011).

The contemporary indigenous perspective in Latin America based on the concept of *buen vivir* (Ecuador) or *vivir bien* (Bolivia) provides a different logic to that dominant in mainstream development thinking and practice and in the Western corridors of power. It is keenly attuned to biodiversity and sustainability rather than the pursuit of private profit above all else. It values reciprocity and sharing rather than self-advancement and greed as indicators of a good life. It is premised on the value of living well in social solidarity and harmony with nature. Central to the current debates around a new indigenous politics of transformation is the question of autonomy. Like the term multiculturalism, it can actually be quite compatible with neoliberalism (Žižek, 1997) but it can also be a very positive value in promoting the autonomy of indigenous peoples. Nor does an affirmation of autonomy as a value resolve the concrete question of political alliances that the indigenous and other movements might enter into.

A critical assessment of the concept of *bien vivir* or *Sumak Kawsay* would need to engage with previous attempts to create an 'Andean utopia' through an invocation of the Incas to rethink colonialism and injustice since the Spanish conquest (Domínguez and Caria, 2014; Marañón, 2014). One of the best known is Alberto Flores Galindo's (2010) *In Search of an Inca*, which stresses the idealization of the pre-colonial Inca past as a period of harmony and prosperity that could become a guide for the future. Flores Galindo himself denied that he was promoting an Andean utopia as a blueprint for socialist or *neo-indigenista* political projects and acknowledged its authoritarian stands. However, this work is a rich repository of ideas and social practices that can inform current debates around transformative alternatives. As Flores Galindo puts it: 'For people without hope, the Andean utopia challenges a history that condemned them to the margins. Utopia denies . . . the illusion of development understood as westernization' (pp. 247–8).

In previous engagements between the socialist and indigenous paradigms for social transformation, it is Peruvian communist thinker and organizer José Carlos Mariátegui (1894–1930) who stands out. Having engaged with the thinking and politics of Antonio Gramsci while in exile in the early 1920s, he returned to Peru with a clear understanding that 'Without the Indian no Peruvianness is possible' (Vanden and Becker, 2011: 141). The self-activity of the Amerindian masses and their move from a regional to a national level of organization would play a key role in that process. Thus, the making of the nation, encapsulated in this slogan *Peruanicemos el Perú* (let us Peruvianize Peru), is inseparable from a recovery of the indigenous past of the 'hidden Peru' in which an indigenous non-market logic of reciprocity and communalism was core to the meaning of society.

In terms of the politics of globalization and contestation, the notion that 'another world is possible' in a philosophical and a practical sense is key to understanding the prospects for alternative development models. It is only Western ethnocentrism that could imagine other human worlds were not possible. Other world views and cosmologies have always existed that are opposed or quite independent from what Polanyi (1947) called 'our obsolete market mentality'. Market sovereignty is contested daily by social action based on reciprocity. Even 'actually existing capitalism' recognizes that the market could not exist without trust and shared norms of reciprocity. Those expelled from the market society through the various forms of social exclusion characteristic of global capitalism also revert to reciprocity and redistribution in order to survive. These norms are imbued with moral–ethical principles at odds with those of the 'market mentality'. Sustainable economic cultures are being built today seeking ecological sustainability and based on social solidarity. The pre-capitalist and today's non-capitalist worlds show to what extent society as market is a recent and quite limited human innovation.

Against all forms of economic determinism, and the 'class reductionism' of classical Marxism, Polanyi stresses that social class is not always determinant. This critique resonates with the contemporary transition towards 'new' social movements mobilized around non-class issues. For Polanyi, '[c]lass interests offer only a limited explanation of long-run movements in society. The fate of society is determined by the needs of classes' (Polanyi, 2001: 159). Certainly, Polanyi recognized the essential role played by class interests in social change, but he refuses to adopt a narrow class logic: 'There is no magic in class interest which would secure to members of one class the support of members of other classes' (p. 160). This is particularly the case in times of social crisis – 'those critical phases of history when a civilization has broken down or is passing through a transformation' (p. 163) – when new options for society are being debated, sometimes in extremely short periods of time. In this dramatic situation, no narrow class interest can even defend its own interests: 'Unless the alternative to the social set-up is a plunge into utter destruction, no crudely selfish class interest can maintain itself in the lead' (p. 163). These are precisely the types of consideration lying behind current concerns with 'global governance' from above and they should inform any articulation of 'good globalization' from below.

The critique of economism implicit in Polanyi's work also has a contemporary ring, as when he stresses the 'cultural' element in social dislocation and resistance. A cataclysmic event such as the Industrial Revolution in the 19th century and the 'Globalization Revolution' today are, in Polanyi's words, 'economic earthquakes' that transform the lives of vast multitudes of people. But, 'actually, of course', argues Polanyi, 'a social calamity is primarily a cultural phenomenon that cannot be measured by income figures or population statistics' (p. 164). When people are dispossessed of their traditional means of livelihood, when customs and ways of life are disrupted, and 'alien' cultural values are imposed, this affects the very way in which people ascribe meaning to their condition.

To conclude, the search for societal protection against the ravages of the self-regulated market is diverse and complex, appearing in a number of forms in different societies. As Polanyi put it for his era, '[t]he great variety of forms in which the "collectivist" counter-movement appeared [was due to] the broad range of the vital social interests affected by the expanding market mechanism' (p. 151). Common examples may be bottom-up, for example in the form of workers' unions, or top-down, with responses such as the welfare state. However, in the Global South, the search for development has been the most prevalent form of counter-movement, or mechanism of defence against the self-regulating market. The developmental state of the 1950s and 1960s was a conscious bid to temper the free market through the creation of national developmentalism based on state-led industrialization behind protectionist barriers. In the current era, the political and economic exclusion generated by neoliberalism has provided the inspiration for a number of actors and institutes to search for new development alternatives appropriate for the current conjuncture. Latin America is a rich laboratory for the study of a wide range of counter-movements, offering in differing ways alternative development models in keeping with the current era and the needs of the people.

Recommended reading: García Canclini (1995), Munck (2012), Polanyi (2001), Silva (2009).

References

Acosta, A. (2012). *Buen Vivir. Sumak kawsay. Una oportunidad para imaginar otros mundos*. Quito: Abya Yala.

Acosta, A. and Martínez, E. (2009). *El Buen Vivir – Una vía para el desarrollo*. Quito: Abya Yala.

Bhabha, H. (1994). *The Location of Culture*. London/New York: Routledge.

Cardoso, F.H. (1979). *Dependency and Development in Latin America*. Berkeley, CA: University of California Press.

Cardoso, F.H. and Faletto, E. (1969). *Dependencia y Desarrollo en América Latina*. Mexico: Siglo XXI.

Castañeda, C. (1993). *Utopia Unarmed. Latin America after the Cold War.* New York: Vintage Books.

Choquehuanca C.D. (2010). 'Hacia el reconstrucción del Vivir Bien'. *Revista América Latina en movimiento, Sumak Kawsay: recuperar el sentido de vida.* Quito: ALAI, pp. 8–13.

Dagnino, E. (1998). 'Culture, citizenship, and democracy: changing discourses and practices of the Latin American left'. In S.E. Alvarez, E. Dagnino and A. Escobar (eds), *Cultures of Politics, Politics of Cultures: Re-Visioning Latin American Social Movements.* Boulder, CO: Westview Press, pp. 1–29.

De Oliveira, F. (1973). 'A Economia Brasileira: Crítica à Razão Dualista'. *Cadernos CEBRAP*, 2: 3–82.

Domínguez, R. and Caria, S. (2014). 'La ideología del buen vivir: La metamorfosis de una "alternativa al desarrollo" en desarrollo de toda la vida'. *Pre-textos para el Debate* 2. Quito: Universidad Andina Simón Bolívar.

Farah, I. and Vasapollo, L. (eds) (2011). *Vivir bien: ¿Paradigma no capitalista?* La Paz: CIDES-UMSA.

Flores Galindo, A. (2010). *In Search of an Inca: Identity and Utopia in the Andes.* Cambridge: Cambridge University Press.

Frank, A.G. (1970). *The Development of Underdevelopment in Latin America.* New York: Monthly Review Press.

García Canclini, N. (1995). *Hybrid Cultures: Strategies for Entering and Leaving Modernity.* Minneapolis, MN: University Minnesota Press.

García Canclini, N. (2002). *Latinoamericanos buscando lugar en este siglo.* Buenos Aires: Paidós.

Gudynas, E. (2011). 'Buen Vivir: today's tomorrow'. *Development*, 54(4): 441–7.

Gudynas, E. and Acosta, A. (2011). 'El buen vivir más allá del desarrollo'. *Qué Hacer*, 181: 70–81.

Houtart, F. (2011). 'El concepto de sumak kawsay (buen vivir) y su correspondencia con el bien común de la humanidad'. *Ecuador Debate*, 84: 57–75.

Kapoor, I. (2008). *The Postcolonial Politics of Development.* London: Routledge.

Kay, C. (1989). *Latin American Theories of Development and Underdevelopment.* London: Routledge.

Marañón, B. (ed.) (2014). *Buen vivir y descolonialidad: crítica al desarrollo y la racionalidad instrumentales.* Mexico: UNAM – Instituto de Investigaciones Económicas.

Munck, R. (2012). *Rethinking Latin America: Development, Hegemony and Social Transformation.* New York: Palgrave.

Polanyi, K. (1947). 'Our obsolete market mentality'. In G. Dalton (ed.), *Primitive, Archaic and Modern Economics: Essays of Karl Polanyi.* Boston, MA: Beacon Press, pp. 59–77.

Polanyi, K. (2001). *The Great Transformation: The Social and Political Origins of Our Time.* Boston, MA: Beacon.

Silva, E. (2009). *Challenging Neoliberalism in Latin America.* Cambridge: Cambridge University Press.

Vanden, H. and Becker, M. (eds) (2011). *José Carlos Mariátegui: An Anthology.* New York: Monthly Review Press.

Zamosc, L. (2007). 'The Indian movement and political democracy in Ecuador'. *Latin American Politics and Society*, 49(3): 1–34.

Žižek, S. (1997). 'Multiculturalism, or, the cultural logic of transnational capitalism'. *New Left Review*, 1(225): 28–51.

35

PEASANT ALTERNATIVES TO NEOLIBERALISM

Leandro Vergara-Camus

It is rarely acknowledged, but the history of the idea and process of development has always been haunted by the spectre of the peasantry. Indeed, during the Cold War, peasant-based armed guerrilla movements more than working-class organizations were the main adversaries of Western-supported regimes in the Third World. With the defeat or exhaustion of most guerrilla struggles and the implementation of neoliberal policies in the 1980s, the great majority of studies switched their focus to the process of restructuring that neoliberalism was triggering in the countryside of the Global South. But the resurgence of peasant struggles for land across the developing world in the 1990s brought back discussions on the nature and potential of peasant-lead rural movements. With the rise of the alter-globalization movement and the World Social Forum of Porto Alegre, in which rural movements through *La Vía Campesina* have always played a crucial role, scholars and activists moved from talking about 'resistance to neoliberalism' to 'alternatives to neoliberalism'.

Those of us who consider ourselves critical scholars use the term *alternative* a lot. By this term, we want to signal that capitalism or neoliberalism is not inevitable or the only form of organizing our societies. But considering the diversity and fragmented nature of subaltern classes, we should recognize that there are all kinds of 'alternatives' to neoliberalism. They can be nationalist, populist, anti-neoliberal, anti-capitalist, anti-modernist or modernist and developmentalist, or a complicated mix of all of that. While acknowledging this diversity, the main objective of peasant alternatives is to defend and promote the interests of a particular peasantry and establish the conditions for the survival, reproduction and (ideally) prosperity of poor rural households as peasants.

What kind of class is the peasantry?

The first theme to address when attempting to study, understand and assess peasant alternatives to neoliberalism is obviously the characteristics of the peasantry as a class. Within agrarian studies, there has been a long debate about the nature of the peasantry and its prospects within the development of capitalist societies, which had one of its defining moments in the debate between Alexander Chayanov and Vladimir Ilyich Lenin at the beginning of the 20th century (Bernstein, 2009). Chayanov argued that the peasant household functioned under a distinctive logic because it was organized around the need to balance out production and the use of family labour with the demographic cycles of the household. For him, food production of the peasant households was dictated more by the subsistence needs of the family unit than by the possibility of making profits on the market. In contrast, Lenin looked at the peasantry as a class that was made of three strata: rich, middle and poor peasants. He argued that internal class differentiation would turn the upper stratum into an agrarian capitalist class, while the lower strata would either become rural proletarians or migrate to the city. In sum, the peasantry was doomed to disappear. The 20th century saw numerous replays of this debate in many countries of the Third World. Surprisingly, some of the assumptions accepted by the opposed camps of this debate seem to be making a comeback within agrarian studies (Bernstein, 2014; Boltvinik and Archer Mann, 2016; McMichael, 2015).

Peasants are indeed an anachronistic social category for modernist social scientists because the term does not comply with the images that they have of the individuals or collective subjects, and their persistence also does not comply with their concept of the pathways that societies are supposed to take. For liberal political economists in particular, peasants do not seem to follow individualistic profit-maximizing rationality when they take decisions about agricultural production. For the Marxist political economist, because peasants still control their means of production (land, agricultural tools and inputs), they are not a proletariat. However, because peasants traditionally tend not to control enough land (or have access to it through patron–client relationships with landlords), use their own family labour instead of wage labour, do not produce solely for the market and are subjected to exploitation from dominant classes, they are not fully capitalists either. Furthermore, for Marxists who believed in the need of a proletarian socialist revolution, peasants were an ambiguous class because being in some sense 'two classes at the same time', they could join the working class in favour of a socialist revolution or the landed oligarchy against it (Akram-Lodhi and Kay, 2010).

On the basis of Lenin's 'three class in one' typology, many have preferred to use the term peasants to refer to the poorest sectors of the peasantry, which reproduced themselves partly through non-capitalist relations, and the term farmers for those who reproduced themselves mainly through capitalist relations irrespective of the size of their plot (Boltvinik and Archer Mann, 2016: 18–19). The authors that continue to use the term peasants today tend to follow these distinctions, and see them as part of a class:

1. that has (or fights to reclaim its) access to land, but does not control enough land to accumulate wealth in order to turn it into capital;
2. whose control of land allows it to secure part of its subsistence by producing food for self-consumption and to partly avoid the market for its social reproduction;

3. that is able to mobilize unpaid family labour from the household and rely on sociocultural practices of solidarity, reciprocity and redistribution from its kinship network or community (Halperin and Dow, 1977); and

4. that reproduces a collective identity, based on a particular experience of class, racial, ethnic or national difference associated to a given territory.

Some of these practices are non-capitalist social relations because they are not mediated by money or commodities. Hence, these practices provide some level of peasant autonomy from the market, not that they exist outside of capitalism. The discussion on the existence or disappearance of the peasantry is in essence a debate about whether these practices still persist and provide some degree of autonomy (Van der Ploeg, 2010) or if these practices have been subsumed by capitalism, making rural subjects completely market-dependent (Bernstein, 2001). Those who see class as being determined essentially by economic relations tend to reject the idea of the persistence of the peasantry (Bernstein, 2001), while those who see it fundamentally as a political process (McMichael, 2015) or as a process that combines economic, cultural and political dimensions (Otero, 1999) tend to emphasize its modern reinvention.

Although some of the discussion may seem like an exercise in nitpicking, understanding the class nature of peasants is important because it allows us to identify which institutions and sociocultural practices they tap into when they build their alternatives.

Recommended reading: Akram-Lodhi and Kay (2010), Bernstein (2001, 2009, 2010), Boltvinik and Archer Mann (2016), Halperin and Dow (1977), Otero (1999).

The capitalist transition in agriculture and the impact of the international food regime on peasants

Capitalist expansion triggers processes of de-peasantization and proletarianization, but the incomplete proletarianization that is typical of the Global South often leads a sector of the peasantry to struggle for re-peasantization by getting involved in struggles to regain access to land (Moyo and Yeros, 2005). Hence, although not strictly about peasant alternatives, the research carried out on the global restructuring of agriculture (see Chapter 4 by Kay in this volume) and the international food regime (see Chapter 24 by Akram-Lodhi in this volume) constitute an essential part of any study of peasant alternatives. The changes that have been triggered since the rise of neoliberalism – particularly market deregulation and the privatization of state agencies involved in supporting small-scale producers through guaranteed prices, subsidized inputs, commercialization and technical support in the Global South – have completely transformed the social, economic and political conditions upon which peasants managed to get by. What stands out in these new developments is the growing control of agriculture by private corporate firms upstream – sale of agricultural seeds, fertilizers, herbicides, pesticides and machinery – and downstream – purchase, sale and processing of grains and food (Weis, 2007). Another element that stands out is that the restructuring of the state has been crucial in facilitating the increased control of capital over agriculture. Recent studies are also showing that climate change mitigation policies are affecting peasant agriculture through the creation of ecological reserves or the development of agrofuels projects (Fairhead et al., 2012). There is an important debate about the ability of some small-scale producers to find a space within this new international food regime and about how to turn the tide towards a more socially just outcome. Some authors believe that peasant producers, assisted by new forms of state support, could be linked to agribusiness-led commodity chains through contract farming, while others believe that this is not a viable option.

Recommended reading: Akram-Lodhi and Kay (2009), Fairhead et al. (2012), Moore (2010), Weis (2007).

Control of land, labour, nature and territory

Because they control their means of production, peasants are in a position to choose what, when and how to produce. Compared to other labourers, they are more in control of their labour power and the labour process. But peasants cannot remain peasants without access to land and without some kind of control over a certain territory and its natural resources. Collective struggles for land have always, therefore, been one of the central struggles of peasant movements, redistribution of land (or agrarian reforms) often being the way of translating this demand into state policy. The expansion of certain industries such as mining, oil extraction, forestry, tourism or plantation agriculture (sugar cane, banana, oil palm, etc.) constantly pose a threat for peasant communities. Collective struggles for land have often also been about continued access and control of natural resources (forest, water, fauna, etc.) that access to land and control of a territory implies. When their territories are not encroached by industrial developments, demographic pressure on land is one of the most important problems that peasant families have to face. Getting access to land can take on different forms and involves many actors, institutions and social relationships. At the centre of all this is the power of those that are able to control the mechanisms that determine the access through the state or the community. As mentioned, some of the cultural practices within peasant communities are based on practices of solidarity, reciprocity and redistribution, but many of them are also patriarchal and exploitative, socially enforcing what men and women can or cannot do. No study of peasant alternatives can be complete without exploring the power relations that exists within households and analysing the racial, ethnic and gender relations within and among rural communities, as well as the ecological foundations, upon which a particular type of peasant agriculture is carried out in a particular region of the Global South.

Disentangling the foundations of these practices and their consequences for the different members of peasant households and communities can allow us to assess if peasant alternatives to neoliberalism are indeed 'alternative' or the extent to which they tackle the issues that reproduces inequality and exploitation not only of peasant communities and within peasant communities, but also within peasant households. The issue here is about assessing how 'democratic' a peasant alternative is by examining how all forms of inequalities are tackled, how social mobilization is organized, and how political consciousness is acquired through the political prac-tices that the peasant organization reproduces on the inside.

Codified in what is often called 'traditional knowledge', generation after gener-ation, peasants reproduced and modified their methods of farming and of using and conserving natural resources. Considering their precarious dependence on nature, the main objective of this traditional knowledge is to maintain a balance between the exploitation and conservation of nature. This agricultural knowledge, how-ever, is not static, and is subject to trial and error of new methods, as well as the use of modern science and technology. The agroecology movement has emerged recently with the conscious objective of drawing from, supporting, and enhancing the accumulated peasant agricultural knowledge in order to build an alternative to the fossil-fuel-dependent technologies used by industrial and green revolution agriculture (Altieri and Toledo, 2011; Holt-Gimenez, 2006). An assessment of a peasant alternative to neoliberalism would have to also determine how environ-mentally sustainable and economic feasible this alternative is.

Recommended reading: Akram-Lodhi *et al.* (2008), Altieri and Toledo (2011), Fernandes Mancano (2005), Holt-Gimenez (2006), Vergara-Camus (2014), Wolford (2010), Zibechi (2012).

Alternative to what? Avoid, integrate or create markets

In their attempts to carve out a space for themselves within the process of capitalist development that is controlled by large capitalist farmers and corporate oligopolies, peasants have often sought to find ways to deal with market forces in ways that would be more beneficial to them. These coping strategies can be classified in three types: market avoidance, market integration and market creation (see Van der Ploeg, 2010, for a different, though complementary, approach).

These strategies are not mutually exclusive, and can be combined and inter-twined in complex ways. Strategies of market avoidance are those that imply a conscious decision of retreating from market relations into subsistence production by concentrating efforts on food crops for self-consumption (rice, maize, beans, potatoes, yam, cassava, etc.), replacing agricultural inputs that have to be bought by those produced 'for free' by nature and humans (what Van der Ploeg calls self-pro-visioning and co-production), or by tapping into collective sociocultural practices of solidarity, reciprocity or redistribution that do not involve monetary exchange. Strategies of market integration are those that imply a deeper involvement with the market, either as seller of agricultural products, as wage worker in agriculture or other industries, or as member of a larger producer organization that will allow the peasant household to yield better negotiating power vis-à-vis market intermediar-ies. Those that have sufficient and adequate access to land and natural resources can do the former as a household by switching from food crops to cash crops (coffee, cacao and bananas) or cattle. The option of selling their labour power in exchange for a wage is something that peasant households tend to do periodically, but cannot be considered a collective response. The option of joining forces in order to benefit from what economists call 'economies of scale' at the level of production or simply economic leverage in terms of purchasing power for inputs or for setting the price of a given commodity continue to be at the heart of countless experiences of producers associations and cooperatives. Finally, the creation of new markets for their products has recently become an important coping strategy for a minority of organized peasant producers since the 1980s. These new markets take the form of a fair trade network, organic production, local farmers markets, alternative labelling and certification schemes, etc. Many of these initiatives have sought to provide an alternative to the capitalist market by guaranteeing a just price for producers, linking producers and consumers in more ethical ways, supporting local development, etc. However, a great deal of discussion has been triggered by the market-friendly approach adopted in particular by the fair trade movement, its problematic certification mechanisms, and its mainstreaming into (or cooptation by) the global food industry (see Fridell, 2015; Raynolds *et al.*, 2007).

To understand the nature of peasant alternatives to neoliberalism, students of development would have to assess the ways in which households and collective strategies are intertwined and reinforce each other, and to determine if a particular initiative of a peasant movement can provide a decent livelihood for them by protecting their control of land and natural resources and contributing to a democratization of peasant household and communities.

Recommended reading: Bernstein (2014), Fridell (2015), McMichael (2015), Otero (1999, 2004), Raynolds *et al.* (2007), Van der Ploeg (2010), Vergara-Camus (2014).

Peasant movements and politics today: outside, within or through the state

As mentioned earlier, peasants have been key social subjects of radical politics. They have also been the social basis of quite a few reactionary and right-wing movements. But 2007 marked the moment in which the majority of the world's population was no longer rural. Considering the complexity of the rural areas of the Global South, peasants are probably the majority in only a few less developed countries and there are many countries in which they are actually not even the majority of the rural population. This poses the question of the power that peasant movements can mobilize on their own, but also, and more importantly, of the kind of peasant demands and proposals that can coincide with those of other subaltern groups of society. How can peasant movements convince other groups to join forces with them to either build alternatives to neoliberalism outside of the state, or pressure the state to implement certain alternative policies, or occupy the state to carry out an anti-neoliberal project, or build transnational networks to build a common view and coordinate campaigns (Borras *et al.*, 2008)?

To my limited knowledge, the Zapatista movement in Chiapas is probably the only peasant movement that has taken the first path, though to a great extent on its own. The second path is taken by most peasant movements across the Global South. The third path is taken by peasant movements that are strong enough to yield some political influence or have links to political parties. The fourth path is what the rural transnational movement *La Vía Campesina* has been about for more than three decades now.

Out of all the discussion and alternative proposal that have emerged in the last three decades of resistance to neoliberalism, none have had more visibility than those of *La Vía Campesina*. Its global campaign for agrarian reform contributed to putting redistributive agrarian reform back on the international agenda. Its idea of food sovereignty, which challenges the current corporate-driven global food system, has established itself as a competing paradigm and is generating heated discussions on the left. One of the least explored issues is the role of the state in food sovereignty. Indeed, many principles of food sovereignty require strong state or societal control over private corporations, but the food sovereignty movement does not seem to have a clear conception of what the capitalist state is and how it can be transformed or controlled to put its principles in action. Some of the ideas behind the food sovereignty movement have been put to the test of policy recently in Latin America. In Bolivia and Ecuador, peasant and indigenous movements played a key role, first in bringing down neoliberal governments, then in electing left-of-centre nationalist government, and finally inserting pro-peasant principles (such as food sovereignty, the social function of land or communitarian forms of production and exchange) into the Constitution of these two countries. However, the results have not been impressive (Zibechi, 2012). In none of the countries governed by leftist governments in Latin America was there an extensive redistributive agrarian reform. In all cases, their policies have continued to promote agribusiness, only funnelling comparatively very few financial resources to small-scale producers. Only in Brazil did the state promote family agriculture through its programme of buying food for school meals from agrarian reform settlers. However, this pales in comparison to all the resources and policies that were mobilized in the promotion of agribusiness. In almost all the cases, the needs of rural workers were ignored (Kay and Vergara-Camus, 2017). Hence, any study of peasant alternatives to neoliberalism would have to venture into a complex critical analysis of the power of peasant movements and their strategies towards the state and other sectors of their civil society to see which sector of the peasantry they have benefited in last instance.

Not in a fortuitous way, this last discussion brings us back to the question of what kind of class the peasantry is. This underscores the need to examine the peasantry in all its complexity and as much as possible free from preconceived assumptions. The peasantry is not by essence anti-capitalist, although it reproduces itself partly through non-capitalist sociocultural practices. Consequently, the orientation of a particular peasant alternative will depend on the contradictory political struggles that peasant movements are involved in. Peasant alternatives will not simply be determined by the 'economic class positions' of the peasants involved (smallholders or semiproletarians), but also by their attempt to politically transcend these, find a basis for unity and reach out to other sectors.

Recommended reading: Akram-Lodhi *et al.* (2008), Borras *et al.* (2008), Deere and Royce (2009), Kay and Vergara–Camus (2017), Petras and Veltmeyer (2001), Zibechi (2012).

References

Akram-Lodhi, H. and Kay, C. (eds) (2009). *Peasants and Globalization: Political Economy, Rural Transformation and the Agrarian Question*. London/New York: Routledge.

Akram-Lodhi, H. and Kay, C. (2010). 'Surveying the agrarian question (part 1): unearthing foundations, exploring diversity'. *Journal of Peasant Studies*, 37(1): 177–202.

Akram-Lodhi, H., Borras Jr., S.M. and Kay, C. (eds) (2008). *Land, Poverty and Livelihoods in an Era of Globalization*. London: Routledge.

Altieri, M. and Toledo, V.M (2011). 'The agroecological revolution in Latin America: rescuing nature, ensuring food sovereignty and empowering peasants'. *Journal of Peasant Studies*, 38(3): 587–612.

Bernstein, H. (2001). 'The "peasantry" in global capitalism: who, where and why?' In L. Panitch and C. Leys (eds), *Socialist Register 2001: Working Classes, Global Realities*. London: Merlin Press, pp. 25–51.

Bernstein, H. (2009). 'V.I. Lenin and A.V. Chayanov: looking back, looking forward'. *The Journal of Peasant Studies*, 36(1): 55–81.

Bernstein, H. (2010). *Class Dynamics of Agrarian Change*. Halifax: Fernwood.

Bernstein, H. (2014). 'Food sovereignty via the "peasant way": a sceptical view'. *The Journal of Peasant Studies*, 41(6): 1031–63.

Boltvinik, J. and Archer Mann, S. (eds) (2016). *Peasant Poverty and Persistence in the 21st Century: Theories, Debates, Realities and Policies*. London: Zed Books.

Borras Jr., S.M., Edelman, M. and Kay, C. (eds) (2008). *Transnational Agrarian Movements Confronting Globalization*. London: Wiley-Blackwell.

Deere, C. and Royce, F.S. (eds) (2009). *Rural Social Movements in Latin America: Organizing for Sustainable Livelihoods*. Gainesville, FL: University Press of Florida.

Fairhead, J., Leach, M. and Scoones, I. (2012). 'Green grabbing: a new appropriation of nature?' *Journal of Peasant Studies*, 39(2): 237–61.

Fernandes Mancano, B. (2005). 'The occupation as a form of access to land in Brazil: a theoretical and methodological contribution'. In S. Moyo and P. Yeros (eds), *Reclaiming the Land: The Resurgence of Rural Movements in Africa, Asia and Latin America*. London: Zed Books, pp. 311–40.

Fridell, G. (2015). *Alternative Trade: Legacies for the Future*. Halifax: Fernwood.

Halperin, R. and Dow, J. (1977). *Peasant Livelihood: Studies in Economic Anthropology and Cultural Ecology*. New York: St. Martin's Press.

Holt-Gimenez, E. (2006). *Campesino a Campesino: Voices from the Farmer-to-Farmer Movement for Sustainable Agriculture in Latin America*. Oakland, CA: Food First.

Kay, C. and Vergara-Camus, L. (eds) (2017). 'The agrarian and agricultural policies of left-wing governments in Latin America'. Special issue of *Journal of Agrarian Change*, 17(2).

McMichael, P. (2015). 'A comment on Henry Bernstein's way with peasants, and food sovereignty'. *Journal of Peasant Studies*, 42(1): 193–204.

Moore, J. (2010). 'The end of the road? Agricultural revolutions in the capitalist world-ecology, 1450–2010'. *Journal of Agrarian Change*, 10(3): 389–413.

Moyo, S. and Yeros, P. (eds) (2005). *Reclaiming the Land: The Resurgence of Rural Movements in Africa, Asia and Latin America*. London: Zed Books.

Otero, G. (1999). *Farewell to the Peasantry: Political Class Formation in Rural Mexico*. Boulder, CO: Westview Press.

Otero, G. (ed.) (2004). *Mexico in Transition: Neoliberal Globalism, the State and Civil Society*. London: Zed Books.

Petras, J. and Veltmeyer, H. (2001). 'Are Latin American peasant movements still a force for change: some new paradigm revisited?' *Journal of Peasant Studies*, 28(2): 83–118.

Raynolds, L., Murray, D. and Wilkinson, J. (2007). *Fair Trade: The Challenge of Transforming Globalization*. London: Routledge.

Van der Ploeg, J.D. (2010). 'The peasantries of the twenty-first century: the commoditisation debate revisited'. *Journal of Peasant Studies*, 37(1): 1–30.

Vergara-Camus, L. (2014). *Land and Freedom: The MST, the Zapatistas and Peasant Alternatives to Neoliberalism*. London: Zed Books.

Weis, T. (2007). *The Global Food Economy: The Battle for the Future of Farming*. London: Zed Books.

Wolford, W. (2010). *This Land Is Our Land: Social Mobilization and the Meaning of Land in Brazil*. Durham, NC: Duke University Press.

Zibechi, R. (2012). *Territories in Resistance: A Cartography of Latin American Social Movements*. Oakland, CA: AK Press.

36

SOCIALISM AND DEVELOPMENT

A Latin American perspective

Claudio Katz

The Latin American Left once again is discussing how to construct a path towards socialism – the socialism of the 21st century, as understood by Hugo Chávez. The correlation of forces has changed through popular action, the crisis of neoliberalism and US imperialism's loss of offensive capability. It is no longer relevant to juxtapose a revolutionary political period of the past with a conservative present. The weakness of the industrial proletariat, destroyed by forces of capitalist development, and the weakness, if not absence, of the labour movement in many countries in the current context are not likely to impede anti-capitalist progress in the class struggle, which depends on the exploited and the oppressed uniting in common struggle.

What is crucial is the level of popular consciousness. In the current context of what some see as a new phase in capitalist development – extractive capitalism, based more on the plunder of society's natural resource wealth and the destructive operations of 'resource-seeking' or extractive capital than the exploitation of labour – the forces of resistance and the activism of the anti-capitalist social movements has forged a new anti-neoliberal and anti-imperialist alliance. However, an anti-capitalist link in this alliance with an open debate about how to bring about 21st-century socialism is still missing. The liberal democratic constitutional framework that replaced the dictatorships of the 1970s has not impeded the development of the political left, which received a major boost from the activism of the anti-neoliberal peasant-based and indigenous social movements of the 1990s (Petras and Veltmeyer, 2009, 2013). This activism was a major factor in the 'red' and 'pink' tide of regime change in the turn into the 21st century. This change in the political tide brought the political class on the centre-left to power, initiating a 'progressive cycle' in Latin American politics, which, by many accounts, is coming to an end with the ascension of the far right to power in Argentina and its advances in a number of other countries (Petras and Veltmeyer, 2009, 2017; Webber and Carr, 2013).

This apparent swing in the pendulum back from the left towards the right reflects an evident change in the correlation of force in the class struggle, which poses for the Left a serious dilemma, although – I would argue – not an impossible situation in regard to rebuilding socialism.

Recommended reading: Petras and Veltmeyer (2017).

Five reasons why Latin America is fertile ground for the rebuilding of socialism

The call by Hugo Chávez (2007) to build the socialism of the 21st century has resurrected the debates on the way forward, the path to follow and the alliances needed to form a non-capitalist society. This discussion has reappeared when most of the Left and the forces of progressive change had become accustomed to omitting any reference to socialism. The recovery of the socialist project's credibility is not yet visible in political circles, but the goal of emancipation from exploitation and oppression is once again debated by the popular organizations seeking a strategic compass for the struggle of the oppressed. What is the current meaning of the socialist project?

Latin America has become for several reasons a privileged scenario for a reconsideration of the socialist project. First, the region is at the centre of the international resistance to imperialism and neoliberalism. A number of popular uprisings in recent years led to the defenestration of several neoliberal presidents (Bolivia, Ecuador and Argentina) and reinforced the activism and forceful presence of the social movements on the political landscape. At the level of class struggle – including setbacks or repression (Peru, Colombia) and also reflux or disappointment (Brazil, Uruguay) – a number of new contingents have joined the popular movement. These have contributed to a renewal of the youth base of the movement (Chile), as well as very combative forms of self-organization (the Oaxaca Commune in Mexico). Socialism offers a strategic aim for these actions and could be transformed into a subject of renewed reflection.

Second, socialism has begun to achieve a certain street presence in Venezuela, providing a popular struggle bulwark against concerted efforts by the far right and the US state to provoke a middle-class uprising and the overthrow the project of the Bolivarian Revolution (to bring about the socialism of the 21st century). The vital presence of the idea of socialism on the streets among workers and the popular classes confirms the ideological alignment of the Bolivarian process with the Left absent in other nationalist experiences. In the days of the Soviet Union, some Third World leaders adopted a socialist identity purely for geopolitical purposes (to counteract the pressure of US imperialism) or for economic advantage (to obtain subsidies from the Soviet state). As these motivations and interests have entirely disappeared, current efforts to revive the socialist project reverberate are more genuine. The resurgence of an interest in socialism is also evident in Bolivia, and it is still alive and well in Cuba despite 45 years of an embargo, sabotage and imperialist aggression. If the collapse of actually existing socialism in the USSR and

Eastern Europe had extended to the island, no one today would be proposing an anti-capitalist agenda in Latin America. The political impact would have been too devastating for the cause of progressive change in the region.

In the third place, socialism is a flag taken up by the Left opposition to the social liberal presidents, who abandoned any allusion to socialism in order to ingratiate and accommodate themselves to the capitalist class and its political functionaries. Bachelet, Lula and Tabaré Vázquez eschewed all references to socialism in their discourse, refused to implement social reforms and placed themselves in opposition to the popular masses. Bachelet does not remember the name of her party (the Socialist Party of Chile) when she presides over the *Concertación* regime that has recycled the neoliberal model. In privileging the bankers and kowtowing to the ruling class, Lula totally forgot his youthful flirtation with socialism, and Tabaré repeats this same pattern when seeking to sign a free trade agreement with the United States. In the three countries, socialism is a banner against this desertion of a project, which reappears in a regional context very different from the one that prevailed in the 1990s. The stage of right-wing uniformity has ended, with the most emblematic characters of extreme neoliberalism having been forced to abandon the political stage. The imperialist politics of military coups are no longer viable and the mobilization of the forces of resistance by the social movements has opened up large democratic spaces for the construction of a social and solidarity economy from below. Under these conditions, conservative politicians and leaders coexist with the centre-left presidents brought in by a 'pink' wave of progressive regimes (Lula in Brazil, the Kirschners in Argentina, Tabré Vasquez in Uruguay) and with governments of a nationalist populist complexion swept in with a 'red' wave of regime change (Barrett *et al.*, 2008; Petras and Veltmeyer, 2009).

Fourth, in Latin America, a change of economic context favours a renewed debate on alternative models of development (neodevelopmentalism, the social and solidarity economy), including alternatives to (capitalist) development itself (in the form of a proposal for *Bien Vivir*, a model for living in solidarity and harmony with nature) and socialism. In several sectors of the dominant classes, after a traumatic period of extra-regional competition, denationalization of the productive apparatus and loss of international competitiveness, there has been a neodevelopmental turn towards the goal of inclusive development to the detriment of neoliberal orthodoxy (Bresser-Pereira, 2006, 2007, 2009; Katz, 2006a).

Neodevelopmentalism is one pillar of the economic model used by most governments in South America to make public policy in the area of national development. It is based on the post-Washington Consensus on the need to bring the state back into the development process and 'establish a better balance between the market and the state' and a more inclusive form of capitalism (Fine *et al.*, 2001). The other pillar is 'neo-extractivism' – the extraction of natural resources for export in primary form – what in some contexts is described as 'reprimarization' (Cypher, 2010).

This approach has generated powerful forces of resistance against the destructive operations of extractive capital, and an ongoing debate on how to combine extractivism with socialism (García Linera, 2013). But this turn towards neo-developmentalism and neo-extractivism ('inclusionary state activism') has challenged all the economic dogmas that have dominated development thinking over the past decade, particularly as regards the viability and the form taken by capitalism under these conditions. This rethinking has exposed several cracks within the dominant mindset regarding the virtues of capitalism, allowing the Left space to counter the neodevelopment model of choice for many governments with a socialist alternative.

In fifth place, there is a widespread tendency to conceive of programmes of national development in regional terms. This stance also permeates popular organizations that perceive the need to evaluate their proposals in regional terms. This new spirit allows us to face the debate on the now defunct FTAA with a regionalist reformulation of socialism. The three regional integration projects in play include the strategic aim of relaunching the neoliberal project (FTAA), a project for regulation regional capitalism (MERCOSUR) and experimentation with a partnership for trade and development that is compatible with socialism (ALBA).

The current Latin American context therefore encourages the resumption of anti-capitalist programmes in various fields. But these orientations are embodied in different strategies. One possible way for doing so would involve developing popular struggle, encouraging social reforms and radicalizing the transformations propitiated by the nationalist governments. This would require unmasking the duplicities of the centre-left leaders, questioning the neodevelopment project, promoting ALBA as a link to post-capitalist regional integration, and above all supporting both Cuba and Venezuela in their efforts to advance the socialist project and keep it alive.

Recommended reading: Barrett *et al.* (2008), Munck (2013), Petras and Veltmeyer (2009).

Constructing socialism: a question of strategy

After several years of silence, a strategic discussion regarding socialism is re-emerging on the Latin American Left, which once again is analysing assessments and courses of action in order to advance towards socialism. This reflection and debate includes six major themes: material conditions, the correlation of force in the class struggle, social subjects, popular consciousness, institutional frameworks and organizing the oppressed.

The first debate revisits a classic controversy. Have the productive forces in Latin America matured enough to permit undertaking an anti-capitalist transformation? Are the existing resources, technologies and skills sufficient to initiate a socialist process?

First, the countries of the region are less prepared than the developed nations – but more pressed – to confront this challenge. They suffer more intense nutritional, educational and sanitary disasters than the advanced economies, but have fewer material resources at their disposal to solve these problems. This paradox is the consequence of Latin America's peripheral situation and its resulting agricultural backwardness, fragmentary industrialization, and financial dependence.

On the Left, there have been two traditional responses to this dilemma: promote a progressive capitalist stage (a more humane and inclusive form of capitalism), or initiate a socialist transition adapted to the region's shortcomings. In a recent article, I advocated the second option (Katz, 2005). But another equally important debate concerns the timeliness of this course. Recovering from a traumatic period of industrial slump and bank meltdown, Latin America is experiencing a phase of growth, an export boom and a recovery of entrepreneurial and corporate profits. One could object that, under these conditions, there is no likelihood of a collapse that would justify anti-capitalist transformation. But the socialist option is not a Keynesian programme to turn around recessive market trends. It is a platform to overcome the exploitation and inequality inherent in capitalism. It seeks to abolish poverty and unemployment, eradicate environmental disasters and put an end to the nightmares of war and the financial cataclysms that enrich a minuscule percentage of millionaires at the expense of millions of individuals.[1]

No socialist revolution ever coincided with the depths of a financial crisis. In the majority of cases, it erupted as a consequence of war, colonial occupation or dictatorial oppression. It was under such conditions that the Bolsheviks took power in Russia, Mao succeeded in China, Tito prevailed in Yugoslavia, the Vietnamese drove out the United States, and the Cuban Revolution triumphed. Many of these victories were consummated at the height of a post-war boom, that is, during a stage of intense capitalist growth. No mechanism, therefore, shackles the debut of socialism to an economic collapse. The misery that capitalism generates is sufficient to inspire the overthrow of this system in any phase of its periodic fluctuations.

Only catastrophist theorists see an unwavering link between socialism and financial meltdown. This supposed connection forms part of their habitual portrayal of capitalism as a system that always operates on the verge of final collapse. Waiting for this fall, they identify any banking slump as a global depression, and they confuse a simple stock market downturn with a general crash. These exaggerations ignore the basic workings of the system that they intend to uproot and make it impossible to tackle any of the problems of socialist transition.[2]

Recommended reading: Katz (2005).

Globalization and socialism, and small countries

One objection to the initiation of socialist processes emphasizes the impediments that globalization creates. It argues that the current internationalization of capital makes an anti-capitalist challenge impracticable in Latin America (Harnecker, 2000). But where exactly is the obstacle rooted? Globalization does not constitute a barrier to the socialist project, which has a universal reach. Expansion across borders amplifies capitalism's imbalances and creates greater objective bases for overcoming it.

Only those who conceive of the construction of socialism as a 'competition between two systems' can view globalization as a great obstacle. This approach is a remnant of the theory of the 'socialist camp' proclaimed by supporters of the old Soviet model. They gambled on defeating the enemy by means of a series of economic successes and geopolitical achievements, forgetting that one cannot defeat capitalism at its own game.

Peripheral – or less industrialized – economies in particular can never triumph in a competition with imperialist powers that have controlled the world market for centuries. The success of socialism requires a continuous sequence of processes that undermine global capitalism. Achieving socialism in a single country (or single bloc) is an illusion that repeatedly has led to subordinating the possibilities of revolutionary transformation to a diplomatic rivalry between two blocs of nations.

The portrayal of globalization as blocking the development of other models is an offshoot of the neoliberal vision, which proclaims the non-existence of alternatives to the right-wing path. But if one accepts this premise, one must also discard any scheme of regulated or Keynesian capitalism. It is incongruent to affirm that the totalitarianism of globalization has buried the anti-capitalist project, but that it tolerates interventionist regimes of accumulation. If one closes the first option, one also rules out chances for neodevelopmentalist endeavours (since these depend on the power of the national state to resist externally imposed measures).

Since globalization is not in reality the end of history, every alternative remains open. What we are witnessing is merely a new period of accumulation, sustained by recovery of the rate of profit that the oppressed of every country pay. This regressive flow makes socialism an immediate necessity as the sole popular response to the new stage. Only socialism can correct the disorders created by the global expansion of capital in the current framework of financial speculation and imperialist polarization.

Many theorists recognize the global viability of the socialist option but question its feasibility in small Latin American countries. They believe that this beginning ought to be postponed – for example, in Bolivia – some 30 or 50 years, to allow the prior formation of an 'Andean-Amazonian capitalism' (García Linera, 2005, 2006a, 2006b). But why 30 years and not 10 or 150? In the past, these time frames were associated with calculations of the emergence of national bourgeoisies in charge of carrying out the pre-socialist stage. But currently, it is evident that the impediments to developing a competitive capitalist system in countries such as Bolivia are at least as great as the obstacles to initiating socialist transformations. One need merely imagine the concessions that the large foreign corporations would demand for participation in their project, and the conflicts that these commitments would generate with the popular majorities.

The difficulty is even greater if one conceives of 'Andean-Amazonian capitalism' as a model compatible with the reconstruction of indigenous communities (García Linera, 2006a). In any scheme that is driven by commercial competition, the abuses against these communities would persist. The step to socialism in countries as peripheral as Bolivia is complex, yet possible and desirable. It requires promoting a transition together with similar programmes and alliances in other countries of Latin America.

Recommended reading: García Linera (2006a), Harnecker (2000), Katz (2006b).

The correlation of class forces

Socialist change depends on a balance of forces favourable to the oppressed. The popular majority cannot prevail over its antagonists if this balance is negative. But how does one evaluate this parameter?

The correlation of forces in Latin America is determined by the positions that are won, threatened or lost by three sectors: the local capitalist classes, the mass of the oppressed and US imperialism. During the 1990s, capital carried out a global offensive against labour. This offensive weakened in the last few years, but it left a climate adverse to wage earners on an international scale. Nonetheless, in Latin America, one can note several peculiarities.

The capitalist class has actively participated in the neoliberal assault, but ended up suffering various side effects of this process. They lost competitive positions with the opening of markets and relinquished defences against their external competitors with the denationalization of the productive apparatus. The financial crises also battered the establishment and reduced its direct political presence. The Right thus ended up in the minority, and the centre-left governments formed in conditions of the 'progressive cycle' have replaced many conservative governments in national administrations (especially in the Southern Cone). The capitalist elites no longer set the entire region's agenda with impunity. A crisis of neoliberalism, which could lead to the structural decline of this project, has affected them.

Great popular upheavals, which precipitated the fall of several heads of state in South America, have also modified the regional relationship of forces. Uprisings in Bolivia, Ecuador, Argentina and Venezuela have affected the totality of the dominant classes. They have challenged ruling-class aggressiveness and have imposed in many countries a certain degree of accommodation with the masses.

The combative impulse differs widely. In certain countries (Bolivia, Venezuela, Argentina and Ecuador), one finds popular initiative (*protagonismo*), but in others (Brazil and Uruguay) there has been an ebb brought about by disappointments. What is new is the awakening of union and student struggles in countries that led the neoliberal ranking (Chile) and in countries asphyxiated by social abuses and the haemorrhage of emigrants (Mexico). The correlation of forces in Latin America varies greatly, but one can affirm a general surge of popular initiatives in the entire region.

The correlation of forces in Latin America has therefore undergone several significant changes and continues to do so. As a generalization, the dominant classes can no longer rely on their strategic neoliberal compass; the popular movement has recovered its street presence; and US imperialism has forfeited its capacity to intervene.

Recommended reading: Katz (2005).

The issue of class consciousness

The eradication of capitalism is a project entirely dependent on the level of consciousness of the oppressed. Only their convictions can guide a process of struggle towards socialism. The primitive view of this transformation as a historically inevitable process has lost intellectual consensus and political appeal. No pattern of historical evolution of this type exists. Either socialism will be a voluntary creation of the great majorities, or it will never emerge. The experience of 'actually existing socialism' illustrates how damaging it is to substitute the paternalism of functionaries for the initiative of the people.

But the consciousness of the oppressed is subject to strong mutations. Two opposing forces influence its development: the lessons learned by the exploited in their resistance to capital, and the discouragement they suffer as a result of burdensome labour, survival anxieties and everyday alienation.

The inclination of wage earners to question or accept the established order arises from the changing outcomes of this conflict. Under certain circumstances, the critical view predominates, and at other moments resignation prevails. These attitudes depend on many factors and are reflected in very different generational perceptions of capitalism. The bulk of contemporary youth, for example, grew up without the expectation of improvement in labour conditions and education that prevailed in the post-war period, and view exclusion, unemployment or inequality as normal operating patterns of the system. This outlook on the established order has not prevented the new generation of Latin Americans from resuming the combativeness of its predecessors.

The predominant image of capitalism influences socialist consciousness, but does not determine its continuity. In this regard, what is essential are the conclusions drawn from the class struggle and the impact generated by great revolutions in other countries. These benchmarks determine the existence of certain 'average degrees of socialist consciousness' that translate into levels of greater enthusiasm or disappointment about the anti-capitalist project. The victories achieved in Russia, China, Yugoslavia, Vietnam and Cuba, for example, promoted a positive socialist perception, which did not dissipate with the numerous defeats that occurred in those periods.

The present generation of Latin Americans did not grow up like their parents in a context marked by revolutionary triumphs. This absence of a successful anti-capitalist referent – close to their immediate personal experiences – explains their spontaneously distancing themselves further away from the socialist project.

The great differences between the current period and that of 1960–1980 lie more on this plane of political consciousness than in the realm of relationships of force or in the change of the popular subjects. It is not the intensity of the social conflicts, the willingness of the oppressed to struggle, or the capacity of the oppressors to control that has substantially changed, but the visibility of – and confidence in – a socialist model.

Recommended reading: Webber (2016).

Responses of the Left to the current conjuncture

The constitutional framework significantly alters the context of leftist activity. For one thing, in some contexts it has induced socialists to proclaim the end of 'revolutionary utopia' and the beginning of a new era of gradual advances towards a post-capitalist future. They returned to the gradualist scheme and proposed to embark on the road to socialism through an initial consensus with the oppressors. They advocated taking this path to gaining hegemony for the workers.

But the vast trajectory of social democracy has proved the unreality of this option. The dominant classes do not give up power. They only co-opt partners to recreate the pillars of an oppression based on private ownership of the big banks and corporations. They will never permit this control to be corroded by the political or cultural weight of their antagonists. For this reason, any policy that indefinitely postpones the anti-capitalist goal ends up reinforcing oppression. Socialism requires preparing and consummating anti-capitalist ruptures. If one forgets this principle, the strategy of the Left lacks a theoretical compass – a strategy and tactics adequate to the situation faced by the Left in the project to build socialism.

But the confrontation with constitutionalism has also generated positive effects in recent years. It has allowed, for example, debate on the Left about the form that a genuine democracy under socialism would adopt. This reflection introduced a significant change in the way of conceptualizing the anti-capitalist perspective. In the 1970s, democracy was a topic that the critics of the Soviet bureaucracy omitted or barely put forth. Now almost no one skirts this problem. Socialism has ceased to be imagined as a prolongation of the tyranny that reigned in the Soviet Union, and has currently begun to be perceived as a regime of growing participation, representation and popular control.

But this future also depends on the immediate responses to constitutionalism. Two positions prevail on the Left: one proposes to gain space within the institutional structure and the other promotes parallel organs of people's power (Petras and Veltmeyer, 2005: Chapter 6). The first argues for advancing by climbing from the local to the provincial level to subsequently reach the national governments. It follows from the experiences of community administrations that the Brazilian Workers' Party (*Partido dos Trabalhadores*) and the Broad Front (*Frente Amplio*) of Uruguay pursued in the early 1990s. It recognizes the bitter concessions granted to the Establishment during these administrations (business commitments and postponement of social improvements), but it construes the final outcome as positive. Undeniably, this 'municipal socialism' led to old activists turning into confidence men of capital. They debated at city halls, exhibited hostility towards the social movement and ended up governing on behalf of the dominant classes. First they moderated programmes, then they called for responsibility, and finally they changed sides.

An opposite strategy to the institutional path exists that encourages social mobilization and rejects electoral participation. It denounces the corruption of the Workers' Party or the passivity of the Broad Front and advocates the emergence of direct options for people's power. It also questions the electoral traps, which in the Andean countries have led to channelling resistance through the system.

This vision ignores the influence of the electoral arena and minimizes the negative consequences of abandoning it. Citizenship, voting and electoral rights are not just instruments of bourgeois manipulation. They are also popular conquests achieved against dictatorships, which under certain conditions allow one to take a stand against the Right. If elections were pure trickery, they would not have been able to fulfil the progressive role that they have played, for example, in Venezuela.

Participation in the constitutional framework fosters the political practices necessary for future socialist democracy. Rejecting electoral participation is as pernicious on a tactical level (isolation) as it is in terms of strategy (preparing this socialist future). In the face of the false dilemma of accepting or ignoring the rules of constitutionalism, there is a third viable path: to combine direct action with electoral participation. With this approach, the expressions of people's power – which any revolutionary process requires – would be made compatible with the maturation of socialist consciousness, which to a certain extent takes place in the constitutional arena.

Recommended reading: Petras and Veltmeyer (2017).

Social movements and political parties?

Popular consciousness translates into organization (Harnecker, 2011). The grouping of the oppressed is essential to creating the instruments of an anti-capitalist transformation, since without their own organizations, the exploited cannot form another society. Movements and parties constitute two modes of contemporary popular organization. Both are essential to the development of socialist convictions. They reinforce confidence in self-organization, and they develop the norms for the future exercise of people power.

Movements sustain the immediate social struggle, and parties fuel a more fully developed political activity. Both are necessary for facilitating direct action and electoral participation. But this complementarity is frequently questioned by exclusivist advocates of movement or party. Some movement-oriented theorists – who subscribe to autonomist points of view – believe that party organization is obsolete, useless and pernicious.

But their objections apply only to the actions of certain parties, and not to the general operation of these structures. No emancipatory project can evolve exclusively in the social realm, nor can it do without the specific platforms – the links between demands and power strategies – that party groupings provide. These groupings help overcome the limitations of a spontaneous rebellion. The party facilitates the maturation of an anti-capitalist consciousness that does not emerge abruptly from protest actions, but requires a certain processing in order to transform the battle for immediate improvements into a struggle for socialist objectives.

Parties are important organizations in the electoral process. Some people on the Left have argued that the electoral process is a system rigged in favour of the dominant and ruling classes that are able to manipulate the process in their class interest. They argue that people power can best be exercised in the form of social movements that mobilize the forces of resistance against both capital and the state. Others, however, counter this with the argument that participation in electoral politics can be made compatible with the promotion of people's power – that the Left must avoid institutional co-optation without turning its back on the electoral process. Movements and parties fulfil a complementary function since social struggle is not self-sufficient and partisan organization is necessary. But it is essential to avoid sectarian posturing and to include immediate improvements as part of a revolutionary agenda. This principle governs socialist strategy, although the political left has yet to find a way of incorporating it into its political practice.

In this regard, the political left has a lot to learn from studying the dynamics of the social movements, which in recent years have coalesced and come together in the search of a unified agenda in opposition to both neoliberalism and capitalism. On the other hand, these social movements are very localized and 'subterranean' in form (on this, see Bebbington and Bury, 2015) – mostly on the expanding frontier of extractive capital, and focused on protesting the negative socioenvironmental impacts of extractivism with a relatively limited concern or ability to connect to the broader class struggle based on the capital–labour relation.

The critics of political parties as a democratic instrument for achieving power (for example, Harnecker, 2011) have drawn support from the favourable attitude towards social movements that has predominated at the World Social Forums in recent years. Nonetheless, from Seattle (1999) to Caracas-Bamako (2006) and Bolivia (2000–2003),[3] much has changed (on this, see Harnecker, 2002; Webber, 2016). Confidence in the self-sufficiency of movements has declined, especially in the current Latin American scenario marked by electoral defeats of the Right. The foundational 'utopian moment' of the forums has shrunk, clearing the way for debating strategies that include parties. This change also reflects the turn of various movement-oriented theorist, who continue to aggressively question leftist organizations while defending Lula or Kirchner (Cocco, 2006; Negri, 2005; Negri and Cocco, 2006). The rejection of parties also persists among authors who propose 'changing the world without taking power' (Holloway, 2002). They dissent from political organizations that defend the need to conquer state power, but without ever clarifying how a post-capitalist society lacking governmental forms would emerge. The state is the target of all social demands, and its transformation is the condition for any anti-capitalist transition. Not even the most basic democratic changes that we currently see in Latin America are conceivable without the state. This instrument is necessary to implement social reforms, create constituent assemblies, and nationalize the basic means of social production and society's wealth of productive and natural resources. Those who deny this are disconcerted by the new scenario that exists in some countries such as Venezuela and Bolivia in regard to post-development, resource nationalism, inclusionary state activism and socialism (Katz, 2016).

Recommended reading: Veltmeyer (2011).

Hugo Chávez and the socialism of the 21st century[4]

A major lesson that can be drawn from political developments in the 20th century is that both capitalism and socialism require the agency of the nation state. As for socialism, the role of the state is to socialize the means of production and nationalize the strategic heights of the economy, as well as to ensure an equitable distribution of the social product. In the current regional context of a global capitalist system in crisis and a model (neoliberal globalization) that has clearly exhausted its limits, and the apparent end of a 'progressive cycle' of post-neoliberal regimes in Latin America, the only country in Latin America – apart from Cuba, which is actively engaged in 'updating' its socialist model – currently pursuing a socialist path towards national development is Venezuela. Since Hugo Chávez was swept into office and state power at the end of 1998, this path has been charted by the Socialist Party of Venezuela (PSUV), which at the moment is desperately seeking to stay on course under conditions that have reached crisis proportions, raising serious questions about the viability of the socialist project.

One of the first measures taken by Venezuela under Chávez's presidency was to nationalize or renationalize key firms in strategic sectors of the economy, this in contrast to the privatization agenda of the neoliberal regimes that dominated Latin American politics throughout the 1990s. As in Mexico, one of several countries in the region that has stayed the course of the neoliberal policy agenda into the 21st century, the oil industry in Venezuela's energy sector had already been nationalized in the era of the developmental state, the heyday of developmentalism and protected from the drive towards privatization under the neoliberal model of the Washington Consensus. Its hegemony in the energy sector allowed the government to advance the project of the Bolivarian Revolution with the agency of state power, the key instrument and motor of socialist development. Bringing key firms, particularly in the energy (oil and electricity) and telecommunications sectors, under state control provided the government with an important lever in its project to advance towards socialism.

As for the matter of ensuring a more equitable distribution of the social product, a major socialist principle, the Venezuelan government under Chávez's presidency implemented the same policy as that prescribed by the post-Washington Consensus on the need for a more inclusive form of national development – a new social policy targeted at poverty reduction. In this respect, the Bolivarian Revolution assumed the mantle of inclusionary state activism, which has characterized the other centre-left, or 'progressive', post-neoliberal regimes formed in a red – or, to be more precise, pink – tide of regime change that hit the region in the first decade of the new millennium. Although Chávez's conception of socialism was rather different from that of Rafael Correa and Evo Morales, two other presidents who espoused socialism, at the level of rhetoric if not in political practice, his model of the Bolivarian Revolution was constructed on the basis of the same pillar that Correa and Morales used as a cornerstone of their national development plan. This was neo-extractivism, an amalgam of neodevelopmentalism as conceived of by the economists at ECLAC and an extractivist strategy of capitalist development (Gudynas, 2010; Veltmeyer and Petras, 2014).

In regard to these three pillars of socialist development in the current context – nationalism, neodevelopmentalism and inclusionary state activism – we could add ALBA, the Bolivarian (intra-regional trade) Alliance for the Americas, also conceived of by Chávez as a 'motor' of socialist development. With the exception of ALBA, a mechanism of socialist development as well as regional integration, the socialist project advanced in the form of the Bolivarian Revolution does not differ greatly from other 20th-century socialist experiments, including Cuba. What set the Chavista project apart from these experiments was what Chávez described as the fifth motor of his project to advance towards the socialism of the 21st century, namely popular participation in the form of communalism and the agency of the communal council.

In January 2005 at the World Social Forum, Hugo Chávez explicitly called for the reinventing of socialism in a different way from what existed in the Soviet Union. 'We must reclaim socialism as a thesis, a project and a path, but a new type of socialism, a humanist one, which puts humans and not machines or the state ahead of everything' (cited in Sojo, 2005). Six months later, Chávez argued the importance of building a new communal system of production and consumption – in which there is an exchange of activities determined by communal needs and communal purposes, not just what Marx described as the 'cash nexus' or the profit motive, the incentive to make money, accumulate capital. 'We have to help to create it, from the popular bases, with the participation of the communities, through the community organizations, the cooperatives, self-management and different ways to create this system' (cited in Sojo, 2005).

The occasion was the creation of a new institution – the *Empresas de Producción Social* (EPS), as the key operational units of a social and solidarity economy – and an organizational pathway towards the achievement of socialist human development (Lebowitz, 2007). Drawn from a number of sources, but particularly from existing cooperatives pledged to commit themselves to the community, these new enterprises of social production incorporated or were organized with reference to the cooperative principles of popular power and workers' participation and self-management.

On Chávez's re-election in December 2006, a new building block was added to this institution: the communal council (based upon 200–400 families in existing urban neighbourhoods and 20–50 in the rural areas). These were established to diagnose democratically community needs and priorities. With the shift of resources from municipal levels to the community level, the support of new communal banks for local projects, and of a size that permits the general assembly rather than elected representatives to be the supreme decision-making body, the councils were envisioned as a basis not only for the transformation of people in the course of changing circumstances, but also for productive activity based upon communal needs and communal purposes. These new councils were identified as the fundamental cell of Bolivarian socialism and the basis for a new state. 'All

power to the communal councils!' Chávez declared. An 'explosion in communal power', designated as the fifth of 'five motors' driving the path towards socialism.
Recommended reading: Azzelini (2016), Katz (2016), Lebowitz (2007).

The prospect of socialism at the end of the neoliberal era

The activism in the 1990s of social movements formed by the peasantry and the rural landless workers – the 'rural poor' in development discourse, or the 'rural semiproletariat' in Marxist discourse – brought about the demise of neoliberalism as an economic doctrine and a policy agenda (Petras and Veltmeyer, 2009, 2013). By the end of the 1990s, neoliberalism was everywhere on the defensive and in some countries, particularly in the Andean highlands and the Southern Cone of South America (Argentina, Bolivia, Ecuador, Venezuela), there emerged a new progressive cycle in Latin American politics characterized by the search for an alternative post-neoliberal form of capitalism ('inclusive development'), and in some contexts 'the socialism of the 21st century' (Chávez, 2007; Harnecker, 2010). However, after a decade and a half of diverse experiments in the direction of inclusive development (the 'new developmentalism') – and in the case of Venezuela, and to some extent Bolivia and Ecuador, socialism and resource nationalism – the 'progressive cycle' is evidently over with the return of the far right in Argentina and Brazil, and with it the restoration of the neoliberal policy agenda. At the same time, notwithstanding widespread disenchantment with neoliberalism (the neoliberal model of capitalist development) in the popular sector and policy circles, all of the governments on the Pacific Rim of Latin America, with the exception of Ecuador, have maintained their alignment with US imperialism, and continue to toe the neoliberal line. Even in Venezuela, the only country in the region – aside from Cuba, which is engaged in a process of 'updating' its socialist model of national development – socialism is very much in question, contested by a resurgent Right emboldened by a deep economic crisis, which they themselves have provoked with the active support and funding provided by the US imperialist state (Petras and Veltmeyer, 2017).

Under these conditions the prognosis in regard to socialism is not favourable. On the other hand, the contradictions of capitalism – particularly as regards extractivism, but also the capital–labour relation in the context of a pendulum swing from the left to the right – are generating powerful forces of resistance in the popular sector, creating new conditions for socialist development. This is the fundamental and urgent challenge of the Left: how to mobilize and organize these forces in a socialist direction.
Recommended reading: Petras and Veltmeyer (2017).

Notes

1 One per cent of the planet's population currently controls 40 per cent of the wealth (Aizpeolea, 2006).
2 An extreme example of this conception – which assumes catastrophe as a quality – is set forth by Rieznik (2006).

3 *Editors' note*: Katz is referring here to the class struggles in Bolivia in the form of what has become known as the 'water war' (1999–2000) and the 'gas war' (culminating in 2003). For an analysis of the dynamics of these struggles, see Webber (2011).

4 This chapter is an edited amalgam of several essays authored by Claudio Katz over the past three years. But rather than asking him to update his discussion of the prospects of socialism in the 21st century with regard to developments in Venezuela – particularly Hugo Chávez's timely contribution – the editors have leaned heavily on a discussion provided by Michael Lebowitz in his *Monthly Review* article (Lebowitz, 2007), as well as a talk presented at Saint Mary's University in November 2015 (Lebowitz, 2015).

References

Aizpeolea, H. (2006). 'Como se reparte la torta'. *La Nación*, 15 September.

Azzelini, D. (2016). *Communes and Workers' Control in Venezuela: Building 21st Century Socialism from Below*. Social Sciences E-Books online, Brill Historical material book series. Available at: http://booksandjournals.brillonline.com/content/books/9789004331754.

Barrett, P., Chávez, D. and Rodríguez Garavito, C. (eds) (2008). *The New Latin American Left: Utopia Reborn*. London: Pluto.

Bebbington, A. and Bury, J. (eds) (2015). *Subterranean Struggles: New Dynamics of Mining, Oil and Gas in Latin America*. Austin, TX: University of Texas Press.

Bresser-Pereira, L.C. (2006). 'El nuevo desarrollismo y la ortodoxia convencional'. *Economía UNAM*, 4(10): 7–29.

Bresser-Pereira, L.C. (2007). 'Estado y mercado en el nuevo desarrollismo'. *Nueva Sociedad*, 210, July–August.

Bresser-Pereira, L.C. (2009). *Developing Brazil: Overcoming the Failure of the Washington Consensus*. Boulder, CO: Lynne Rienner.

Chávez, H.R. (2007). 'El socialismo del siglo XXI'. In N. Kohan (ed.), *Introducción al pensamiento socialista*. Bogotá: Ocean Sur, pp. 243–8.

Cocco, G. (2006). 'Los nuevos gobiernos no se entienden sin los movimientos sociales'. *Página*, 12, 20 March.

Cypher, J. (2010). 'South America's commodities boom: developmental opportunity or path dependent reversion?' *Canadian Journal of Development Studies*, 30(3–4): 635–62.

Fine, B., Lapavitsas, C. and Pincus, J. (eds) (2001). *Development Policy in the Twenty-First Century: Beyond the Post-Washington Consensus*. London: Routledge.

García Linera, A. (2005). 'Somos partidarios de un modelo socialista con un capitalismo boliviano'. *Clarín*, 23 December.

García Linera, A. (2006a). 'El capitalismo andino-amazónico'. *Enfoques Críticos*, 2, April–May.

García Linera, A. (2006b). 'El evismo'. *OSAL*, 19, January–April.

García Linera, A. (2013). 'Once again on so-called "extractivisim"'. *Monthly Review*, 29 April. Available at: https://mronline.org/2013/04/29/gl290413-html/.

Gudynas, E. (2010). 'The new extractivism of the 21st century: ten urgent theses about extractivism in relation to current South American progressivism'. Americas Policy Program, 21 January. Available at: www.iadb.org/intal/intalcdi/PE/2010/04716.pdf.

Harnecker, M. (1998). 'Haciendo posible lo posible: La izquierda en el umbral del siglo XXI'. *Rebelión*. Available at: www.rebelion.org/docs/95166.pdf.

Harnecker, M. (2000). *La izquierda en el umbral del siglo XXI*. Madrid: Siglo Veintiuno Press.

Harnecker, M. (2002). *La izquierda después de Seattle*. Madrid: Siglo Veintiuno Press.

Harnecker, M. (2010). 'Twenty-first century socialism'. *Monthly Review*, 62(3), July–August II: 3–78.

Harnecker, M. (2011). 'The political instrument'. In H. Veltmeyer (ed.), *Socialism of the 21st Century: Possibilities and Prospects*. Toronto: Fernwood, pp. 78–99.

Holloway, J. (2002). *Change the World Without Taking Power*. London: Pluto Press.

Katz, C. (2005). 'Strategies for the Latin American left: problems of autonomism'. *International Socialist Review*, 4, November–December. Available at: www.isreview.org/issues/44/autonomism.shtml.

Katz, C. (2006a). *El porvenir del socialismo*. Caracas: Monte Ávila.

Katz, C. (2006b). 'Socialismo o Neo-desarrollismo'. 1 December. Available at: www.lahaine.org.

Katz, C. (2016). 'Is South America's "progressive cycle" at an end?' *The Bullet*, E-Bulletin No. 1229, 3/13/2016. Available at: www.socialistproject.ca/bullet/1229.php9/18/.

Lebowitz, M. (2007). 'Venezuela: a good example of the bad left of Latin America'. *Monthly Review*, 59(3), July–August. Available at: http://monthlyreview.org/2007/07/01/venezuela-a-good-example-of-the-bad-left-of-latin-america.

Lebowitz, M. (2015). 'The path towards the socialism of the 21st century in Venezuela'. *IDS Working Paper*, 20 November. Halifax: Saint Mary's University.

Munck, R. (2013). *Rethinking Latin America: Development, Hegemony and Social Transformation*. Basingstoke: Palgrave Macmillan.

Negri, T. (2005). 'La derrota de EEUU es una derrota política'. *Página*, 12, 1 November.

Negri, T. and Cocco, G. (2006). 'América Latina está viviendo un momento de ruptura'. *Página*, 12, 14 August.

Petras, J. and Veltmeyer, H. (2005). *Social Movements and State Power: Argentina, Bolivia, Brazil, Ecuador*. London: Pluto Press.

Petras, J. and Veltmeyer, H. (2009). *What's Left in Latin America?* Farnham: Ashgate.

Petras, J. and Veltmeyer, H. (2013). *Social Movements in Latin America: Neoliberalism and Popular Resistance*. Basingstoke, UK: Palgrave Macmillan.

Petras, J. and Veltmeyer, H. (2017). *The Class Struggle in Latin America*. London: Routledge.

Rieznik, P. (2006). 'En defensa del catastrofismo'. *En defensa del marxismo*, 34, 19 October.

Sojo, C. (2005). *Venezuela's Chavez Closes World Social Forum with Call to Transcend Capitalism*. Available at: https://venezuelanalysis.com/news/907.

Veltmeyer, H. (2011). *Socialism of the 21st Century: Possibilities and Prospects*. Toronto: Fernwood.

Veltmeyer, H. and Petras, J. (2014). *The New Extractivism: A Model for Latin America?* London: Zed Books.

Webber, J. (2011). *Red October: Left-Indigenous Struggles in Modern Bolivia*. Chicago, IL: Haymarket.

Webber, J. (2016). *The Last Day of Oppression, and the First Day of the Same: The Politics and Economics of the New Latin American Left*. Chicago, IL/London: Haymarket/Pluto.

Webber, J. and Carr, B. (eds) (2013). *The New Latin American Left: Cracks in the Empire*. Lanham, MD: Rowman & Littlefield.

37

CONFRONTING THE CAPITALIST HYDRA

The Zapatistas reflect on the storm that is upon us[1]

Sergio Rodríguez Lascano

The Zapatista Army of National Liberation (EZLN) has in different ways high-lighted the existence of widespread tendencies regarding both the changes that have taken place in the world capitalist system and the form of organization by and from below (what they call 'the Others'). For the Zapatistas, the current phase of capitalism is not simply a change of economic model, but a reconfiguration of the system in its entirety:

> We keep asking and we are told that, as with [capitalist] production, the 'new' goods [based on pillage and plunder, rather than labour exploitation] also generate profit.
>
> And this is one of the favourite foods of the hydra.
>
> And that appropriation of profit, made possible by exploitation and plun-der, is based on private ownership of the means of production . . . and, maybe we could add, dispossession.
>
> Is that the motherhead of the hydra?
>
> Is private ownership of the means of production, dispossession, circula-tion and consumption the head without which the system perishes, unable to reproduce itself? Well, of course I [the unindentified author of the text] say that this is where so much noise is made. Some say yes, some say no, and some say 'yes' or 'no' but add 'not only'.
>
> But new data from other observation posts that are collated through the exchange of seeds are coming: there is an increase in gender violence, child-hood is also prey to the beast, in its insatiable appetite the hydra [capitalism] not only tightens the yoke on those who produce the wealth and make turn the wheel of history, also vomit millions of unemployed, dispossessed, outcasts and the undead.

The musicians, poets and artists agree, each in their own way, send their views, either in *décimas* (song in 10 verses), in *gráfica* (orally transmitted song), or in *rolas* (band songs). High culture and communication make out as if it were nothing unusual, but those below cry out.

Economists have started their analysis, but early results show that the fundamentals remain, while new modalities arise that say that they could be responsible for a global economic catastrophe.

Nature is assaulted in an effort to turn it into commodities: food and medicinal plants . . . expropriated by the market.

The storm threatens the city and countryside.

It is not national, they tell us. In various parts of the world we find the same symptoms.

Zapatismo, they say, 'captures' the essence, and judgement: a war, a world war, a war whose only enemy is humanity.

The warship of the system navigates with its slogan as a declaration of principles, a programme and plan of action.

Bellum Semper. Universum Universum Exitium Bellum (War forever. World War. Universal destruction).

(*EZLN – Comisión Sexta, 2015: 301, 302*)

So, it appears that Zapatismo links political economy with war. In a somewhat abusive interpretation of Zapatista thinking, we could say that it raises two possibilities or a combination of these two possibilities: political economy is the continuation of war by other means, or war is the continuation of political economy by other means. Either war is political economy or political economy is war:

If it is true that capitalism not only produces wealth and scientific and technological advances, but also produces misery, destruction and death, then we must point out things by their name: capitalism produces for and by means of war. Its progress, its development depends on war; it articulates its genealogy, it is the main line of tension, its spinal column.

In the classical sense, the goal of this war has been plunder and conquest. With that war, capitalism 'liberated' those who work with their belongings and only left them their capacity – manual and intellectual – to produce. And it also 'freed' them to be hired, employed, enslaved 'by their own choice', while 'freeing' them of any other options other than choosing to become a commodity. A commodity that like any other is sold, purchased, circulates; but it is also 'special' because it is able to produce goods with added value, surplus value. This is what makes the commodity 'labour' different from other commodities. The worker creates something new that is worth more than the sum of the values of the things that were used to produce it.

Well, that part is better explained and more fully in the scientific books of history and economics. Here, the author(s) of the text bring it up because the war that was at the origin of capitalism as the dominant system continues. The so-called 'periods of peacetime' are not such at all. 'At all times and in all places the system destroys and kills. It is not its existence that causes wars, it exists for war.'

And one of the things that we find in the new stage of this capitalist war, what the Zapatistas term 'world war', now seeks the destruction of a country in order to rebuild it. Or to be clearer: creating disorder in order to reorder society. Capitalism causes chaos and is nourished by it.

But let us step back (into the text) a bit:

> In the origins of its development, capitalism takes whatever serves its advance and discards what does not. For example, in the Industrial Revolution the mechanization of production discarded not only manual production, but also those who produced it.
>
> In capitalism there is a displacement of qualified labour that becomes useless or obsolete, and is replaced by another new skilled workforce ... The space of production is filled and emptied continuously; this is true but it leaves residues: the old and the newly qualified.
>
> Aid and social programmes tend to alleviate this phenomenon. The same applies to the financing programmes for nano-, micro- and small companies. But they are not enough. While generating employment, the system produces unemployment.
>
> As if it were a great vacuum cleaner, capitalism absorbs labour power in abundance, extracts all what it can, leaving only bones barely covered by skin. Then it presses the button 'expel' and millions of workers are thrown into [the ranks of the] unemployed. As in the great wars that absorb products, soldiers, weapons, territories. And they disgorge rubble and corpses. That is why we say that the capitalist machinery is also, and above all, a war machine against the workers.

Thus, from the Zapatista, perspective capitalism is war. And in its current stage, capitalism is a war against the whole of humanity, against the entire planet:

> War is not only the origin of the capitalist system, it is present in each and every one of its 'qualitative leaps'. War is the medicine that capitalism administers to the world to cure it of the evils imposed by capitalism itself.

Now then – the text notes:

> It is said and repeated that in the wars nobody wins.
> False.
> And there are not only those who are victorious in a conflict. There are also those who win, no matter who the winner and who the loser ...
> And we are not referring only to the great armaments industry, which can produce deadly goods that demand continual renewal; which needs wars

to maintain its production, its sales, its profits. By following the genealogy of capital we discover that not rarely has military war been the way out of its crises. The market of that industry is war, it gains gain from destruction and death.

Of course it now appears that thanks to this terrible creative machine the armaments companies are the same ones that offer to rebuild what has been destroyed. This destruction that Zapatismo has indicated as one of the characteristics of the ongoing war, unlike in the past, is not only a matter of destroying or defeating what opposes it, it is also necessary to destroy the conquered territory completely. The wasteland of war is also a commodity. And so is reconstruction.

But 'territory' should not only be laid waste by the agents of capitalism, the instruments of war: 'it must also be depopulated', it is noted in the text, thus 'eliminating not only the undesirable, the rebellious, others – also those who have nothing to do with it'.

Long ago, the armies of the great powers developed much of their so-called 'special forces' and precision weapons. The sense of these troops and weapons was to be able to deliver 'surgical' blows, that is to say, to be able to eliminate the threat without the trauma of an attack that brings along the protests of the always annoying pacifists and defenders of human rights.

Well, not anymore:

Now what interests them is to produce the greatest possible destruction, the greatest number of dead, missing and displaced. The so-called 'collateral victims' are not such. They are also military targets, 'targets' as told in the manuals of the various capitalist armies.

After depopulating a territory of its inhabitants, big companies arrive with their skilled and domesticated cadres, and the local population that remains is used for the lowest paid jobs and will be treated as a foreigners in their own land. And society in that territory is reorganized [nation building, reconstruction], thus completing the other element that Zapatismo points out as a characteristic of [capitalism as] world war: reconstruction/reorganization/reordering.

In short, from a Zapatista perspective, capitalist war seeks destruction/depopulation – and, simultaneously, reconstruction/reordering.

Earlier, it was noted that in their reference to war that the Zapatistas were not just referring to armed force and the arms industry. Regardless of who is victorious and who is defeated, the winner is financial capital: 'For almost 20 years we have followed the development of this criminal. The most ferocious, inhuman and cruel that the world in all its history has known . . .' (pp. 314–19).

We could add – as the text of *El pensamiento crítico frente a la hidra capitalista* notes – that the hydra has mutated in recent years, which makes it necessary to study its genealogy. But if everything changes, what does not change? What is the primary head of the hydra? Or is the entire hydra precisely what does not change, regardless of the stage or stage the system reaches?

And these questions are no less because war is not only economic:

> From what we have heard here and for all we know, war also comes with the shields and billy clubs of the police deployed in the eviction of local inhabitants; with the Israeli missiles that fall on schools, hospitals and civilian neighbourhoods of Palestine; in the media campaigns that precede invasions and then justify them; in the patriarchal violence that invades the most intimate corners [of social life]; in the heterosexual intolerance that stigmatizes difference; as religious fanaticism; in the modern markets of the organs of live human beings; in the chemical invasion of the field in the countryside; in the content of the media; in organized and disorganized crime; in enforced 'disappearances'; in the impositions of governments; in the spoils disguised as 'progress'. In short, in the destruction of nature and humanity.
>
> *(p. 326)*

At the same time, the Zapatistas do not see an exclusion between exploitation and what is now known as financialization. Although they trace the level to which this financialization has reached to the excesses of capitalism, such as the fact that the total world debt represents 286 per cent of the world's GDP, they link this fact to exploitation:

> A few days ago we heard in this seedbed that you are getting profit without exploiting the workforce. We also hear that profit is only obtained from the exploitation of the labour force. We can assume that someone lies because one assertion is exactly the opposite contradictory of the other. What Zapatismo sees is that it is remuneration, money, that hides the apparent contradiction. Profits derived from speculation do not represent wealth, which is obtained from labour itself. This difference is hidden behind the form of "money" . . .
>
> *(p. 322)*

The other key thesis of Zapatismo has to do with the question of the nation state. Not of the state as such, but the nation state, i.e. the concrete form that arose along with the emergence of capitalism, first as an absolutist state linked to the 'original accumulation' and later as a nation linked to the accumulation of capital:

> The hydra has not only mutated in its modes and poisons, it also extended its empire of war to childhood, guessing perhaps that subjugation is also inherited, like fear, like poverty, like rebellion.
>
> And beyond. The land receives fierce and irremediable *tarascadas* (snappy answers). Wounded, the first mother stumbles, fragile, helpless, vulnerable.

At the foot of the hydra, on the lifeless bodies of its past heads (the nation state, the domestic market, classical politics, national boundaries, local political classes, small and medium enterprises) lie their favourite victims: truth and justice.

(*p. 232*)

A further note:

In other words, do fundamental decisions, which guide the course of a national society, continue in the sphere of the state, of government, of public administration? Even palliatives, short-term consolations, are possible? In much of the world, the problem has been located in public administration. And the diagnosis is almost unanimous that it is a matter of corruption of the government apparatus. But the point here is that in order to contest the fight against corruption there is no politically defined flag. Against administrative corruption can be found the Right, the Left and "independent" politics. Everyone strives to offer probity and honesty . . . and all end up being [touched or brought down] by some scandal.

And here comes a fundamental question:

Do we, the Zapatistas, think that the nation state, i.e. the state as we know it, has remained untouched in the war of the system? Or are we in front of a hologram . . .

Neither one thing nor the other: the nation state is no longer what it was. But does it maintain some resistance to supranational powers? When representatives of a European state, let us say Greece, sit down and talk to Angela Merkel, are they talking to the Bundestag or the International Monetary Fund . . . or the European Central Bank . . . or the European Commission . . . or with the four of them . . . or none?

We need to reconstruct the genealogy of the nation state and confront the result with the current reality. And then ask these questions: What were their bases, which ones are maintained, which have disappeared, and which have mutated? What were its functions, its place, its area of influence, its area of interest?

At first glance it seems evident that some of its main features already lie as victims of the ongoing war. And it is increasingly difficult to speak of sovereignty, territory, authority, monopoly of violence, legal domination, independence. Of course, we must take care of the evidence, but the clarification of the state is necessary – and urgent.

(*pp. 309–10*)

Of course, one might think that there is something apocalyptic in Zapatista thought. But I think they have recovered an old tradition of critical thinking:

things have to be called by their name and not located with a completely irresponsible optimism. The assault, the storm, is terrible, and besides we are hardly talking about its first expressions. The thinktanks of the Deutsche Bank tell us that we must prepare for 35 years of crisis.

But the very metaphor of the hydra, being very strong, is of great importance in that the hydra was defeated by an alliance between Hercules and Yolao.

Yes, the vision that Zapatismo has painted, almost from its first public appearance, is that we are in the middle of a war against humanity, not against a class or a fraction of class, but against humanity as a whole. Space is too short to understand the deep meaning of the concept. But we do understand that the so-called neoliberalism does not consist of a simple economic model; it is a way of organizing-disorganizing people's lives. That is, the whole of social relations, economics, politics, state, ideology, culture, international relations and, of course, the concept and practice of war are arriving at the approach of total war.

But in the face of this total war rises an equally total resistance globally, with many pockets of resistance around the world. One of those pockets of resistance is expressed in the mountains and the jungle of the Mexican southeast and is represented by the EZLN, who tells us that:

the classic beginnings of the Zapatista reflections: disconcerting, anachronistic, misplaced, absurd. Like not wanting, or just like it, like 'there we leave them', like 'there they see', like 'how it goes in their account'. As if they were looking at a piece of a puzzle and waiting for it to be understood that they are not describing a part of reality but are imagining the whole picture. As if they are looking at the puzzle already completed, with its figures and full colours, but with the edges of the pieces visible, indicating that the whole is due to the parts, and of course, each part acquires its meaning in their relationship with the others. It is as if the Zapatista reflection allows them to see that what is missing is lacking, and not only what exists, what is perceived as immediate.

Something like what Walter Benjamin did with Paul Klee's 'Angelus Novus'. In reflecting on a painting Benjamin 'completes' it: he sees the angel, but he also sees what the angel sees, sees where he is thrown by what he sees, sees the force that assaults him, sees the brutal footprint. Sees the completed puzzle:

There is a picture of Klee that is called Angelus Novus. In it is shown an angel who seems about to move away from something that has paralyzed him. His eyes stare, his mouth open and his wings spread. This is how one imagines the Angel of History. The face is turned to the past. Where we perceive a chain of events he sees a unique catastrophe that heaps ruin upon ruin and throws it at his feet. He would like to stop, awaken the dead and recompose what is torn apart, but from Paradise there is a hurricane that is entangled in its wings, and it is so strong that the angel can no longer close them. This hurricane pushes him irresistibly toward the future, to which he turns his back, while the debris rises before him to the sky. That hurricane is what we call progress.

(Marx, 10th Thesis on the Philosophy of History)

In the end, the most important element of of the text (*Confronting the Capialiust Hydra*) is the reflection that leads us to a key question:

But if the greed of the hydra is infinite, the earth and humanity are not. And it is here, friends and enemies, where critical thinking compels us to do something. It is here that critical thinking slaps us and asks us: What about you?

(p. 326)

The Zapatistas have their answer; they have decided to create new social relations in their territories. They have to do not only with what we would call the relations of production, but also with all the mechanisms to be able to construct a democracy from below. In the book of Marras, the Zapatista comrades explicitly point out, in relation to the new forms of social relations that have created the Zapatista women: 'No, the problem is that the object of the science of history is not ONLY to explain its object of knowledge, but to transform it'.

OK, but in order to do it you need to be able to explain it. And to explain it is also, and above all, to reconstruct his genealogy. Could the Zapatistas explain their struggle as women we are if they did not listen to Miriam, Rosalinda, Dalia, Lizbeth, Selena, Lupita, Zapatista Defence?

Zapatismo cannot be explained by itself; it needs concepts, theories and critical thinking to give an account of itself. You have heard or read the wonderful genealogy of the struggle of Zapatista women, yes, their heroism, yes, their stubborn commitment, but something was missing.

What is lacking is political economy. Yes, because that rebellion and resistance could grow, develop and expand to what now surprises and terrifies us, only when there were the material bases that made them concrete. It was not until women were released from economic dependence on men that we pass from theory to reality.

It was not till cooperatives emerged, constructed their own projects, appropriated the economy, that they took off. It was because of the tireless work of the Ramonas, Susanas and all Zapatista women who . . . infected other women, and these others and so on that they could do it, and they can do it because they do not depend economically on men.

And let me tell you that this was only possible when at least two fundamental developments took place: one was a change in ownership of the means of production, and the other was people taking and executing their own decisions, i.e. politics.

In explaining this (the thinking embodied in the text of *El pensamiento crítico frente a la hidra capitalista*), we have used the toolkit of political economy. Without these tools, one could come to think that everything was and is one, and that it is merely a question of will, of firmness, of commitment, of militancy. But Heracles-Yolao must fulfil this work or suffer the condemnation of always starting again: cutting off one head and giving birth to two more. Tear the wall until the crack is gone and end up hurting it irreparably.

And before confronting to destroy, they have to see the way to survive, to resist. So what might help is to ask for the origin of both who confronts and what is confronted. So it is a matter of tracking the hydra, to follow its trail, to know its manners, its times, its places, its history, its genealogy (p. 282).

Therefore, they are advancing in the process of building their own path. And that was why it was so timely to pose the question. And you, what?

The Zapatista response is theirs; but for us the question is how to find ours. In that sense, the book *Critical Thinking in Confronting the Capitalist Hydra* is first and foremost a site for building together – accepting our differences – an anti-capitalist way forward.

Recommended reading: Estrada Saavedra (2007).

Note

1 *Editors' note*: In this chapter, Sergio Rodriguez Lascano, the director of and columnist with the Zapatista journal *Rebeldía*, provides insights into the thinking of the Zapatista movement. In so doing, he relies on extensive material from the Zapatista movement itself, believing that presenting their own words is the most appropriate form of testament. The words of the Zapatistas themselves are either presented in quotation marks or paraphrased by Lascano with an occasional commentary.

References

Estrada Saavedra, M. (2007). *La Comunidad Armada Rebelde y el EZLN*. Mexico City: El Colegio de México.

EZLN – Comisión Sexta (2015). *El pensamiento crítico frente a la hidra capitalista*. Mexico: Comisión Sexta Adherente.

INDEX

Page numbers followed by 't' and 'n' refer to information found in tables and notes respectively. The number following an 'n' refers to the note number.